The AMERICAN REVOLUTION

A VISUAL HISTORY

SMITHSONIAN

The
AMERICAN REVOLUTION

A VISUAL HISTORY

DK UK

Senior Editor Helen Fewster
Senior Art Editor Sharon Spencer
North American Editor Margaret Parrish
Managing Editor Angeles Gavira Guerrero
Managing Art Editor Michael Duffy
Jacket Design Development Manager Sophia MTT
Jacket Editor Claire Gell
Pre-Production Producer Nikoleta Parasaki
Producer Mary Slater
Publisher Liz Wheeler
Art Director Karen Self
Publishing Director Jonathan Metcalf

DK DELHI

Senior Editor Anita Kakar
Project Art Editor Vaibhav Rastogi
Art Editors Shreya Anand, Konica Juneja
Assistant Art Editor Simar Dhamija
Managing Editor Rohan Sinha
Managing Art Editor Sudakshina Basu
Jacket Designer Dhirendra Singh
Managing Jackets Editor Saloni Singh
Picture Researcher Deepak Negi
Manager Picture Research Taiyaba Khatoon
DTP Designers Nand Kishore Acharya, Anita Yadav
Senior DTP Designers Harish Aggarwal, Sachin Singh
Pre-Production Manager Balwant Singh
Production Manager Pankaj Sharma

TOUCAN BOOKS

Managing Editors Sarah Bloxham, Ellen Dupont
Senior Editor Dorothy Stannard
Senior Art Editor Thomas Keenes
Assistant Editor Abigail Mitchell
Editors John Andrews, Cathy Meeus, Donald Sommerville, Constance Novis
Additional Picture Research Sarah Smithies, Jo Walton
Cartography Merritt Cartographic
Proofreader Caroline Hunt
Indexer Marie Lorimer

First American Edition, 2016
Published in the United States by DK Publishing
345 Hudson Street, New York, New York 10014

Copyright © 2016 Dorling Kindersley Limited
DK, a Division of Penguin Random House, LLC

16 17 18 19 10 9 8 7 6 5 4 3 2 1
001–288639–April/2016

DK books are available at special discounts when purchased in bulk for sales promotions, premiums, fund-raising, or educational use. For details, contact: DK Publishing Special Markets, 345 Hudson Street, New York, New York 10014 or SpecialSales@dk.com

Printed in China

A WORLD OF IDEAS:
SEE ALL THERE IS TO KNOW

www.dk.com

CONTENTS

1

FROM RESISTANCE TO REBELLION BEFORE 1775

2

THE START OF THE WAR 1775

NEWPORT, RHODE ISLAND

3

BIRTH OF A NATION
1776

4

THE STRUGGLE
FOR MASTERY
1777

THE DEATH OF MONTGOMERY

BRITISH ENCAMPMENT

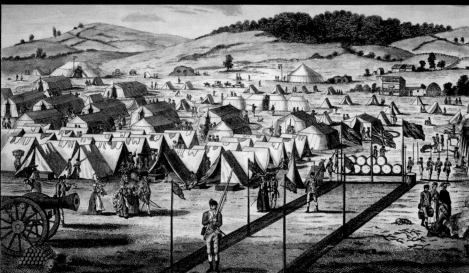

5
A WIDENING
WAR 1778

6
CONFLICT
SPREADS 1779

7
THE CONTINUING
STRUGGLE 1780

TUG-OF-WAR

DEATH OF PULASKI

AMERICA VICTORIOUS 1781–83

AFTERMATH: A STRONGER UNION

WASHINGTON BIDS FAREWELL TO HIS OFFICERS

A FRAME OF GOVERNMENT

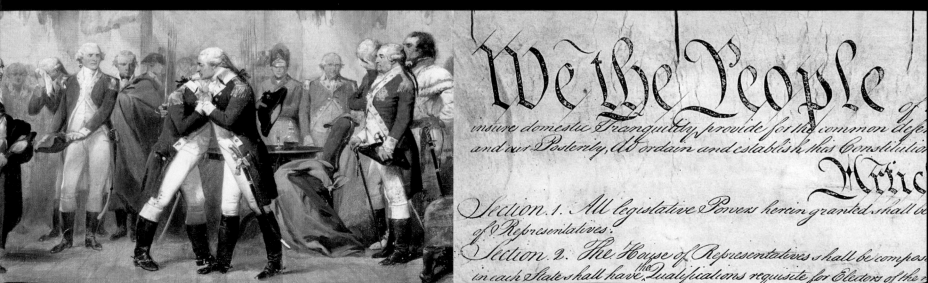

George Washington at Princeton
George Washington sat for this portrait, by Charles Willson Peale, to celebrate his victory at Princeton in 1777. Painted from life, this definitive image is thought to be a true likeness of the American hero.

Foreword

Americans went to war to win their independence from Great Britain. Just weeks after fighting broke out at Lexington and Concord, the Continental Congress appointed George Washington commander in chief of an army "for the Defense of American Liberty." Outmatched American troops often retreated, but returned to fight again, frustrating British efforts to crush the rebellion. A stunning American victory at Yorktown finally sapped Britain's will to fight, and in 1783, both parties signed the Treaty of Paris. America had won its independence.

Two hundred years later, during the bicentennial events at Yorktown, Virginia, in October 1981, I witnessed Americans again dressed in the brightly colored uniforms of George Washington's Continental Army, as well as those of militia units and guards of the original Thirteen Colonies. They reenacted the battles that finally won our independence, and spectators were able to experience the sounds, the smells, and the feel of the battle. It took thousands of spectators back in time to give us all a small glimpse into the era when our forefathers fought to secure our freedoms and form a new nation.

The objects of history, and their stories, have fascinated me ever since. That experience led me to ask questions about the material culture of the past, and would lead me to a career at the Museum of American History, where many of those tangible pieces of history have been preserved and exhibited. The gunboat *Philadelphia* is one of them: serving in the Battle of Valcour Island, it sank on its maiden voyage, but the battle helped to delay the British advance, and allowed the fledgling American army to reinforce itself and come back stronger. Also among the museum's artifacts are many from George Washington: the uniform of blue and buff, which he wore for many of his formal portraits by Charles Willson Peale; a pair of epaulettes; his battle sword with green-dyed ivory handle, which he bequeathed to his nephew with the promise to draw the sword only "in self-defense or in the defense of [the] country and its rights"; and several pieces for field use, including canteen items, his marquee tent, and his folding camp stool. Washington took to the field with his men and army and used these objects, making a point to be among his soldiers.

This book serves as a visual survey of the American Revolution, our War of Independence, but indeed, a war that included the world. Many countries with colonies and interests in the "new world" fought in the conflict, along with Native Americans. Finally, through revolution, a new nation—the United States—was formed. The book draws on collections throughout the world, and most especially from the Smithsonian Institution. The Smithsonian has been collecting and preserving Revolutionary War materials since its founding in 1846. Most of the Washington material came to the Institution from the Patent Office collections; other materials came to us as family heirlooms, passed down from generation to generation and given to the National Museum to be preserved for future generations.

The objects, art, and documents of the period are key to telling and illustrating the story of our founding—from engravings by Paul Revere, to paintings and portraits by Peale, to original documents, drawings, maps, illustrations, and first-person accounts. Illustrated timelines, colorful maps, and gallery spreads filled with vintage military materiel further help the reader to visualize and understand the war.

Every page offers a visual tour of this history, with many personal touchstones and glimpses of how those before us forged a new nation, and won our independence.

Jennifer L. Jones

JENNIFER L. JONES
EDITORIAL CONSULTANT

EVROPA.

SEPTENTRION

GROENLANDIA

AMERICA

OCEA.

SEPTEN

TRIONA

MAR

NUS OCCIDENTA

LIS

DEL

Tropicus Cancri

MAR

NOR

LIS

ARCHI

B d S Bartol

Id So Petro

DEL

PELAGO

DE S. LAZARO

CIRCULUS ÆQUINOCTIALIS

ZUR

AMERICA

NOVA
GUINEA

MERIDIONALIS

PERUVI

LI ANA

MARE

Tropicus Capricorni

PACIFI

CUM

Zelandia

nova

Tierra del

Fretum Magellanicum
Fretum le Maire
Staten land

*America primum detecta a Christophoro Columbo.
anno 1492 at ab Americo Vespucio latius retecta año
1499 deg suo nomine eam dicit hinc á 1520 á
Ferdinando Magellano, Fretum quod denomine
suo Magellanicum dictum, ... est Idem
præstiterunt Franciscus Draco á 1579 Tomas Can-
disch ann ... Oliverius á Nort á 1600 Sebal
dus de Weert á 1600 Georgius Spilbergh
á 1614 commodius vero et citius fretum de-
prehensum anno 1616 á Iacobo le Mayre
quod et ab ipsius nomine dictum fretum
le Mayre.*

MERIDIES

AFRICA

Lands of opportunity
The Age of Discovery in the 15th century opened
imperial possibilities for Europe. This map (c. 1657)
details the discovery of the Americas at the foot of
the left hemisphere.

1

FROM RESISTANCE TO REBELLION

BEFORE 1775

In the mid-18th century, at the end of the French and Indian War, Britain had debts to pay and tried to raise revenue by increasing taxes in its American colonies. Resentment grew with the imposition of each new tax and many colonists began to question America's subordination to Britain.

≪Tinder box in Boston
In March 1770, the violent suppression of unarmed protesters by British Redcoats in Boston left five people dead. News of the so-called Boston Massacre spread through the colonies, provoking outrage and

BEFORE 1775

By 1750, Britain had 13 North American colonies, which had developed at an astonishing pace since the first, Virginia, was founded in 1607. In 1754, the French and Indian War broke out on North American soil between Britain and its old enemy, France. The Treaty of Paris, ending the war in 1763, gave the victorious British new North American territories—but the colonial boundaries that once stretched to the Mississippi were considerably curtailed when George III conceded all land west of the Proclamation Line to Native Americans, inciting anger among the colonists. Furthermore, to pay debts incurred by the war, parliament turned to the Thirteen Colonies for funds, sparking protests over "taxation without representation." This dissent would become loud, violent, and ultimately revolutionary.

1 Sir William Johnson, Britain's agent to the Iroquois, worked with the Native Americans at Albany. 2 The Battle of the Plains of Abraham in September 1759 was a key British victory in the French and Indian War. 3 In 1768, British troops occupied Boston in an attempt to quell unrest.

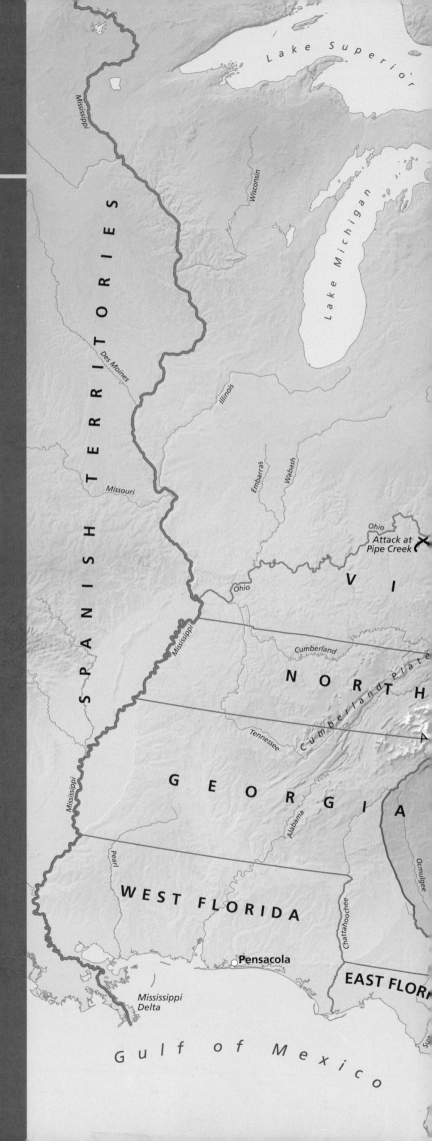

Newfoundland

Magdalen
Islands

Prince
Edward
Island

Siege of Louisbourg
Louisbourg

Sable
Island

NOVA SCOTIA

Bay of Fundy

Halifax

Saguenay

Saint-Maurice

St. John

Battle of the
Plains of Abraham
Quebec
2

Montreal

St. Lawrence

Penobscot

Ottawa

MASSACHUSETTS

Fort Frontenac

Lake
Champlain

Fort
Carillon

White
Mountains

NEW HAMPSHIRE

Lake Ontario

Siege of
Fort William
Henry

Treaty of Fort Stanwix

Georgian Bay

Lake Huron

Lake Erie

Detroit

NEW YORK

Mohawk

Albany
1

Hudson

Green Mountains

Connecticut

Catskill
Mountains

Boston
MASSACHUSETTS
3
Boston
Tea Party
Cape
Cod

ATLANTIC OCEAN

Susquehanna

Delaware

CONNECTICUT

Newport
**RHODE
ISLAND**

Yellow Creek
Massacre
Fort Duquesne
Battle of the Monongahela

PENNSYLVANIA

Allegheny

**NEW
JERSEY**

New York City

Stamp Act Congress

Treaty of
Camp Charlotte

Fort Necessity

Princeton
First
Continental
Congress
Philadelphia

Battle of Point Pleasant

Ohio

Kanawha

APPALACHIAN MOUNTAINS

Potomac

DELAWARE

Baltimore

MARYLAND

Chesapeake Bay

KEY

— Border of Spanish territories

— 1763 Proclamation Line

— Colonial boundaries

○ Town / settlement

✕ Battle / siege

🏰 Fort

⛵ Naval battle

🖋 Treaty / convention

VIRGINIA

James

Yorktown

Norfolk

Roanoke

Dan

Blue Ridge

CAROLINA

Wateree

Pee Dee

Cape Fear

Camden

Wilmington

SOUTH CAROLINA

Santee

Cooper

Augusta

Savannah

Charleston

annah

N

0   100 km
0   100 miles

Mohawk

**NEW
HAMPSHIRE**

NEW YORK

Albany
1

Hudson

Green Mountains

Connecticut

Catskill
Mountains

Boston
3
Boston
Tea Party
MASSACHUSETTS
Boston Massacre
Cape
Cod

Susquehanna

Delaware

CONNECTICUT

Gaspee
Affair

Newport
**RHODE
ISLAND**

PENNSYLVANIA

Battle of Golden Hill
Treaty of Easton
New York City
Stamp Act Congress

Long Island

Princeton

First Continental Congress
Philadelphia

**NEW
JERSEY**

**ATLANTIC
OCEAN**

Baltimore

MARYLAND

DELAWARE

0   100 km
0   100 miles

TIMELINE BEFORE 1775

Britain's Thirteen Colonies ▪ The French and Indian War ▪ **Treaty of Paris** ▪ Stamp Act crisis ▪ **Taxation without representation** ▪ Troops occupy Boston ▪ **Boston Massacre** ▪ Tax on tea ▪ **Boston Tea Party** ▪ Punitive legislation ▪ **First Continental Congress**

BEFORE 1750

MAY 14, 1607
The Virginia Company founds the first permanent English settlement in North America at Jamestown.

DECEMBER 21, 1620
The Pilgrims land at Plymouth Rock, founding the Plymouth Colony.

JUNE 9, 1732
George II grants James Oglethorpe a charter to found Georgia—Britain's 13th American colony.

1609–46
English settlers fight three wars with the Native American Powhatan Confederacy.

C.1730–50
The First Great Awakening, an evangelical Protestant movement, spreads through the colonies.

FEBRUARY 22, 1732
George Washington is born.

≫ King George III

JUNE 4, 1738
The future British monarch George III is born to Frederick, Prince of Wales, and Princess Augusta of Saxe-Coburg.

1750–59

≫ British General Braddock is mortally wounded in the Battle of the Monongahela

JULY 9, 1755
British forces are defeated near the Monongahela River.

MAY 8–9, 1756
Britain and France declare war in America. The conflict spreads to Europe on May 17, beginning the Seven Years' War.

AUGUST 8, 1757
The British surrender Fort William Henry.

SEPTEMBER 13, 1759
The British take Quebec after victory on the Plains of Abraham.

DECEMBER 12, 1753
Major George Washington, Adjutant General of the Virginia militia, orders the French to evacuate the Ohio Valley.

MAY 28, 1754
Washington attacks the French at Jumonville Glen, sparking the French and Indian War.

JULY 3, 1754
Washington surrenders Fort Necessity to the French and their Native American allies.

1760–69

OCTOBER 25, 1760
George III accedes to the throne and becomes King of Great Britain and Ireland.

MARCH 24, 1765
The Quartering Act requires colonists to provide barracks for British soldiers.

NOVEMBER 1, 1765
The British Parliament passes the Stamp Act; protests break out in the colonies.

≪ Teapot protesting the Stamp Act

FEBRUARY 10, 1763
Britain, France, and Spain conclude the Treaty of Paris, ending the French and Indian War in North America and the Seven Years' War in Europe.

MARCH 18, 1766
Parliament repeals the Stamp Act and passes the Declaratory Act.

JUNE 15–JULY 2, 1767
The Townshend Acts are passed, provoking uproar among the American colonists.

≫ Treaty of Paris

"We ask but for **Peace, Liberty, and Safety.** We wish not a **diminution of the prerogative,** nor do we solicit the grant of **any new right** in our favor."

PETITION TO THE KING FROM THE FIRST CONTINENTAL CONGRESS, OCTOBER 25, 1774

0	1771	1772	1773	1774	»

JUNE 9
Colonists burn the schooner HMS *Gaspee,* which had run aground off Rhode Island.

JANUARY
Parliament convenes a commission to investigate the *Gaspee* incident.

MARCH 31
Parliament passes the first Intolerable (Coercive) Act, which closes Boston Harbor.

SEPTEMBER 5
Colonists convene the First Continental Congress in Philadelphia.

⥥ First Continental Congress

NOVEMBER 2
Samuel Adams and Joseph Warren establish a permanent Committee of Correspondence in Massachusetts.

MARCH 12
Virginia's House of Burgesses establishes a permanent Committee of Correspondence.

MAY 10
Parliament passes the Tea Act to help the struggling East India Company.

⌃ The Boston Massacre

MARCH 5
Five civilians are killed by British troops under Captain Thomas Preston in the so-called Boston Massacre.

APRIL 12
Parliament repeals the Townshend Acts.

MAY 16
The Battle of Alamance takes place between North Carolina militia and settlers protesting against taxation.

DECEMBER 16
The Sons of Liberty dump tea chests into Boston Harbor to protest the Tea Act—an incident known as the Boston Tea Party.

MAY 20
Parliament passes another two Intolerable Acts: the Massachusetts Government Act, and the Administration of Justice Act.

OCTOBER 7
General Gage dissolves the Massachusetts legislature, called the General Court.

⌄ The Boston Tea Party

SEPTEMBER 7
British soldiers involved in the Boston Massacre are arraigned.

OCTOBER 30
Captain Preston is acquitted of murder.

OCTOBER 10
In Lord Dunmore's War, Virginia militia defeat Native Americans at the Battle of Point Pleasant.

DECEMBER 2
All but two soldiers involved in the Boston Massacre are acquitted.

OCTOBER 25
The First Continental Congress concludes.

17

« BEFORE

Before the Europeans arrived, North America was home to many Native American peoples.

EARLY TROUBLES
European colonization of the Americas had begun in the late 15th century. The first British settlement was established in 1585, when Sir Walter Raleigh founded a colony on **Roanoke Island**. The settlers clashed with local Native Americans, and when John White, one of the original settlers, returned to Roanoke in 1590, he found it **abandoned**: the word "CROATOAN," the name of a nearby island, carved into a tree, was the only clue to the fate of the colonists.

THE LOST COLONY OF ROANOKE

The **Thirteen Colonies**

The foundations of Britain's North American empire were laid in the 17th century as separate ventures—or colonies—established to exploit the vast resources of these new lands. Each colony had its own economic and political structure.

B ritain was not the only European nation in the business of empire-building: France founded a colony in Quebec in 1606, and there was a Dutch settlement in New Amsterdam, which would later become New York. Britain's first permanent colony—Virginia—was founded in 1607, and the twelfth settlement, Pennsylvania in 1682. Georgia, the thirteenth, was founded by James Oglethorpe in 1732.

The Thirteen Colonies each had separate agreements from the British government. The colonies started as risky ventures, whether by collective charter, individual proprietorship, or

Trading hub
The settlement at Newport, Rhode Island, was founded in 1639. Over the succeeding century, the township rid itself of the many pirates who had used it as a base, and Newport grew rich both from the slave trade and from distilleries making rum from Caribbean molasses.

as royal colonies. Also called Crown colonies, royal colonies were directly administered by an official chosen by the Crown. Charter colonies, on the other hand, were chartered by the Crown to a company or individual, and administered themselves. The status of a colony could be subject to change: the Virginia Company, for example, had its charter revoked in 1624 and became a Crown colony governed by an official appointed by the king.

The settlers had diverse origins. The majority were English, but there were around 200,000 Scots-Irish, and some 100,000 Germans accounted for one-third of Pennsylvania's population. Most colonists had gone to America seeking better opportunity: whether political, social, religious, or economic.

> Colonists sailed to America on long, crowded voyages. The *Mayflower*, carrying 135 people, took four months to reach Cape Cod in 1620.

Early challenges
The 17th century had seen bloody religious wars in Europe, and thousands had left the Old World to escape persecution. Going to America, however, was not an easy option. The colonists frequently clashed with the indigenous peoples: settlers in Virginia fought several wars with the Powhatan Confederacy through the 17th century. But this was only one of the dangers they faced. During the winter of 1609–10, Jamestown's first colonists endured a "Starving Time"—a period of low agricultural production fatally combined with the failure of relief sent from Britain to reach them.

Other settlements had their own problems and their own wars: the Massachusetts Bay Colony, which

witnessed the "Great Migration" of thousands of Puritans, beginning with the Puritan Fathers in 1620, was ravaged by King Philip's War against local Native Americans in the 1670s. The war was led by the intertribal leader Metacom, also known by the English name of King Philip.

In the Province of Carolina, the colonists battled Native American tribes, such as the Tuscarora and the Yamasee, from 1711 to 1717. The colony also struggled under ineffective government by the founding Lords Proprietors. Despite enjoying some years of prosperity, the colonists eventually petitioned parliament to replace these governors. In response, the Crown bought out seven of the eight Lords and in 1729 took control of the separated colonies of South Carolina and North Carolina.

Colonies flourish

The early challenges in colonial settlement could not, however, stop the tremendous development and growth witnessed in the 18th century. The population, approximately 250,000 in 1700, was roughly doubling every 25 years and in 1770 had grown to more than 2 million, about a third of the population of Great Britain. By the 1770s, African slaves accounted for about 20 percent of the population, some 42 percent of them in Virginia.

Each colony was unique, but there were three general groupings with shared economic, and therefore political interests, largely shaped by geography and climate. The New England colonies of Massachusetts, Connecticut, New Hampshire, and Rhode Island faced long, harsh winters and a short growing season. As a result, they relied on the sea for their livelihood in shipping and fishing, including trading and whaling. The middle colonies of New York, New Jersey, Pennsylvania, and Delaware had, by contrast, milder weather and a longer growing season. Grain farming and animal husbandry were the basis of their economies.

"I look upon **Virginia** as a **rib taken** from **Britain's side.**"

ALEXANDER SPOTSWOOD, GOVERNOR OF VIRGINIA, 1720

Select chamber
In the 18th century, the British House of Commons represented only narrow vested interests, based on the ownership of land. Neither American colonists nor great British cities such as Manchester elected representatives.

The southern colonies—Virginia, North Carolina, South Carolina, Georgia, and Maryland—had hotter climates and even longer growing seasons. Their plantations focused on cash crops—tobacco, indigo, and rice—producing quantities well in excess of what they needed for their own use. Slaves put in the hard labor to make these cash crops viable.

Economies of the 18th century were dominated by mercantilism. This system aimed to augment a nation's wealth by maximizing exports and limiting imports. A major imperial power, Britain expected the American colonies to support the economy of the mother country. The colonies were sources of raw materials and unfinished goods, which were then traded for finished products that were manufactured in Britain. While the British had a regulatory system of trade laws and duties in place, they did not strictly enforce these on the Thirteen Colonies, preferring to concentrate on European trading challenges. This policy of "salutary neglect" allowed the American colonies to trade with whomever they liked and still buy goods from Britain and provide it with raw materials.

Evolving institutions

British politics at the time were fractious; long-established factions often rested upon aristocratic families. The restructuring of the parliamentary constituencies was long overdue. Voting rights depended on the property qualifications of a small minority of Protestant males. Less than 3 percent of the British population could vote.

Across the Atlantic, a different system had developed. Every colony had a governor, usually appointed by the Crown. A council in each colony, a senior advisory body if not exactly an upper house, was also appointed by the Crown, but each colony also had an assembly elected by the people, which involved a much wider electorate than in Britain. As in Britain, the right to vote depended upon property qualifications, but the thresholds were considerably lower.

Most significant, however, was that until the middle of the 18th century, the British government left the Thirteen Colonies to attend to their own affairs. Colonial assemblies could and did initiate legislation—notably for financial issues—and by the 1760s the Thirteen Colonies had become self-governing societies with well-developed representative institutions.

AFTER »

Relations between Britain and its colonies were thrown into disarray when the Crown imposed new taxes.

UNITED FORCE
In the 1760s, wartime expense pushed Britain into tightening its grip on the North American colonies. The imposition of new taxes gave the Thirteen Colonies a collective grievance against Britain and a reason to pull together, leading to the Stamp Act Congress of 1765 **28–29** ». Seeing how they might benefit from an intercolonial body, the colonists then formed the **First Continental Congress** **44–45** » in 1774. The delegates reconvened at the **Second Continental Congress** **62–63** » in May 1775, to debate the moral, practical, and constitutional consequences of going to war against Britain.

Colonial Society

The Thirteen Colonies succeeded in creating miniature versions of the Old World. However, life in America was very different, and colonial societies showed great diversity compared both to Britain and to one another.

During the 18th century, the Thirteen Colonies enjoyed phenomenal growth, as a result of plentiful land and mushrooming trade. Class stratification existed, but took a different shape from that in Europe, being less rigid in its hierarchy and offering more social mobility. The scarcity of labor helped, and many landless workers sought to become tenants or take on leases in order to improve their prospects.

The majority of colonists lived in small towns and villages, each with their own tradesmen, merchants, farmers, and artisans. These categories encompassed an array of occupations— from apothecaries to printers and wig-makers—who were all specialized craftsmen, as well as being versed in business and trade.

Despite the social mobility, it paid to be wealthy, white, and male. White men could, and might be expected to, lead public lives, involving themselves with political affairs. Women, however, were usually relegated to the private domain of the home. Few would have questioned the traditional gender roles. In an anonymous letter printed in the *Boston Gazette* in 1740, "A Lady" postulated that "If Women were train'd up to Business from their early Years 'tis highly probable they would in general be more industrious, and get more Money than Men." Such opinions were not widely held, but

social mobility, demographics, labor shortages, and high mortality rates did open opportunities for some women in trade, crafts, and general medical practices.

White women were not equal to white men, but the colonies were also home to a large enslaved population, subordinate to both, which grew rapidly through the importation of new slaves and by childbirth. Slaves had no rights and were treated as personal property. In the South, slaves worked to increase their masters' yields on the plantations, and in the North in distilleries, shipyards, and stores.

23 Average age by which women were married.

7 Average number of children women bore.

Religious influences

The Church also had a powerful influence over colonial society, which, thanks to the large number of different religious groups that had settled the

Human bondage

Shackled on their legs, necks, and mouths, slaves were sent en masse to the American colonies. Many died on the slave ships; the survivors were sold at auction, some branded with hot irons.

BEFORE

Twelve of the Thirteen Colonies were founded in the 17th century. This initial period of settlement presented many challenges.

JOSTLING FOR SUPREMACY
The **Thirteen Colonies ‹‹ 18–19** were British territories established along the east of the North American continent. Other European powers with colonies on the continent were **France and Spain**. Many settlers were looking for new economic opportunities, but others, such as the **Pilgrim Fathers**, were seeking a place where they could freely practice their religion.

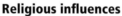

> " The place **is free for all Persuasions ...** they live **Friendly** and **Well** together."

GABRIEL THOMAS, *AN ACCOUNT OF WEST JERSEY AND PENNSYLVANIA,* 1698

land, was home to myriad Christian denominations—Anglicans, Baptists, Congregationalists, Episcopalians, Lutherans, Puritans, Presbyterians, Quakers, and Roman Catholics— and to communities of Jews. Despite varied ideologies, the colonists as a whole had a strong faith in divine will, which profoundly influenced their understanding of the world around them. For this reason, colonial society saw a close relationship between religious, political, economic, and social spheres.

However, by the 18th century colonial religion had begun to move away from the narrower orthodoxy of the previous century. Massachusetts

no longer resembled the strictly Puritan New England of old—and in the 1730s and '40s, the colonies were rocked by a religious revival movement: the Great Awakening.

A diverse movement, the Great Awakening spread among several Protestant sects. The emphasis was on individual spirituality, not doctrine, even to the point of encouraging interdenominational cooperation. Itinerant preachers helped the movement to spread, gaining celebrity status as newspapers announced and reported on their movements.

Preachers such as Gilbert Tennent, Jonathan Edwards, and George Whitfield were immensely skilled orators, and appealed to the hearts of their assembled crowds, inspiring thousands of colonists to convert and a new generation to follow their rhetorical lead. Reporting on the religious revival in 1737, Edwards wrote: "Our public assemblies were beautiful; the congregation was alive in God's service, everyone earnestly intent on the public worship."

Edwards really did mean "everyone." The personal nature of conversions appealed even to the colonists who were illiterate. African Americans were converted in large numbers, and Edwards's account described crowds overcome by feeling: "some weeping with sorrow, others with joy."

Educating the colonies

By 1760, the colonies shared a literacy rate that was higher than the mother country. The states in New England

Burgeoning congregations

Colonial church attendance rose significantly in the early 18th century, to 75–80 percent of the populace between 1700 and 1740. Religion played an important role in colonial life.

Putting down roots

By 1790, farmers made up 90 percent of the colonial labor force, yet farming methods differed according to region. For example, the thin soil of New England required more intensive work to yield sufficient crops.

had rates of around 85 percent for white males, reaching close to 100 percent in Boston. The lowest levels of literacy were in the Southern Colonies; Virginia's rate was 54–60 percent. However, there was variation even within these geographical categories: female literacy was about half that of males, and rates in urban areas far surpassed those in rural towns and villages.

By the middle of the century, the emphasis in elementary education was on reading, writing, and arithmetic—for practical purposes, such as Bible reading, as well as skills for trade and business. This took place in a growing number of local schools—small, usually one-room buildings in towns, which often doubled as a meeting house. Children of all ages attended, with boys and girls—if the latter were included—segregated. However, these schools were not attended by all children. Wealthier parents frequently employed tutors to teach their sons, while the poorest children received no schooling at all, and were expected to contribute to their family's income.

Beyond the white males of the elite governing classes, only a few colonists attended college, There were nine colleges by 1775, all with some major religious influence, including Anglican, Baptist, Puritan, and Presbyterian. The first "colonial college" was Harvard University, founded in the Massachusetts Bay Colony in 1636 as "New College." Thomas Jefferson's alma mater—the College of William and Mary—was founded in Virginia nearly 60 years later. All nine institutions had formal charters and granted degrees, mostly to student bodies numbering fewer than 100.

Mixed fortunes

The few large cities were home to about 10 percent of the colonial population. In 1760, the top five were Boston, Charleston (then called Charles Town), New York, Newport, and Philadelphia. Cities around major seaports acted as entry points to the New World from Britain, and had the largest concentration of "middling classes" who were enjoying increasing wealth.

As part of the British mercantile system, imports and exports to Britain and its colonies were constant.

Farmers growing crops for local and family consumption would sell the surplus to raise funds for buying British and West Indian imports, such as textiles, homewares, and luxuries.

Not everyone could afford these luxuries. A minority of the colonial population—the hardiest colonists—lived on the western frontier, in the backcountry. Close to the wilderness, and regularly encountering Native American threat, they led very different, often less prosperous and much harsher lives than those of the city-dwellers in the east.

Such variety in experiences led to the evolution of diverse local and regional

identities, as colonists confronted issues that were unique to their economy, status, or land. In spite of these identities, colonists had one thing in common: prior to the War of Independence, they still considered themselves to be British. They were mostly loyal subjects of their king, tied to their motherland by economy, government, friendship, and blood.

Little luxury
The colonists enjoyed hot chocolate, served from a long-handled pot sometimes made from copper. The low duties enjoyed by the colonists made this drink affordable.

AFTER

The Thirteen Colonies were parochial, with distinct perspectives. The colonies communicated with each other only on a limited basis.

BUILDING A UNION
Unified approaches to challenges were rare, even against the **French and Indian threat 24–25 »**. However, after 1763 the **debate over taxation** with Britain would breed a spirit of cooperation previously believed to be impossible **28–29 »**. Such community of purpose would lead to the **First Continental Congress** of 1774 **44–45 »** and later to the creation of a standing **Continental Army 64–65 »**. Eventually, the Thirteen Colonies would declare themselves to be an independent nation.

The **French** and **Indian War**

In the 1750s, the British and French became embroiled in a war in North America over control of the Ohio Country. The war was costly and had disastrous consequences for many colonists living on the frontier, as well as repercussions in Europe.

BEFORE

Major European and world powers, Britain and France had been at war intermittently for centuries.

IMPERIAL DOMINANCE
The 18th century was a time of **shifting diplomatic relationships** in Europe. Wars—rarely fought between two single belligerents and often about succession—pitted alliances of multiple European nations against each other. Britain and France were always on opposing sides. Both countries were **empires** with colonial possessions across the known world, and longstanding North American territories. Britain had the **Thirteen Colonies << 18–19**, while Canada and Louisiana belonged to France. The European colonies had been taken, by force or by agreement, from the Native American settlers.

In 1754, simmering tensions between Britain and France in America erupted in the French and Indian War, which escalated into a worldwide conflict, known in Europe as the Seven Years' War, from 1756. The major source of this tension was disputed land in the Ohio River Valley, which was largely settled by Native Americans. British colonists generally wanted to increase the security of the frontiers by pushing west with further settlement while settlers in French territories in modern-day Canada sought expanded trade, not land, as a basis for control.

Native Americans were not united in their allegiances. The most influential alliance, the Six Nations of the Iroquois Confederacy, mostly allied themselves with the British, with whom they had a relationship dating back to the early 17th century, formalized in a treaty known as the Covenant Chain. Other Nations, mostly enemies of the Iroquois people, chose to side with the French. Native American leaders chose carefully when deciding which side to align with—and when. They had to balance their increasing dependence upon trade goods against their desire to limit encroachment on their lands.

The fatal spark

In 1753, 21-year-old Lieutenant Colonel George Washington was sent to tell the French to evacuate the Ohio Country near Lake Erie, where French officials were building forts on land already claimed by the British. The French refused to leave, and over the course of the following year built Fort Duquesne (present-day Pittsburgh) near the strategic confluence of the Allegheny and Monongahela rivers. Washington returned to the Ohio Country in May 1754, now with reinforcements: 160 men, Seneca chief Tanaghrisson—known as Half King—and 12 warriors as guides.

On May 28, Washington's party crept up on 35 Frenchmen under the command of Ensign Joseph Coulon de Villiers de Jumonville. Details remain unclear, but the encounter became a bloody and lopsided ambush in which de Jumonville was killed, along with many of his men. Anticipating retribution, Washington withdrew to open ground called Great Meadows and built a small fortification, aptly

> ## "In this country a thousand men could **stop three thousand.**"
>
> CHEVALIER DE MONTREUIL TO PIERRE DE RIGAUD, JUNE 17, 1756

named Fort Necessity. He was right to be cautious. On July 3, a force of some 600 French and 100 Native Americans overwhelmed them. Washington surrendered, despite receiving reinforcements, after signing a capitulation badly translated from French in the soaking rain. Without Washington realizing it, the document included a clause placing responsibility for de Jumonville's death on him. This skirmish in the woods was the spark that ignited a new war between Britain and France.

War on many fronts

The American colonies were not prepared for war. Military operations were expensive and disruptive; supplying food and arms to British forces was also problematic. Early British operations fared badly—the defeat and death of Commander in chief Major General Edward Braddock,

Conquered stronghold
This engraving amalgamates three distinct stages of the Battle of the Plains of Abraham— the amphibious landing of British forces, their scaling of the cliffs, and the arrival of French troops.

in battle by the Monongahela River on July 9, 1755, was a devastating blow.

By 1756, hostilities had spread worldwide. Britain struggled to allocate resources to North America, the Caribbean, northern Europe, the Mediterranean, and India, and further British defeats followed. A British expedition to Louisbourg in Nova Scotia foundered, and the French siege of Fort William Henry, on Lake George, New York, ended with the garrison's surrender in August 1757. An assault on French-held Fort Carillon (later known as Ticonderoga) also ended in disaster in July 1758. At the same time, the western frontiers of Pennsylvania, Maryland, and Virginia saw much bloodshed resulting from Native American raids. Britain was losing the war.

The tide turns

The rise in 1757 of William Pitt the Elder as the principal British strategist began to pay dividends from August 1758. Pouring money into the conflict, Pitt sent thousands of British regulars to fight, and even reimbursed the colonies for the troops they had raised.

The French could not match this concentration of land and naval power, and the tide turned in Britain's favor. Both Fort Frontenac on Lake Ontario, and Fort Louisbourg, in distant Nova Scotia, fell to the British in August 1758. Fort Duquesne, in western Pennsylvania, fell in November. On December 4, British Lieutenant Colonel Henri Bouquet held a conference with the Delaware Nation in Duquesne, exhorting them to "send the French away out of your Country … they are a restless, mischievous People and the Disturbers of your Peace."

The following year became known as an *Annus Mirabilis* (Miraculous Year) for Britain, victorious against France on several continents. In parliament, Horace Walpole claimed that "Our bells are worn threadbare with ringing for victories." In North America, after months of trying to lure the French forces at Quebec into battle, the British General James Wolfe and his men landed at L'Anse-au-Foulon in the early hours of September 13 and made their way to the Plains of Abraham to take the fortress of Quebec. Receiving word of the British landing, the Marquis de Montcalm, the French commander, ordered his men to attack. Wolfe's army pushed forward with a close-range discharge of musket

fire, and the French army retreated. Both Montcalm and Wolfe were killed in the battle. Their victory allowed the British to lay siege to Quebec, which surrendered on September 18, 1759, thereby taking control of Canada.

Spain entered the war in 1762, but its alliance with France failed to deliver Portugal, as it had hoped, and led to additional losses around the world. British expeditions went on to end France's influence in India, seize the French Antilles and Spanish Cuba in the Caribbean, and take Spanish Manila in the Philippines. With the British victorious across several continents, Britain, France, and Spain signed the Treaty of Paris with Portuguese agreement on February 10, 1763. The terms included the cession of French territory in North America to Britain, including lands inhabited by Native Americans east of the Mississippi.

> **THE TREATY OF PARIS (1763) saw King Louis XV of France cede "in full right, Canada, with all its dependencies" to George III.**

The Proclamation Line

In October 1763, George III issued a royal proclamation to set out how the territories acquired by the peace treaty with France were to be governed. In particular, it set a boundary along the Appalachian Mountains for the Thirteen Colonies, designating this land as "Indian Reserve." Only the British Crown could buy or grant land to the west of this line, and colonists were forbidden from settling there. This was not well received by the colonists—many, including George Washington, held old grants west of the line that were now in doubt.

Military training
This drawing from a French drill manual shows soldiers how to present arms. During the time of the French and Indian War, infantrymen carried flintlock muskets to which they could attach a socket bayonet, allowing soldiers to charge the enemy when needed.

AFTER ❯❯

The French and Indian War left victorious Britain with difficult choices to make.

THE COST OF VICTORY
The **elimination of the French empire** in North America and acquisition of certain Spanish holdings gave the British the resources to develop even greater economic power. However, Britain's immediate concern was the **massive debt 28–29 ❯❯** incurred in achieving victory. The Thirteen Colonies seemed a natural source of necessary funds.

IMPACT ON NATIVE AMERICANS
The French and Indian War changed how Britain dealt with the Native Americans. British Commander in Chief Sir Jeffrey Amherst built larger garrisons, allowed fewer trading posts, and **treated the Native Americans like a conquered people**. The Native peoples realized that British rule posed a threat to their lands; while the French had concentrated on trading, many British colonists were more **eager to expand their land holdings**. As a result, within months of the end of the French and Indian War a confederation of Native peoples rose up to drive out the British in a war known as **Pontiac's Rebellion 36–37 ❯❯**.

French military map case
Maps were vital for exploration, colonial expansion, and waging war. Battle sites were carefully chosen, with detailed plans drawn up to take advantage of the hills, bridges, rivers, and terrain.

Testing Loyalties

The French and Indian War stretched loyalties to new limits. Some British officers, such as Robert Orme, the aide-de-camp to the British commander in chief Major General Edward Braddock, were openly disdainful of the American troops who fought alongside them. Many colonists, on the other hand, resented the failures of the British Army to protect them from the effects of war, as indigo plantation pioneer Eliza Pinckney explained to a friend in England.

"The General had now frequent opportunities of seeing and hearing of the appearance and disposition of the Virginia Recruits and companies. Mr. Allen had taken the greatest pains with them, and they performed their evolutions and firings as well as could be expected, but their languid, spiritless and unsoldierlike appearance considered with the lowness and ignorance of most of their Officers, gave little hopes of their future good behavior.**"**

FROM THE DIARY OF ROBERT ORME, 1755, PUBLISHED IN WINTHROP SARGENT'S *HISTORY OF AN EXPEDITION*, 1856.

"[The] Cherookees [have] become extreamly troublesome to us … and highland troops under Col. Montgomery, sent us by Genl. Amherst, have not done much more than exasperated the Indians to more cruel revenge, and they are now about to leave us to the mercy of these Barbarians. I hope the good people of England won't give all their superfluous money to French prisoners and to build foreign Churches, but reserve some for their poor fellow subjects in America for if they go on to make new conquests in America and neglect the protection of their old colonies they may have importations of distressed people from the Southernmost part of North America to exercise their charity upon.**"**

ELIZA LUCAS PINCKNEY, PLANTER, TO THE HONBLE. MRS. KING OF OCHAM COURT, SURREY, ENGLAND, JULY 1760

Allies out of control

The French had problems controlling their Native American allies. This engraving shows French commander Louis-Joseph de Montcalm, who had agreed to allow the safe withdrawal of British forces, failing to stop the Native American fighters under his command from attacking as the British evacuated Fort William Henry in 1757. Women, children, servants, and slaves were all caught up in the massacre.

BEFORE

The inhabitants of the Thirteen Colonies were proud to be British, but their relationship with the mother country was put under strain during the French and Indian War.

COMMERCIAL ORIGINS
The **Thirteen Colonies** ‹‹ **18–19** had been established in North America for commercial gain. The first, Virginia, was **established in 1607** by a charter granted to the Virginia Company. The colonies were governed by their own assemblies, but had **no representation** in the British House of Commons ‹‹ **22–23**.

SPOILS OF WAR
Britain had emerged victorious from the **French and Indian War** ‹‹ **24–25**. The Treaty of Paris, which ended the conflict in 1763, provided **substantial territorial gains** for Britain. However, the war with France had been costly, and had also angered many American colonists, who felt that the British had **failed to protect them** ‹‹ **26–27** from the adverse effects of a war fought on colonial soil.

BRITISH PRIME MINISTER 1712–70

GEORGE GRENVILLE

Author of the Sugar and Stamp Acts, George Grenville became prime minister after more than 20 years in parliament. His ministry, which began in 1763, was short-lived. Not only did his tax policies upset the colonists, but he was also unpopular at home, clashing with radical John Wilkes over freedoms established in the Bill of Rights, and with the king over the Regency Bill. He was dismissed in July 1765; Grenville never held office again, but supported colonial taxation until his death in 1770.

"If this be treason, make the most of it."
Patrick Henry's rousing speech on May 30, 1765 defended the Virginia Resolves, but his criticism of the king had contemporaries crying treason. He soon apologized, professing loyalty to George III.

Raising Revenue

After the French and Indian War, parliament had debts to pay. But when the British government introduced the Stamp Act in 1765 to raise revenue, colonial criticism was united, rational, and swift—triggering debate about the legality of "taxation without representation."

In the course of the French and Indian War, Britain's national debt had roughly doubled, from about £72 million in 1756 to well over £130 million in 1763—$15.3 billion to $27.2 billion in today's money. Postwar debt reduction was necessary, and parliament sought greater administrative and fiscal effectiveness—looking first to Britain itself and then to Ireland, India, the Caribbean, and North America.

A source of funds

As the considerable war debts had been incurred in the American colonies, parliament sought to raise money by taxing the colonists. George Grenville, prime minister in April 1763, began with the Sugar Act—technically, the American Revenue Act—which parliament approved on April 5, 1764. This replaced the expiring Molasses Act, which customs officials and the Royal Navy had already begun to enforce more

Sold to the Thirteen Colonies
British merchants were quick to capitalize on colonial opposition to the Stamp Act, manufacturing teapots like this one—thought to have been made in the Cockpit Hill Factory in Derby, England.

an increase in the number of peacetime troops in the Americas. Two-thirds of these troops would be stationed on the colonies' western frontier, the rest in the Caribbean—all areas vulnerable to French and Spanish encroachment, and Native American attacks. The act—passed

representation. The Virginia House of Burgesses passed a series of Resolves written by Patrick Henry on May 30, 1765, asserting that only Virginia's own assembly had the right to tax colonists in Virginia. Maryland and Rhode Island soon passed their own resolutions to this effect. Meanwhile, from May 1764, Bostonian Samuel Adams (see pp.34–35) became a leading critic of the Stamp Act. After joining the Massachusetts legislature in September 1765, he wrote that the act was "calculated to enslave and ruin us."

Decisive action

In Britain, the American crisis had already contributed to Grenville's departure from office, but in October, colonial leaders decided to come together to discuss a solution. Meeting in New York, the Stamp Act Congress, which included 27 delegates from nine colonies, crafted a "Declaration of Rights and Grievances" arguing that only colonial assemblies had the right to tax. The declaration was sent to both the king and parliament.

Opposition to the Stamp Act turned into a rallying cry for agitators across the colonies. The Sons of Liberty, comprising concerned citizens from all sections of colonial society, formed in Boston in 1765. Meeting secretly in small groups, the organization would grow considerably in the years ahead. Meanwhile, on the streets, reactions to the Stamp Act became increasingly violent. The bulk of it centered on the much-hated customs officials. Angry, unruly mobs intimidated local tax commissioners, rendering the officials increasingly ineffective. In Boston, for example, protesters hung up an effigy of Governor Hutchinson's brother-in-

law, the local Stamp Act commissioner. Protesters cut down the crude effigy and paraded it through the streets, shouting "Liberty, Property and No Stamps," before wreaking havoc on the local stamp office.

Too little, too late

The Stamp Act, clearly unenforceable, was repealed in March 1776 by the new prime minister, Lord Rockingham. Not only had the act generated little revenue, but it had also incited some unprecedented colonial resentment. Yet what most surprised the British was the unity of the opposition. Perplexed as well as thwarted, British officials were back to square one.

The Stamp Act planted a seed of dissent among the colonists. The British ignored these warning signs.

STUBBORN MINISTRIES
Although they repealed the Stamp Act, Rockingham's ministry also passed the **Declaratory Act** in 1766, asserting the right of parliament to tax the American colonies. The British tried taxing the colonists in 1767, when a new ministry under William Pitt the Elder introduced the **Townshend Acts 30–31** ».

KEY AGITATORS
For Samuel Adams and the Sons of Liberty, the Stamp Act was **only the beginning**. As they protested the Townshend Acts, their hometown became a hotbed of simmering tension. This would lead to the **Boston Massacre 30–31** » in 1770, while the tax on tea led to members of the Sons of Liberty **dumping tea in Boston Harbor 38–39** » in 1773.

> ## "It is ... the **undoubted right of Englishmen**, that **no taxes** be imposed on them but with **their own consent.**"
>
> DECLARATION OF RIGHTS AND GRIEVANCES OF THE COLONISTS IN AMERICA BY THE STAMP ACT CONGRESS, OCTOBER 7, 1765

rigorously. The Sugar Act lowered the tax on foreign molasses with the aim of increasing its collectability—and by extension the revenue. However, it also included, among other things, a list of goods that could only be exported to Britain. Merchants and traders were required to have detailed shipping documents, subject to strict inspection; Grenville also replaced all absentee customs officials and those prone to accepting bribes with new appointments.

The colonists objected strenuously to the Sugar Act. It came at a time of economic depression in the colonies, as lucrative contracts to provide British expeditions with food, supplies, and transportation had ended. To make matters worse, the newly appointed customs officials initially demonstrated an unprecedented dedication to duty in collecting the new tax.

Not just sugar

It soon transpired that the Sugar Act was only the beginning. The Stamp Act of 1765 was intended to pay for

on March 22, 1765—decreed that legal papers, periodicals, and documents would be required to use officially stamped paper from November of that year. The paper must be paid for in British, rather than colonial, currency.

The colonists had been debating early proposals for the Stamp Act since 1764, and its passage caused outrage throughout the territories. Lawyers cited the illegality of taxation without

Ousted by the mob

An effigy of Boston's Stamp Act commissioner, Andrew Oliver, was raised on the "Liberty Tree" in August 1765. The mob beheaded the figure and plastered it with "stamps." Within days, Oliver resigned from his post.

A VIEW OF PART OF THE TOWN OF BOSTON IN NEW ENGLAND AND BRITTISH SHIPS OF WAR LANDING THEIR TROOPS! 1768

1 Beaver 5 Mermaid   On friday Sept. 30th 1768. the Ships of War, armed Schooners, Transports, &c Came up the Harbour and Anchored round the Town: their Cannon loaded,   A Long Wharf
2 Senegal 6 Romney   a Spring on their Cables, as for a regular Siege. At noon on Saturday October the 1st the fourteenth & twentyninth Regiments, a detachment from the 59th Regt.   B Hancock's Wh.
3 Martin 7 Launceston and Train of Artillery, with two pieces of Cannon, landed on the Long Wharf: there Formed and Marched with insolent Parade, Drums beating, Fifes   C North Batter
4 Glasgow 8 Bonetta   playing, and Colours flying, up KING STREET. Each Soldier having received 16 rounds of Ponder and Ball.

Peacekeepers

Patriot Paul Revere witnessed the arrival of British troops at Boston. They were instructed to quell unrest and restore order in 1768. Revere later described how they "formed and marched with insolent parade, drums beating, fifes playing, and colors flying."

Boston Erupts

Britain's efforts to tax the colonies hit the colonists hard. Little heed was paid to their growing sense of identity, and British enforcement was heavy-handed. Resentment grew, particularly in Boston, which was becoming a powder keg of opposition to colonial rule.

« BEFORE

Britain needed to raise funds and believed greater control over its American colonies to be part of the solution.

ORGANIZED RESISTANCE

The introduction of the **Stamp Act** in 1765 **« 28–29** to raise funds in the Thirteen Colonies outraged the colonists. Some took to the streets to protest, and a **Stamp Act Congress** met in New York to discuss the matter. In July 1765, George III replaced George Grenville with a **new prime minister**, the Marquess of Rockingham, who repealed both the Stamp and Sugar Acts.

COMMEMORATIVE TEAPOT OF 1766

Stamp Act Repeal'd

Although Britain repealed the troublesome Stamp and Sugar Acts, parliament still asserted its right to tax the colonists. It passed the Declaratory Act in March 1766, stating that parliament had "full power and authority to make laws and statutes of sufficient force and validity to bind the colonies and people of America ... in all cases whatsoever." The act directly opposed the freedoms espoused by the *Declaration of Rights and Grievances* written by the Stamp Act Congress, which stated that "All resolutions, votes, orders, and proceedings ... whereby the power and authority of the parliament of Great Britain to make laws and statutes ... is denied ... are hereby declared to be utterly null and void."

Despised duties

Many in parliament believed that the repeal of the Stamp Act had been too conciliatory toward the colonists. After the Marquess of Rockingham's ministry fell in July 1766, William Pitt the Elder, recently made Earl of Chatham, became leader of a coalition government. Pitt delegated the matter of taxing the American Colonies to Charles Townshend, his Chancellor of the Exchequer.

Townshend proposed four new acts of parliament, passed in June 1767. The first of the four Townshend Acts, as they became known, shut down the New York assembly for refusing to execute the governor's instructions to house British troops, as required by the Quartering Act of 1765. The colony had instead paid £3,000 ($552,000 today) toward the soldiers' upkeep. The other Townshend Acts taxed lead,

glass, paints, paper, and tea, and were met with a slow-burning fury among the American colonists.

Colonial outcry was multifaceted. In December 1767, the first of John Dickinson's *Letters from a Farmer in Pennsylvania* was published. This was one in a series of 12 essays by the Philadelphia lawyer—later a member of the First Continental Congress—criticizing the Townshend Acts. The letters, which were widely circulated and reprinted, played a vital role in uniting colonial opinion against the legislation and prompted the Massachusetts House of Representatives to take up the case.

Samuel Adams's Massachusetts Circular Letter, passed by the colony's House of Representatives in 1768 and sent to the other 12 colonies, argued that the Townshend duties were not just bad, but unconstitutional. The letter infuriated the British, and when Massachusetts refused to revoke it, the assembly was dismissed.

As these "official" responses to the acts gathered attention, so did the reactions of the everyday colonist. Citizens gathered, assemblies met, and merchants agreed to stop importing British goods. Likewise, many colonists ceased purchasing taxed items, and instead made their own paper and spun their own cloth. But the response to the duties was not just economic. Some colonists turned to violence against the officials enforcing the duties, while the Sons of Liberty, a secret society formed to fight taxation, erected "liberty poles" as symbols of their dismay.

> **LIBERTY POLE** A tall wooden staff, mounted with a Phrygian cap, liberty poles were both meeting places and symbols of dissent.

Uneasy occupation

Townshend established a Board of Customs Commissioners for America, with incentives to convict violators. He intended to use some of the funds raised to pay the salaries of the colonial governors, previously the responsibility of the colonial assemblies. Another British reorganization in 1768 created a new ministerial position, Secretary of State for the Colonies. Until then, the colonies, along with southern England, Wales, and Ireland, had fallen under the jurisdiction of the Secretary of State for the Southern Department. Now, one minister, the Earl of Hillsborough, appointed in February 1768, could concentrate on

Tackling Boston

Hillsborough instructed the British commander in chief in America, Major General Thomas Gage, to leave his headquarters in New York City and go to Boston to take command. Gage immediately sent 4,000 troops to Boston, but when the regiments arrived in the city's harbor, officials announced that there were no facilities available to house them, leaving the Redcoats to camp on commons and in public buildings. This set the scene for serious friction between the inhabitants of Boston and the British troops. In addition, in the first few months after the Redcoats' arrival, Gage lost as many as 70 soldiers to desertion, as men slipped away from the army and into the civilian population. Private Richard Ames was executed on Boston Common to set an example against desertion in October 1768.

Tensions in Boston were likely exacerbated by those in New York, where the Sons of Liberty had published a pamphlet *To the Betrayed Inhabitants of the City*, leading to clashes in the streets between colonists and soldiers. In January 1770, the British cut down a New York liberty pole in a deliberate act of provocation—the fifth such pole to fall at the hands of British

"Our City is yet a Garrison filled with armed Men."

COMMITTEE OF THE BOSTON SONS OF LIBERTY TO JOHN WILKES, NOVEMBER 4, 1769

soldiers. This action sparked the Battle of Golden Hill outside New York City on January 19, 1770. It was more a brawl than a battle—no one was killed in the clash—but further disorder on the streets followed. Rising tempers and fraying nerves added to the underlying tension.

Boiling point

Boston had an uneasy winter. While multiple factions debated the Townshend Acts, civilians and soldiers shared a mutual antipathy. The *Journal of Occurrences*, a series of news accounts, reported many offenses made by soldiers against citizens; although tales of rapes and beatings were highly exaggerated, they nonetheless fueled the colonists' anger.

Boston then witnessed two major incidents that stirred the cauldron of resentment. First, in February 1770, a young boy named Christopher Seider was killed by a customs official. The *Boston Gazette* made much of his death, and his funeral was impressively attended. The second incident occurred on the night of March 5, when the British were unprepared for action, having transferred two regiments, half of the infantry strength, to Halifax in Canada. Popular anger boiled over when a British sentry became embroiled with a civilian who had insulted an officer. A small squad under Captain Thomas Preston went to the sentry's rescue. A menacing crowd soon gathered and pelted the soldiers with whatever they could lay their hands on. In the chaos, one soldier was hit by ice, then slipped. As he recovered, he fired his firelock, and other shots rang out in answer. Five civilians, starting with Crispus Attucks, were killed, and six were wounded. Boston was on the brink of anarchy.

Arriving on the scene, Lieutenant Governor Thomas Hutchinson restored calm. Preston and his soldiers were jailed and later stood trial for murder, represented by Patriots John Adams and Josiah Quincy. The case resulted in acquittals and two minor sentences, but the so-called "Boston Massacre," was not forgotten. Five civilians had died at the hands of His Majesty's troops. The damage to the British cause had been done.

Inflammatory account

The obituaries of Samuel Gray, Samuel Maverick, James Caldwell, and Crispus Attucks—four of the five men killed by British troops in the Boston Massacre—were published in the *Boston Gazette* on March 12, 1770, fanning the flames of outrage.

AFTER »

The events in Boston helped to stoke anti-British sentiment throughout the colonies. Meanwhile, the unpopular Townshend Acts failed to resolve the dispute over taxation.

ALL BUT TEA
British politicians were stupefied by the **colonial reaction** to the Townshend Acts—the assemblies' petitions and resolutions, the large-scale intimidation, and increased political violence. Eventually, another new British ministry, under **Lord North**, repealed the acts on April 12, 1770, but retained the **tax on tea**.

TROUBLED CITY
The Boston Massacre was not the end of the unrest in Boston. The **Boston Tea Party 38–39 »** of 1773 set the stage for the entire War of Independence—and led to the punitive **Intolerable Acts 42–43 »**, which sparked further dissent. The first battles of the War of Independence were fought in the area around Boston, at **Lexington and Concord 54–55 »** in April 1775 and at **Bunker Hill 58–59 »** a few months later.

MASSACRE VICTIM 1723–70

CRISPUS ATTUCKS

Born around 1723 to a slave father and Native American mother, Crispus Attucks was raised in Framingham, Massachusetts. Sold to Deacon William Brown at 16, Attucks ran away on September 30, 1750; three notices about the escape were posted in the *Boston Gazette*, offering a £10 ($2,250 today) reward—to no avail. Attucks became "Michael Johnson," working in Boston as a seaman and ropemaker for about 20 years. On March 5, 1770, he responded to calls to demonstrate against British troops. He was felled by two musket balls, making him the first casualty of the War of Independence.

The **Boston Massacre**

Enmity between the people of Boston and occupying soldiers peaked in March 1770 when a mob attacked a British sentry. Captain Thomas Preston's men, arriving on the scene, fired at the jeering crowd. Three people were killed instantly—two died later from wounds—inflaming anti-British sentiment. That October, thanks to the evidence of eyewitnesses such as apothecary Richard Palmes, Preston and his men were put on trial: two were found guilty of manslaughter.

"I immediately went there and saw Captain Preston at the head of six or eight soldiers with guns breast high and bayonets fixed ... that instantly I saw a piece of snow or ice fall among the soldiers on which the soldier at the officer's right hand stepped back and discharged his gun. At the space of some second the soldier at his left fired next, and the others one after the other. After the first gun was fired, I heard the word 'fire,' but who said it I know not. Turning myself to the left I saw one man dead, distant about six feet; I having a stick in my hand made a stroke at the soldier who fired, and struck the gun out of his hand. I then made a stroke at the officer, my right foot slipped, this brought me on my knee, the blow falling short ... I saw the soldier that fired the first gun endeavoring to push me through with his bayonet, on which I threw my stick at his head, the soldier starting back, gave me an opportunity to jump from him into Exchange Lane, or I must have been inevitably run through my body.

I looked back and saw three persons laying on the ground, and perceiving a soldier stepping round the corner as I thought to shoot me, I ran down Exchange Lane ... and followed Mr. Gridley with several others persons with the body of Captain Morton's apprentice up to the prison house, and saw he had a ball shot through his breast; at my return I found that the officers and soldiers were gone.**"**

RICHARD PALMES, AT THE TRIAL OF CAPTAIN THOMAS PRESTON, OCTOBER 1770

Fueling the fire
Propagandists such as the engraver Paul Revere (see pp.56–57) seized on the massacre to justify the Patriot rebellion. Revere copied this engraving, to reproduce in print, from a drawing by Henry Pelham.

PATRIOT ACTIVIST Born 1722 Died 1803

Samuel **Adams**

> "**All** might be **free** if they **valued freedom,** and defended it as they ought."
>
> SAMUEL ADAMS, ON HEARING THE GUNFIRE AT LEXINGTON, APRIL 19, 1775

Boston radical Samuel Adams was the leading theoretician and activist in the early stages of the War of Independence. An admiring Thomas Jefferson once called him "the patriarch of liberty." Modern historians have queried whether Sam Adams was really, as was once believed, the hidden hand behind major events such as the riots that led to the Boston Massacre in 1770 or the Boston Tea Party of 1774. None, however, have denied the impact of his polemical writings or his efforts to invent new forms of political resistance.

Puritan values

Adams was born the son of a prosperous Boston merchant who was also a deacon in the Congregationalist Church and a significant figure in the city's political life. Sam Adams inherited from his father a firm belief in the Puritan virtues of honesty and austerity, and a critical attitude toward British royal officials.

In 1739, Deacon Adams was involved in a land speculation project that failed through the actions of the Massachusetts' royal governor and the British parliament. Financially disastrous for the Adams family, the fiasco added a personal bitterness to their distrust of Britain and its agents.

Sam Adams followed in his father's footsteps by entering the Boston Caucus, a radical political club with considerable influence in the city. Not having his father's aptitude for business, however, he proved barely capable of earning a living. All his energy was devoted to public issues. His cousin John Adams, future second president of the United States, once wrote of Sam that he was perhaps "too attentive to the public and not enough so to himself and his family." Money problems were a permanent feature of his life.

Until the 1760s, Sam Adams was known only in the world of politically disaffected Bostonians. It was the dispute over British taxation following the Sugar Act of 1764 that brought him to wider notice, when the Boston

Defender of rights
Samuel Adams points at the Massachusetts charter, a document he argued protected the rights of the colony's citizens against abuse of royal power. This portrait was made by John Copley around 1772.

Making a stand
The statue of Adams outside Boston's Faneuil Hall shows him standing resolute with folded arms, as he supposedly stood after demanding the withdrawal of British troops from the city in 1770.

Trade wars
British soldiers watch over the unloading of supplies at Boston in this period engraving. In 1774, the harbor was the scene of the Boston Tea Party, an act of sabotage backed by Samuel Adams.

Town Meeting—the city's assembly—asked him to write instructions for its representatives to the Massachusetts assembly. These contained a statement of the principle of "no taxation without representation." The following year he was elected to the Massachusetts House of Representatives.

Forming a united front
Between 1765 and 1774, Adams was tireless in organizing resistance to measures that he regarded as offenses to the colonists' rights and freedoms. A gifted propagandist, he wrote articles in opposition to British rule in Massachusetts. In his political texts, he formulated a principled justification of rebellion, minting phrases that were later used by Jefferson in the Declaration of Independence.

Adams advocated novel tactics of resistance, such as trade boycotts, and grasped the need for the colonies to unite. His idea of sending a circular letter from the Massachusetts assembly to other colonies in 1768 drew a repressive response from the British authorities. With even sharper subversive intent, his Committee of Correspondence, set up in 1772, established communication between radicals in the different colonies.

The British authorities denounced Adams as a rabble-rouser who used mob violence for political ends.

Harnessing the press
In spring 1768, Adams circulated a letter attacking the revenue-raising Townshend Acts to the assemblies of the 13 colonies. The *Boston Gazette* featured the text on its front page.

In 1765, they accused him of inciting Boston mobs to attack the home of Governor Thomas Hutchinson, and in 1770 they detected his hand behind the disorders that led to the Boston Massacre of civilians by British soldiers. In both cases, Adams defended the rioters in print but denied incitement.

Whatever the truth, it is hard to believe he was not involved in organizing the Boston Tea Party in December 1773 (see pp.38–39), when a shipment of tea was dumped into Boston Harbor following his address to the Boston Town Meeting. Although it is no longer believed that his closing words—"This meeting can do nothing further to save the country"—was a signal to attack the ships, he is likely to have known that a plan was afoot to take action.

After the Boston Tea Party, Adams led the defiant response to the Coercive Acts (see pp.42–43) in Massachusetts. He was a prime mover in organizing the Continental Congress in Philadelphia and attended as a delegate—the first time he had traveled outside his own state. It was believed that the British military expedition to Lexington in April 1775 was designed to capture Adams and his colleague John Hancock. Forewarned by Paul Revere, the pair escaped. This incident enhanced Adams's reputation: when his cousin John Adams went to France in 1776, the French were disappointed that he was not "the famous Adams."

Postwar role
After 1775, Sam Adams played a less prominent role in the War of Independence and the construction of the United States. He was, however, a signatory of the Declaration of Independence, and did solid work on congressional committees. In 1779, he helped draft a constitution for Massachusetts. He advocated a minimal central government for the United States but supported adopting the Constitution. Despite his rebellious past, he backed the use of force to suppress uprisings against the republic. The chief concern of his later years was the spread of corruption, which ran counter to the austere virtue that he exemplified in his own life.

> "It is a good **maxim** in politics… to put and keep the **enemy** in the **wrong**."
>
> SAMUEL ADAMS, LETTER TO RICHARD HENRY LEE, MARCH 21, 1775

SAMUEL ADAMS'S GRAVE

Westward Expansion and the **Frontier**

For many American colonists, the expulsion of France from Canada and its lands east of the Mississippi cleared the way for the colonies to expand inland. However, the British government and the Native American peoples of the region had different expectations.

« BEFORE

Colonial expansion had led to numerous conflicts, both with competing European empires and the Native peoples they dispossessed.

FRONTIER CLASHES
Britain had been engaged in **frontier warfare «« 18–19** with Native American tribes from the beginning of their settlement of North America. By the 18th century they were benefiting from an **increasing dependence** on trade goods among several Native tribes, but such interaction did not preclude war.

PEACE TERMS
The Treaty of Paris of February 10, 1763, ended the **French and Indian War «« 24–25**, and effectively eliminated the French empire in North America. Britain won New France east of the Mississippi as well as Spanish Florida, to add to the Thirteen Colonies that they already possessed.

EARLY COLONIAL MATCHLOCK MUSKET, USED BY MILITIA AND NATIVE AMERICANS

The Thirteen Colonies had experienced decades of costly warfare with Native American tribes. Each peace treaty brought not peace, but relief. Culture clashes continued to breed hostility, which became increasingly uncompromising.

Pontiac's Rebellion
The demise of the French empire worried Native leaders. Even the Iroquois, stalwart British allies, understood the colonists' hunger for land. These concerns, combined with a reduction in "gifts" to tribal chiefs—a cost-cutting measure of British commander in chief Sir Jeffrey Amherst—sparked the Pontiac's Rebellion, a Native American upheaval, unforeseen and extensive, that lasted from 1763 until 1766.

Pontiac, an Ottawa war chief, and his supporters achieved devastating early success. Some eight British forts fell. As the Pennsylvania, Maryland, and Virginia frontiers were set aflame, Amherst commented, "We must use every stratagem in our power to reduce them." But the larger British posts held out, including Detroit and Fort Pitt. Detroit was besieged but never cut off, as British vessels still operated on nearby Lake Erie. On July 31, 1763, however, Pontiac scored a notable victory at the Battle of Bloody Run, defeating an attack on his camp, near Detroit. This

period of Indian success ended with the Battle of Bushy Run on August 5–6, when Colonel Henry Bouquet came under attack as he led a relief column of 450 men toward Fort Pitt. Feigning military weakness, Bouquet provoked an all-out charge by the Native American warriors, who were then shredded by British volleys. Fort Pitt was relieved and Pontiac soon abandoned the siege of Detroit.

Enforcement of the Proclamation Line of 1763, drawn by the British to define Native American territory west of the Appalachian Mountains, helped conciliate the Native tribes, and Pontiac agreed to peace, but not surrender, in July 1766. However, the proclamation was not meant to set a permanent boundary. It was modified to colonial advantage in the 1768 Treaty of Fort Stanwix, negotiated with the Iroquois by William Johnson.

Lord Dunmore's War
No treaty withstood the pressures of colonial expansion for long. In 1773–74, colonists began to settle in Kentucky, in territory that had been allocated to the Shawnee people at Fort Stanwix. The first attempt by trapper Daniel Boone in September 1773 was abandoned after a group of Delaware, Shawnee, and Cherokee tribesmen captured his son and tortured him to death. But the following year, in April 1774, settlers struck back. A group under Captain Michael Cresap attacked the Shawnee at Pipe Creek, and later that month some of Cresap's associates murdered a group of Mingo at Yellow Creek.

These events sparked "Lord Dunmore's War," in which Virginia's royal governor called upon militia to neutralize the Native threat. They succeeded in doing so: after the Battle of Point Pleasant, on October 10, 1774, the Shawnee were forced to cede lands in the Treaty of Camp Charlotte. But again, peace would not last.

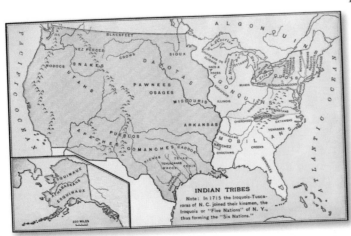

Tribal lands in 1715
From the time of the earliest European settlement, Native American peoples were pushed steadily west. Many tribes in the east of the tribal areas went to war with the encroaching Europeans.

Burning of Deerfield
Frontier skirmishes were by no means new. In 1704, Deerfield, Massachusetts, then an English border settlement, was attacked by French troops and Native Americans during Queen Anne's War.

COLONIAL OFFICIAL, 1715–74

WILLIAM JOHNSON

For many years, Johnson was Britain's Superintendent of Indian Affairs for the northern colonies. From the late 1730s he developed a large property in the north of New York province and became an honorary Mohawk chief. He persuaded many Iroquois to fight for Britain in the French and Indian War. He then opposed the policies of General Amherst that led to Pontiac's Rebellion and tried to prevent the growth of a general anti-British alliance among Native American peoples.

AFTER

Expansion of the colonies was an issue at the very heart of America's rebellion.

QUEBEC EXPANDS
The shifting western boundaries of the Thirteen Colonies continued to generate disagreement. The **Quebec Act of 1774 42–43 ≫** stirred up more anger, when vast tracts of old New France, west of the Proclamation Line, were allocated to Quebec.

NATIVE AMERICAN ALLIES
When war broke out between Britain and the rebel colonists, the majority of **Native American tribes** supported the British **228–29 ≫** because they were seen to be more likely to **limit expansion** of the colonies. Kentucky and the Carolinas saw extensive attacks by Native Americans.

The **Boston Tea Party**

Boston was once again at the center of colonial unrest in the wake of the Tea Act of 1773, which was intended to help the struggling East India Company. As the Sons of Liberty targeted commissioners, 5,000 colonists met at the Old South Meeting House to plot their next step.

Copycat tactics
In 1772, the colonists who boarded HMS *Gaspee* disguised themselves as Native Americans: in 1773, participants in the Boston Tea Party followed suit.

« BEFORE

Relations between Britain and its American colonies had been cordial for the first half of the century. This all changed during the 1760s.

UNPOPULAR LEGISLATION
A series of acts that attempted to **tax the Thirteen Colonies «« 28–29** caused uproar—especially in Boston—and culminated in the **military occupation «« 30–31** of that city in 1768. The British, hoping to pay off debts from the **French and Indian War «« 24–25,** had become increasingly frustrated by colonists' insistence upon "no taxation without representation."

BRITISH TROOPS OCCUPIED BOSTON FROM 1768

In the early 1770s, British political attention mainly focused on the deteriorating situation in Europe. Britain had few allies. Its popularity on the Continent following the Seven Years' War, in which it gained new territories, was virtually nil. While the Royal Navy, in reality whittled down by postwar austerity, flexed its strength in "naval demonstrations," the other major powers watched, waited, and plotted for the opportunity to cut Britain down to size.

Meanwhile, the Thirteen Colonies were preoccupied with a host of internal issues. In Massachusetts, a furore blew up over the discovery of letters to the British government written by Governor Thomas Hutchinson. The correspondence revealed little sympathy for the complaints of his fellow colonists; in fact, the letters could have been written by the members of the British cabinet themselves.

The *Gaspee* affair

By 1772, imports from Britain to the Thirteen Colonies were at an all-time high. The repeal of the Townshend Acts had left the tax on tea standing, though this had not caused much of a stir up to that point. However, the apparent truce between Britain and the colonies had not altered the ongoing battle between customs officials, Royal Navy enforcers, smugglers, and merchants, some of whom worked for both sides.

In early 1772, the Royal Navy transferred the schooner HMS *Gaspee* to the waters around Rhode Island in order to deal with these seasoned law-breakers. The *Gaspee*'s Lieutenant William Dudingston and his men harassed the local merchants, delaying them with extra and unnecessary customs inspections.

In June 1772, the *Gaspee* gave chase to a packet sloop, the *Hannah*, as it left Newport. The sloop's captain, Benjamin Lindsay, lured Dudingston's vessel over a sandbar off nearby Namquad Point, running the *Gaspee* aground. When Lindsay landed at Providence, Rhode Island,

with news of his success, an excitable mob gathered, boarded the *Gaspee*, and burned it, taking Dudingston and his men captive. This focused parliament's attention more firmly on the colonies. As George III commented to Lord North in August 1772: "We must get the colonies into order before we engage with our neighbor."

A government commission convened in January 1773 to investigate the *Gaspee* affair, but it could not identify and prosecute any perpetrators. The commission still managed to enrage the colonists when word leaked out that they were authorized to transport suspects to England for trial.

Colonial communication

For the colonists, the *Gaspee* affair provided the necessary incentive to organize permanent Committees of Correspondence—local bodies set up to address specific issues. Massachusetts assembled its permanent committee on November 2, 1772, and Virginia followed suit on March 12, 1773. Members of the Virginia committee took on the responsibility of encouraging contact between the Thirteen Colonies.

These committees comprised the most influential men in the colonies, such as lawyers, notable businessmen, and former military men. They ensured information circulated within each colony, and between colonies. The committees also functioned as shadow governments in the event that a governor dissolved a colonial legislature. In New Hampshire, the colonial assembly was dissolved several times by Governor Wentworth, largely because it kept voting to establish a Committee of Correspondence.

Tea controversy

The British parliament had more to worry about than the *Gaspee*. The East India Company, which governed British colonies on the Indian subcontinent, was in trouble. Accused of greed and corruption, hindered by a European credit crisis, and facing war and famine on the subcontinent, in 1772 the East India Company appealed for help to avoid bankruptcy.

Parliament responded by passing the Tea Act of May 10, 1773, abolishing tax on tea in Britain imported by the East India Company, which made it even cheaper than tea smuggled from the Netherlands. However, although

Loathsome commissioners
This Philadelphia newspaper, written under the pseudonym "Scaevola," compared the newly appointed tea commissioners to Stamp Act officials. If they enforced the Tea Act, Scaevola argued, they would prove "detestable and infamous."

TO THE
Commiffioners
APPOINTED by the *EAST-INDIA* COMPANY, for the SALE of
TEA, in America.
GENTLEMEN,

removed the tea tax at home in Britain, it was maintained in the American colonies.

These developments cast the British in a negative light—and confirmed colonial claims that the small tax retained on tea after the repeal of the Townshend Acts was essentially direct

waged war in the press, but by November they had begun to employ more threatening tactics, hoping the power of the mob would cow the consignees into abandoning their commissions. However, the officials, some of whom were relatives of Governor Hutchinson, stood firm.

Public opinion
The Boston Tea Party was witnessed by a crowd of like-minded colonists. Although this 1846 lithograph suggests otherwise, the spectators were largely silent and sober in the face of such a serious statement of colonial dissent.

"This **Destruction** of the Tea is so bold, so daring, so firm".

THE DIARY OF JOHN ADAMS, DECEMBER 17, 1773

taxation. Debate turned into action in Philadelphia and New York. Activists such as the Sons of Liberty would not wait for parliament to reconsider, and threatened violence. As a result, no tea was landed in either colony.

Boston, meanwhile, was once again a hotbed of tension. The Sons of Liberty directed their attention to the officials, or "consignees," who awaited deliveries at the harbor, hoping to convince them to turn back incoming tea shipments. At first, the activists

Notorious protest
Customs regulations obliged ships to follow various procedures upon docking in port, and this set a clock ticking. The first ship to arrive in Boston Harbor was HMS *Dartmouth*. Hearing of its impending arrival, about 5,000 Boston colonists convened at the Old South Meeting House, and resolved not to pay the duties on the tea. The political activist Samuel Adams asked the assembled crowd, "Is it the firm resolution of this body

that the tea shall not only be sent back, but that no duty shall be paid thereon?" The crowd replied with a resounding "Yes."

Boston was at an impasse. The owner of the *Dartmouth* could not obtain official permission to return to England with unloaded cargo; and Governor Hutchinson refused to allow the ship to leave without paying duty. The Boston colonists reacted on December 16. At the Old South Meeting house, Samuel Adams reportedly declared: "This meeting can do nothing more to save the country." They would not allow the tea to be landed. That same night about 50 colonists, disguised in Native American dress, boarded three tea ships. In a premeditated act of protest, they dumped some 90,000 lbs (40,800 kg) of tea into Boston Harbor.

AFTER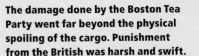

The damage done by the Boston Tea Party went far beyond the physical spoiling of the cargo. Punishment from the British was harsh and swift.

COLONIES UNITE
Despite widespread frustration with the British authorities, colonial sympathy for a nighttime raid that had shown utter disregard for the respect of private property was still quite limited. Only the **severity of British retribution**, carried out in a series of economic, legal, and political clampdowns, changed colonial attitudes significantly in Boston's favor 42–43 ».

READY FOR WAR
Britain's retribution led the colonists to discuss taking up arms, readying **local militias** 64–65 ». The British, meanwhile, had their eye on the leading activists, particularly Bostonians Samuel Adams and John Hancock.

The Tea Saboteurs

The 200 or so men who took part in the Boston Tea Party were proclaimed as the "Boston Boys." Years later, some of the participants, including George Hewes, a Boston shoemaker, recalled the night they boarded the tea ships disguised as Native Americans and threw the cargo overboard.

"It was now evening, and I immediately dressed myself in the costume of an Indian, equipped with a small hatchet, which I and my associates denominated the tomahawk, with which, and a club, after having painted my face and hands with coal dust in the shop of a blacksmith I repaired to Griffin's wharf. When we arrived at the wharf, there were three of our number who assumed an authority to direct our operations, to which we readily submitted. They divided us into three parties, for the purpose of boarding the three ships which contained the tea at the same time ... We then were ordered by our commander to open the hatches and take out all the chests of tea and throw them overboard, and we immediately proceeded to execute his orders, first cutting and splitting the chests with our tomahawks, so as thoroughly to expose them to the effects of the water. In about three hours from the time we went on board, we had thus broken and thrown overboard every tea chest to be found in the ship, while those in the other ships were disposing of the tea in the same way, at the same time. We were surrounded by British armed ships, but no attempt was made to resist us.

We then quietly retired to our several places of residence, without having any conversation with each other, or taking any measures to discover who were our associates. There appeared to be an understanding that each individual should volunteer his services, keep his own secret, and risk the consequence for himself. No disorder took place during that transaction, and it was observed at that time that the stillest night ensued that Boston had enjoyed for many months."

GEORGE HEWES, A PARTICIPANT IN THE BOSTON TEA PARTY, FROM *A RETROSPECT OF THE BOSTON TEA-PARTY, WITH A MEMOIR OF GEORGE R. T. HEWES,* 1834

Popular heroes
In time, people came to view the Boston Boys as triumphant heroes, as this lithograph shows. The British, however, responded with the so-called Intolerable Acts, which, among other things, closed the port of Boston to commerce.

The **Intolerable Acts**

Shocked by the audacity of the Tea Party, parliament passed a series of acts in 1774 to punish Boston for its disobedience. They proved incendiary: colonies once critical of Boston changed their tune and joined together to discuss their grievances.

« **BEFORE**

Higher taxes and a greater use of British military muscle to control protest had served to alienate the colonists. Boston had become a focus of colonial dissent.

THE TAX DEBATE
Britain had angered colonists in the aftermath of the **French and Indian War** by increasing taxation « **28–29**—first through the **Stamp Act of 1765** and later with the **Townshend Acts of 1767** « **30–31**—in order to pay its debts.

COLONIAL DISSENT
British troops had arrived in Boston to maintain order in 1768. Tensions in the town had then reached boiling point in 1770, when five colonists were killed in the **Boston Massacre** « **30–31**. The contentious tax on tea had remained in place—even after the repeal of other disputed duties—and had resulted in an infamous act of rebellion in Boston's port, the **Boston Tea Party** « **38–39**, in 1773.

London learned of the Boston Tea Party in January 1774. Demands for swift, punitive action came from all quarters in Britain: the wanton destruction of private property silenced the government's opponents, swung moderates, and empowered hardliners. As a result, five Acts of Parliament—the Coercive Acts, known in the Thirteen Colonies as the "Intolerable Acts"—were passed between March and June 1774.

Punitive measures

The first measure—the Boston Port Act—shut down Boston Harbor from June 1, an economic strangulation that aroused widespread colonial sympathy. The second statute—the Massachusetts Regulatory Act—gave the openly loyalist governor, Thomas Hutchinson, the power to approve all appointments to the council, plus those of judges and local officials, and stipulated that jurists would no longer be elected but be appointed by sheriffs instead. The act also overturned the Massachusetts charter of 1691. The colonial assembly remained, but the governor had to approve the calling of town meetings.

Third, the Impartial Administration of Justice Act—sometimes called the Murder Act—granted British officials the right to extradite accused criminals to England or another colony for trial, in order to avoid juries that might show too much sympathy toward colonists. The fourth measure, an updated Quartering Act, granted General Thomas Gage, commander

> " A most wicked System for **destroying** the **liberty of America.**"
>
> RICHARD HENRY LEE OF VIRGINIA, 1774

in chief of British forces, the authority to billet troops in private dwellings, not just in barracks or public buildings.

The fifth act—the Quebec Act, passed in June 1774—was not directly related to Boston but provoked colonial anger

Dressing down
In July 1774, Benjamin Franklin endured an hour-long verbal attack from British Solicitor-General Alexander Wedderburn for illegally obtaining letters written by Thomas Hutchinson, the governor of Massachusetts.

the House of Lords, as did Edmund Burke—critic of George III—from the House of Commons. And Benjamin Franklin, in London to represent the Pennsylvania assembly, petitioned the Privy Council—the King's closest advisors—against them.

Meanwhile, the Intolerable Acts unleashed far more direct action in America against British policy than any previous interventions. Other colonies publicly denounced the British and pledged their support to beleaguered Boston, led by Virginia's legislature, the House of Burgesses. On September 9, Suffolk County in Massachusetts adopted the Suffolk Resolves, written by Boston physician Joseph Warren, which rejected the Massachusetts Government Act. Replete with provocative language, the Suffolk Resolves called for the entire colony to cut off all trade and taxes with Great Britain, Ireland, and the West Indies.

Coordinated dissent

September 1774 marked a new era in colonial organization, as the colonies met to form the First Continental Congress. Delegates from all colonies except Georgia—needing British support in its fight against Native Americans—convened in Philadelphia from September 5 through October 26 and, through compromise and mutual, sometimes grudging, respect, came to agreements. Bostonian silversmith and recruited courier Paul Revere brought the Suffolk Resolves to the assembled delegates, who endorsed the document on September 17. Then, by approving the Declaration and Resolves of the First Continental Congress on October 14, they laid the foundations of colonial rights on the law of nature, the British constitution, and colonial charters. Delegates agreed that the British parliament could regulate external trade but had no rights to tax them as it did not represent them.

Regarding a boycott of trade with Britain, the proposed Continental Association was far harder to develop, but the delegates persevered, even creating local committees to enforce the association's dictates. It was eventually agreed that consumption of East India Company tea would cease immediately, and imports from Britain would be prohibited from December 1. The Congress also agreed that it would

> General Gage was soon ordered to capture the leaders of the rebellion, but the rebels got word of his plans.

THE CRACKDOWN BEGINS
Hearing that the Provincial Congress was attempting to raise militiamen, Gage ordered around 700 British regulars to **destroy local militia supplies** and called for the capture of rebel agitators Samuel Adams and John Hancock.

READY TO FIGHT
Paul Revere warned the rebels of the incoming British troops, giving local militias—minutemen—time to assemble. Their first clashes with the British were at **Lexington and Concord 54–55 >>**.

MASSACHUSETTS MINUTEMEN

meet in May 1775, to determine if exports to Britain would cease in September that year. Finally, it petitioned George III to repeal the Intolerable Acts, but received no formal response from Britain to the petition.

Meanwhile, General Gage had returned to Boston as military governor and in May 1774 ordered his troops to seize the powder stocks in Charlestown, near Boston. He suspended the General Court, the Massachusetts legislature, on October 7. Massachusetts then organized the first Provincial Congress at Concord, where debate included discussion about war and the state of local militias. By late September 1774, Gage had pulled troops from New York and Halifax and informed his superiors that enforcing Boston's closure would require reinforcements. He even advocated suspension of the Intolerable Acts, stating that resistance came not merely from Boston's dregs but across the colony's citizenry.

nonetheless. It established religious toleration for the Roman Catholics of Quebec. The aim of this move was to reconcile French Catholics to Britain's control of Canada and negate the possibility of them undermining that authority from within. In fact, the Quebec Act did much more than this. By joining the western lands between the Mississippi and Ohio rivers under the provincial rule of Quebec, it effectively dashed colonial aspirations for westward expansion.

Outspoken critics

The five acts did not go completely unchallenged in parliament. Pitt the Elder spoke against them from

---

SUSPECTED PATRIOT SPY 1734–1824

MARGARET KEMBLE GAGE

Born into a wealthy, influential family in East Brunswick, New Jersey, Margaret Kemble nevertheless married an Englishman, Brigadier General Thomas Gage, in December 1758. The couple played a prominent role in New York society, but the struggle for independence divided their loyalties.

In 1775, when an informant warned the Patriots of the incoming British troops (see pp.54–55) suspicion fell on Kemble. Gage wrote to a fellow officer, "I had communicated my design to one person only." Although he sent his wife away to England, they reunited, and had their last child in London in 1777.

56 Number of delegates to the First Continental Congress.

4 Number of delegates who represented Massachusetts.

The First Continental Congress

Delegates met at Carpenters' Hall, Philadelphia, in 1774 to formulate a unified response to the Coercive Acts (see pp.42–43), but their opinions were divided. Virginia's Patrick Henry, for example, asserted the right of the colonies to challenge parliament. Others, such as Pennsylvania's Joseph Galloway, later a prominent Loyalist, wished to find a compromise with the British.

"Government is dissolved. Fleets and Armies and the present state of things show that government is dissolved ... The distinctions between Virginians, Pennsylvanians, New Yorkers and New Englanders are no more. I am not a Virginian, but an American ... I go upon the supposition that Government is at an End ... All America is thrown into one mass.**"**

PATRICK HENRY, DELEGATE OF VIRGINIA, AS RECORDED IN THE DIARY OF JOHN ADAMS, SEPTEMBER 6, 1774

"Desirous as I am to promote the freedom of the Colonies ... I beseech you, by the respect you are bound to pay to the instructions of your constituents, by the regard you have for the honor of your country, and as you wish to avoid a war with Great Britain, which must terminate, at all events in the ruin of America, not to rely on a denial of Parliament ... because whatever protestations may be made to the contrary, it will prove to the world that we intend to throw off our allegiance to the State, and to involve the two countries in all the horrors of a civil war.**"**

JOSEPH GALLOWAY, DELEGATE OF PENNSYLVANIA, FROM THE JOURNALS OF THE CONTINENTAL CONGRESS, SEPTEMBER 28, 1774

The First prayer in Congress
Congress began with a prayer led by Reverend Jacob Duché, who beseeched God to "give them wisdom ... to settle things on the best and surest foundation." This painting by the patriotic American artist T. H. Matteson shows Patrick Henry, eyes closed, bottom left.

BRITISH PRIME MINISTER Born 1732 Died 1792

Lord **North**

"I wish for **harmony;** but I see **no prospect** of **obtaining it.**"

LORD NORTH, SPEECH IN DEBATE ON THE TOWNSHEND DUTIES, MARCH 5, 1770

Britain's prime minister both before and during the American War of Independence, Lord Frederick North has often been represented as a dull, incompetent bully, and the servile agent of King George III. The reality was more nuanced: North was a principled politician and a skilled administrator, excelling in debate in the House of Commons. In the American colonies, however, he faced a situation for which he had no solution, military or political. As a result, North has gone down in history as the man who lost America.

North was the eldest son of the Earl of Guilford, an undistinguished member of the British aristocracy. While his father occupied the family's hereditary seat in the House of Lords, Frederick was eligible for the House of Commons, to which he was elected unopposed at the age of 22 in a constituency effectively owned by his father.

"Oh God! **It is all over.**"

LORD NORTH, ON LEARNING OF BRITISH SURRENDER AT YORKTOWN, NOVEMBER 25, 1781

Loyal conservative

North was not a physically attractive man. He was overweight, nearsighted, and clumsy, with a voice both boomingly loud and indistinct. But he impressed his fellow members of parliament with his lucid mind, his grasp of public affairs, and his good nature—he was rarely personally disliked even by opponents. North was fiercely loyal to the throne, and always eager to defend George III against his radical critics, believing firmly that the British system of rule by king and parliament provided the best guarantee of freedom and prosperity.

North's popularity with George III and his evident talent, especially for financial administration, led to his rise to Chancellor of the Exchequer in 1767, and in 1770 to First Lord of the Treasury. Combining these two posts, he became head of government and created a post that is now known as prime minister, although this was not a term he himself acknowledged.

North was not an ambitious man and took on the burden of leading the British government with some reluctance. He scored notable successes in

The Gordon Riots

The anti-Catholic Gordon Riots of 1780 were the worst domestic disorders of North's ministry. London was devastated by violent mobs for a week. The unrest had a damaging effect on the British attempt to gain foreign support for its struggle against the American rebellion.

The State Tinkers

James Gillray's 1780 cartoon shows members of the British government—North on his knees, Sandwich and George Germain on a block—trying to repair the "national kettle." Meanwhile, George III, hands raised, marvels at their futile efforts.

foreign policy, facing down a Spanish attempt to occupy the Falkland Islands (a British territory off South America), and reforming the administration of India and Ireland. But his chief interest was government finance. He showed great ingenuity in measures to reduce the national debt, including introducing a lottery that contributed to government coffers. Despite a reputation for indolence he was a tireless speaker in parliament, making some 800 speeches in the Commons between 1770 and 1774, many of them lengthy.

Misunderstanding America

His hold on power, which was to last through 12 difficult years, depended equally upon the support of the king and of members of parliament. Unfortunately, devotion to the authority of king and parliament and a desire to cut expenditure were not the best attitudes with which to face the mounting crisis in the American colonies. North failed to understand the situation in America and was slow to appreciate its seriousness. He was genuinely astonished when

his policy on tea imports to the colonies provoked American wrath (see pp.38–39). He considered the punitive measures taken against Massachusetts after the Boston Tea Party a mild response to an intolerable outrage and believed the American rebels must be a minority without widespread support. He was a practical politician whose life was spent making deals and compromises, but he could see no way of finding agreement with colonists who rejected the rule of king and parliament.

When it was too late, he sought peace on the basis of concessions over taxation, yet he himself recognized that more fundamental issues were at stake, the question being, as he put it, "whether we have or have not any authority in that country."

North's chief concern during the war in America was always to cope with the adverse financial and political impact of the conflict on Britain; he left the conduct of the war to others, such as the Secretary of State for America Lord Germain,

and the Earl of Sandwich. After the British defeat at Saratoga in 1777 (see pp.162–63), North attempted another peace initiative but it was too little, too late. His will to govern had in effect evaporated.

North's decline

With dwindling support in parliament, North was eager to resign, but George III insisted he stay in office. After the British defeat at Yorktown in 1781 North knew the American war was lost but continued to hold out for a peace on the most favorable terms possible. In 1782, after losing a vote of confidence in the House of Commons, he finally persuaded the king to let him go. His brief return as home secretary in a coalition with the radical Charles James Fox, whom George III detested, irreparably damaged his relationship with the king.

From 1784, in declining health and with his sight failing, North retired. After visiting North at home, Horace Walpole wrote that "if ever loss of sight

could be compensated, it is by so affectionate a family." North finally entered the House of Lords after his father's death in 1790, but made only two speeches before he died in August 1792. He was interred in the family tomb at Wroxton, Oxfordshire.

Loyal premier

Head of the British government for 12 years, in this portrait by Nathaniel Dance-Holland Lord North wears the Chancellor's gown and riband of the Garter, an honor bestowed by the king.

TIMELINE

- **1732** Born April 13 in Albemarle Street, Piccadilly, London, first son of Francis North, Earl of Guilford, and Lady Lucy Montagu.

- **1742–48** Educated at Eton College and at Trinity College, Oxford.

- **1754** Elected unopposed as member of parliament for Banbury, a "pocket borough" controlled by his family.

- **May 1756** Marries Anne Speke, daughter of a Somerset landowner; the couple will go on to have seven children.

- **1759** Appointed to the Treasury Board, a well-paid government post.

- **1765** Supports the passage of the Stamp Act.

- **1767** Appointed Chancellor of the Exchequer.

- **1769** Plays a leading role in the political crisis caused by the expulsion of radical MP John Wilkes.

- **January 1770** Becomes head of government as First Lord of the Treasury and Chancellor of the Exchequer.

LADY NORTH, NORTH'S WIFE FROM 1756

- **1770** Repeals the Townshend duties on imports to the American colonies, but insists on retaining the duty on tea.

- **1771** Defeats a Spanish attempt to seize the Falkland Islands from Britain.

- **1772** As a sign of royal favor, King George III awards him the Order of the Garter.

- **1774** In response to the Boston Tea Party, promotes punitive legislation aimed at Massachusetts—the "Intolerable Acts."

- **1775** A general election confirms his parliamentary majority; he delegates conduct of the American war to his ministers.

- **1777** Following the British defeat at Saratoga, sends a peace commission to America, but the Patriots reject his proposals.

- **June 1780** Suppresses the anti-Catholic Gordon Riots in London.

- **September–October 1780** A general election reduces his majority in parliament.

- **November 1781** Accepts that American colonies must be granted independence after British defeat at Yorktown.

- **March 1782** Resigns after a vote of no confidence in parliament.

- **February 1783** Allies with Charles Fox in vote on peace terms with the United States.

- **April–December 1783** Serves as home secretary in the Fox-North coalition, until the king dismisses that ministry.

- **August 1790** Succeeds his father as Earl of Guilford.

- **1792** Suffering from edema, dies on August 5, at home in London.

2
THE START OF THE WAR
1775

In spring 1775, tensions reached breaking point. Conflict erupted in New England and the colonies voted to raise an army. In August, ignoring a last-ditch petition for peace by moderates, King George III issued an open declaration of war.

《 Drama at Bunker Hill
Events at Bunker Hill in the summer of 1775 encouraged the rebels to hold their nerve in the face of British aggression. The damage inflicted by rebel forces during early skirmishes took the British by surprise and bolstered their opponents' resolve.

ACTION IN 1775

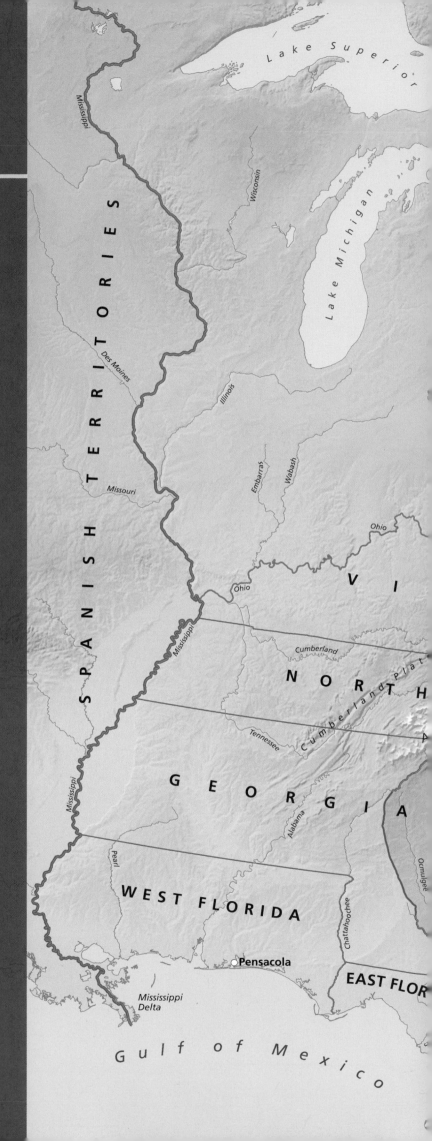

The focal point of military operations in 1775 was New England, where the first rebel army—formed after skirmishes at Lexington and Concord—laid siege to Boston, the main British garrison in the Americas. Britain failed to break through the encirclement, and suffered heavy losses at Bunker Hill in June. Once the Second Continental Congress took control of the Patriot war effort, and the remaining colonies joined the rebellion, the scope of the war expanded. In the Carolinas, Patriot and Loyalist militias engaged in a civil war without much British involvement, but Patriot grievances against Lord Dunmore in Virginia brought the war to the South by the fall. In the northeast, the Patriots launched a two-pronged invasion of Canada via Montreal and Quebec against British commander Sir Guy Carleton.

1 The Second Continental Congress met at the Pennsylvania State House. 2 The first major battle of the war was fought in June between the British Army and colonial militia at Bunker Hill. 3 General Sir Guy Carleton defeated Continental Army forces at Quebec in December.

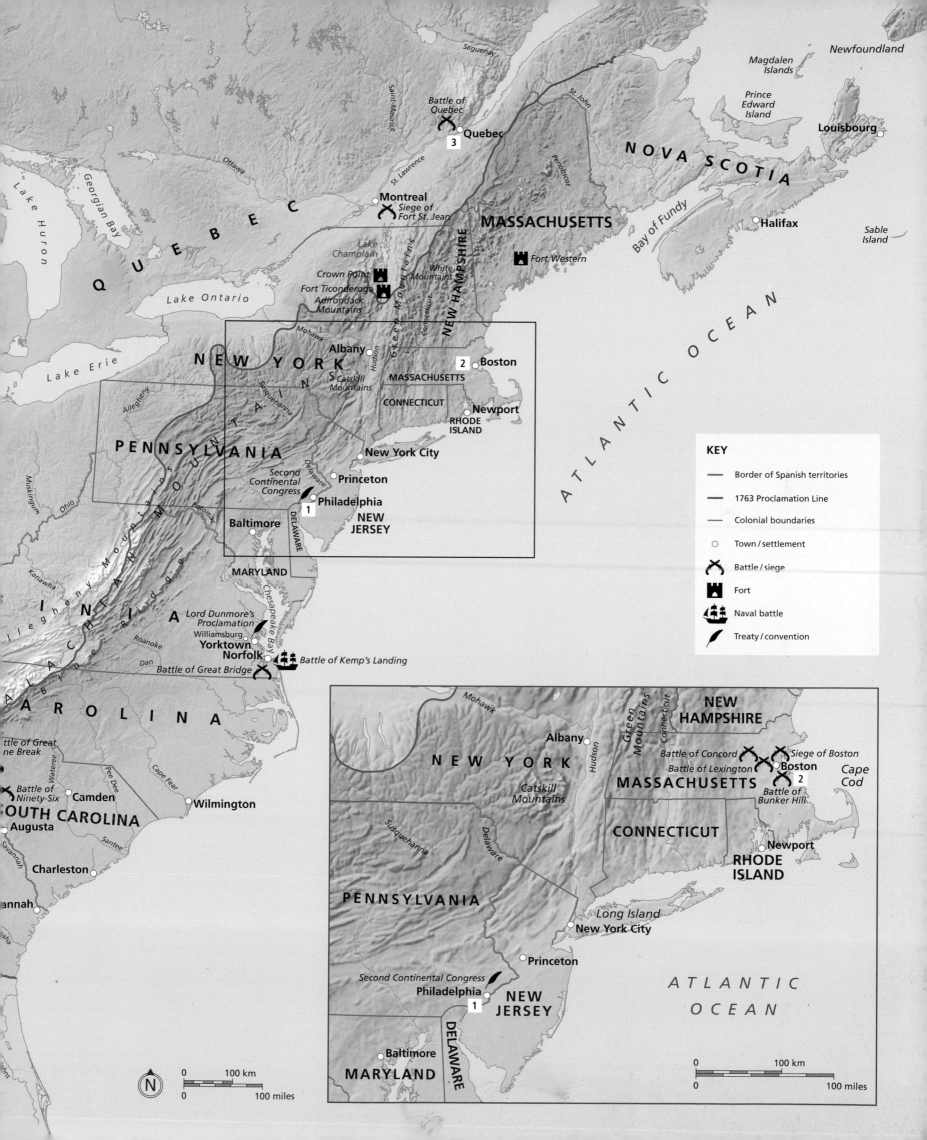

Newfoundland

Magdalen Islands

Prince Edward Island

NOVA SCOTIA

Louisbourg

Sable Island

Saguenay

Ottawa

Saint-Maurice

St. John

St. Lawrence

Penobscot

Battle of Quebec
3 Quebec

Q U E B E C

Montreal
Siege of Fort St. Jean

Lake Champlain

Crown Point
Fort Ticonderoga
Adirondack Mountains

White Mountains

NEW HAMPSHIRE

Fort Western

MASSACHUSETTS

Halifax

Bay of Fundy

ATLANTIC OCEAN

Lake Huron

Georgian Bay

Lake Ontario

Lake Erie

Mohawk

N E W   Y O R K

Albany

2 Boston

MASSACHUSETTS

Catskill Mountains

CONNECTICUT

Newport

RHODE ISLAND

Allegheny

Susquehanna

Hudson

Green Mountains

Connecticut

P E N N S Y L V A N I A

Delaware

New York City

Second Continental Congress
1 Philadelphia

Princeton

Baltimore

NEW JERSEY

Ohio

Muskingum

DELAWARE

Potomac

MARYLAND

Chesapeake Bay

KEY

— Border of Spanish territories

— 1763 Proclamation Line

— Colonial boundaries

○ Town / settlement

✕ Battle / siege

▉ Fort

⛴ Naval battle

✒ Treaty / convention

Kanawha

A P P A L A C H I A N   M O U N T A I N S

Blue Ridge

Lord Dunmore's Proclamation
Williamsburg
Yorktown
Norfolk
Battle of Great Bridge

Battle of Kemp's Landing

Roanoke

Dan

C A R O L I N A

ttle of Great
ne Break

Battle of Ninety-Six

Camden

OUTH CAROLINA

Augusta

Wateree

Pee Dee

Santee

Cape Fear

Wilmington

Charleston

annah

Savannah

ATLANTIC OCEAN

Mohawk

NEW HAMPSHIRE

Albany

Hudson

Green Mountains

Connecticut

Battle of Concord
Battle of Lexington

Siege of Boston

2 Boston

Cape Cod

N E W   Y O R K

Catskill Mountains

MASSACHUSETTS

Battle of Bunker Hill

CONNECTICUT

Susquehanna

Delaware

P E N N S Y L V A N I A

Newport

RHODE ISLAND

Long Island

New York City

Princeton

Second Continental Congress
1 Philadelphia

NEW JERSEY

DELAWARE

Baltimore

MARYLAND

ATLANTIC OCEAN

N

0   100 km
0   100 miles

0   100 km
0   100 miles

TIMELINE 1775

A state of rebellion ▪ **Fort Ticonderoga** ▪ Paul Revere's ride ▪ **Second Continental Congress** ▪ Continental Army established ▪ **The Battle of Bunker Hill** ▪ Boston besieged ▪ **Olive Branch Petition** ▪ Invasion of Canada ▪ **Dunmore's Proclamation**

JANUARY	FEBRUARY	MARCH	APRIL	MAY	JUNE
JANUARY 20 In the Fincastle Resolutions, Virginia Patriots profess sympathy for the Continental Congress and opposition to the Intolerable Acts.				**MAY 10** The Second Continental Congress convenes in Philadelphia.	**JUNE 14** The Second Continental Congress authorizes the creation of the Continental Army. **JUNE 15** The Congress appoints George Washington as commander in chief of the Continental Army.
	FEBRUARY 9 Parliament declares that Massachusetts is in a state of rebellion against Britain.	**MARCH** William Howe, Henry Clinton, and John Burgoyne leave for America, to put down growing unrest in the colonies.	**APRIL 18** British troops march from Boston toward nearby Lexington and Concord; Paul Revere and William Dawes warn Massachusetts Patriots of their approach.	**MAY 10** Ethan Allen and his Green Mountain Boys, along with Benedict Arnold, capture the British outpost at Fort Ticonderoga, New York.	**JUNE 16** Rebel troops outside Boston fortify Breed's Hill after seizing the heights of Charlestown.
JANUARY 23 A group of London merchants ask parliament to reconsider its punitive policies in the colonies, claiming financial distress from the stoppage of trade with America.	**FEBRUARY 26** British troops attempt to seize military stores in Salem, Massachusetts, and are opposed by local militia.			≪ Patriots seize Fort Ticonderoga	**JUNE 17** The Battle of Bunker Hill is fought on the heights of Charlestown, outside Boston. The British drive the rebels back but suffer heavy losses.
	FEBRUARY 27 Parliament passes the Conciliatory Resolution, offering tax concessions to the colonies in the hope of forestalling insurrection.	**MARCH 22** Edmund Burke applauds the Americans' "love of freedom," and urges the British parliament to reconcile its differences with the colonists.	**APRIL 19** British troops and Massachusetts militiamen clash at Lexington, and along the road from Concord to Charlestown. The Patriot Siege of Boston begins.		
		MARCH 23 In the Virginia House of Burgesses, Patrick Henry proposes raising troops, in anticipation of armed conflict with Britain.	**APRIL 20** General Artemas Ward arrives in Cambridge to take command of the rebel forces there. **APRIL 23** The Massachusetts Provincial Congress authorizes the raising of an army.		

≪ Paul Revere rides through the night to alert the Patriots

≫ Battle of Bunker Hill

≫ William Diamond's drum

> "Gentlemen may cry, Peace, Peace—but **there is no peace.** The **war is actually begun!** ... Why stand we here idle? ... Give me **liberty,** or give me **death!**"
>
> PATRICK HENRY TO THE VIRGINIA CONVENTION, MARCH 23, 1775

JULY	AUGUST	SEPTEMBER	OCTOBER	NOVEMBER	DECEMBER

JULY 3
George Washington assumes command of the rebel army at Cambridge, Massachusetts.

AUGUST 22
George III, shocked by news of the carnage at Bunker Hill, issues a proclamation, declaring America to be in a state of open insurrection.

« King George's proclamation

SEPTEMBER 11
Benedict Arnold sets out from Cambridge with an invading force to attack the British in Quebec.

SEPTEMBER 25
Ethan Allen is captured by the British while trying to attack Montreal.

OCTOBER 10
British General Thomas Gage leaves Boston for Britain; General Sir William Howe takes command of British forces in North America.

NOVEMBER 3
Fort St. Jean surrenders to rebel forces under Richard Montgomery.

DECEMBER 2
Montgomery and Arnold's armies rendezvous outside of Quebec.

AUGUST 25
General Richard Montgomery leads a rebel army from Fort Ticonderoga toward Fort St. Jean, to invade Canada.

SEPTEMBER 27
General Montgomery's army lays siege to Fort St. Jean.

OCTOBER 13
The Congress authorizes the establishment of the Continental Navy.

⌄ The flag used by the Second Continental Congress in 1775

JULY 5
The Second Continental Congress issues the Olive Branch Petition to affirm its loyalty to the king.

OCTOBER 18
British naval forces raid and burn Falmouth, in present-day Maine.

NOVEMBER 7
Lord Dunmore, the royal governor of Virginia, declares that any slave belonging to a rebel master will be freed if he offers to serve the king.

DECEMBER 5
Henry Knox begins an expedition to transport captured British siege cannon from Fort Ticonderoga to Boston.

JULY 6
The Second Continental Congress accuses parliament of extending its authority into America illegally, defending the rebels' military actions against British forces.

DECEMBER 31
Patriot forces under Benedict Arnold and Richard Montgomery attack Quebec.

OCTOBER 27
George III declares his intention to put down the American insurrection with armed force, leading to the raising of new Loyalist regiments.

» Continental officer's coat

» Loyalist of the Queen's Rangers

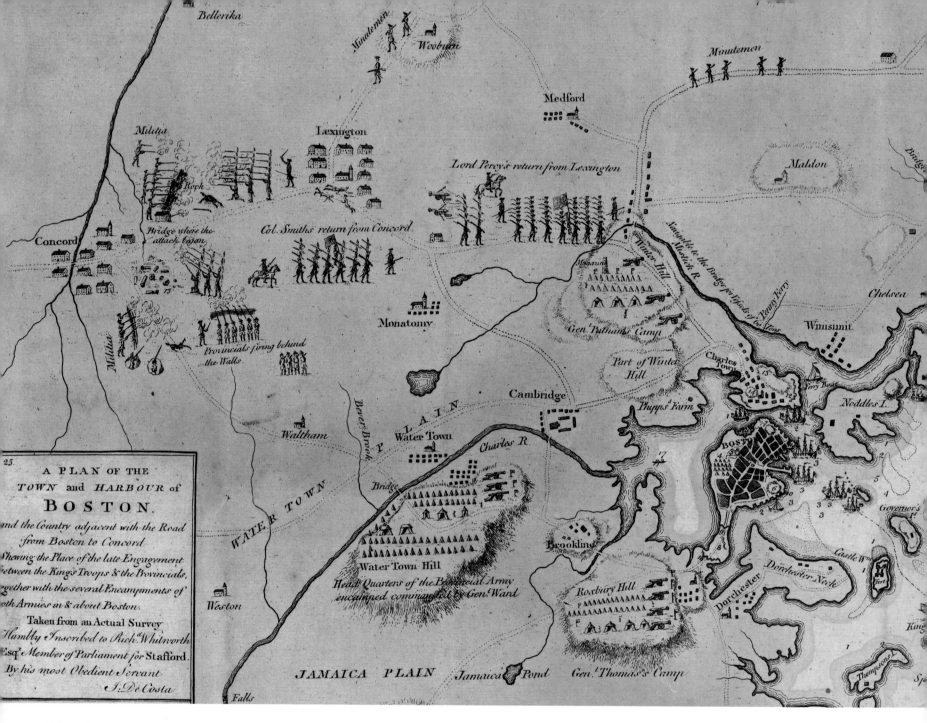

A PLAN OF THE
TOWN and HARBOUR of
BOSTON.
and the Country adjacent with the Road
from Boston to Concord
Shewing the Place of the late Engagement
between the King's Troops & the Provincials,
together with the several Encampments of
both Armies in & about Boston.

Taken from an Actual Survey
Humbly Inscribed to Rich.ᵈ Whitworth
Esq.ʳ Member of Parliament for Stafford.
By his most Obedient Servant
J. De Costa.

Hot pursuit
This plan of Boston and the surrounding area
shows assorted Patriot militia units in pursuit of
British forces as they fled from Lexington and
Concord to Cambridge on April 18, 1775.

 BEFORE

**New taxes and punitive acts
of parliament had provoked protest
in Boston.**

THE PATRIOTS PREPARE
The **Intolerable Acts of 1774 ≪ 42–43**,
intended by the British to punish Boston for the
Tea Party ≪ 38–39, aroused great hostility
in eastern Massachusetts. At the **First
Continental Congress ≪ 44–45**, held in
fall 1774 to formulate a unified response to
these acts of parliament, delegates from 12 of
the Thirteen Colonies agreed to petition for the
repeal of the acts and to boycott British goods.

Lexington and Concord

**When General Gage made moves to clamp down on rebel activities in Lexington, word
quickly spread. Within hours, Redcoat enforcers found themselves facing a small band
of nervous but armed militia refusing to disperse.**

As tensions mounted in eastern
Massachusetts in spring 1775,
the rebels and the British
prepared for conflict. Patriots took
control of the colonial militia and
stockpiled munitions in secret locations,
while the British sent military patrols
into the countryside to assert the
authority of the Crown.

In April, General Thomas Gage,
the British commander in Boston,
received orders to disarm likely rebels
and apprehend their leaders. The best
plan, he decided, was to send a British
detachment under the command of

Lieutenant Colonel Francis Smith
across the Charles River to march on
Lexington and arrest the rebel leaders
Samuel Adams and John Hancock.
Smith would then continue to
Concord, some 20 miles (32 km) west,
to destroy rebel stockpiles of weapons
and ammunition hidden in the town.
Gage scheduled the attack for April 18.

Patriot spies in Boston caught wind
of Gage's intention and took action to
frustrate it. Their first task was to get
the warning out, but this was no easy
task: British sentries guarded Boston
Neck, the narrow spit of land that

attached Boston to the mainland, and
British warships patrolled the Charles
River ferryway that separated Boston
from Charlestown and Cambridge.

Raising the alarm
On the night of April 18, two of
the leading rebels, silversmith Paul
Revere and a tanner named William
Dawes, set off to spread the alarm
among their fellow Patriots: the
British were on the move, and would
soon reach Concord. To minimize the
danger of them both being caught,
the pair traveled separately. Dawes

took the road out of Boston via the Boston Neck, just before the British could seal it off, while Revere rowed across to the other side of the Charles River and set off from there.

While Revere and Dawes each traveled westward on their legendary "midnight rides" (see pp.56–57), Gage's military expedition set off from Boston. Late that evening, around 700 British infantrymen boarded boats for the short passage to Cambridge, arriving in the town at around 2 a.m. From there, an advance guard led by Major John Pitcairn set out on foot for Lexington, their shoes and uniforms sodden from disembarking in water that was waist-deep.

To add to their discomfort, the men could hear the sounds of the Massachusetts countryside coming to life around them. The success of their mission depended on stealth, but thanks to the warnings provided by Revere and Dawes, the inhabitants of Massachusetts were prepared.

In Lexington, a band of 80 colonial militia were armed and waiting when the British advance guard marched into the village. Adams and Hancock, whom Pitcairn had orders to arrest, had fled, having been warned of British intentions by Revere and Dawes.

The fatal shot

The leader of the militia, Captain John Parker, a veteran of the French and Indian War, had no desire to start a fight. He arranged his men so that they would not hinder the British advance, and in his thin, raspy voice told his terrified men to stand their ground.

Parker hoped that the Redcoats would pass them by, but Pitcairn took the presence of the militia as a challenge. Attempting to surround Parker's company, he ordered the Patriots to disperse. A few tense moments passed, and it appeared that Parker's men fully intended to back away peacefully, until suddenly a shot—later called the "shot heard round the world"—rang out.

To this day, it is uncertain who fired that first shot. No order to fire had been given on either side, but Pitcairn's men—believing either that they had been fired upon or that they had been ordered to shoot—let loose a devastating volley of musketry. Parker's men fired back and tried to retreat. Although their officers attempted to hold them back, the British forces lunged forward with fixed bayonets, scattering what was left of Parker's militia. When the smoke cleared, eight Patriot militiamen lay dead or dying on Lexington Green.

British forces advance
The battle on Lexington Green pitted heavily armed British soldiers against a band of lightly armed volunteers. This mismatch only added to the outrage felt throughout New England at the loss of life.

Clash at Concord
Pitcairn and his troops then moved on to Concord. Initially, on reaching the township, the British met no resistance. They discovered cannon and stores of ammunition, flour, and various other provisions, and destroyed whatever they could. However, the local militia had begun to gather, alerted and angered by reports of the bloodshed at Lexington. A firefight broke out between the British Redcoat infantry and the Patriots at Concord's North Bridge. But when Smith decided to take his troops back to the safety of Boston, the battle began in earnest.

Within minutes of leaving Concord, Smith's Redcoats were attacked. Militia from all over the county—and from neighboring counties, too—had rushed

300 British Redcoats died at Lexington and Concord.
100 Patriot militia lost their lives in both engagements.

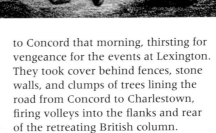

Inscription "Battle of Lexington April 19th, 1775"

Minuteman's drum
This drum was used by 16-year-old drummer boy William Diamond to summon the minutemen to the green at Lexington on April 19, 1775.

to Concord that morning, thirsting for vengeance for the events at Lexington. They took cover behind fences, stone walls, and clumps of trees lining the road from Concord to Charlestown, firing volleys into the flanks and rear of the retreating British column.

Smith sent out flankers—patrols to sweep the ground adjoining the road—and, although the Patriot militia soon fell back, they quickly resumed their attack elsewhere along the road. The British, meanwhile, left a trail of destruction in their wake: looting and burning the villages en route to Boston in retaliation. Exhausted by the long night's march, however, the Redcoats could gain no advantage.

Fighting retreat
Fortunately for the British, a column of 1,000 Redcoats under the capable command of Brigadier General Hugh Percy was waiting at Lexington when Smith's shattered force arrived, still pursued by Patriot militia. Reinforced, the British now had a fighting chance of escaping catastrophic defeat, but Patriot forces hounded them in ever greater numbers, as word of the insurrection at Lexington spread.

At the town of Menotomy (present-day Arlington), the Patriots took cover in houses and barns along the road, forcing the British to engage in bloody house-to-house fighting. The Patriot militia contested every step of the retreat, even into Cambridge itself, and the fighting only ended when the British, many of whom had marched more than 40 miles (64 km) in 24 hours, found refuge in Charlestown, as the daylight failed.

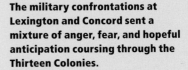

AFTER

The military confrontations at Lexington and Concord sent a mixture of anger, fear, and hopeful anticipation coursing through the Thirteen Colonies.

THE PATRIOTS ASSEMBLE
Neither incident could be called a pitched battle, and the losses were light. But the consequences went beyond the statistics. Over the ensuing weeks, rebel militia from all over New England streamed into the Boston area to **guard against further moves** by the British **58–59 »**.

There was, as yet, little talk of independence. Still, the Patriots had learned that they could indeed fight, and win, against the British Army. And as leaders from the Thirteen Colonies prepared to journey to Philadelphia for the meeting of the **Second Continental Congress 62–63 »**, news of the triumph at Concord undoubtedly bolstered the argument that the time for action had arrived.

MEMORIAL TO THE MINUTEMEN AT LEXINGTON

> "Don't fire unless fired upon, but if they **mean to have a war,** let it **begin here.**"
> CAPTAIN JOHN PARKER TO HIS MINUTEMEN, APRIL 19, 1775

Paul Revere's Ride

When Patriot leaders in Boston caught wind of British plans to destroy their arms depot in Concord, they sent Paul Revere to alert the countryside. On April 18, 1775, Revere crossed the Charles River—under the guns of the British man-of-war HMS *Somerset*—and rode to Lexington to meet William Dawes and Dr. Samuel Prescott. Together the three men rode for Concord, rousing each household along the way.

"Mr. Daws and the doctor stopped to alarm the people of a house. I was about one hundred rods [550 yards or 503 meters] ahead when I saw two men ... I called for the doctor and Mr. Daws to come up. In an instant I was surrounded by four ... The doctor ... came up and we tried to get past them; but they being armed with pistols and swords, they forced us into the pasture. The doctor jumped his horse over a low stone wall and got to Concord.

I observed a wood at a small distance and made for that. When I got there, out started six officers on horseback and ordered me to dismount. One of them, who appeared to have command, examined me, where I came from and what my name was. I told him ... and added that ... there would be five hundred Americans there in a short time, for I had alarmed the country all the way up. He immediately rode towards those who stopped us, when all five of them came down upon a full gallop. One of them ... clapped a pistol to my head, called me by name and told me he was going to ask some questions, and if I did not give him true answers, he would blow my brains out ... We rode till we got near Lexington meeting-house, when the militia fired a volley ... which appeared to alarm them very much. The [British] major inquired of me how far it was to Cambridge, and if there were any other road ... [Then] they all rode towards Lexington meeting-house. I went across the burying-ground and some pastures and came to the Rev. Mr. Clark's house, where I found [John] Hancock and [Samuel] Adams. I told them of my treatment, and they concluded to go from that house towards Woburn.**"**

PAUL REVERE, IN A LETTER TO HIS FRIEND JEREMY BELKNAP, C. 1798

Poetic license
Paul Revere has been celebrated in art and literature, including Henry Wadsworth Longfellow's poem *Paul Revere's Ride* of 1861. Longfellow heightened the drama by setting the ride at midnight, inspiring Charles Green Bush in this 19th-century illustration to do the same.

Siege of Boston and Bunker Hill

Word of the bloodshed on Lexington Green spread like wildfire through Massachusetts and the neighboring colonies. Soon militiamen from all over New England crowded the roads that led to Boston. Gage prudently sat tight and waited for reinforcements: the Siege of Boston was on.

The mob of militia that trudged into the rebel positions guarding Boston could hardly be called an army. Some of the men had received rudimentary military training, but there was little organization or discipline. Since few of these amateur soldiers thought they were signing up to fight an actual war, they had no reservations about leaving whenever they felt like it. Yet they had the invaluable advantage of good leaders: John Thomas of Massachusetts, Israel Putnam of Connecticut, John Stark of New Hampshire, and Nathanael Greene of Rhode Island. Above them was their commander in chief, Artemas Ward. Hardly an inspiring leader, Ward was nonetheless dedicated and patient, and without personal ambition.

Thanks to Artemas Ward, and to Dr. Joseph Warren—the president of the Massachusetts Provincial Congress— the armed mob outside Boston gradually came to resemble an army. It lacked weapons and ammunition, and had virtually no artillery, but Ward, Warren, and the army's leaders at least kept the army well fed and housed.

Best-laid plans

General Gage, the royal governor of Massachusetts, dared not send another expedition into the countryside to search for arms. Britain could not afford another Concord. But within a month of that event, the British would have the advantage. Transports full of fresh, well-equipped Redcoats were already on the way from Britain and Ireland, and with them three new and aggressive generals: William Howe, Henry Clinton, and John Burgoyne. When their ships began to arrive at Boston in mid-May, British spirits soared and Gage resolved to take the war to the enemy.

Meanwhile, the rebels did their best to make life miserable for the British. In late May, militia led by generals Stark and Putnam raided Noddle's Island and Hog Island; the British response was confused and ineffective, and they lost a warship in the process. The events at Noddle's Island boosted

BEFORE

Bunker Hill was not the first time Boston had witnessed violence between rebels and the British.

HOTBED OF DISSENT
Boston had seen its fair share of conflict. **After occupation by British forces ‹‹ 30–31** in 1768, tensions escalated, culminating in the **Boston Massacre** In the wake of the Tea Act of 1773, its port was also the setting for colonial dissent in the **Boston Tea Party ‹‹ 38–39**. The British **punishments ‹‹ 42–43** that followed pushed the rebels to discuss training and readying their own militias.

EARLY SKIRMISHES
In the first battles at **Lexington and Concord ‹‹ 54–55**, local militiamen had defeated British regulars. Even then, war between Britain and the colonies was not considered inevitable.

BRITISH GENERAL THOMAS GAGE

Patriots retreating to Cambridge

Patriot redoubt defended by men under Dr. Warren

24-pound British artillery pieces

Battle commences
This British sketch of troop movements, published in August 1775, shows the rebel army (blue) taking up positions on Breed's Hill, while the British Army (red) move in two distinct flanks.

Ward's headquarters at Cambridge, while a smaller force under John Thomas held onto Roxbury, at the base of Boston Neck. Weighing up their options, the British generals decided on an all-out assault on the weaker position at Roxbury. They could overrun Thomas's force, they reasoned, before Ward would be able to respond, and then the Redcoats could turn north and roll right over Ward's main

Ward and Dr. Warren took a desperate gamble. They decided to seize the high ground overlooking Charlestown, right across the Charles River from Boston itself. This, they hoped, would draw Gage's attention away from Roxbury and force the British to make battle on terms more favorable to the rebels.

Risky choice
On the night of June 16, little more than a day before the British planned to attack Roxbury, Putnam and Patriot Colonel William Prescott—the officer chosen for the task—led a small force to Charlestown under cover of darkness. They had orders to fortify the largest rise on the Charlestown peninsula, known as Bunker Hill.

After arriving on site, though, Prescott and Putnam changed their minds. They marched their men instead to a smaller height called Breed's Hill. Breed's was much closer

> ## "I cannot answer for his men, but **Prescott will fight you** to the **gates of Hell.**"
>
> ABIJAH WILLARD, AIDE TO GENERAL GAGE, JUNE 1775

colonial morale and humiliated the British, strengthening Gage's determination to crush the rebels.

In mid-June 1775, Gage sat down with his generals to plan an offensive. Rebel forces, they knew, were concentrated in two places. The larger rebel army centered on Artemas

army. Confident of success, they scheduled the attack for early morning on Sunday June 18, 1775.

However, in Boston, the British could keep no secrets. Word of Gage's plan found its way to Ward's headquarters. To buy time and prevent the complete destruction of their army, General

to the British ships in the harbor and well within range of British guns. It would be harder to defend, but taking possession of the hill would be a challenge that Gage could not possibly ignore. From midnight to dawn, Prescott's men labored stealthily to dig a four-sided earthen fort atop Breed's. At daybreak, watchful British sentries realized the rebels' intentions. Soon British ships and shore batteries began to pound the exhausted rebels with incessant artillery fire.

Gage also responded promptly. Scrapping the plans for a Roxbury assault, he approved General Howe's proposal: an immediate and direct assault on the rebels. Howe's plan was a solid one. While the British artillery kept up their bombardment, Howe would lead a force across the Charles River by boat. The center of his assault force would pin the rebel forces in front, and his right wing would roll up the rebel left. It took several hours for the British to gather boats for the

The eyes of Boston

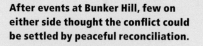

Spectators crowded on hills, rooftops, and steeples to watch the war's first major conflict. Winslow Homer's engraving shows Copp's Hill, where British General John Burgoyne also watched the battle.

new plan; during that time, the rebels strengthened their fortifications on Breed's Hill.

Hollow victory

The British assault, conducted in the afternoon of June 17, did not go according to plan. Howe's assault on the rebels' left flank faltered and fell apart. The rebel militia repulsed the British attack, inflicting heavy casualties, and the Redcoats withdrew after a botched attempt to renew the British assault.

Howe, shocked by the extent of his losses, regrouped his army and sent it forward in a final push, focused on the Breed's Hill redoubt. In this attack, too, the British suffered severe casualties, but the Redcoats were determined. The colonial militiamen were running low on ammunition, and finally the rebels gave way. Howe's badly bruised army drove the remaining rebels from the heights of Charlestown, which had been set alight in the fray. There, the Redcoats finally stopped—victorious but bloodied. British casualties—those killed, injured, or lost—numbered 1,000 men, or 40 percent of the force.

Born in 1727, Artemas Ward was the son of a successful merchant, and later a graduate of Harvard College. A tax assessor and magistrate, Ward was one of the more prominent Patriots in 1775. Although sick at the time of the Lexington alarm, he nonetheless rode 40 miles (64 km) from his home in Shrewsbury to join the army at Cambridge. He commanded the rebel army from that day until the arrival of George Washington in July.

After the Siege of Boston, Ward's military career was over, but he continued to serve in public life, including a stint in the US House of Representatives from 1791 to 1795.

AFTER

After events at Bunker Hill, few on either side thought the conflict could be settled by peaceful reconciliation.

HEAVY LOSSES

Bunker Hill had been a **British victory**, but it was purchased at a **tremendous cost**. The battle marked the end of Gage's career in America, and William Howe soon replaced him as senior British commander.

PETITIONING THE KING

In a last-ditch attempt at peace, in June 1775 the Second Continental Congress sent the **Olive Branch Petition 72–73 »**. to King George. At the same time, however, they sent a seemingly contradictory document: the **Declaration of the Causes and Necessity of Taking up Arms.**

FORMING AN ARMY

After Bunker Hill, Patriot forces settled down to mount a **long-term Siege of Boston 100–01 »**. The experience of battle, though, **bolstered American confidence**. They saw it as proof that militia could be equal or even superior to well-disciplined professionals: a belief that would later prove problematic for George Washington, in his quest to **create a standing army 64–65 »**.

The **Battle** of **Bunker Hill**

As the Siege of Boston continued and the British made plans to break out of the city, colonial forces took a desperate gamble and seized the heights of nearby Charlestown to force the British to attack. The next day, the British responded, attacking the American fortifications on and around Breed's Hill. Those watching from rooftops and the surrounding hills experienced the full gamut of emotions, from excitement and pride to fear and trepidation.

"We sought the highest window we had as soon as the light of advancing day gave us reason to hope for a sight of the expected contest. There they were, the audacious rebels! hard at work, makeing what seemed to me a monstrous fence. 'What is it they are going to do, aunt, and what are they makeing that big fence for?' 'They mean to shoot our King's soldiers, I suppose,' she said, 'and probably the fireing is intended to drive them away.'

... The glittering host, the crashing music, all the pomp and brilliance of war moved up toward that band of rebels, but they still labored at their entrenchment; they seemed to take no heed. The bullets from the ships, the advanceing column of British warriors were alike unnoticed ... Every available window and roof was filled with spectators, watching the advanceing regulars ... the troops drew nearer and the rebels toiled on.

At length one who stood conspicuously above the rest waved his bright weapon; the explosion came attended by the crash of music, the shrieks of the wounded, the groans of the dying. My aunt fainted ... I screamed with all my might. The roar of artillery continued, but the smoke hid the havoc of war from our view ... O, how wild and terrific was that long day!

... Uncle came home and said the rebels had retreated. Dr. Warren was the first who fell that day. Then came the loads of wounded men attended by long lines of soldiers, the gay banners torn and soiled, a sight to be remembered a lifetime."

DOROTHEA GAMSBY, DESCRIBING THE SCENE IN A LETTER TO HER GRANDDAUGHTER
MANY YEARS LATER

Valor in defense
Despite being driven from the field of battle, the militia's performance against the British regulars and the high number of casualties they inflicted on their red-coated foes gave heart to the rebellious colonists.

The Second Continental Congress

On May 10, 1775, when delegates gathered in the Pennsylvania State House, the situation in Massachusetts was top of the agenda. Tensions had escalated into battle, leaving delegates faced with a serious question: should they make the conflict in Massachusetts their own?

There was not much talk of independence in early 1775, and many Patriots still held onto the hope that George III would be open to reconciliation and compromise. In the spring of that year, one matter towered over all the others: war. Many in the Congress were eager to take up arms. The confrontations at Lexington and Concord in April had shown that the colonial militia could stand up to British Redcoats.

On the opening day of the Second Continental Congress in May, this optimism was boosted by events at Fort Ticonderoga and Crown Point, both vital strategic points controlling passage of Lake Champlain. A ragtag group led by Ethan Allen and Benedict Arnold seized the fort and forced the surrender of the British garrison on May 10, without firing a shot. As militia companies paraded in town squares, delegates in Philadelphia celebrated the victory.

Forming a government

The Second Continental Congress was not technically a government, but the rebel assembly in Massachusetts was asking it to act as one. The Massachusetts Provincial Congress sent repeated petitions to the delegates in Philadelphia, requesting "direction and assistance." Their cries for help, which followed so closely in the wake of the battles of Lexington and Concord, won over the majority of delegates, and the Continental Congress gradually assumed the burden of directing the war effort. As Benjamin Franklin, writing on May 13, claimed, "Britain has found means to unite us … a War is commenc'd, which the youngest of us may not see the End of."

First, the Congress asked the colonies to send all the gunpowder they could spare to Artemas Ward, commander of militia in Massachusetts, Connecticut, and New Hampshire, for the "use of the Continent." Then, on June 14, 1775, it authorized the recruitment of ten companies of riflemen from the frontier. Although they would be recruited from Pennsylvania, Virginia, and Maryland, they were to be jointly funded by the rebel colonies and would serve them as a

« BEFORE

In September 1774, delegates from 12 of the Thirteen Colonies met to form the First Continental Congress.

THE SITUATION CHANGES
Delegates to the First Continental Congress resolved to meet again in May 1775, should parliament not repeal the **Intolerable Acts** **« 42–43**. But battles at **Lexington and Concord « 54–55** in April 1775 put the rebels onto a war footing. Preparing for further armed conflict, Benedict Arnold joined Ethan Allen and his Green Mountain Boys, who were plotting to capture artillery from **Fort Ticonderoga** for the rebel cause.

FORT TICONDEROGA

Dressed for the part
Washington (center) made a point of wearing his military uniform at the Second Continental Congress—the only delegate to do so—to show his readiness to serve as commander in chief.

group. The Continental Army—the first national army of what would become the United States—was born.

Emerging leader

Equally pressing was the question of command. Creating generals presented thorny political issues. Each one of the delegates wanted to make sure that the colony he represented was rewarded with a generalship or two. It was the issue of the commander in chief, however, that was most fiercely debated. The army at Boston already had a commander in Artemas Ward; although Ward was no great military

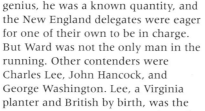

12 COLONIES The number represented at the opening of the Second Continental Congress. Georgia did not send any delegates until July 1775.

genius, he was a known quantity, and the New England delegates were eager for one of their own to be in charge. But Ward was not the only man in the running. Other contenders were Charles Lee, John Hancock, and George Washington. Lee, a Virginia planter and British by birth, was the most experienced soldier in the Thirteen Colonies, having held high-ranking positions in the British and Polish armies for much of his life. He was also a touchy, vain man with eccentric habits, which meant that he was not a popular choice. John Hancock, a prominent Massachusetts Patriot,

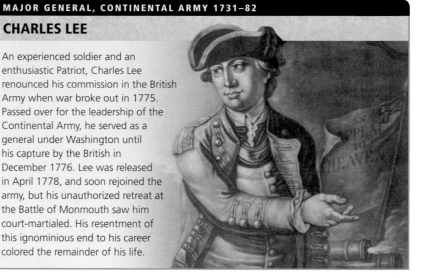

CHARLES LEE

An experienced soldier and an enthusiastic Patriot, Charles Lee renounced his commission in the British Army when war broke out in 1775. Passed over for the leadership of the Continental Army, he served as a general under Washington until his capture by the British in December 1776. Lee was released in April 1778, and soon rejoined the army, but his unauthorized retreat at the Battle of Monmouth saw him court-martialed. His resentment of this ignominious end to his career colored the remainder of his life.

had no military experience, and was easily ruled out of the race.

The final candidate, George Washington, was the most compelling. He could not boast a military record equal to that of Charles Lee—in fact, his martial skills were by no means proven, despite three years of service in the Virginia Regiment during the French and Indian War. But he had a commanding presence, and a humble manner. Eliphalet Dyer of Connecticut characterized him as "no harum Starum ranting Swearing fellow but Sober, steady, and Calm."

Washington's southern origins also worked to his advantage, as did the fact that he was born in Virginia—a native of the colonies. He was not from New England, so he represented the rest of the colonies in a way that Ward and Hancock could not. Best of all, while Washington was ready to serve the cause, it was clear that he did not crave power for himself.

Roman ideal

Many in the Congress feared that a professional army, in the hands of an ambitious general, could easily become an instrument of tyranny. Their model for the perfect commander in chief was Cincinnatus: a Roman statesman who had taken up the sword when his country called him to service in wartime and retired to private life as soon as the crisis had passed. In Washington, delegates such as John Adams of Massachusetts saw

a modern-day Cincinnatus—a military leader without political ambition, and a man they could trust.

Adams nominated Washington for supreme command of the Continental Army on June 14. The next day, the Congress unanimously voted to offer Washington the appointment. Refusing pay for his service, Washington accepted, and a week later the new commander in chief left Philadelphia, accompanied by his chosen second-in-command, Charles Lee. Washington was already on his way to Boston when he received news of the battle brewing at Bunker Hill (see pp.58–59).

AFTER »

The war with Britain was now America's war, not just New England's. Washington set to work creating an army, while the Congress debated its next move.

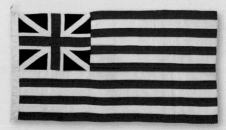

GRAND UNION FLAG

RAISING THE FLAG

While Washington set about transforming the ill-disciplined armed mob into a **real army 64–65 »** in August 1775, the Congress debated how to respond to George III's **Proclamation of Rebellion 72–73 »**, an open declaration of war on the Thirteen Colonies. A new flag, the **Grand Union Flag**, also known as the Congress flag, was created to represent the united colonies in December 1775.

"He seems discreet and virtuous."

ELIPHALET DYER, DESCRIBING GEORGE WASHINGTON, 1775

BEFORE

From the founding of the very first English colonies in North America, settlers relied on local militias for self-defense.

MILITIA ORIGINS
The colonists' notion of militia service came from the "trained bands" of Elizabethan England. In the **early colonies ≪ 22–23** where clashes with Native Americans were commonplace, the militia was vital, but by the time of the **French and Indian War ≪ 24–25**, much of the burden of **colonial defense** was taken up by regular British forces.

Militia and the Continental Army

Throughout the War of Independence, American rebels would rely on two distinctly different types of military organizations on land: a standing, professional Continental Army, and less permanent bands of amateur citizen-soldiers—the militia.

The concept of the militia was a very simple one. It required every free man of military age—from 16 to 60 years old—to serve when called upon, to attend regular training sessions called "musters," and to provide his own weapons and ammunition. In the volatile existence of the early colonies in New England and Virginia, the militia ensured the safety of the settler populations. Even after the 1760s, when regular British forces offered protection, the militias remained in existence, often on more formal terms.

In Massachusetts, all men of military age were enrolled in the regular militia; older, less vigorous men, were grouped into the so-called "alarm companies." The youngest, fittest men could volunteer for service in special "first-responder" units. They pledged to be ready for action "on a minute's notice"—and so members of these units were known as minutemen.

Throughout the colonies, militia units declined in quality in the 18th century, and militia musters became social gatherings rather than training sessions. Heightened tensions with Britain, however, breathed new life into the militia, especially in Massachusetts after 1774. The men who stood up to the British at Lexington and Concord, those who came to Boston in the days following, and those who fought and died at Bunker Hill were militiamen. Clearly, militia units had their advantages. They could be raised and sent home quickly, and mobilizing them did not require a huge outlay of cash. But the militia had disadvantages, too. These units were democratic institutions that elected their officers; they were unlikely to be as obedient as regular soldiers. The colonists, as they admitted themselves, were not bred to habits of deference.

> **25** PERCENT of the militia in Concord's 1775 muster rolls served in minutemen units.

Local resistance

The militiamen outside Boston in 1775 came and went as they pleased, often disregarding orders and ignoring officers they didn't know. They were, in other words, not soldiers. Militia units were reluctant to fight outside their home colony and, while they had some rudimentary training in drill, they did not have the kind of discipline that characterized professional forces such as the British Army. On the western frontier, where fighting Native Americans and hunting wild game were common, the colonists were often skilled marksmen, but in the more settled areas, men were more likely to be unfamiliar with firearms.

Farmer to fighter
Daniel Chester French's statue of a Concord minuteman stands ready for action, having abandoned his coat and plow to defend his land with the local militia.

Militia success
The Battle of Bennington in August 1777 saw militia units and the Green Mountain Boys win a decisive victory against a detachment of the British army under General Burgoyne.

Washington's ideal of a professional, European-style army prevailed, but it was not easily achieved, and did not make significant progress until 1778.

IMPROVING THE ARMY

Baron von Steuben revolutionized the training and organization of the Continental Army at **Valley Forge 184–85 »** but militia units continued to play a vital role. In 1780, it was Patriot militia who won the day at **Kings Mountain 280–81 »**.

ARMING A NEW NATION

At **war's end**, military leaders understood that Americans would not support a large, permanent army. Their solution—a **small professional army and navy**, supplemented by a trained militia in time of war—became the guiding principle of the American military establishment.

Call to arms

This 1776 poster encouraged men to join the Continental Army in the fight against the "hostile designs of foreign enemies." The final rallying call is "God save the United States."

Professional rivals

Following Bunker Hill, many Patriots were fully convinced that American militia units were as good as, and possibly better than, British regulars. However, most rebel military leaders knew otherwise. George Washington, among others, understood that the militia had its uses, but that a professional army would still be necessary if the united colonies were to defeat the British.

Militia units might be able to hold off a British attack as they had at Bunker Hill, fighting defensively behind fortifications, or as they did when ambushing the Redcoats retreating from Concord, but in an open fight they could not stand toe-to-toe with the British. It would take training—and lots of it—to perfect the intricate maneuvers that were part of battle tactics in the late 18th century. It would also take iron discipline and obedience to orders to keep an army intact amid the stresses of combat. The "technical" branches of service, such as artillery and engineers, required professionally trained officers and men.

Army established

A militia army that shrank from open combat might be able to provide resistance to the British, but only a professional army—like the Continental Army as Washington envisaged it—could actually defeat the British on equal terms. A professional army would be necessary in another way as well: if the fledgling United States did in fact win its independence from Britain, only a standing army would inspire respect from the nations of Europe.

Army established

Not everyone agreed with Washington. The Second Continental Congress would never entirely get over its fear of standing armies. A professional army, they worried, might be more obedient to its generals than to the Congress, and was potentially a tool of future tyranny. Standing armies were also expensive. They required pay, uniforms, equipment, and weapons, and the Patriots' finances were limited. Some Patriot leaders, notably General Charles Lee, simply believed the militia to be superior.

In spite of this, the Second Continental Congress voted in 1775 to establish a standing Continental Army for the defense of the colonies. Washington was appointed its commander soon after (see pp.62–63). With its high turnover rate and short enlistment periods, this first army lacked, Washington noted, "the order, regularity, and discipline of veterans." In 1775, Washington's inexperienced and untrained army, had plenty of room for improvement. Both the Continental Army and militia units had distinct strengths and weaknesses; but both, for all their faults, would soon prove vital to American success in the War of Independence.

A variety of uniforms

In 1775, his men ragged and lacking proper clothing, Washington wrote to the Congress to request simple, inexpensive outfits. The "hunting shirt" was adopted as the uniform for New England regiments in mid-1776.

"We have a most **miraculous militia** in this city."

JOHN ADAMS TO JAMES WARREN, JUNE 1775

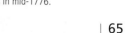

[1] TRICORNE HAT

[2] DRAGOON HELMET

[5] COLONEL'S EPAULETTE

[6] OFFICER'S EPAULETTE

[7] SWORD BELT TIP

[3] BAYONET AND SHOULDER BELT

[4] RUMLET

[8] CARTRIDGE BOX AND SHOULDER STRAP

Patriot Uniforms

The Continental Congress tried to establish a uniform for its soldiers—by 1779, blue coats with white vests had become the official dress for the infantry— but militiamen wore civilian clothing, which varied from region to region.

[1] **Tricorne hat** A fashionable item of civilian attire, tricornes were worn by soldiers on both sides. This hat belonged to Colonel Jonathan Pettibone of the 18th Regiment Connecticut Militia. [2] **Dragoon helmet** Those who fought on horseback, such as dragoons, wore helmets for protection. This helmet is made of leather with brass trim. [3] **Bayonet and shoulder belt** Bayonets were held in a leather scabbard and carried on the left side to make them easily accessible. [4] **Rumlet** This barrel-shaped wooden canteen would have been used to carry hard liquor—likely rum. [5] **Colonel's epaulette** Ornamental shoulder pieces were worn singly, or in pairs for those who had gained the rank of colonel or higher. This was one of the two worn by Colonel Anthony Wayne of the 4th Pennsylvania Regiment. [6] **Officer's epaulette** This silver epaulette would have been fastened to the coat of an infantry officer. [7] **Sword belt tip** Discovered in New Jersey, this brass sword belt tip's design features a liberty cap mounted on a pole. [8] **Cartridge box and shoulder strap** This box, a modified version of the British cartridge pouch, held 29 cartridges. [9] **Bearskin knapsack** Although not official issue, animal-skin knapsacks were relatively common. This one belonged to Elisha Gross of the 3rd Continental Artillery. [10] **Officer's coat** Made of blue wool and faced with red trim, this coat was worn by Colonel Peter Gansevoort Jr. of the 3rd Regiment of the New York Continental Line during his command at Fort Stanwix, New York, in 1777. [11] **Vest** Many militiamen wore vests, which were usually made of linen or wool. Infantrymen in the Continental Army also wore them; officially these were white, but in practice soldiers wore vests in any color, as uniforms were scarce. [12] **Breeches** Made of leather and reaching to the knee, breeches were worn with gaiters that covered the shoes and the lower leg.

[9] BEARSKIN KNAPSACK

10 OFFICER'S COAT

11 VEST

12 BREECHES

The Loyalists

The American War of Independence was not just a struggle for freedom and national self-determination, but a civil war as well. The conflict divided loyalties throughout the Thirteen Colonies.

Before the outbreak of hostilities in the spring of 1775, many colonists did not share in the spirit of resistance that permeated places like Boston. Even when the war had begun, a substantial portion of the colonial population—as much as 20 percent—remained steadfastly loyal to the British Crown, despite the dangers of being labeled "Tories." Like any civil war, the divisions tore apart neighborhoods and families. Lieutenant Colonel William Stark, a commander of Loyalist forces, for example, was the older brother of prominent New Hampshire Patriot John Stark, the victor of the Battle of Bennington.

A diverse alliance

Many factors persuaded colonists to remain loyal to Britain. For some, close family ties with the mother country, or trading links with British merchants, influenced their decision. For others, it was traditional respect for the authority of the Crown, and the stability that British rule represented. They did not want to be associated with those who were seen as acting illegally. Others had settled in America after fighting in the French and Indian War, having been awarded land grants for their service by the British government. The Scottish Loyalists who fought in the Battle of Moore's Creek Bridge (see pp.106–07) fell into this category. Other groups, such as the Quakers, sympathized with the Patriots and their grievances, but were repelled by the use of violence and the tactics that Patriots often used to intimidate their Loyalist neighbors.

Non-Europeans in America—overwhelmingly Native Americans and African Americans—found that the Patriot cause had little to offer them. For many Native Americans, British authority was the only thing that kept the white colonists from encroaching deeper into their lands. Likewise, African American slaves had no reason to support the cause of "liberty" when Patriot landowners showed no inclination to include freedom from slavery in the rights and liberties they sought to achieve through war (see pp.78–79).

Loyalist units

British military commanders overestimated the size of the Loyalist population; and more importantly, they overestimated the willingness of Loyalist men to rally to the king's banner. Even so, Loyalists did make significant contributions to the British war effort. In the southern campaigns, much of the fighting was done by Loyalist militia units rather than by British regular troops.

Loyalists were welcomed into the ranks of the British Army, but on the whole, colonists who wanted to fight for the king enlisted in one of a number of "Provincial" battalions attached to the British Army, such as Butler's Rangers (mostly from New York) and the King's Royal Regiment (raised in Canada). Robert Rogers, a Massachusetts-born hero of the French and Indian War (see pp.24–25), established and commanded the Queen's American Rangers. (Butler had originally offered his services to the Continental Congress but had been rejected by Washington, who thought he might be a spy.) In total, at least 50,000 American volunteers served in British military forces during the course of the war.

Life as a Loyalist

Some locations were friendlier toward Loyalists than others. In towns under British occupation, Loyalists could live quite comfortably. New York City, held by the British until the end of the war, had perhaps the most significant loyal population. But for Loyalists who did not enjoy the immediate protection of British troops, life during the war could be difficult. The harassment of high-placed officials loyal to the king had been bad enough in places such as Boston in the decade before the war, but once open hostilities began, Patriots often went out of their way to intimidate Loyalists. The tarring-and-feathering of ordinary colonists, often for no greater an offense than just not being enthusiastic about the Patriot cause, became a common occurrence for Loyalists, the majority of whom simply wanted to get on with their lives quietly.

Open persecution was the primary reason that compelled a sizable number, probably close to 10 percent of the colonial population, to pack their belongings and seek a more peaceful life elsewhere. Some Loyalists sought refuge in Britain itself, others moved to Florida, and large numbers settled in the king's loyal provinces in Canada.

Many pro-British families undertook the northward trek to Canada at the start of the fighting, but they left in far greater numbers at the end of the war, when British military forces withdrew from their posts in the new American republic. Nova Scotia was the most popular destination for these Loyalist émigrés. The numbers of new settlers in this territory was so large that in 1784 Britain created a new province—New Brunswick—just for them.

> The term "Tory" was derived from the British political party that represented the interests of the upper classes. In America, it was often used to describe colonists who remained loyal to the British Crown. It carried connotations of wealth and privilege.

BEFORE

In the mid-18th century, most American colonists had British origins and even the most ardent Patriots thought of themselves as British.

LIMITED OBJECTIVES

At the outset, the rebellion was a **fight for rights and liberties** that the Patriots claimed belonged to all the king's subjects—in particular, protection **against arbitrary taxation ≪ 28–29**. To many colonists, even those who disagreed with Britain's treatment of the colonies, thoughts of **taking up arms against their king**, still less ideas of demanding independence, were **inconceivable**.

Drummed out of town
Pro-British colonists were often persecuted by their Patriot neighbors. This unfortunate Loyalist—by his dress a wealthy man—is literally being drummed out of town by a group of rebel militia, clearly made up of farmers and working men.

Inducements to fight
This British recruitment poster for the First Battalion of Pennsylvania Loyalists offered to supply clothing and equipment to volunteers as well as financial rewards for service in the name of the king.

TEUCRO DUCE NIL DESPERANDOM.
First Battalion of PENNSYLVANIA LOYALISTS, commanded by His Excellency Sir WILLIAM HOWE, K.B.

ALL INTREPID ABLE-BODIED

HEROES,

WHO are willing to serve His MAJESTY KING GEORGE the Third, in Defence of their Country, Laws and Constitution, against the arbitrary Usurpations of a tyrannical Congress, have now not only an Opportunity of manifesting their Spirit, by affisting in reducing to Obedience their too-long de-luded Countrymen, but also of acquiring the polite Accomplishments of a Soldier, by serving only two Years, or during the present Rebellion in America.

Such spirited Fellows, who are willing to engage, will be rewarded at the End of the War, besides their Laurels, with 50 Acres of Land, where every gallant Hero may retire. . . . .

Each Volunteer will receive, as a Bounty, FIVE DOLLARS, besides Arms, Cloathing and Accoutre-ments, and every other Requisite proper to accommo-date a Gentleman Soldier, by applying to Lieutenant Colonel ALLEN, or at Captain KEARNY's Ren-dezvous, at PATRICK TONRY's, three Doors above Market-street, in Second-street.

Loyal frontiersman
Robert Rogers (1731–95) was an American colonial frontiersman, who served in the British Army during both the French and Indian War and the American War of Independence. He raised and led the Queen's American Rangers, a Loyalist brigade famously known as Rogers' Rangers.

> **"Brandish your swords** and … sing Success to our **Troop,** our **Country,** and **King."**
>
> "THE VOLUNTEERS OF AUGUSTA," A LOYALIST SONG FROM GEORGIA

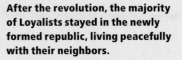

AFTER

After the revolution, the majority of Loyalists stayed in the newly formed republic, living peacefully with their neighbors.

LOYALISTS AFTER INDEPENDENCE
Although many Loyalists felt it wise to **live discreetly**, a tiny number rose to **positions of prominence** in the newly independent nation. One of these was Tench Coxe of Philadelphia, a political economist and businessman nicknamed "Mr. Facing Bothways," who served in the Second Continental Congress from 1788.

CHANGES IN SOCIETY
Some prominent Loyalist families in areas such as New York City, where support for the British had been strong, chose to leave America. Their positions of power and influence were filled by Patriots. These **newly empowered citizens** often came from the "lower classes." Even before the war ended, one rich Bostonian commented, in 1779, that "fellows who would have cleaned my shoes five years ago, have amassed fortunes and are riding in chariots."

Loyalists Under Pressure

As tensions increased, in some areas Americans with Loyalist sympathies came under severe pressure from their Patriot countrymen. Those regarded as working with the British, such as customs officials and tax collectors, were often subjected to physical retribution—notably tarring and feathering, a traditional punishment for traitors. Others had their land and possessions confiscated as David Fanning—a leading Loyalist militiaman from North Carolina, captured by the Patriots 14 times, recalled in his memoirs.

"[Loyalists] in the interior parts of North Carolina ... have been induced to brave every danger and difficulty ... rather than render any service to the Rebels, had their properties real and personal taken to support their enemies, the fatherless and widows stripped, and every manner of support taken from them, their houses and lands and all personal property taken, and no resting place could be found for them. As to placing them in their former possessions, it is impossible—stripped of their property, driven from their homes, deprived of their wives and children, robbed of free and mild government, betrayed and deserted by their friends, what can repay them for this misery?

Dragging out a wretched life in obscurity and want, Heaven, only, which smooths the rugged paths, can reconcile them to misfortune. Numbers of them left their wives and children in North Carolina, not being able to send for them owing to the distresses, and now in the West Indies and other parts of the world for refuge, and not returned to their families yet.**"**

DAVID FANNING, *THE NARRATIVE OF COLONEL DAVID FANNING*, 1865

Tarred and feathered
British propaganda aimed to keep the Loyalist population on the side of the king with reminders of their suffering at Patriot hands. *The Bostonians Paying the Excise-man* shows how a rebel mob attacked customs official John Malcolm in 1774 and then threatened him with hanging.

Galloping toward war
In this British cartoon of 1775, George III and Lord Chief Justice Mansfield drive a chaise with two horses labeled "Obstinacy" and "Pride" into an abyss, trampling established rights underfoot.

<< BEFORE

The **Proclamation** of **Rebellion**

Relations between Britain and its American colonies deteriorated rapidly in the spring of 1775.

ESCALATING TENSIONS
Opposition to **punitive laws and taxation << 42–43** in New England turned into **violent confrontations** between Britain and its colonies at **Lexington and Concord << 54–55** and **Bunker Hill << 58–59**. Nonetheless, while firebrands in the **Second Continental Congress << 62–63** wanted independence whatever the cost, moderate delegates advised caution. At the same time, the Congress took the precaution of **preparing for war**, stockpiling **gunpowder** and organizing its **own army << 64–65**.

Over the summer of 1775, delegates at the Second Continental Congress in Philadelphia searched for a solution to the brewing conflict with Britain—some wanted war, others did not. In London, King George raged against the rebels' flagrant insubordination.

John Dickinson of Pennsylvania, a respected moderate at the Second Continental Congress, took a leading role in searching for a peaceful reconciliation with King George. On July 5, 1775, the Congress approved Dickinson's Olive Branch Petition, a direct appeal to King George that made it clear that the colonists'

quarrel was with parliament, not with Britain or with him. Dickinson's petition maintained that the Thirteen Colonies wanted nothing more than reduced taxes and more favorable trade arrangements.

Dickinson was sincere in his hope for a peaceful redress of grievances, but after the violent confrontation at

Bunker Hill there were few delegates in Congress who shared his optimism. Thomas Jefferson (see pp.116–17) preferred a much more provocative approach and John Adams privately believed that war was not only unavoidable but also desirable if the American colonies were to achieve full independence.

according to the Declaration, and the Patriots would not stand down until "Hostilities shall cease on the part of the Aggressors." Thomas Jefferson was one of the document's principal authors. Curiously, so was John Dickinson, the author of the Peace Petition. Congress sent both documents on to Britain.

The final straw

Only a few days before the documents reached Lord Dartmouth, the first ships to leave Boston after Bunker Hill arrived in Britain, bringing news of the June battle. Their human cargo made a piteous sight—the grieving widows of slain British soldiers stationed in the colonies, wounded men and officers, and the remains of the many dead. Lexington and Concord had been minor humiliations for the British, but the heavy losses incurred at Bunker Hill were, to George III, an unforgivable insult. This was no minor disagreement with loyal colonists; this was a full-fledged rebellion, and the king would not stand for it. "The dye is cast," he wrote after learning of Bunker Hill.

Colonial Secretary Lord Dartmouth received both the Congress's Petition and the Declaration on the same day. When Dartmouth attempted to present the two documents to the king, George refused to read them. In George's opinion, they had been written by rebels against the Crown, represented by an illegitimate assembly.

On August 23, 1775, the king issued "A Proclamation for Suppressing Rebellion and Sedition," his formal response to the insurrection in Massachusetts. "Many of Our Subjects in divers Parts of Our Colonies … in America," the Proclamation declared, "misled by dangerous and ill-designing Men, and forgetting the Allegiance which they owe to the Power that has protected and sustained them … have at length proceeded to an open and avowed Rebellion … and levying War against Us." Britain would, the king asserted, bend all its energies toward the suppression of this rebellion, and any Briton corresponding with the rebels would be considered a traitor. Just in case the message was unclear, the king reiterated its sentiments in his Speech from the Throne at the opening of parliament in October 1775. Proclaiming that "to be a subject of Great Britain, with all its consequences, is to be the freest member of any civil society in the known world," George III accused the rebels of wanting to establish "an independent empire." He vowed to crush the rebellion in the colonies with every means at his disposal, including, "friendly offers of foreign assistance."

British peacemaker
Despite being the stepbrother of Lord North, William Legge, Lord Dartmouth, King George's colonial secretary, initially sympathized with the colonists and opposed a military solution.

Doves and hawks

The colonists took the proclamation to be the king's response to the petitions George had refused to read. It overjoyed zealots, such as John Adams, who welcomed war, and disappointed the shrinking band of moderates who had been confident the king would see reason.

There were objections to the royal proclamation within Britain. The Whigs—the political coalition in parliament that tended to oppose the king—sympathized with the disaffected colonists and were generally against the war. Even the leading British commanders appointed to suppress the rebels, notably generals William Howe and Henry Clinton (see pp.108–09), expressed doubts about the prospects of British success, not least in view of the logistical difficulties of fighting a rebellion thousands of miles away, when resources in the empire were already stretched. But the king's will prevailed, and by the end of the year he had fully committed his realm to war.

Causes and necessity

The day after approving the Olive Branch Petition, the Congress agreed to another, seemingly contradictory document, the "Declaration of the Causes and Necessity of Taking Up Arms." The Declaration did not call for independence, but it was worded in a way guaranteed to provoke the king, listing all the offenses the Congress believed Britain had committed against the colonies. Not only had Britain treated the colonies unfairly, the Declaration alleged, but it had also stubbornly refused to listen to grievances and appeals for a decade. Freedom was the "Birthright" of all British subjects,

> ## "In defense of the **freedom** that is our birth-right … we have **taken up arms.**"
>
> DECLARATION OF THE CAUSES AND NECESSITY OF TAKING UP ARMS, 1775

declaring independence 112–13 » ... southern colonies 76–77 » ... African American support 78–79 » ... Hesse-Kassel 154–55 »

Once the king had made his position clear, moves toward a declaration of independence accelerated in the Thirteen Colonies. Meanwhile, Britain set about rallying support.

PATRIOTIC FERVOR
With the king pushing for punishment of the rebellion, the Second Continental Congress edged closer to **declaring independence 112–13 »**. Delegates from the **southern colonies 76–77 »** united behind their New England colleagues.

THE BRITISH PREPARE
In addition to recruiting additional troops in Britain to send to America, the British began enlisting the **support of Loyalists** in America, especially in the southern colonies, where tensions between Loyalists and Patriots already existed.

The British also explored the possibility of exploiting **African American support 78–79 »**, promising freedom to slaves, and set about **hiring auxiliary troops** from the independent principalities of Germany, such as **Hesse-Kassel 154–55 »**. These German mercenaries would play a significant role in the British attempt to suppress American resistance.

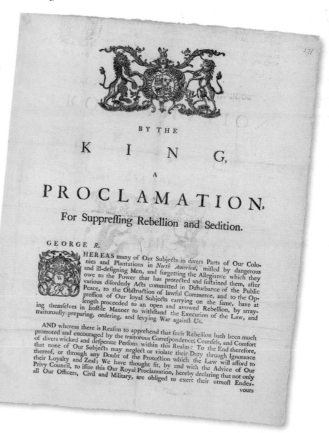

Royal threats
The "Proclamation for Suppressing Rebellion and Sedition" not only threatened severe penalties for those guilty of rebellion but also for anyone who failed to report knowledge of such.

BRITISH KING Born 1738 Died 1820

King **George III**

"**Born** and **educated** in this **country**, I **glory** in the name of **Briton.**"

GEORGE III, OPENING HIS FIRST PARLIAMENT, NOVEMBER 18, 1760

George III was the ruler against whom the American colonists rebelled. They viewed him as a monstrous figure, a ruthless and arrogant oppressor of the people. Modern historians have on the whole taken a more sympathetic view of the king, seeing his determination to compel the obedience of his subjects and hold onto the territory of his empire as being no more than would be expected of any 18th-century monarch.

George III was a member of the Hanoverian dynasty that had been imported from Germany to rule Britain after the death of the childless Queen Anne in 1714. He was the first Hanoverian king to be born and bred in Britain, speaking English as his native language, of which he was inordinately proud. A tall, dignified young man—only 22 years old at his accession in 1760—he had a regal bearing, yet turned out to have little taste for monarchical grandeur and display.

A sense of duty

George appreciated the quiet pleasures of domesticity, enjoying a contented union with his wife Queen Charlotte. He was an affectionate father to his children, a devout Christian who loved music, had a keen interest in science, especially astronomy, and earned the nickname "Farmer George" for his down-to-earth attitude toward new agricultural techniques.

George took his role as a constitutional monarch seriously and

Martial king

This portrait of George III by Benjamin West, painted in 1783, shows the king improbably clad in plate armor. His father, George II, was in fact the last British monarch to lead an army into battle.

George's German queen

Charlotte of Mecklenburg–Strelitz fretted over the War of Independence in letters to her brother Charles. She was concerned for Britain, but also for the German mercenaries fighting in the war.

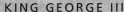

"Monstrous craws"
The British press frequently ridiculed the royal family. This James Gillray caricature from 1787 depicts them gorging on golden guineas. The Prince of Wales (center) was a notorious spendthrift.

did not see his position as that of a mere figurehead. He regarded it as his right and duty to appoint the government and to exercise influence over its policies. Though radicals in Britain and American rebels accused the king of plotting to extend his personal rule to the point of tyranny, he generally respected the need for the support of a majority in parliament and accepted that he would sometimes have to appoint ministers he disliked. The system worked most smoothly when he was able to rely on a prime minister of his own choosing, as was the case with both Lord North and later William Pitt the Younger.

Facing rebellion
George did not wish to trample upon established freedoms or constitutional practice, but he was determined not to tolerate any resistance to the authority of king and parliament. When the radical MP John Wilkes made scurrilous attacks on him in the newspaper *The North Britain* in 1763, George insisted he be arrested for libel, triggering a long sequence of legal and political battles in which Wilkes was supported by angry London mobs. During the anti-Catholic Gordon Riots of 1780, it was the king who insisted soldiers should be sent to fire on rioters to restore order.

The initial disturbances in the American colonies were viewed by the king in the same light as riots in London: as the work of an unruly

minority. He did not consider colonial objections to taxation without representation justified, and did not support attempts at compromise that did not involve American submission to parliament and the Crown.

This attitude undoubtedly limited the ability of his ministers to respond flexibly to the crisis, encouraging intransigence and the use of military force against the rebellious colonists.

After the British defeat at Saratoga in 1777 (see pp.162–63), George pressed for the continuation of war, even though his government wavered. He was slow to agree that the surrender at Yorktown in 1781 (see pp.306–07) must lead to an end of hostilities, or to the recognition of America's independence. However, the lack of bitterness in his subsequent attitude to the United States was striking. Receiving John Adams as the first US ambassador to Britain in 1785, he frankly admitted he had been

Failing mind
In the later years of his life, when this engraving was made, George III was debilitated by blindness and by the episodes of "madness" that medical science still struggles to explain.

"the last to consent" to independence, but gladly declared himself "the first to meet the friendship of the United States as an independent power."

Deteriorating health
The later years of his long reign were darkened by family problems and poor health. His sons failed to inherit their father's domestic virtues, proving profligate in their spending and dissolute in their sex lives. George III had improved the public image of the monarchy but his offspring brought it into disrepute, inflicting damage that was not repaired until the virtuous reign of Queen Victoria.

The decline of the king's mental health was probably an even more disturbing blow to a political order in which authority ultimately resided in the monarch in person. From 1788 George III was subject to periods of insanity for which he underwent degrading treatments. The cause of his illness remains uncertain, though the rare disease porphyria has been suggested as the culprit. He also went blind and sank into dementia from 1810, the collapse of his reason hastened by grief at the death of his favorite daughter, the young Princess Amelia.

The king's illness did not always elicit sympathy. This is evident from Shelley's famous poem *England* in 1819, which refers savagely to the "old, blind, despised and dying king." Yet for most of his reign George had clearly commanded the respect of the majority of his British subjects, the degree of their attachment to their monarch matched only by the degree of virulent hatred felt by his radical political enemies at home and in America. Living until 1820, George III occupied the British throne for 59 years, making him the longest-serving British monarch up to that time. His record has since been surpassed by Queen Victoria and Queen Elizabeth II.

> "He has **plundered** our **seas**, **ravaged** our coasts, **burnt** our towns and **destroyed** the **lives** of **our people**."
>
> THOMAS JEFFERSON, DECLARATION OF INDEPENDENCE, 1776

see pp.162–63

TIMELINE

- **1738** Born May 24 at Norfolk House, St. James's Square, London, son of Frederick, Prince of Wales, and Augusta of Saxe-Gotha.
- **1751** The death of his father at age 44 leaves George immediate heir to the British throne.
- **1755** The Earl of Bute, a close associate of George's mother Augusta, is appointed his tutor.
- **October 1760** Accedes to the throne on the death of King George II.
- **September 1761** Marries German princess Charlotte of Mecklenburg-Strelitz, six hours after meeting her for the first time.
- **1762** Appoints the Earl of Bute as prime minister, but Bute's tenure of office lasts less than a year.
- **August 1762** The future King George IV is born, first of George III's 15 children.
- **1763** End of the French and Indian War.
- **1770** Duke of Grafton resigns; Lord North becomes Britain's prime minister.
- **1774** Insists a hard line be taken against American rebels in Massachusetts in the wake of the Boston Tea Party.
- **1778** Urges Lord North to stay in office and continue the fight against the American rebellion after the British defeat at Saratoga.
- **April 1780** A parliamentary motion denouncing the increasing influence of the Crown, put forward by MP John Dunning, is passed by the House of Commons.
- **June 1780** Orders the use of military force to suppress the anti-Catholic Gordon Riots in London.
- **1782** Unwillingly accepts the resignation of Lord North and the need to recognize American independence.
- **1783** Appoints William Pitt the Younger as First Minister of Great Britain, a post he holds for the next 17 years.
- **1788** Suffers his first attack of "madness," possibly the effect of porphyria.
- **1793** Denounces the execution of French King Louis XVI by revolutionaries; Britain becomes involved in the French Revolutionary and Napoleonic Wars.
- **1804** Further bout of mental incapacitation is followed by almost total blindness.
- **1810** George descends into his final illness, becoming incapable of fulfilling the functions of a monarch.
- **February 1811** The future George IV takes over as Prince Regent.
- **1818** Queen Charlotte dies, the second longest serving consort in British history.
- **1820** George III dies at Windsor on January 28, and is buried in St. George's Chapel at Windsor Castle on February 15.

1806 COPPER HALFPENNY COIN

The South

Class rivalries and resentments ran deep in the Southern Colonies. The emerging conflict with Britain was the very thing to stir up trouble, which the British believed could be exploited to their advantage in the war.

BEFORE

In the South—Virginia, Georgia, and the Carolinas—the rumblings of discontent were just as audible as those in New England.

PATRIOT SYMPATHIES
Most southern colonists were in sympathy with **Patriots in Boston << 30–31**, but needing British protection from Indian attack, Georgia did not send any delegates to the **First Continental Congress << 42–43**, and did not join the **Second Continental Congress << 62–63** until July 1775. The other southern colonies, especially Virginia— "the Old Dominion"—contained many eager Patriots from the start.

DUNMORE THE WARMONGER
Before the outbreak of armed rebellion in the colonies, the Virginia militia had recent experience of war. In 1774, they had fought the Shawnee people under their royal governor in **"Lord Dunmore's War" << 36–37**. Dunmore emerged the victor, but was accused of waging the war as a distraction, in the face of growing dissatisfaction with British rule in Virginia.

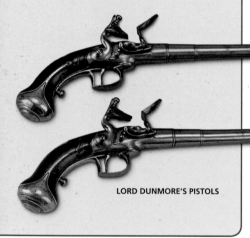

LORD DUNMORE'S PISTOLS

I n the early years of the War of Independence, the main military confrontations between the rebels and the British forces took place in the North. The southern colonies were bitterly divided. In particular, divisions within Georgia delayed the decision to join the rebellion until July 1775.

The wealthy planter class of the tidewater regions of Virginia and North Carolina had largely Patriot sympathies, while the less well-off farmers of the backcountry tended to be loyal to the Crown, as were the large numbers of settlers who were of Scots–Irish or German descent. This pool of potential support attracted the attention of the British authorities, who wanted to find ways to exploit this rift to defeat the rebels.

Rebellion in Virginia
Although there was clear evidence of resistance to British taxation in Virginia, the British high command did not immediately take meaningful action, as there was much to do in Boston. In early 1775, support for the Patriots was growing in the South. In March, many in Virginia were swayed by Patriot Patrick Henry's address to the Virginia Convention at St. John's church in Richmond, in which he cried: "Give me Liberty, or give me Death!"

In April 1775, the royal governor of Virginia, Lord Dunmore, tried to quash Patriot resistance. Only one day after the clashes at Lexington and Concord (see pp.54–55) and acting without warning, Dunmore seized colonial stockpiles of gunpowder stored at Williamsburg, giving orders for their transfer to a waiting British warship.

Virginia Patriots quickly rallied, mustering the militia and forcing Dunmore to flee the capital. By June, fearing for his life, Dunmore took refuge on a British man-of-war, but continued to attempt to hold the colony. After months of small skirmishes, between Dunmore's modest force of Redcoats and Patriot militia, the governor made a daring and controversial move. On November 7, 1775, Dunmore issued a proclamation declaring Virginia to be in a state of rebellion and imposed martial law.

> **After 11 days of skirmishing, the Battle of Great Bridge forced Dunmore to leave Virginia. The battle itself lasted only 30 minutes.**

The Virginia legislature was vocal in their outrage, but bold as Dunmore's Proclamation was, it was not enough. Although Dunmore's small force of British regulars scored a minor victory against Virginia militia at Kemp's Landing one week after the Proclamation, only a month later, on December 9, a Patriot army of Continental troops and local militia repulsed and shattered an attack by Dunmore's mixed force of Redcoats, Loyalists, and sailors at Great Bridge. Dunmore withdrew, and the British would not pose a serious threat to Virginia until 1779.

War in the backcountry
Elsewhere in the South, trouble mounted between Patriots and Loyalists. News of Lexington and Concord also stirred up trouble in Georgia, inspiring the Sons of Liberty (see pp.28–29) to steal gunpowder from the magazine in Augusta.

In South Carolina, Patriots took control of the coastal city of Charleston, driving out the last royal governor. However, the most serious action took place inland in the backcountry. During the summer of 1775, both Patriots and Loyalists in South Carolina raised large militia forces and tried to enlist the aid of

Native American tribes to the west. In November 1775, the warring factions came to blows, when Loyalist militia seized gunpowder that the Patriots had tried to send to their Cherokee allies.

Patriots under Andrew Williamson took possession of Ninety Six, a frontier settlement some 150 miles (240 km) northwest of Charleston. On November 19, a Loyalist force surrounded them there and eventually drove them off after an intense three-day skirmish.

Snow patrol
Meanwhile, a larger Patriot army under Colonel Richard Richardson pushed deep into the South Carolina backcountry, in an expedition that came to be known as the "Snow Campaign." Richardson's growing Patriot force captured several prominent Loyalist leaders and pounced on a Loyalist encampment beside the Reedy River. On December 22, 1775, in the Battle of Great Cane Brake, Richardson's men defeated the Loyalists, before retiring— through a snowstorm—to Charleston. The numbers engaged may have been small, and the operation short, but the Snow Campaign neutralized Loyalist strength in the Carolina backcountry.

AFTER

Patriot triumphs in the South in 1775 laid the groundwork for resistance to the British advances in 1776.

LOYAL SCOTS CONTINUE THE FIGHT
British hopes of utilizing the Loyalist settlers, notably the Scots, to counter Patriot strength in the Carolinas remained alive in early 1776. Highland Scots fought at the Battle of **Moore's Creek Bridge 106–07 >>** off the mouth of North Carolina's Cape Fear River.

CHANGE OF FOCUS
In mid-1776, the arrival of a British fleet off the coast of South Carolina changed the focus of the war in the South. A key battle was fought at **Sullivan's Island 110–11 >>**, and in 1778, the British laid siege to the coastal town of **Savannah 210–11 >>**.

ROYAL GOVERNOR 1730–1809
LORD DUNMORE

John Murray, the 4th Earl of Dunmore, was appointed royal governor of New York and of Virginia in 1771. His rule in Virginia was fraught with tension, in large part because he failed to consult the legislative assembly, the House of Burgesses. Dunmore's clashes with the colonial assembly brought him into conflict with the Virginia militia and eventually led him to make his famous proclamation of 1775, which offered emancipation to slaves who fought for the British (see pp.78–79). His efforts to retain British control of Virginia ended in failure after his forces were defeated at the Battle of Great Bridge in December 1775. Dunmore returned to Britain in July 1776. He later served as governor of the Bahamas.

The Edenton Tea Party
North Carolina's own "tea party" took place on October 25, 1774, when wealthy Penelope Barker organized a boycott of British goods. British cartoons mocked the women's effort.

‹‹ BEFORE

The notion that people of African birth were born to serve the white population was pervasive in 18th-century America.

SLAVE-OWNING CULTURE

Slavery played a significant role in the economy of the **Thirteen Colonies ‹‹ 18–19**. As the practice of indentured servitude declined, wealthy colonists looked to buy slaves, especially to work the large, labor-intensive indigo, rice, and tobacco **plantations in the South**.

Many key revolutionary figures owned slaves: **George Washington** had slaves from the age of 11, while **Thomas Jefferson** owned more than 600 slaves during his lifetime.

DOUBLE STANDARDS

Ardent Patriots who believed passionately in the **equality of all men** did not often extend that equality to people of color. Nevertheless, some free black men did serve the Patriot cause, especially in the early days of the war. Twenty-one free African Americans took part in the **Battle of Concord ‹‹ 54–55**, while 88 fought at **Bunker Hill ‹‹ 58–59.**

Avenging his master's death

Pompey, the servant of Major Peirson, the commander of the 95th Regiment of Foot, fought with the British on the island of Jersey in 1781. The artist painted him wearing the colors of the Royal Ethiopians, although that regiment never fought in Jersey.

African American Loyalists

In 1770, around 20 percent of the colonial population was of African origin, the vast majority of them enslaved. Aware of this pool of potential support, the British turned to African Americans to boost their ranks, enticing slaves to fight to earn their freedom.

The African Americans serving with the rebels in the northern colonies were, for the most part, free men. In the South, however, where the majority of African Americans were slaves, there was little opportunity, or motivation, for them to support the Patriot cause. The British understood this and made it part of their strategy to widen the rift between Patriot masters and their slaves.

> **Dunmore's Royal Ethiopian Regiment had close to 300 soldiers by December 1775.**

The call goes out

The most famous expression of this policy was the issue of the Emancipation Proclamation in November 1775 by John Murray, Lord Dunmore. The last royal governor of Virginia, Dunmore was fighting a losing battle against the Virginia rebels, and by June that year had been forced to seek refuge on a British warship (see pp.76–77).

His proclamation officially declared martial law in Virginia, denounced those who opposed his authority as traitors, and included the remarkable assertion that all indentured servants and African American slaves capable of fighting for the king would be freed from bondage. Dunmore was no idealist; his motivation was to drive a wedge between slaves and their owners, raise the potent fear of a slave insurrection, and tap into a previously unused source of recruits for the Loyalist side.

Successful recruitment

Dunmore's proclamation set the tone for British policy for much of the war. General William Howe, the principal British commander from 1775 to 1778, disliked the idea of African Americans in his army, but his successor, Sir Henry Clinton, revived Dunmore's policy with the Philipsburg Proclamation of 1779, promising freedom—and land—to any escaped slave of a Patriot. Slaves of Loyalists were specifically excluded.

Ads for runaway slaves during the period attest to the effectiveness of Dunmore's strategy. One posted in the *Virginia Gazette* in 1775, by a Robert Brent of Stafford County, Virginia, claimed that his former slave Charles had run away "from no cause of complaint … but from a determined resolution to get Liberty, as he conceived, by flying to Lord Dunmore."

African Americans sought freedom with the British in great numbers. They served in racially-mixed British units and figured prominently in Loyalist units, some of them all black. Lord Dunmore raised a full regiment—known as the Royal Ethiopian Regiment—in 1775, comprising many escaped slaves. In the southern campaigns, former slaves made up a large proportion of British forces. One in 10 Redcoats in the British Army at Savannah in 1779 was black.

Many African Americans served as noncombatants. Units such as the "Black Pioneers" were tasked with digging trenches, building fortifications, and other manual labor. A memorandum from William Howe's orderly book shows that in 1778 the Black Pioneers were ordered to "Attend the Scavengers, Assist in Cleaning … Removing all Newsiances being threwn into the Streets" in Philadelphia following the British capture of the city.

Loyalist belt plate
The Butler's Rangers regiment contained about a dozen former slaves, but only one—Richard Pierpoint, who signed the Petition of Free Negroes in Canada in 1794—is known by name.

> ## "They have been **flattered with their freedom,** if they be **able to bear arms.**"
>
> **LETTER FROM THE *VIRGINIA GAZETTE*, NOVEMBER 25, 1775**

African Americans also served as boatmen and wagon drivers to transport supplies, while others used their skills as carpenters and blacksmiths in the army. In some positions, African Americans found themselves integrated with their white counterparts, but laborers were often kept segregated into black units, such as the Virginia Company of Black Laborers.

The Black Brigade

African Americans fighting for the British could not generally aspire to officer status; even in the Royal Ethiopian Regiment. Titus Cornelius—known to the British by the honorary title of Colonel Tye—was a rare exception. After a period of service in the Royal Ethiopian, Tye led a band of African American guerrilla fighters—the elite "Black Brigade"—in a series of successful raids in New Jersey in 1779 and 1780.

Call to arms
In his proclamation, Dunmore called on all able-bodied men—including servants and slaves of rebels—to "report to his Majesty's standard" as soon as possible.

AFTER »

The promise of freedom was not always fulfilled: at the end of the war the British government agreed to return any slaves in their possession.

HONORING PROMISES
Although some generals, including Lord Cornwallis, abandoned the African American troops under their command, others, such as Sir Guy Carleton, did their best to honor their debt to African American Loyalists. When **British forces evacuated New York in 1783, 310–11** », the British took some 3,000 former slaves to settle in Canada.

LIFE IN CANADA
For those African American Loyalists who managed to escape to Canada, **freedom did not translate into an easy life**. Nova Scotia was not good farmland, and white Loyalists—some of them former slave owners—did not react well to the presence of so many former slaves. In 1784, the resentment of **landless white Loyalists** in Shelburne, Nova Scotia, boiled over into a series of brutal attacks on black homesteads, the **first recorded race riots** in North America.

BEFORE

Before 1763, Canada was called New France, and was the largest American territory in France's colonial empire. The 1763 Treaty of Paris handed Canada to Britain.

TRADITIONAL ENEMIES
The **old rivalry** between Britain and France led to war in their American colonies. French settlers and allied Native American groups **frequently attacked** British settlements in New England and other colonies. Britain's victory in the **French and Indian War ‹‹ 24–25** changed all that.

RELIGIOUS DIMENSION
Patriot leaders saw French-Canadians as **likely partners** in an anti-British rebellion. Catholic Canadians, however, had seen how New England Protestants opposed the 1774 **Quebec Act ‹‹ 42–43** establishing religious tolerance. They did not welcome an independent, possibly anti-Catholic, America.

The Invasion of Canada

The Congress authorized its generals to invade Canada in 1775, hoping to win the population over to their side and block a possible British invasion of New England from the north. The Patriots believed that Canada was not well defended and could be captured easily.

The Continental Congress had high hopes that the people of Canada would cast their lot with the rebels. The First Continental Congress had made overtures to Canada, and the Second continued to press the case. Pointing out how the traditional liberties associated with living under British rule were being systematically crushed, the Congress tried in vain to persuade the inhabitants of Quebec, Nova Scotia, and St. John's Island (present-day Prince Edward Island) to join them. Delegates hoped that at least the French-speaking Canadians would regard their American neighbors as brothers and embrace their cause.

When Benedict Arnold and Ethan Allen, Patriot heroes of the capture of Fort Ticonderoga in May 1775, proposed an invasion of the territories to the north, the Congress listened. In late June, it gave its stamp of approval, and offered command of the expedition to General Philip Schuyler of New York—much to the chagrin of the ambitious Arnold, who had entertained hopes of getting the position himself.

Twin attack plans
The basic plan was ambitious but straightforward. Schuyler, with General Richard Montgomery as his second in command, would push

north from Ticonderoga to Lake Champlain and eventually on to Montreal. Once Montreal had fallen, Schuyler would lead his force to Quebec, arriving there well before winter set in. However, Benedict Arnold, who clung tenaciously to the prospect of finding glory in a Canadian invasion, did not want to let Schuyler and Montgomery take an assignment that he was convinced should be his.

The Quebec Expedition
This 19th-century engraving depicts Benedict Arnold's troops crossing the St. Lawrence to begin the Siege of Quebec. The attackers eventually had no option but to try to storm the city's defenses.

Arnold approached George Washington, then commanding the army at Boston, with another plan. If Washington could spare the men, Arnold would lead them through the Maine wilderness, via the Kennebec and Chaudière rivers, to the banks of the St. Lawrence and the gates of Quebec. There he would await Schuyler, and together the two American armies would attack the thinly defended town. He assumed that the French Canadians would flock to the rebel standard, and therefore that success would be all but guaranteed.

March on Fort St. Jean

Schuyler's invasion was cursed with bad luck and bad planning. Overcautious, Schuyler wasted valuable time while preparing his army. Eventually Montgomery took the initiative. In late August 1775, while Schuyler was busy in negotiations with potential Native American allies, Montgomery set out

from Ticonderoga to attack the British garrison at Fort St. Jean on the Richelieu River. Meanwhile, Schuyler, a notorious hypochondriac, resigned his command.

Montgomery pushed on, and somehow his sick and disheartened army held together. After a 55-day siege, St. Jean fell on November 3, 1775. The campaign almost wrecked the Patriot army.

The "set of pusillanimous wretches," as Montgomery called his own troops, ransacked the countryside. The New Englanders and New Yorkers, who made up the bulk of Montgomery's army, were mostly Protestant, and the French settlers were mostly Catholic; so many Patriot soldiers therefore had no reservations about treating the French roughly. The behavior of many rebels alienated the very population they were supposed to win over.

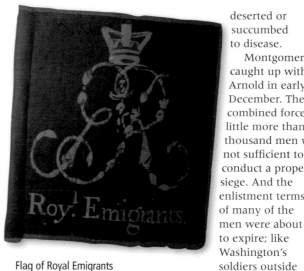

Flag of Royal Emigrants
Camp colors such as this marked the streets in British Army campsites so that the soldiers could identify their regimental areas. Recruited in North America in 1775, the Royal Highland Emigrants played a leading role in the defense of Quebec City that year.

deserted or succumbed to disease.

Montgomery caught up with Arnold in early December. Their combined force of little more than a thousand men was not sufficient to conduct a proper siege. And the enlistment terms of many of the men were about to expire; like Washington's soldiers outside Boston, they had committed to serve only until the end of the year. Faced with the complete dissolution of their armies, the two Patriot generals felt compelled to act.

Last-ditch assault

On December 31, 1775, in the teeth of a raging blizzard, the rebels launched an all-out attack on the heavily fortified city. Montgomery was killed outright in the very first moments of the assault; most of his troops retreated once word of their commander's death spread through

BRITISH GENERAL 1724–1808

SIR GUY CARLETON

Carleton saw service in the British Army from the 1740s. He came to North America in 1759 and was wounded in the capture of Quebec. Appointed Governor of Quebec in 1768, Carleton supported the 1774 Quebec Act.

In 1775, Carleton prepared to defend the colony against rebel attack but was nearly captured when Montreal fell to the rebels, only escaping in disguise. After General Burgoyne was appointed to lead the invasion of New York in 1777, Carleton left Canada. He commanded British forces in North America briefly at the end of the war and was Governor-General of Canada in the 1780s and 1790s.

" the most … **unparalleled …** **sufferings …** of any nation."

DR. ISAAC SENTER ON THE RETREATING PATRIOTS, FROM HIS DIARY, 1775

Six days after the fall of St. Jean, Montgomery's army reached Montreal, which surrendered on November 13. But winter was setting in, Quebec was still a long way off, and Montgomery's sullen men were deserting in droves.

Advance on Quebec

To the east, Arnold didn't have it much better. With Washington's blessing, Arnold marched out of Cambridge in September with a thousand men. Among them were perhaps the best troops for the job: a body of Continental riflemen, frontiersmen recruited from the backcountry, led by the legendary Daniel Morgan.

Arnold ran into problems right from the outset, however. Leaky boats and spoiled provisions made the passage up the Kennebec River and down the Chaudière a genuine nightmare of toil, disease, and near starvation. By mid-November when Arnold's forces approached Quebec, only half of his men remained, the rest having either

the ranks. Arnold, with Daniel Morgan by his side, made it into the Lower Town. Here they found themselves trapped. Arnold was wounded, Morgan surrendered, and only a handful of Arnold's men managed to escape.

The Canadian campaign had been an unmitigated disaster, the Continental Army's first significant defeat, but it was not over. Arnold laid siege to Quebec—to no effect. The British commander, Sir Guy Carleton, was content to sit tight and wait it out. His men were well-supplied, sheltered, and warm. What was left of Arnold's army went hungry, and was soon ravaged by one of the worst smallpox epidemics of the war.

For a very brief while, the Patriot forces maintained their toehold in Canada. At the turn of the year, Montreal remained under rebel occupation and the pitiful remnants of Arnold's once-proud army held their positions outside Quebec.

AFTER »

By the spring of 1776, the Patriot campaign in Canada was over. Canada would no longer be a strategic objective for the rebels.

WITHDRAWAL AND INVASION

In May 1776, rebel troops pulled out of Montreal and Quebec to begin the disheartening march back to Fort Ticonderoga. The arrival of **fresh regiments of Redcoats 92–93 »** emboldened Carleton, who pursued the retreating Patriots. In 1776 and again in 1777, British armies **advanced into New York** via Montreal, Lake Champlain, and Fort Ticonderoga **152–53 »**.

LESSONS FOR THE FUTURE

The 1775 invasion of Canada consumed manpower and resources that might have been better employed closer to home; it demonstrated **the folly of conquest** when self-defense needed everything that the rebels could muster. Several participants in the 1775 campaign also played a key role in later battles, notably **Benedict Arnold**, who fought inspiringly on the Patriot side in the battles of 1776–77.

Heroic failure
General Montgomery expires in the arms of his compatriots in *The Death of Montgomery at the Attack on Quebec* (1775) by war artist John Trumbull (1756–1843).

3
BIRTH OF A NATION
1776

The Patriots grappled with the challenges of creating a credible army, while Britain struggled to deliver "decisive action." The British had the edge in Quebec and New York City, but were driven back at Charleston. The end of the year brought the Patriots a morale-boosting development at Trenton.

«The toppling of King George
In July 1776, the Continental Congress declared independence from Britain. On hearing the news, New Yorkers attacked a statue of King George on the Bowling Green, slinging ropes around the

ACTION IN 1776

For the British, 1776 was a year of missed opportunities. Logistical difficulties—lack of shipping and a stormy Atlantic—delayed the dispatch of reinforcements and supplies, and the cautious generals, William Howe and Guy Carleton, too often failed to press their advantage. Nevertheless, British forces raised the siege of Quebec, cleared Canada of rebels, captured New York City, and nearly destroyed George Washington's army—all before winter arrived. For Patriots, despite receiving a tranche of artillery from Henry Knox that enabled them to push the British out of Boston, and a victory at Charleston, 1776 was mainly a year of military disaster. Two events lifted rebel spirits: the Declaration of Independence in July and the surprise attack at Trenton, New Jersey, on Christmas Day.

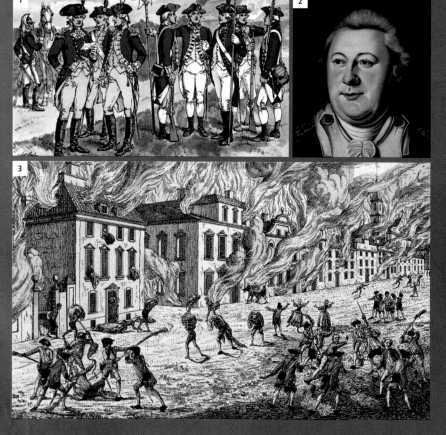

1 The Congress reorganized the army, creating the Southern and Middle Departments in February. 2 General Henry Knox's delivery of artillery enabled the Patriots to drive the British out of Boston in March. 3 British-occupied New York City was ravaged by fire in September.

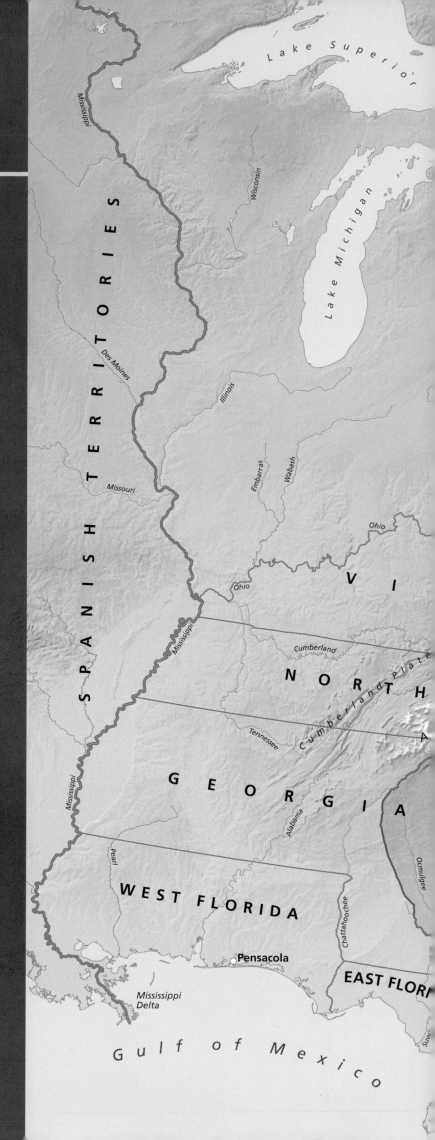

Newfoundland

Magdalen Islands

Prince Edward Island

Louisbourg

Saguenay

NOVA SCOTIA

St. Maurice

Quebec

Battle of Trois Rivieres

Penobscot

St. John

MASSACHUSETTS

Bay of Fundy

○ **Halifax**

Sable Island

Ottawa

QUEBEC

St. Lawrence

Montreal *St. Jean*

Lake Champlain

Battle of Valcour Island

Fort Saint-Frédéric

Fort Ticonderoga

Skenesboro

White Mountains

Green Mountains

NEW HAMPSHIRE

Connecticut

Lake Huron

Georgian Bay

Lake Ontario

Lake Erie

Mohawk

NEW YORK

Albany

Hudson

Catskill Mountains

MASSACHUSETTS

[2] **Boston**

Cape Cod

CONNECTICUT

Newport

RHODE ISLAND

ATLANTIC OCEAN

Allegheny

PENNSYLVANIA

Battle of Princeton

[3] **New York City**

Princeton

Philadelphia **NEW JERSEY**

Battle of Trenton

[1]

Muskingum

Ohio

Kanawha

Baltimore

DELAWARE

MARYLAND

Chesapeake Bay

James

Yorktown

Roanoke

Dan

Norfolk

KEY

— Border of Spanish territories

— 1763 Proclamation Line

— Colonial boundaries

○ Town / settlement

✕ Battle / siege

🏰 Fort

⛵ Naval battle

🪶 Treaty / convention

⛺ Loyalist winter camp

⛺ Patriot winter camp

CAROLINA

Pee Dee

Wateree

Cape Fear

Battle of Moore's Creek Bridge

SOUTH CAROLINA

Camden

Wilmington

Governor Martin's Proclamation

Augusta

Charleston Fort Sullivan

Battle of the Rice Boats ⛵ *Battle of Sullivan's Island*

annah

Hutchinson Island ○ *Tybee Island*

oha

Johns

0   100 km
0   100 miles

N

0   100 km
0   100 miles

Mohawk

NEW HAMPSHIRE

Green Mountains

Connecticut

NEW YORK

Albany

Hudson

Catskill Mountains

MASSACHUSETTS

[2] **Boston**

Siege of Boston

Cape Cod

CONNECTICUT

Newport

RHODE ISLAND

Susquehanna

PENNSYLVANIA

Delaware

Battle of Fort Washington

Battle of Harlem Heights

Morristown

Battle of White Plains

Long Island

Battle of Long Island

New York City [3] ⛵ *Landing at Kip's Bay*

New Brunswick

Attack on HMS Eagle

Princeton

Perth Amboy

Second Continental Congress (I) *Battle of Trenton*

Philadelphia

[1]

NEW JERSEY

DELAWARE

Second Continental Congress (II)

🪶 **Baltimore**

MARYLAND

ATLANTIC OCEAN

0   100 km
0   100 miles

TIMELINE 1776

Evacuation of Boston ▪ **European alliances** ▪ Patriot success in South Carolina
▪ **The Declaration of Independence** ▪ Battle of Long Island ▪ **Howe takes**
New York ▪ Washington crosses the Delaware ▪ **Battle of Trenton**

JANUARY	FEBRUARY	MARCH	APRIL	MAY	JUNE
JANUARY 1 Four British warships open fire on Norfolk, Virginia.	**FEBRUARY 12** A 44-ship convoy leaves Ireland for the Cape Fear River to rendezvous with North Carolina Loyalists.	**MARCH 12** British General Sir Henry Clinton arrives off Cape Fear but is unable to land his troops.	**APRIL 3** The Second Continental Congress authorizes privateers to attack British vessels.	**MAY 3** The last ships from Clinton's fleet arrive off the Cape Fear River.	
JANUARY 9 An agreement is signed between Britain and Brunswick-Wolfenbuettel, securing auxiliary troops. It is the first of several treaties with the German principalities.	**FEBRUARY 27** Loyalists suffer a decisive defeat at the Battle of Moore's Creek Bridge, North Carolina.				⌃ Thomas Jefferson **JUNE 10** The Congress appoints a committee—including Thomas Jefferson—to draft the Declaration of Independence.
JANUARY 10 Thomas Paine's pamphlet *Common Sense* is published in Philadelphia.					**JUNE 28** Patriot Colonel William Moultrie defeats British forces under Clinton and Parker at the Battle of Sullivan's Island, in South Carolina.

⌄ Contemporary cartoon satirizing revolutionary ideas

⌃ Howitzer of the type used to lift the Siege of Boston

		MARCH	APRIL	MAY	
		MARCH 17 Under the threat of artillery bombardment, General William Howe evacuates British forces from Boston and ships his troops to Halifax, Nova Scotia.	**APRIL 7** The main convoy of Hessian reinforcements for the relief of Quebec sets sails from England and Ireland.	**MAY 6** The British warship HMS *Surprize* breaks through the ice of the St. Lawrence River to raise the siege of Quebec.	
		MARCH 21 A British flotilla, carrying 700 troops intended to raise the siege of Quebec, sails from England.		**MAY 15** The kings of France and Spain agree to provide secret financial assistance to the American rebels.	

≫ General Sir Henry Clinton

"When I was talking to him I observed him to play with pen and ink on several small pieces of paper ... I was struck by the inscription ... 'Victory or Death.'"

DR. BENJAMIN RUSH, ABOUT GEORGE WASHINGTON, RECALLING THE NIGHT OF DECEMBER 23, 1776

JULY	AUGUST	SEPTEMBER	OCTOBER	NOVEMBER	DECEMBER
JULY 3 General William Howe disembarks 10,000 men on Staten Island. **JULY 4** The Congress revises and issues the Declaration of Independence.		**SEPTEMBER 6** Patriot Sergeant Ezra Lee attempts to sink Admiral Lord Howe's HMS *Eagle* with the submersible *Turtle*.	**OCTOBER 11** General Benedict Arnold's forces are defeated at the Battle of Valcour Island.	**NOVEMBER 16** The Dutch governor of St. Eustatius, in the West Indies, orders a 13-gun salute honoring the Patriot flag—the first official acknowledgment of American sovereignty.	**DECEMBER 12** A British patrol captures General Charles Lee in a New Jersey tavern.

≫ Washington crossing the Delaware

JULY 9
A crowd on New York's Manhattan Island, excited by the Declaration of Independence, pulls down a statue of George III.

« *Turtle* submersible

OCTOBER 26
Benjamin Franklin sails for France to raise support for the Patriot cause.

AUGUST 22
The first British and Hessian troops land on Long Island.

SEPTEMBER 11
The Staten Island Peace Conference collapses as Britain refuses to recognize American independence.

OCTOBER 28
British and Hessian forces engage the Patriots in the Battle of White Plains.

NOVEMBER 28
Washington and his army retreat to the west bank of the Delaware River.

DECEMBER 25
Washington recrosses the Delaware to mount a surprise attack on a Hessian garrison at Trenton, New Jersey.

≫ The surrender of Hessian Colonel Johann Rall at Trenton

≪ Crowds topple a statue of George III on Bowling Green, Manhattan Island

AUGUST 27
General Howe's forces overwhelm Washington's Continentals in the Battle of Long Island.

SEPTEMBER 15
British troops land at Kips Bay on Manhattan Island and attack Washington's troops at Harlem Heights.

JULY 20
George Washington rebuffs peace overtures made by General Howe and his brother, Admiral Lord Richard Howe.

AUGUST 29
Washington starts the evacuation of the Brooklyn lines to Manhattan Island, across the East River.

SEPTEMBER 26
Congress authorizes a commission to sail to France to negotiate for loans, ships, and supplies.

Headquarters of the Empire
George III directed his American policy from St. James's Palace in London, where he met "grand strategist" Lord George Germain and other ministers several times a week.

BEFORE

Most British people did not relish war with America. Many feared that a struggle there might provoke another war with France. But to King George III the prestige of the Empire was at stake.

A FARAWAY REBELLION
After **Lexington and Concord 《 54–55**, where a war of words became one of bullets, the only British army in the Thirteen Colonies found itself **bottled up in Boston by a rebel force 《 58–59**. Britain had stamped out previous rebellions, but those had been in Scotland and Ireland. The American colonies comprised a vast extent of territory some 3,000 miles (4,800 km) away.

IMPLEMENTING POLICY
The king ruled the country through his cabinet, a small group of ministers who made policy. From November 1775, matters concerning the **Thirteen Colonies 《 18–19**, were entrusted to Lord George Germain, the secretary of state for the American department. His portfolio included implementing strategy for the coming war.

British Strategy

As 1776 began, King George III's ministers debated how best to halt the gathering rebellion in Britain's North American colonies. They decided to overthrow the seditious Congress, defeat its army, and promote those still loyal to the Crown.

Lord George Germain may have been welcome at St. James's Palace, the official residence of the king, but he was merely tolerated at Horse Guards, the headquarters of the British Army. The American secretary had been declared unfit to serve "in any military capacity whatsoever" after failing to follow an order at the Battle of Minden in 1759. Now he was in charge of running the war.

Germain had inherited from his predecessor, Lord Dartmouth, the top commanders in North America—General Guy Carleton in Quebec and General William Howe, who was responsible for expanding Britain's American territories from Nova Scotia to Florida during the French and Indian War. More importantly, he also inherited the strategic plan his predecessor had devised to scotch the

rebellion in 1776—a plan Germain by and large approved, hoping that with this strategy the war could be quickly ended by one decisive campaign.

Superior forces
Britain's main advantage was its professional army and renowned navy. Some armchair strategists thought that

4 The average number of months it took to cross the Atlantic in 1776. If conditions were good, the time could sometimes be cut by half.

the navy alone might win the war, by choking the life out of the colonies with a blockade. But in higher circles that plan was deemed impracticable, the navy being in disrepair after the

Seven Years' War in Europe and the American coastline being too long to patrol. Furthermore, to be effective a blockade would have to be maintained on neutral ports in the West Indies, which provided the rebels' principal supply base. Such an action might provoke a war with France or the Netherlands—Britain's worst fear.

Instead, the army and the navy would combine in joint operations to subdue the colonies. Boston, to begin with, was deemed untenable and Howe was ordered to evacuate it. New York City, with its spacious harbor, offered a better base, and Howe and his brother—Admiral Richard Howe, now in charge of their combined operations fleet—were ordered to seize the port. Command of the city might lead to control of that colony's principal river, the Hudson, potentially

"I should be for **exerting** the **utmost force ...** to finish the rebellion in **one campaign.**"

LORD GEORGE GERMAIN TO GENERAL JOHN IRWIN, SEPTEMBER 13, 1775

navigable by British warships as far as Albany, over 130 miles (210 km) upstream. An expeditionary force sent up the Hudson could meet one coming down from Montreal via Lake Champlain—thereby cutting off New England, the seedbed of revolt, from the rest of the colonies.

Isolating insurrectionist New England by land and by sea was the primary goal of Britain's war strategy. Severed from its supply base, the rebel army would either be starved into submission or forced to hazard a major battle against trained regulars. It might also be outflanked if the British seized Newport, Rhode Island. Local militia would have to break away to meet the new threat.

Germain changed nothing in Carleton's plan, except perhaps placing more emphasis on securing the Hudson, especially after receiving news of the Patriot defeat at Quebec (see pp.80–81). If Carleton could seize Lake Champlain, the only transportation corridor in that roadless wilderness, he might link up with Howe at Albany by early summer. The end of the rebellion might then be in sight.

On the other hand, the American Secretary took a dim view of a plan to sweeten the armed coercion with a little conciliation. The Howe brothers had also been appointed peace commissioners, official bearers of the king's "olive branch" to the rebels. Germain saw to it that the envoys could only offer amnesties, rendering the mission—undertaken after the Declaration of Independence—an inevitable failure.

Loyalists in the South

While the main push to isolate New England was being planned, another front opened, offering the opportunity to rally Loyalist support. Few Loyalists might be found in New England, but it was confidently believed that at least a third of the population in the South— Georgia, the Carolinas, and Virginia—and upward of half in the middle colonies—New York, New Jersey, and Pennsylvania— sided with the king. These Loyalists, it was decided, should be recruited and their families protected. Their legions might then garrison the reconquered colonies, it being impossible for the overstretched British Army.

Loyalists in the South, at least according to the report of former royal governors there, were already believed to be on the march, and a second task force had been dispatched there in November 1775. This force was to rendezvous with loyal backcountry frontiersmen off North Carolina's Cape Fear River, from where it could explore

950	The number of horses shipped to America in 1776.
400	The number of horses that died en route in 1776.

The capture of New York

In September 1776, General William Howe achieved his first strategic goal, occupying New York City and the mouth of the Hudson River. The British would retain the port for the rest of the war.

targets of opportunity, even, perhaps, sailing into Charleston, the region's leading seaport.

Storm clouds

Lord Germain would later be criticized for issuing overly detailed and conflicting instructions to his generals, but in early 1776 his judgment was sound. The subsequent campaigns were impeded not by his interference but rather by vagaries of the weather, the caution of his commanders, and staggering logistical challenges.

Germain had to arrange the transportation across the Atlantic of more than 20,000 troops, including the first detachments of soldiers hired from Germany, along with their ordnance, supplies, provisions, tents, baggage, horses, ammunition, and wagons, all of which needed assembling at various embarkation ports. Everything the troops needed— from axes to water buckets, rum casks to drum cases—had to be shipped from the home islands. The 1776 campaign marked the beginning of a British seaborne logistical effort that would not be exceeded until World War II, and it was maintained for eight years.

Finally, Germain's hope for a short decisive campaign in 1776 was thrown into sharp relief by events across the English Channel. Those in charge of Britain's war policy realized that a protracted struggle in America would be likely to result in the rebels reaching out to France for assistance. Their fears were well founded; in June of 1776, British spies reported that the Comte de Vergennes, the leading French minister, had won permission to offer secret aid to the Americans—and authorization to begin building up the French navy to a war footing.

AFTER

In the end, British strategy in 1776 was undone by various delays and diversions. Fleets were scattered by Atlantic storms, and troops and supplies were rerouted to Canada to help defeat a Patriot invasion there.

FATAL DELAYS

General Howe took **New York City 118–19 ≫**, secured the lower Hudson River, and pushed the rebels off Manhattan. But he could not open his campaign until August, fatally delaying any attempt to meet General Carleton in Albany.

Carleton, meanwhile, was detained at Lake Champlain, on the border with Canada, by the need to build a naval fleet to counter an American flotilla in the **Battle of Valcour Island 128–29 ≫** in October 1776.

SOUTHERN STRATEGY

The British **southern strategy** also foundered. North Carolina Loyalists were defeated at the **Battle of Moore's Creek Bridge 106–07 ≫** and the foray into Charleston was repulsed at the **Battle of Sullivan's Island 110–11 ≫**.

BRITISH FIELD GUN

Redcoats

On the winning side of every major war since 1689, the British Army was considered by many contemporaries to be the best in the world, and the regiment of foot, as the red-coated infantry was called, was its heart and soul.

An officer and a gentleman
Richard St. George Marsergh, of the 4th Regiment of Foot, commissioned this portrait of himself before leaving for America. Toward the end of the war, he served as an aide-de-camp to Sir Henry Clinton.

« BEFORE

Until the French and Indian War, the colonial militia—pools of men called on to provide defense—was the only military most colonials knew, and it was only mustered when war flared up with the French and their Indian allies.

INTO THE WILDERNESS
Large numbers of British regulars traveled to North America to fight in the **French and Indian War « 24–25**. Many colonists fought alongside them in the conflict, including the young George Washington.

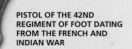

PISTOL OF THE 42ND REGIMENT OF FOOT DATING FROM THE FRENCH AND INDIAN WAR

FIRST IMPRESSIONS
The Patriots' success in the fight along the road back from **Lexington and Concord « 54–55** and the damage they inflicted at **Bunker Hill « 58–59** boosted their confidence. Yet the reality of fighting troops, whom Boston urchins called "lobsterbacks," would prove a **formidable challenge**.

I n 1776, there were 70 regiments of foot and 28 of horse in the British Army in different parts of the empire. With few exceptions, members of these regiments wore the famous red coat, the color of the "facings"—collar, lapel, and cuffs—being the only thing to distinguish soldiers of one regiment from another.

Each regiment in the British Army contained around 600 officers and men. On campaign, a regiment was divided into ten companies. Two of them, the grenadiers and the light infantry, were elite units. The remaining eight were line companies, so called because they were deployed in long battle lines two or three ranks deep.

The officer class
Regiments operated as proprietary concerns, owned by a colonel who could augment his income by dipping into the regimental budget. Most officers purchased their commissions, working their way up the ladder of promotion by selling, for example, a lieutenancy in order to buy a captaincy. Because only gentlemen could afford to buy commissions, the class system was preserved. An ambitious young officer might serve as an aide-de-camp (assistant in the field) to a high-ranking officer.

The rank and file
There were many reasons why a young man would accept the "king's shilling" and join the army, but poverty was chief among them. Half of the recruits came from the Scottish Highlands and Ireland, the poorest parts of the British Isles at that time.

> **8 PENCE the amount a British Army private earned per day.**
> **6 PENCE how much a soldier might pay each week for laundry.**

Soldiering brought little improvement to the lives of these men. They subsisted on salt pork and biscuit, and marched heavily burdened by blanket, knapsack, canteen, and ammunition. They fought in inhospitable climates and were often ravaged by disease. Some looted; others were accused of atrocities. Yet surprisingly few soldiers deserted, despite temptations. For many of the men, the army was their only home.

The hatmen
In the open field, the line infantry bore the brunt of the fighting. These "hatmen"—for they wore tricorne hats—hoisted Brown Bess muskets with fixed bayonets, and advanced shoulder to shoulder on the enemy, closing up when a comrade was killed or wounded. Because commands could not be heard above the din of battle, drums conveyed all orders: at a distance of about 35 yd (32 m), they beat out orders to halt, level muskets, and fire.

The resulting volley was not a haphazard pulling of triggers; on the

> "**I do not think that there exists a more select corps.**"
>
> CAPTAIN FRIEDRICH VON MUENCHHAUSEN, GENERAL HOWE'S AIDE, JUNE 1777

contrary, volley firing by platoon meant that a portion of the battalion was always shooting while others were reloading, the flash and smoke and thunder rolling up and down the line in a disciplined fashion. One sustained volley might be enough to demoralize the foe. If any enemy survivors then heard three resounding cheers and the pounding of hundreds of feet, they would know that a bayonet charge was coming.

Feared grenadiers
The dreaded bayonet charge, a British specialty, was all the more terrifying when giant grenadiers came storming through the smoke. Although these units had once thrown grenades, only their name survived by the late 18th century. The grenadiers were still the largest and most physically imposing soldiers in a regiment—often standing at 7 ft (2.1 m) tall when wearing their signature bearskin hats.

The volley and charge helped the British win nearly every pitched battle in the War of Independence, while most Patriot victories were made over small detachments isolated from a main army. Only at the battles of

Frontal assault
At the Battle of Bunker Hill in 1775, Redcoat grenadiers marching in formation made a frontal assault into the fire of the Patriot defense. In later battles, British commanders, having learned the lessons of Bunker Hill, made better use of flanking tactics.

Saratoga and Yorktown—where the Redcoats were trapped—did the Patriots win resoundingly. The Patriot strategy was usually to make the conflict a war of attrition and raids, always retreating to the hills and forests. The British grenadiers on the battalion's right may have won honor on European battlefields, but this new form of war in America favored the other elite company: the light infantry.

Light infantry

Composed of lithe, agile men, the "light bobs" were Britain's answer to the frontier-style bush fighting of the Patriots. Wearing short jackets and skullcaps—the better to maneuver through undergrowth—they acted as scouts or flankers. Ranging ahead of the main body, they climbed fences and trees, and fired from behind cover. Unlike line soldiers, who obeyed orders instinctively, they were trained to be self-reliant—which sometimes made them insubordinate.

Supply chains

"You cannot conquer America," former prime minister William Pitt once said. It was too big; it was too far away; it had too few roads. For this reason, British forces were rarely more than 15 miles (24 km) from a navigable river. Nearly all their food traveled 3,000 miles (4,800 km) from England, so baggage trains could be immense: in 1778, one numbered 1,500 wagons and stretched for 12 miles (20 km). The trains not only carried rations, tents, and ammunition but also camp followers, mostly wives and women, who cooked, washed, sewed, and helped tend to the wounded. Baggage trains also used up the army's supply of horses, already impaired by inadequate forage, which was another reason why it was an infantryman's war. The best known cavalry unit, Tarleton's Legion, was raised locally. Its baggage train was limited to 35 wagons.

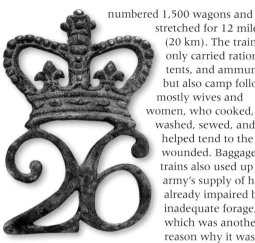

Redcoat badge
A detachment of the 26th Regiment of Foot, consisting of 45 officers and men, was defending Fort Ticonderoga when it was captured by Patriots in 1775. This brass badge was found in the ruins.

The American War of Independence was undoubtedly a defeat for the British Army, but it won some notable battles along the way.

BRITISH SUCCESS
The battles of **Long Island 118–19 »** and **Camden 274–75 »** rank among the most devastating British victories of the age, while their capture of **Charleston 266–67 »** in 1780 was a model of siegecraft.

IGNOMINIOUS DEFEAT
The **Battle of Saratoga 162–63 »** saw the first surrender of a British army in its history, and **Yorktown 304–05 »** the second. There would not be another defeat on this scale until the surrender of Singapore in 1942 during World War II.

[4] BRITISH GRENADIER OFFICER'S COAT

[1] INFANTRYMAN'S LEATHER CAP

[2] GRENADIER'S BEARSKIN CAP

[3] INFANTRYMAN'S ROUND COAT

British Uniforms

Eighteenth-century European military uniforms were designed to impress rather than for the practicalities of warfare. British soldiers' bright red coats enabled their commanders, and enemies, to see them during battle.

[1] **Infantryman's leather cap** This light, foldable leather cap, adopted mid-war, improved upon the original standard-issue hat, which was heavy, hot, and unsuitable to the campaigns in America. [2] **Grenadier's bearskin cap** Tall bearskins added to the imposing appearance of the grenadiers. The royal motto, *ec aspera terrent*, meaning "difficulties be damned," is engraved on the front plate. [3] **Infantryman's round coat** Many Americans fought on the British side during the war. Some Loyalist regiments received green jackets; they later fell out of favor except among light infantry. [4] **British grenadier officer's coat** The wings on the shoulders of this scarlet jacket indicate that this officer also wore epaulettes. [5] **Ankle gaiters** Redcoats wore brown, gray, or black gaiters when on campaign: white gaiters were reserved for parade. [6] **2nd Battalion officer's coat** These were lighter and more comfortable than the coats worn by common soldiers, because officers could usually afford to have their uniforms made to order

by military tailors. [7] **44th Regiment of Foot officer's coat** The coat facings were used to identify the soldier's regiment: yellow represented the 44th Regiment of Foot. [8] **Officer's epaulette** Fastened to the coat shoulders by straps or laces, these were worn by officers as an insignia of rank. [9] **Gilt gorget** British officers wore breast plates called gorgets around the neck while on duty. They were also a mark of rank. [10] **Silver gorget** Gorgets were made of gold, silver, and gilt; the Warrant of 1768 decreed that the metal should match that of the regiment. [11] **Haversack** Usually made from canvas or coarse linen, the haversack was used by soldiers to carry equipment and rations. [12] **Belt with bayonet** This belt belonged to a soldier of the 15th Regiment of Foot who fought at the Battle of Ridgefield in 1777. [13] **Belt with cartridge box** Embossed with the royal insignia of King George III, the box contained powder and lead shot. [14] **Tin canteen** Hung from the shoulder, canteens were used to carry water.

[5] ANKLE GAITERS

6 2ND BATTALLION OFFICER'S COAT

7 44TH REGIMENT OF FOOT OFFICER'S COAT

8 OFFICER'S EPAULETTE

9 GILT GORGET

10 SILVER GORGET

11 HAVERSACK

12 BELT WITH BAYONET

13 BELT WITH CARTRIDGE BOX

14 TIN CANTEEN

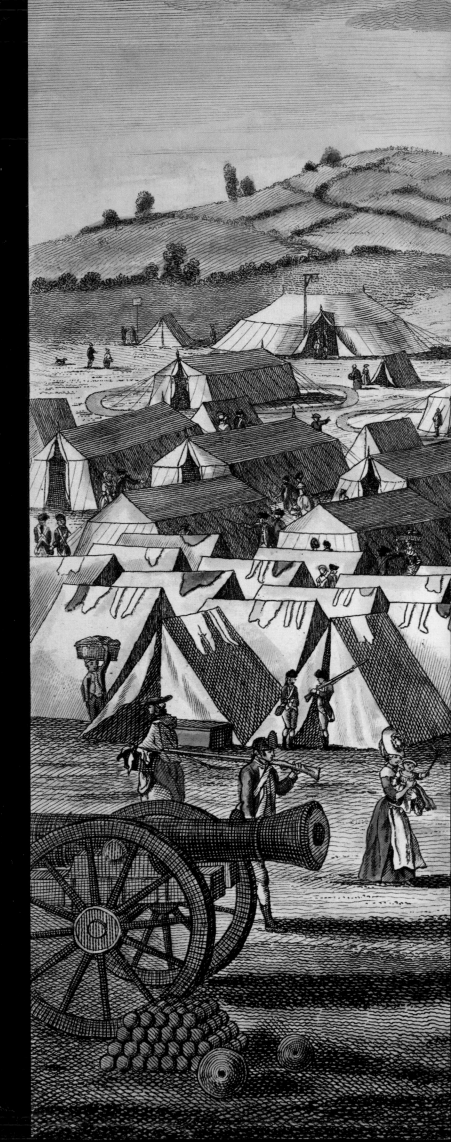

A Serving Redcoat

Redcoat camps in America not only provided sleeping accommodation for the officers, men, and the women (wives and female servants) who accompanied them, but also needed to include provision for eating, laundry, and entertainment. In many cases the facilities were less comfortable than the officers were expecting—as Lord Rawdon describes in a letter to his uncle, the Earl of Huntingdon.

"At our lines neither officer nor man have the smallest shelter against the inclemency of the weather, but stand to the works all night. Indeed in point of alertness and regularity our officers have great merit. I have not seen either drinking or gaming in this camp. If anything, there is too little society among us. In general, every man goes to his own tent very soon after sunset, where those who can amuse themselves in that manner, read; and the others probably sleep. I usually have a red herring, some onions, and some porter about eight o'clock, of which three or four grave sedate people partake. We chat about different topics and retire to our beds about nine. There is not quite so much enjoyment in this way of life as in what ... the troops in Boston enjoy. For some days past it has not ceased raining; every tent is thoroughly wet, and every countenance thoroughly dull. A keen wind which has accompanied this rain, makes people talk upon the parade of the comforts of a chimney corner; and we hear with some envy, of several little balls and concerts which our brethren have had in Boston."

CAPTAIN LORD RAWDON TO HIS UNCLE, OCTOBER 5, 1775

A British encampment

This domestic view of camp life—showing well-dressed wives, laundry drying over tent poles, canine companions, and a baby in its mothers arms—dates from 1780. Although idealized, it does portray the spectrum of camp society: small "common tents" for the rank and file; larger "wall tents" for officers; and "marquees," in the background, for the highest-ranking men.

The **Philosophy** of **Revolt**

The ideas that encouraged colonists to break free from Britain had deep roots. Derived from philosophical principles, ethnic loyalties, and even religious awakenings, they profoundly shaped American concepts of freedom.

BEFORE

British colonists living in North America felt protective of their historic rights and liberties.

THE GOOD LIFE
In their own eyes, the inhabitants of the **Thirteen Colonies ‹‹ 18–19** were just as much **freeborn Englishmen** as their "cousins" back home. Many of them even enjoyed greater prosperity, thanks to burgeoning trade. Apart from experiencing intermittent wars with the French, the colonies basked in the glow of a halcyon age—one that ended with passage of the **Sugar Act in 1764 ‹‹ 28–29**.

WRITER 1737–1809

THOMAS PAINE

British-born Thomas Paine, the most influential political pamphleteer of the late 18th century, was a born propagandist. His best-selling, 47-page *Common Sense* (1776) justified the American struggle for independence, while his *American Crisis* papers boosted low morale. Paine later extolled the virtues of the French Revolution in *The Rights of Man* (1791) and promoted freedom of thought, especially in religious matters, in *The Age of Reason* (1794). Without Paine's pen, said John Adams, "the sword of Washington would have been raised in vain."

It was only natural for transplanted Englishmen who valued their rights as British subjects to turn to the English philosopher John Locke. In *Two Treatises of Civil Government*, Locke asserted that society was not founded as a divinely ordained hierarchy; on the contrary, he maintained that all men are created equal, and all have the right to life, liberty, and property. They also have the right to resist tyranny.

Defending liberty

To the thoughtful colonist of the "Country" persuasion, the social contract involved interlocking relationships between the concepts of property, liberty, privilege, duty, virtue, and resistance. It was the duty of Patriots, as the Country faction styled themselves, to keep vigilant watch on the monarch and his greedy and corrupt court, who might otherwise usurp all ancient liberties. They were opposed to high taxes, suspicious of standing armies, protective of personal freedoms, and preferred the balance of power to lie with the landed gentry. Their favorite exemplars were classical rather than biblical: the ancient Greek city-states and the Roman Republic.

These ideas had crossed the Atlantic via *Cato's Letters*, political pamphlets published in the *London Journal* in 1720–23 and widely reprinted in the Thirteen Colonies. Their authors, John Trenchard and Thomas Gordon, had been inspired by the writings of Algernon Sidney, an English politician known as the English Cato, whose *Discourses* had argued that "free men always have the right to resist tyrannical government." Sidney was executed for holding such views by Charles II in 1683.

To Thomas Jefferson, Sidney was as influential as Locke. So was Scotland's Francis Hutcheson, the most respected moral philosopher in 18th century America, who was read by students at Harvard. Hutcheson's views chimed with those of the Patriots: "For wherever any Invasion is made upon unalienable Rights, there must arise… [a] Right to Resistance."

COMMON SENSE:
ADDRESSED TO THE
INHABITANTS
OF
A M E R I C A.
On the following interesting
S U B J E C T S.
I. Of the Origin and Defign of Government in general, with concife Remarks on the Englifh Conftitution.
II. Of Monarchy and Hereditary Succeffion.
III. Thoughts on the prefent State of American Affairs.
IV. Of the prefent Ability of America, with fome mifcellaneous Reflections.

Written by an ENGLISHMAN.
By *Thomas Paine*

Man knows no Mafter fave creating HEAVEN, Or thofe whom choice and common good ordain.
THOMSON.

PHILADELPHIA, Printed.
And Sold by R. BELL, in Third Street, 1776.

A key text
The title page of Thomas Paine's 1776 revolutionary pamphlet *Common Sense* clearly acknowledges his English origins, while offering philosophical backing to the Patriotic cause.

Shaping influences

Most Americans, however, received their philosophy from the pulpit. The Great Awakening of the mid-18th century had challenged the old Anglican order of priest, bishop, and king. Methodists and Baptists preached an egalitarian brotherhood of man, with preachers drawn from the laboring classes. Presbyterian parsons in the backcountry thundered about the God of Battle's judgment on idolatrous empires. Their elders, largely frontiersmen originating from the Scottish borders and northern Ireland, were clannish and combative, hating Englishmen, Native Americans, and tidewater planters with equal fervor.

New Englanders, on the other hand, remained wedded to their traditional congregational-style town meetings. Their ideology was rooted in their origin story: they did not forget that their forefathers had crossed the storm-tossed Atlantic, leaving England far behind them, to found, in the words of John Winthrop, the first

> **10,000** **Estimated number of copies of Paine's *Common Sense* sold in 1776.**

governor of the Massachusetts Bay Colony, a "city upon a hill," a beacon unto the world.

British actions toward Boston in 1774 had sent a shudder down the backs of many colonists. No one better expressed the "felt necessities of the times" than Thomas Paine. The publication of *Common Sense* in 1776, in which Paine urged "Ye that dare oppose not only the tyranny but the tyrant, stand forth!" captured the imaginations of Americans in every colony. Within weeks, many would take up his challenge.

AFTER

As the war took hold, the desire for independence spread among the majority of people in the Thirteen Colonies.

LAUNCHING A NATION
On July 4, 1776, the Second Continental Congress issued its **Declaration of Independence 112–13 ››**, after nearly a month of deliberation. The moderate, more cautious delegate John Dickinson called it a "skiff made of paper," but the development was widely celebrated in the colonies, with bonfires and firework displays. Within five years the declaration was **officially recognized** by France (1778), Spain (1779), and the **Netherlands** (1781), each of which entered the war against Britain.

LIBERTY AND FREEDOM: THE HEART OF THE US

Revolutionary thinker
The British mocked Thomas Paine for his writings in both America and France. This cartoon depicts him as a jack-of-all-trades trampling on justice and accepted codes of behavior.

Wha WANTS ME

I am Ready & Willing to offer my Services to any Nation or People under heaven who are Desirous of Liberty & Equality

The Liberation of Boston

The arrival of Henry Knox's "noble train" of artillery in Boston gave the Patriots a much-needed boost. Using the cannons to fire on the British from Dorchester Heights, the Patriots forced General Howe to attack.

As the new year dawned on snowbound Boston, it revealed a city choked off by six months of siege, encircled by 14 miles (23 km) of entrenchments. To any British sentry, the rebel militiamen manning those trenches looked no different from usual, but the change in the Patriots' flag indicated that at least one thing was new. On January 1, 1776, Washington raised a banner with 13 alternating red-and-white stripes, and a Union Jack in the corner, over Cambridge's Prospect Hill. The 13-gun salute honoring the Congress flag proved that his army, although low on supplies, was not entirely out of powder.

Washington desperately needed weapons and reinforcements. He had practically disbanded one army—its enlistments having expired—and raised another to take its place. With few muskets at his men's disposal, many were armed with only spears or pikes. This was about to change, though, with the arrival of siege guns brought by Henry Knox.

On January 18, Knox rode into Framingham, a few miles from the army's Cambridge headquarters, with 52 cannons and mortars sledged nearly 300 miles (490 km) from Fort Ticonderoga, a recent Patriot gain. On this journey, Knox had crossed two lakes, one river, and rugged mountain ranges, with the ordnance drawn by slow-plodding oxen. Washington's prayers had been answered.

Cabin fever

Holed up in Boston, General Howe was more than ready to leave the city. He had been ordered to evacuate months ago, but Atlantic storms had scattered the promised transports. Winter gales had then set in, confining him to Government House. At least he had a good supply of firewood. Fuel had become so scarce in the besieged city that wooden fences, dilapidated houses, and frame churches had to be pulled down and used for the fire. Even the elms on Boston Common were felled.

There were also food shortages, resulting in a thriving black market, but the British officers still managed to put on plays, balls, and other diversions. Howe's dragoons took over the venerable Old South Meeting House, ripped out the pulpit and pews, spread tanbark over the floors, and established a riding school. Meanwhile, in the lines and outer works, his troops shivered through the snowstorms, grew bored, and misbehaved. The number of floggings rose.

Intimidation tactics

With Knox's artillery now in his possession, Washington decided to seize Dorchester Heights, a hilltop looming over the city from the southeast. Neither army had fortified the treeless slopes because of the exposure to enemy fire this would have entailed. Washington, though, had no intention of digging earthworks in that frozen ground.

On March 2, using some of the cannons brought by Knox, the rebels began a two-day bombardment of

BEFORE

Two decades of turbulent unrest in New England's leading seaport had shut down its commerce, radicalized many of its citizens, and brought war to its doorstep.

CITY UNDER SIEGE
The 1770 **Boston Massacre ≪ 30–31** and **Boston Tea Party ≪ 38–39** in 1773 inflamed tensions in the Massachusetts capital. Its subsequent occupation by British soldiers fanned the fires to an inferno. After a firefight at **Lexington and Concord ≪ 54–55**, British troops were **besieged in the town of Boston ≪ 58–59**, by a ring of rebellious militia units, soon led by a newly appointed and untried commander in chief: George Washington.

STATUE OF PAUL REVERE, A BOSTONIAN PATRIOT HERO

> "Rows of **barrels** ... rolled ... down the hill ... [might throw] the **assailants** into the **utmost confusion**."
>
> MAJOR GENERAL WILLIAM HEATH, IN HIS MEMOIRS, 1901

Evacuating Boston
The British left the city on a Sunday morning, Howe directing red-coated regulars onto waiting ships. To prevent the Patriots from using them, he ordered laborers to drop cannons into the harbor— where tea chests had been dumped only three years before.

HENRY KNOX

Born in 1750, jovial and rotund Henry Knox did not seem destined to play a soldier's part. He learned his military history from books, owning and operating a popular bookstore before the war. As chief artillery officer, Knox was present at all of Washington's major campaigns—from the Siege of Boston to the Battle of Yorktown—and also succeeded Washington as Senior Officer of the Army from December 1783 to June 1784. Knox was chosen as the first Secretary of War of the United States in 1789. The former bookseller went on to build coastal fortifications and make treaties with Native Americans, before retiring in 1795.

Boston. Then, on the night of March 4, while the cannonading continued, 3,000 men and 300 ox carts carried fascines—bundles of brushwood fitted in wooden frames—bales of hay, and barrels filled with dirt and rocks to the summit of Dorchester Heights. Nearby orchards had been chopped down to create an abatis (a wall of felled trees) to protect the improvised works. By dawn the next day, about 20 pieces of artillery, including 24-pounders and mortars from Ticonderoga, had been heaved into place.

Howe was stunned at what he saw through his spyglass the next morning. The rebels had done more in one night, he muttered, than his army could in a month. The works on Dorchester Heights appeared to be bristling with cannons. Even if the British commander had known that

Washington did not have enough powder or shot to prolong the bombardment, the guns could not be ignored. Howe had to attack.

That rainy afternoon—as the Royal Navy began moving its warships out of range of the Patriots' cannons—Howe's force embarked on the remaining transports and anchored them under the Heights, ready for the offensive. Soon, however, the rain turned into a gale, blowing the transports into each other and fouling their anchors. Howe's attack was called off, while the Americans strengthened their lines.

Bitter retreat

Evacuation was Howe's only option. On March 17, scarlet-coated columns filed out of Charlestown or marched off the Common, tramping down to the wharves. Washington's lines

remained quiet: Howe had threatened to torch the town if the rebels fired a shot. Nearly 9,000 men, and as many horses and stores as possible, were rowed out to the waiting ships. So were 1,000 Loyalists, stunned that a rebel horde had forced the British army to quit the city.

Howe's men left behind nearly 100 pieces of ordnance. Heavier guns were spiked but many others were serviceable. They also left pillaged houses, broken furniture, and "crows-feet"—razor sharp four-pointed metal spikes—scattered over the streets.

The Royal Navy fleet tarried off Boston for another 10 days, its sails disappearing from view on March 27. The ships steered north to the British base at Halifax, Nova Scotia. Washington, the new commander in chief, had won his first victory.

AFTER

When Howe's fleet sailed out of Boston Harbor, it spelled the end of revolutionary conflict in the place where it all began.

THE NEXT CAMPAIGN
Awaiting reinforcements—more than 16,500 troops, including 12,200 Hessians—General Howe turned his attention from Boston to **New York 118–19 ≫**. Anticipating the British attack, Washington ordered his army to Manhattan. Post-evacuation, Boston ceased to be a military theater and remained **in Patriot hands**. Its port was key to Patriot shipbuilding and repairs.

Knox Transports Siege Artillery

The Patriots' transportation of 59 cannons and mortars from captured Fort Ticonderoga to Boston, some 300 miles (500 km) south, was one of the epic feats of the war. Relays of horses and some 80 yoke of oxen dragged the 42 sleds of ordnance across frozen lakes and over mountains. On January 25, 1776, after three months of effort, Colonel Henry Knox delivered his "noble train of artillery" to the Patriot lines—without losing a single piece.

"10th [January 1776] reach'd No. 1, after have Climb'd mountains from which we might almost have seen all the Kingdoms of the Earth.

11th [January 1776] went 12 miles thro' the Green Woods to Blanford. It appear'd to me almost a miracle that people with heavy loads should be able to get up & down such Hills as Are here with any thing of heavy loads ... at Blanford we overtook the first division who had tarried here until we came up, and refus'd going any further on accott that there were no snow beyond five or six miles further in which space there was the tremendous Glasgow or Westfield mountain to go down. But after about three hours perseverance & hiring two teams of oxen ... they agreed to go.**"**

DIARY ENTRY OF CONTINENTAL ARMY GENERAL HENRY KNOX, 1776

"We then reached Westfield, Massachusetts and were much amused with what seemed the quaintness and honest simplicity of the people. Our armament here was a great curiosity. We found that very few, even among the oldest inhabitants, had ever seen a cannon ... We were great gainers by this curiosity, for while they were employed in remarking upon our guns, we were, with equal pleasure, discussing the qualities of their cider and whiskey.**"**

HORSE HANDLER JOHN BECKER, *THE SEXAGENARY, OR REMINISCENCES OF THE AMERICAN REVOLUTION*, 1883

Arrival of the artillery
This 19th-century colored engraving depicts
Henry Knox, on horseback, directing one of his
59 disassembled cannons into an American camp
near Cambridge, Massachusetts.

[1] SMALL CANNONBALL

[2] LARGE CANNONBALL

[3] GRAPESHOT

[4] BRITISH BRONZE 6LB CANNON

[5] FRENCH 24LB CANNON

[6] HOWITZER

Artillery

Although most artillery was imprecise at long range, it played an important role in many battles, especially sieges—often with devastating effects.

[1] **Small cannonball** The standard projectile was a cast-iron sphere. When fired it bounced lethally through enemy ranks, mowing down anyone in its path. [2] **Large cannonball** Larger projectiles were deployed against enemy batteries and to destroy opposing fortifications. [3] **Grapeshot** Used to scythe down closely grouped adversaries, grapeshot consisted of bundles of large lead or iron balls, held together by quilting and a wooden base. [4] **British bronze 6lb cannon** Bronze cannons were less powerful than the iron equivalents, but much lighter. This cannon was captured by the Continental Army in the 1775 Siege of St. John's. [5] **French 24lb cannon** The French used heavy artillery like this piece during the Siege of Yorktown; it proved vital in forcing the British surrender. [6] **Howitzer** Short-barreled artillery pieces, howitzers combined a high trajectory shot with the maneuverability and power of a field cannon.
[7] **Mortar** Mounted on a flat wooden bed, the mortar barrel was elevated to produce a high trajectory shot, capable of striking targets behind fortifications and trenches. [8] **9-inch mortar shell** Mortar shells were filled with black powder, timed to explode once they landed behind enemy lines. [9] **13-inch French mortar shell** Heavy mortar was used in siege warfare. This French shell was found at the Yorktown battle site. [10] **10-inch Spanish mortar** The size of a mortar was based on the width in inches across the mouth of the bore. [11] **British 8-inch howitzer shell** Howitzers were capable of firing these hollow, explosive shells, as well as anti-personnel projectiles like grapeshot. [12] **French mortar** The French supplied arms to the Patriots, and later sent artillery units to North America, helping to tip the contest in the Patriots' favor.

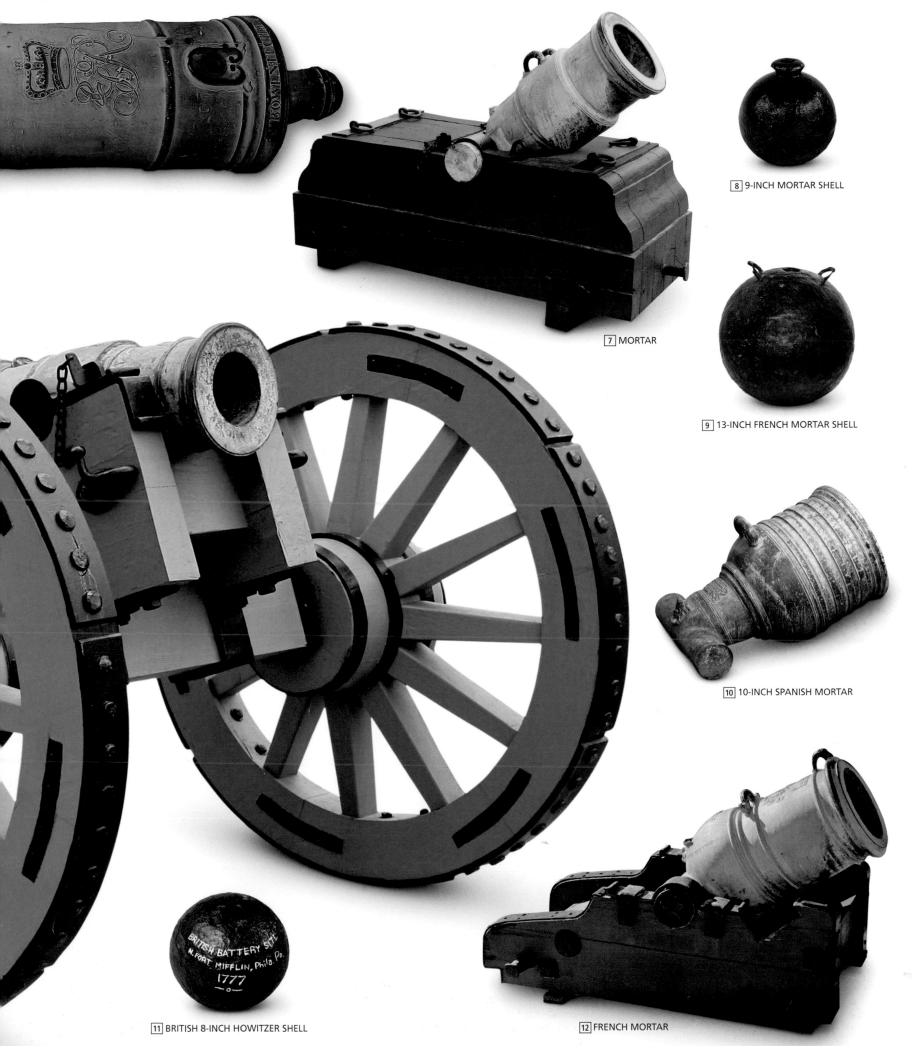

8 9-INCH MORTAR SHELL

7 MORTAR

9 13-INCH FRENCH MORTAR SHELL

10 10-INCH SPANISH MORTAR

11 BRITISH 8-INCH HOWITZER SHELL

BRITISH BATTERY SITE
N. FORT. MIFFLIN, Phila. Pa.
1777

12 FRENCH MORTAR

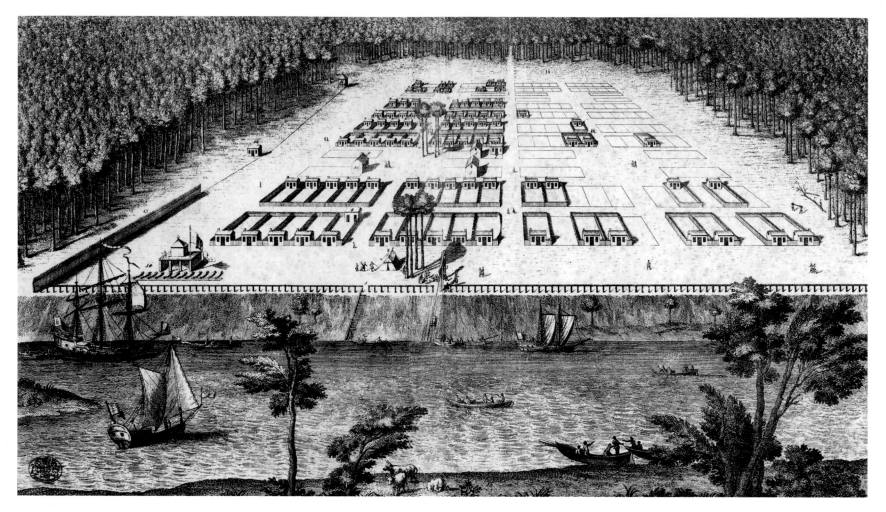

Bird's-eye view
The town of Savannah sits on bluffs above its river. In 1776, the cliffs provided the ideal place for the Patriots to mount cannon and fire on the British ships below.

« **BEFORE**

For most of 1775, the war in the North focused on the rebellion in Massachusetts. In the South, it centered on bitter conflicts between Patriots and Loyalists.

OUSTED FROM OFFICE
In 1775, royal governors in the southern colonies—Georgia, Virginia, and the Carolinas—were driven from office by Patriot mobs. In Virginia, the former governor, **Lord Dunmore**, sought to recruit **Loyalists « 68–69** as well as **African Americans « 78–79**.

LEAVING BOSTON
British General Sir Henry Clinton left **Boston « 100–01** at the end of 1775 and sailed south to join a larger fleet from Ireland.

The **South** Chooses Sides

At the start of the war, the British were confident they could rely on the support of Loyalists in the South. It was not until 1776 that they put the theory to the test, in Savannah, Georgia, and in a campaign led by Scottish settlers on North Carolina's Cape Fear.

Scottish basket-hilted broadsword
Developed to protect a warrior's hand in close combat, the basket-hilted broadsword was often wielded in the "Highland Charge," a favorite Scottish tactic in the 17th and 18th centuries.

Basket hilt

Blade

Convinced that the southern colonies held many men and women loyal to the Crown, the former governors of Virginia, the Carolinas, and Georgia persuaded the king and his ministers that the appearance of a fleet off those shores would rally Loyalist support. Such assurances were given even though Patriot mobs had forced three of the four former governors to take refuge in British warships.

Skirmish in Savannah
Although Georgia's governor, James Wright, had been stripped of his powers by the Provincial Congress in 1775, he still occupied the official mansion in Savannah. However, on January 12, 1776, when the first Royal Navy vessels appeared off Tybee Island, at the mouth of the Savannah River, he was put under house arrest. Three weeks later, on February 11, Wright escaped, and with the help of a

Loyalist plantation owner found sanctuary on HMS *Scarborough*, which took him to Halifax, Nova Scotia.

On the night of March 2, some 2,000 Redcoats aboard the remaining Royal Navy fleet off Savannah landed on Hutchinson Island, opposite the town. They secured 11 boats loaded with rice at anchor there, with the aim of taking the supplies to besieged Boston. Over the next few days, however, Patriot militia mustered. They dragged cannons onto the bluffs to shoot at the warships, and loosed burning boats downstream, setting several of the rice barges ablaze. Luckily for the British, they got most of the cargo safely out to sea and eventually to Boston.

Rallying the Scots

Things looked more promising for the British off the mouth of North Carolina's Cape Fear River, where exiled Governor Josiah Martin rocked in his floating sanctuary, HMS *Scorpion*. On January 10, 1776, Martin had issued a proclamation calling for all loyal subjects to rally to "His Majesty's Royal standard" and assemble at Brunswick, near the port of Wilmington. There they would meet the ships carrying General Sir Henry Clinton and his troops from Boston, the vanguard of a larger fleet that was on its way from Ireland.

Martin hoped for a sizable turnout by Highland Scots, who lived by the thousand in the upper Cape Fear region. Most of these settlers had been living there since 1763, having received land grants for their military service in the Seven Years' War.

Marching to the pipes
More than 48,000 Scottish Highlanders served in the British Army between 1756 and 1816. They were accompanied into battle by the skirl of pipers.

Among them were a former British army officer named Allan MacDonald and his wife, Flora (see box).

Moore's Creek Bridge
On February 18, the Loyalists assembled at a village crossroads called Cross Creek (today's Fayetteville) for the march to Wilmington. Only 7 miles (11 km) away, however, the Patriots were quietly gathering as well. Armed with muskets and dragging two old cannons—called "Old Mother Covington and her daughter"—these militiamen decided to block the Highlanders' path at a place deep in the swamps called Moore's Creek Bridge. Led by colonels John Lillington and Richard Caswell, the militiamen first erected trenches on the west bank of the bridge, then decided to pull back to the east side. They also pulled up the bridge planks, leaving only the log stringers in place, which they then greased liberally with lard.

Loyalist scouts detected the Patriots, however, and the Highlanders held a conference of war. They decided to attack before dawn, assaulting with broadswords. Eighty men, led by Captain John Campbell, would deliver the blow. General Donald McLeod would accompany them.

Highlanders swamped
In the pre-dawn gloom of February 27, the Highlanders, many sporting plaids or kilts and wearing dirks (long daggers), crept forward, stumbling

1,500 Loyalists marched to Moore's Creek Bridge.

500 of these men carried firearms.

FLORA MACDONALD

A famous Scottish heroine, Flora MacDonald was celebrated for helping Charles Edward Stuart, Bonnie Prince Charlie—last claimant to the British throne of an exiled Scottish dynasty—to escape following his defeat at the Battle of Culloden in 1746 by disguising him as a maid. After emigrating to North Carolina, MacDonald probably aided her soldier-husband, Allan, to rally the Highlanders in support of the British before the Battle of Moore's Creek Bridge. Eventually she returned to Scotland and lived out her days on the Isle of Skye.

upon the abandoned trench on the west bank. Perhaps they thought their foes had fled, or were still asleep, because they charged the bridge, drums beating, bagpipes skirling, and crying "King George and the broadswords!" Halted by the slippery bridge, they began inching their way over the treacherous timbers, Campbell leading on one stringer and McLeod on the other. They were only 30 paces from the other side when Old Mother Covington and the Patriot trench erupted with a crashing volley of fire.

The ensuing melee could not have lasted long. Thirty Highlanders were killed or wounded by musket balls or canister, some falling into the creek from the bridge, others—including Campbell and McLeod—shot while gaining the east bank. McLeod, hit by nine bullets and 24 pellets of swan shot somehow managed to sit up and point his broadsword at the rebel trenches. It was McLeod's final act of defiance.

In the darkness and confusion of battle the surviving Highlanders took to their heels. For the next two days the Patriots rounded them up in the nearby woods and swamps—850 men in all, including Allan MacDonald. Lillington's Patriots, who had suffered only two casualties during the skirmish, spent most of the time looting the captured wagon train, taking some 1,500 rifles, 350 muskets, and 150 broadswords, as well as a treasure chest. Some of the victors pranced around in triumph, wearing Scottish plaids.

It was now clear that the Loyalist cause was doomed in North Carolina. Arriving off Wilmington in March, Clinton was crestfallen at the news. He and his soldiers remained stewing on their transport vessels or swatting mosquitoes in camps off Cape Fear until May 1776, when the fleet from Ireland finally arrived and the joint force set sail for Charleston.

AFTER

Cowed by the debacle at Moore's Creek Bridge, most North Carolina Loyalists kept a low profile for the rest of the war.

A SPUR TO THE PATRIOT CAUSE
News of victory at Moore's Creek Bridge, alongside reports of the triumph over the Royal Navy at **Sullivan's Island** near Charleston **110–11 »** in June 1776, encouraged the Continental Congress to issue the **Declaration of Independence 112–13 »** in July. Ironically, North Carolina was the first of the Thirteen Colonies to instruct its delegates to **vote for separation from Britain**.

LOYALISTS VERSUS PATRIOTS
Loyalists farther south would only bide their time. In 1780, when the British finally captured Charleston **266–67 »**, they would emerge to wage a furious and **bloody civil war** with Patriot militia in the South Carolina backcountry **268–69 »**.

> "The battle lasted **three minutes ...** This, we think, will effectually put a **stop to Toryism** in North Carolina."
>
> ANONYMOUS NEWSPAPER REPORT, CITED IN FRANK MOORE'S *DIARY OF THE AMERICAN REVOLUTION*, 1860

Full of promise
This portrait was painted when Clinton was a promising young guards officer during the Seven Years' War. His undoubted military competence was undermined by a gloomy indecisive temperament.

BRITISH COMMANDER Born 1730 Died 1795

Henry **Clinton**

"A **dear bought victory,** another such would have **ruined us.**"

SIR HENRY CLINTON DESCRIBING THE BATTLE OF BUNKER HILL, 1775

Among the British generals who held command during the War of Independence, Sir Henry Clinton was the most accomplished soldier. He was a skillful and courageous field commander and a clear-sighted strategist. Unfortunately, defects of character undermined his performance, ruined his relationship with other generals, and made him waver in executing his own strategic plans.

Born to fight

Clinton was the son of an admiral and the grandson of a general on his mother's side. The only question ever posed about his career was whether he would choose the army or the navy. He spent part of his youth in New York, where his father was serving as royal governor.

Returning to Britain, he gained a respectable position as a guards officer through the patronage of the Duke of Newcastle but depended for further advancement upon his own talents. During the Seven Years' War in Europe (1756–63) he served as the aide-de-camp of the Duke of Brunswick, one of the most respected commanders of his time. He could have received no better education in European military practice. He also gained direct experience of combat—a leg wound suffered at the Battle of Nauheim in Germany in 1762 troubled him for the rest of his life. Clinton's pleasure in his rise through the military and social hierarchy—promotion to major general, election as an MP in 1772—was blighted by

personal tragedy. The death of his wife, also in 1772, hit him hard, his grief regarded by some of his contemporaries as inappropriately excessive. He was still seeking escape from the pain of bereavement when he was sent to America in spring 1775.

Arriving in besieged Boston, Clinton was soon on prickly terms with his fellow officers. He had no respect for the abilities of either Thomas Gage or William Howe, the generals under whom he served. He regarded their handling of the Battle of Bunker Hill in June 1775 as disastrous and believed he could have done much better. In early 1776, Howe sent him to the Carolinas with an expedition. He was not allowed to organize it as he would have liked, and it proved abortive. Returning north to take part in the attack on New York in August, he masterminded a victory over Washington's army at Long Island, but then saw the fruits of victory squandered by Howe's inertia.

From Howe's point of view, Clinton was no doubt an irritating subordinate, prone to ideas that involved an unacceptable level of risk. In early 1777, Howe selected Burgoyne over Clinton to lead a planned expedition from Canada (see pp.152–53).

On leave in Britain, the offended Clinton tried to resign his American command but was ordered back across the Atlantic. Feeling sidelined, he was left with a small force defending New York City while Howe struck at Philadelphia and Burgoyne advanced down the Hudson valley. Poor relations between the commanders contributed to the disaster that followed at Saratoga. Clinton could see that Howe's strategy left Burgoyne's force in danger. Attempting to come to Burgoyne's aid, however, he allowed himself to be distracted by a dispute with Howe over reinforcements and in the end did too little too late.

Command base
In 1779, Clinton established his headquarters as British commander in chief at Philipsburg Manor in the Hudson Valley, New York State. It was here that he issued the Philipsburg Proclamation, granting freedom to all slaves owned by Patriot masters.

Picking up the pieces

In the wake of Burgoyne's surrender Clinton again tried to resign, but instead it was Howe who left America and Clinton was appointed commander in chief in his place. He had a distinct lack of enthusiasm for the job, complaining that he would "have wished to avoid the arduous task of attempting to retrieve a game so unfortunately circumstanced." Yet he soon demonstrated the military

competence that justified his elevation to the commanding role. Forced to abandon Philadelphia in June 1778, he faced the challenge of carrying out a withdrawal across New Jersey to New York City, encumbered with an enormous baggage train and pursued by superior Patriot forces. He coped admirably with a difficult supply situation and, by skillful placement of his troops, defeated a Patriot attack at Monmouth Court House. Clinton

claimed, with pardonable exaggeration, to have reached New York without losing a wagon. The same ability to organize military operations in the field distinguished his capture of Charleston in 1780, where he commanded the siege in person.

Fatal flaws

Clinton had a clear grasp of the strategic situation, which presented him with two desirable goals. One was to win back individual states and secure them in collaboration with Loyalists, "enabling His Majesty's faithful subjects to resume their civil government," as he wrote. This policy was pursued, with some limited success, in the southern states. He also needed to engage and defeat Washington's Continental Army with his own forces based in New York. Unfortunately, in the execution of his wider duties as commander in chief his

defects of character came to the fore and he vacillated between these two strategies. He spent long periods passively in New York, blaming inadequate resources. Consumed with self-doubt and self-pity, he vainly begged the British government to relieve him of his command.

Clinton's relationships with other generals did not improve when they were his subordinates. General Charles Cornwallis, leading the British campaign in the South, took to largely ignoring Clinton's orders, which constantly changed as Clinton was buffeted by his hopes and fears. Instead of controlling strategy, the commander in chief wavered between options. In summer 1781, he chose to concentrate Cornwallis's army in a defensive position by the Chesapeake Bay, but failed to send promised reinforcements. He bore much of the blame for the subsequent surrender at Yorktown (see pp.304–05).

In 1782, Clinton returned to England, his active military career at an end. He devoted his later years to a defense of his record in North America and to a complicated private life—he had five children by his mistress from the American war, Mary Baddeley, whom he brought back with him to London. In 1794, Clinton was appointed governor of Gibraltar, but he died in 1795 before taking up the post. Two of his legitimate sons followed in their father's footsteps, serving as generals in the Napoleonic Wars.

Bombarding Fort Moultrie
In 1776, Clinton's forces joined Sir Peter Parker's in a failed attack on Fort Moultrie, guarding Charleston harbor from Sullivan's Island. Parker and Clinton blamed each other for the defeat.

"Clinton is the only man who might still save America."

KING GEORGE III, 1779

The **Battle** of Sullivan's Island

A British fleet arrived at Sullivan's Island, South Carolina, in June 1776, hoping to capture Charleston. The only thing standing in their way was Fort Sullivan, a makeshift palmetto-log redoubt.

O n the morning of June 1, 1776, lookouts in the mastheads of a Royal Navy fleet under the command of Admiral Sir Peter Parker, spied the entrance to Charleston Harbor. Aboard the fleet's flagship, the 50-gun HMS *Bristol*, was South Carolina's exiled royal governor, Lord William Campbell, who was largely responsible for the fleet being in those waters. While in London the previous

fall, Campbell had convinced the king and his ministers that a show of strength in the South would rally the settlers of the Tory backcountry and win back Virginia, the Carolinas, and Georgia to the Crown.

Plan of attack

Sent in response to Campbell's idea, Parker's convoy of warships and transports, had arrived off North Carolina's Cape Fear River in May 1776, where it rendezvoused with the fleet of General Clinton, the expedition's commander. Clinton, knowing that the Loyalists of North Carolina were in disarray and could not be relied upon for effective support, had wanted to turn north toward the Chesapeake Bay, but Parker and Campbell made a case for taking Charleston, the chief port of the South and the wealthiest city on the continent. Reluctantly, Clinton acquiesced.

While adverse winds kept the fleet inactive, Parker and Clinton pored over charts and squinted through spyglasses. Two low-lying coastal islands, crowned with palmetto trees, guarded the entrance to Charleston Harbor. To the south was James Island, its north shores protected by a large sandbank called the Middle Ground. That shoal forced ships to pass close to the neighboring Sullivan's Island,

BEFORE

Loyalist support had been strong among settlers in the South, but by the spring of 1776 the Patriot cause was gaining momentum.

SOUTH DIVIDED

In South Carolina, a civil war had broken out in 1775. Attacks on Loyalist recruiting centers—the "Snow Campaign"—effectively **silenced local Loyalists ‹‹ 76–77**. In February 1776, Loyalist militias in North Carolina were heavily defeated at **Moore's Creek Bridge ‹‹ 106–07**. A British fleet commanded by Sir Henry Clinton, which had arrived too late to support the Loyalist struggle at Moore's Creek Bridge, stayed in the waters off Cape Fear, awaiting the fleet of Admiral Sir Peter Parker to arrive from Ireland.

where men could be seen raising a large palmetto-log redoubt, dubbed Fort Sullivan.

While bad weather kept the warships at anchor 3 miles (5 km) from the fort, Clinton took a sloop and reconnoitered Sullivan's Island. He planned to land troops on Long Island, just to the north, where only a narrow channel called the Breach, which he believed to be fordable at low tide, separated the two islands. He assumed that his men could just splash across the Breach, brush aside whatever militia opposed them, and take the fort from its undefended rear.

However, on June 16 Clinton and 2,200 soldiers found that the Breach was not fordable. In some places it remained too deep even at low tide. To his "unspeakable mortification and disappointment," Clinton sent a note to Parker explaining his unhappy predicament. The attack would have to be made by the Navy alone.

Ready and waiting

Weather favored the Patriot commander of the fort, Colonel William Moultrie, and his 435 men. It bought them time to strengthen the palmetto-log walls—spaced 8 ft (2.5 m) apart, the gap filled with sand—and position their 31 guns. Moultrie knew the odds were steep, but not to what degree: the fleet opposing him mounted 260 guns. On the morning of June 28 the British fleet weighed

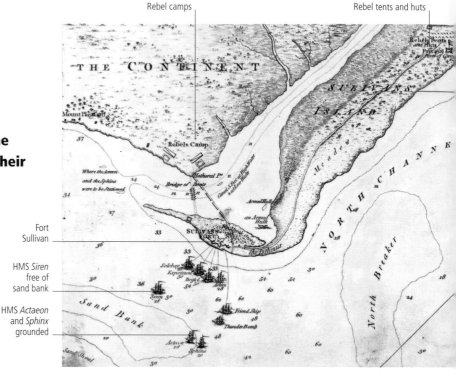

Rebel camps

Rebel tents and huts

Fort Sullivan

HMS *Siren* free of sand bank

HMS *Actaeon* and *Sphinx* grounded

Obstacle course
Sullivan's Island is surrounded by treacherous sand banks as shown by this plan of the battle drawn up soon after. Such detailed information may not have been available to the British before the engagement.

A battle misremembered
Despite of the mayhem depicted here, there was little hand-to-hand fighting in the battle, and casualties inside the fort were few. The fort's flag, designed by Colonel Moultrie, can be seen (top left).

PATRIOT GENERAL 1730–1805

WILLIAM MOULTRIE

Born in Charleston, William Moultrie was set to be a planter but became a soldier instead. His brother later became the Loyalist lieutenant governor of British East Florida, but Moultrie sided with the Patriots from the outset of the rebellion. Commissioned colonel of the 2nd South Carolina regiment in 1775, he was lionized for his victory at Fort Sullivan—renamed Fort Moultrie in his honor. He was captured in Savannah in 1778, but promoted to major general in 1782. Moultrie later served two terms as governor of South Carolina.

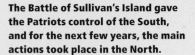

anchor. Led by Parker in the *Bristol*, seven warships, made the attack, anchoring in two lines just south of Sullivan's Island. By noon 100 guns fired at the fort. Yet most did little damage: the spongy palmetto wood absorbed the cannonballs' impact. Bad decision-making also hampered

submerged sandbars in the Middle Ground. Eventually *Siren* and *Sphinx* worked free, withdrawing to repair damage, but *Actaeon* remained grounded.

While the British attack failed to go according to plan, Moultrie's men defending the

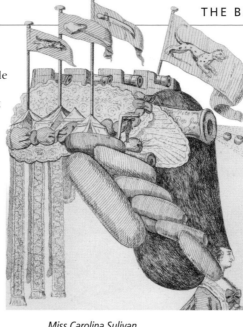

"**Never** did men **fight more bravely** and never were men more **cool.**"

WILLIAM MOULTRIE, *MEMOIRS OF THE AMERICAN REVOLUTION*, 1802

the British attack. HMS *Thunder*, which carried heavy 10-inch mortars, was anchored over a mile away, forcing its gunners to use extra powder to gain the necessary range. The resulting recoil cracked the ship's decks; the *Thunder* had put itself out of action.

Meanwhile, HMS *Actaeon*, *Siren*, and *Sphinx* maneuvered toward the passage between Sullivan's Island and the mainland, intending to fire on the fort from its rear. But the ships made too wide an arc and stuck fast on

fort had some success. They aimed their firepower primarily at the *Bristol*, literally shooting it to splinters. One deadly shard pierced Governor Lord Campbell's side and would eventually kill him.

The final score

The battle continued until twilight brought it to a close. At least 64 sailors had been killed and several hundred wounded, mostly on the *Bristol*. The flagship had been holed no fewer than

Miss Carolina Sulivan
This British cartoon of 1776 ridiculed the loss of Sullivan's Island, South Carolina, depicting the Island as an apparently feeble woman—with cannons and flags concealed in her hair.

70 times. Conversely, the 7,000 cannonballs that hit the fort had killed only 12 men and wounded 25 others.

Just before midnight the warships slipped away. *Actaeon*, still stuck on the Middle Ground, was burned. Moultrie and his men had won a tremendous victory—at very little cost.

AFTER

The Battle of Sullivan's Island gave the Patriots control of the South, and for the next few years, the main actions took place in the North.

TABLES TURNED
After Moultrie's successful defense, Charleston became the principal port through which food and supplies reached the Continental Army. Meanwhile, the defeated British expedition finished its repairs, picked up Clinton's men, and sailed to New York for the **Battle of Long Island 118–19 »**.

SOUTHERN THEATER
Sullivan's Island was not the last British attack on the South. A detachment of Clinton's forces were involved in the **assault on Savannah 244–45 »** in December 1779, and in April 1780, Clinton's army **besieged Charleston 266–67 »**, confronting Moultrie again. These engagements were followed by key battles in South Carolina: notably **Camden 274–75 »** in June 1780, **Kings Mountain 280–81 »** in October 1780, and **Cowpens 290–91 »** in January 1781.

« BEFORE

Two developments helped persuade Americans that the time was ripe for independence: one was a proclamation from London, and the other was the publication of a political pamphlet.

THE KING DECLARES WAR
The **Proclamation of Rebellion** **« 72–73** in August 1775, leading to the **Prohibitory Act** in December, notified the world that a state of war existed between Britain and its American colony. Legally that made America a foreign nation.

ROUSED BY PAINE
Thomas Paine's political pamphlet **Common Sense « 98–99** had an electrifying impact in Britain's colonies. Its closing lines were particularly rousing: "Every thing that is right or natural pleads for separation. The blood of the slain, the weeping voice of nature cries, 'TIS TIME TO PART.'"

Ringing endorsement
The Second Continental Congress met at the Pennsylvania State House in Philadelphia, where the Liberty Bell was rung on July 8 to announce that independence had been declared.

The Declaration of Independence

Until 1776, the word "independence" was barely whispered in the Pennsylvania State House, for the purpose of the Continental Congress was to influence Britain's parliament, not replace it. But change was in the air, and not even the staunchest Loyalist could stop it.

On the morning of Friday, June 7, 1776, delegates to the Second Continental Congress entered the Pennsylvania State House through a doorway surmounted by the royal arms. Seated in the Assembly Room, they listened as Richard Henry Lee of Virginia introduced a resolution "that these United Colonies are, and of right ought to be, free and independent States."

The long-expected moment had at last arrived. But a furious debate lasted well into the evening and the whole of the next day, with Pennsylvania's John Dickinson, a respected moderate, bravely battling against the tide running toward independence. His delegation was supported by those of other colonies with strong Loyalist populations—namely New York, New Jersey, Maryland, Delaware, and South Carolina—but their delegates were also starting to lean toward separation.

Congress recessed on Sunday. The next morning it agreed to postpone the vote for three weeks.

The vote is cast
On June 11, a five-man committee—including Benjamin Franklin, John Adams, and Thomas Jefferson—was appointed to draft a document defining the legal and moral justification for independence, should the vote go that way. The burden of writing fell chiefly on Jefferson, partly because he had helped John Dickinson draft the "Declaration of the Causes and Necessity for Taking Up Arms" in 1775, and partly for what Adams called his "gift of composition."

The young Virginian spent most of the next three weeks seated in his rented second-floor lodgings, scratching away with his quill and pen. Adams and Franklin offered a few emendations, and on Friday, June 28, the first draft was read before Congress and then left on a table for delegates to peruse at their leisure. There was no discussion; everything was adjourned until Monday, July 1.

That fateful Monday was a stormy day, both inside and outside the State House. While claps of thunder rattled the tall windows, the delegates argued for nine straight hours. John Dickinson continued to plead for moderation; John Adams argued the case for "independency." All agreed that the vote had to be unanimous. Eventually, South Carolina motioned for the decision to be postponed until the next day: it wanted time to reconsider.

On Tuesday, July 2, South Carolina announced it would vote for independence. Argument was increasingly fruitless. John Dickinson, for one, stayed away so that the rest of the Pennsylvania delegation might vote as it pleased. When the roll call came, Pennsylvania voted for independence, as did every other delegation—although many members did so with a heavy heart. The deciding "aye" for Delaware came from Caesar Rodney, who walked into the chamber still booted and spurred, having ridden 80 miles (130 km) through the dark and rain.

Choosing the right words
On Wednesday, July 3, the delegates finally turned to the document still lying on the table. As thunder continued to rumble, they spent the day arguing, editing, and revising the text. The words that finally emerged were aimed partly at the delegates' fellow Americans— they had a right to "life, liberty, and the pursuit of happiness"—and partly at foreign powers. No European monarchy would countenance rebellion. Americans were not rebels, the Declaration intimated; they were freeborn men with a heritage of self-government, who were

70 The age of the oldest signer, Benjamin Franklin.

26 The age of the youngest signer, Edward Rutledge.

Down with the king
Independentists in New York City pulled down the statue of King George III on July 9, 1776, in a symbolic toppling of the Crown's authority. Francis Xavier Habermann's illustration was one of many artworks to record the event.

LEGISLATOR STATESMAN 1732–1808

JOHN DICKINSON

Born in 1732, John Dickinson became the "Penman of the Revolution," famed for his hand in drafting key documents. His *Letters from a Farmer in Pennsylvania*, opposing the Townshend Acts, were widely disseminated. As a delegate to the Continental Congresses, Dickinson hoped for reconciliation, and wrote the 1775 Olive Branch Petition. Although he later fought in the war, Dickinson abstained from voting on the Declaration of Independence, believing America was not ready for revolution. At the end of the war, he became president of both Delaware and Pennsylvania.

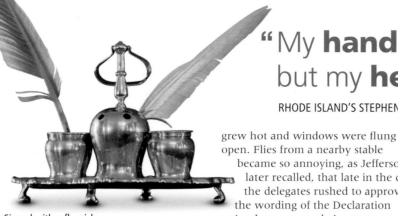

"My hand trembles, but my heart does not."

RHODE ISLAND'S STEPHEN HOPKINS UPON SIGNING THE DECLARATION, 1776

Signed with a flourish
All 56 delegates used the inkwell and quills from the Syng inkstand to sign the Declaration of Independence. The largest and most flamboyant signature belonged to the Congress's president, John Hancock.

struggling against tyranny—a tyranny enumerated in 19 grievances lodged against King George.

That night, a massive thunderstorm flashed and roared over Philadelphia. The morning of Thursday, July 4, however, brought a cooling north wind. In the State House there was more tedious editing while the afternoon grew hot and windows were flung open. Flies from a nearby stable became so annoying, as Jefferson later recalled, that late in the day the delegates rushed to approve the wording of the Declaration simply to escape their tormentors.

Public reaction

The Declaration was sent off to the printers with the date—July 4—at the top. The broadside soon reached townships up and down the seaboard, where it was widely celebrated with firework displays, bonfires, and the pealing of church bells.

On July 8, General Washington had it read to his assembled troops in New York while the gilded lead statue of King George from Battery Park was melted down into 42,000 musket balls. In Philadelphia, the royal arms were struck off the entrance to the State House.

In London, King George III—indicted in the Declaration as "unfit to be the ruler of a free people"—was hurt and annoyed. One Tory MP groused that a "more impudent, false, and atrocious Proclamation was never fabricated by the hands of man," but opposition politicians defended it. The historian Edward Gibbon confided to a friend that the Americans "have now crossed the Rubicon."

AFTER »

"Damn the consequences, give me the pen!" said New York's delegate Lewis Morris upon signing the Declaration. Yet he endorsed a very consequential document.

SIGNED AND SEALED
A suitably engrossed, or official, copy of the Declaration was made on parchment but it was not ready to sign for another month. Most of the **56 delegates** who appended their signature did so on **August 2, 1776**, the remainder signing over the following few weeks.

ENDURING LEGACY
It is hard to overestimate the impact of the Declaration of Independence. Today, the engrossed copy is in the US National Archives. The immediate effect, however, was to secure foreign **recognition by France, Spain, and the Netherlands**, who all entered the war against Britain 188–189 ».

Crafting the Declaration

Once the Continental Congress had decided to declare independence from Britain, the details of the resolution had to be agreed. The subcommittee appointed to draft the formal announcement presented the result of their joint labors to the Congress, which continued to tinker with it. Years later, Thomas Jefferson, the Declaration's main author, recalled the clauses that were struck out.

"Congress proceeded the same day [Thursday, July 4] to consider the declaration of Independence which had been reported & lain on the table the Friday preceding, and on Monday referred to a committee of the whole. The pusillanimous idea that we had friends in England worth keeping terms with, still haunted the minds of many. For this reason those passages which conveyed censures on the people of England were struck out, lest they should give them offense. The clause, too, reprobating the enslaving of the inhabitants of Africa, was struck out ... The debates having taken up the great parts of the 2d 3d & 4th days of July were, in the evening of the last, closed, the declaration was reported by the commee, agreed to by the house and signed by every member present except Mr. Dickinson ... The parts struck out by congress shall be distinguished by a black line drawn under them; & those inserted by them shall be placed in the margin or in a concurrent column."

THOMAS JEFFERSON IN HIS AUTOBIOGRAPHY, 1821

The Declaration of Independence
John Trumbull's famous painting of the event depicts the five-man drafting committee presenting the Declaration of Independence to the Congress's president, John Hancock, who ordered that it should "lie on the table" for delegates to study.

AMERICAN STATESMAN Born 1743 Died 1826

Thomas Jefferson

"The **God** who **gave us life,** gave us **liberty** at the same time."

THOMAS JEFFERSON, *A SUMMARY VIEW OF THE RIGHTS OF BRITISH AMERICA*, 1774

Prominent among the Founding Fathers of the United States, main author of the Declaration of Independence, and the country's third president, Thomas Jefferson was a consistent advocate of individual freedom and the power of the people to make or unmake governments. More than any other individual, he formulated the ideals upon which the United States was built, expressing the principles underlying the War of Independence in the language of universal human rights. Jefferson is admired not only for his political acumen, but also for his talents as a philosopher, architect, amateur scientist, and promoter of public education.

Radical thinker

Brought up on a Virginia plantation, Jefferson inherited land, slaves, and debts. Yet, believing that talent, not birth, should justify a man's place in society, he never showed much interest in his family origins. His ideas were heavily influenced by the principles of the rationalist Enlightenment, learned about from books in his father's library and also from George Wythe, a lawyer and teacher who became his mentor. As a young man Jefferson established a successful legal practice and entered politics as a representative to the Virginia assembly in 1769.

In 1774, joining in the widespread outrage at Britain's Intolerable Acts (see pp.42–43), Jefferson wrote a treatise entitled *A Summary View of the Rights of British America*. In clear, direct but elevated language, it proposed the radical view that Americans had a natural right to govern themselves. A year later, as a delegate to the Second Continental Congress in 1775, Jefferson formed a friendship with the prominent Massachusetts' radical John Adams. It was Adams who proposed Jefferson write the Declaration of Independence in 1776. Although

An American abroad

Thomas Jefferson had this portrait painted by American-born artist Mather Brown during a visit to London in 1786, when he was serving as US Minister to France.

"**Men** may be **trusted** to **govern themselves** without a master."

THOMAS JEFFERSON, LETTER TO GEORGE WASHINGTON, JANUARY 4, 1786

Word perfect
Jefferson spent 17 days in June 1776 working on his first draft of the Declaration of Independence. He then presented it to fellow Congress members Benjamin Franklin and John Adams for correction and amendment.

much of Jefferson's original draft was revised by Congress, the declaration's opening paragraphs were his alone.

Jefferson spent the war years in Virginia. Many of his proposals for radical reform, such as the notion of creating a public education system, met stubborn resistance from his fellow delegates in the Virginia assembly. Serving as state governor, he suffered the ignominy of fleeing in the face of a British invasion, successively abandoning the state capital and his estate at Monticello to the enemy soldiers.

The death of Jefferson's wife in 1782 was the culmination of his misfortunes, and he returned to national politics as a refuge from a deep depression. As a prominent delegate to the Confederation Congress from 1783, he pushed through the policy that territory in the West should eventually be organized into new states rather than controlled by existing ones. He also won acceptance for a decimal currency.

International envoy
In July 1784, Jefferson was sent to Europe, where he was to help Benjamin Franklin and John Adams negotiate a trade deal with France. He did not return to the United States for five years. The lively social and cultural atmosphere of Paris thoroughly revived his spirits. Although he never ceased to be an American patriot, Jefferson found in France a second homeland. He welcomed the outbreak of the French Revolution in 1789 and intended to continue living there as the US's Minister to France. However,

while making a visit to the United States in 1790, he received an irresistible invitation from newly installed President George Washington to run the country's international affairs as the first secretary of state. For the next two decades Jefferson was a dominant figure in American politics, and a founder of the Democratic-Republican Party, which opposed the growing power of the federal government and its chief executive.

President Jefferson
Although twice elected president, Jefferson was never entirely comfortable with a post that he felt veered toward monarchy. As president he avoided the trappings of power, showing modesty at all times in his dress and behavior. He was, on the other hand, vigorous in pursuing the territorial expansion of the United States. In international affairs, his instinct was always to support the French in their prolonged wars with the British, whom he abhorred. A notable moment in Jefferson's presidency was the ban on the import of slaves to the United States, effective from 1808. Jefferson had long opposed the international slave trade, writing a denunciation of Britain's role as a slave-trading nation in his original draft of the Declaration of Independence. Yet he remained a slaveholder all his life. Jefferson was aware of the contradiction between

slavery and his principles of freedom and equality, but argued that emancipation would pose insuperable problems unless linked to the expatriation of freed slaves to Africa.

Jefferson was on the whole a popular president, although his attempt to wage an economic war on Britain in 1807 was disastrous and rapidly abandoned. In 1809, after completing his second term, he retired from

politics, after which his chief interest became the establishment of the University of Virginia. Declining health and failing finances blighted his final years. In one of history's strangest coincidences, Jefferson died on the 50th anniversary of the signing of the Declaration of Independence.

Folding writing surface

Inkwell

Jefferson's portable writing desk
This small mahogany "writing box" was made to Jefferson's own design in 1776. He drafted the Declaration of Independence on it and continued to use it through most of his life.

Among the greats
The heads of four presidents were famously carved out of Mount Rushmore, South Dakota, in the 1930s. They are (l–r): George Washington, Jefferson, Theodore Roosevelt, and Abraham Lincoln.

TIMELINE

- **1743** Born April 13 at Shadwell in Albemarle County, Virginia, son of farmer and surveyor Peter Jefferson and Jane Randolph Jefferson.
- **1760–62** Studies at the College of William & Mary in Williamsburg, Virginia.
- **1767** Qualifies to practice as a lawyer.
- **1768** Starts building his house at Monticello.
- **1769–75** Represents Albemarle County in the Virginia House of Burgesses.
- **1772** Marries Martha Wayles Skelton; she bears six children, of whom two survive to adulthood.
- **1774** His tract on the rights of British America is debated by the First Continental Congress.
- **June 1775** Selected as a delegate to the Second Continental Congress.
- **June 1776** Writes the first draft of the Declaration of Independence.
- **September 1776** Elected to the Virginia House of Delegates.
- **1777** Drafts Statute of Religious Freedom, proposing complete freedom of worship.
- **1779–81** Serves as Governor of Virginia.
- **June 1781** Flees Monticello as it is captured by British soldiers.
- **1782** His wife Martha dies at the age of 33.
- **1783–84** Serves as a Virginian delegate to the Confederation Congress.
- **May 1785** Takes over from Benjamin Franklin as US Minister to France, serving until 1789.
- **1790** Appointed the first US Secretary of State under President George Washington.
- **1792** Forms the anti-administration Republican Party (also called the Democratic-Republican Party) with James Madison and others.
- **December 1793** Resigns as secretary of state.
- **1797** Narrowly loses to John Adams in the presidential election; becomes vice-president.
- **1798** Writes the Kentucky Resolutions, affirming states' rights to reject federal laws.
- **1801** Elected president of the US after a prolonged deadlock in the electoral college.
- **1803** Extends US territory through the Louisiana Purchase of land from France.
- **1804** Sends Captain Meriwether Lewis and Lieutenant William Clark to explore the West.
- **1805** Inaugurated for a second term as US president.
- **1807** Promotes a ban on the import of slaves to the US.
- **1809** Retires from political life.
- **1819** Founds the University of Virginia in Charlottesville.
- **1826** Dies on July 4, on the same day as fellow Founding Father John Adams.

JEFFERSON'S GRAVESITE AT MONTICELLO

The Battle of Long Island

In June 1776, a massive army of British Redcoats and German mercenaries converged on New York City. By isolating the strategically vital port from New England, they hoped to achieve the "one decisive action" that would end the war.

When the first Royal Navy masts came into view outside New York Harbor on June 25, 1776, it was no surprise to George Washington. The American commander had expected General William Howe and his brother, Admiral Richard Howe—joint commanders of a British expeditionary force—to make a move upon New York City. By August 12, 32,000 soldiers, including 8,000 Hessians, had landed on nearby Staten Island. Watchers in the city counted ten ships of the line, 20 frigates, and hundreds of transports anchored in the harbor. It was the largest expeditionary force Britain had ever sent abroad. Washington took a risk by dividing his 19,000-man force between Manhattan Island and neighboring Long Island. Brooklyn Heights on Long Island, just across the East River from Manhattan, dominated New York City, and Washington realized that artillery placed there could destroy the city. In order to draw fire away from Manhattan, he fortified the Heights. His men dug a jagged line of breastworks—protected by ditches, and sharpened stakes—above Gowanus Creek. Nevertheless, he still worried that the British would attack the city instead.

Mass invasion

On August 22, 15,000 British soldiers began to come ashore on Long Island. Three brigades of Hessians soon joined them, the camps spreading for nearly 6 miles (10 km). From a low range of wooded hills to the north, nearly 10,000 Patriot infantrymen watched. Most of them were stationed behind the Brooklyn Heights fortifications, but other units guarded four passes through the hills, all of which linked up to the main Brooklyn road.

The Patriots had dug rudimentary works, but the pass at the easternmost end of the hills, Jamaica Pass, had only a small band of five mounted militiamen for defense. This was not a well-known pass, and Washington's officers did not expect Howe's men to use it.

Shortly after midnight on August 27, a 2 mile- (3 km-) long column of Redcoats led by General Henry Clinton quietly took the road to Jamaica Pass. Well before dawn they had captured the five-man outpost. From there, they turned left, preparing to roll up the unsuspecting American line.

As the sun rose, all across the Patriot front the British made a great show of advancing, cannon roaring. Soon panic-stricken Patriot militiamen were pouring out of woods and across fields, fleeing not the feints to their front but

After liberating Boston, Washington had moved his army to New York in anticipation of Britain's next step.

Army scattered
The unexpected arrival of the British at Brooklyn Heights caused pandemonium in the Continental Army as its largely untested soldiers broke rank around Cortelyou House, shown here on the right.

Crossing the East River
After the battle, the Patriots retreated across the East River to the safety of Manhattan, using every available boat. The last man to step into the last vessel was reputedly Washington himself.

rather General Clinton's onslaught coming up the road from Jamaica Pass. As morning wore on, even the feints became real attacks, and long lines of Jaegers and grenadiers began pushing hard against the collapsing positions of Washington's army. The Patriots, now eager to retreat, were routed.

Those who were able ran for the safety of the Brooklyn fortifications. If they made it, it was due to a smart-looking set of troops dressed in brown hunting shirts or blue coats with red facings: the Maryland and Delaware Lines. They made up the Continental Army's western flank, under General William Alexander, known as Lord Stirling. Anchored on Gowanus Creek, these stalwart troops, had held off British attacks for much of the day, even though they were heavily outnumbered, withstanding hours of heavy cannonading.

Eventually, the leading elements of Howe's flank attack—Cornwallis's troops—reached a battlefield landmark, the Cortelyou House, and cut off the Patriots' line of retreat. Some of the Delaware troops crossed Gowanus Creek to reach the Brooklyn lines, but more than 250 Marylanders stayed behind to buy time for the retreating troops. The last Marylanders assaulted Cornwallis's lines five times, but the sixth attempt foundered. "Good God! What brave fellows I must this day lose!" lamented Washington, watching from the Heights.

BEFORE

WAR ENDS IN BOSTON
In March 1776, Washington forced General William Howe's army out of the **besieged city of Boston ‹‹ 100–01**, bringing the city under Patriot control for the rest of the war. The lifting of the siege left Howe free to focus on New York City, a vital port and springboard, which the British were eager to bring under their control. Anticipating this move, Washington ordered the building of defenses around New York's harbor.

Midnight retreat

The Battle of Long Island was over. Washington had been thoroughly outgeneraled, with more than a thousand men left dead, wounded, or captured. Howe's losses were less than half that. Yet Washington still had 9,500 men on the Heights, including reinforcements from the city, behind the Brooklyn fortifications. Luckily, a stiff northeast wind kept the Royal Navy out of the East River at Washington's back, but it also brought two days of drenching rain. With water waist-deep in their trenches, and all their gunpowder soaked and useless, the rebels could have been overrun by a single charge of grenadiers.

Howe, though, missed that opportunity and prepared to besiege the rebel works. Realizing the clock was ticking, on August 29 Washington issued orders to take all boats to the East River and assemble them at Manhattan's wharves after dark. That night, an array of barges, skiffs, and sloops—manned by skilled Massachusetts boatmen from the maritime towns of Marblehead and Salem—began ferrying troops, guns, horses, and supplies from Brooklyn to the city. The six-hour operation took place in total silence. British sentries grew suspicious, but dawn brought a thick fog that masked the final embarkations. The British now controlled Long Island, but Washington had saved his army.

Anticipation builds

London was ecstatic over the news of Howe's victory at Long Island, and George III promptly conferred a knighthood upon the British general. But the battle for control in New York was far from over.

For about three weeks, New York saw little activity. Adverse winds prevented the Royal Navy from crossing the East River to the city, which was still held by the Patriots. As August turned to September, from his Manhattan stronghold at Harlem Heights, Washington waited, anticipating Howe's next move.

During the lull in hostilities, the Patriots decided to try something new. On September 7, a submersible ship named *Turtle* was sent to attack Admiral Howe's flagship, HMS *Eagle*. It was the first submarine to be used in naval warfare. However, Sergeant Ezra Lee, pedaling the *Turtle*, was unable to attach explosives to the *Eagle*, or to keep the *Turtle* submerged. The attack was abandoned with the *Eagle* unharmed, and the standoff continued.

Meanwhile, Patriot General Nathanael Greene and New York's John Jay began arguing for the city to be burned, to keep it out of British hands. The Second Continental Congress soon vetoed this plan, declaring that "it should in no event be damaged." Nonetheless, a fire broke out on September 21. By then, however, Washington had plenty of other things to worry about.

City ablaze

The Great Fire destroyed around 300 buildings in New York City. The British believed it was started deliberately, but the culprit was never caught. Dozens were questioned, including Patriot spy Nathan Hale.

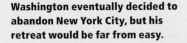

Washington eventually decided to abandon New York City, but his retreat would be far from easy.

IN BRITISH CONTROL

In September, Washington's army faced Howe's forces again in the **Battle of Harlem Heights 124–25 »**, and in October at both **White Plains** and **Fort Washington**. These engagements left the British in control of New York. Although weakened, the Continental Army had not been destroyed, and retreated to Pennsylvania.

WAR IN NEW JERSEY

In late 1776, Washington took the offensive, and crossed the Delaware from Pennsylvania into New Jersey to attack **Trenton and Princeton 132–33 »**. New Jersey remained the focus of the conflict at the beginning of 1777, with the **Forage War 140–41 »**—a war of attrition that sought to cut off supplies—lasting until spring.

> "The **time is now near** at hand, which must … **determine** whether **Americans** are to be freemen or slaves."

GEORGE WASHINGTON TO HIS ARMY, AUGUST 26, 1776

AMERICAN COMMANDER IN CHIEF Born 1732 Died 1799

George Washington

"First in war, first in peace, and first in the hearts of his countrymen."

HENRY LEE, US MILITARY OFFICER AND CONGRESSMAN, 1799

George Washington contributed more than any other individual to the success of the War of Independence. Calm, firm, and incorruptible, he was a man who loved neither war nor power and was never happier than when cultivating his family estate at Mount Vernon in Virginia. Yet he won the armed conflict with the British as commander in chief of the Continental Army and, as the first US president, endowed the American government with a dignity and authority it would otherwise have struggled to achieve.

A member of the Virginia landowning class, as a young man Washington served Britain as an officer in the

The Continental Army
Founded by Washington in 1775, the Continental Army suffered a host of problems, ranging from desertion to lack of pay, food, and clothing. It became nonetheless, in Washington's words, "a patriotic band of brothers," who were capable of beating British regulars.

Impressive stature
The portrait *George Washington at Princeton*, painted by Charles Peale Polk in 1788, captures Washington's air of authority. At more than 6 feet (1.8 m) tall, he was every inch the heroic figure.

colonial militia, making his mark on American history with his first entry into combat. On May 28, 1754, militia led by Washington clashed with French troops in the backwoods of the Ohio Valley, firing the first shots of what was to become the French and Indian War.

First command
Fourteen months later, returning to Ohio country as aide to British General Edward Braddock, Washington distinguished himself by his calm conduct amid the mayhem of defeat at the Battle of Monongahela. He

The art of retreat
This painting by Junius Brutus Stearns (1810–85) depicts Washington on horseback fighting for the British at the Battle of the Monongahela (1755), in which he learned the value of an orderly retreat.

"I have heard the **bullets whistle...** there is something **charming** in the **sound.**"

GEORGE WASHINGTON, LETTER TO HIS BROTHER, 1754

was rewarded with command of the Virginia Regiment, a role that gave him experience in organizing, training, and leading troops. Nonetheless, the British declined to offer him an officer's commission in their army—a decision they would have cause to regret.

Rebel with a cause

When peace returned in 1758 Washington married wealthy widow Martha Dandridge Custis, and settled down to farm at Mount Vernon—in his words, "the most delectable of pursuits." As a member of the Virginia House of Burgesses he opposed the Stamp Act and the Townshend Acts in the 1760s, but it was not until 1774 that he shook off a lifelong loyalty to Britain. Sharing in the widespread indignation at the Coercive Acts, he was elected as a Virginian delegate to the rebel Continental Congress. In the following year, when the confrontation with Britain turned to armed conflict, his previous experience of command made him an obvious choice to lead the new Continental Army.

Washington used stratagems suitable to inferior forces, avoiding pitched battle where possible. His victory over British Hessian mercenaries at Trenton over Christmas 1776 (see pp.132–33) was effectively a guerrilla raid. Political considerations often obliged him to stand and fight when he thought it unwise. In August 1776, he was forced to defend New York City, leading to a defeat on Long Island from which he removed his troops with skill. In September 1777, the defeat of his army at Brandywine near Philadelphia (see pp.170–71) gave him another unwanted chance to show how he could handle an army in retreat.

Military setbacks fueled political machinations against Washington and encouraged opponents who aspired to replace him. At the Battle of Monmouth in June 1778, his ambitious second-in-command Charles Lee failed to implement Washington's plan of attack. The incident erupted into a violent argument between the two men, and Lee was later court-martialed for insubordination.

Washington could, however, rely upon the support of his chief of staff Alexander Hamilton and the French volunteer the Marquis de Lafayette. He also collaborated comfortably with French nobleman the Comte de Rochambeau. In 1781, their joint armies marched 450 miles (700 km) south to besiege Yorktown, Virginia. The surrender of Lord Cornwallis at Yorktown convinced Britain that the war was lost.

From soldier to president

Most European observers expected Washington to assume leadership of the new United States as a military ruler. Instead, as soon as peace was agreed, he resigned his post and went home to Mount Vernon. He returned in 1787 to oversee the convention that drew up a federal Constitution, and accepted the post of president when elected in 1789. His two terms of office ensured that the United States would have a central government that was strong enough to hold the fractious states together.

Purple heart
Washington introduced the Badge of Military Merit in the form of a purple heart in 1782. The US government revived the decoration, bearing Washington's profile, on the 200th anniversary of the commander's birth in 1932.

TIMELINE

- **1732** Born February 22 into a prosperous family of English descent in Westmoreland County, Virginia.

- **1754–58** Serves in the French and Indian War, reaching the rank of brigadier general.

- **1759** Marries Martha Dandridge Custis and begins improving his estate at Mount Vernon.

WASHINGTON'S ESTATE AT MOUNT VERNON

- **August 1774** Elected as a Virginia delegate to the rebel First Continental Congress.

- **June 15, 1775** Appointed commander in chief of the newly created Continental Army by the Second Continental Congress.

- **March 1776** His troops force the British to leave Boston after an 11-month siege.

- **August 1776** Faces defeat at the Battle of Long Island but manages to withdraw with his army into Pennsylvania.

- **December 25–26, 1776** Raids the Hessian garrison at Trenton, New Jersey, then defeats British forces at Princeton eight days later.

- **September 11, 1777** His defeat at the Battle of Brandywine enables the British to occupy Philadelphia.

- **December 1777–June 1778** Encamped at Valley Forge, Pennsylvania, his army endures great hardship. He survives political plots to remove him from his post.

- **June 28, 1778** Fights the British as they withdraw from Philadelphia at the Battle of Monmouth.

- **January 1781** Suppresses mutinies in the Pennsylvania and New Jersey regiments.

- **August–September 1781** The Continental Army joins forces with the Comte de Rochambeau's French expeditionary force, marching south from New York to Virginia.

- **September 28–October 19, 1781** His forces besiege British troops under Lord Cornwallis at Yorktown and force them to surrender.

- **December 23, 1783** Resigns his commission at the end of the War of Independence.

- **1787** Presides over the Constitutional Convention.

- **April 30, 1789** Sworn in as the first president of the United States under the Constitution.

- **1797** Retires to Mount Vernon.

- **1798** Appointed commander in chief of the provisional army in the face of a perceived threat from France.

- **December 14, 1799** Dies at Mount Vernon.

BEFORE «

After Boston, Washington had set his sights on New York City. The British reacted quickly to stop the Patriots from controlling this key port.

A STRONG BEGINNING

Washington had been victorious in his first campaign after taking command of the Continental Army: in March 1776, his tactical thinking had intimidated Howe's men into **evacuating Boston** « **100–01**.

PATRIOTS ROUTED

In August 1776, a combined force of British regulars and Hessians drove the Patriots out of **Long Island** « **118–19**. The novice Patriot recruits, many of whom were **militiamen** « **64–65**, had shown fear in the face of the trained British Redcoats « **92–93**. Washington took his surviving army across the East River into New York City.

Fields of war

The 42nd (Highland) Regiment—known as the Black Watch—made their stand against the Patriots from behind a fence during the fierce battle of September 16, on present-day Morningside Heights.

Retreat from New York

After the Patriots' disastrous performance at the Battle of Long Island, Washington's army retreated in the dead of night. Although it was temporarily secure behind the fortifications of Harlem Heights, Washington knew that another British advance was imminent.

As he waited in New York City for the British attack, Washington made a difficult decision. The ability of the Royal Navy to outflank the Patriots via both the East and the Hudson rivers made it clear that he must abandon the city. On September 8, he informed the Continental Congress, "On every side there is a Choice of difficulties," and confessed to "some Apprehension that all our troops will not do their duty."

The Patriots had very little time to act. On September 15, a thundering barrage told Washington that

General William Howe had begun the next phase of his campaign. Galloping southward from his headquarters at Harlem, Washington spotted five Royal Navy warships off Kips Bay on the East River firing 70 guns at his defenses. Soon, more than 12,000 enemy troops were pouring ashore, routing his militiamen. Smacking them with his

riding cane, Washington tried to rally his men. The Hessians were nearly upon him when an aide-de-camp grabbed his bridle to turn his horse.

Battle of Harlem Heights

As Howe's regulars surged north along the Post Road, pushing Washington's main body toward Harlem, General

> "It caused my **heart to ache** to see **so many** of the **slain and wounded.**"
>
> WILLIAM BURKE, 45TH REGIMENT OF FOOT, ON THE BATTLE OF WHITE PLAINS, FROM HIS MEMOIR, 1837

PATRIOT SOLDIER 1755–76

NATHAN HALE

On September 8, 1776, George Washington asked for a volunteer to leave Harlem Heights and slip behind enemy lines on a scouting mission. That man was 21-year-old Nathan Hale, a schoolteacher from Connecticut who had joined the Patriot army after the Siege of Boston. Hale had accepted a commission as a first lieutenant in the Continental Army and in the following spring had gone with his regiment to New York. Until this point, Captain Hale had not yet fought in any battles, yet he was the only man brave enough to volunteer to undertake Washington's dangerous mission.

The handsome and athletic officer, disguised as the civilian schoolteacher he had once been, was soon discovered. On the evening of September 21, he was captured and interrogated. The following day he was hanged as a spy—on the scaffold. His last words, "I only regret that I have but one life to give for my country," went down in history.

Isaac Putnam led the Patriot rearguard out of the city. Although Putnam abandoned more than 50 cannons, his column still stretched out for 2 miles (3 km), making them vulnerable to attack. With this in mind, he followed a little-used farm lane screened from the Post Road by thick woods, where today's Central Park now stands. It was a hot, dusty, and nerve-wracking 12 mile (19 km) march, but the column arrived safely, joining Washington's lines at Harlem Heights just after dark, having had only one brush with British troops.

That night, the opposing armies bivouacked 2 miles (3 km) apart, facing each other across the valley. Howe's tents stretched all the way from the Hudson to the Harlem River, while Washington's men lay on their arms, without blankets, in previously prepared fortifications on the crest of Harlem Heights.

In the early hours of September 16, a detachment of Patriot rangers crept down into the valley and up the forested southern escarpment. By dawn, they were in combat with detachments of British light infantry and the 42nd Highlanders, called the "Black Watch." Sent scrambling back into the woods, the rangers heard the taunting notes of a bugle horn—the rallying cry for a fox chase.

This deliberate insult provoked a ferocious Patriot counterattack later that morning. Initially, this drove back the British, but the Redcoats then rallied, and for the next few hours battle raged over buckwheat fields and fenced orchards. Grenadiers, Hessian Jaegers, and artillery were brought into play, and the Continentals—including some routed survivors of Kips Bay—disengaged. Yet the Battle of Harlem Heights boosted the confidence of the Patriots, who had distinguished themselves in a stand-up fight with British regulars.

Armies on the move

Howe stayed in place on the Heights for four weeks. On October 12, he outflanked the rebel left again, landing 4,000 troops first at Throg's Neck on Long Island Sound—where they were halted by unexpectedly marshy conditions and 25 riflemen behind a woodpile—and then six days later at nearby Pell's Point. Meanwhile, Washington's army, lacking tents and even kettles, had quit Manhattan Island and began falling back to the heights above White Plains. The Patriots had so few horses that they were forced to roll their cannons and wagons by hand.

At White Plains, Howe caught up with Washington. The British commander, studying his counterpart's positions, saw 14,500 rebels strongly entrenched between a millpond and the Bronx River. But just across the river, overlooking the rebel line, Howe could see Washington's men, exposed to attack, busily digging defensive works on Chatterton's Hill.

Battle of White Plains

On October 28, nearly 20,000 British and Hessian soldiers lounged about the autumnal wheatfields, enjoying the weather, as their commanders held an open-air council of war. Soon enough, however, 4,000 of them were on their feet. Supported by a dozen guns, they attacked Chatterton's Hill.

The Battle of White Plains began with a cannonade and then seesawed back and forth between assault and repulse, volley and bayonet. Gradually, the Hessians and the British dragoons forced the Patriots off the summit of the hill. Howe dug in and again the British troops began to outflank their opponents. Then, on October 31, the Patriots slipped away, entrenching 5 miles (8 km) away, on the heights of North Castle. Their defensive works were so hurried that some of the sharpened stakes bristling along the front were just uprooted cornstalks.

Howe chose not to follow the Patriot commander. Instead, his army turned southwest toward the Patriot garrison Fort Washington—which its namesake had left isolated 15 miles (24 km) behind the lines. That stronghold, high above the Hudson, anchored a chain of sunken hulks and *chevaux-de-frise*, spiked obstacles designed to prevent enemy warships from ascending the river. But one Royal Navy frigate after another had passed these barriers with ease, and thousands of British and Hessian troops assailed the river's cliffs.

On November 15, the fort surrendered, and with it went 2,600 men, 146 cannon, 12,000 shot, 2,800 muskets, and 400,000 cartridges. Overlooking events on the far bank of the Hudson stood a distraught figure on a horse. Washington had galloped south along the river to watch the fort fall.

Washington's army fled west. Many of his 5,400 remaining soldiers lacked shoes, shirts, and coats, and slept without tents or blankets. As winter rains set in, turning the New Jersey roads into quagmires, the men began deserting in droves.

Lord Cornwallis, ordered by Howe to pursue Washington, was gaining on the Patriot commander every day. With only one more river to cross—the Delaware—Washington expected the worst. On December 18, 1776, he wrote to a relative: "I think the game is pretty near up." Morale was low throughout the army. That December, Thomas Paine, a volunteer with the Patriots picked up his pen and, using the head of a drum as a makeshift desk, began the series of articles that became *The Crisis* with his most famous line, "These are the times that try men's souls."

> **2,600** men surrendered at Fort Washington and were taken prisoner by the British. Only 600 survived.

Fight to the death
The men of the 17th Light Dragoons, who served in the New York campaign, styled themselves the "Death or Glory Boys." Their cap badge sported a skull and crossbones.

Regimental badge

Horsehair crest

AFTER ≫

After New York, Washington knew he had to act boldly if the Patriots were not to be defeated.

A GROWING WAR

At the end of 1776, the war's focus shifted to New Jersey, where the British had built a chain of forts. At Christmas, Washington **recrossed the Delaware River 130–31 ≫** to mount a **surprise attack on the Hessian garrison 132–33 ≫** followed by an attack on the British garrison at **Princeton** in early January 1777.

While the British held on to New York City after Long Island and Harlem Heights, the rest of the colony continued to see conflict. During 1777, battles raged in the **Hudson highlands 160–61 ≫**, and in 1779, New York saw battles at Minisink, Newtown, Stony Point, and Paulus Hook.

Running the Hudson River Barricade

In the fall of 1776, Patriot forces seeking to block British warships from ascending the Hudson River built Fort Washington on Manhattan Island and Fort Lee on the North Jersey cliffs opposite. They then spanned the river with a barricade of sunken ships studded with iron-speared *chevaux de frise*. Even so, on October 9, British Admiral Hyde Parker—helped by a traitorous pilot—led HMS *Phoenix, Roebuck*, and *Tartar* through the barricade.

"Having previously considered what would be best to be done in the Event of the Guide proving Treacherous, Capt Parker had pistols laying on the Binnacle, telling the guide that would be his Fate if the ships should stop in their passage. On the near approach, the Pilot, in great confusion, told him the marks which then appeared were not those that had been described to him, and he was totally at a loss.

Fortunately this had been so strongly suspected that Capt Parker immedty hauld up to the side where it was known the deepest water lay—and the ships all passed within 40 yards of the Muzzles of the Enemy's Guns in the Batterys of Fort Washington—amidst the fire of 100 Cannon from both sides of the River—in little more time than about 20 minutes.

The shots that did the ships the most damage were from the Jersey shore. The guns from those batteries were so well served that very few missed striking some part of the ship ... Eight men were killed in the three ships, four of which unfortunately came to my share, who could least spare them, as indeed is generally the case. Among them was poor Leake, my first lieutenant."

JOURNAL OF CAPTAIN ANDREW SNAPE HAMOND, ABOARD HMS *ROEBUCK*

Family pride
The family of Admiral Hyde Parker, who captained HMS *Phoenix* in the Hudson River attack, commissioned the artist Dominic Serres to commemorate the daring feat. The painting inspired many copies, including this one by William Joy in around 1835.

The **Threat** from **Canada**

Early in 1776 it was a priority for the British to secure their hold on Canada. The territory was a vital base for a move through upstate New York against the rebel forces. Control of lakes and rivers, which provided the best way to move men and supplies, was key to success.

As predicted by General Guy Carleton, governor of Quebec, the siege of that city ended with the breakup of the ice in the St. Lawrence River. On May 6, 1776, the sails of three Royal Navy ships carrying General John Burgoyne's relief force hove into view, and the threadbare troops of the Continental Army retreated toward Montreal.

Retreat along the Richelieu

The Continental Army's Canadian campaign was ending disastrously. The scattered rebel posts along the St. Lawrence River began falling back southward to their former invasion route along the course of the Richelieu River, flowing out of Lake Champlain. With their ranks depleted by smallpox and dysentery, on June 5 the rebels made a final forlorn attack, targeting the nearby settlement of Trois-Rivières. It was not enough. The British spotted their forces crossing the St. Lawrence

and lured them into a swamp within range of the grapeshot of Royal Navy vessels and the massed volleys of British regulars. Many of the rebel soldiers surrendered.

Carleton had reversed the tide of war in Canada. With Burgoyne as his second-in-command, he now took the offensive, driving for the distant Hudson River to join with another British contingent—General William Howe's army—at Albany, hoping that this decisive move might end the rebellion. The Continental troops opposing him were dying of disease so rapidly that 900 of them were shoveled into mass graves on the Richelieu River's Île aux Noix. The survivors torched every outpost as they retreated, as well as destroying

every boat that might be of use to the British on Lake Champlain. Bordered by the steep Adirondacks and forested Green Mountains, Lake Champlain was the only good route leading south. Without boats, an advancing army would have to hack roads out of the wilderness. Making the British pause long enough to assemble new

BEFORE

The siege of the city of Quebec by Patriot forces in the winter of 1775–76 was the main focus of the early months of the war.

STRATEGIC WATERWAY
In May 1775 Ethan Allen and Benedict Arnold captured **Fort Ticonderoga** **«** **62–63** for the Continental Army, winning control of the strategic waterway of Lake Champlain. The rebels dragged artillery seized from Ticonderoga over the mountains to Boston, **forcing the British** to leave that city **«** **100–01**.

THE MARCH ON QUEBEC
In September 1775, the Patriots started their advance into Quebec province, General Richard Montgomery driving north from Lake Champlain, and Arnold crossing the mountains of Maine. Both were **defeated at the gates of Quebec** **«** **80–81** but Arnold kept the city besieged. While the siege continued, the British forces within the city were unable to join with other detachments to isolate the rebel forces in New England.

Mast for square-rigged sail and topsail

One of two 9-pound guns

Swivel gun

Anchor

12-pound bow gun

Hawsehole for anchor cables

Oak planking

The gunboat *Philadelphia*
Sunk in the battle and found in 1935 sitting upright on the bed of Lake Champlain, the *Philadelphia* was one of Benedict Arnold's gundalows, a type of flat-bottomed gunboat built specially for the Battle of Valcour Island.

boats would clearly interrupt their momentum and buy the Patriots enough time to muster their defense.

In July, General Horatio Gates took over the sickly and ill-supplied Patriot force at Crown Point and Fort Ticonderoga. Under his command, the men's health and morale improved and new recruits began to arrive. Meanwhile, Carleton had rebuilt the shipyard at St. Jean and was building hundreds of bateaux (shallow boats) to ferry British forces down the lake.

Preparing naval forces

The only thing that could stop or delay Carleton now was a navy and the Continental Congress set out to get one. They already had a 12-gun schooner, *Royal Savage*, captured at St. Jean, plus a sloop and two eight-gun schooners. There was also a boatyard at Skenesboro, at Lake Champlain's southern end, where it was possible to build a small flotilla of oar- and sail-propelled gunboats. To command the operation, Gates picked the most determined officer in the Patriot army—Benedict Arnold. Although wounded at Quebec, Arnold had spent the winter fighting in Canada. Now he urged on the felling of trees and the hewing of ribs, planks, and keels. He imported tools and supplies over forest trails, and offered good money to attract craftsmen from New England.

Word of these activities soon reached the British, who continued to strengthen their fleet. The British task was easier, for they controlled the mighty St. Lawrence—with its shipyards and naval vessels. Three warships came up that great river, were then dismantled and portaged over 10 miles (16 km) of Richelieu River rapids, and finally rebuilt at St. Jean.

Battle of Valcour Island

Both fleets were ready by the fall. While 17,000 Redcoats pitched their tents on banks of Lake Champlain, Carleton's fleet commander, Commodore Thomas Pringle, with 25 armed vessels, hunted Arnold and his flotilla. He found him on October 11, lurking behind Valcour Island—with four ships and 11 armed galleys. For five hours the fleets dueled. The smaller Patriot navy suffered most damage; nearly 60 men were killed or wounded and all the sails and rigging were shredded. The *Royal Savage* was

set on fire and exploded. Pringle, the British commander—who had lost one gunboat and about 40 casualties—then arranged his fleet in a cordon stretching from the island to within a mile of the lake's western shore. He planned to finish Arnold at dawn the next day.

Night brought fog. The British lookouts could see nothing and the battered rebel fleet was able to slip away, creeping in single file so close to the western shore that its crews could see the campfires of Carleton's Native Americans in the woods. Pringle caught up with Arnold two days later on October 14, and all but destroyed the Patriot flotilla; only three ships and one galley reached safety at Fort Crown Point. Judging even this haven to be insecure, Arnold burned the fort and retreated to Fort Ticonderoga, where the Patriots were preparing for an attack that never came.

"Our **attack** … became very **fierce;** and, close quarters, very **animated.**"

HESSIAN CAPTAIN GEORG PAUSCH, IN HIS JOURNAL, PUBLISHED 1886

Engagement on Lake Champlain

This print shows the British ships in a neat line of battle on October 11, off Valcour Island. As the day went on, this arrangement gave way to small groups of ships targeting Patriot vessels.

The snow was already capping the Adirondack peaks. Carleton had spent three months building a fleet and now he judged it too late in the year for campaigning. To the incredulity of some of his officers he returned his army to winter quarters in St. Jean. "Gentleman Johnny" Burgoyne sailed for London, there to plead for a more powerful invasion in 1777.

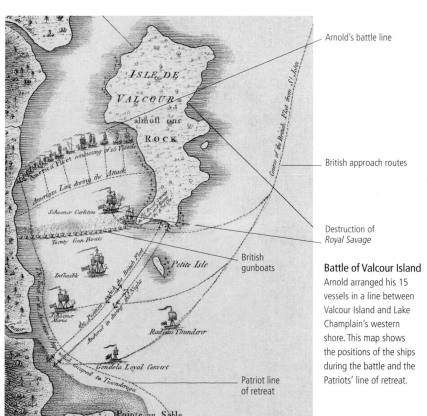

Arnold's battle line

British approach routes

Destruction of *Royal Savage*

British gunboats

Battle of Valcour Island

Arnold arranged his 15 vessels in a line between Valcour Island and Lake Champlain's western shore. This map shows the positions of the ships during the battle and the Patriots' line of retreat.

Patriot line of retreat

AFTER

This tactical defeat for the Patriot forces in fact marked a strategic victory for the cause of American independence.

BREATHING SPACE

Carleton's caution in refusing to advance on the fortifications at Ticonderoga and Mount Independence enabled **General Horatio Gates** to reinforce Washington's forces. Some of those troops fought in the **Battle of Trenton 132–33** ❯❯. This pause also allowed Gates, General Philip Schuyler, and General Arthur St. Clair to strengthen Patriot forces in the Lake Champlain–Hudson River corridor.

THE CONSEQUENCES OF DELAY

Carleton's halt ensured that one of the key British military goals—linking up forces from New York and Canada to isolate Patriot forces in New England—would not be realized in 1776. This hiatus meant that General Burgoyne and his 6,000 British and German soldiers would attempt that strategy in 1777, a path that eventually led to the battles of **Saratoga 162–63** ❯❯.

Washington crossing the Delaware
On December 25, 1776, Washington led his troops across the icy Delaware River to deliver a surprise attack at Trenton. Emanuel Leutze's iconic painting captures Washington's sense of mission.

Trenton and Princeton

Driven across the Delaware River in November 1776, the Continental Army was all but beaten. In a desperate gamble, Washington rallied his demoralized troops and recrossed the river to mount a surprise attack on the British post at Trenton.

« BEFORE

By the fall of 1776, the British seemed to have gained the upper hand.

FLIGHT FROM DISASTER

The Patriots had lost ground on several fronts. In Canada, Sir Guy Carleton had vanquished Benedict Arnold's fleet at the **Battle of Valcour Island « 128–29** on Lake Champlain. The Continental Army also lost **Long Island « 118–19**. After these defeats, Washington fled west across the Hudson and Delaware rivers, pursued by Lord Cornwallis.

PEACE REJECTED

In September 1776, the British initiated the **Staten Island Peace Conference**. Discussions broke down over the issue of American independence, which the Patriots insisted upon.

In early December 1776, the 6,000 officers and men of Washington's army were spread thinly along the banks of the frozen Delaware River, huddled behind earthworks with few guns and no tents. To every eye it was a defeated army and its general a beaten man. In the wake of a series of British victories, George Washington was expecting to be relieved of command, a mortal blow to his pride.

It was also an army about to dissolve: after December 31, when most enlistments expired, just 1,400 men would remain. Without more men, there was a danger that General Howe's troops would be able to walk across the frozen river and win the war without firing a shot.

Howe had let Lord Cornwallis take Christmas leave and put the bulk of the British forces into winter quarters in New York. But he had also established a chain of posts along the highway from New York to Philadelphia—at Amboy, New

Brunswick, Princeton, and Trenton, on the banks of the Delaware.

Pondering those dispositions, Washington devised a desperate plan: he would recross the river and risk everything in a surprise raid on Trenton, garrisoned by 1,400 Hessians. On December 23, Washington wrote to his aide-de-camp, Colonel Reed, that "necessity, dire necessity, will, nay must, justify my attack."

Launching the offensive

On Christmas night, 2,400 handpicked men, commanded by Washington himself and General Nathanael Greene, slogged to McKonkey's Ferry on the Delaware. In bitterly cold weather, the men, horses, and cannons were loaded onto flat-bottomed Durham boats manned by John Glover's "Marbleheaders," who had rescued the army from Brooklyn Heights (see pp.118–19), and ferried across the icy waters. It was 3 a.m. when the last man stepped onto the enemy shore, and it was another hour before the army began to march.

They hurried down the rutted roads to Trenton, expecting to meet disaster: the day was dawning, the gunpowder

> " …use the **bayonet.** I am resolved to **take Trenton.**"
>
> GEORGE WASHINGTON, DECEMBER 26, 1776

was wet, and the shoeless men were leaving bloody footprints in the snow. The Patriots could only hope that the Hessian forces in charge of the British post at Trenton had imbibed too much Christmas cheer. Certainly their commander, Colonel Johann Rall, had tarried late at wine and cards. A message sent to alert him about the Patriot attack—"Rebels approaching in force"— was later found in his pocket, probably unread.

Just before 8 a.m. Washington's forces overran the Hessian pickets. Soon they were pouring into the snowbound town. At first, few muskets were heard

firing, so drenched were the flintlocks. Then the big guns were unlimbered and the roar of cannons echoed through the streets. While a stupefied Rall hastily formed his lines, Patriot soldiers broke into the houses, dried their flints, and began shooting out of windows. Within an hour, Rall had been shot off his horse, mortally wounded, and the Patriots had taken 948 prisoners, six field pieces, 1,000 muskets, 14 drums, and 15 stands of colors. Twenty-two Hessians lay dead in the snow, while 92 others were wounded. Washington did not lose a single man.

It was nightfall before the last Patriot soldier was ferried back across the river. The exhausted men had marched and fought continuously for nearly 50 hours.

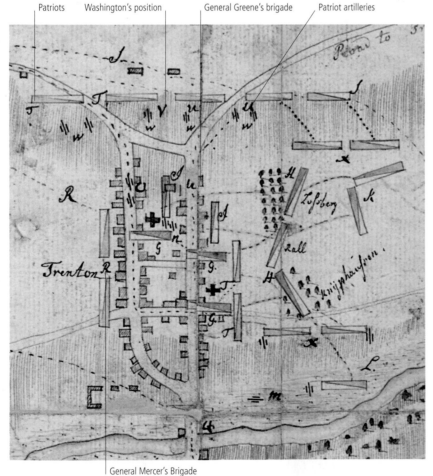

Patriots | Washington's position | General Greene's brigade | Patriot artilleries

General Mercer's Brigade

Plan of attack

This contemporary map of the Battle of Trenton shows the positions of the Patriot forces under their generals Washington, Greene, and Mercer.

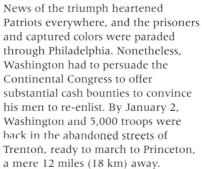

MILITARY LEADER 1732–97

JOHN GLOVER

John Glover hailed from Marblehead, Massachusetts, a seaport north of Boston. The town's militia company under his command won fame as the "amphibious regiment" because every member was a skilled boatman. They took up oars on two memorable occasions, assisting the Patriot retreat after the Battle of Long Island, and ferrying Washington's men across the Delaware River before the Battle of Trenton. After the war Glover returned to Marblehead, where he died in 1797.

News of the triumph heartened Patriots everywhere, and the prisoners and captured colors were paraded through Philadelphia. Nonetheless, Washington had to persuade the Continental Congress to offer substantial cash bounties to convince his men to re-enlist. By January 2, Washington and 5,000 troops were back in the abandoned streets of Trenton, ready to march to Princeton, a mere 12 miles (18 km) away.

A furious clash

After the Patriot victory at Trenton, Howe withdrew every British post on the Delaware and recalled Cornwallis from leave. At the head of 8,000 men and a train of artillery, Cornwallis advanced on Trenton.

Another battle loomed. But heavy rains and sodden roads delayed Cornwallis's approach, and Washington, making a night march over rough trails, circled around the British left flank. His goal, Princeton, was only lightly guarded.

Dawn found Washington at the town's outskirts, where he sent

The Death of General Mercer
Unhorsed, clubbed by a musket butt, and stabbed by seven bayonets, General Mercer died in the Battle of Princeton. This painting by John Trumbull commemorates his bravery in battle.

General Hugh Mercer to seize a stone bridge on the nearby Trenton Road. A force of 1,200 Redcoats under Colonel Charles Mawhood was approaching that very spot.

The furious battle that followed lasted only 15 minutes, but the losses were great. When Mercer's horse went down, Washington galloped through the maelstrom rallying his men. Mawhood's troops, outnumbered, fought bravely but eventually broke.

The battle ended when 194 Redcoats, holed up in the College of New Jersey's Nassau Hall, surrendered. But the Patriots didn't occupy the field, and when Cornwallis entered the town he found they had already gone. The earl didn't follow them; instead he pushed into New Brunswick to protect a supply depot there. Washington headed north for Morristown and its protective circle of hills.

Washington's success at Trenton and Princeton revitalized the Continental Army and forced the British to revise their plans.

CLEARING NEW JERSEY

After Trenton and Princeton, General Howe pulled all British forces back to the outskirts of New York for winter, effectively clearing New Jersey of British and Loyalist forces. Howe spent the winter planning a **spring offensive**, aiming to capture **Philadelphia** via **Chesapeake Bay** and the **Brandywine Valley 170–71 »**.

FRUITS OF VICTORY

Patriots celebrated as news of Trenton and Princeton spread through city, town, and countryside. Encouraged by the Patriot victories, the **French increased financial aid** to the Continental Congress **188–89 »**, and shipped military supplies to the Continental Army.

4
THE STRUGGLE FOR MASTERY
1777

As the momentum of war increased, major military campaigns gripped the North and South. The British relied on the support of American Loyalists and German mercenaries; the Patriots—desperately short of funds and supplies—appealed to Britain's traditional enemy, France.

≪ Sold into service
Several German margraves made money by loaning their troops to Britain. The Hessians, as they were known, fought in major battles in the North and South, including Saratoga in 1777.

ACTION IN 1777

T he year 1777 started badly for the British, who had seemed tantalizingly close to victory toward the end of 1776. While Washington embarked upon the Forage War in New Jersey, to cut off British supplies, British strategists dithered over the best way forward. As General John Burgoyne's combined force of British regulars and German mercenaries advanced down the Hudson Valley from Canada, capturing Fort Ticonderoga, Fort Edward, and Fort George, General Howe embarked on a plan to march on Philadelphia, leaving Burgoyne without expected reinforcements. Howe met with success at Brandywine and Germantown but neither victory was decisive. After capturing Philadelphia, the British were driven back at the Battle of Red Bank on the Delaware River, south of the city.

1 Britain recruited increasing numbers of German mercenaries in 1777. Many fought at Germantown in October. 2 British General John Burgoyne led a major offensive down the Hudson Valley. 3 HMS *Augusta* was destroyed by fire at the Battle of Red Bank.

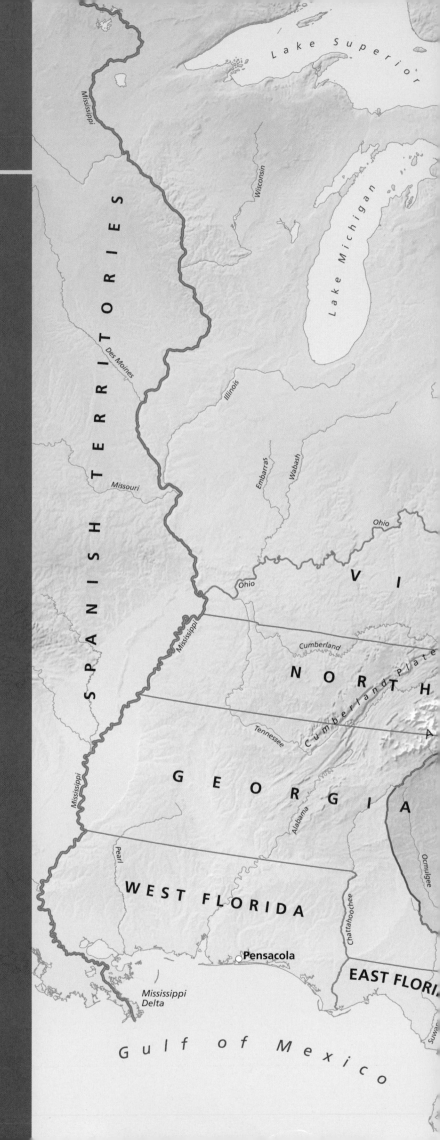

Newfoundland

Magdalen Islands

Prince Edward Island

Louisbourg

NOVA SCOTIA

Sable Island

Quebec

Saguenay

St. John

Saint-Maurice

Ottawa

St. Lawrence

Montreal

Penobscot

MASSACHUSETTS

Bay of Fundy

Halifax

Q U E B E C

Georgian Bay

Lake Huron

Lake Ontario

Lake Champlain

Lake Erie

Fort Ticonderoga
Adirondack Mountains
White Mountains
Green Mountains
NEW HAMPSHIRE

Siege of Fort Stanwix
Fort Oswego
Battle of Oriskany

2

Saratoga

Fort Constitution

N E W Y O R K

Albany
MASSACHUSETTS

Boston
Cape Cod

Catskill Mountains
CONNECTICUT
RHODE ISLAND

Hudson

Newport

ATLANTIC OCEAN

Allegheny

P E N N S Y L V A N I A

Susquehanna

Battle of Germantown **1**
Valley Forge **Princeton**
Battle of Brandywine **3** **Philadelphia**

New York City

DELAWARE

NEW JERSEY

Baltimore

MARYLAND

Muskingum

Ohio

Kanawha

Potomac

V I R G I N I A

James

Yorktown
Norfolk

Roanoke
Dan

Chesapeake Bay

C A R O L I N A

KEY

— Border of Spanish territory (1763)
— 1763 Proclamation Line
— Colonial boundaries (1763)
○ Town / settlement
⚔ Battle / siege
🏰 Fort
⛵ Naval battle
🖋 Treaty / convention
⛺ Loyalist winter camp
⛺ Patriot winter camp

SOUTH CAROLINA

Wateree
Pee Dee
Cape Fear
Camden
Wilmington

Augusta
Santee
Cooper
Savannah
Charleston

annah
Ogeechee
Altamaha
St. Johns

N
0 — 100 km
0 — 100 miles

Battle of Oriskany
Battle of Bemis Heights
Battle of Freeman's Farm
Saratoga
Battle of Bennington
Green Mountains
Connecticut
NEW HAMPSHIRE

Fort Constitution

Albany
Hudson

N E W Y O R K

Catskill Mountains

MASSACHUSETTS

CONNECTICUT

Long Island

Boston
Cape Cod

Newport
RHODE ISLAND

Battle of Forts Clinton and Montgomery
Battle of Ridgefield

Delaware
Susquehanna

P E N N S Y L V A N I A

NEW JERSEY

Morristown
Battle of Bound Brook
Battle of Millstone
New Brunswick
Battle of Spanktown
Perth Amboy
Princeton
New York City

Second Continental Congress (III)
Second Continental Congress (IV)
Valley Forge **1**
Battle of Germantown
Battle of Brandywine **3**
Philadelphia
Fort Mercer
Fort Mifflin
Second Continental Congress (II)

Second Continental Congress (I)
Battle of Red Bank

Baltimore

MARYLAND

DELAWARE

ATLANTIC OCEAN

Fort Constitution

0 — 100 km
0 — 100 miles

TIMELINE 1777

Battle of Princeton ▪ **The Forage War** ▪ Burgoyne's offensive ▪ **Fall of Fort Ticonderoga** ▪ British take Philadelphia ▪ **Battle of Saratoga** ▪ Surrender of Burgoyne's army ▪ **Articles of Confederation**

JANUARY	FEBRUARY	MARCH	APRIL	MAY	JUNE
JANUARY 3 Washington and his Continentals defeat the British at Princeton and force them back toward New Brunswick, New Jersey.	**FEBRUARY 6** Parliament issues letters of marque and reprisal, authorizing attacks on Patriot ships by privateers.	**MARCH 6** Representatives of New York pass an act allowing the confiscation and sale of Loyalist property. The proceeds are allocated to the Patriot war effort.	**APRIL 13** A surprise attack by British and Hessian troops forces General Benjamin Lincoln to abandon the outpost at Bound Brook, New Jersey.	**MAY 20** The Cherokee make peace with colonists in South Carolina, ceding land in the Treaty of Dewitt's Corner.	
JANUARY 6 The Continental Army retires to its winter quarters at Morristown.		**MARCH 12** The Continental Congress returns to Philadelphia from Baltimore.	**APRIL 27** Patriot forces under General Benedict Arnold defeat the British at Ridgefield, Connecticut.		

≫ Marquis de Lafayette

≪ Finding forage

≫ Mercenaries embark from Hesse-Kassel to America

JANUARY 7 In the Forage War, General Maxwell's militia forces the British evacuation of Elizabethtown, New Jersey.	**FEBRUARY 23** Patriot militia inflict heavy losses on the British in the Battle of Spanktown during the Forage War in New Jersey.			**MAY 27** The Congress authorizes formation of the northern department of the Bureau of War, under General Philip Schuyler's command, which consists of "Albany, Ticonderoga, Fort Stanwix and their dependencies."	**JUNE 13** The French Marquis de Lafayette lands near Charleston, South Carolina, to aid the Patriots.
JANUARY 20 Patriot Brigadier General Philemon Dickinson and his militia surprise and drive off a British foraging force near Somerset Court House, Pennsylvania.	**FEBRUARY 26** The Continental Navy sinks five British supply vessels near Amboy, New Jersey.				**JUNE 17** General John Burgoyne's army strikes south from Canada, sailing down Lake Champlain.
					JUNE 30 General Howe's army evacuates New Jersey and crosses to Staten Island.

≫ General Benjamin Lincoln's sword and scabbard

"Yonder are **the Hessians** … **Are you worth more?** Prove it! Tonight the **American flag** flies from yonder hill or **Molly Stark sleeps a widow!**"

PATRIOT GENERAL JOHN STARK TO HIS TROOPS, BEFORE THE BATTLE OF BENNINGTON, AUGUST 14, 1777

JULY	AUGUST	SEPTEMBER	OCTOBER	NOVEMBER	DECEMBER
JULY 6 Burgoyne's troops capture Fort Ticonderoga after it is abandoned by the Patriot garrison.	**AUGUST 1** Burgoyne's troops reach the Hudson. **AUGUST 2** St. Leger's troops lay siege to Fort Schuyler.	**SEPTEMBER 9** Washington and his army are driven back toward Philadelphia in the Battle of Brandywine.	**OCTOBER 4** Washington's army is defeated at Germantown and forced to resume its retreat.	**NOVEMBER 10** The British begin their bombardment of Fort Mifflin in Pennsylvania.	**DECEMBER 5** British and Continental forces start a three-day skirmish around Whitemarsh, Pennsylvania.

« Battle of Germantown

JULY 7 Forces under General Simon Fraser and Baron von Riedesel attack the Patriot rearguard at Hubbardton, after pursuing them from Fort Ticonderoga.	**AUGUST 6** On their way to relieve Fort Schuyler, General Nicholas Herkimer and his militia are ambushed by St. Leger's troops at Oriskany.				**DECEMBER 19** Washington and the Continental Army fall back to their winter quarters at Valley Forge.
JULY 25 British Lieutenant Colonel Barry St. Leger and his troops reach Fort Oswego.	**AUGUST 16** Vermont militiamen, with the aid of some troops from Massachusetts, wipe out Hessians dispatched on a foraging expedition in battle at Bennington.	**SEPTEMBER 19** General Gates, although defeated, delays Burgoyne's advance along the Hudson River with an attack at Freeman's Farm.	**OCTOBER 7** Burgoyne loses the Battle of Bemis Heights.	**NOVEMBER 15** The Congress adopts the Articles of Confederation.	

⯈ Battle of Bennington

NOVEMBER 25
A Patriot war council decides against attacking Philadelphia.

		SEPTEMBER 21 General Anthony Wayne's Patriots, ordered to harass the British, are surprised in a nighttime attack on their camp at Paoli.	**OCTOBER 17** Burgoyne and his army surrender to Gates at Saratoga.		

» General John Burgoyne

JULY 27 General William Howe sets sail from New York for the Chesapeake Bay with 15,000 men, intending to defeat Washington in the field and capture Philadelphia.	**AUGUST 22** General Benedict Arnold advances to relieve Fort Schuyler, so St. Leger retreats to Fort Oswego. **AUGUST 25** Howe's troops land at the Head of Elk, Maryland.	**SEPTEMBER 26** General Howe's troops enter Philadelphia. The Congress, which had left the city for Lancaster, retires further, to York, Pennsylvania.	**OCTOBER 22** Hessian troops fail to capture Fort Mercer at the Battle of Red Bank.		

BEFORE

In the fall of 1776, Washington's army looked all but beaten. The British commanders began to think they were close to delivering a decisive victory that would end the conflict.

ADVANTAGE BRITAIN

British **Redcoats ‹‹ 92–93 had proved themselves strong** in the face of an untrained Patriot army. The year 1776 had seen British victories and advances, with General Howe's **invasion of New York ‹‹ 118–19** and **success in Canada ‹‹ 128–29**.

PATRIOT RESURGENCE

After the Patriot defeats in battles at **Long Island** and **Harlem Heights**, Washington retreated across the Delaware River. He fought back in December 1776, **routing the Hessians** in a surprise attack at **Trenton ‹‹ 132–33**, and then defeating the British garrison at **Princeton**.

WINTER QUARTERS

After Trenton and Princeton, the **Continental Army** retired to take up its winter quarters in **Morristown, New Jersey**, while General Howe's Redcoats fell back to Perth Amboy and New Brunswick.

> "Though it was … the fashion … to treat them in the **most contemptible light,** they are now become a **formidable enemy.**"
>
> COLONEL WILLIAM HARCOURT, MARCH 1777

New Jersey arena

Patriot militias, occasionally reinforced by Continental troops, launched raids from their base at Morristown and met the British in some 58 skirmishes—some very minor indeed— across New Jersey's Raritan Valley.

The **Forage War**

Following his victories at Trenton and Princeton, Washington ordered Patriot militiamen to harass British communications and supply columns in New Jersey. This campaign of attrition became known as the Forage War.

Newark (January 5)

Morristown (Patriot base)

Boundbrook (April)

New Brunswick (British base)

Somerset (June)

Millstone (January 20)

Rahway, known as Spanktown (February 23)

Woodbridge (January 20–23)

Amboy (British base)

Elizabethtown (January 5–7)

The Patriot successes at Trenton and Princeton meant that even after a full year of successful campaigns the British were on the defensive at the beginning of 1777. Although General James Grant, in command of the British garrisons in New Jersey, bragged that he could hold down the state "with a corporal's guard," Washington had proved that his Continentals were far from finished as an effective fighting force.

However, with winter upon them, a full-scale resumption of the war was out of the question. Washington also faced two major problems. First, many of his men's enlistment periods had come to an end, temporarily reducing his fighting strength to around 2,500 Continental troops, who were now established in camps around Morristown; second, smallpox was spreading rapidly through the ranks.

Laissez-faire commander

The British commander in chief, General Howe, did not intend to renew the New Jersey campaign immediately. Indeed, Justice Thomas Jones, a New York Loyalist angered by Howe's lackadaisical conduct, claimed that the commander in chief "was diverting himself in New York in feasting, gunning, banqueting, and in the arms of Mrs. Loring."

PATRIOT SOLDIER 1739–1809

PHILEMON DICKINSON

Lawyer-turned-soldier Philemon Dickinson's success in leading Patriot militia at the Battle of Millstone led to his promotion to major general in command of the New Jersey militia. Dickinson also saw success at Monmouth in 1778, and in 1782 he became a delegate to the Continental Congress, representing Delaware. After the war, Dickinson served as senator for New Jersey from 1790 to 1793, before retiring to his country estate near Trenton.

Washington swiftly recognized the importance of harassing the British supply lines. In particular, he was determined to stop the British from foraging for feed for their horses. He explained in a letter to Major General Joseph Spencer that "the Enemy … are much distressed for Provision and Forage, and, unless they make a push to extricate themselves, they must in a Manner perish this winter."

A local struggle

Washington urged the militia to launch pinprick attacks on British and Hessian foragers and supply columns whenever they had the opportunity. In addition to interrupting supply lines, the aim of this constant attrition was to prevent the opposing army from consolidating control of an area. Soldiers on both sides had to be alert and ready for action at any time.

From early January to the end of March 1777, armed clashes and skirmishes took place between Patriot militiamen, sometimes supported by small Continental Army detachments, and the British forces. Actions largely centered on New Jersey's Raritan Valley, running north and west of New Brunswick to the Millstone River. Many of the militiamen came from villages in New Jersey, and although both sides laid traps for each other in the countryside, their superior knowledge of the local area gave the Patriot troops a distinct advantage.

The first skirmish took place on January 4, 1777, when Patriot militiaman Captain John Stryker, leading the Somerset Horse, captured a supply train near Ten Mile Run, a tributary of the Millstone River. The train's five wagons were filled with warm winter woolens, which Stryker promptly sent to Washington to help clothe his ragged army. Further attacks on British and Hessian foraging parties followed at Newark, Rahway (known as Spanktown), and around Elizabethtown, which the British then abandoned on the orders of General Howe, who was conducting the campaign from the safety of New York. Washington told the Continental Congress that the British had evacuated Elizabethtown "with so much precipitation" that they lost 100 prisoners, two regiments' baggage, and a whole host of provisions.

Spoils of war

The skirmishing intensified. On January 20, Brigadier General Philemon Dickinson led around 400 New Jersey militiamen and

2,887 British soldiers killed or captured January–April 1777.

1,510 British soldiers killed or captured in the whole of 1776.

In search of forage
The old saying "an army marches on its stomach" applied as much to the horses of the British troops as it did to the soldiers themselves. Washington understood this well, as he disrupted and cut off vital supply lines.

50 Connecticut riflemen into action at the Battle of Millstone, about 8 miles (13 km) west of New Brunswick. The 20-minute skirmish against 500 British regulars and the Hessians resulted in a clear victory for the Patriots. According to Washington, Dickinson's men acquired "107 horses, 49 wagons, 115 cattle, 70 sheep, 40 barrels of flower, and 106 bags among other things." They also took 49 prisoners.

In New York, General Howe became increasingly concerned as the Patriot attacks persisted. Charles Stedman, a British commissary officer, noted that "the excursions which the garrison… made for forage, were often attended with fatal consequences."

Bigger prizes

Although minor skirmishes continued in New Jersey throughout the war, by March 1777 Washington and Howe's Forage War was over. The coming of spring brought relief for the hard-pressed British, as attentions turned to the year's bigger campaigns. In April, the British saw victory at Boundbrook, returning to New Brunswick after looting the town and capturing supplies. Washington's army took up positions at Middle Brook. In June, Howe marched his army to Somerset, hoping to draw out the Patriots, but Washington did not fall for the feint. After minor skirmishes, Howe set sail for Chesapeake Bay, refocusing his attention on capturing Philadelphia, America's largest city.

AFTER

Once General Howe made the capture of Philadelphia his primary objective, he moved his army out of New Jersey. At the same time, General John Burgoyne, commanding troops in Canada, hatched his own plan.

CHANGING PRIORITIES
Wary of crossing the Delaware, Howe wrote to Lord George Germain, in charge of British strategy in London, **"I propose to invade Pennsylvania by sea."** Meanwhile, General John Burgoyne prepared to **march down the Hudson Valley** from Canada **152–53 ≫**.

POLITICAL MANEUVERS
In Philadelphia, George Washington briefed the Continental Congress on the state of the war. He was joined by a **new military ally**, French volunteer the Marquis de Lafayette. British advances on Philadelphia forced the Congress to move, first to Lancaster, and then to York, Pennsylvania, where, seeking to strengthen cooperation between the Thirteen Colonies, it finalized and issued **the Articles of Confederation 324–25 ≫**.

FIRST MEETING OF LAFAYETTE AND WASHINGTON, AUGUST 5, 1777

The **British** in New Jersey

Strategically situated between the British stronghold of New York City and the Patriot capital in Philadelphia, wealthy New Jersey was one of the most fought-over territories in the War of Independence. Its citizens—themselves divided between Patriots and Loyalists—were often caught between the two armies. During the Forage War of 1776–77 (see pp.140–41), soldiers on both sides confiscated crops, burned houses, and killed those suspected of giving comfort to the enemy.

"No sooner had the army entered the Jerseys than the business (we say business for it was a perfect trade) of plunder began. The friend and the foe shared alike. The people's property was taken without being paid for or even a receipt given. The British Army foraged indiscriminately, procuring considerable supplies of hay, oats, Indian corn, cattle, and horses, which were never or but very seldom paid for.

The people of the Jerseys were well effected to his Majesty's government, but when the people found that the promised protection was not afforded them, that their property was seized and most wantonly destroyed, that in many instances their families were insulted, stripped of their beds with other furniture—nay, even of their very wearing apparel—they then determined to try the other side, trusting that they would at least, at one period or another, receive compensation for the supplies taken from them for the use of the American side.

And it is but justice to say that the Americans never took anything from their friends but in case of necessity, in which cases they uniformly have receipts for what they did take, always living as long as they could upon their enemies and never suffering their troops to plunder their friends with impunity. But, at the same time, it is to be noticed that the American troops were suffered to plunder the Loyalists and to exercise with impunity every act of barbarity on that unfortunate class of people, frequently inflicting on them scourges and stripes."

LOYALIST OFFICER CHARLES STEDMAN, IN HIS *HISTORY OF THE ORIGIN, PROGRESS, AND TERMINATION OF THE AMERICAN WAR*, 1794

The British invasion
On November 20, parties of Redcoats sailed up the Hudson and landed below Fort Lee. This contemporary watercolor attributed to serving British officer Thomas Davies shows them climbing the cliffs to capture the fort.

European Assistance

Even before the break with Britain, Patriot leaders were on the hunt for possible European allies. France, with its historic connection to Canada and its long rivalry around the world with the British, was the most likely country to provide help.

In May 1776, the French King Louis XVI dismissed Anne-Robert-Jacques Turgot, the main obstacle to France joining a war against Britain. As the French comptroller-general of finance, Turgot had opposed all-out war on the grounds of cost. With Turgot out of the way, Louis was free to lend the Patriots one million livres ($8 million today) to buy military essentials. Silas Deane, a delegate of the Continental Congress, and Caron de Beaumarchais, a French secret agent who later became a playwright, agreed the deal.

« BEFORE

Even before the outbreak of war, France was conspiring with Patriot factions, promising to help if they proclaimed independence.

NEGOTIATING REVENGE
The French attitude to America's bid for independence was colored by the defeats the country had suffered in the **French and Indian War « 24–25** and the loss to the British of its territories in Canada.

Secret negotiations with France started in late fall 1775, when the Comte de Vergennes, the French foreign minister, dispatched Julien de Bonvoulois, a former naval officer posing as a merchant, undercover to America to open discussions with the leaders of the Patriot cause.

Both sides were anxious to keep the arrangement secret. Some delegates to the Congress still believed in the possibility of reconciliation with Britain, but this would have meant accepting harsh British terms. The other choices were equally stark. The Americans could fight alone, knowing they lacked the resources to win a protracted war, or they could declare independence and seek French military assistance. The Congress chose to take the latter course of action. John Adams, who earlier had warned his fellow delegates that a French alliance ran the risk of "exchanging British for French tyranny," was one of the many who changed his mind.

Loans and arms

It seems more than likely that the revolution would have foundered had it not been for the massive assistance the Patriots received from France. Washington's victories at Trenton and Princeton at the end of 1776 saved their cause from military collapse, but the Patriots were also teetering on the verge of financial disaster. Somewhat surprisingly, the Congress had failed to anticipate the fact that its overseas and domestic suppliers would require payment in cash once hostilities had begun. Hard currency vanished from circulation, while the paper promissory notes the Congress and the individual colonies issued in its place depreciated so quickly that at one point economic collapse became a real possibility.

Fortunately, the French were prepared to continue backing the Patriots. The Patriot capture of Fort Ticonderoga in 1775 had persuaded them that American independence was not a lost cause. In January 1777, they

Bankrolling the rebels
Loans from France and the Netherlands played a large part in financing the war effort of the American rebels. This type of French gold coin of 1777, showing a portrait of King Louis XVI and known as a *Louis d'or*, was equal to 24 livres ($190 today).

loaned the rebels another four million livres ($32 million today) and promised them an annual subsidy of two million livres ($16 million today), secured by shipments of tobacco to France. Surplus military supplies were shipped in bulk across the Atlantic.

Yet French Foreign Minister Comte de Vergennes was not at this point prepared to declare war on Britain.

Hammer

Flint

Flash pan

Frizzen

Trigger

Trigger guard

Stock

US stamp

Carrying ring

French musket
"Charleville" naval muskets, named after one of the armories in France where they were made, were imported and brought into American military service. They were usually of 0.69-inch (18 mm) caliber (diameter of the barrel) and a trained soldier would be able to fire three or four rounds per minute.

The French navy insisted that it was unready for combat with its massive rebuilding program as yet incomplete. This caution was reinforced by the unwillingness of Spain, a potential ally, to join France. Accordingly, Vergennes turned down American pleas to send them ships of the line and "an immediate Supply of twenty or thirty Thousand Muskets and Bayonets, and a large Quantity of Ammunition and brass field Pieces." Nor was Vergennes prepared to extend diplomatic recognition to the infant republic or agree to a trade treaty with it. The most he would do at this stage was to encourage French army officers to go to America of their own volition.

Lending expertise

The young Marquis de Lafayette (see pp.146–47) was one of the first French officers to volunteer. Other soldiers seasoned in recent European wars included François-Louis Teissèdre de Fleury, who later fought with distinction at the Battle of Brandywine, the Marquis de Tuffin, who was anxious to disguise his aristocratic origins by taking the name "Armand," and the Irish-born Frenchman Thomas Conway. Importantly, Baron von Steuben, a Prussian recommended to Benjamin Franklin by the Comte de Saint-Germain, the French war minister, eventually played a leading role in training the Continental Army.

Friendless in Europe

The British were fully aware of the French intrigues with the Patriots. One Member of Parliament cynically remarked that "France to us sends most fair words, to America, stores and officers." It was also clear to the British government that it had precious few friends in Europe it could look to for support against the rebels.

Raising revenues

The Patriots used profits from the tobacco trade to pay the French, but production was disrupted by the fighting. Many of the slaves who harvested and processed the tobacco crop escaped during the war or ran off to join the Loyalist armies.

Spain, next to France, was considered the most likely to provide active support to the Patriot cause. Although the Spanish attitude to the conflict was ambivalent, their Bourbon king was allied to the French royal dynasty by family ties. Austria, also allied to France, was resolutely neutral. Catherine the Great of Russia, having refused to supply troops to fight for the British as mercenaries, remained aloof. Eventually, Russia, Sweden, and Denmark were to form the League of Armed Neutrality to resist British attempts to stop and search their merchant shipping.

This left Germany—or rather its patchwork of electorates and principalities—as a potential source of support for Britain. Frederick the Great, the Hohenzollern ruler of Prussia, had been Britain's most important ally in the French and Indian War, but the British decision to make peace with France without consulting him had left him outraged. There would be no Prussian assistance. When the British looked to Germany for the mercenaries they needed to hire to complement their own army, they were obliged to look to the various smaller states.

AFTER

While German mercenaries continued to pour in to help the British, developments in the fall of 1777 tipped France into formalizing its alliance with the Patriots.

BOOTS ON THE GROUND

German mercenaries 154–55 》 played a huge part in the British war effort. The German states continued to send soldiers right through to the end of the war.

THE ALLIES

British General Burgoyne's **defeat at Saratoga 162–63 》** in October 1777 was the catalyst that persuaded France that the Patriot cause was worth supporting in a more direct way **188–89 》**. French, and later Spanish, naval intervention turned the war into a **worldwide conflict 218–19 》**.

KEY AIDE

The **Marquis de Lafayette** became one of Washington's most trusted men, especially when others in the Continental Army were plotting against the Patriot commander. The relationship was cemented at **Valley Forge 186–87 》** in the winter of 1778–79.

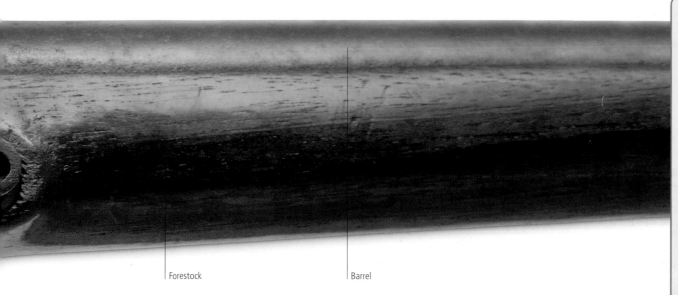

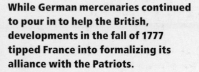

Forestock   Barrel

" England is the **natural enemy** of France. She is a greedy enemy, **ambitious, unjust, and treacherous.** "

COMTE DE VERGENNES, 1776

FRENCH COMMANDER Born 1757 Died 1834

Marquis de Lafayette

> "The **welfare** of America is intimately **connected** with the **happiness** of all **mankind.**"

MARQUIS DE LAFAYETTE, IN A LETTER TO HIS WIFE, 1777

Gilbert du Motier, Marquis de Lafayette was a French aristocrat who dedicated his life to the cause of freedom. He was a dashing military commander and a political activist of unshakable integrity. After volunteering his services to the nascent United States in 1777, he became one of General George Washington's most trusted officers and a hero of the American struggle for independence. Back in France, he fought for liberty, human rights, and representative government in the French Revolution of 1789.

Born into an undistinguished branch of France's provincial nobility, before the age of two Lafayette suffered the

loss of his father, who was killed fighting the British in the Seven Years' War. The deaths of his mother and grandparents left him at adolescence a wealthy orphan, the sole inheritor of the family estates. Aged 16, he married into the de Noailles family, powerful figures at the French court. He was guaranteed the pleasures of privilege and rapid promotion to high rank in the French army.

Pursuit of glory

Instead of pursuing this easy course, however, the young Lafayette became caught up in a plan hatched by an American agent in France, Silas Deane, to recruit volunteers to fight in the struggle for independence. The details of this plot were murky, but Lafayette's motivation was transparent and honorable. He wanted to win military glory, and to do so fighting in a cause that had captured his romantic imagination. Defying orders from his superiors to stay in France, he paid for a ship to transport himself and a number of other officers to America.

Eager to engage French support for their war effort, the

Courage under fire

In his first experience of battle, at Brandywine on September 11, 1777, Lafayette received a leg wound. He nonetheless continued fighting, and succeeded in rallying the fleeing American troops.

Continental Congress confirmed the rank of major general conferred on Lafayette by Deane. The position he attained in the Continental Army, however, depended upon the personal relationship he established with Washington. Initially fazed by the arrival of a teenaged general with no experience of senior command, Washington soon adopted Lafayette as a surrogate son, while Lafayette found in Washington a father figure. The shared privations of the terrible winter at Valley Forge in 1777–78 sealed the bond between them.

Clashing personalities

Military glory was in short supply in the War of Independence and Lafayette suffered his share of frustration. In 1778, ordered to carry out an invasion of Canada, he had to abort the mission, which was hopelessly under-resourced. At the Battle of Monmouth (see pp.196–97) in June, General Lee's retreat denied Lafayette the chance to lead a daring attack on British forces.

His chief value to the United States was his potential to mobilize French support for the cause. Although France had gone to war with Britain, its aid to the Americans remained very limited. Returning home in 1779, Lafayette at first pushed for a French invasion of Britain, which he hoped

Revolutionary general

A wealthy idealist, Lafayette pursued military glory in the fight for freedom. This portrait by Joseph-Désiré Court shows Lafayette as a lieutenant general in the French Revolutionary Army in 1791.

Hero's welcome

Crowds lined the waterfront in New York City to greet Lafayette on his triumphant return to the United States in August 1824. He visited every state of the Union, and was received with enthusiastic celebrations wherever he went.

to lead. When this failed to materialize, he secured the agreement of the royal government to send an expeditionary force to fight alongside Washington's Continental Army. He returned to America ready to act as a liaison between the American and French forces.

Impulsive and impatient, Lafayette soon found himself at odds with the commander of the expeditionary force, the Comte de Rochambeau, who arrived in America with no intention of rushing into action. Ordered by Washington to defend Virginia against British attack in early 1781, Lafayette had the impression he was being sidelined. Instead he found himself at the focal point of the war. At first, commanding inferior forces, he had to evade contact with the army of General Charles Cornwallis. But in June, as Cornwallis withdrew toward Chesapeake Bay, Lafayette pursued him, harassing the British rearguard. At Green Spring on July 6, Lafayette's rashness and inexperience showed when the vanguard of his force was caught in a trap set by Cornwallis for his pursuers. Still, undeterred by this setback, Lafayette followed the British to Yorktown, fixing Cornwallis in that position until Washington and Rochambeau arrived from New York. As the Siege of Yorktown (see pp.304–05) approached its climax, he led one of the most important assaults on the British redoubts. Overall he had proved himself among the most effective commanders in the field.

Hero of two worlds

Lafayette was still only 25 years old when the War of Independence ended. A hero both in France and the United States, he devoted himself to further pursuit of political freedom, joining a French organization dedicated to the abolition of slavery, and also getting behind the cause of liberal reform in monarchical France. When King Louis

> ## "He made our cause his own."
>
> THOMAS JEFFERSON, 1824

XVI summoned the Estates-General, an archaic form of parliament, in 1789, Lafayette was among those who transformed it into a revolutionary national assembly. He put forward the first draft of a Declaration of the Rights of Man and, that year, took command of the National Guard militia in Paris. Later, he served in the French Revolution as a general in the field. But in France the revolution fell into the hands of radical extremists who had no time for liberal aristocrats. Accused of being a traitor, Lafayette fled the country.

Uncaged spirit

Ironically, Lafayette was caught and imprisoned by France's enemies, Prussia and Austria, as a dangerous revolutionary, and spent five years in various prisons. His American friends provided what help they could, giving asylum to his family and eventually arranging for his wife and daughters to join him in Olmuetz, Austria. Lafayette was at last released as part of the peace deal between France and Austria in 1797. For most of the following two decades he lived quietly in France, but in the 1820s he returned to a public role, supporting freedom movements wherever they formed. Making a long visit to the United States in 1824, he was received with adulation, his heroic status confirmed. In 1830, at the age of 72, he once more found himself in the vanguard of a revolution in Paris. That year, the Chamber of Deputies offered to proclaim Lafayette the new ruler of France following the abdication of Charles X in the July Revolution. Instead, Lafayette supported the crowning of the relatively liberal Louis Philippe, although he soon became disillusioned by the new king's acts of oppression. Lafayette died in 1834 after a battle with pneumonia, unreconciled to a world in which the pure freedom he craved proved always too elusive.

TIMELINE

- **1757** Born Marie Joseph-Paul-Yves-Roch-Gilbert du Motier on September 6 at Chavaniac, in Auvergne, France, son of the Marquis de La Fayette.
- **1759** His father is killed fighting at the Battle of Minden; he inherits the family title.
- **1771** Commissioned as an officer in the Royal Musketeers at 13 years of age.
- **1773** Becomes a dragoons officer.
- **1774** Marries Adrienne de Noailles; they will have three children.
- **April 1777** Sails for America as a volunteer to fight in the War of Independence.
- **July 1777** Commissioned as a major general in the Continental Army.
- **September 1777** Wounded at the Battle of Brandywine in Pennsylvania.
- **December 1777–March 1778** Shares the privations of winter at Valley Forge.
- **June 1778** Fights in the Battle of Monmouth.
- **January 1779** Travels to France.
- **April 1780** Returns to America. A French expeditionary force is promised to follow.
- **January 1781** Ordered by Washington to lead troops south to Virginia.
- **August–October 1781** Plays a leading role in the defeat of British forces at Yorktown.
- **December 1781** Congress sends him to France to advance the American cause.
- **1789** Active in the opening stages of the French Revolution.
- **1791** Resigns from command as the revolution becomes more illiberal.

THE OATH OF LA FAYETTE AT THE FÊTE DE LA FÉDÉRATION

- **April 1792** Commands an army in France's war against Austria and Prussia.
- **August 1792** Captured fleeing France to avoid arrest by the radical Jacobin government.
- **1792–97** Held prisoner at various locations in Prussia and Austria.
- **1800** Returns to France, living at the chateau of La Grange in the Seine-et-Marne region.
- **1818–30** Leads the opposition to the restored Bourbon monarchy in France.
- **1824–25** Tours every state of the United States.
- **1830** Heads the revolution that overthrows the Bourbon King Charles X.
- **1834** Dies in Paris on May 20, aged 76.

« **BEFORE**

Many enslaved and free African Americans had served in the local militias of the Thirteen Colonies. Nonetheless, when war broke out, Patriots feared they might enlist with the British.

PATRIOT FEARS

When George Washington took command of the newly formed Continental Army in 1775, he **banned African American recruitment**. As a slaveholder, he held the view that blacks were inferior and would not perform well in battle. There was also concern that slaves might try to enlist in the Continental Army without the consent of their masters. These fears were compounded in November 1775, when Virginia Governor Lord Dunmore issued a **proclamation** granting **freedom to any slaves** « 78–79 who ran away from their Patriot masters and joined the Loyalists.

KILLED IN THE BOSTON MASSACRE, CRISPUS ATTUCKS WAS AN EARLY PATRIOT CASUALTY

"No regiment is to be seen in which there are not **Negroes in abundance** and among them are **able-bodied** and **strong fellows ...**"

HESSIAN OFFICER, 1777

Saluting the soldiers

Five hundred African American soldiers served under George Washington at Valley Forge (see pp. 184–85). A monument to them is located where an all-African American Rhode Island Regiment was encamped.

African American Patriots

In total, around 5,000 African Americans served in the Continental Army during the course of the war—but they were not always welcomed. Although some proved their worth in early battles in New England, African Americans were only reluctantly admitted to the army's ranks.

In 1777, George Washington reluctantly consented to the renewal of African American enlistment in the Continental Army. The need for more men outweighed the many entrenched fears associated with arming African Americans. Yet by summer 1778, there were still only some 750 African Americans serving with the Patriots. In 1780, Rhode Island and Connecticut both raised all-African American contingents, but they were still commanded exclusively by white officers.

The North enlists
New England tacitly ignored the earlier ban on African American recruitment in 1775, and continued to allow African Americans to serve in their militias. When the prohibition was lifted, Rhode Island compensated owners of the slaves who enlisted in the First Rhode Island Regiment with £120 (around $22,000 today) "for the most valuable Slave and in proportion for those of less Value." The state also stipulated that all African American volunteers would be "made free and entitled to all the Wages, Bounties, and Encouragement given by Congress to any Soldier inlisting into their service." Massachusetts and Connecticut soon followed suit.

Still, African American recruitment was a policy largely forced on the Patriots by the difficulty of raising enough white soldiers to fill the ranks, and this recruitment did not take place

Double standards
Although they fought alongside white soldiers, enslaved African American recruits remained their owner's "property." This 1777 receipt makes reference to a "Negro soldier belonging to" another soldier.

PATRIOT SPY c.1760–c.1832

JAMES ARMISTEAD

James Armistead underwent a transformation from slave to double agent. He joined the Continental Army in 1781 with the permission of his master. Posing as an escaped slave, he was sent by the Marquis de Lafayette into the camp of Benedict Arnold, a former Patriot general who had gone over to the British. Asked to spy for the British himself, Armistead traveled easily between the two sides, giving Lafayette information that allowed the Patriots to besiege the British at Yorktown. After the war, Lafayette wrote to the Virginia legislature requesting Armistead's freedom.

without protest. Six members of the Rhode Island assembly opposed its 1778 decision to allow the formation of an African American regiment; they argued that they could not consistently recruit "a band of slaves." Some of Washington's generals were equally disapproving. General Philip Schuyler asked Brigadier General William Heath if it was "consistent with the Sons of Freedom to trust their all to be defended by Slaves?" Heath agreed that it was not.

Although small, the increase in African American numbers over the course of the war was significant. Some of the recruits were slaves who purchased or were granted their freedom. Others, such as Jack Arabus, the slave of wealthy Connecticut merchant Captain Ivers, struck deals with their masters. Arabus agreed to join the Continental Army in place of his master's son. In exchange, Arabus was promised his

freedom once the war ended. However, ultimately the deal turned sour. Ivers went back on his word and refused to let Arabus go. He kept the £10 bounty (around $1,800 today) that he had received from the town of Stratford for enlisting Arabus, even though Arabus had been caught and imprisoned in New Haven for deserting the army. Ivers even sued for the return of his "property." Luckily for Arabus, Yale-educated lawyer Chauncey Goodrich took up the case and Judge James Wadsworth ruled in his favor. Many of the 300 other African Americans who also fought for Connecticut secured their freedom as a result of this groundbreaking judgment.

The stubborn South
In the southern colonies, the "dread of instigated insurrections" was extreme. Some Patriots there were vehemently opposed to any notion of allowing African Americans to fight. Even when

threatened by British invasion, the southern Patriots remained adamant. "We are much disgusted here at the Congress recommending us to arm our Slaves" wrote delegate Henry Gadsen in 1779. The South Carolina planters reacted poorly to the idea, while in 1781 Major Edward Giles wrote that arming African Americans was "the child of a distempered imagination."

Colonel John Laurens and his friend Alexander Hamilton tried to persuade South Carolina to allow an African American regiment to be raised there. In 1779, Hamilton argued that "the Negroes will make very excellent soldiers." He urged his fellow Patriots to overcome "the contempt we have been taught to entertain" for African Americans, to see past "prejudices and self-interest." The appeal fell on deaf ears. Only a handful of South Carolina legislators supported the idea, and Washington refused to back it. In 1780, South Carolina finally allowed 1,000 African Americans into their regiments— but they were given only menial tasks, and no weapons with which to fight.

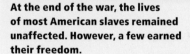

AFTER

At the end of the war, the lives of most American slaves remained unaffected. However, a few earned their freedom.

LITTLE CHANGE
Around 500,000 African American slaves lived in America throughout the War of Independence. In most cases, their **status remained unchanged** after the war. The 5,000 or so African Americans who joined the Continental Army were more fortunate: although most were enslaved when the war began, many were declared free at its end. Nevertheless, in 1783, the **Virginia assembly condemned owners** for continuing to keep slaves who had served as soldiers in bondage.

PROGRESS IN THE NORTH
Some northern states provided for the **gradual emancipation of slaves**. Pennsylvania, Rhode Island, and Connecticut passed laws stipulating that children born into slave families must be freed at a young age. Massachusetts **abolished slavery**.

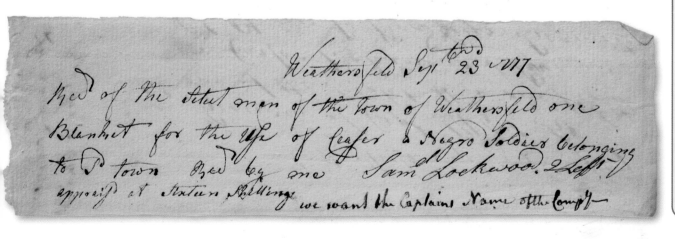

An **African American Militiaman**

Although African Americans fought on the Patriot side at Lexington, Concord, and Bunker Hill, many Patriots were against African American enlistment. Some thought it would encourage slaves to run away from their masters, endanger the social order, or even that African Americans would be too cowardly to fight. Of course, this wasn't the case, as the bravery of men such as former slave Boyrereau Brinch proved.

"I drove my horse as fast as possible, stabbed him with my sword and gun, kicked my heels in his side, but having no spurs and not being so good a horseman, they gained on me. I looked forward and saw my Captain in full view, almost a mile distant. This encouraged me. And the long shanked Negro soldier with a leather cap, mounted on an elegant English gelding light horse, made all whistle again.

When I came in about 20 or 30 rods, I heard the Captain say 'There comes one of our leather caps. It is Jeffrey. Reserve your fire so as not to kill him.' However, the men fired and three balls cut my garments. One stuck my coat sleeve, the next hit my bayonet belt, and the third went through the back side of my leather cap. They were so close upon me that the same fire killed four of the British and five horses and wounded some more. I did not stop for this salute, but pulled on for headquarters. When our men fired, the enemy were within two or three jumps of me, but being so handsomely saluted upon surprise, as our men were concealed from their view, they made the best retreat possible.

I made no halt until I arrived within our camp. When I dismounted, tied my horse and went to set up my gun, I found I could not open my hand, which was the first time I discovered that I was wounded. A slight fear and precipitation had turned me almost as white as my fellow soldiers."

BOYREREAU BRINCH, A CONNECTICUT MILITIAMAN AND FORMER SLAVE, KNOWN AS JEFFREY BRACE, FROM HIS MEMOIR *THE BLIND AFRICAN SLAVE*, 1810

Shooting of Major Pitcairn
An African American named Peter Salem is said to have shot Major Pitcairn at the Battle of Bunker Hill on June 17, 1775. While it is uncertain that a soldier by that name took part in that battle, two early 19th-century accounts attributed Pitcairn's death to an African-American soldier.

Battle of Bennington
On August 16, Patriot militiamen led by Brigadier John Stark routed British and Hessian soldiers at the small town of Bennington. The British had gone to Bennington to capture much-needed provisions.

Burgoyne's Offensive

General John Burgoyne's complex and audacious plan to attack from Canada was intended to give him the advantage of surprise over the Patriots. It would also, he thought, allow him to achieve his ultimate aim—to isolate rebellious New England from the rest of the colonies.

BEFORE

Following their failure to force Washington into total defeat in 1776, the British military commanders proposed a number of strategies to crush the rebellion.

HOWE'S PLANS
British strategy revolved around one basic assumption. To win the war against the American colonies, Commander in Chief General Howe argued, the British must fight a **single decisive battle** in which the Continental Army would be destroyed. Howe proposed expeditions to **gain control of the Hudson River** and **seize control of Philadelphia**, a Patriot stronghold.

BURGOYNE'S TWO-PRONGED ATTACK
On leave in London after taking part in **offensives in Canada** in the fall of 1776 **≪ 128–29**, General John Burgoyne persuaded George III and Lord George Germain, the government minister in charge of war strategy, to include in their plans for the coming year an audacious **two-pronged attack from Canada**, which would be led by him.

The attack the British had tried to mount from Canada in 1776 failed, said General Burgoyne, only because of its commander's caution and indecision. He was sure the determined attack he proposed to mount in 1777 would turn the tide of the campaign.

Burgoyne was brimming with confidence. The strategy he proposed was to advance with 7,000 of his best troops from St. John's in Quebec and cross Lake Champlain to capture the key Patriot stronghold at Ticonderoga. His forces would then push down the Hudson Valley toward Albany in Upper New York, where they would rendezvous with 2,000 men commanded by Lieutenant-Colonel Barry St. Leger, who by this time would have marched eastward from Oswego to meet him.

Misguided threats
Burgoyne arrived back in Canada in the summer of 1777, ready to begin his planned offensive. The day before he set out, he issued a proclamation addressed to the Patriot forces under the commander in chief of the north, General Philip Schuyler. He warned him that if they did not abandon "the Phrenzy of Hostility," the British would create "Destruction, Famine and every conmitant Horror" wherever they went. The proclamation backfired.

Rather than acting as a deterrent to the Patriots, it simply stiffened their resolve. The speech Burgoyne made to 400 of his Native American allies was even more unfortunate. "Warriors, you are free," he harangued them. "Go forth and strike at the common enemies of Great Britain and America."

DECISIVE MOMENT

THE MURDER OF JANE McCREA

Among the scalps that Burgoyne's Native American allies brought back to his camp was that of Jane McCrea. She lived near Fort Edward and was engaged to one of Burgoyne's own Loyalist officers. Although she was only one out of the 11 frontier dwellers slaughtered by the Native Americans that day, the fate of this female civilian caused uproar. Within days, newspapers were full of the story and hitherto neutral frontiersmen quickly took up arms to defend their families against Britain and her allies.

AFTER

> " The great **bulk** of the **countryside** is ... **with the Congress** in principle and in zeal."

GENERAL JOHN BURGOYNE, AUGUST 1777

Burgoyne decided to persist with his advance rather than order a retreat, refusing to accept his offensive was foundering.

FURTHER SETBACKS
Although Bennington was not a major battle, it marked a turning point. **Recruits flooded to join the Patriot forces** as news of the successes there spread. A **new Patriot commander** emerged. On August 19, Major General Horatio Gates replaced Schuyler in overall command of the rebel army. The stage was now set for the final showdown between Burgoyne and his rebel American opponents.

A LAST GAMBLE
Burgoyne thought failure to continue his advance would lead to disgrace and loss of his command, so he decided to press on. The well dug-in Patriots were more than ready to meet him 162–63 >>.

Although he then went onto tell his audience, "I positively forbid bloodshed when you are not opposed in arms" and that he would permit the scalping only of those who were already dead, the provisos were too little and too late. The Native Americans failed to obey this directive. Unleashed, they were practically uncontrollable. Their "enthusiasm" for the fight resulted in numerous brutal killings of civilians.

Initial British success
The actual offensive started well enough. By July 6, the outnumbered and outgunned Patriots had retreated from Fort Ticonderoga and then surrendered their defensive position on Mount Independence. One flabbergasted Hessian officer noted that they left "more than 50 field pieces, extraordinarily large supplies of ammunition, muskets, tents, rice, coffee, sugar, and even a new flag."

10,000 The size of Burgoyne's army.
6,000 The number of men who surrendered.

As ordered by Major General Arthur St. Clair, Ticondeoga's recently appointed commander, the rebels fell back to Hubbardton some 24 miles (39 km) away with the British advance guard in hot pursuit. There, the Patriot rearguard put up a spirited resistance, which allowed St. Clair to make his getaway. Meanwhile, Colonel Pierce Long, who had been put in charge of the Patriot evacuation of the fort, was making his way up Lake Champlain to Fort Edward, 16 miles (26 km) farther to the south. He was pursued by Burgoyne himself.

Tactical errors
Had Burgoyne pressed on with his pursuit, harrying the Patriot forces before him to prevent them from reorganizing, he might have won a notable victory. Instead, he waited for his supply wagons and cumbersome artillery train to catch up, by which time General Schuyler's forces had been reinforced.

This was Burgoyne's first mistake. The second was to decide to take the land route to Fort Edward. This involved building a road over miles of inhospitable country. Nor were his sappers allowed to get on with the task unimpeded. Patriot tree felling and other acts of sabotage slowed their progress to a crawl. At best, Burgoyne was now managing to advance just a mile a day. It took him three weeks to get to Fort Edward and a further ten days to gather his supplies together. Only after that was he ready to start the journey south again, aiming to cross the Hudson River at Fort Miller, 47 miles (75 km) above Albany.

Confrontation at Bennington
On August 14, the British commander ordered a 600-strong combined force of Hessians, Loyalists, and Native American scouts to split off from the main body of the army and march southeast toward Bennington, a Patriot supply depot. Lieutenant Colonel Frederick Baum, the force's commander, had instructions to carry off "large supplies of cattle, horses and carriages." Instead, on August 16, he walked into a Patriot trap sprung by Brigadier John Stark. His 2,000 New England militiamen routed Baum's heavily outnumbered troops outside the township. Stark's forces went on to destroy a column of Hessian reinforcements. The two engagements cost Burgoyne almost 1,000 men.

As Burgoyne continued southward, Howe wrote to say he would not be advancing to support him. It was clear that Burgoyne's plan was unravelling before his eyes. In addition, he would not be reinforced by St. Leger and his forces, who were marching back to Canada after having been forced to lift the siege of Fort Schuyler.

Heroic general
General John Burgoyne arrived in America with a glowing reputation gained in the Seven Years' War in Europe. This 1766 portrait by Sir Joshua Reynolds was painted at the height of his fame.

German Mercenaries

Manpower shortages forced the British to recruit German auxiliaries to fight on the Loyalist side. The Declaration of Independence denounced the king's use of such troops to complete his "works of death, desolation, and tyranny."

◀◀ BEFORE

In the 18th century it was not unusual for the major European powers to hire foreign troops to supplement their armies at times of war.

A HISTORICAL ALLIANCE
Britain had employed troops from the German principality of **Hesse-Kassel** in many of its wars. The British had previously been allied with forces of other German states in the Seven Years' War—the American theater of which was the **French and Indian War ◀◀ 24–25**.

FRENCH ALIGNMENT
The French, who had opposed Britain during the Seven Years' War, began to **support the Patriot cause ◀◀ 144–45** by lending the Continental Congress money to buy **supplies and ammunition**.

SWELLING THE RANKS
In addition to hiring Hessian auxiliaries, the British endeavored to increase the size of their army by enlisting the help of **American Loyalists**. They also actively looked to recruit slaves. **Lord Dunmore's Proclamation ◀◀ 78–79** encouraged slaves to desert Patriot masters by promising liberty to those who earned it fighting in British uniform.

While the Patriots could muster more than 50,000 volunteers, the British had only around 20,000 troops stationed in the British Isles, half of whom were manning garrisons in Ireland. Britain turned first to Catherine the Great to make up the shortfall, but she refused. An attempt to hire the "Scots Brigade" from the Dutch also failed before the British turned to the German principalities.

Striking a deal
The man in charge of the negotiations for the British was Colonel William Faucitt. His instructions reflected the urgency of the situation as far as parliament was concerned. "Great activity is necessary," they read, "as the King is extremely anxious to be at Certainty one Way or another as to the Possibility of obtaining Foreign Troops for America."

commanding officers. The wore their own uniforms and took their own weapons, the manufacture of which created employment at home.

Mutual benefit
The contracts between Britain and the German states served the interests of both sides. The principalities needed the money. Hesse-Kassel, poor and agricultural, became increasingly

Pommel

Prussian design
Hessian infantrymen carried this standard sword with a double-edged blade of Prussian design. Hesse-Kassel's ruler, Frederick II, strictly regulated the weapons and dress of his soldiers.

Heavy cast brass hilt

> **"the Hessians ... long ... to have a Brush with the Rebels,** of whom they have a ... **despicable opinion."**
>
> CAPTAIN LORD FRANCIS RAWDON, AUGUST 1776

Faucitt set to work, making his first agreement with Charles I, Duke of Brunswick-Wolfenbuettel. The Duke agreed to supply Britain with 3,964 infantrymen and 336 "unmounted" dragoons—the British were to provide them with horses. Similar agreements were subsequently made with other German states: Ansbach-Bayreuth, Anhalt-Zerbst, Hesse-Hanau, Hesse-Kassel, and Waldeck. The German auxiliaries, often conscripted, were supplied as entire units with their own

Departing Europe
Hired units traveled to America on overcrowded ships. One fleet carrying troops from Ansbach-Bayreuth faced mutiny over the cramped conditions; the ruler of Ansbach had to coax soldiers back on board.

militarized, as the hiring out of soldiers became its main way of raising money; seven percent of its population were under arms.

The British, of course, needed troops. As Lord North told the British House of Commons, hiring troops from the German states was "the best and most speedy way of reducing America to a proper constitutional state of obedience." Whigs in parliament were less certain. Lord Camden denounced the treaty with Hesse-Kassel, which agreed a payment of 20 million talers (around $180 million today), as "a mere mercenary bargain for the hire of troops on one side, and the sale of human blood on the other." Such protests were to no avail. In August 1776, Hessian contingents landed on Staten Island, ready to take part in the Battle of Long Island (see pp.118–19).

Hired hands

An estimated 30,000 German mercenaries fought for the British during the course of the war. Hesse-Kassel supplied by far the greatest number of troops—so many that the term "Hessian" became synonymous with auxiliaries from any and all German states. Hesse-Kassel sent

Poor mercenaries

Campaign life brought challenges for the Hessians. Some 5,000 soldiers from Hesse-Kassel alone would perish in the War of Independence, and as many as 80 percent of them died of diseases—Captain Georg Pausch, who commanded an artillery unit, wrote that many of his soldiers encamped with the British Army at Montreal suffered from dysentery. Smallpox and typhus were also rife among the ranks.

Pausch's regiment was not only sick, but also poor. While his men found comfort in Canadian girls, Pausch complained about the lack of pay and resources: "Officers have to add money of their own, or else live poorly. A bombadier, for example, has to pay for a pair of boots 20 florins; for a coat, five times as much as in Hanau." But worst of all, to Pausch, was his own

Many Hessians preferred to stay in North America after the war rather than return to Germany.

NEW HOMELAND

Around 5,000 Hessians **settled in North America**—in Nova Scotia, thanks to British incentives **310–11 ⟫**, and in the United States, due to land grants from **Congress 334–35 ⟫**. Many were claimed lost or dead by Brunswick-Wolfenbuetttel, whose treaty provided for compensation in such circumstances.

The war failed to provide long-term solutions to the financial problems faced by the German states. The **French Revolution**, however, would have a transformative effect on these principalities.

THE FLAG OF THE PRINCIPALITY OF ANSBACH-BAYREUTH, WHICH WAS STILL IN DEBT AFTER THE WAR

"Landgraviate of Hesse" engraved on blade

·FRIEDERICH·LANDGRAFF·ZU·HESSEN·

four grenadier battalions and 15 infantry battalions, including those of Carl von Donop and Karl von Truembach, who led the 8th infantry regiment. Most Hessian regiments were named for their commander, and thus changed names during the course of the war; von Truembach's unit became the Regiment von Bose after General Carl von Bose took command in 1778.

Hesse-Kassel also sent artillery, grenadiers, and fusiliers—notably the fusilier regiments of von Lossberg and von Knyphausen, and Johann Rall's grenadiers. The most sought-after

> **60** PERCENT **of mercenaries came from Hesse-Kassel.**
>
> **40** PERCENT **of Burgoyne's army at Saratoga were "Hessians."**

German regiments were the Jaeger corps, "hunters," who were marksmen and woodsmen. By 1781, there were 821 Jaegers from Hesse-Kassel and 245 from Ansbach in the British Army in New York; they were also deployed on the Canadian border.

treatment by the British. "The National pride and arrogant conduct of these people allow them to command my men, while I am not permitted to command theirs!"

Looking to exploit such discontent, the Continental Congress tried to persuade as many as they could to defect. One proclamation from April 1778 promised 50 acres (20 ha) of land to every soldier who deserted, while any Hessian captain who brought 40 men over to the Patriot side was promised 800 acres (320 ha) of woodland, four oxen, one bull, two cows, and three sows. Such attempts to lure the Hessians were not in vain: some German prisoners even deserted to join their former captors upon their release.

From victory to defeat

The Alt von Lossberg Regiment from Hesse-Kassel fought at Long Island, White Plains, and Fort Washington, before their humiliating defeat at the Battle of Trenton in 1776.

Hessian losses

The Hessians saw action in almost every major battle. They fought with distinction in New York and at the Battle of White Plains in October 1776, but in Rhode Island and during the opening stages of the advance into New Jersey things did not go as well for them. Colonel Johann Rall was mortally wounded at Trenton (see pp.132–33) at the end of 1776, and Colonel Carl von Donop, perhaps the Hessians' most respected leader, was killed at the Battle of Red

Bank (see pp.170–71) in October 1777. Also in 1777, Hessians were trounced at the Battle of Bennington in August (see pp.152–53), where they lost 900 men, including Lieutenant Colonel Friedrich Baum.

After General John Burgoyne's surrender at Saratoga, large numbers of Hessians formed part of the Convention Army, as the prisoners of war from Saratoga were known, in their march to the Albemarle Barracks; in Charlotesville, Virginia; they were kept prisoner in America until peace was formalized in 1783.

The German Experience in America

Many of the mercenaries employed by Britain were conscripts from Hesse-Kassel (in modern-day Germany). Although unruly—provoking many neutral Americans into supporting the Patriot cause—they showed courage on the battlefield. Johann von Ewald of the Schleswig Jaeger Corps, recorded the bravery of his compatriots at the Battle of Red Bank in 1777.

"The battery began to play and the three battalions advanced against the fort with incredible courage. But they were received so hotly by the garrison and by the vessels ... that they were repelled with great loss, although several officers and a number of grenadiers scaled the breastwork. Colonel Donop himself and his adjutant, Captain Wagner, were mortally wounded at the edge of the ditch. Captain Stamford, who commanded the Linsing Battalion, was shot through the chest, Minnigerode through both legs and the gallant Colonel Schieck, who commanded the Regiment von Mirbach, was shot dead at the barred gate.

Colonel Wurmb immediately ordered the Jaeger Corps to move up to the edge of the wood to cover the retreat. He personally took the Grenadier Battalion Lengerke, who had protected the rear ... and hurried with the battalion to the passing of the Timber Creek Bridge to occupy it.

Night ended the battle and the attacking corps reassembled at the spot from which it had departed for the attack ... no retreat [had been] thought of, and no wagons brought to transport the wounded. The seriously wounded officers were carried on the guns and horses, and all the privates who could not drag themselves away on their wounded limbs fell into enemy hands. But since the enemy took the retreat for a trap, and had expected a new attack during the night, the men had to remain on the battlefield a whole night in the most deplorable condition without the slightest care, whereby the majority died of their wounds.**"**

JOHANN VON EWALD, CAPTAIN OF THE SCHLESWIG JAEGER CORPS, 1791

Conscription of a Hessian soldier
Most German mercenaries fighting in America were peasants uprooted from poor agricultural communities. Pressganged into military units and then leased to the British Crown, they had no choice but to serve.

1 BRUNSWICK
MITER CAP

2 HESSIAN
MITER CAP

3 BRUNSWICK
SERGEANT'S PARTIZAN

4 BRUNSWICK
OFFICER'S SPONTOON

5 HESSIAN JAEGER UNIFORM

German Equipment and **Uniforms**

In the 18th century, Germany was divided into numerous archbishoprics, kingdoms, and principalities. Hired regiments went to America equipped with their own weapons, uniforms, and insignia, unique to their various homelands.

[1] **Brunswick miter cap** Miters were named for their similarity to the miters worn by bishops. This example was captured at Bennington in 1777. [2] **Hessian miter cap** This fusilier's cap is made of cloth with brass fittings and plate. [3] **Brunswick sergeant's partizan** A spearhead mounted on a long pike, partizans could defend the regimental flag from enemy cavalry. [4] **Brunswick officer's spontoon** Symbols of authority, spontoons were also utilized in hand-to-hand combat. [5] **Hessian Jaeger uniform** The Hessian Jaegers, an elite light infantry corps, wore distinctive green jackets. [6] **Hessian flag pole finial** Made to adorn

the top of a flag pole, this finial bears the initials of Hessian ruler Frederick II. [7] **Brunswick cartridge box plate** Found near Saratoga, this regimental badge belonged to a solider from Brunswick. [8] **Hessian cartridge box plate** The lion on this badge denotes the Hessian Regiment von Bose. [9] **Dragoon's cartridge box and shoulder strap** Dragoons—light cavalry capable fighting as infantry when dismounted—were equipped with shoulder-arms. [10] **Brunswick drum and sling** Drums communicated commands over the din of war. [11] **Brunswick officer's gorget** This gorget signified its wearer's officer status.

[6] HESSIAN
FLAG POLE FINIAL

[7] BRUNSWICK
CARTRIDGE BOX PLATE

[8] HESSIAN
CARTRIDGE BOX PLATE

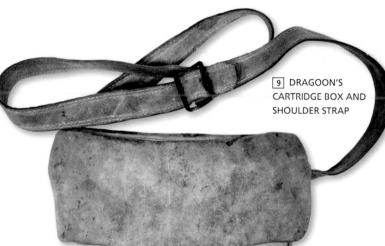

[9] DRAGOON'S
CARTRIDGE BOX AND
SHOULDER STRAP

[11] BRUNSWICK
OFFICER'S GORGET

[10] BRUNSWICK
DRUM AND SLING

The British in Upper New York

In the summer of 1777, General Burgoyne's army advanced down the Hudson Valley toward Albany. Although he was initially confident of assistance from British commanders in the region, Burgoyne's offensive was soon put in jeopardy.

BEFORE

The British hoped that an attack on the Hudson Highlands in Upper New York would drive a wedge between New England and the southern colonies.

TICONDEROGA TO BENNINGTON
After the defeat of the American attack on **Quebec** in late 1775 « **80–81**, the British **advanced south from Canada** « **128–29**. General John Burgoyne took command of the British offensive in 1777, capturing the Patriot stronghold of **Fort Ticonderoga** « **152–53** in early July. However, in early August, the offensive ran into trouble, when a force sent to raid a Patriot supply depot at **Bennington** was routed by militiamen.

US GENERAL 1718–90

ISRAEL PUTNAM

Born in 1718, Israel Putnam served with distinction in the French and Indian War, rising to the rank of lieutenant colonel. When the War of Independence broke out, he joined the Patriot side, playing a leading role at Bunker Hill in 1775 and achieving the rank of general the same year. Putnam had less success at Long Island during 1776, and failed to defend the Hudson Highlands from the British in 1777, although a court of inquiry exonerated him for his conduct in this. Putnam's military career was ended by a paralytic stroke in 1779.

The certain knowledge that General Howe's army was bound for Philadelphia and would no longer be meeting his own army at Albany in Upper New York placed General Burgoyne in an uncomfortable position. Without backup, it was unclear how he would achieve the objective of his offensive, to march on Albany. Howe, the British commander in chief, had left instructions for General Sir Henry Clinton in command in New York City to "act as occurrences would direct."

Although Clinton had been in London at the same time as Burgoyne the previous winter, he had not been consulted about the feasibility of Burgoyne's offensive. Nor had Howe taken Clinton into his confidence before planning his 1777 campaign.

Lord George Germain, who was responsible for the conduct of the war, would have done well to seek Clinton's advice before agreeing to Howe's and Burgoyne's attacks. Clinton knew America and the Americans well—having lived there with his family for some years—and as a general, Clinton had already demonstrated substantial

"I have too **small** a force to make any **effective** diversion in your favor."

GENERAL CLINTON TO GENERAL BURGOYNE, AUGUST 1777

strategic capability. Upon hearing of Burgoyne's plan, he began to worry that dividing his forces might give the Patriots the opportunity to strike at New York and so reverse all the gains the British had made there the previous year.

This fear was at the back of Clinton's mind when he received an appeal from Burgoyne, asking him to confirm that he was going to march to his support.

Failed siege
The harassed Burgoyne had already learned that Lieutenant Colonel Barry St. Leger was unable to rendezvous with him near Albany. St. Leger had set out from Fort Oswego on Lake

Ontario immediately after hearing the news of the British capture of Ticonderoga. Entering the Mohawk Valley in mid-July, St. Leger had headed for Fort Schuyler, reaching it on August 2. Previously known as Fort Stanwix, Fort Schuyler was occupied by about 800 Patriots under Colonel Peter Gansevoort.

Accompanied by British and Hessian regulars, Loyalist volunteers, and Canadian militia, St. Leger laid siege to the fort, but was only able to bring up his artillery to begin bombarding it on August 8. His force included around 800 Native American warriors, mostly Mohawk and Seneca, led by Mohawk leader Joseph Brant; these warriors played a key role in the siege by winning a bloody encounter with Brigadier General Nicholas Herkimer's 800 Patriot militiamen at Oriskany on August 6. The ambush prevented Herkimer's men from marching to relieve the garrison at Fort Schuyler. However, St. Leger's siege eventually proved unsuccessful. Discovering that Continental reinforcements, under the command of General Benedict Arnold,

6,617 Troops served with Burgoyne during the campaign. Gates led 11,469 troops in total.

were on their way to confront him, St. Leger decided to fall back. By August 23, when Arnold reached the fort, St. Leger had already begun a roundabout journey back toward Lake Ontario and on to Canada.

Burgoyne's problem
Burgoyne now depended solely on Clinton. Earlier, Clinton had agreed to "try something at any rate, if it might be of use to you." He had promised that, around September 22, he would "make a push" to get past the Patriot forts guarding the southern end of the Hudson Highlands, and move up the river toward Burgoyne with 2,000 men. However, he added a caveat.

Beltplate of Emmerich's Chasseurs
This Loyalist regiment, raised by a Hanoverian officer called Andreas Emmerich, fought in Clinton's successful attack on Fort Montgomery in 1777. After serving effectively near New York City in 1778, it was disbanded in 1779 after quarrels among its officers.

Should it prove impossible to reach Burgoyne quickly, he warned that he would retire to Manhattan "to save this important post."

Burgoyne wasted no time in replying to Clinton. "Do it, my dear Friend, directly," he wrote. In the meantime, he would hold his ground in the

Hudson Valley and wait for Clinton to appear. But days went by without a sign from Clinton, and with no further news of his whereabouts. Burgoyne was soon forced to cut his army's daily rations by a third.

That same day, Clinton finally moved out of New York City with 3,000 men and several warships. After a feint toward Verplanck's Point on the eastern bank of the Hudson to distract the Patriot forces, he moved west of the river and took Fort Clinton and Fort Montgomery in just 72 hours, even though his attacking force had no artillery. The troops garrisoning Fort Constitution, 3 miles (5 km) upstream, were so unnerved that they abandoned it without further ado, leaving all their guns and stores behind. General Israel Putnam, commanding Patriot militiamen against seasoned regulars, was forced to fall back from the river, although he maintained control of the surrounding countryside.

Lacking support

Clinton's advance guard got as far as Esopus but then the offensive came to a sudden halt. Clinton had received a demand from Howe for reinforcements and had to accede to the commander in chief's request. Even more to the point, a courier from Burgoyne had managed to make his way through the Patriot lines to reach him. The news he brought was alarming. Burgoyne,

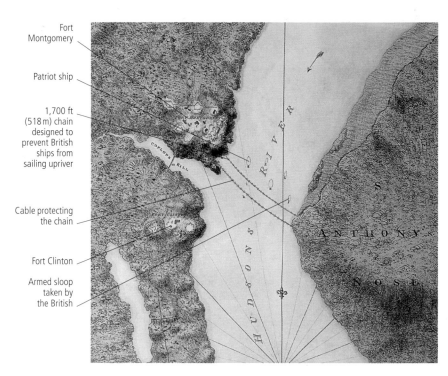

Fort Montgomery

Patriot ship

1,700 ft (518 m) chain designed to prevent British ships from sailing upriver

Cable protecting the chain

Fort Clinton

Armed sloop taken by the British

Down by the river

Burgoyne's army reached the Hudson River at the beginning of August after a grueling march through the wilderness. They camped on the banks of the river—difficult hilly and wooded terrain.

the courier reported, was pinned down by the Patriots—now commanded by General Horatio Gates—and cut off from his main supply base. By this stage his army was outnumbered by nearly three to one.

Astonishingly, Burgoyne, who had previously made much of his independent command, now asked General Clinton for orders. Clinton immediately realized that Burgoyne, staring defeat in the face, was trying

Inadequate defenses

More than half of the 600 men at forts Montgomery and Clinton were killed when the British captured these positions in October 1777. The British also broke the defensive boom, before continuing upriver.

to pass the buck, in the event of a calamity. Clinton was determined not to attract blame. "Sir Henry Clinton cannot presume to give any orders to General Burgoyne," he replied stiffly. "I sincerely hope this

Burgoyne continued his advance. He crossed the Hudson near Saratoga on September 13, to attack a Patriot force that outnumbered his army.

TWO-STAGE BATTLE

The British made two unsuccessful attempts to break through the Patriot encirclement— at the Battle of **Freeman's Farm** on September 19 and at **Bemis Heights 162–63 »** on October 7, sometimes known as the first and second battles of Saratoga. Meanwhile, General Howe took his army to **Philadelphia**.

THE WAR TRANSFORMED

After Saratoga the British held only New York City, Philadelphia, and part of Rhode Island. The United States was winning friends overseas; an **alliance with France 188–89 »** would soon follow.

little success of ours may facilitate your Operation." He immediately readied his troops to return to Manhattan, destroying the recently captured forts before they left.

What Burgoyne would have made of this reply is unknown, for he never received it. Clinton sent three different couriers back to him, but not one managed to make it past the Patriots. It was Gates, not Burgoyne, who would read Clinton's careful message.

The Battle of Saratoga

When the British army of General John Burgoyne found itself cornered by forces of General Horatio Gates on the Hudson River in October 1777, the stakes were high. The armies were huge, the strategic goals were crucial, and France, the Patriots' ally, was watching.

On September 13, 1777, General John Burgoyne's army crossed the Hudson River near Saratoga. As it did so, the forces of General Horatio Gates took up positions on Bemis Heights, dominating the main road from Saratoga to Albany.

Gates's position was a strong one, carefully selected for him by Thaddeus Kosciuszko, a gifted Polish military engineer who had arrived in Philadelphia in 1776 to volunteer his services to the Patriots. Anchored on the right by the Hudson River and on the left by thick woods and craggy, steep bluffs, it was protected by fortifications designed by Kosciuszko—a U-shaped breastwork stretching for about three-quarters of a mile (1.2 km). Gates personally

Long shot
Daniel Morgan led a Provisional Rifle Corps in the Saratoga battles. He and his unit are credited with making the decisive attack on the British right wing at the Battle of Bemis Heights.

commanded the Continentals he stationed on the right overlooking the river. More Continentals, led by Brigadier General Ebenezer Learned, held the center, while a mixed force of Continentals and militia, under Brigadier General Benedict Arnold, was deployed on the left. Gates's plan was to hold his ground and let Burgoyne come to him. The British general obliged.

The first encounter

Prior to the attack, Burgoyne divided his army into three columns, with Baron von Riedesel and his Brunswick regiments on the left moving along the Hudson, Brigadier-General James Hamilton marching down the rutted road in the center, and Brigadier-General Simon Fraser in the woods to the right. At 10 a.m. on September 19, a single cannon shot signaled the start of Burgoyne's advance.

By mid-afternoon, the British center had reached Freeman's Farm. Gates had been persuaded by Arnold to move troops to block the advance. The resulting battle was fought with fury. Alexander Scammel, a colonel in the Patriot militia, said it was "the hottest Fire that ever I heard" while one of Burgoyne's veterans recorded that "the fire was much heavier than ever I saw it anywhere."

It was a brutal slogging match from start to finish. The British twice came close to disaster. The first time, they were saved by von Riedesel, whom Burgoyne ordered to attack the Patriot right flank, and the second by Major-General William Phillips, who led the 20th Regiment into action through a cornfield on the eastern side of the farm and so prevented a rout. The fighting went on for three hours until the fading daylight brought it

Only the brave
General Arnold is wounded at the Battle of Bemis Heights. Arnold insisted on fighting in the battle even though he had been relieved of duty by Gates after the earlier engagement at Freeman's Farm.

to an end. The Patriots then fell back, leaving Burgoyne in possession of the field. It was, however, a hollow victory. The Patriots had prevented a British breakthrough. Moreover, British casualties amounted to more than 600 men killed and wounded—double the losses on the Patriot side. Thanks to a generous injection of military supplies by the French earlier in the year, which had encouraged new recruits to sign up to the Patriot cause, Gates was able to replenish his army fairly rapidly. Burgoyne, on the other hand, could not.

A decisive battle

Burgoyne was in no hurry to resume the action. He ordered his men to dig in, hoping to provoke Gates into making an attack. He thought, too, that General Sir Henry Clinton might still be moving up the Hudson to

relieve him. He was wrong on both counts. Gates, whose army was growing stronger by the day, was more than ready to play a waiting game. His approach, however, infuriated Arnold, who made it clear he disapproved of his superior's caution. Gates responded by relieving Arnold of his command.

For his part, Burgoyne had to choose between two options. Either he could retreat while he was still able to do so, as von Riedesel and Fraser both urged him, or he could renew the attack. He chose the latter course. On the afternoon of October 7, his army moved forward,

« 152–53

BEFORE

The British plan to isolate New England from the rest of the rebel states depended on a complex series of maneuvers by several forces. None worked out as planned.

GATES TAKES COMMAND
General **Horatio Gates** replaced General Philip Schuyler as commander of the Patriots' northern department following the loss of **Fort Ticonderoga** « 152–53 in July 1777. Samuel Adams said: "Gates is the man of my choice. He has the Art of gaining the love of his Soldiers." The Continental Congress voted for the takeover by eleven to one.

DOGGED DETERMINATION
The British setback at **Bennington** and Lieutenant Colonel Barry St. Leger's **forced retreat from Fort Stanwix to Fort Oswego** « 160–61 did not deter General Burgoyne from pursuing his advance down the Hudson. However, his **confidence began to wane** when he learned that General Clinton would not be supporting him.

signaling the start of the Battle of Bemis Heights. They advanced in three columns for about three-quarters of a mile (1.2 km) and then deployed to form a single line stretching for about half a mile (900 m). Burgoyne's aim was simple. It was to take the bluffs that dominated the Patriot position, bring up his artillery to bombard Gates's defenses remorselessly, and then to break through the Patriot left.

Gates continued to watch and wait—much to the fury of Arnold, who appeared uninvited at the Patriot headquarters. When Gates finally sent reinforcements forward to harass the British right, they laid down a deadly fire and the British started to fall back in confusion. At this point Arnold took a hand. Without orders, he rode into the heart of the action, leading his men in an all-out assault on a key British redoubt. The Hessians holding it broke ranks and fled. Although

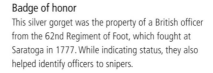

Badge of honor
This silver gorget was the property of a British officer from the 62nd Regiment of Foot, which fought at Saratoga in 1777. While indicating status, they also helped identify officers to snipers.

British royal arms

Arnold himself was seriously wounded in the moment of triumph—his leg was shot by enemy fire and then badly broken when his horse fell on him—the battle was over. It was a major Patriot victory.

That night, Burgoyne withdrew his beaten troops back toward Saratoga. He had lost 894 men at Bemis Heights, including two generals. The dispirited British soldiers huddled in their camp under constant Patriot fire while their commanders debated their best course of action. Having dismissed the

possibility of retreating successfully, Burgoyne made the decision to ask Gates for terms.

Terms of surrender

On 17 October, the negotiations were finally concluded when Burgoyne formally signed the articles of surrender. Gates's first act after the surrender was to invite Burgoyne and his officers to dinner. According to a newspaper report, the meal "consisted of a ham, a goose, some beef and some boiled mutton." Under the terms of surrender, Gates agreed that Burgoyne's British and Hessian troops would march to Boston from where they would be free to return to Britain or Canada, in return for a promise never to fight in America again.

News that the Continental Army had beaten a major British force in open battle reached Europe in December. It convinced French leaders that the Americans were worthwhile allies.

TREATY AND WAR
American representatives in Paris agreed a **treaty with France 188–89 »** in February 1778. This recognized the **independence of the United States** and established a military alliance. After hearing of the treaty Britain declared war on France in March.

BETRAYAL AND BAD FAITH
Quarrels between Patriot generals would eventually lead Benedict Arnold, the hero of Saratoga, being passed over for promotion and ultimately to his **defection to the British 256–57 »** in 1780.

Burgoyne's captured troops, the so-called **Convention Army**, languished in America for the rest of the war.

MONUMENT TO ARNOLD

"Both armies seemed determined to conquer or die."

PATRIOT GENERAL JOHN GLOVER, OCTOBER 1777

Surrender at Saratoga

When attempts to break through the Patriot noose at Saratoga failed, General Burgoyne had little choice but to negotiate an honorable surrender. In a ceremony governed by military protocol, Burgoyne proffered his sword to General Horatio Gates, while his men watched somberly from the sidelines. Among them was Lieutenant William Digby.

"About 10 o'clock, we marched out, according to treaty, with drums beating and the honors of war, but the drums seemed to have lost their former inspiring sounds, and though we beat the Grenadier's March, which not long before was so animating, yet then it seemed by its last feeble effort, as if almost ashamed to be heard on such an occasion.

As to my own feelings, I cannot express them. Tears (though unmanly) forced their way, and if alone, I could have burst to give myself rent. I shall never forget the appearance of their troops on our marching past them; a dead silence universally reigned through their numerous columns, and even then, they seemed struck with our situation and dare scarce lift up their eyes to view British troops in such a situation. I must say their decent behavior during the time (to us so greatly fallen) merited the utmost approbation and praise ...

The meeting between Burgoyne and Gates was well worth seeing. He paid Burgoyne almost as much respect as if he was the conqueror, indeed, his noble air, the prisoner, seemed to command attention and respect from every person. A party of Light Dragoons was ordered as his guard, rather to protect his person from insults than any other cause. Thus ended all our hopes of victory, honor, and glory."

LIEUTENANT WILLIAM DIGBY, 53RD (SHROPSHIRE) REGIMENT, IN *THE BRITISH INVASION FROM THE NORTH. THE CAMPAIGNS OF GENERALS CARLETON AND BURGOYNE FROM CANADA, 1776–1777*, 1887

Surrender of General Burgoyne
This painting by John Trumbull, dating from 1821, depicts the moment General Burgoyne stepped forward to offer his sword to General Gates (center), who refused to take it. Instead, Gates respectfully directed Burgoyne toward his tent to take refreshment.

Prisoners of War

Thousands of soldiers and sailors were taken prisoner during the war. Officers generally received reasonable treatment—living in private houses on parole—but many enlisted men faced cold, hunger, and disease as they battled to survive the rigors of enemy imprisonment.

Prisoners on parade
Hessian soldiers taken at Trenton in 1776 were marched to Philadelphia and then to Virginia, where "the people flocked to see them." Many of the soldiers were sent to work as farmhands.

« BEFORE

It was standard practice to take enemy soldiers captive in times of war, and both sides took prisoners from the outset of hostilities.

REBEL STATUS
George III's 1775 **Proclamation of Rebellion « 72–73** declared the Patriot forces traitors; as such, Patriot captives were considered to be "the king's misguided subjects." Naming them prisoners of war was to acknowledge that they came from an independent foreign state.

NUMBERS SWELL
At the end of 1776, the number of Patriot prisoners in British hands was 4,854, of which 204 were officers. The Patriots had captured only 2,800 British prisoners. However, after their victory at **Saratoga « 162–63** the victorious Patriots took more than 300 officers—including seven generals—and in excess of 5,000 other servicemen prisoner.

The prisoners who were Patriots suffered the most hardship during the War of Independence. It is estimated that, out of 18,154 Patriot combatants taken prisoner by the British, at least 8,500 died between 1775 and 1783. Some estimates put the figure as high as 11,000.

Patriot prisoners were confined in a number of places across the British Empire from Caribbean islands, such as Antigua and St. Lucia, to Senegal in Africa. Captives were also held in Ireland, Scotland, and Wales, as well as in America itself, in New York City, Savannah, Philadelphia, and Florida. However, by far the largest number of prisoners were shipped to Britain.

If they did not die on the sea voyage, they were taken to a detention center. The most important of these were Forton prison, near Portsmouth, and Old Mill prison, near Plymouth.

Inhuman conditions

All the prisons were extremely overcrowded. In New York City, 23 new prisons were put into service. In addition to Provost and New Bridewell—the city's official jails—warehouses, abandoned buildings, churches, King's College, and even the City Hall were all used as lockups. The Liberty Street prison, housing some 500 prisoners, was one of several sugar warehouses that were turned into jails.

In order to cope with the ever-growing number of prisoners, the British even converted old naval and merchant vessels into prison ships: there were at least 28, mostly moored in the bays and rivers around New York, with one anchored off Charleston harbor.

Conditions—particularly on the prison ships—became so bad that, on January 13, 1777, Washington wrote to Admiral Lord Howe, the brother of

Put to work
An old copper mine in Connecticut was converted into a prison in 1773, and used to house Loyalist prisoners during the war. According to the prison records, they lived alongside "thieves, counterfeiters, and murderers." Most were set to work making nails.

A PROSPECTIVE VIEW OF OLD NEWGATE Connecticut's STATE PRISON.

The subterranean Vault, over which this place is built was wrought about the middle of the 17 Century for the purpose of obtaining Copper Ore, the opening into those Gloomy Caverns is a Descent of 35 feet, from thence Descending in various Serpentine Directions 70 Yards, opens to the Well is in depth 74 feet from the Surface to the Water

1 The Commandant's apartment 2 the Guard Room 3 the work shop 4 the store for Nails 5 the Bake house 6 the Cole house 7 the Smiths shop 8 the Well 9 the gate for Entrance 10 the Pickets & inclosure of the Prison 11 the path leading from the work shop to the Caverns

PATRIOT PRISONER 1724–92

HENRY LAURENS

Born in 1724, Henry Laurens rose through the ranks to become first a delegate to the Continental Congress, and then its president. In 1780, the leading Patriot statesman was captured by the British on his way to the Netherlands to negotiate a $10 million loan for the Continental Congress. Laurens was imprisoned in the Tower of London—the only American ever to be held there—until his parole and eventual exchange in return for the release of Lord Cornwallis, the British commander captured at Yorktown in 1781. Laurens's health suffered in captivity, but he was never in danger of execution.

At the end of the war, some Hessian prisoners—and some deserters—remained in America rather than returning to their homelands. Some British escapees followed suit.

NEW LIVES
Scores of British soldiers married Americans and settled down to work as farmers after the war. The majority of escaped prisoners returned to Great Britain—or, in the case of Loyalists, sought a new life abroad. About 80,000 Loyalists chose to leave America after **peace was declared 312–13 >>**.

ACHIEVING RECOGNITION
Patriots held captive in Britain were not **recognized as prisoners of war** until an act of parliament was passed in 1782—six months after the war ended.

settlements in the Wyoming Valley, Pennsylvania, in 1777. Loyalist officers unlucky enough to be captured by the Patriots were often tried and executed on the spot.

Winning freedom
Many captives on both sides tried to escape, but it was not the only way to achieve freedom. Both the Continental Congress and the British offered inducements to persuade prisoners to change sides, though the Congress put an end to the practice in March 1778, due to its lack of success. After that, parolees had to pledge not to soldier again until a formal exchange was completed. The British favored such arrangements—late in 1777, they exchanged Jabez Field for a British officer who had been captured six months earlier—but, despite Washington's wishes, the Congress did not concur. It was only after the surrender at Charleston in 1780, when as many as 5,700 Patriot soldiers and 1,000 sailors fell into British hands, that it finally conceded the principle.

This, at least, was progress. The Continental Congress had previously intervened to prevent the October 1777 agreement concluded by General Horatio Gates and General Burgoyne as part of the terms of surrender after the Battle of Saratoga from coming into effect. The two commanders had agreed that Burgoyne's army—some 5,900 men—would be repatriated to Britain, having given their word never to serve in America again.

Horatio Gates was criticized for this generosity, and the Continental Congress repudiated the deal. The fear was that if Burgoyne's men were allowed to sail home the British government would deploy them for domestic garrison

Two Patriot prisoners—Isaac Hayne and Joshua Huddy—were executed during the war, Hayne by the British for breaking parole and Huddy by Loyalists in revenge for the death in custody of a Loyalist farmer.

duties—allowing the troops they were replacing to be shipped to America. A Connecticut Congressmen declared bluntly that should the Patriots allow repatriation, Burgoyne's men would be "more dangerous to us than if we never had accepted of his Surrendry."

Accordingly, the Convention Army, the name given to the soldiers captured at Saratoga, was marched 50 miles (80 km) inland to Cambridge, Massachusetts, where they were billeted. Some 1,300 prisoners escaped over the course of the following year, after which the men were moved to Charlottesville in Virginia, 700 miles (1,126 km) south. It took the prisoners 12 weeks to march to their destination, during which time another 600 prisoners escaped. After nearly two years in Virginia, they were moved again—first to Maryland, then to Philadelphia, and ultimately to the aptly named Camp Security, near York in the same state. The Convention Army was finally repatriated in 1783 after the Treaty of Paris.

the British commander in chief General William Howe, to protest. "You may call us rebels, and say that we deserve no better treatment," he wrote. "But, remember, my Lord, that supposing us rebels, we still have feelings as keen and sensible as Loyalists, and will, if forced to it, most assuredly retaliate upon those upon whom we look as the unjust invaders of our rights, liberties, and properties."

On the whole, officers were better treated than their men. Almost every officer was paroled—freed on the

The unfortunate prisoners christened it Newgate, after the London prison of the same name.

Like their Patriot counterparts, enlisted men faced a tough life as prisoners, particularly when it came to food and shelter. Thomas Aubrey, a lieutenant in the 4th Foot regiment, who was taken prisoner at Saratoga, recorded that "the soldiers have been so indifferently supplied with provisions, the barracks swarm with rats of an enormous size. "For this reason, the captives were often

"We have now **more English prisoners** than you have **American**."

BENJAMIN FRANKLIN, 1779

condition that they did not take part in the war again—and allowed to live in private homes in exchange for paying room and board. For example, Lieutenant Jabez Field, captured at the Battle of Long Island in 1776, recorded how he was treated with the "greatest humanity & Tenderness" and always "dwelt in Affluent Circumstances."

British and Loyalist prisoners
Initially, each colony was responsible for any prisoners taken within its borders. However, following the Declaration of Independence, the Continental Congress took charge. Its practice was to scatter prisoners around in remote locations as far from the coast as possible, housing some in prisons and others in hastily constructed barracks. Some were even housed in an abandoned copper mine in Simsbury, Connecticut.

allowed to work to earn money to buy food and other necessities. They labored on farms, in shipyards, at forges, and in mines.

Despite their hardships, British and Hessian regulars were generally better treated than their Loyalist allies, who had a much harder time. The latter were punished for the sins of their fellow Loyalists, especially for atrocities committed against the frontier population, such as the attack by a group of New York Loyalists and their Native American allies on

Death boat
Living conditions aboard the British prison ship HMS *Jersey* (see pp.168–69), moored off New York, were particularly harsh. Every morning, the captured Patriots held on board were woken by the gruesome cry, "Rebels, bring out your dead!"

Life on a British Prison Ship

The British prison ships moored in Wallabout Bay on New York's East River were riddled with deadly diseases and infested with vermin. Christopher Hawkins, a young prisoner who managed to escape from the notorious HMS *Jersey*, later recalled his incarceration in the prison known as "hell."

"We were all put between decks ev'ry night before dark, the number being great our situation here was extremely unpleasant. Our rations were not enough to satisfy the calls of hunger. Although the British had a hospital ship near us for the accommodation of the sick yet we had a great deal of sickness on board the *Jersey*, and many died on board her. The sickness seemed to be epidemic and which we called the bloody flux or dysentery.

After the prisoners had been driven below at dusk of the evening and the boat had ceased conveying the sick to the hospital ship, many of the prisoners would become sick the fore part of the evening and before morning their sufferings would be ended by death—such was the malignancy of the disease. My situation amongst others after being stowed away for the night was on the larboard side of the ship with our heads near the wall or side, and the two bots before mentioned either side of me. Thus situated, but one gangway to the upper deck was open, from which my place of rest was about 20 feet, and, as only two prisoners were allowed to visit the upper deck at the same time in the night, the calls of nature be never so violent, and there was no place between decks provided to satisfy these calls. This induced an almost constant running over me by the sick, who would smear myself and others with their filthy and loathsome filth."

CHRISTOPHER HAWKINS, IN HIS MEMOIRS, *THE ADVENTURES OF CHRISTOPHER HAWKINS*, 1864

Death trap
Over the course of the war some 10,000 prisoners died of disease on the prison ships. This engraving of 1855 by the American illustrator F. O. C. Darley depicts the squalid conditions that allowed disease to spread. Ironically, before the war, the *Jersey* had served as a hospital ship.

« BEFORE

General Washington fought back from defeats in the battles around New York City in 1776, with victories in New Jersey at the end of the year.

PATRIOT VICTORIES IN NEW JERSEY

Many New Jersey citizens supported the Loyalist side in 1776, but Washington's victories at **Trenton and Princeton** « **132–33** at the turn of the year gave Patriot forces the upper hand in the state. British garrisons were pulled out and Patriot militia sought out and punished Loyalists.

HOWE'S PLAN

During the spring and summer of 1777 the British commander in chief General Howe attempted to bring Washington into open battle in **New Jersey**. Unsuccessful, Howe withdrew, setting his sights instead upon Philadelphia—which Washington would be forced to defend with his main army.

Howe's commitment to this new strategy meant that he was **not able to support General Burgoyne's plan** to form a "junction" on the Hudson with other British regiments « **160–61**.

The Philadelphia Campaign

When General Sir William Howe landed his army in Maryland in July 1777, his plan was to force Washington and his Continental Army into open battle for the Patriot capital. It was a confrontation he was confident he could win.

It was July—perilously late in the campaigning season—before British commander in chief General Howe decided on the best route to take to the Patriot capital. After changing his mind several times, he made plans to sail up Chesapeake Bay and land on the west side of the Elk River not far from Head of Elk (now Elkton) in Maryland. His intelligence service told him that this was a safer route because the Delaware River was extensively fortified.

The sea voyage lasted 32 days—four times longer than anticipated. But in the wake of Howe's landing in August, Washington finally determined Howe's objective. The Patriot commander in chief took only 36 hours to get his Continentals moving south. He had around 14,000 men with him, 2,000 fewer than his adversary, but militia reinforcements later raised the Patriot total to some 18,000 men.

Plans of attack

After his landing in Maryland, Howe took three weeks to ready his army for battle and Washington put this time to good use. Abandoning the cautious tactics that he had previously favored, Washington marched to confront Howe at Brandywine Creek, which the British needed to cross to approach Philadelphia. He concentrated the best of his troops and most of his artillery centrally at Chadd's Ford and along the wooded slopes above it. Three brigades of militia were deployed on his left and three divisions were stationed at Buffington's Ford to guard his right. Skirmishing riflemen were ordered to take up position west of the creek to harass Howe's men as they advanced.

Had Howe then launched a full-scale frontal assault, Washington might well have won the victory he sought, but the British commander did not oblige. Instead, Howe split his forces. While General Wilhelm von Knyphausen readied an assault against the Patriot center, Howe ordered Lord Cornwallis

to march the remaining 8,000 men the 18 miles (30 km) to Jeffries Ford, to turn Washington's right flank and fall on the Continentals from the rear.

Battle of Brandywine

The battle began at 10 a.m. on a foggy September 11. Knyphausen took nearly five hours to drive the Patriot skirmishers back over the Brandywine, suffering heavy casualties in the process. He then paused, waiting for news of Cornwallis's flanking movement while his artillery dueled with the Patriot guns.

Washington chose to reinforce the center of his line in preparation for a counterattack. At 4 p.m., however, the battle on the Patriot right began in earnest. After 90 minutes of desperate fighting, superior British numbers prevailed and the Patriots reeled back in disarray.

It was time for Knyphausen to cross the Brandywine and complete the envelopment of the Patriots. But at Dilworthtown, stubborn Patriot resistance brought the British advance

Cavalry flag
Few cavalry units were deployed by either side, but the 2nd Continental Light Dragoons, whose flag is shown here, fought at Germantown. Their motto reads "the country calls its sons to respond in tones of thunder."

to a halt. Under cover of darkness, Washington managed to retreat to safety. He had lost around 1,100 men: Howe's casualties were half as many.

Taking Philadelphia

Howe marched on Philadelphia the following day, shadowed and harassed by a troop led by Patriot General Anthony Wayne. On the night of September 20, Wayne set up camp near the Paoli Tavern, where they were taken by surprise by 2,000 of Howe's men. A total of 272 Patriots were killed, wounded, or missing after the attack. Only four British soldiers were killed and 11 wounded.

Philadelphia now lay open. The Congress fled to Lancaster some 50 miles (80 km) to the west, decamping, as one Loyalist put it, "with the utmost precipitation and in the greatest confusion." On September 26, Howe's troops entered the Patriot capital.

It was a major success for Howe, but not the complete triumph for which he had hoped: Washington was still in the field. Reinforced by militia from New Jersey, Maryland, and Virginia as well as Continentals from the Hudson Highlands, he planned to strike another blow against Howe at Germantown, some 5 miles (8 km) north of Philadelphia.

The attack began at 5 a.m. on October 4. At first, the Patriots met with success, but in the fog several units got lost and two of Washington's brigades opened fire on each other by

Battle of Germantown
Victory at Germantown ensured that Philadelphia, the capital of the newly formed United States, remained in British hands through the winter of 1777–78. This picture of the battle was painted by the Italian artist Saverio (Xavier) della Gatta in 1782.

> **"I see gathering thick and fast the darker frown and a blacker storm of Divine indignation."**
>

mistake. The Patriot commander also wasted valuable time trying to storm the Chew House, home of the city's chief justice, which the British had turned into a makeshift fortification.

After three hours, the fighting ceased. As British reinforcements arrived, Washington beat a retreat. The campaign was over. While the British concentrated on capturing the Patriot forts on the Delaware—to open up the river as a route for seaborne supplies—Washington pulled his army back to Valley Forge for the winter.

AFTER

The loss of Philadelphia caused some in the Continental Congress to question the army's leadership.

ATTACHING BLAME
Howe had taken Philadelphia, but the Continental Army remained a significant threat, particularly with the French poised to **join the Patriot cause 188–89 »**. Some Patriots, however, **turned on Washington** as a result of the loss of Philadelphia. Jonathan D. Sergeant, Attorney General of Pennsylvania, said: "Thousands of lives and millions of property are yearly sacrificed to the **insufficiency of our commander in chief**. Two battles has he lost for us by two such blunders as might have disgraced a soldier of three months standing." Washington fought on regardless, and the tide soon turned in his favor.

FRENCH SERGEANT'S HALBERD

5

A WIDENING WAR

1778

Washington's army began the year weak and hungry. Many soldiers deserted. But news that France had joined the war revived Patriot spirits. Money, men, and supplies poured in to help the rebels, forcing the British to rethink their strategy.

≪Winter encampment
En route to Valley Forge in January 1778, General Washington's army reached its lowest ebb. With food in short supply and the extreme weather taking a heavy toll in death and desertion, Washington appealed to the Congress for more

ACTION IN 1778

Despite three years of fighting, the war was no closer to conclusion. Washington's Continentals were brought to a low ebb in their winter encampment at Valley Forge before the military training of German volunteer Baron von Steuben turned them into a more professional fighting force. In February, a formal alliance between the United States and France raised the stakes for Britain, which changed its strategy and deployments to counter its old enemy. Washington seized the opportunity to attack the British as they withdrew from Philadelphia, and attempted the first joint Franco-Patriot action in an attack on British-held Newport, in Rhode Island. While war in the North returned to stalemate, Britain turned to the southern colonies, assaulting vulnerable Georgia and successfully opening a southern theater.

[1] Baron von Steuben transformed the Continental Army at Valley Forge in February. [2] Britain's evacuation of Philadelphia in June led to many Loyalists leaving the city. [3] The Patriots and French mounted a joint attack on the British at Newport, Rhode Island, in August.

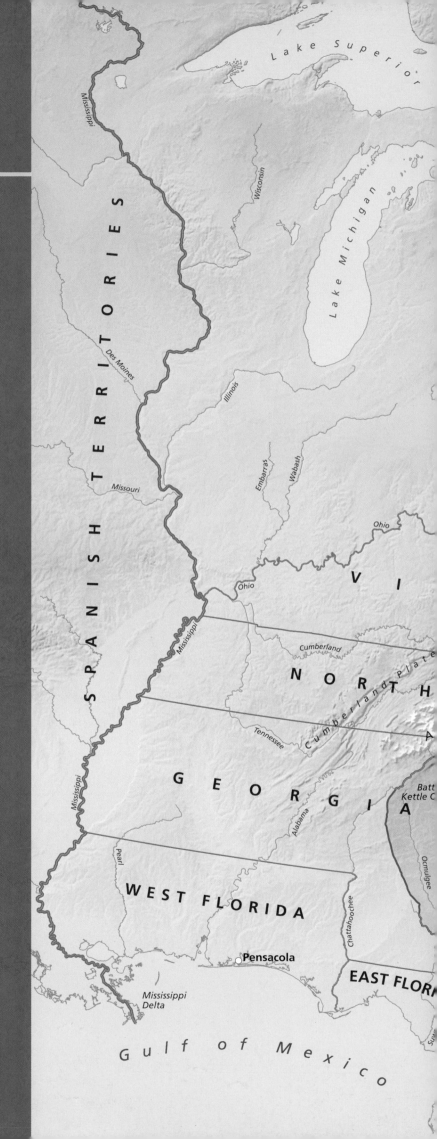

Newfoundland

Saguenay

Magdalen Islands

Prince Edward Island

Louisbourg

NOVA SCOTIA

Quebec

Saint-Maurice

St. John

Penobscot

MASSACHUSETTS

Bay of Fundy

Halifax

Sable Island

Montreal

Ottawa

St. Lawrence

Lake Champlain

White Mountains

NEW HAMPSHIRE

Lake Huron

Georgian Bay

Q U E B E C

Lake Ontario

Adirondack Mountains

Green Mountains

Connecticut

ATLANTIC OCEAN

Lake Erie

Mohawk

Allegheny

N E W   Y O R K

Albany

Hudson

Catskill Mountains

Boston
MASSACHUSETTS

Cape Cod

CONNECTICUT

3

Newport
RHODE ISLAND

Susquehanna

Delaware

PENNSYLVANIA

New York City

Princeton

Valley Forge   1

Second Continental Congress

2 **Philadelphia**

NEW JERSEY

Muskingum

Ohio

KEY

	Border of Spanish territories
	1763 Proclamation Line
	Colonial boundaries
○	Town / settlement
✕	Battle / siege
▯	Fort
🚢	Naval battle
🖋	Treaty / convention
⛺	Loyalist winter camp
⛺	Patriot winter camp

DELAWARE

Baltimore

MARYLAND

Patomek

James

Chesapeake Bay

A P P A L A C H I A N   M O U N T A I N S

Yorktown

Norfolk

Roanoke

Dan

Kanawha

V I R G I N I A

C A R O L I N A

Pee Dee

Cape Fear

Waterree

Camden

Wilmington

OUTH CAROLINA

Santee

Augusta

Charleston

Battle of Brier Creek

✕ *Battle of Beaufort*

✕ *Capture of Savannah*

▯ *Fort Morris*

annah

Mohawk

NEW HAMPSHIRE

NEW YORK

Albany

Hudson

Green Mountains

Connecticut

MASSACHUSETTS

Boston

Cape Cod

Catskill Mountains

CONNECTICUT

🚢 *Battle of Rhode Island*

3 **Newport**

RHODE ISLAND

Susquehanna

Delaware

PENNSYLVANIA

Long Island

New York City

Princeton

Second Continental Congress

✕ *Battle of Monmouth Courthouse*

Valley Forge   1

Philadelphia   2 **NEW JERSEY**

🖋 *Philadelphia*

ATLANTIC OCEAN

DELAWARE

Baltimore

MARYLAND

N

0   100 km

0   100 miles

0   100 km

0   100 miles

TIMELINE 1778

Hardships at Valley Forge ▪ **France joins the war** ▪ Carlisle Peace Commission ▪ **The British leave Philadelphia** ▪ Battle of Monmouth ▪ **John Paul Jones raids England** ▪ Native American alliances ▪ **Battle of Rhode Island** ▪ Savannah falls to the British

JANUARY	FEBRUARY	MARCH	APRIL	MAY	JUNE
		MARCH 2 Major General Nathanael Greene is appointed quartermaster general of the Continental Army at Valley Forge.	**APRIL** Baron von Steuben begins to train the army at Valley Forge.		

⌃ Winter at Valley Forge

JANUARY
The Continental Army suffers supply shortages at their winter camp at Valley Forge.

FEBRUARY 5
South Carolina ratifies the Articles of Confederation.

FEBRUARY 6
France and the newly declared United States sign a Treaty of Amity and Commerce and a Treaty of Alliance.

❯ British Light Dragoon pistol

APRIL 12
Carlisle's Peace Commission, a group of British delegates, is dispatched to the Second Continental Congress.

MAY 4
The Congress ratifies treaties with France—signed in February 1778—embracing the alliance.

JUNE 13
Carlisle's commission submits peace proposals to the Congress which do not include recognition of the Declaration of Independence.

JANUARY 28
The Second Continental Congress refuses the reconciliation terms presented to Benjamin Franklin by the British in December 1777.

❯ The allies carve up British commerce

MAY 20
British forces from Philadelphia unsuccessfully attempt to trap 2,200 Continentals defending Valley Forge, in the Battle of Barren Hill.

JUNE 18
British forces under General Sir Henry Clinton evacuate Philadelphia.

JUNE 19
The Continental Army breaks camp to follow the retreating Clinton.

MARCH 17
Britain officially declares war on France.

APRIL 13
French Admiral Comte d'Estaing's fleet sails from Toulon for American waters.

APRIL 23
John Paul Jones, on the *Ranger*, attacks the port of Whitehaven, England.

MAY 30
The first official Oath of Allegiance to the United States is sworn by soldiers at Valley Forge, including Benedict Arnold.

❯ Molly Pitcher at the Battle of Monmouth

JUNE 28
The British Army clashes with the Patriots at Monmouth Courthouse.

❮ Benjamin Franklin

> "The British King and Council have determined to **offer Independence to America,** provided she will break her Treaty with France ... a **symptom of Despair.**"
>
> AMERICAN COMMISSIONERS TO THE MASSACHUSETTS COUNCIL, JULY 29, 1778

JULY	AUGUST	SEPTEMBER	OCTOBER	NOVEMBER	DECEMBER

OCTOBER 6
British and Patriot forces clash at Chestnut Neck, New Jersey.

NOVEMBER 4
D'Estaing's fleet sails from Boston for the West Indies.

DECEMBER 9
D'Estaing's fleet arrives in the West Indies.

OCTOBER 8
Continental soldiers and frontier militia burn the Iroquois town of Unadilla, in revenge for the burning of German Flatts.

» Comte d'Estaing

⌃ Iroquois raiders massacre settlers in the Wyoming Valley

JULY 2
The Congress returns to Philadelphia from its temporary quarters at York, Pennsylvania.

AUGUST 10
A major storm breaks out in Rhode Island, scattering British and French ships as they prepare for battle.

SEPTEMBER 13
Loyalists and Native Americans, led by Joseph Brant, burn the town of German Flatts, New York.

SEPTEMBER 14
Franklin is appointed to represent the Continental Congress in France.

OCTOBER 18
A British fleet commanded by Captain Henry Mowat burns the coastal town of Falmouth, Massachusetts.

NOVEMBER 11
A combined Loyalist and Native American force attacks Cherry Valley, New York. Patriot propagandists describe it as a massacre.

DECEMBER 17
British forces under Lieutenant Governor Henry Hamilton recapture Fort Sackville in the Illinois country (now Indiana).

JULY 3
Many Patriots are killed by Loyalists and their Iroquois allies in the Wyoming Valley Massacre, near Wilkes-Barre, Pennsylvania.

JULY 4
Patriot George Rogers Clark takes Kaskaskia.

AUGUST 29
General Pigot attacks Continental forces in the Battle of Rhode Island.

SEPTEMBER 17
The Patriots sign the Treaty of Fort Pitt with the Lenape (Delaware) people.

NOVEMBER 27
The Carlisle Peace Commission departs for England, convinced of the impossibility of bringing about a peaceful settlement to the conflict.

DECEMBER 28
The British capture St. Lucia with a victory in the Battle of Morne de la Vierge.

⌄ British and French fleets battle off Rhode Island

JULY 27
The British and French fleets do battle near the island of Ushant off the French coast.

DECEMBER 29
British forces capture Savannah, Georgia, beginning their campaign to return the province to royal control.

BEFORE

The year 1777 ended in a military impasse for Patriot and British forces, as defeats and victories canceled each other out.

MIXED FORTUNES

Generals Gates and Arnold had led a force of Continental regiments and New England militias to victory at **Saratoga ≪ 162–63** in the fall of 1777, capturing General Burgoyne's entire army of regulars and Hessians and securing French support for American independence. To the south, however, Washington's losses at the battles of **Brandywine** and **Germantown ≪ 170–71** left the victorious British firmly in control of Philadelphia.

HESSIAN MITER

Facing Stalemate

As a new year dawned in 1778, the combatants stared at a troublesome impasse. Despite years of fighting and wide-ranging campaigns, neither side had been able to crush the other—but both had learned key lessons. A new kind of conflict demanded fresh tactics.

The nature of war in the rebellious American colonies was very different from that of earlier colonial wars or from wars in Europe. Unlike the seemingly endless wars of 18th-century Europe, the War of Independence saw few major set-piece engagements. After his defeats around New York and Philadelphia, Washington was wary of endangering

Tug of war

In a cartoon of 1778, *The Curious Zebra*, George Washington holds the tail of a zebra inscribed with the names of the 13 colonies, while Lord North grips its reins, as the two men struggle for control.

his army by pitting them against the highly trained British regulars on an open battlefield.

As for Britain's commanders, Sir William Howe and Henry Clinton had seen the carnage of Bunker Hill in 1775 and thereafter dared not take a chance on launching assaults on strongly fortified Patriot positions. British generals could not afford to lose their soldiers in risky engagements or pyrrhic victories. Their red-coated regulars and Hessian auxiliaries were irreplaceable—reinforcements were an ocean away. Although Washington's Continental regiments were

perennially understrength, at least he could rely on short-term assistance from local militia forces and was able to replace soldiers lost to disease, desertion, or death with new recruits.

Challenging terrain

The scale and shape of the landscape imposed its own limits on the combatants—physical constraints were fundamental to plans for the continuing war. Roads were few and unimproved, slowing the movement of armies and supplies. Rivers could prove useful conduits or impassable barriers: water transportation was

THE CURIOUS ZEBRA.
alive from America! walk in Gem'men and Ladies, walk in.

London, Printed for G. Johnson as the Act directs 3 Sep.r 1778, and Sold at all the Printshops in London & Westminster.

often a better option than the poor roads. The bridges and fords across rivers or creeks were few and far between, however, restricting or impeding army maneuvers.

Beyond the eastern shores, Britain's navy could move soldiers and supplies up and down the coast with near impunity, but it also had to carry supplies for weeks or months across the Atlantic Ocean from depots in Ireland. Worse, the defeat at Saratoga in 1777 (see pp.162–63) showed the

"Our **soldiers** are in a **wretched condition.**"

JAMES THACHER, M.D., REVOLUTIONARY ARMY SURGEON, *MILITARY JOURNAL*, MARCH 1780

danger British armies faced if they were cut off inland. The terrain provided ready-made fortifications for the Patriot cause: north and west of British-occupied New York, the combination of the Hudson Highlands and ranges of steep hills in New Jersey helped the Continentals keep the King's forces contained.

A time of terror

British regulars and Washington's Continentals also discovered they were not the only combatants. Throughout the war, local groups in contested zones such as New York City, Philadelphia, Georgia, and the Carolinas took advantage of the chaos to further their own interests and persecute their opponents. Some were merely thugs and thieves or outlaw bands who stole or destroyed property. Others had declared political allegiances.

Irregular warfare

A 19th-century wood engraving depicts a skirmish between British soldiers and colonists. Many localized groups joined the conflict to uphold their own beliefs or political aims.

The legitimacy of these combatants was in the eye of the beholder. To the British occupying New York, James DeLancey was a daring captain of light horse, leading loyalist refugees. The Patriot victims of his raids, however, considered his men to be "cow-boys" and rogue "skinners."

By 1778, the most notorious zone for this irregular war of "all against all" was the "Neutral Ground" north of British-occupied New York. The inhabitants, exposed to depredations from armies and militias on both sides, suffered greatly. Timothy Dwight, the president of Yale College noted how they "feared everybody whom they saw, and loved nobody." Although the road between Boston and New York" had heretofore seen a continued succession of horses and carriages and life and bustle,"

Stretched supply lines

Most of the goods needed to supply British soldiers in America were shipped across the Atlantic from homeland ports such as London, and took several months to reach their destination.

wrote Dwight, "not a single solitary traveler was visible from week to week, or from month to month."

Lure of liberty

Despite the chaotic nature of the conflict, George Washington desired "a respectable army" of proper soldiers to advance the political legitimacy of their cause. In fact, it may have been political ideology that marked the largest difference between wars in Europe and the events unfolding in America. Continental soldiers and Patriot militias heard constant exhortations about the righteousness of their cause. Late in the war, Johann Ewald, a Hessian captain, noted the effect of this: "What soldiers in the world could … do what was done by these men, who go about nearly naked and in the greatest privation? Deny the best disciplined soldiers of Europe what is due them and they will run away in droves, and the general will soon be alone. But from this one can perceive what an enthusiasm—which the poor fellows call 'Liberty'—can do!"

AFTER

Both Patriot military operations and Britain's strategy to secure the rebellious colonies were transformed during the course of 1778.

FRANCE JOINS THE FRAY

After years of secretly sending the Americans guns and ammunition, the **French made an open alliance** with the Patriots and **declared war on Britain 188–89 》**. In the wake of the American victory at Saratoga (thanks, in part, to the availability of French weaponry), France feared Britain would grant concessions to the Patriots, join forces with them, and attack French possessions in the West Indies. Great Britain responded by **evacuating Philadelphia** and reinforcing its vulnerable islands in the West Indies.

AN ARMY GROWS IN CONFIDENCE

With the support of the Continental Congress, Washington set about revitalizing the Continental Army, improving lines of supply, maintenance of equipment, and the whole army's system of logistics. He also appointed **Baron von Steuben**, a Prussian military man, to oversee the **training and drilling** of Patriot soldiers **184–85 》**.

American wilderness
Upper New York was an impenetrable wilderness.
The hostile conditions made troop movement
virtually impossible without recourse to waterways,
as General Burgoyne found in 1777.

At the end of 1777, Washington and his army in Pennsylvania suffered setbacks and were forced to retreat from Philadelphia.

A DIFFICULT YEAR

General Howe's victory over Washington's Continental Army at **Brandywine** in September 1777 allowed the British to march into **Philadelphia ‹‹ 170–71**, forcing the Continental Congress to flee. Washington had moved his forces to the northwest of the city. In the ensuing months the situation in Pennsylvania was at **stalemate ‹‹ 180–81**. Small-scale raids and maneuvers designed to secure supply lines and disrupt those of their opponents characterized the operations of both sides.

POSITIVE SPIN

When Benjamin Franklin, in France, heard the news of the reversals in the fall of 1777, he quipped, "Say not that the British army has taken Philadelphia, but rather that Philadelphia has taken the British army."

Winter at Valley Forge

At the start of 1778, the Continental Army was worn down by a long campaign of hard fighting and near-endless maneuver. Yet Washington still led 11,000 soldiers and officers, with 8,200 fit for duty—a far sight better than the dark days at the end of 1776.

With winter deepening, Washington believed the inadequate supply situation a more dangerous and pressing enemy than the British. To lessen the burden, he had hoped to split his army into a number of small camps spread in an arc west of Philadelphia. Politicians in the Congress and state legislatures, however, demanded that Washington keep the army together to block the British occupying Philadelphia.

As a consequence, the Continental Army took up winter quarters at Valley Forge. Just 20 miles (32 km) from Philadelphia, the site's position west of the Schuylkill River and its wooded hills made it easily defensible. There, Washington explained to his soldiers,

they would be able to protect the rest of Pennsylvania from "the ravages of the enemy."

Taking stock

The rich farmland of eastern Pennsylvania was densely settled, but Valley Forge initially looked bleak. The two contending armies in the Philadelphia campaign had already stripped the countryside. Equally discouraging, Valley Forge had no barracks and the Continentals had to build their own shelters to escape the winter cold. They built orderly formations of one-room huts, 14 ft by 16 ft (4.3 m by 4.9 m), constructed from rough-hewn logs, notched and stacked, and chinked with clay to seal the gaps.

Each hut housed 12 men. In solidarity with his men, Washington refused to shift his quarters from a tent to a nearby house until his soldiers completed their huts—an operation that took more than a month. To the political theorist Thomas Paine, the flurry of construction looked like "a family of Beavers; every one busy."

Food and supplies in Washington's army had already reached critical levels by the end of 1777's Philadelphia campaign. When the army arrived at Valley Forge, the commissary had only flour—no meat or dried fish—to disperse to the men. Late December 1777 and early January 1778 saw the army's hungriest days, and by mid-February Washington reported that

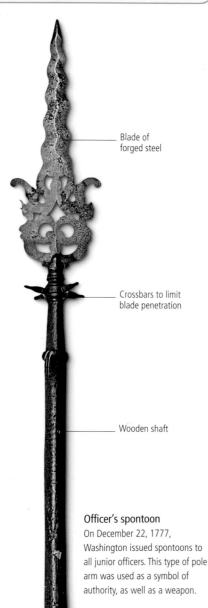

Blade of forged steel

Crossbars to limit blade penetration

Wooden shaft

Officer's spontoon
On December 22, 1777, Washington issued spontoons to all junior officers. This type of pole arm was used as a symbol of authority, as well as a weapon.

"This **army** must **inevitably be reduced to one** or other of these three things: **starve, dissolve, or disperse.**"

WASHINGTON IN A LETTER TO THE PRESIDENT OF THE CONGRESS, DECEMBER 23, 1777

his "starving" soldiers faced famine. At least 3,000 men were "barefoot and otherwise naked," Washington told the Congress. "I much doubt the practicability of holding the Army together much longer, unless some great and capital change suddenly takes place."

Nevertheless, Washington rejected calls to seize supplies from local inhabitants. Trying to maintain the legitimacy of their cause in the eyes of wary civilians, his officers tried to offer fair compensation to farmers. Washington's orders insisted their struggle was to protect "Rights, Liberty, and Property"—so the army could not risk being seen as "plunderers instead of protectors." Forage parties had to range as far as southern New Jersey, Delaware, and Maryland for food and supplies.

Conditions at Valley Forge were trying: disease killed more than 2,500 soldiers at the encampment that winter. Contrary to myth, the weather was not terribly cold but it was wet, which turned the roads into muddy mires. More cold and snow would, in fact, have firmed up the roads and eased transport of food and supplies.

Ultimately, Washington proved astute in his communications with the Congress, using reports of the dire situation to reform the supply chain, and to encourage the unfolding myth of his soldiers' stalwart suffering and brave self-sacrifice.

As spring approached and the supply situation improved, the army began to stir. Friedrich von Steuben, a European volunteer who styled himself "Baron" and claimed to have served Frederick the Great as an aide-de-camp and quartermaster, arrived at Valley Forge with a commission from the Congress. Experiences in the 1777 campaign had shown Washington and his generals the necessity of "Establishing one uniform Sett of Manoeuvres and Manual Exercise."

Drilling the men

Von Steuben set about building a training program and new drill routine for the Continental. First, he took a 100-man model company and personally trained them, casting aside the class-based expectations that only lowly corporals or sergeants would concern themselves with training the common soldiers. Von Steuben's shaky grasp of English necessitated his aides translating his commands—and curses—for the soldiers. Those men then "spread the instruction," teaching others in their respective regiments. Von Steuben explained that the success of his methods rested on his realization that "the genius of this nation is not in the least to be compared with the Prussians, the Austrians, or French. You say to your soldier, 'Do this,' and he doeth it, but I am obliged to say, 'This is the reason why you ought to do that:' and then he does it."

Fit for a commander

The camp bed used by Washington was made from canvas, wood, and iron. It consisted of three folding stools. The bed measured 6½ ft (2 m) to accommodate the army leader's 6 ft 2 in (1.9 m) frame.

AFTER »

Washington's army remained in its Valley Forge encampment until the spring of 1778, by which time the outlook had changed for the Patriots in Pennsylvania.

WASHINGTON IN PURSUIT

Perceiving a new threat in the North from the Patriots' French ally, British forces **withdrew from Philadelphia** to reinforce their stronghold in New York **196–97 »**. Washington's retrained and reinvigorated army marched out of Valley Forge to confront the British on their progress across **New Jersey**.

TIGHT FINANCES AND DISSENT

Declining economic conditions, especially **depreciation of the Continental currency**, and squabbles and rivalries between the Patriot generals posed new threats to the war effort. Despite three years of fighting, the Patriots' path to victory and independence still looked long and full of dangers.

Training the troops

Baron von Steuben picked out particular men to demonstrate his maneuvers to the other troops. His reformed "manual exercise" became the standard for the Continental Army.

CABINS IN VALLEY FORGE TODAY

185

The Army at Valley Forge

As January took hold, conditions in Washington's winter quarters at Valley Forge, Pennsylvania, grew increasingly harsh. The difficult weather, severe food shortages, and disease took their toll on the soldiers physically and mentally. More than 2,000 men died in the camp, but those who survived came out of Valley Forge belonging to a more effective, more disciplined fighting force.

❝The Army which has been surprisingly healthy hitherto, now begins to grow sickly from the continued fatigues they have suffered this Campaign ... I am Sick—discontented—and out of humor. Poor food—hard lodging—Cold weather—fatigue—Nasty Cloaths—nasty Cookery—Vomit half my time—smoak'd out of my senses—the Devil's in't—I can't Endure it. Why are we sent here to starve and Freeze—What sweet Felicities have I left at home; A Charming Wife—pretty Children—Good Beds—good food—good Cookery—all agreeable—all harmonious. Here all Confusion—smoke and Cold—hunger and filthyness—A pox on my bad luck. There comes a bowl of beef soup—full of burnt leaves and dirt, sickish enough to make a Hector spue—away with it Boys—I'll live like the Chameleon upon Air.

Poh! Poh! cryo Patience within me—you talk like a fool. Your being sick Covers your mind with a Melancholic Gloom, which makes everything about you appear gloomy. See the poor Soldier, when in health—with what cheerfulness he meets his foes and encounters every hardship—if barefoot, he labors thro' the Mud and Cold with a Song in his mouth extolling War and Washington—if his food be bad, he eats it ... seeming content—blesses God for a good Stomach and Whistles it into digestion.❞

DIARY ENTRY OF CONTINENTAL ARMY SURGEON DR. ALBIGENCE WALDO

The limits of endurance
George Washington and the young French volunteer, the Marquis de Lafayette (far left), formed a strong bond during the encampment at Valley Forge. Their concern for the men in their charge raised the soldiers' spirits and helped them get through the bitter winter.

French Intervention

France, although sympathetic to the fledgling United States, had avoided direct involvement in the American war. By 1778, however, Patriot military success and the chance to exploit British weakness persuaded the French that it was time for action.

The century-long contest between Britain and France cast a long shadow over the American struggle for independence. Despite three years of open war between the Thirteen Colonies and their mother country, the English historian Edward Gibbon wrote that he still thought England and France were "fairly running a race for the favor of America." In early 1778, Britain lost that race.

Making treaties

Their dramatic victory at Saratoga in 1777 promised a change in Patriot fortunes. Lafayette (pp.146–47) had joined the Patriots in 1777, but news of Saratoga combined with two other factors to push the French court toward an formal alliance. First, the refitting of France's fleets was due to be complete by the spring of 1778. Second, Patriot diplomats in France,

HOW DO YOU LIKE IT MONSIEUR.

Poking fun at old foes
A British cartoon, captioned "How do you like it Monsieur," shows a well-fed Briton kicking and pulling at a skinny, effete Frenchman, reflecting the traditional British contempt for France, now in alliance with the Patriots.

including Benjamin Franklin, had met with a secret emissary from the British government, to discuss peace, independence, and a formal alliance between Britain and the colonies.

Fear of such an alliance forced the French foreign minister, Comte de Vergennes, to act while the British empire was still distracted and divided. He pushed for French King Louis XVI to accept the Patriots' overtures and move toward declaring war on Great Britain.

Two treaties, drafted quickly in January and February 1778, forged the alliance between "His Most Catholic Majesty" and the young republic of the United States: a Treaty of Commerce and Amity, focused on trade, and a formal Treaty of Alliance. This second agreement was vital. As the Patriots

had hoped since 1776, France pledged in its alliance to maintain the liberty and independence of the United States. For both France and the Patriots, the treaty's key article looked to the end of the war: "Neither of the two Parties shall conclude a Truce or Peace with Great Britain, without the formal consent of the other first obtained." The new allies swore "not to lay down their arms" until the independence of the United States was assured by victory and a formal treaty. The French fought to humble Britain—it would not do to have their Patriot allies make a separate peace. As for the United States, it could not risk abandonment. The French crown also renounced all claim to Canada, implicitly promising the new republic it would not compete for control over North America.

Astute self-presentation by Franklin and the demands of practicality had done their work. Word of the treaty

« **BEFORE**

France and Britain were old adversaries; it was only natural that the French would take advantage of disorder in their enemy's colonies.

LONGSTANDING ENMITY
During the 18th century, Britain and France were engaged in a series of conflicts, collectively called the **Second Hundred Years' War**. After the Seven Years' War, which formed part of that larger struggle, concluded with **Britain's victory in 1763**, France began rearming in expectation of renewed conflict. When Britain went to war with its American rebels, France began **supplying the rebels with weapons**. In 1776, Benjamin Franklin went to Paris in pursuit of an **open alliance** between the Patriots and France.

FRENCH MOLD FOR MUSKET BALLS

> ## "Washington's negotiations
> have done more in Europe, than
> all our **ambassadors.**"
>
> JOHN ADAMS TO HENRY KNOX, SEPTEMBER 19, 1779

CHARLES-HECTOR, COMTE D'ESTAING

The Comte d'Estaing was a vice admiral of the French navy when his ships sailed into American waters in 1778. This was his first naval command—he was known more as a soldier, having fought in India during the Seven Years' War. After setbacks off New York and Newport in 1778, he captured British territory in the Caribbean, but in 1779 failed to drive the British from Savannah. Wounded in the attack, the Comte returned to France. He supported the French Revolution but would not break with the royal family and so was executed during the Reign of Terror that ensued.

reached American shores and the ears of the Congress in May 1778. The Continental Army, emerging from the harsh winter at Valley Forge (see pp.184–85), marked the news with a long day of celebration. Washington praised Divine Providence for "raising us up a powerful Friend among the Princes of the Earth, to establish our liberty and Independence upon lasting foundations." He ordered, in celebration, a "feu de joie" salute—soldiers sequentially discharging their muskets. The hills echoed with the sound of cannons and shouts of "Long Live the King of France!"

France enters the fray

On April 13, 1778, the Comte d'Estaing's squadron sailed from Toulon for America—the first time since France's defeat in the Seven Years' War that French ships had sailed into combat. The fleet of 12 ships of the line and four lighter frigates carried 4,000 soldiers and aimed to tip the balance of power, but uncooperative winds set them back and the fleet did not arrive in American waters until early July.

The British were thankful for their luck. The French fleet had narrowly missed both the chance to destroy the vessels evacuating Philadelphia and the opportunity to trap General Clinton's army in New Jersey as it withdrew to New York. The Whig politician Charles Fox complained in parliament that had "the French fleet arrived but six days sooner" the price would have been "the naval power and glory of Great Britain." Instead, d'Estaing attempted to advance on a reinforced, British-occupied New York City, stationing his fleet off Sandy Hook at the mouth of the lower bay.

Washington knew that a successful French and Patriot assault on this key stronghold might signal the beginning of the end for the British. Unable to take warships over the tricky sandbars, however, the French commander was forced to withdraw. D'Estaing and his new Patriot allies would have to look for another opportunity to strike against their now-shared British enemy.

The prospect of French reinforcements was welcome news to American rebels.

COMMAND OF THE SEAS
The **reinvigorated French navy** promised to change the tide of the war. British warships had dominated the Atlantic, moving men and material unopposed up and down the North American coast. Now Britain would have to **guard against invasion** of their own shores, and prepare to counter threats against their islands in the **Caribbean**, forcing Britain to **rethink its strategy** in North America **194–95 »**.

SPAIN WADES IN
French attempts to bring Spain into a wider war against Britain bore fruit in 1779, with the **Treaty of Aranjuez**, a secret alliance between France and Spain that led to attacks on Britain itself.

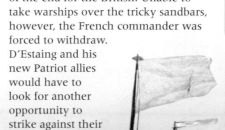

Battle of the giants
The first major encounter between British and French forces occurred off Rhode Island in August 1778 when British ships under the command of Lord Howe clashed with the French squadron of the Comte d'Estaing.

AMERICAN STATESMAN Born 1706 Died 1790

Benjamin Franklin

"Make yourselves sheep and the wolves will eat you."

BENJAMIN FRANKLIN, IN A LETTER TO THOMAS CUSHING, 1773

Often referred to as "The First American," Benjamin Franklin combined the hardworking entrepreneurial ethos of the Puritan tradition with the rational open-mindedness of the European Enlightenment. Leaving his native Massachusetts for good at the age of 17, he always saw beyond colonial boundaries, working to build a unifying sense of American identity that was a necessary precondition for the founding of the United States. His influence was pervasive, while his negotiation of a military alliance with France in 1778 was key to securing an American victory in the War of Independence.

From printer to politician

Franklin was proud of being a man who rose from lowly origins through his own efforts and abilities. A late arrival in a large, cash-strapped Boston family, he had little formal education. Starting work aged 12 as an apprentice in his brother's print shop in 1718, by 1730 he was running his own printing business and an influential newspaper in Philadelphia.

Franklin's journalistic writing made him famous throughout the colonies, especially the folksy wisdom of his *Poor Richard's Almanack*. He popularized aphorisms that permanently entered the language—"a penny saved is a penny earned," and "an ounce of prevention is worth a pound of cure." Tirelessly energetic, he left his mark in many areas of public life, from the US postal service to hospitals, from higher education to fire insurance. He also achieved renown as an inventor and a scientist, studying areas as diverse as electricity, meteorology, and ocean currents.

From the 1750s, Franklin took an active role in politics. When a congress of colonial delegates met at Albany in 1754 to discuss coordinated action against the

Elder statesman

Franklin was 79 years old and serving as president of Pennsylvania when French artist Joseph Siffred Duplessis began painting this portrait. Duplessis continued to work on the painting even after Franklin's death.

Franklin's bifocals
One of Franklin's inventions was a pair of bifocal eyeglasses designed for his own use. This drawing, showing the top and bottom lenses for near and far sight, was included in a letter he wrote in 1785.

French, Franklin proposed a Plan of Union that would have created a unified government for the colonies. Ahead of its time, the proposal was rejected by colonial assemblies, who were later described by Franklin as "narrowly provincial in outlook, mutually jealous, and suspicious of any central taxing authority." Franklin's unity plan was not in any sense anti-British. From 1757 to 1775 he spent most of his time in Britain, where he was respected as a man of notable talents and achievements, invited to join learned societies and showered with honorary degrees.

"Rebellion to tyrants is obedience to God."

BENJAMIN FRANKLIN, MOTTO PROPOSED FOR US GREAT SEAL, AUGUST 1776

Franklin was slow to pick up on the mounting tide of resistance to British rule in America. He was living in London when the passage of the Stamp Act triggered outrage in the colonies in 1765. Underestimating the popular hostility to the measure, he sought a lucrative post as Pennsylvania stamp distributor for a friend. Radicals responded by threatening to destroy his house in Philadelphia. Momentarily wrong-footed, Franklin retrieved his reputation by testifying against the stamp tax in front of a committee of the House of Commons.

Breaking with the British
Over the following years, acting as the agent of Pennsylvania and other colonies, Franklin repeatedly expressed colonial discontent at British policy,

both in print and in parliament. He made himself the recognized spokesman for the colonial position, and by 1773 Franklin's frustration at British government policy had undermined his sense of loyalty. When he gained possession of private letters from royal Governor Thomas Hutchinson of Massachusetts that seemed to threaten the province's traditional freedoms, Franklin sent them to Boston where extracts were leaked, further inflaming anti-British feeling. After admitting responsibility for the leak, in January 1774 Franklin was subjected to a humiliating dressing-down in front of the British Privy Council. At that point his loyalty to Britain was at an end.

By the time Franklin returned to Philadelphia, fighting with the British had already broken out. A man of immense prestige, he was an obvious choice as Pennsylvania's delegate to the Continental Congress. He was appointed a member of the five-man committee selected to draw up the Declaration of Independence.

As the Patriot leader with the greatest personal experience of Europe and the highest reputation on the other side of the Atlantic, in December 1776 he was sent to France to seek support for the rebellion against

Rounce: moves bed of press

Lifelong interest
Printing was Franklin's trade and he ran a printing business for a large part of his life. He used this wooden printing press, now in the National Museum of American History in Washington, D.C., when he worked as a printer in England in the 1720s.

Britain. Although his grasp of the French language was far from perfect, he was welcomed by the French intellectual elite as a fellow disciple of the Enlightenment and widely praised for the republican simplicity of his dress and manners. Initially seeking a deal on finance and trade, he ended by concluding a full military alliance.

After the British defeat at Yorktown, Franklin found himself at the center of the peace negotiations conducted in France. He failed to achieve his goal of adding Quebec to the United States but signed the highly satisfactory Treaty of Paris in 1783 (see pp.312–13).

Honorable homecoming
When Franklin returned to America for the last time in 1785, he stood second only to George Washington in honor and fame. His advanced age prevented him from playing a dominant role in the new government, though he was key to the acceptance of the "Connecticut compromise" at the Constitutional Convention in 1787, which solved the ongoing debate over fair representation in Congress. Signing the US Constitution was Franklin's last major political act. He died of pleurisy on April 17, 1790, aged 84, and around 20,000 mourners attended his funeral in Philadelphia.

Platen: presses paper to type

1956 COMMEMORATIVE FRANKLIN STAMP

TIMELINE

- **1706** Born January 6 in Boston, Massachusetts, the fifteenth child of candle and soap maker Josiah Franklin.
- **1718–23** Learns a printer's trade as apprentice to his brother James.
- **1721** Writes for his brother's newspaper, the *New England Courant*.
- **1724–26** Moves to London, England, and works as a printer.
- **1727–30** Establishes his own printing house in Philadelphia and takes over the *Pennsylvania Gazette*.
- **1730** Deborah Read becomes his common law wife; they have two children.
- **1732** Begins publishing his famous *Poor Richard's Almanack*.
- **1737** Appointed postmaster of Philadelphia.
- **1741** Invents the Franklin stove.
- **1746** Begins experiments with electricity.
- **1749** Founds the College of Philadelphia.
- **1751** Elected as a representative to the Pennsylvania assembly.
- **1754** Proposes the Albany Plan of Union for a unified government of the Thirteen Colonies at the start of the French and Indian War.
- **1757–62** Sent to England by the Pennsylvania Assembly to contest the influence of the Penn family in the colony.
- **1764–75** Dispatched a second time to Britain, where he becomes a spokesman for the American colonies.
- **1773** Leaks private letters written by Massachusetts Governor Thomas Hutchinson.
- **1775** Returns to Pennsylvania; is selected as a delegate to the Second Continental Congress.
- **July 1775** Congress appoints him the first Postmaster General.
- **1776** Serves on the Committee of Five that draws up the Declaration of Independence and signs the Declaration on July 4.
- **December 1776** Sent to France to secure French government support for the American independence struggle.
- **1778** Secures a military alliance with France.
- **1782–83** Negotiates the Treaty of Paris with Britain, ending the War of Independence.
- **1785–88** Serves three one-year terms as president of Pennsylvania.
- **1787** Serves as a delegate to the Constitutional Convention, signing the US Constitution.
- **1788** Retires from public life.
- **1790** Dies in Philadelphia on April 17, aged 84; interred at the Christ Church Burial Ground.

BEFORE «

After defeats at New York in 1776, the American states and the Continental Congress had realized they needed a professional army.

SUCCESS AND DEFEATS

Although Washington's army had notable successes under his command, such as the battles of **Trenton** (1776) and **Princeton** (1776) **« 132–33**, Washington also experienced serious setbacks, including the **Battle of Long Island « 118–19** (1776) and **Brandywine « 170–71** (1777). The Patriot victory at **Saratoga « 162–63**, in October 1777, was won under the command of Washington's rival, General Horatio Gates.

FIGHTING FIT

Washington believed that success lay in having a professional army, so he had organized training for the troops from Prussian volunteer Baron Friedrich von Steuben during their encampment at **Valley Forge « 184–85**.

American Options

The United States faced difficult questions as the war approached its fourth year. They had declared their independence and secured an alliance with the French, but internal divisions remained and the ill-clothed army was starving.

As the army suffered at Valley Forge in the winter of 1777–78, Washington weighed his options for the coming year's campaign. They could attack the British in Philadelphia or strike against long-occupied New York. Alternatively, as he explained to his officers, he thought his troops could remain "quiet in a secure, fortified Camp … arranging the army," while waiting for the British to make

An independent army

This chart is believed to show the organization of the Continental Army's northern department in around 1778–80, with "thirty-three battalions in the front line and fifteen battalions in the rear line."

a move, and then "govern ourselves accordingly." Delegates from northern states, however, looked again to another campaign in Canada. With General Burgoyne's army captured at Saratoga (see pp.162–63), the huge province was vulnerable. The Congress proposed Lafayette lead the "irruption" into Canada, hoping the French-speaking inhabitants would rally to his flag. A victorious offensive could finally end the war.

Washington objected: the Congress's plan was a "child of folly" that would be "productive of capital ills." He was convinced the proposed invasion

Cap in hand

Supplies were so short that at one point Washington distributed uniforms by lottery. Soldiers often wore their own hats and breeches.

would suffer the same fate as the effort in 1775–76—or worse, expose the invading Continentals to the fate of Burgoyne's army.

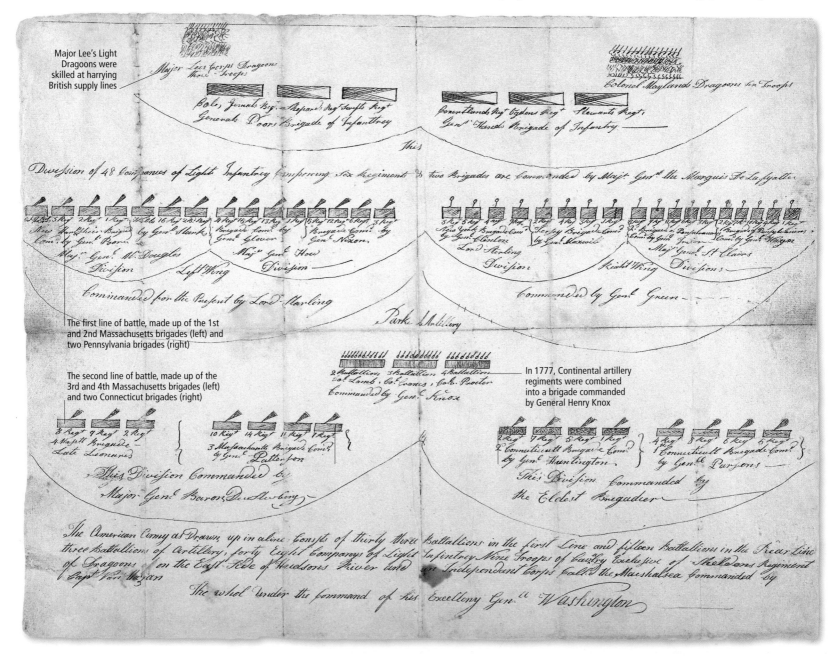

Major Lee's Light Dragoons were skilled at harrying British supply lines

The first line of battle, made up of the 1st and 2nd Massachusetts brigades (left) and two Pennsylvania brigades (right)

The second line of battle, made up of the 3rd and 4th Massachusetts brigades (left) and two Connecticut brigades (right)

In 1777, Continental artillery regiments were combined into a brigade commanded by General Henry Knox

In part, Washington objected to the plan because he perceived General Horatio Gates's fingerprints on it. Gates had ended 1777 as the hero of Saratoga; Washington, by contrast, had lost Philadelphia, and the war dragged on. Washington's allies passed along rumors that Thomas Conway—a volunteer recently arrived from France whom the Continental Congress had made a general—was plotting against Washington. "Heaven has been determined to save your Country," Conway allegedly wrote to Gates, "or a weak General and bad Counselors would have ruined it."

Internal feuds

Washington's underlings encouraged their commander's suspicions that some in the Congress were "holding up General Gates to the people," and "making them believe that you have done nothing." Washington quickly became convinced a cabal of officers was plotting to replace him with Gates as commander in chief.

Conway was, indeed, not alone in criticizing Washington: General Johann de Kalb, a German volunteer, thought

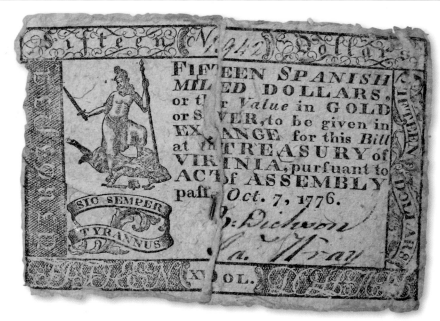

Paper promise
A sword-brandishing Liberty adorns a "fifteen dollar bill," the highest denomination in a series of bills issued by the state of Virginia to help to fund the war. The holder of this flimsy piece of paper would hope to redeem its value at a later date.

questions of seniority and promotions. John Adams complained that "Jealousies, Envy, and Distrust" alone drove these soldiers: "I am wearied to Death with the Warfare between military officers, high and low."

In fact, many officers had served since 1775 or 1776 and had suffered danger and deprivation without, they thought, adequate compensation. In

paper without sufficient gold or silver coinage to back it. Farmers resisted trading provisions to the Continental Army for paper currency doomed to depreciate in value, deeming it "no better than oak leaves and fit for nothing but Bum fodder."

Economic disruption and the collapse of the Continental currency limited the Patriots' military options. By May 1778, the Congress realized it had to reorganize its army. Not only did it reduce the total number of infantry regiments supplied by the states to 80, but it also cut the size of each regiment by one-third. Under the new organization, gradually implemented across the rest of the year, well-organized Massachusetts was responsible for raising 15 regiments, while populous Virginia and Pennsylvania each had to field 11. On the other end of the scale, tiny Delaware and thinly-populated

Georgia were required to raise only a single regiment apiece.

Hiring soldiers proved arduous, as enlistment bounties and pay fell in value while wartime labor shortages pushed civilian wages up. Supplying the army with food, fodder, and clothes also became difficult. The Congress and the states rushed to keep up, offering more rewards for service. As a result, soldiers who had enlisted in 1776 or 1777 not only saw the value of their bounties evaporate but also encountered new recruits who received far more to enlist than they had themselves. In the meantime, the Patriot cause would suffer defections, mutinies, crushing supply shortages, and desperately low morale among both soldiers and civilians.

AFTER

Even with French backing the Continental Army continued to suffer from a shortage of funds, but Washington's leadership was unshakable after 1778.

MONEY PROBLEMS
The currency crisis would reach its nadir by 1780, when inflation reached 1,000 percent and wagon-loads of currency were required to purchase one wagon of food for the army. Trade out of Philadelphia fell to one-seventeenth of its prewar levels by 1779, and Virginia's **tobacco exports**, which had been 100 million pounds a year in the 1770s, dropped to 1.6 million pounds a year by the end of the war. An accelerating currency crisis necessitated drastic reforms in 1781.

UNORTHODOX TACTICS
Although Washington believed success lay in having a disciplined army, **Patriot militia bands and guerrilla fighters 268–69 ❯❯** played a significant role in the latter stages of the war, especially in the South.

"They worry one another like Mastiffs. **Snarling for Rank and Pay** like Apes for Nutts."

JOHN ADAMS, COMPLAINING ABOUT CONTINENTAL ARMY OFFICERS, MAY 1777

Washington "the weakest general" under whom he had served. De Kalb suspected that if Washington achieved "anything sensational he will owe it more to his good luck or his adversary's mistakes than to his own ability." Some American politicians agreed. Benjamin Rush, a signatory of the Declaration of Independence and the army's surgeon general, anonymously denounced Washington to Patrick Henry, governor of Virginia. A different general at the head of the army—perhaps Charles Lee or Horatio Gates—would, he claimed, "in a few weeks render them irresistible." Henry, though, sent the letter to Washington, who recognized the handwriting, and Rush resigned from the army.

Washington had a sharp eye for political opportunity. He defended himself and slandered his critics as "concealed enemies" and "secret traitors," driving them out of the service. Feelings of suspicion and agitation were not confined, though, to Washington. His officers in the Continental Army had also felt increasing disaffection as the war lengthened, wrangling constantly over

1778, their proposed solution looked to the practices followed in the British Army, whereby officers who served to the end of the war would receive an annual pension of half their army pay, while those who returned to civilian life could sell their commissions.

The proposals, though, struck against the republican spirit of the cause. Worse, the officers threatened to resign if the Congress did not meet their demands. Washington argued that without these inducements his officers had "no sufficient ties" to keep them in the field. Despite worsening financial conditions in the states, the Congress caved in and voted to provide officers with half-pay pensions for seven years after the war.

Financial squeeze

A far greater threat to the Patriot cause than infighting at headquarters or squabbles between officers and the Congress was, however, posed by the growing economic crisis. By 1778, the Continental dollar had fallen to a quarter of its 1775 value. The Congress had printed too much

Flawed hero
After Horatio Gates's victory at Saratoga in 1777, the Congress appointed him president of the Board of War, effectively making him Washington's superior. Gates resigned from the post when his part in moves to undermine Washington were exposed.

In 1776–77, Britain failed to execute a successful strategy to win the war in North America. Although Britain won most of the battles, the Patriots' few successes proved very damaging.

ONE DECISIVE ACTION
After rejecting the Congress's **Olive Branch petition** in August 1775 « 62–63, British politicians chose to believe they could deliver "one decisive action" that would bring the colonies to heel. In summer 1776, even as they attacked **New York City** « 118–19, the Howe brothers tried to negotiate a compromise for peace. Patriot leaders, however, had already committed themselves to fight with their **Declaration of Independence**, and rejected the approach.

By the end of 1777, despite the weakness of Washington's army, Britain's search for a decisive battlefield victory had proved vain. Britain had bases in New York and Philadelphia but needed a plan for what to do next.

THE OLIVE BRANCH PETITION, DATED JULY 8, 1775

Rethinking British Strategy

With neither side achieving a decisive military breakthrough and France on the verge of entering the war, the British were forced to review their aims. Their focus now turned toward the valuable Caribbean islands, protection of home soil, and gaining control of the South.

The capture of General Burgoyne's army at Saratoga shocked the British at the end of 1777. To make things even worse, there were reports from spies of negotiations between the American rebels and the French. Voices in Britain, including that of the historian and Member of Parliament Edward Gibbon, doubted the sanity of continuing "a war whence no reasonable man entertains any hope of success."

Overtures of peace
Desperate to bring an end to the fighting before French meddling widened the war, in early 1778, Prime Minister Lord North proposed a peace mission to America. Led by the young Earl of Carlisle, the commissioners were empowered to meet with the Congress "as if it were a legal body" and to offer a treaty to bring the war to a close. Britain would agree to stop imposing taxes, remove troops, and act in future only with the consent of colonial legislatures. However, although Lord North's plan offered Americans peace and self-rule within the empire, the emissaries could not under any circumstances recognize American independence.

The British may have hoped to make a secret deal. One of Carlisle's colleagues was William Eden, in effect head of the British secret service, who had been in contact with Benjamin Franklin in Paris in 1777 and 1778, and also had several of his associates on the British payroll.

In the end, as far as the Congress was concerned, it was too little, too late. The Congress had ratified the treaties with France a month before the Commission arrived in America in June 1778. When the commissioners asked for a meeting, the Congress instead demanded the withdrawal of British forces and recognition of independence before any negotiation could take place, pinning their hopes on the strength of their arms—and on their alliance with France.

War with France posed a heavy, but familiar threat to the British. King George described the old French enemy as "Faithless and insolent," while Secretary of State Lord Sandwich insisted to Lord North that the Bourbon powers of France and Spain were "at bottom our inveterate enemies." As a result, while the Franco-Patriot alliance complicated Britain's strategic situation, it clarified the politics of the war, making it harder to make peace with the Patriots. The Whig opposition party may have been uncomfortable with conducting a war against their kin in America, but,

> " Fifty thousand **veteran troops have not,** in three years … **secured possession of 50 miles of ground in America!**"
>
> ESSAY IN *THE PUBLIC LEDGER*, LONDON, DECEMBER 12, 1777

as one French observer saw it, the British as a whole were "shamelessly eager" to fight France.

Allocating resources
With the entry of the French into the war, Britain faced threats in new theaters and could no longer afford to focus exclusively on the rebellious colonies in North America. France had at least 33 ships of the line ready in its Atlantic and Mediterranean squadrons, forcing Britain to allocate at least half of its 40 ships of the line to a Channel Fleet to defend its own shores. Further division of its naval forces would invite invasion at home or defeat in North American or Caribbean waters. Britain could either protect the home islands or maintain naval superiority on the American side of the Atlantic.

Despite calls to reinforce the squadron in America, the British ministry kept the fleet near England.

This proved prescient: when a French squadron sailed from the Brittany port of Brest that summer, a British fleet, under Admiral Augustus Keppel, was able to confront it on July 27, 1778, off the tiny French island of Ushant. The collision of the old foes was indecisive.

Change of plans
While the British government awaited a response to its peace overtures to the Continental Congress and prepared to counter a renewed French threat, it also reassessed its strategy against the rebels. Even if America could not be conquered, the strength of the empire

| The Battle of Ushant had no clear winner—the British lost 133 men, the French 161—yet both sides claimed they had the advantage.

Head of the commission
Frederick Howard, the 5th Earl of Carlisle, was only 30 years old when appointed to lead Britain's ill-fated peace commission to the Continental Congress in 1778, carrying Lord North's promises for self-rule.

No deal
A French print mocks parliament's attempt to reconcile with its colonies. The envoy, riding on an ass, is driven back to Britain by angry Americans. Only one Loyalist attempts to tie the British ass to American shores.

Changes in Britain's tactics following French intervention and the Patriots' growing self-belief were inevitable. The new strategies, though, would lead to new problems.

BRITISH FOCUS SHIFTS
As Britain redeployed its soldiers and ships to confront the French enemy, the war would now **extend into the Caribbean 218–19 »**, with both sides attacking valuable enemy-held sugar islands. Ports in Georgia and the Carolinas were a thousand miles nearer the sugar islands than New York, making bases in the South more important in British eyes.

VICIOUS CIVIL WAR
The Southern Strategy, however, would bring **civil war to Georgia and the Carolinas 268–69 »**, with Patriot and Loyalist partisans and guerrillas falling on each other like wolves, and the number of Loyalists never meeting British expectations. The British won almost all the major battles in the South during 1779–81 but this was not decisive. Able and utterly ruthless Patriot guerrilla commanders such as Thomas Sumter and Francis Marion ensured that the areas under British control were increasingly limited.

might still prevent full independence. To the north, Canada remained safely under British control. In the West, Britain's Native American allies were fighting fiercely to maintain their independence and keep back encroaching American settlers. After the evacuation of Boston and the defeat at Saratoga, rebellious New England was a lost cause and would be ignored for now. British forces were secure in lower New York, dominating the middle colonies even if they could not reconquer them. However, the sprawling, sparsely settled slave colonies of the South—Virginia, the Carolinas, and Georgia—were rich from the export of tobacco and rice, and far too valuable to the empire to lose without a fight.

Britain's new plan for 1778 therefore rested on two pillars: a renewed focus on regaining the southern colonies and on harnessing the support of loyal Americans—including those afraid that

war would disrupt their hold over a massive population of slaves. In theory, small British armies, strengthened by a suppressed Loyalist majority ready to spring to arms, would be able to restore royal authority in the southern colonies.

Heading south
This "Southern Strategy" would define the rest of the war. As news of the developing Franco-Patriot alliance trickled back to London, the British

ministry set the new plan in motion, accepting General William Howe's resignation and reassigning the commanders. Although he was mistrusted by Lord North, General Henry Clinton was elevated to command almost by default and ordered to reinforce his position in New York.

While Clinton was instructed to fight Washington's army if a good chance arose, the mid-Atlantic states would cease to be a zone for British offensives. Clinton was to redeploy 10,000 of his soldiers—half to reinforce the West Indies and target the rich French island of St. Lucia; the rest to man stations in Canada and Florida. A smaller force of 3,500 soldiers, from Hessian, Highland, and Loyalist regiments, would sail for Georgia to attack Savannah. If the redeployment of troops made holding Philadelphia impossible, then that city could be abandoned to the rebels. The Southern Strategy was underway—but with no clear plan on how to follow up successful action.

War comes to Europe
The Battle of Ushant, which took place in the western approaches to the English Channel, was the first major naval engagement between British and French fleets following the Franco-Patriot alliance in 1778.

The **March** from **Philadelphia**

British occupation of Philadelphia proved brief, as the prospect of war with France forced a change in tactics and the evacuation of the Patriots' capital. The Continental Army now had an opportunity to attack British forces on the march.

The British had enjoyed an easy winter in Philadelphia. Ample food, comfortable shelter, and the pleasant company of the city's fairest marked a stark contrast with the conditions suffered by Washington's Continentals merely 40 miles (65 km) away at Valley Forge. Although a third of the captured city's population had fled, 20,000 inhabitants remained and cooperated with the occupying force.

Rounds of parties for the king's dashing officers, as well as concerts, entertainments, and parades for the rank and file, were the order of the day. It was perhaps little wonder that at least 1,100 Continentals deserted to join their more comfortable opponents. However, Loyalists in the city were outraged that General William Howe was neglecting offensive operations against the adversary at Valley Forge.

British retreat

Howe had, in fact, tendered his resignation in October 1777. He was relieved by General Henry Clinton, who arrived in Philadelphia in May 1778 carrying new instructions: British forces were to evacuate Philadelphia and turn their attention to the South. George III himself had realized the new strategic situation. With a war against France coming, he had told Lord North in March, "It is a joke to think of keeping Pennsylvania."

Word of the imminent evacuation filled Philadelphia's Loyalists with terror. Both honor and policy required Clinton to aid them, so he promised passage to New York by sea. Three thousand people lined up to depart for exile in June.

With his fleet overloaded with Loyalist refugees, Clinton was forced to push his army overland across New Jersey to the safety of New York City. Washington's spies noted their preparations and reported the British march on June 18.

Progress proved painfully slow. With 10,000 soldiers, plus artillery pieces and 1,500 wagons, the column of Clinton's army stretched 12 miles (19 km). It took almost a week to cover the first 35 miles (56 km) of the 100-mile (160 km) route from Philadelphia to the relative safety of the New Jersey coast, especially

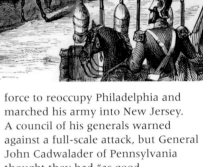

The general's send-off
Howe's departure from Philadelphia was celebrated with a *meschianza* (Italian for "medley"), in the style of a medieval tournament. The event cost more than £12,000, in excess of $2 million today.

with Patriot militias hindering the march by downing trees and destroying bridges along the way.

Plan of action

Washington was eager to attack Clinton's column. He knew their numbers were well matched—his regiments fielded 13,000 soldiers—and Patriot skills and spirits had recovered at Valley Forge. He dispatched a small

force to reoccupy Philadelphia and marched his army into New Jersey. A council of his generals warned against a full-scale attack, but General John Cadwalader of Pennsylvania thought they had "as good an opportunity as we shall probably have during this Contest to strike a

The British had spent three years trying to crush the rebellion in North America but the Patriots had proved surprisingly resilient and had grown in confidence.

WASHINGTON'S CAMP CHEST

LIMITED CONTROL
Despite the capture of major cities, British generals had been **unable to destroy the Continental Army** in the northern states. British sovereignty existed only in occupied areas, extending no farther than the range of their guns.

AMERICAN RESOLVE
The rallying of the Continental Army in its winter camp at **Valley Forge** « 184–85 gave the rebels renewed vigor and, away from the main armies, Patriot militia were terrorizing Loyalists and crushing resistance.

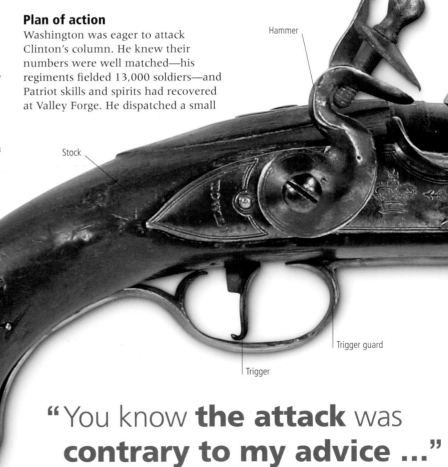

Hammer

Stock

Trigger guard

Trigger

> "You know **the attack** was **contrary to my advice …**"
>
> GENERAL CHARLES LEE TO WASHINGTON ON THE ACTION AT MONMOUTH, 1778

decisive Blow." General Anthony Wayne agreed: even if an attack ended in defeat, the public would note the British withdrawal and believe Washington's men had done their part at "Burgoyning Clinton."

Unconvinced the Patriots could stand against British regulars, General Charles Lee—recently returned to the army via a prisoner exchange—strongly advised against attack. Steuben, the driller of troops at Valley Forge, offered the wisest advice: launch an attack on Clinton's vulnerable baggage train. The Continentals now moved quickly, drawing near the British column in central New Jersey in the last week of June.

Washington's initial plan detached 1,500 soldiers for a probing attack; Lee declined the command as unworthy of a major general. As command passed to Lafayette, Washington revised his design, increasing the force to more than 5,000 men. Lee now "viewed it in a very different light" and assumed command of the attack. Washington hoped this enhanced force would destroy Clinton's rear guard, an elite, but outnumbered force of 2,000 men.

Rearguard action

On the morning of June 28, Lee advanced his three divisions—led by Lafayette, Wayne, and Maxwell—toward the British rearguard which was departing Monmouth Courthouse after a 40-hour rest stop there. The Patriots had no sense of the terrain before them, however, and Lee became greatly worried when they

soldiers into the fight. Despite realizing his numerical superiority was melting away, Lee continued the attack, which began to fall into disorder. Although the Continental soldiers fought well, their officers showed far less polish. Lee's orders were ignored or changed by the commanders of the three divisions, each acting for himself. Lafayette began to withdraw, creating a cascade. Lee had not ordered a retreat, but his

as he heard (untrue) rumors that Lee's men had fired only a single volley.

Reaching Lee's position, Washington raged at the general, calling him "a damned poltroon" and demanding an explanation of the "unaccountable retreat." Before Lee could reply Washington relieved him of command.

Assuming control, Washington rallied the Continentals into the defensive position Lee had begun at the western

266 The number of days the British forces occupied Philadelphia, from marching in on September 26, 1777, to the day they evacuated the city on June 18, 1778.

Heat of battle
Washington, surrounded by officers, rallies the forces of the Continental Army at the Battle of Monmouth in 1778. Fierce fighting took place in temperatures in excess of 100°F (38°C)—37 Continentals and 59 British troops died of heat stroke.

go, relieved to count only 360 Patriot dead against 500 British soldiers. He knew, though, that he had lost an opportunity and blamed Lee, who was court-martialed and dismissed from the army. Clinton's army was shipped across from New Jersey to New York at the start of July.

Barrel

British fire power
The Elliot pattern flintlock pistol was used by the 16th (Queen's) Regiment of Light Dragoons—cavalry soldiers who fought at the Battle of Monmouth. The gun had a 9-inch (22.9 cm) barrel firing a .62-inch (15.7 mm) caliber metal ball.

came to three deep ravines that would slow reinforcements or complicate a retreat. He pressed on, though, confident in his numerical superiority.

As Lee's divisions began to skirmish with the rear guard commanded by Cornwallis, Clinton threw 4,000 more

Ramrod

army was wavering and he began to pull the men back, hoping to forestall a disorderly panic. He aimed to take up a strong defensive position on the far side of the westernmost ravine.

Washington, at headquarters 7 miles (11 km) from the fighting, was in the dark. Lee had failed to update him on the situation. Instead the commander in chief learned of the withdrawal from a boy walking away from the fighting. The shocking news left him "exceedingly surprised and rather exasperated." Washington's rage grew

ravine, pulling up reinforcements. During the rest of the afternoon, Clinton launched three assaults despite the intolerably hot conditions, while Patriot and British artillery dueled for hours. As darkness fell, Clinton withdrew his men "fainting with fatigue, heat, and want of water."

Washington and his men slept on the battlefield, determined to renew the attack in the morning, only to find Clinton's force had slipped away in the night. His political and strategic purpose fulfilled, Washington let them

AFTER ›

Monmouth proved the war's last major engagement in the northern states. The British—and the conflict—became focused on the South.

JOINT HONORS
Both sides insisted they had met their goals at Monmouth, the longest day of fighting and the largest exchange of artillery since the war began. Washington had attacked the British and for the first time had held the battlefield; Clinton had successfully **delivered his army to New York**. The **stalemate** that had begun the year would continue.

GLOBAL CONFLICT
Under pressure to **protect its European and Caribbean interests 218–19 ››** from the French, Britain concentrated on Georgia and the Carolinas. In so doing, Britain hoped to weaken rebellious Virginia and protect its most valuable assets.

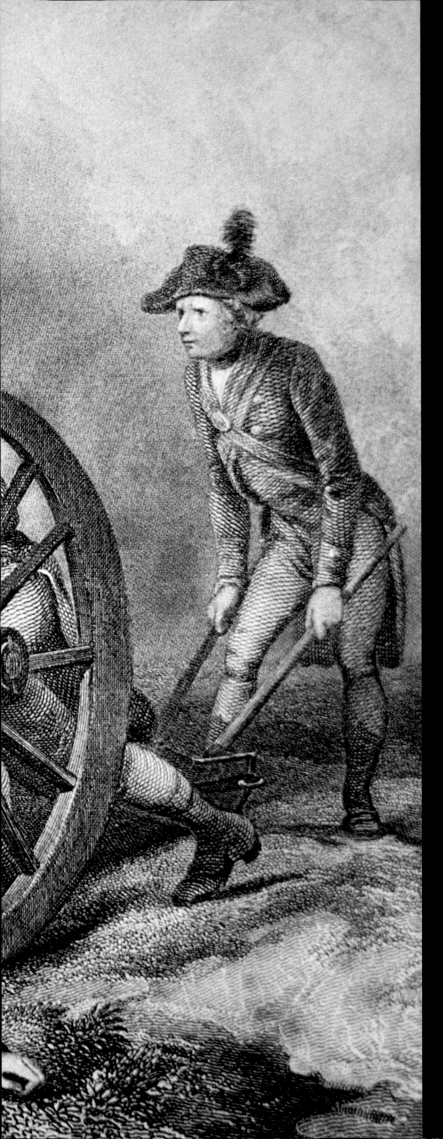

Molly Pitcher

Throughout the War of Independence, women stood on battlefields, working beside their soldier husbands. The legendary "Molly Pitcher"—a woman who carried water to soldiers and the artillery, then manned her fallen husband's cannon—is a composite character based on at least two eyewitness accounts of a woman identified by some as Mary Ludwig Hays McCauly at the Battle of Monmouth as well as other recollections of the war.

"One of the camp women I must give a little praise to. Her gallant, whom she attended in battle, being shot down, she immediately took up his gun and cartridges and like a Spartan heroine fought with astonishing bravery, discharging the piece with as much regularity as any soldier present. This a wounded officer, whom I dressed, told me he did see himself, she being in his platoon, and assured me I might depend on its truth.**"**

DIARY ENTRY OF CONTINENTAL ARMY SURGEON DR. ALBIGENCE WALDO

"One little incident happened, during the heat of the cannonade, which I was eye-witness to, and which I think would be unpardonable not to mention. A woman whose husband belonged to the Artillery, and who was then attached to a piece in the engagement, attended with her husband at the piece the whole time; while in the act of reaching a cartridge and having one of her feet as far before the other as she could step, a cannon shot from the enemy passed directly between her legs without doing any other damage than carrying away all the lower part of her petticoat—looking at it with apparent unconcern, she observed, that it was lucky it did not pass a little higher, for in that case it might have carried away something else, and ended her and her occupation.**"**

JOSEPH PLUMB MARTIN IN HIS MEMOIR, *A NARRATIVE OF SOME OF THE ADVENTURES, DANGERS, AND SUFFERINGS OF A REVOLUTIONARY SOLDIER*, 1830

Fighting on the frontline
The story of a woman taking over from her fallen husband to load cannons and man artillery caught the Patriots' imagination. After the war, "Molly Pitcher" inspired numerous paintings and engravings.

Women and the Revolution

Colonial America was a patriarchal society which expected women to be subservient to men. For women of all classes, the war brought, for its duration, new dangers, but also new freedoms and opportunities to influence events.

Under the legal principle of "coverture" that applied in both Britain and its colonies, women did not possess an independent legal identity. They were "covered," first by their fathers, then by their husbands. This usually blocked them from signing contracts or owning property. The proper place and status of women was well-defined. While men could engage in "public" life, for example participating in politics, a woman's "proper sphere" was a private, domestic one. Political action was considered to be contrary to a woman's natural place and ability.

The War of Independence tested the limits of colonial gender roles. The success of boycotts, protests, and the economic sanctions introduced by the Continental Association in 1774, relied on the participation of colonial women willing to act in defense of American liberties. One example of this rising female politicization appeared in North Carolina in 1774, when the women of Edenton published an agreement to forgo British goods "until … all acts which tend to enslave our Native country shall be repealed."

> **The British allowed only female visitors on their prison ships. In 1778, Elizabeth Burgin helped some 200 Patriot prisoners escape from ships in New York's harbor.**

On the home front
War increased the political and material demands on women, especially when it came to domestic production. The growing of crops, raising stock, spinning thread, and weaving cloth all became political acts by which women supported the cause. As the men marched to war, wives and daughters were left to run farms and trades. Their correspondence reveals a change in attitudes, with reports to absent husbands beginning to refer to "our farm," or even "my farm" rather than "your farm."

Women took other actions to support the revolutionary cause. In July 1777 a riot erupted in Boston when a group of female shopkeepers attacked "an eminent, wealthy, stingy Merchant," breaking into his warehouse to punish him for hoarding and inflating prices.

"A large concourse of men stood amazed, silent spectators of the whole transaction," Abigail Adams wrote.

In 1779, elite women in Philadelphia took action in a different way, organizing a fundraising campaign for soldiers of the Continental Army. These women were not only persistent—one Loyalist complained that "people were obliged to give them something to get rid of them"—but they were also effective, collecting more than $300,000 ($6 million today) with a view to giving each man $2. When Washington protested, fearing his men would spend it on alcohol, the "Ladies of Philadelphia" obtained shirts for the army instead, proving themselves more effective supporters of their soldiers' welfare than the Continental Congress.

Mission of mercy
During the Battle of Bemis Heights British camp follower Lady Harriet Acland courageously crossed the Hudson River into rebel territory in search of her wounded husband, Colonel John Dyke Acland.

◀◀ **BEFORE**

The traditional order in the colonies blocked women from political life and mocked those who ventured beyond their expected role.

A WOMAN'S PLACE
Society viewed women and men as physically, intellectually, and emotionally different, but complementary. Women were **defined in relation to the men** in their lives. Obedient daughters were expected to become good wives—life partners who balanced their husbands manly qualities and labors. Political discourse defined virtue—the key attribute that enabled a community to defend its liberty—as a quality pertaining to men. Times of crisis, however, regularly tested these commonplace expectations.

Liberty cap

Heroines and spies
When war threatened their families or communities, women began to act with a new independence. Sybil Ludington was only 16 when she rode 40 miles (65 km) through the night to warn colonial forces in Connecticut about a British raid on Danbury in April 1777. Women also proved to be invaluable messengers and spies. Many took great risks to gather intelligence on the enemy—sometimes opportunistically, but also

Symbol of the nation
A late-18th-century banner depicts Lady Liberty, or Columbia, wielding a liberty pole adorned with a liberty cap. Like the eagle and snake also featured, Lady Liberty was taken up as a key symbol of the new republic.

as members of organized spy rings. A mysterious "Agent 355" in the so-called Culper Spy Ring, formed by Washington to report on the British in New York, is believed to have played a key role in uncovering the deception of Benedict Arnold.

While this woman's true identity is unknown, the names and feats of many spy heroines have become part of the history of the war. In South Carolina, 18-year-old Emily Geiger turned her hand to espionage. Captured by the British while carrying a message for General Greene, Geiger was let free when her inquisitors could find no papers on her: Geiger had memorized the message, and then eaten it to destroy the evidence. Geiger went about her missions in her usual dress, but many others went undercover to gather intelligence. In October 1775, Deborah Champion claimed she had eluded a British patrol by disguising herself as an old woman

PATRIOT SOLDIER 1760–1827

DEBORAH SAMPSON

Disguising herself as a man, Deborah Sampson enlisted in a Massachusetts regiment in 1782 under the name of Robert Shurtliff. Sampson fought the British in several skirmishes, taking a sword cut to her head and two musket balls in her thigh near Tarrytown, New York. To avoid detection, she cut out one ball herself. Deborah served for 17 months before a doctor discovered her true sex. He informed General Peterson, and Sampson recieved an honorable discharge. After the war Sampson gave a lecture tour detailing her experiences.

DEBORAH SAMPSON.

in order to pass a message to George Washington from her father—a commissary general.

In a similar vein, during the Siege of Ninety-Six, Patriots Grace and Rachel Martin dressed in their husbands' clothes and borrowed their pistols to successfully accost a British dispatch as it passed through their town. The Martins intercepted key intelligence, sending it on to General Greene, before changing their clothes and

" You will **not consider** yourself as **commander in chief** of your **own house.** "

LUCY KNOX, WIFE OF CONTINENTAL ARMY GENERAL HENRY KNOX, 1777

returning home, only to find the men they had attacked at their kitchen table, looking for shelter. Feigning ignorance, the Martins were able to avoid detection.

On the front lines

While many women stayed at home, it was also quite common for them to travel with armies. At least 400 women lived with the army at Valley Forge, cooking, mending, and

Behind the lines

A 1782 print shows two camp followers doing laundry. Although camp followers were mostly wives and relatives of the troops, some were "lewd women," prostitutes.

washing. However, revolutionary women did more than just laundry—some acted as nurses, and others found themselves on the frontlines. A few bound their breasts, cut their hair, and enlisted under male names, including Ann Bailey and Deborah Sampson. Bailey was promoted to corporal before being discovered, arrested, and imprisoned. Real women—Margaret Corbin and Mary Hays McCauley—even gave rise to a legendary figure called Molly Pitcher (see pp.198–99).

Some women were thanked for their service in the War of Independence, awarded pensions, and recognized as war heroines. Margaret Corbin, or "Captain Molly," was the first woman to receive a pension in the United States. Many more women, however, saw their contributions go unnoticed—their names and deeds lost to history.

AFTER »

Women's expectations increased after the war, but it took another 50 years to achieve significant changes for women in law or custom.

BORN TO RAISE SONS

After the war, reformers in the United States campaigned to expand **education for women**. Only a woman who could read and reason, it was argued, would be able to raise virtuous sons to defend the republic. This ideal of **"republican motherhood"** was, however, counterbalanced by a backlash that reserved full citizenship and the right of suffrage for (white) men.

PROGRESS AT LAST

In the 1830s, women contributed to a raft of **social reform movements**, including anti-alcohol temperance societies and, in the northern states, activism against slavery. Women were not entitled to vote in elections, and despite some state referendums, did not **achieve suffrage** until after the 19th Amendment was passed 1919.

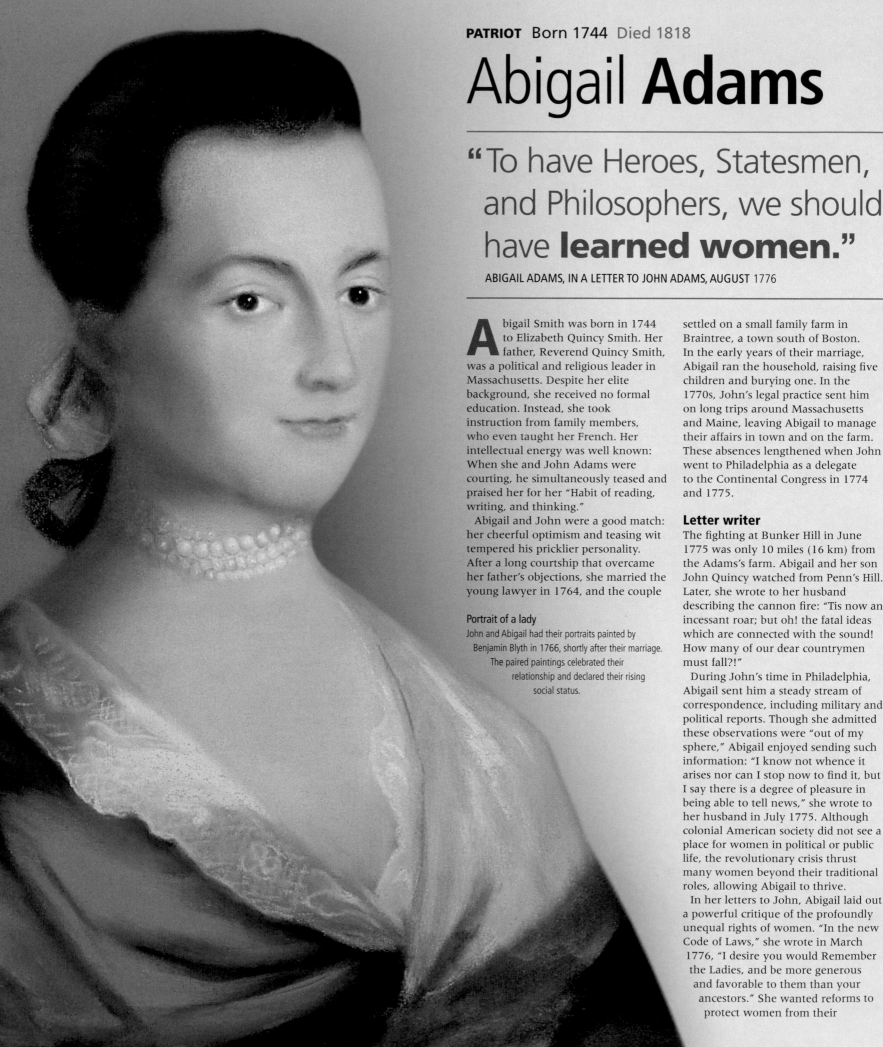

PATRIOT Born 1744 Died 1818

Abigail **Adams**

"To have Heroes, Statesmen, and Philosophers, we should have **learned women.**"

ABIGAIL ADAMS, IN A LETTER TO JOHN ADAMS, AUGUST 1776

Abigail Smith was born in 1744 to Elizabeth Quincy Smith. Her father, Reverend Quincy Smith, was a political and religious leader in Massachusetts. Despite her elite background, she received no formal education. Instead, she took instruction from family members, who even taught her French. Her intellectual energy was well known: When she and John Adams were courting, he simultaneously teased and praised her for her "Habit of reading, writing, and thinking."

Abigail and John were a good match: her cheerful optimism and teasing wit tempered his pricklier personality. After a long courtship that overcame her father's objections, she married the young lawyer in 1764, and the couple

Portrait of a lady
John and Abigail had their portraits painted by Benjamin Blyth in 1766, shortly after their marriage. The paired paintings celebrated their relationship and declared their rising social status.

settled on a small family farm in Braintree, a town south of Boston. In the early years of their marriage, Abigail ran the household, raising five children and burying one. In the 1770s, John's legal practice sent him on long trips around Massachusetts and Maine, leaving Abigail to manage their affairs in town and on the farm. These absences lengthened when John went to Philadelphia as a delegate to the Continental Congress in 1774 and 1775.

Letter writer
The fighting at Bunker Hill in June 1775 was only 10 miles (16 km) from the Adams's farm. Abigail and her son John Quincy watched from Penn's Hill. Later, she wrote to her husband describing the cannon fire: "Tis now an incessant roar; but oh! the fatal ideas which are connected with the sound! How many of our dear countrymen must fall?!"

During John's time in Philadelphia, Abigail sent him a steady stream of correspondence, including military and political reports. Though she admitted these observations were "out of my sphere," Abigail enjoyed sending such information: "I know not whence it arises nor can I stop now to find it, but I say there is a degree of pleasure in being able to tell news," she wrote to her husband in July 1775. Although colonial American society did not see a place for women in political or public life, the revolutionary crisis thrust many women beyond their traditional roles, allowing Abigail to thrive.

In her letters to John, Abigail laid out a powerful critique of the profoundly unequal rights of women. "In the new Code of Laws," she wrote in March 1776, "I desire you would Remember the Ladies, and be more generous and favorable to them than your ancestors." She wanted reforms to protect women from their

Shrewd trader
This ivory fan is believed to have belonged to Abigail Adams. During the war, Abigail conducted a lively trade in imported luxuries such as fans, ribbons, handkerchiefs, and fabric.

husbands—laws that would "put it out of the power of the vicious and Lawless to use us with cruelty and indignity with impunity." While her demand was serious—her sisters suffered abuse and neglect from their husbands—she was also delighting in the revolutionary spirit of the age. If John and his colleagues didn't act, Abigail warned, "we are determined to foment a Rebellion, and will not hold ourselves bound by any Laws in which

In John's absence, Abigail successfully managed the household and family finances, and took decisive economic actions to protect her family and advance their prospects. Starting early in the war, she saw opportunities to use shortages to her personal advantage. In 1776, for example, she noted the lack of pins in eastern Massachusetts and asked John to ship a supply from Philadelphia. John accordingly sent 6,000 for her to sell and barter.

In early February, 1778, John left America to take up a diplomatic posting in France. He returned to his home in Braintree in early August 1779, but in November, after the

> # " …write me **more letters!** They are **my food** by day and **my rest** by night."
>
> ABIGAIL ADAMS, IN A LETTER TO JOHN ADAMS, OCTOBER 1778

we have no voice, or Representation." With this language, Abigail repeated the political arguments that Patriots had employed against the British.

Taking charge
In the upheaval of the war and during John's long absences, Abigail matched her words with many independent actions. She made decisions that went far beyond her normal "sphere," although she hid them from anyone who might disapprove. In July 1776, when dangerous wartime epidemics threatened her family's health, Abigail herself made the decision to inoculate the children against smallpox, writing to her husband after the event from Boston. She also took charge of her children's education, and adjusted John's instructions from afar as she thought fit.

Giving credit
Abigail speculated in risky government securities similar to this bond—a state of Massachusetts Bay promissory note— in the hope of achieving a higher return after the war.

conclusion of the Massachusetts Constitutional Convention, went back to Paris. He didn't see Abigail again for five years. During this long separation, Abigail implored her husband to write more frequently. Upon receiving a packet of three letters, she claimed, "Cheerfulness and tranquility took the place of grief and anxiety."

As the war progressed, Abigail began to import and sell scarce luxury items from Europe. With her profits, she even speculated in risky government securities. She also used her own judgment regarding her husband's instructions for buying land. Her information and insight were more up-to-date than his, which thousands of miles and months of travel time invariably made obsolete.

As the war drew to a close, Abigail stood by her demand for women's rights, complaining in 1782 that women were "deprived of a voice in Legislation" and "obliged to submit to those Laws which are imposed upon us." Even as America had won her independence, and her sons secured their rights, Abigail noted the denial of political and legal status to women.

Political powerhouse
In 1784, Abigail traveled to Europe to join her diplomat husband at the British court and on August 7, she and her daughter Nabby were reunited with him in London. There and in the early American republic, her keen observations of people and factions proved valuable contributions to the family business of politics. In 1789, John Adams became the first vice president of the United States, and in 1797 he took up the office of president. Their son, John Quincy Adams, would also hold that office.

After John's presidential term ended, the family retired to Braintree (now Quincy, Massachusetts). In a move defying contemporary custom, at the end of her life she boldly wrote her own will. Although it would not be recognized by the state, she laid out detailed instructions for the dispersal of her money and property to her granddaughters, nieces, and female servants. When she died in 1818, John and her sons carried out her wishes.

TIMELINE

- **November 22, 1744** Born in Weymouth, Massachusetts to William Smith and Elizabeth Quincy Smith.
- **Late 1761** Begins a courtship with lawyer John Adams.
- **October 25, 1764** Aged 19, marries John Adams in Weymouth.
- **July 14, 1765** Birth of first child, Abigail, called "Nabby" by the family, just short of nine months after her wedding day.
- **July 11, 1767** Birth of John Quincy Adams.
- **September 1774** Resumes a life-long habit of corresponding with husband John when he attends the first Continental Congress in Philadelphia.

ABIGAIL MARRIED JOHN ADAMS IN 1764. THEIR MARRIAGE WAS A REMARKABLE PARTNERSHIP.

- **1775** Appointed by Massachusetts Colony General Court, along with Mercy Otis Warren and Hannah Winthrop, to question women in the colony accused of loyalty to the Crown.
- **July 1777** Sixth and final pregnancy ends with the stillbirth of a daughter, Elizabeth.
- **February 1778** Stays behind with her younger children when John Adams sails for France on a diplomatic mission, taking eldest son John Quincy with him.
- **November 1779** John, selected as French Minister, departs once again for France.
- **June 1784** Takes Nabby to England to join John.
- **April 1788** Returns to the United States with her husband and children.
- **March 1789** John is inaugurated as first vice president of the United States.
- **March 1797** John inaugurated as second President of the United States. Caring for John's dying mother, she does not attend the ceremony in Philadelphia.
- **January 1800** Moves with John into the newly constructed White House in the new national capital of Washington, D.C.; lives there for five months.
- **March 1801** Returns to the home in Massachusetts following the election of Thomas Jefferson as president.
- **October 28, 1818** Dies of typhoid fever.

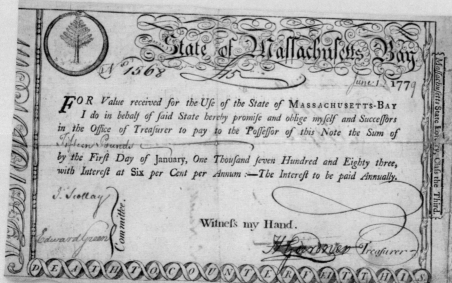

The **War** in the **North**

With the arrival of the French fleet, Washington hoped to break the stalemate around New York. A joint French and Patriot force targeted British-held Newport, Rhode Island, but bad weather, poor planning, and British reinforcements dashed hopes of victory.

« BEFORE

With the new threat from France, Britain rethought its tactics and abandoned the recently captured city of Philadelphia. The Continental Army sensed it was time to attack.

HEADING BACKWARD
Britain **evacuated Philadelphia** « 196–97 on June 18, 1778, to consolidate its forces at New York and free ships and soldiers to defend its valuable sugar islands in the Caribbean. Despite three years of campaigning, Britain appeared no closer to bringing its rebellious colonies to heel.

STANDOFF IN THE NORTH
Washington's army had remained in the field and the Continentals attacked General Clinton's withdrawing army in New Jersey at **Monmouth Courthouse** on June 28, 1778. Although both sides fought hard and well, the battle proved a draw—and would be the **last major engagement** in the northern theater of the war.

Siege of Rhode Island
A depiction from a British magazine shows General John Sullivan's troops advancing on the British at Newport during the Americans' failed siege.

By summer 1778, the British were strongly entrenched in New York; without help, Washington lacked the forces to attack the city. The French fleet, under the Comte d'Estaing, arrived on July 8, just too late to intercept the British ships that had evacuated Philadelphia. Had the French captured these ships, it would almost certainly have ended the war.

New line of attack
D'Estaing's fleet dramatically outnumbered the British squadron, tipping the balance of power, and Washington wanted to exploit the "most interesting advantages" offered by this new French force before British reinforcements, already under sail from Britain, arrived. With d'Estaing's extra men and naval strength, Washington could break his enemy's stronghold in Manhattan. The recapture of New York, Washington thought, "would have reduced to a moral certainty, the ruin of Great Britain."

D'Estaing, who had been blockading the harbor since July 11, was also eager to strike a blow against the British, but the simple physics of buoyancy thwarted the will to fight. With the French fleet poised outside New York harbor, d'Estaing's pilots reported that the channel was too shallow for their heavy warships.

Still eager, Washington and d'Estaing decided to strike the British at Newport, Rhode Island. Occupied by the British since 1776 and garrisoned by 6,700 men commanded by General Robert Pigot, the valuable port city had been invulnerable to a Patriot assault. The British position in Newport threatened southern New England and its shipping lanes. The arrival of the French fleet, however, trapped Pigot's garrison. Again, Washington sensed

the "certainty of success" and dispatched reinforcements to General John Sullivan, whose Continentals had been monitoring the occupied town. Sullivan called out the New England militia and prepared for an offensive.

Joint venture
On paper, Sullivan had 10,000 men, but they were mostly militia who were only slowly assembling, and d'Estaing had to tarry for two weeks as his

PATRIOT GENERAL 1740–95

JOHN SULLIVAN

Dispatched to pull back the failing invasion of Canada in 1776, Sullivan almost became the scapegoat for the bruising Patriot loss. At the Battle of Long Island in 1776, he fought bravely but was captured, and his failed raid on Staten Island in August 1777 provoked a Congressional inquiry. His regiments were flanked at Brandywine and fell to friendly fire at Germantown in 1777.

Dubious military success came in 1779 when he led an army through Iroquois lands, burning cornfields, houses, and orchards to punish Britain's allies. He followed his mixed military career with political success, serving in Congress, as state governor, and as a federal judge.

Patriot counterparts completed their muster. Britain's Pigot, nevertheless, fearing an imminent French attack, scuttled four frigates before they could fall into enemy hands.

Sullivan and d'Estaing proposed a joint attack on Newport beginning with simultaneous landings on August 9. The plan was for French marines to land on the west side of Aquidneck Island, while Sullivan's Continentals and militia crossed the bay and approached from the east.

However, the plan quickly fell apart. Sullivan sent his men across a day too soon, a mistake that d'Estaing, already suspicious of his new allies' competence, saw as sloppy and an affront to French honor. Worse, on the day of the French landing, British reinforcements arrived, canceling France's temporary naval superiority. D'Estaing reembarked his marines and sailed out for battle. For two days, the fleets maneuvered for favorable position, only for both to fall victim to a gale that scattered and damaged their ships before a shot could be fired.

Vulnerable isolation

Expecting the French to return after dealing with the British, Sullivan pressed ahead with the attack, digging entrenchments against Newport's defenses. His militia, though, began to melt away as deserters headed for home. Fearing the British fleet would return with even more reinforcements, d'Estaing declared on August 20 that his force would withdraw to Boston to repair its ships. The Patriot officers raged at this desertion, although the absconding of more than half of their own militia soldiers was perhaps equally damaging.

LE DESTIN MOLESTANT LES ANGLOIS.

France comes to the rescue
Comte d'Estaing presents the palm frond of victory to America, here imagined as a Native American who holds a staff topped with a liberty cap and sits on a throne of produce destined for France.

Without French aid, Sullivan turned from the attacker to the attacked. Spies reported that Clinton in New York was preparing a force to trap the Patriots in Rhode Island. On August 29, Pigot launched an attack on the retreating Continentals, who fought desperately as they escaped back to the mainland. The First Rhode Island Regiment, a battalion open to "every able-bodied Negro, mulatto or Indian man slave" in the state, fought off three attacks by British and Hessian soldiers.

Luckily for Sullivan, the British forces found it as difficult to cooperate as the French and the Patriots did. Rather than trap the Continentals, the British fleet sailed out in a fruitless effort to confront d'Estaing's battered squadron.

After the confusion at Newport, Washington was left viewing the British strength in New York from "an awkward, and disagreeable state of suspense." Rather than mounting a new combined offensive, in November, d'Estaing steered his forces toward Britain's sugar islands of the Caribbean—setting sail without even writing to Washington to tell him of his destination.

AFTER »

The invervention of the French, and Comte d'Estaing's fleet, had promised much but did not deliver in the first joint action. Washington would have to wait for the alliance to bear fruit.

MIXED FORTUNES

After the failure at Newport in 1778, the French sailed south to take France's war with Britain to the Caribbean sugar islands, where **Grenada fell** to d'Estaing's fleet. Not only was the Newport campaign a missed opportunity for Washington and the Patriot cause, but it also showed how difficult combined operations could be for the unfamiliar allies. In 1779, d'Estaing launched another ill-fated attack on the British at **Savannah 244–45 »**.

THE TAKING OF GRENADA

"An unfortunate storm ... blasted ... the fairest hopes that ever were conceived."

WASHINGTON IN A LETTER TO HIS BROTHER, JOHN AUGUSTINE, SEPTEMBER 23, 1778

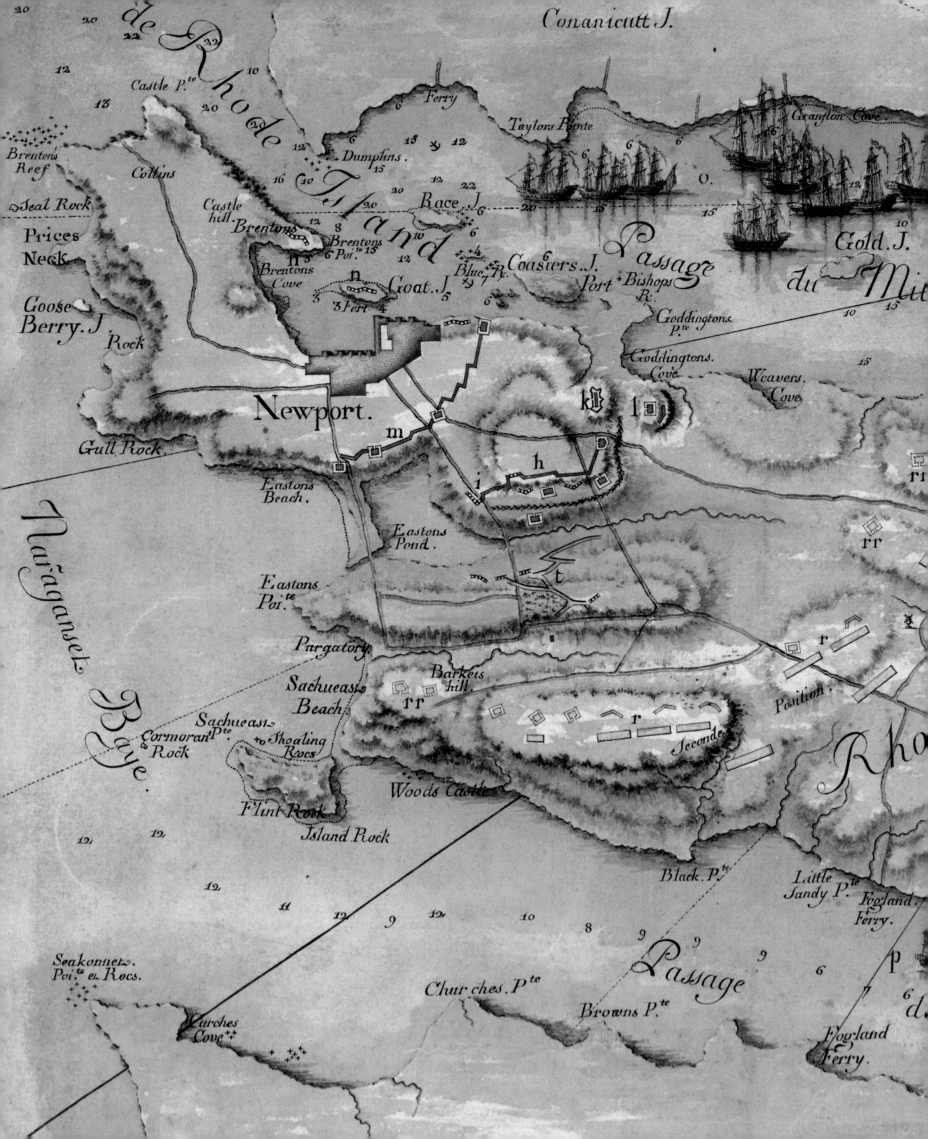

Prudence J.

Dyres. J.

Popasquash Neck

Popasquash. P.^te

Goggershall . P.^te

Redwoods.

Arnold's. P.^te

Bristol Baye.

Island.

Chemin de l'Ouest.

Almey's hill.

Hog. J.

Bris- tol Ch. de Bristol

Denfeys hill.

Basfonds dont parties a Sec dans les Grandes Marées.

Neck

Chemin de

Turkey. hill.

Premiere. Position.

Butt's hill.

Ferry de Bristol.

Ch. de Bristol.

l'Est.

a

d

Quakers. hill.

b

c

Sandy Pte

Black. P.^te

Bridge

Hon^r Thurmans P.^te

Quay

Pocasset River.

Howlands. Ferry.

l'Est.

Goulds. J.

Common Sense Pointe

Vantons Cove. Tiverton.

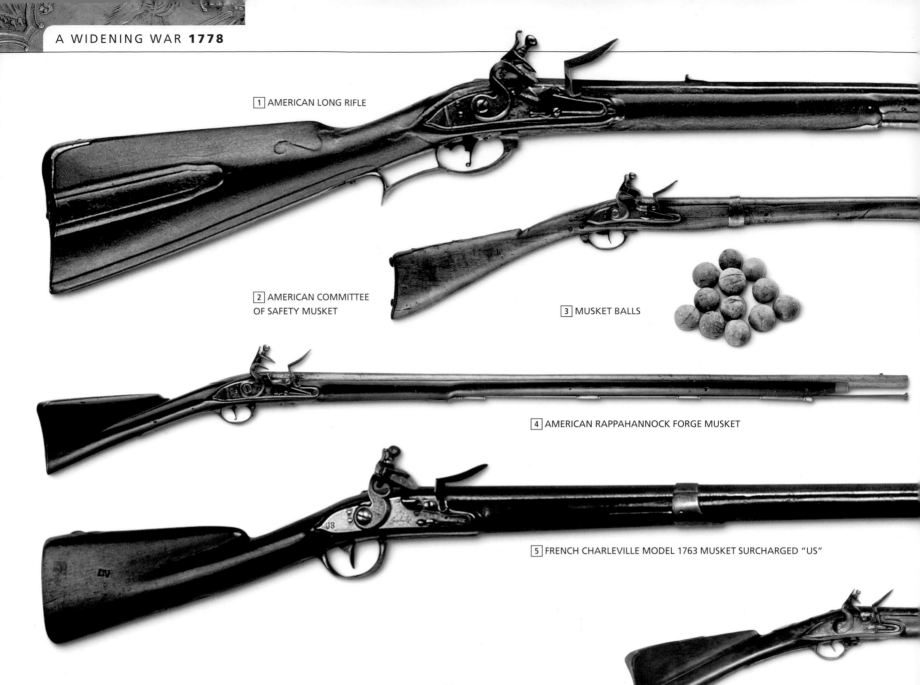

[1] AMERICAN LONG RIFLE

[2] AMERICAN COMMITTEE
OF SAFETY MUSKET

[3] MUSKET BALLS

[4] AMERICAN RAPPAHANNOCK FORGE MUSKET

[5] FRENCH CHARLEVILLE MODEL 1763 MUSKET SURCHARGED "US"

Muskets and Rifles

Most infantrymen on both sides in the War of Independence were armed with muskets—slow to load and very inaccurate. Rifles, used by some light infantry and specialized marksmen, were more accurate but took even longer to load.

[1] **American long rifle** The long rifle was popular among hunters and frontiersmen. This .54 caliber example dates from around 1760. [2] **American Committee of Safety musket** Copied from existing designs, these were produced by private gunsmiths for Patriot militia forces. [3] **Musket balls** Made of solid lead, these early bullets were packed into the barrel of the musket. [4] **Rappahannock Forge musket** Rappahannock Forge in Virginia was one of several private manufactories employed by the Continental Congress to arm its soldiers. [5] **French Charleville Model 1763 musket surcharged "US"** This example is stamped "US" on the metal lock plate. Arms of this type were supplied to the Patriots by their French allies. [6] **American socket bayonet** Bayonets were fitted around the barrel of the musket to ensure they did not interfere with the flight of the musket ball. [7] **British short land musket** This variant of the "Brown Bess" type became the standard British infantry weapon in the 1760s. This example is fitted

with a socket bayonet. [8] **American officer's fusil** This light flintlock musket was made for a Connecticut militia officer by Elijah Buell, himself a militiaman. [9] **Hessian musket** German muskets such as this one from Hesse-Kassel were modeled on the Prussian Model 1740 Potzdam Musket. [10] **Hessian Jaeger rifle** Made in Hesse-Kassel by Bernard Pistor in 1769, this was for use by marksmen from elite light infantry units, known as Jaegers, who were often deployed as skirmishers. [11] **Musket flints** Eighteenth-century muskets used a "flintlock" mechanism to fire. The necessary spark was created when the flint impacted upon steel. [12] **Powder horn** Cattle horns were used by some soldiers to store gunpowder. Soldiers often carved names, dates, and images onto the horn. [13] **Bullet mold** This Hessian example was used to create lead musket balls. [14] **Tin canister** Designed to carry 36 paper cartridges, this would originally have had a strap attached. Tin provided greater protection from rain than the more common leather cartridge pouches.

6 AMERICAN SOCKET BAYONET

7 BRITISH SHORT LAND MUSKET

8 AMERICAN OFFICER'S FUSIL

11 MUSKET FLINTS

9 HESSIAN MUSKET

12 POWDER HORN

10 HESSIAN JAEGER RIFLE

13 BULLET MOLD

14 TIN CANISTER

British Resurgence

With New York City its only significant possession and France now an active belligerent, it was time for Britain to put its new strategy to the test, with attacks in the South meant to provide the springboard for a British comeback.

⟪ BEFORE

Since the abortive British attack on Charleston in June 1776, there had been no major military operations in the South—only some increasingly disturbing guerrilla fighting.

EVACUATING PHILADELPHIA

To free up resources for a return to the South, Clinton **left Philadelphia** in June 1778, **⟪ 196–97** and headed overland across New Jersey to New York. The British forces' long wagon train carried supplies and baggage, and thousands of Loyalists left the city.

LOYALISTS AND BRITISH TROOPS CROSSING NEW JERSEY

Philadelphia had been evacuated, and New York City was safely reinforced, so in November 1778, British General Henry Clinton began executing his orders to focus his offensive actions on the southern colonies and secure these economically valuable assets for the British Crown. The new British strategy was to crush the rebellion by conquering the southern colonies and then expanding to the north.

Georgia was easily the weakest of the 13 rebellious colonies and the obvious place to begin. The most recently founded colony, its white population was small and matched in number by the population of enslaved Africans. Georgians also faced strong Indian opponents along their extensive backcountry frontier. In addition, the British had a well-defended base nearby around Saint Augustine in East Florida. British forces there, led by Brigadier General Augustine Prévost, had beaten off several attacks by Georgia militia in 1777 and 1778.

Targeting Savannah

The British identified Georgia's port and capital at Savannah as the compelling first objective. Clinton dispatched a force of 3,500 soldiers under the command of Lieutenant Colonel Archibald Campbell with clear orders: "attempt the reduction of Georgia." This force was as diverse as it was compact: Campbell led fellow Scots of the 71st Highlanders, two regiments of Hessians, and four battalions of northern Loyalists now in arms to fight for their king. His transports reached the Savannah River just before Christmas 1778.

A flawed defense

Georgia's Patriots made fatal mistakes in their defense. The British force made its way upriver toward the town, landing at a rice plantation and advancing along a causeway nearly ½ mile (0.8 km) long. "This narrow Passage led up to a House situated on an Eminence very steep," wrote

Loyalist officer's button
The King's American Regiment was raised in 1776 and fought in New York and Rhode Island before being sent south to join the campaigns in Georgia and Florida.

Howe's rear, killing nearly 100 men and capturing over 400. With just seven dead and 17 wounded in the entire operation, Campbell's force took the town and a stockpile of weapons and supplies. The fighting was all over in a matter of hours.

> ## "I have **ripped one star and one stripe** from the **rebel flag** of America."
>
> BRITISH LIEUTENANT COLONEL ARCHIBALD CAMPBELL, 1779

Stephen DeLancey, a Loyalist officer from New York. "Had the Rebels been there in Force with Cannon, it would in my opinion have been impracticable to have made good the Landing … But from great want of Generalship they had but thirty men at this strong Post."

General Robert Howe, Campbell's Patriot counterpart, was, however, vastly outnumbered with a force of just 700 Continentals and 150 Georgia militia. They were also inexperienced: only a few of Howe's Continentals had seen action earlier in the war.

Howe's officers rejected a retreat, thinking it better to make a defensive stand at the town. They deployed, Campbell would later report, "in the style of an Half Moon," blocking the main road into Savannah.

Campbell himself spied out the enemy lines from the top of an oak tree and expected a tough fight. He proved lucky a second time, however. An enslaved man—perhaps the exiled royal governor's still-loyal servant Quamino Dolly—guided Campbell's soldiers on "a private way" through a swamp to pierce the American right flank. The next day, December 29, the rebels' defeat was total: Campbell's Highlanders and Germans attacked

BRITISH ARMY OFFICER 1739–91

LIEUTENANT COLONEL ARCHIBALD CAMPBELL

Commissioned into the Royal Engineers in 1758, Campbell was wounded in General Wolfe's Siege of Quebec in 1759. Captured in 1777 on his journey to America to head Fraser's Highlanders, Campbell spent two years as a prisoner in Massachusetts before he was exchanged for Ethan Allen, leader of the Green Mountain Boys. Despite his long captivity, Campbell did not try to take revenge on the rebels during the Savannah campaign. An American officer thought he "had too nice a sense of honor to be made an instrument of injustice or oppression." In poor health, he returned to Britain in 1779. His service to the British Empire continued; he later became governor of Jamaica and then of Madras.

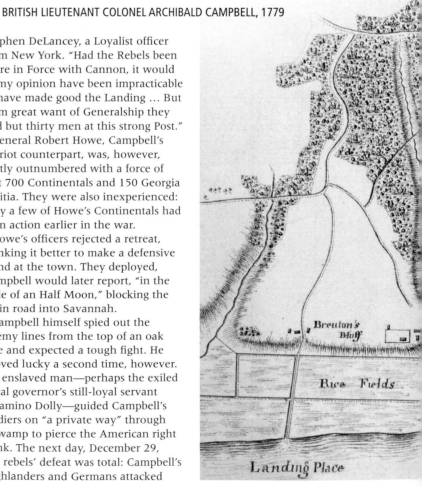

Breuton's Bluff

Rice Fields

Landing Place

German support

Hessian troops contributed to the campaign in Georgia and South Carolina. During an engagement at John's Island, South Carolina, they seized cannons and flags taken from them at Trenton at the end of 1776.

The South stumbles

Meanwhile, General Prévost invaded from East Florida to complete the reconquest of Georgia, eventually reaching Savannah in January 1779 and taking over command from Campbell. Resistance by the weak Patriot forces proved futile. "You cannot be ignorant that four armies are in motion to reduce this Province," one British officer warned the Patriots in Fort Morris, a key defensive point south of Savannah. "The resistance you can or intend to make will only bring destruction upon this country." If they surrendered their arms, however, and undertook to remain neutral "until the fate of America is determined," the British promised that former rebels would be allowed to "remain in peaceable possession of your property."

The response of John McIntosh, the Georgian commander, was bold: "We have no property compared with the object we contend for … and would rather perish in a vigorous defense than accept your proposals. We, sir, are fighting the battles of America, and therefore disdain to remain neutral till its fate is determined.

As to surrendering the fort, receive this laconic reply, 'Come and take it!'" The British did just that, bombarding the doomed fort into surrender in January 1779.

After the fall of Savannah, Sir James Wright returned to his office as royal governor—the first time during the conflict that a civilian official returned to exercise British sovereignty in a rebellious province. DeLancey, the Loyalist officer, crowed in a letter to his wife that rebels were "daily coming in and receiving Protections for their Persons and Property. The Government here established is to the greatest Degree lenient, so that I conclude … they will be sooth'd into a Change of Sentiments and receive Money and Property as Greater Goods than Rebellion and Poverty."

This promise of stability and order under a Loyalist government was the key to Britain's unfolding southern strategy. Whether they could extend these successes into the rebellious Carolinas and put themselves into a position to regain lost ground in the northern states would, they believed, determine the outcome of the war.

It would not be easy, however. In January 1779, Campbell advanced inland to occupy Augusta but had to abandon it in mid-February, leaving local Loyalists vulnerable to the usual vicious reprisals from the Patriots.

British control in Georgia survived a siege of Savannah by French and Patriot forces in 1779. Patriot defeats at Charleston and Camden in South Carolina followed in 1780.

MIXED FORTUNES

French naval power gave the Patriots the chance to recover from their initial defeats in Georgia. After capturing British possessions in the West Indies, the **Comte d'Estaing** headed north to **besiege Savannah 244–45 ❱❱**, but returned home to France in the fall of 1779, worried about the possibility of severe weather. **Victory at Camden 274–75 ❱❱** helped the British to extend their zone of control but they and their Loyalist allies pressed too hard on the captured or defeated Patriots, provoking renewed resistance.

Taking of Savannah

This contemporary map shows the British approach to the town from the southwest (south is at the top) as well as the rebels' half-moon defense line that the British outflanked.

6
CONFLICT SPREADS
1779

The American, French, and British navies took the war to Europe and even Africa, while Native American allies on both sides harassed settlements along the western frontier. At the end of the year, the main armies converged on Savannah, in a bid to control the South.

« Frontier fear
Both British and Patriot forces enlisted the help of Native American scalping parties to mount war on enemy settlements. One of the most brutal attacks was the Battle of Wyoming in Pennsylvania, depicted here by Alonzo Chappel. Iroquois warriors and Loyalists killed around 300 people.

ACTION IN 1779

As the war spread to the Caribbean, Africa, and Europe, Britain had to divert troops abroad, consolidate forces, and abandon some earlier gains. The year began well for the Patriots in the west, with Virginia militiaman George Rogers Clark leading a march on Vincennes and capturing Fort Sackville. The Patriots met with mixed fortunes later in the year. In July, a major naval expedition to take Fort George on Penobscot Bay failed, as did a joint Franco-Patriot attempt to retake Savannah in October, and although General Anthony Wayne captured Stony Point for the Patriots in July, they soon abandoned it. Meanwhile, Spain's declaration of war on Britain in April led to Bernardo de Gálvez evicting the British from Bayou Manchac, Baton Rouge, and Natchez in the fall, as well as to Spain's siege of British Gibraltar.

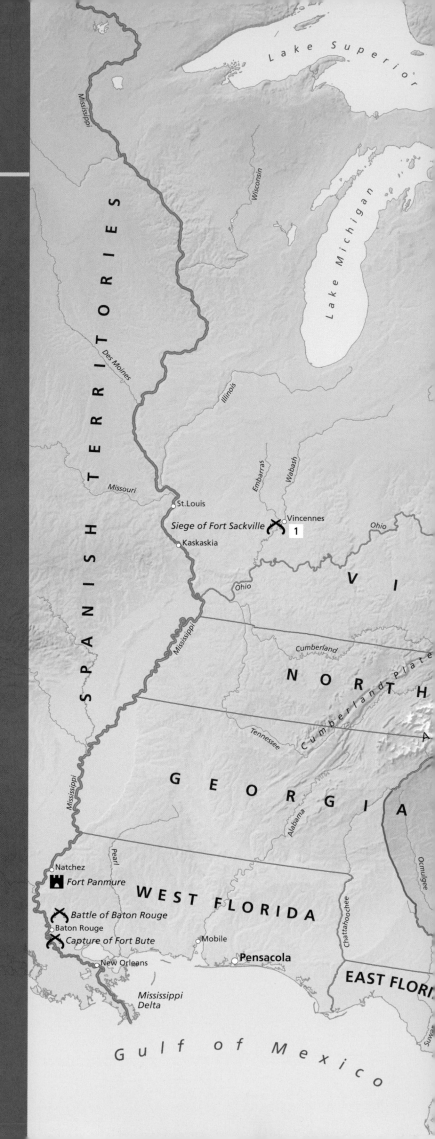

[1] George Rogers Clark and his men marched on the British garrison at Vincennes in February. [2] In July, Brigadier General Anthony Wayne launched an attack at Stony Point. [3] Franco-Patriot forces tried to take Savannah back from the British in October.

214

Newfoundland

Magdalen Islands

Louisbourg

Prince Edward Island

Quebec

Saguenay

St. Lawrence

Saint-Maurice

St. John

NOVA SCOTIA

Ottawa

Montreal

MASSACHUSETTS

Penobscot

Fort Penobscot

Bay of Fundy

Halifax

Sable Island

Lake Huron

Georgian Bay

Lake Ontario

NEW HAMPSHIRE

Penobscot Expedition

Detroit

Lake Erie

Lake Champlain

Adirondack Mountains

White Mountains

Green Mountains

Connecticut

ATLANTIC OCEAN

NEW YORK

Mohawk

Albany

Hudson

Boston

MASSACHUSETTS

Cape Cod

Battle of Newtown

Catskill Mountains

CONNECTICUT

Newport

West Point

RHODE ISLAND

2

Susquehanna

Battle of Minisink

KEY

Border of Spanish territories

1763 Proclamation Line

Colonial boundaries

○ Town / settlement

✗ Battle / siege

🏰 Fort

⛵ Naval battle

🪶 Treaty / convention

⛺ Patriot winter camp

PENNSYLVANIA

Allegheny

Morristown

New York City

Fort Pitt

Delaware

Second Continental Congress

Princeton

Muskingum

Ohio

Philadelphia

NEW JERSEY

Potomac

Baltimore

DELAWARE

MARYLAND

Kanawha

Blue Ridge

James

Chesapeake Bay

Roanoke

Yorktown

Dan

Norfolk

APPALACHIAN MOUNTAINS

ALLEGHENY MOUNTAINS

CAROLINA

Camden

Pee Dee

Cape Fear

Wilmington

SOUTH CAROLINA

Augusta

Wateree

Santee

Savannah

Cooper

Charleston

Beaufort

3

✗ Siege of Savannah

annah

Sunbury

Johns

Brunswick

N

0   100 km
0   100 miles

Mohawk

Cherry Valley Massacre

Albany

Hudson

Green Mountains

Connecticut

NEW HAMPSHIRE

NEW YORK

Battle of Newtown

Catskill Mountains

MASSACHUSETTS

Boston

Cape Cod

Susquehanna

Battle of Minisink

West Point

Fort Lafayette

New Haven

West Haven

CONNECTICUT

Newport

RHODE ISLAND

Wyoming Valley Massacre

Battle of Stony Point

Fairfield

Green's Farms

Norwalk

Greenwich

2

Lloyd's Neck

PENNSYLVANIA

Morristown

Battle of Paulus Hook

Long Island

New York City

Delaware

Princeton

NEW JERSEY

ATLANTIC OCEAN

Second Continental Congress

Philadelphia

Baltimore

MARYLAND

DELAWARE

0   100 km
0   100 miles

Native American allies ▪ **The Siege of Fort Sackville** ▪ Spain enters the war ▪ **War in the West Indies** ▪ Global possessions seized ▪ **Skirmishes in New York** ▪ Franco-Patriot Siege of Savannah ▪ **War rages at sea** ▪ The British evacuate Rhode Island

JANUARY	FEBRUARY	MARCH	APRIL	MAY	JUNE
JANUARY 9 A British and Native American force captures Sunbury, Georgia, after a three-day siege.			**APRIL 12** France and Spain sign the secret Treaty of Aranjuez formalizing their alliance against Britain.	**MAY 9–24** The Royal Navy raids Chesapeake Bay plantations and towns. **MAY 10** The British burn Norfolk, Virginia.	**JUNE 1** The British take Stony Point and Verplanck's Point on the Hudson River. **JUNE 18** French forces capture St. Vincent, in the West Indies.
JANUARY 9 British forces occupy Vincennes in the West. **JANUARY 29** A Native American and Loyalist force occupies Augusta, Georgia.	**FEBRUARY 1–2** The British occupy Port Royal Island, South Carolina. **FEBRUARY 23–25** The Siege of Fort Sackville ends in a victory for the Patriot militia.	**MARCH 3** The British abandon Augusta, Georgia, but defeat pursuing American militia at the confluence of Brier Creek and the Savannah River.		**MAY 22** A Franco-American plan to attack Liverpool, England, is canceled.	
JANUARY 31 The French take Senegal, West Africa, from the British.	**FEBRUARY 26** British forces burn property and steal cattle in West Greenwich, Connecticut.	**MARCH 6** General John Sullivan is offered command of an expedition against the Iroquois in the North. **MARCH 12** The Chasseurs-Volontaires de Saint-Domingue are established in Haiti.			
			APRIL 19 Patriot raiders led by Goose van Schaick burn the principal settlement of the Onondaga in New York.	**MAY 23** Patriot General Benedict Arnold sends intelligence to the British.	**JUNE 21** Spain declares war on Great Britain. **JUNE 24** Spanish forces besiege Gibraltar. The siege continues until 1783.

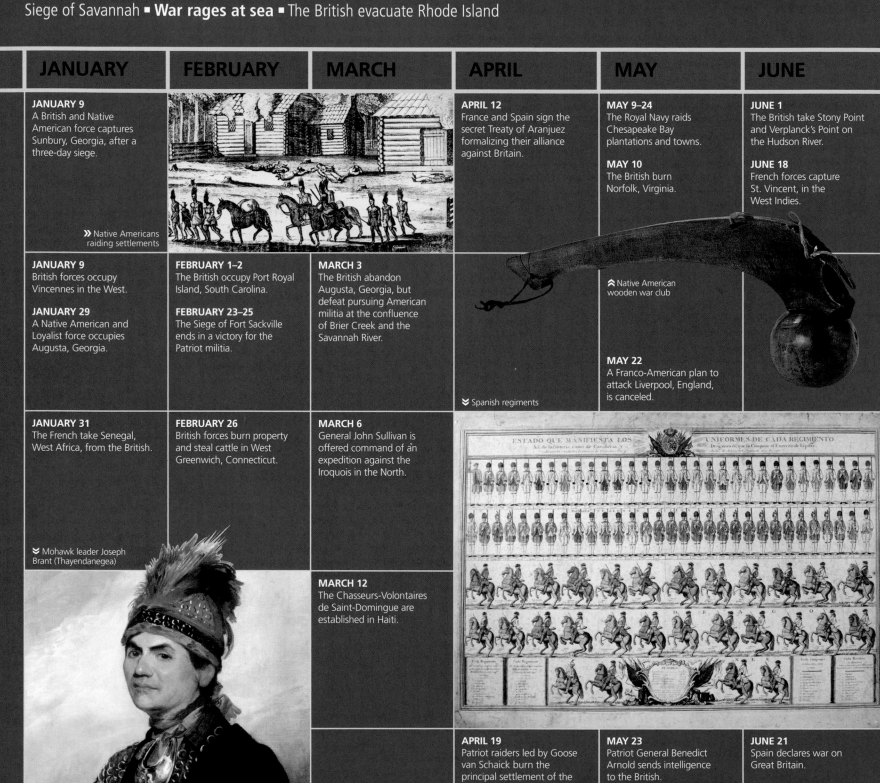

» Native Americans raiding settlements

⌃ Native American wooden war club

⌄ Spanish regiments

⌄ Mohawk leader Joseph Brant (Thayendanegea)

"Our enemies will not get aid from any power in Europe to carry on the war ... Yet ... nothing but ... the last necessity can inspire wisdom."

RICHARD HENRY LEE TO THOMAS JEFFERSON, MARCH 15, 1779

JULY	AUGUST	SEPTEMBER	OCTOBER	NOVEMBER	DECEMBER
		SEPTEMBER 3 The Franco-Spanish fleet abandons its planned invasion of England, and returns to Brest, France. **SEPTEMBER 7** The Spanish capture Fort Bute, Louisiana.	**OCTOBER 1** The Patriots take 111 Loyalists prisoner at Savage Point, Georgia.	**NOVEMBER 10** Snow begins to fall in the Northeast, beginning a harsh winter. Rivers and waterways freeze solid. Snow will continue to fall almost every day until March 1780.	**DECEMBER 1** The Continental Army enters winter quarters at Morristown, New Jersey.
⌃ D'Estaing captures Grenada in the West Indies. **JULY 1** The French capture Grenada from the British. **JULY 8–9** British raiders loot and burn Fairfield and Green Farms, Connecticut.		**SEPTEMBER 16** The Siege of Savannah begins. French and Patriot forces, including 500 from Saint-Domingue, attempt to retake Savannah.			
JULY 22 Loyalists and Native Americans led by Joseph Brant defeat Patriot militia at Minisink, New York.	**AUGUST 14** The Penobscot Expedition is destroyed by a British relief force. » Patriot fleet defeated in the Penobscot Bay		**OCTOBER 18** The Franco-Patriot Siege of Savannah ends.		
JULY 25 A Franco-Spanish fleet unites and sails for the south coast of England.	**AUGUST 14** John Paul Jones sails from France on a diversionary cruise around Britain.			**NOVEMBER 11–20** Minor skirmishes off the coast of Lisbon, Portugal take place between British and Spanish frigates.	⌃ New York Harbor **DECEMBER 26** A British fleet sets sail from New York, to Charleston, South Carolina.
« The "Pirate" John Paul Jones	**AUGUST 29** Patriot forces defeat Native Americans and Loyalists at Newtown, New York.	**SEPTEMBER 23** John Paul Jones, aboard the *Bonhomme Richard*, defeats Britain's HMS *Serapis* in battle off Flamborough Head, England.	**OCTOBER 25** The British evacuate Newport, Rhode Island.		**DECEMBER 31** British and Dutch fleets engage off the Isle of Wight, near England's south coast.

PENOBSCOT RIVER

PENOBSCOT BAY

« BEFORE

Britain's victory in the French and Indian War had upset the European balance of power, which France was keen to redress.

BRITAIN VERSUS FRANCE
Eager to restore its dominion and to regain the West Indian islands ceded to Britain in the **Treaty of Paris in 1763 « 24–25**, France had provided covert aid to the rebelling colonies and signed the **Franco-American Alliance of 1778 « 188–89**. The British reacted by **declaring war on France** and moved warships and troops to the Caribbean, in anticipation of conflict there.

GLOBAL REPERCUSSIONS
When France entered the war reverberations spread far and wide. In August 1778, for example, British forces besieged and **captured the French port of Pondicherry**, in India.

War on the Periphery

In 1779, Spain entered an alliance with France, a supporter of the Patriot cause. A local rebellion against colonial rule in America had become a worldwide conflict, as hostilities spread through Europe, Africa, and Asia.

France had long been trying to draw Spain into the war against Britain. Eventually, following extended negotiations, France and Spain signed the Treaty of Aranjuez on April 12, 1779. This secret alliance asserted that, in return for French help in capturing Gibraltar, Florida, and the Mediterranean island of Minorca from the British, Spain would support France in recovering Senegal, Newfoundland, and Dominica from Britain.

French and Spanish military leaders soon began making plans for a series of ambitious joint operations against the British mainland, envisaging an audacious attack on the port of Liverpool in northwest England followed by a Franco-Spanish invasion of the south.

War in the Sugar Islands

Meanwhile, Britain and France had been fighting for supremacy in the Caribbean. Admiral Samuel Barrington was stationed with a fleet at Barbados when the British sent him an additional 5,000 troops from New York. In December 1778, Barrington's enlarged force had captured St. Lucia, aided by a storm that delayed the arrival of the French fleet. In January 1779, the Royal Navy occupied St. Barthélemy (St. Barts) and St. Martin, an island jointly occupied by the French and Dutch since 1648.

Britain's gains set off a bitter struggle for supremacy. In June, French Admiral Charles-Hector, Comte d'Estaing, fought back. Reinforced by 10 ships of the line, he seized the island of St. Vincent on June 18 and Grenada on July 5. The following day, d'Estaing defeated a British fleet commanded by Admiral John Byron. Both sides sustained serious damage, forcing Byron to make repairs at St. Kitts

" Houses are blazing ... parents lament the loss of sons ... "

SAMUEL ANCELL, *JOURNAL OF THE SIEGE OF GIBRALTAR*, 1793

Power broker
Catherine the Great's main concern was to protect Russian trade, especially the sale of naval stores and grain to France. She formed the League of Armed Neutrality to protect Russian shipping.

before returning to England in August. Comte d'Estaing, on the other hand, sailed back to America in July, planning to join up with Patriot forces and attack the British-held city of Savannah (see pp.244–45).

War in Africa

On the other side of the Atlantic, the war spread to the west coast of Africa in April 1779, when a French fleet paused en route to the Caribbean to seize Senegal and Gambia from the

British. The French controlled these slave-trading areas until the end of the war, when the Gambia region—but not St. Louis, the L'île de Gorée, or the Senegal River region—was restored to Britain.

Spain wades in

On June 21, 1779, Spain formally declared war on Britain. Three days later it attacked Gibraltar, a British territory that controlled the gateway to the Mediterranean at the southern end of the Iberian peninsula. At this time, a vast French fleet was already standing off Iberia waiting to link up with Spanish forces for the long-planned attack on Britain itself. The Franco–Spanish strategy called for occupation of the Isle of Wight as a

BRITTANIAS RUIN,

Last laugh
This British cartoon of 1779 encapsulates Britain's plight as it battled on all fronts. An American, a Frenchman, and a Spaniard embrace one another and chuckle while a Dutchman looks on, mocking Britannia as she bemoans her fate, her shield and broken lance by her side.

base from which to attack the southern naval base of Portsmouth. According to plans, the French would then take over the port.

On July 25, the Spanish fleet finally joined the French, and together they sailed for the English Channel. Events did not unfold as the allies expected, however. Admiral Sir Charles Hardy, commander of Britain's Channel Fleet, successfully evaded his attackers for more than a month and refused to be drawn into an engagement with the superior combined fleet.

By late August, the Franco-Spanish crewmen and troops were suffering from starvation and scurvy. Forced to admit defeat, on September 3 they abandoned the enterprise and sailed for home.

Spain enjoyed far greater success in America. There, in September 1779, Louisiana Governor Bernardo de Gálvez led Spanish troops and local militia in capturing Baton Rouge and Fort Bute on Bayou Manchac. By October, de Gálvez was also able to take possession of Fort Panmure at Natchez on the Mississippi River.

The Russians and the Dutch

Back in Europe, British interference with merchant shipping began to arouse hostility from the Netherlands and Russia, both of which wished to avoid involvement in the widening conflict. The French and British both depended on naval stores and materials from the Baltic region to sustain their war effort, including masts, spars, tar, and turpentine. In

late 1779, Empress Catherine II of Russia began organizing what would become the League of the Armed Neutrality, an alliance of European maritime nations designed to defend neutral shipping against Britain's navy.

The Dutch did not immediately join the League, but in December they assigned warships to protect their merchant fleet, a move that resulted in a brief engagement between Dutch and British warships off the Isle of Wight. By 1780, a suspicion that the Netherlands would join the League, together with other grievances, led Britain to declare war on the Dutch.

AFTER

In early 1780, Britain found itself embroiled in a major conflict without any allies for the first time in more than a century.

WEAKENING RESOLVE
With hostilities endangering so many and such scattered territories of the British Empire, Britain was forced to spread its resources in America more thinly. The British government in London began to question not only whether the war was sustainable but also whether peace would last in the event of a British victory. Was it really **worth the cost to the empire** as a whole to continue a distant battle in order to subdue 13 rebellious American colonies?

Rocking Gibraltar
Spain and France tried to bring the British colony of Gibraltar to its knees with a four-year siege that began in June 1779 and ended in February 1783. Under the terms of the Treaty of Paris in September 1783, Britain retained control of Gibraltar.

BEFORE

British naval superiority was well established; for the Patriots, defeating the Royal Navy was a daunting but necessary prospect.

COMBINED EFFORT
In June 1775, Rhode Island formed the first of a dozen state navies with the purchase of two sloops. A few months later, shortly after forming the **Continental Army** ⟪ **64–65**, the Continental Congress established the Continental Navy. Privateering—legitimizing attacks on enemies by private ships—was authorized by the Congress in March 1776.

BRITISH NAVAL POWER
Britain's naval dominance gave it the strategic flexibility to evacuate its army from **Boston** ⟪ **100–01** and occupy **New York** ⟪ **118–19** in 1776, capture **Philadelphia** ⟪ **170–71** in 1777, and take **Savannah** ⟪ **210–11** in December 1778.

PATRIOT NAVAL RECRUITMENT POSTER

The War at Sea

Ultimately, leaders on both sides of the Atlantic knew that control of the seas would be the key to victory. That key appeared to be firmly held in British hands—until the French and Spanish fleets entered the war.

The arrival of French naval forces in American waters in 1779, and the entry of Spain into the war that same year changed the dynamic of the war at sea. Until then, Britain's Royal Navy had possessed a clear advantage over the Patriots at sea.

British strength
When war broke out, Britain possessed 131 ships of the line—two or three-decked battleships that could mount between 64 and 90 cannons depending on their size. Once deployed in a line of battle, these ships traded volleys called broadsides with an enemy fleet, until one side, usually the side with greater firepower, prevailed. In addition to these leviathans, Britain possessed 139 other naval vessels, including versatile frigates—smaller ships carrying a minimum of 28 guns—and some nimble sloops that mounted at least 20 guns. They also had a variety of bomb ketches, which carried mortars. Although only a fraction of the Royal Navy was stationed in North America when war broke out, it nonetheless posed a formidable threat.

> "Without a, **decisive naval force** we can do **nothing.**"
>
> GEORGE WASHINGTON TO THE MARQUIS DE LAFAYETTE, OCTOBER 1781

Patriot inexperience
The Continental Navy never had more than 60 ships of any type. Most were merchantmen, armed with cannons, although in 1775 the Continental Congress commissioned 13 frigates from shipyards along the east coast. Only seven of these vessels ever went to sea—all eventually captured or sunk—and the other six were burned to prevent their seizure.

John Adams lifted the Continental Navy's first regulations almost entirely from those of the British service, but this did not make up for its lack of experience. In 1779, for example, poor coordination between land and naval forces led to the failure of the Penobscot Expedition, a bid by Massachusetts to capture a British fort in the Penobscot Bay. The Patriots were outgunned by the British and forced to burn or abandon their ships in a humiliating defeat.

The Patriots were more successful as privateers. The Congress and state governments issued around 2,000 "letters of marque" during the war. These allowed private shipowners to seize enemy vessels—meaning that the British would be subjected to naval attacks without costing the Congress either men or resources. Since about the same number of British privateers were sent to prey on American ships, and French corsairs stalked the British, the Atlantic swarmed with sloops and schooners, often manned by crews motivated by the prospect of plunder. They could lawfully claim captured ships and their contents as prizes.

In the course of the war, Patriot privateers seized an estimated 2,208 British vessels, the majority merchant ships plying the West Indies trade routes. The American raiders seen in British waters were often based in French ports, where they were openly welcomed, armed, and supplied.

The bulk of American success at sea in 1779 was thanks to Continental Navy Captain John Paul Jones (see pp.227–28), who prowled the British Isles on board the *Bonhomme Richard*. The clash between Jones and Captain Richard Pearson, on the Royal Navy frigate *Serapis* (see pp.224–25), was one of the epic naval battles of the war.

Naval phase begins
The threat of a Franco-Spanish invasion of England in 1779 compelled Lord Sandwich to keep his best ships in home waters, while British forces in America

Victorious allies
In July 1779, a British fleet commanded by Admiral John Byron (grandfather of the poet Lord Byron) was defeated in the waters off Grenada by French warships under the command of the Comte d'Estaing.

were depleted to reinforce the West Indies. Fleet actions were fought from the Mediterranean to the Caribbean, long files of ships-of-the-line streaming past one another, each firing terrific broadsides at its opponent.

AFTER

While Spanish fleets also saw success, French naval efforts would prove decisive in the war's final stages.

BRITAIN VERSUS FRANCE
In 1780, the British Navy helped land forces **capture Charleston 226–27** ⟫. In the following year, however, the French fleet fought back in the **Battle of the Chesapeake 300–01** ⟫.

SPANISH SIEGE
An invading Spanish squadron provided key support when forces led by Bernardo de Galvez **captured Pensacola** from the British in 1781.

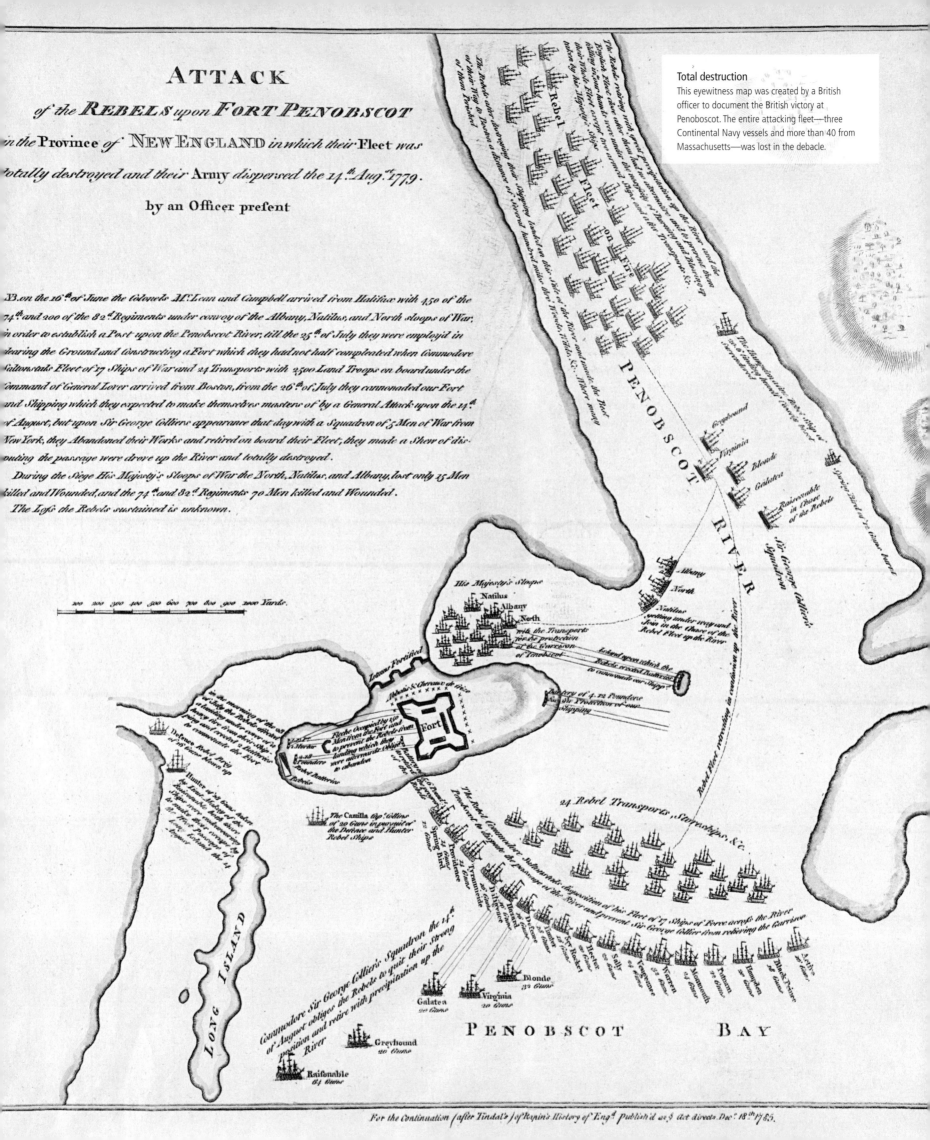

ATTACK
of the REBELS upon FORT PENOBSCOT
in the Province of NEW ENGLAND in which their Fleet was
totally destroyed and their Army dispersed the 14th Augst 1779.
by an Officer present

N.B. on the 16th of June the Colonels McLean and Campbell arrived from Halifax with 450 of the 74th and 200 of the 82d Regiments under convoy of the Albany, Natilus, and North sloops of War, in order to establish a Post upon the Penobscot River, till the 25th of July they were employd in clearing the Ground and Constructing a Fort which they had not half compleated when Commodore Saltonstals Fleet of 17 Ships of War and 24 Transports with 2500 Land Troops on board under the Command of General Lover arrived from Boston, from the 26th of July they cannonaded our Fort and Shipping which they expected to make themselves masters of by a General Attack upon the 14th of August, but upon Sir George Colliers appearance that day with a Squadron of 5 Men of War from New York, they Abandoned their Works and retired on board their Fleet, they made a Shew of disputing the passage were drove up the River and totally destroyed.

During the Siege His Majesty's Sloops of War the North, Natilus, and Albany, lost only 15 Men killed and Wounded, and the 74th and 82d Regiments 70 Men killed and Wounded.

The Loss the Rebels sustained is unknown.

100 200 300 400 500 600 700 800 900 1000 Yards

PENOBSCOT RIVER

PENOBSCOT BAY

LONG ISLAND

Fort

His Majesty's Sloops
Natilus
Albany
North

24 Rebel Transports, Storeships, &c.

Galatea
20 Guns

Virginia
20 Guns

Blonde
32 Guns

Greyhound
20 Guns

Raisonable
64 Guns

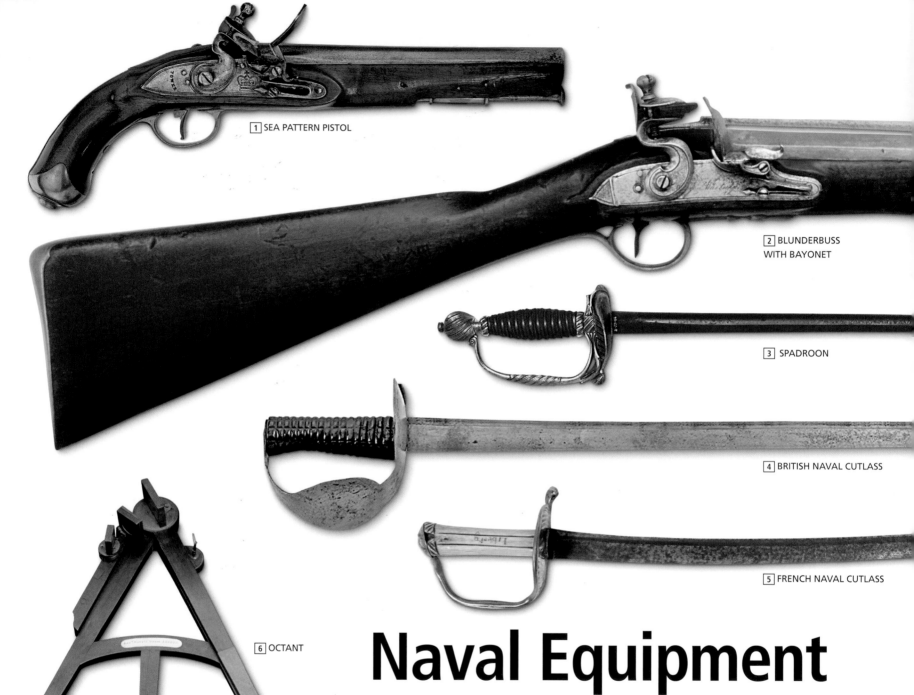

[1] SEA PATTERN PISTOL

[2] BLUNDERBUSS
WITH BAYONET

[3] SPADROON

[4] BRITISH NAVAL CUTLASS

[5] FRENCH NAVAL CUTLASS

[6] OCTANT

[7] COMPASS

Naval Equipment

Unable to compete with British battleships bristling with cannon, the Patriots used privateers to target British merchant vessels. After boarding a ship, the privateers engaged in hand-to-hand combat using a variety of weapons.

[1] **Sea Pattern pistol** This model was made in Belgium for use by the Royal Navy. Flintlock weapons were highly inaccurate and took a long time to reload. [2] **Blunderbuss with bayonet** The blunderbuss had an extended muzzle, allowing it to spray projectiles over a wide area. It could be deployed with devastating effect both at close range and in confined spaces. [3] **Spadroon** A light thrusting sword, the spadroon was popular with naval officers. This British example belonged to Captain Morris of HMS *Bristol*, who was mortally wounded at Fort Moultrie in June 1776. [4] **British naval cutlass** A heavy broad-bladed sword effective for slashing at opponents, the cutlass was popular among seaman due to its sturdiness and simplicity. [5] **French naval cutlass** This cutlass has a bone grip and a profile of King Louis XV on the hand guard. [6] **Octant** A navigational device used to help calculate longitude, the octant had a 45 degree arc. This one was made by Andrew Newell, a mathematical instrument maker in Boston.

[7] **Compass** In a mahogany case, this pocket compass has an inset paper card, printed with the 32 cardinal points. [8] **Hand grenade** Made of iron and filled with black powder—and sometimes nails—grenades could be thrown onto the enemy's deck. [9] **Brass swivel gun and ramrods** A swivel gun was a miniature cannon usually attached to a fixed platform. The pivoting stand enabled a wide arc of fire, but the swivel mechanism was unable to withstand heavy recoil, so such guns had to be small in size. [10] **Chainshot** Consisting of two cannonballs connected by a chain, this projectile was used in naval warfare to damage and destroy the masts and rigging of an enemy vessel. [11] **16-pound bar shot** With a similar purpose to chainshot, this comprised two projectiles connected by a bar. It was used to target enemy rigging. [12] **Boarding ax** Used as close combat weapons during boarding actions, axes were also used to remove heated iron shot from the deck—which could quickly engulf a wooden vessel in flames.

8 HAND GRENADE

9 BRASS SWIVEL
GUN AND RAMRODS

10 CHAINSHOT

12 BOARDING AX

11 16-POUND BAR SHOT

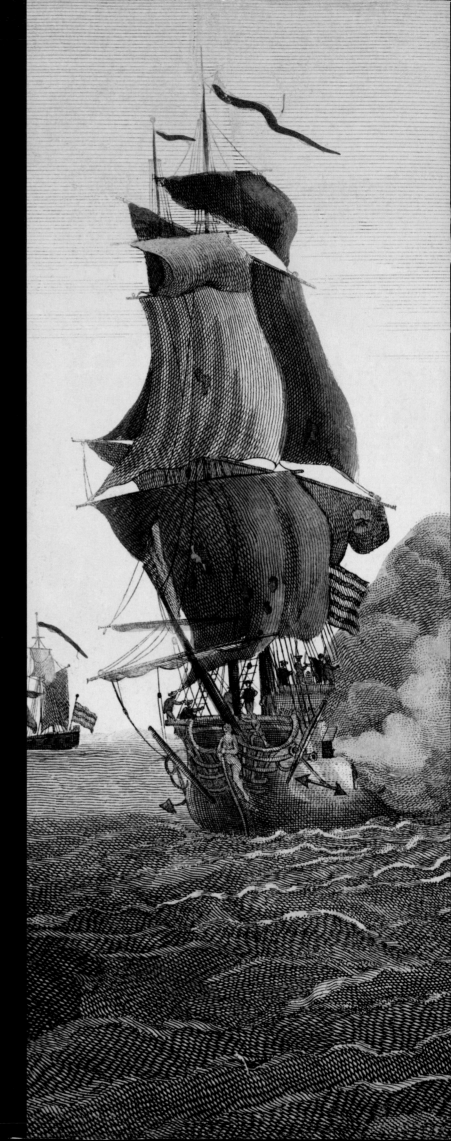

Serapis versus *Bonhomme Richard*

The American vessel *Bonhomme Richard*, captained by John Paul Jones, lay in wait off Flamborough Head, northeast England, for a convoy carrying naval supplies from the Baltic Sea. Spotting the *Bonhomme Richard*, Captain Richard Pearson on the Royal Navy's *Serapis* tacked to meet it. At about 7 p.m. on September 23, 1779, one of the most deadly one-on-one naval battle in the age of sail began.

"The enemy hailed thus: 'What ship is that?' [and] 'What are you laden with?' The answer returned was '[With] Round, grape, and double-headed shot.' And instantly, the *Serapis* [opened fire].... We returned the fire, and thus the battle began ... [Each ship poured cannon fire into the other until both were afire]. Both crews were [now] employed in stopping the progress of the flames, and the firing on both sides ceased. The enemy now demanded of us if we had struck ... 'If you have ... why don't you haul down your pendant[?]' Said Jones, 'We'll do that when we can fight no longer, but we shall see yours come down the first ... Yankees do not haul down their colors until they are fairly beaten.' The combat recommenced again [until at 12:35 a.m.] a single hand grenade having been thrown by one of our men ... fell between their decks, where it [ignited] loose powder [blowing] up about twenty of the enemy. This closed the scene, and the enemy ... bawled out 'Quarters, quarters, quarters, for God's sake!' [Captain Richard Pearson] hauled down the very flag which he had nailed to the flag-staff a little before the battle [at which time he] swore he would never strike to that famous pirate J. P. Jones. The [British] officers now came on board our ship [where Pearson surrendered his sword to Jones]."

NATHANIEL FANNING, *FANNING'S NARRATIVE, BEING THE MEMOIRS OF NATHANIEL FANNING, AN OFFICER OF THE REVOLUTIONARY NAVY*, 1912

Naval engagement
Damage to the *Bonhomme Richard* was so great that Jones and his crew transferred to the captured *Serapis* after their victory. This engraving, based on a painting of 1780 by Richard Paton, shows a third ship, the Patriots' *Alliance* firing a broadside as it sails past.

Father of the US Navy
America's first naval war hero, Commodore John Paul Jones is honored by this handsome bronze memorial sculpted by Charles Henry Niehaus in 1912. It stands in West Potomac Park, Washington, D.C.

PATRIOT NAVAL OFFICER Born 1747 Died 1792

John Paul Jones

"I ... have **no connection** with any **ship that does not sail fast;** for I intend to go in **harm's way.**"

JOHN PAUL JONES, IN A LETTER TO FRENCH SUPPORTER JACQUES-DONATIEN LE RAY DE CHAUMONT, NOVEMBER 16, 1778

Scottish-born sailor John Paul Jones fought for the Patriots during the War of Independence. Taking the war to Britain, he spread panic by raiding the English mainland and fought an epic naval duel with a 44-gun Royal Navy warship in the North Sea. His actions gave a boost to American morale and founded the naval tradition of the United States.

Child runaway
Jones, whose original name was John Paul, was the son of a gardener on an estate close to the Solway Firth, the waterway separating southwest Scotland from England. The lowly life of a landowner's servant did not appeal to him, so at the age of 13 he ran away to sea. Working on ships trading with the West Indies, he rose to be a captain entrusted with running a ship and buying and selling cargo. This was a lucrative position, but his unstable temperament led him to throw it away.

Slight of build, John Paul was more elegant in his manners and dress than the average sea captain, but he was also edgy, quick-tempered, and violent. On one of his voyages, a flogging—standard punishment on ships at the time—resulted in the death of a man. Returning to Scotland, John Paul was briefly jailed but cleared of murder. Three years later, he killed a sailor in a dispute over pay in

the West Indies. Fearing that this time he would not escape prosecution, he fled to Virginia, adopting the addional name "Jones" to cover his tracks.

Captain Jones
The War of Independence offered Jones a new avenue for his ambitions. When the Congress created a Continental Navy in 1775 he went to

Raising the first US Navy flag
In December 1775, as first lieutenant of the *Alfred*, Jones was the first man to raise a US ensign over a naval ship. He hoisted the Grand Union flag, precursor of the Stars and Stripes.

Never surrender
On board *Bonhomme Richard* at the Battle of Flamborough Head, John Paul Jones is said to have shot dead a crewman who was attempting to strike the colors, the traditional gesture of surrender in a naval engagement.

Philadelphia to lobby for a position and was commissioned as a first lieutenant. Although the infant navy was tiny, the Congress was eager to engage in offensive operations that would raise American confidence in the war. Rapidly promoted to captain, Jones gave them what they wanted in late 1776. Voyaging north to Nova Scotia, he raided a port and intercepted transport ships that were carrying British military supplies.

Eager to build on this success, Jones bombarded Congress with plans for ambitious expeditions, including an attack on Britain's African colonies, while advising on the formulation of naval regulations. Finally, in November 1777, he was allowed to sail to France, where he hoped to command a European-built frigate in raids into British home waters.

The frigate never materialized, so in April 1778 Jones set out from a French port to raid Britain on board his sloop *Ranger*. He chose to attack Whitehaven on the Solway Firth, the very port from which he had set out to sea as a 13-year-old. Despite a near mutinous crew, he executed

"I have **not** yet begun to **fight!**"

JOHN PAUL JONES, THE BATTLE OF FLAMBOROUGH HEAD, SEPTEMBER 23, 1779

a successful hit-and-run raid, landing under cover of darkness and damaging two small forts and some shipping.

Bolstered by his success, he attempted to kidnap a local lord, the Earl of Selkirk, from St. Mary's Isle on the Scottish side of the Solway Firth. Finding the earl away from home, Jones stole the family silver—which he politely returned after the war ended. Finally, he defeated the sloop HMS *Drake* in a fight off Carrickfergus, Ireland. It was the first time an American warship had beaten a British ship of its own size.

Although Jones had inflicted negligible damage, his exploits shook British public opinion and in America firmly established his reputation as a Patriot hero.

Impressed by Jones, the French provided him with the resources for a more substantial operation. In August 1779, he set sail on the converted merchantman *Bonhomme Richard* as commodore of a seven-ship squadron. The voyage showed Jones's strength and weakness as a commander. He quarreled bitterly with the captains of the other ships in the squadron and failed to inspire the respect or loyalty of his senior officers. Yet as a fighter in the savage chaos of a sea battle he was unsurpassed.

Jones led his squadron around Scotland into the North Sea. An attempt to raid the port of Leith was aborted, but the mere presence of Jones's ships in the Firth of Forth caused panic ashore. Sailing southward, Jones then chanced upon a convoy of merchant ships off Flamborough Head. *Bonhomme Richard* engaged the larger of the two British warships escorting the convoy, HMS *Serapis*. Although outgunned, Jones won an unlikely victory in a brutal close-quarters encounter, while losing his ship and a large part of his crew. Jones transferred to the captured *Serapis*—heavily damaged but still seaworthy—and sailed to a port in the Netherlands.

The Battle of Flamborough Head confirmed Jones's status as a hero. But his temperament did not inspire trust. No further command materialized before the war's end. After the peace was signed, he was sent to France to collect prize money owed to American sailors for sinking enemy vessels.

Last adventures
In 1787, Jones was signed as an admiral by the Russian Empire to engage the Turkish navy in the Black Sea. He did this with flair, but as usual he made more enemies than friends. His indiscretion with a young girl in St. Petersburg enabled his enemies to bring an accusation of rape. The charge was dropped but he was obliged to leave Russia in a hurry.

Jones spent the last years of his short life in Paris, apparently indifferent to the French Revolution, which was raging all around. In poor health, he died of pneumonia in 1792. His body lay in a neglected cemetery until, in the early 20th century, US President Teddy Roosevelt brought his body back to the United States. Carried across the Atlantic on board USS *Brooklyn* in 1905, John Paul Jones was eventually interred in a marble tomb at Annapolis Naval Academy in Maryland.

TIMELINE

- **July 6, 1747** Born at Kirkbean, Scotland, the son of a gardener.
- **1760** Goes to sea as an apprentice.
- **1768** Becomes master of a brig trading with the West Indies.
- **1770** Briefly imprisoned in Scotland after the death of a sailor flogged on his orders.
- **October 1773** After killing a mutinous sailor in Tobago, takes refuge in Fredericksburg, Virginia, where he adopts the name "Jones."
- **December 1775** Appointed a first lieutenant in the newly formed Continental Navy.
- **March 1776** Serves on the warship *Alfred* and takes part in a raid on Nassau in the Bahamas.
- **May 1776** Given command of the sloop *Providence* with the rank of captain.
- **August–September 1776** Captures British ships cruising off the Bahamas and Nova Scotia.
- **October–December 1776** Commanding *Alfred*, attacks enemy shipping off Nova Scotia and raids Canso.
- **June 1777** Given command of *Ranger*.
- **November 1777** Sails for Europe.
- **April 1778** Raids the British Isles and captures HMS *Drake* off Carrickfergus, Ireland.
- **February 1779** Takes command of the 42-gun *Bonhomme Richard*.
- **August 1779** Leads a squadron around the west of the British Isles and into the North Sea.
- **September 23, 1779** Fights the battle of Flamborough Head against HMS *Serapis*.
- **April 1780** Makes a trimphant return to Paris.
- **1781** Travels to America. The promise of a ship to command fails to materialize.
- **1783** Sent to France to collect prize money owed to American sailors.
- **April 1787** Enters the navy of Empress Catherine II of Russia as a rear admiral.
- **1788** Commands the Russian sailing ship fleet at the siege of Ochakov on the Black Sea, fighting the navy of Ottoman Turkey.
- **April 1789** Arrested in St. Petersburg for alleged rape.
- **July 1790** Returns to Paris.
- **1792** Dies in Paris on July 18, aged 45.

JOHN PAUL JONES COMMEMORATIVE MEDAL, MADE IN 1789

Native Americans at War

During the war, the British sought assistance from Native Americans throughout the Thirteen Colonies and the adjacent lands. The rebels countered by making alliances with the traditional enemies of Native American nations who had taken the British side.

« **BEFORE**

The Native American nations had never followed a unified approach to the settlers or their colonial masters.

PICKING SIDES

Native Americans had fought on both sides in the **French and Indian War** **‹‹ 24–25**, their allegiances determined by tribal rivalries. In the early years of the War of Independence, the British and the Patriots **both sought allies** among the powerful Six Nations of the Iroquois, but these nations initially voted to remain neutral in April 1775.

As hostilities between Britain and the rebel colonists intensified, Native American peoples came under increasing pressure to take sides. History and geography both played a part in deciding allegiance; tribes chose their alliances both on the basis of old rivalries, and in remembrance of past friendship. Some alliances divided the Native American nations; of the Six Nations of the Iroquois Confederacy, only the Oneida and Tuscarora chose to side with the Patriots.

Once alliances were secured, both sides supplied the Native Americans with firearms and ammunition, as well as traditional gifts such as blankets and tools. They encouraged attacks on enemy settlements, and joined Native warriors in raids against both rival tribes and white settlers. No Native Americans, however, simply followed orders from their white allies—most also had their own scores to settle.

Frontier clashes

The Western frontier of the Thirteen Colonies was particularly contentious, with many Native American nations fighting for homelands that had been encroached on by white settlement. In 1777, Shawnee war parties—under nominal British control—launched raids south of the Ohio River, hoping to drive white settlers from Kentucky and reclaim their traditional hunting grounds. Like many others, the Shawnee failed to take back their former homelands.

While Native Americans raided colonial villages on the frontier, their own settlements also

Mohawk warrior

Warrior dress was determined by ritual and custom. War paint designs, for example, differed by tribe, purpose, amuletic properties, and individual achievement.

A Patriot family massacred
Patriot militia captain William Dietz watched his family killed by Loyalists and Native Americans in Beaver Dam (now Berne), New York. This engraving is based on a painting by Jacob Dietz, the captain's younger brother.

came under attack. Colonel Daniel Brodhead and 600 Patriots left Fort Pitt, the "gateway to the West," in August 1779 and marched up the Allegheny River into Seneca territory, burning crops and destroying ten villages. Their dwellings and stores destroyed, an unknown number of Seneca starved and froze to death.

Northern raids

The most notorious Native American raids took place in the North. In June and July 1778, a force of Loyalists and Iroquois—mainly Seneca—warriors swept through the Wyoming Valley in Pennsylvania, killing around 360 men, women, and children.

A similar fate befell civilians in German Flatts (now Herkimer), New York, in September 1778, and in Cherry Valley, New York, two months later on November 11, when, the town and its small Patriot garrison were

taken unaware by a combined Loyalist and Iroquois force. After an unsuccessful attack on the local fort, the raiders, led by Loyalist Captain Walter Butler and Mohawk war chief Joseph Brant (see pp.232–33), laid waste to the town. Patriot Captain Benjamin Warren wrote in his diary of his horror upon finally leaving the fort: "to see the husband mourning over his dead wife with four dead children lying by her side, mangled, scalpt … flesh [torn] off their bones by their dogs." Patriot Colonel Ichabod Alden, 13 of his soldiers, and about 30 civilians were killed.

Retaliation for such attacks was inevitable. Patriots raided the Iroquois towns of Unadilla and Onaquaga in October 1778—in retaliation for Brant and Butler's attack on German Flatts and Cherry Valley earlier that year—and in April 1779 Patriot Colonel Goose Van Schaick led an expeditionary force from Fort Stanwix that attacked several Onondaga villages.

In summer 1779, Washington ordered General John Sullivan to lead 3,200 troops against the "hostile tribes of the Six Nations." Learning of these plans, in late July Brant led his combined force into the Upper Delaware River Valley, defeating 120 Patriot militiamen at Minisink Ford. Meanwhile, Sullivan stayed in the Wyoming Valley awaiting supplies. He broke camp on July 31, and between then and October 3, executed a scorched earth campaign—destroying more than 40 Iroquois villages, burning crops and stores, and defeating a combined force of 1,000 Loyalists and Iroquois at Newtown, New York, on August 29.

Struggles in the South

The Patriots also had to contend with the Cherokee nation. In May 1776, a delegation of Shawnee and Delaware had convinced many Cherokee to ally with Britain and attack settlements on their former lands. The resulting raids led Virginia, Georgia, and the Carolinas to send militia forces into Cherokee territory—Virginia militiamen alone burned 50 Cherokee towns. This led the Cherokees to sign the Treaty of DeWitts' Corner in 1777, ceding most of their lands in South Carolina to the Patriots. While tribes often fought in the hope of regaining land, many were forced to cede it to achieve peace.

Frontier presence

Formerly British, Fort Pitt stood in Native American territory, west of the Proclamation Line, and became the Patriots' western base of operations. They signed a treaty there with the Lenape (Delaware) in 1778.

Inking alliances
Native American chiefs signed documents on behalf of their tribe with hand-drawn pictures, or totems, that had special significance to the nation or individual. These were drawn by representatives of the Six Nations in 1769.

> **Washington, who ordered Sullivan's attack, was named Conotocaurious, "Town Destroyer," by the Iroquois.**

Cherokee leader Dragging Canoe was especially unhappy about the 1777 treaty, leading many of his people who still favored war south and westward, to settle along the Chickamauga Creek, near the Chattahoochee River. Their militancy proved dangerous. In March 1779, learning that 300 Chickamauga warriors had left the region to raid South Carolina and Georgia, leaders in Virginia and North Carolina dispatched more than 1,000 militia and Continental troops to attack. Left without warriors to defend them, many Chickamauga towns were destroyed by the Patriots in late April and early May, but the attacks failed to stop Dragging Canoe, who pronounced his people "not yet conquered." Raids and skirmishes between the Patriots and Chickamaugas continued over the summer and fall of 1779, with neither side scoring a decisive victory.

AFTER

Participation in the War of Independence proved disastrous for most Native American nations.

A FRUITLESS ALLIANCE

The British continued to seek allies, convincing Chickasaws and Choctaw to fight with them along the Mississippi between 1779 and 1780, and Creek warriors to join them in Mobile and Pensacola in 1780 and 1781—all with little success. Not only were at least 500 Native Americans killed in battle during the war, but many died of diseases, such as **smallpox**, which were spread by the marching armies.

HOMELANDS LOST

At **war's end 312–13 »**, the Congress seized most of the Native American lands east of the Allegheny Mountains. Settlers in **the Ohio 240–41 »**, often Patriot veterans, increased the pressure on Native Americans between the Alleghenies and the Mississippi.

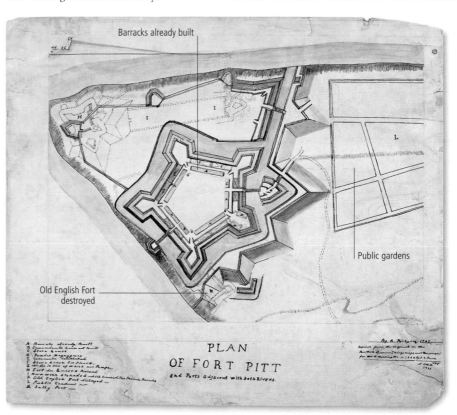

Barracks already built

Old English Fort destroyed

Public gardens

PLAN OF FORT PITT
and Forts adjacent with both Rivers.

Native American Raids

During the War of Independence, Native Americans fought on both sides, sometimes in conjunction with regular troops, but more often, especially as allies of the British, by launching independent raids against isolated white settlements along the frontier. Seneca scalping parties, encouraged by the British, were particularly feared.

"The peltry taken in the expedition will ... amount to a good deal of money ... but we were struck with horror to find among the packages eight large ones containing scalps of our unhappy folks taken in the three last years by the Seneca Indians from the inhabitants of the frontiers ... and sent by them as a present to Col. Haldiman, Governor of Canada ... They were accompanied by the following curious letter to that gentleman:

'At the request of the Seneca chiefs, I send herewith ... eight packs of scalps, cured, dried, hooped, and painted with all the Indian triumphal marks, of which the following is invoice and explanation No. 1. Containing 43 scalps of Congress soldiers, killed in different skirmishes ... 62 of farmers killed in their houses [marked with] a black circle ... to denote their being surprised in the night; and a black hatchet ... signifying their being killed with that weapon.

No. 2. Containing 98 of farmers, killed in their houses; [with] a hoe to mark their profession; great white circle and sun, to show they were surprised in the daytime; a little red foot, to show they stood upon their defence, and died fighting for their lives and families....

No. 3. Containing 97 of farmers...

No. 4. Containing 102 of farmers ... 18 marked with a little yellow flame, to denote their being prisoners burnt alive, after being scalped, their nails pulled out by the roots, and other torments...

No. 5. Containing 88 scalps of women ...

No. 6. Containing 193 boys' scalps ....

No. 7. 211 girls' scalps ...

No. 8. This mixture of ... 122 [scalps includes] a box of birch bark, containing 29 little infants' scalps ...'**"**

EXTRACT FROM A LETTER FROM CAPTAIN COURISH OF THE NEW ENGLAND MILITIA, 1782

Perils of the frontier
Frontier settlements from New York to Georgia were at risk of Native American raids. This colored engraving depicts the aftermath of an attack on a settlement in the Wyoming Valley, Pennsylvania, where Patriot forces were destroying Native American lands.

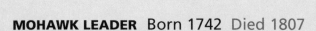

MOHAWK LEADER Born 1742 Died 1807

Joseph **Brant**

"I bow to no man ....
But I will gladly **shake your hand.**"

JOSEPH BRANT, ADDRESSING KING GEORGE III, 1776

The Native American leader Nayendanegea, known to English-speakers as Joseph Brant, was a prominent commander of Native American and Loyalist forces fighting against the Patriots. Unjustly blamed for several massacres, he became a hate figure for many Patriots, who dubbed him "Monster Brant." He is now widely recognized as a skillful leader of irregular troops and an honorable man, who tried to achieve the best outcome for his people despite facing overwhelmingly difficult circumstances.

British connections
A member of the Mohawk people, a tribe adhering to the Iroquois Confederacy, or Six Nations alliance, Brant was born into a Native American world undergoing rapid evolution through contact with Europeans. His stepfather, from whom he received his English name, belonged to a family with close links to the British. An ancestor had visited Britain with a Native American delegation in 1710.

In the 1750s, Sir William Johnson, British Superintendent of Indian Affairs, became a regular visitor to the Brants' home at Canajoharie in the Mohawk Valley. Johnson eventually took Joseph Brant's sister, Molly, as his common law wife, and it was Johnson's influence that opened the way for Joseph—who enjoyed no great status in Mohawk society—to become a figure of historical importance.

As a young man, Brant took part in British military operations in the French and Indian War, including the 1759 expedition against Fort Niagara and the attack on Montreal in 1760.

The following year Johnson sent him to study at Moor's Indian Charity School under the Reverend Eleazar Wheelock. Having expanded his knowledge of the English language and the Christian religion, he became a respected translator and interpreter, working for missionaries and for the British Indian Department.

When the War of Independence broke out in 1775 the Iroquois Council opted for neutrality, but Brant was fully committed to the British side in the conflict. Guy Johnson, who took over as head of the British Indian Department upon the death of his uncle, Sir William Johnson, took Brant first to Canada and then to Britain. The aim was to secure British government support for Iroquois land claims, which would in turn produce Iroquois support for the British war effort. Brant was honored by the British elite, and the diarist and journalist James Boswell interviewed Brant for the *London Magazine*. In early 1776, Brant met King George III and presented his case to George Germain,

Feted by society
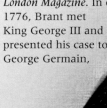
The American artist Gilbert Stuart painted this portrait of Mohawk chief Joseph Brant in London in 1786. While in London, Brant also sat for the British society portraitist George Romney.

Long-term allies
Brant's pro-British sympathies owed much to the relations his mentor, Sir William Johnson, established with the Mohawks. This engraving shows Johnson presenting a peace medal to the Mohawks during the French and Indian War.

"His **manners** are gentle and quiet."

JAMES BOSWELL, DESCRIBING BRANT IN *THE LONDON MAGAZINE*, JULY 1776

the secretary of state for America, but he obtained only empty promises that would never be fulfilled.

From diplomat to warrior

After Brant's return to America in summer 1776, he threw himself wholeheartedly into the war. He took part in the British occupation of New York City and then made his way in disguise through enemy-held territory to reach Iroquois land, where he traveled from settlement to settlement, urging Indians to join the struggle against the American Patriots. He eventually assembled a band of several hundred Native Americans and white Loyalists at Onaquaga in what is now Broome County, New York.

Brant's Volunteers, as they were called, first proved their worth in August 1777 during the British Siege of Fort Stanwix (see pp.160–61), the main strong point of the Continental Army in the Mohawk River Valley. New York militia sent to relieve the siege were ambushed by Brant's force and others in a valley near the village of Oriskany. More than half of the Patriot militiamen were slaughtered.

In the aftermath of the Battle of Oriskany, American Patriots accused the Native American component in the Loyalist force of atrocities, such as torturing and killing prisoners, and even cannibalism. Such

allegations mounted through 1778 as Brant's warriors carried out a series of raids on isolated settlements throughout the Mohawk Valley. Brant led notably destructive attacks on Cobleskill in May and, in collaboration with Loyalist rangers, on German Flatts in September and Cherry Valley in November (see pp.228–29).

Brant's behavior in these and other raids was controversial at the time and has remained so since. Marauding of this kind was certainly meant to be terrifying. Houses and crops were burned, and cattle killed. But eyewitnesses testified that Brant at times intervened to moderate the actions of his warriors—for example, halting the killing of prisoners at Cobleskill. He was not even present at a massacre in Wyoming Valley in July, for which he was blamed, while the Cherry Valley massacre, perhaps the most notorious of the war, was carried out by Seneca warriors nominally under the command of Loyalist Captain Walter Butler. Again, evidence suggests Brant took action to stop the senseless killing of white noncombatants.

Brant fought as a Mohawk war chief but increasingly under the orders of the British army, a reality recognized by his

The Mohawk Chapel
The British Crown gave the Chapel Royal at Brantford, Ontario, to the Mohawks in recognition of their services in the War of Independence. Brant's remains were moved to a tomb there in 1850.

commission as a British officer in 1780. Many white Loyalist volunteers served happily under his command, while his raids were frequently directed against Native Americans fighting on the Patriot side. He took part in some notable actions in the later years of the war, including the defeat of part of George Rogers Clark's militia force invading the Ohio Country in August 1781, a success that saved Fort Detroit from capture. In summer 1782, however, the British ordered Brant to cease operations as peace negotiations proceeded in Paris.

Peace for his people

The terms of the peace treaty were a bitter disappointment to Brant and all Iroquois. Their territory was handed over to the Americans without regard for their rights or their contribution to the war. Brant is said to have exclaimed that the British had "sold the Indians to Congress." Since the Mohawk lands were now under the control of their enemies, Brant persuaded Frederick Haldemand, Governor of Canada, to provide an area north of the Great Lakes where they could live.

In 1785, Brant led about 2,000 Native Americans to a site on the Grand River, now known as the Six Nations Reserve. Brant also visited London, where he secured financial compensation for the Mohawk—and a large pension for himself—but failed to win military support for resistance to American expansion.

In the 1790s, in dispute with the British authorities in Canada over land rights, Brant twice visited Philadelphia, holding talks with President Washington and addressing Congress, though nothing came of these contacts.

Brant experienced personal tragedy in 1795, when he killed one of his sons in a knife fight, but his last years in Canada were at least comfortable, his house on Lake Ontario staffed by some 20 servants. It was there that he died in 1807.

BRANT'S STATUE, VALIANTS MEMORIAL, OTTAWA

1 LONG LAND PATTERN MUSKET

2 POWDER HORN

3 WAR CLUB

4 BALL-HEADED CLUB

5 HAMMERSTONE MALLET

6 POINTED WAR CLUB

7 TOMAHAWK

8 BOW AND ARROWS

Native American Weapons

Native Americans fought on both sides of the war. They brought their own tools to the conflict, but many carried firearms and weapons with European or American-made blades obtained through trade or from raiding.

1 **Long Land Pattern musket** Native Americans did not make their own guns, but used firearms taken from their enemies or supplied by their allies—like this so-called "Brown Bess" musket, a standard-issue British shoulder-arm. 2 **Powder horn** Cattle horns were a popular method of transporting gunpowder. Europeans would use such items to trade with the Native Americans. 3 **War club** Produced throughout the six Iroquois nations—Mohawk, Onondaga, Oneida, Cayuga, Seneca, and Tuscarora—the carved wooden ball-head club was a simple tool used to deliver lethal blows in combat. It could also be thrown at opponents. 4 **Ball-headed club** This club decorated with glass beads comes from a Northeast–Woodland tribe. Carved from a single piece of wood, the ball-head design is very old; these were used against the European settlers in the 17th century. 5 **Hammerstone mallet** A variant of the

wooden war club, this Tuscarora weapon is made of stone. Sharpened deer antlers were also used by the Iroquois to make striking weapons. 6 **Pointed war club** This simple wooden club edged with razor-sharp obsidian was a Lenape Delaware weapon. Pushed west by European settlers, in 1778 the Lenape were the first nation to sign a treaty with the Continental Congress. 7 **Tomahawk** Used as a deadly hacking weapon, the iconic tomahawk could also be thrown short distances. Although traditionally tomahawk blades were made of stone, contact with Europeans resulted in the introduction of iron and steel variants, as in the case of this pipe tomahawk—made of wood, steel, and lead. 8 **Bow and arrows** Mainly used to hunt, bows—like this Seneca design—were made of wood and animal hide. Arrowheads were carved from flint or stone, and the arrows were often fletched with feathers.

Surprise attack
A daring assault by Patriot troops on July 15–16, 1779, led to their recapture of Stony Point. The flag with a star representing each of the 13 colonies, was used by the Congress from 1777.

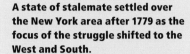

Deadlock in New York

With the British firmly established in the city since 1776, George Washington positioned his Continental Army around New York to monitor their movements. During 1779, each side probed the defenses of the other.

The British were the first to try to break the stalemate that prevailed in New York. In February 1779, William Tryon, the city's royal governor and also the commander of Loyalist military units, led 600 of his troops on a raid against Horseneck Landing in West Greenwich, Connecticut. After driving away the 150 Patriot militiamen who tried to defend the town, the Loyalists burned a saltworks and three coastal vessels, looted Patriot homes and businesses, and carried off 200 head of cattle. Connecticut Patriots reacted by stepping up their destruction of Loyalist farms on Long Island.

Controlling the lower Hudson

On May 30, General Henry Clinton, at the head of 6,000 troops, sailed 25 miles (40 km) up the Hudson River to attack the Patriot fort at Stony Point. Seeing the strength of the attackers, the 40 defenders fled. Clinton then ordered the bombardment of Fort Lafayette, which stood opposite Stony Point, at Verplanck's Point on the other side of the river. The surrender of its 70-man garrison gave Britain control of Kings Ferry, the major crossing point of the Lower Hudson River, and of the river itself as far north as West Point, the impregnable Patriot fortress 17 miles (27 km) farther upstream.

For the next month Clinton tried to lure Washington's army into open battle, but the Patriots remained in the highlands north of New York City. Clinton then sent detachments into Connecticut in the hope that his opponent would leave his defensive positions to protect the towns. Clinton also wanted to punish Connecticut residents for their attacks on supply vessels shuttling between New York City and the British forces at Newport, Rhode Island, as well as for their assaults on Loyalist farms on Long Island.

Midnight assault

In early July 1779, Loyalist forces led by William Tryon landed at New Haven and East Haven and destroyed both public and private property, including vessels in the harbor. They went on to inflict greater damage in the wider area. Connecticut Governor Jonathan Trumbull sought assistance from Washington, but the Patriot commander was planning a raid of his own and refused to take Clinton's bait. On July 15, Brigadier General Anthony Wayne led 1,350 soldiers of the Continental Army in an audacious midnight assault on Stony Point. Approaching with unloaded weapons to avoid a misfire sounding the alarm, they surprised the 625-man British garrison and forced it to surrender. Having inspected its position, Washington decided it would take more men than he cared to risk to hold Stony Point against a counterattack, so ordered his forces to abandon the fort. The Patriots took with them numerous small arms, 15 cannon, and a quantity of badly needed gunpowder before destroying many of the fortifications. The victory at Stony Point also gave the Patriots a badly needed lift to their morale.

A month later, on August 19, Major Henry Lee led 300 men in a second jab at British outposts, this time mounting a midnight attack on Paulus Hook, a small marsh and sand peninsula jutting into New York Harbor from the New Jersey shore. After a 30-minute fight, the 250 British defenders surrendered, and Lee withdrew, taking 158 prisoners with him. Loyalist militia pursued Lee's force for 20 miles (32 km) before abandoning the chase.

Continuing to peck at the British, on September 5, 150 Patriots crossed Long Island Sound from Connecticut to Lloyd's Neck on Long Island, where they surprised 550 Loyalists, took 350 of them captive, and returned to Connecticut without loss.

In October 1779, Clinton decided that the 3,000 troops stationed at Newport, Rhode Island, to prevent the enemy from using Narrangansett Bay as a base from which to attack New York City, would be better employed in the campaign against the rebels in Charleston, South Carolina. By the end of 1779, as the British prepared to move forces south, Washington had moved 12,000 men into winter quarters in Morristown, New Jersey. The impasse in New York was set to continue.

Crack regiment
The elite Continental Light Army Division was employed to seize Stony Point. The division was later commanded by Lafayette, who had special buckles and other insignia made for its officers.

> "We are uncertain ... Whether **the Enemy** mean to make any stand ... or **only plunder, destroy** and make off."
>
> JONATHAN TRUMBULL, GOVERNOR OF CONNECTICUT, TO GEORGE WASHINGTON, JULY 1779

BEFORE

During the winter of 1778–79, the British remained on the defensive around New York City as new threats from other European powers began to take shape.

TENSION MOUNTS
Although in a strong position on Manhattan and Long Island, Britain was on the defensive. Washington continued to **harass the British** around the New York area, while awaiting naval assistance from the French **« 188–89**. By early 1779, interference by the Royal Navy with Dutch merchant shipping had raised **tensions with the Netherlands « 218–19**.

A BRITISH CARTOON OF 1779 SHOWS BRITAIN BEING HARASSED ON ALL SIDES

THE PRESENT STATE OF GREAT BRITAIN.

AFTER

A state of stalemate settled over the New York area after 1779 as the focus of the struggle shifted to the West and South.

WAITING FOR THE FRENCH
The Continental Army endured great hardships in its Morristown base in New Jersey during the winter of 1779–80. Its weakened condition led Washington to await French reinforcements. **French troops arrived in Newport, Rhode Island 244–45 »**, in July 1780, but a British blockade kept the Americans and their allies short of supplies.

MILITARY ACTION DELAYED
During 1780, Washington and his French allies held back from further major attacks in the region, and Clinton's forces did not attack either. **All eyes were on the South**.

PATRIOT GENERAL 1745–96

ANTHONY WAYNE

Wayne led the Pennsylvania Line during the failed 1777 defense of Philadelphia before the recapture of Stony Point in 1779 earned him the nickname "Mad Anthony." After commanding troops at Yorktown in 1781, he settled peace terms with the Cherokees and Creeks in Georgia. Wayne retired from the army in 1784, but a decade later Washington gave him command of the Legion of the United States with orders to subdue the Native Americans. After victory at the Battle of Fallen Timbers, he imposed the Treaty of Greenville (1795) on the defeated Indian nations.

Prized port
Control of New York City and its waterways was essential to the British. The busy Hudson River provided a crucial link to their Canadian bases.

BEFORE

The **Ohio**

The Treaty of Paris of 1763 transferred sovereignty over the lands south of the Great Lakes from France to Britain. The new United States sought to gain control of these territories.

NATIVE AMERICAN OPPOSITION
After the **French and Indian War** **<< 24–25** Native Americans initially opposed British rule. During **Pontiac's Rebellion of 1763–66 << 36–37**, Pontiac, an Ottawa war chief, captured various British forts but failed to take Detroit and Fort Pitt. In 1774, American settlers expanded their territory by winning **Lord Dunmore's War** in what is now Kentucky.

ALLIANCE WITH THE BRITISH
When the war began, the Shawnee and other tribes of the Kentucky area **initially remained neutral**. In 1776, they changed their stance and allied with the British. Lieutenant Colonel George Rogers Clark decided to attack British posts supporting the Shawnee.

While the main armies were fighting in New York, New England, and the southern colonies, smaller forces were engaged in the Ohio region. Even so, the outcome of these battles would shape the territory of the fledgling United States.

By 1777, white settlements in Kentucky, then a western county of Virginia, were being overwhelmed by an onslaught of Native American raids, all of them encouraged from the British fort at Detroit. The fort's commander, the Superintendent of Indian Affairs Lieutenant Governor Henry Hamilton, was even known as "The Hair Buyer" for his policy of paying Native Americans for enemy scalps.

In an attempt to quell Native American attacks, General Lachlan McIntosh, commander of the Western Department of the Continental Army, based at Fort Pitt, near modern-day Pittsburgh, set about erecting a chain of forts. In addition to tackling the Native American problem, McIntosh planned to use the forts to extend supply lines for a march on Hamilton's base at Detroit, 280 miles (450 km) northwest of Fort Pitt.

While McIntosh set his sights on Detroit, a young Virginian named George Rogers Clark recruited 175 of the toughest frontiersmen, crossed the Ohio River in June 1778, and captured the small British garrison at Kaskaskia

Surrender of Fort Sackville
George Rogers Clark accepts Henry Hamilton's surrender at Fort Sackville on February 25, 1779. Clark fooled Hamilton into thinking he was greatly outnumbered.

PATRIOT MILITIAMAN 1752–1818

GEORGE ROGERS CLARK

George Rogers Clark is sometimes described as the "Conqueror of the Old Northwest." From a Virginia planter family, Clark first fought in Lord Dunmore's War in 1774. He was instrumental in having the Kentucky territory recognized as a county of Virginia and then led the Kentucky militia throughout the War of Independence, notably at the capture of Vincennes. Clark fell on hard times after the war. He struggled financially— Virginia delayed repaying him large expenses he had incurred—and lost his command for allegedly being regularly drunk on duty.

on the Mississippi River—without firing a shot. Clark also took Cahokia, Prairie du Rocher, and St. Philippe before sending emissaries to distant Vincennes, an important trading post on the Wabash River. There the French inhabitants and Canadian militiamen garrisoning Fort Sackville quickly declared loyalty to the United States.

The Virginia legislature, meeting in Williamsburg, reacted to the news of Clark's victories by claiming all of the "Old Northwest"—territory north and west of the Ohio River and south of the Great Lakes—for the Old Dominion, as Virginia was sometimes known, and naming it "Illinois County," with Kaskaskia its county seat. When news of Clark's victory reached Detroit, Governor Hamilton gathered a force of 250 men and, on December 17, 1778 recaptured Vincennes, Fort Sackville, and its four-man Patriot garrison.

Frontier warfare
Meanwhile, in eastern Ohio, General Lachlan McIntosh had made good progress building his chain of forts

Spanish influence
The Mississippi valley was an important route for arms and other military goods sent to the Patriots in Illinois from Spain, which controlled the lower Mississippi region.

170 volunteers, many of them militiamen from French settlements heartened by news of the Franco-American alliance. In an epic episode of endurance, Clark's men had marched 180 miles (290 km) across rough country and crossed the rain-swollen Little Wabash River, the

> ## "I knew that to **excel** them in **barbarity** was and is the only way to make **war** upon **Indians** and gain a **name** among them."
>
> GEORGE ROGERS CLARK, *THE CONQUEST OF THE ILLINOIS*

through the wilderness on the way to Detroit. But toward the end of 1778 he had been forced to halt in eastern Ohio at Fort Laurens, his farthest outpost, hampered by supply problems and the onset of winter. Hearing reports that McIntosh had withdrawn most of his force to Fort Pitt and left only 150 troops at Fort Laurens, Hamilton ordered Captain Henry Bird to seize the isolated post. Leading a dozen British infantrymen and some 220 Mingoe and Wyandot warriors, Bird made his way to the fort.

On February 23, 1779, Bird's Indian allies killed 18 of McIntosh's soldiers who were out collecting firewood. The British captain then laid siege to Laurens. Such was the nature of winter frontier warfare, however, that when the siege was raised a month later, on March 23, it was due as much from mutual starvation as it was to the arrival of Patriot reinforcements.

Retaking Fort Sackville
On the very night that Bird's men attacked Fort Laurens, Clark set about retaking Fort Sackville at Vincennes, leading

first of four interlacing rivers that had overflowed their banks and merged into one 20 mile (32 km) wide sea, broken here and there by ridges of dry land. Clark had driven his men through the flooded forests, most of them wading for days through freezing chest-deep waters (see pp.242–43). As they approached Vincennes, they were encouraged to learn from a party of

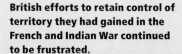

Demand for surrender
On July 24, 1779, George Rogers Clark demanded British Lieutenant Governor Hamilton surrender Fort Sackville. Clark renamed the captured position Fort Patrick Henry.

local hunters that the British were unaware of their advance and that most of the French inhabitants remained loyal to Clark and the Patriot cause.

As evening fell on Vincennes on February 23, Clark's men emerged from the Wabash swamps and fanned out through the streets of Vincennes, which were unusually silent following an advance warning advising all citizens to stay indoors. Hamilton was caught completely by surprise as small parties of Patriot riflemen, under the cover of darkness, crept around the fort and fired through loopholes, wounding several British defenders.

The next morning the British commander refused Clark's demand to surrender; Clark in turn rejected Hamilton's proposal for a three-day truce. While Clark and Hamilton exchanged messages, a party of Canadian militiamen and Native Americans returned to the town, unaware of Clark's attack and were captured by the Patriots. While the Frenchmen were released, Clark determined to make examples of the Native Americans in the party and had them dragged to the front of the fort, tomahawked to death, scalped, and thrown into the river. After that grim warning, Hamilton surrendered Fort Sackville and its 79-man garrison. Clark renamed it Fort Patrick Henry in honor of the Virginia governor.

While Hamilton and his fellow prisoners were marched 850 miles (1,370 km) across the mountains to Williamsburg, Clark attempted to follow up his victories at Kaskaskia and Vincennes with a campaign against Detroit. But he was never able to recruit enough men to make the long and perilous march on the British stronghold.

The summer of 1779 put an end to the idea of taking Detroit by force. General Washington instead unleashed

a massive raid on the Iroquois villages in western Pennsylvania and New York. Colonel Daniel Brodhead, McIntosh's replacement at Fort Pitt, canceled plans to attack Detroit and ordered his troops to abandon Fort Laurens.

Taking scalps
Europeans and Native Americans on both sides in the war took scalps. Although he was later released, Henry Hamilton was initially treated as a war criminal because he participated in such activities.

AFTER »

British efforts to retain control of territory they had gained in the French and Indian War continued to be frustrated.

BRITISH FIGHT BACK
In 1780, British leaders planned a campaign to recapture the Northwest from the Patriots and evict Spain from the lower Mississippi River. Although they managed to seize some Patriot-held forts in the Northwest, **Spain's capture of Mobile** in March 1780 and its seizure of Pensacola, capital of British West Florida, in May 1781 forestalled British designs on Spanish New Orleans.

WILDERNESS WARS
The Old Northwest was ceded to the new United States in the 1783 **Treaty of Paris 312–13 »**, but Britain and her Indian allies renewed their fight for the territory in the **1812 War 342–43 »**.

March on Vincennes

Within a week of learning that the British had taken Fort Vincennes, on the modern border between Indiana and Illinois, Lieutenant Colonel George Rogers Clark left Kaskaskia with some 170 militia to launch a surprise attack on the fort. His aim was to prevent the British from promoting Native American raids in the area and open the passage to the interior. The militia's 17-day journey was hampered by extreme winter weather and abnormal flooding, as Clark recorded in his journals.

"[February 15] We began our march through the water ... By evening we found ourselves encamped on a pretty height in high spirits, each party laughing at the other in consequence of something that had happened in the course of this ferrying business, as they called it. A little antic drummer afforded them great diversion by floating on his drum, etc ... We were now, as it were, in the enemy's country, convinced that the whole of the low country on the Wabash was drowned ...

[February 21] About waist deep one of the men informed me that he thought he felt a path—a path is very easily discovered under water by the feet. We examined and found it so, and concluded that it kept on the highest ground, which it did, and, by taking pains to follow it, we got to the sugar camp ... where there was about half an acre of dry ground ...

[February 22–23] Was the coldest night we had. The ice, in the morning, was from one-half to three-quarters of an inch thick near the shores and in still waters ... We were now in full view of the fort and town at about two miles' distance ... Every man now feasted his eyes and forgot that he had suffered anything.**"**

GENERAL GEORGE ROGERS CLARK, IN HIS JOURNALS, PUBLISHED BY WILLIAM HAYDEN ENGLISH, 1897

Leading the troops
George Roger Clark's determination to retake Vincennes from the British is captured in this popular 19th-century illustration by Frederick Coffay Yohn. It shows Clark and his men trudging through the swollen rivers of Illinois.

The Siege of Savannah

Realizing that the British intended to reconquer America from the South, the Patriots strengthened defenses in South Carolina and called on their French allies for help in ousting Britain from the strategic Georgian port of Savannah.

Lincoln's sword
After Savannah, Benjamin Lincoln retreated to Charleston. Although he was captured there the following year, he was exchanged for a British prisoner and returned to take up his sword at Yorktown.

For eight months after the British capture of Savannah in December 1778, British regulars and their Loyalist and Native American allies skirmished with Patriot militia across the South without either side gaining the upper hand. Meanwhile, the Continental Army's southern department, under the command of Major General Benjamin Lincoln, focused its efforts on strengthening the defenses of Charleston in South Carolina, Britain's next logical target. Lincoln's forces successfully repelled a British advance on the town in May 1779, but then failed at Stono Ferry in June to interrupt the British retreat to Savannah.

French reinforcements

On September 3, Lincoln learned that French Admiral Charles Hector, Comte d'Estaing, was on his way to join him in an attack on Savannah. Six days later, a French fleet of 38 warships carrying 4,000 soldiers sailed into the mouth of the Savannah River. Taken completely by surprise, Britain's commander in Georgia, Major General Augustine Prévost, recalled British and Loyalist troops from outlying posts at Brunswick and Sunbury, in Georgia, and Beaufort, in South Carolina. He also set several hundred slaves to work on a system of breastworks, trenches, and redoubts to protect Savannah from attack.

Discovering that the British had sunk six ships in the river to bar their passage, the French began to disembark troops at Beaulieu, 16 miles (26 km) south of the city on the night of September 11–12. Among them were 500 free blacks of the Chasseurs-Volontaires de Saint-Domingue (modern-day Haiti). Meanwhile, Lincoln advanced on the city from the north with 750 militiamen and 800 Continental troops, including 200 legionnaires under Count Casimir Pulaski, a Polish volunteer.

By September 16, the French and Patriot troops had encircled the city, and d'Estaing demanded its surrender. Playing for time, Prévost requested and was granted 24 hours to discuss terms with his officers. The extension allowed 800 Fraser's Highlanders to reach Savannah from Beaufort, bringing the number of British troops in the city to 3,200. Reinforced, Prévost rejected surrender.

Siege begins

Brigadier General William Moultrie, commanding a Patriot company, pressed for an immediate attack before the British could strengthen their defenses further. Lincoln and d'Estaing decided instead to lay siege to Savannah, and on September 22 the French began offloading cannon from their warships. While the French maneuvered their artillery into position, the British reinforced their earthwork defenses by installing abatis—rows of sharpened stakes anchored at a 45-degree angle—along the ditches running in front of their redoubts.

For two weeks, French artillery poured fire into the British position but failed to breach the defenses or significantly injure the defenders, although the bombardment did do considerable damage to the city itself. During the same two week period, Patriot troops inched closer to the British by digging angled lines of trenches.

Impatient at the slow rate of progress and anxious to return to the West Indies, d'Estaing changed his mind about a siege and pressed for an attack. Lincoln cautioned against launching an assault until allied trenches had been

> "The **Southern** parts of ... **America** are now in Your Lordship's **Power.**"
>
> JAMES WRIGHT, ROYAL GOVERNOR OF GEORGIA, TO LORD GEORGE GERMAIN, NOVEMBER 1779

Honoring the Haitians
This statue in Franklin Square, Savannah, commemorates the Chasseurs-Volontaires de Saint-Domingue, who were charged with covering the allied retreat from Savannah. Twenty-five Haitians were killed or wounded in the battle. Their drummer boy (left) is thought to have been Henri Christophe, who went on to become king of Haiti and a leader in his country's own struggle for independence.

« BEFORE

After the intervention of France in 1778, the British decided to commit more resources to the Caribbean and the American South.

FIRST FRENCH BATTLES
The French fleet under Admiral Charles Hector, Comte d'Estaing, fought an inconclusive battle with the British off **Rhode Island « 204–05** before sailing for the **Caribbean « 218–19** and capturing St. Vincent and Grenada.

BRITISH GAINS
A British expedition **occupied Savannah « 210–11**, Georgia, in December 1778. It set out to reestablish control over the city and surrounding region and to reinstate the royal governor.

extended to reduce the amount of open ground the attackers would have to cross under enemy fire. D'Estaing, however, was worried both by the prospect of bad weather as winter approached and the outbreak of scurvy and other medical problems among his crews. He refused to wait any longer and said his ships had to leave. Lincoln reluctantly agreed to mount a frontal assault, scheduled for October 8.

On the night of October 7, the allies launched diversionary attacks on the British flanks. However, having learned of the allied plan from a spy, Prévost knew that the center-right would be the focus of the main allied attack and did not divert his troops. At 5 a.m. on October 8, after being delayed by fog on their approach march, a combined force of five columns—three of them French and two American—set off. As they crossed open ground, they were felled by withering grapeshot fired from the British Spring Hill redoubt on the western side

of the town; d'Estaing himself was wounded. The redoubt's defenders included some of the best troops of the British garrison, among them Fraser's Highlanders.

Against such opposition, the French were forced to fall back before they could reach the British lines. The South Carolina and Georgia Continentals managed to penetrate the ditch and abatis to mount the walls of the Spring Hill redoubt, but a determined counterattack, spearheaded by the 60th Regiment of Grenadiers and a company of Royal Marines, drove them back.

This phase of the battle continued for an hour, during which 173 Patriots were killed. Among the wounded was Count Curt von Stedingk, a notable Swedish officer in French service.

Savannah River

British ships

Savannah city

Spring Hill redoubt

American camp

Troop camp

Powder store

Plan of attack

The French and Patriot allies placed their trenches and cannons to the southeast of the town but chose to make their attack in five columns against the west side of the defenses.

Death and defeat

As the battle raged, Count Pulaski rode out of the cover of woods to assess the situation. He left behind him, in hiding, 200 French and American cavalrymen waiting for a breach to open in the British lines so they could charge through, spread out, and attack British defenders from the rear. Pulaski was cut down by grapeshot.

By that afternoon, the allies abandoned the assault, and withdrew all along the lines. They maintained a siege for another four days, but on October 15 the Virginia and Georgia

militia units departed, followed on October 20 by the French, who sailed for the Caribbean.

Lincoln's remaining Continental forces were heavily outnumbered by the British, leaving him little choice but to abandon the campaign and return to Charleston. In all, 244 Patriot soldiers died in the failed Siege of Savannah, along with 650 French. In addition, 584 French and Patriot troops were wounded, and 120 captured. The British came off lightly, with some 40 dead, 63 wounded, and 52 missing.

AFTER

British troops taken from Rhode Island and New York headed for Charleston.

TAKING CHARLESTON

With Savannah once again a secure base, the reestablished colonial government continued to launch attacks into South Carolina. In May 1780, **British forces captured Charleston 266–67 ≫** and then in August won a **major victory at Camden 274–75 ≫**.

GUERRILLA STRUGGLE

As well as the major battles, there was extensive **guerrilla fighting in South Carolina 268–69 ≫**, marked by brutality on both sides. Loyalist units led by Banastre Tarleton gained a particularly unsavory reputation.

Hero of Savannah
Polish volunteer Count Casimir Pulaski was fatally wounded by grapeshot while bravely scouting the battlefield at the Siege of Savannah. This memorial to him stands in Monterey Square, Savannah.

7
THE CONTINUING CONFLICT
1780

Although the war in the North had entered a state of deadlock, things were heating up in the South. While the British captured Charleston, the main seaport, and achieved victory at Camden, Patriot militiamen gained the upper hand at Kings Mountain.

« Enter the Overmountain Men
Frontier militiamen from west of the Blue Ridge Mountains had been mustered in October 1778. Skilled at ambush, and armed with long rifles, the so-called Overmountain Men clinched the Patriot

ACTION IN 1780

In the fifth year of the war, the Continental Army was rocked by mutinies as well as the betrayal of Benedict Arnold, whose exposure as a spy led to the capture and execution of the British officer John André. For Britain, however, the year brought the tantalizing prospect of ultimate triumph. While the Patriots clung on in New Jersey and a war of forage and raid prevailed in New York, the British blockaded a French expeditionary force in Rhode Island and won resounding victories at Charleston and Camden. In sweeping two Patriot armies from South Carolina, it seemed the British had secured the South for the Crown—but the presence of British regulars and Loyalist auxiliaries in the Carolina backcountry provoked fierce guerrilla resistance, and Patriot partisans triumphed at Kings Mountain.

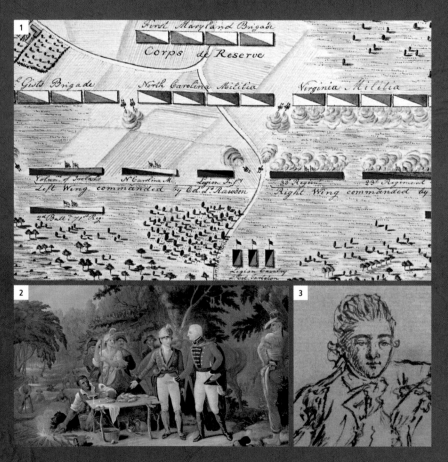

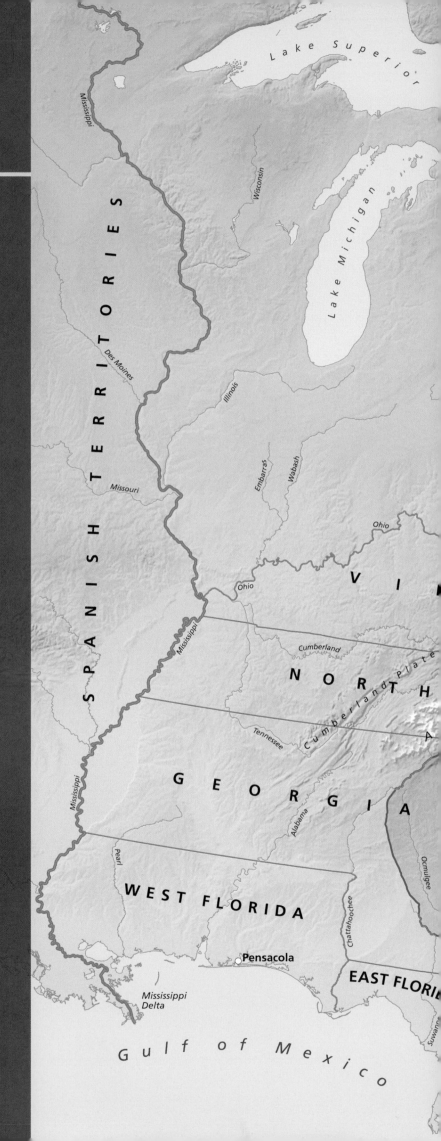

1 The British routed the Patriots at Camden in August. 2 Francis Marion, the "Swamp Fox," mounted guerrilla attacks near Black Mingo Creek in September. 3 In October, Major John André was executed for his part in a plot with Benedict Arnold to surrender West Point.

TIMELINE 1780

The Continental Line mutiny ▪ **Lincoln surrenders Charleston** ▪ Cornwallis routs Gates at Camden ▪ **Treachery at West Point** ▪ Partisan warfare in South Carolina ▪ **Militia victorious at Kings Mountain** ▪ General Greene takes command in the South

JANUARY	FEBRUARY	MARCH	APRIL	MAY	JUNE
JANUARY 1 Patriot troops from the Massachusetts Line mutiny at West Point, on the Hudson River, dissatisfied with the lack of pay and food.		**MARCH 11** Catherine II of Russia forms the League of Armed Neutrality with Denmark and Sweden, opposes British strictures on maritime commerce.	**APRIL 1** General Clinton begins digging siege lines 800 yards (731 m) north of Charleston's defenses. **APRIL 8** A British flotilla enters Charleston harbor.	**MAY 12** Patriot General Benjamin Lincoln surrenders Charleston and its garrison to General Clinton.	**JUNE 3** Henry Clinton issues a proclamation ordering those who had previously fought for the Patriots and had been granted "parole," to swear an oath of allegiance to the Crown.
» Badge of the 71st Regiment of Foot, who fought at Charleston		**MARCH 14** Spanish General Bernardo de Gálvez captures Mobile, in British West Florida. **MARCH 15** The Congress devalues its currency, angering French merchants.	**APRIL 14** British and Loyalist troops under Lieutenant Colonel Banastre Tarleton rout Patriot forces at the start of the Siege of Charleston.		
	FEBRUARY 11 General Clinton's light infantry and grenadiers begin landing on Simmon's Island, just south of Charleston.		**APRIL 17** British and French fleets engage in the West Indies, in the inconclusive Battle of Martinique.	⌃ Battle of Waxhaws **MAY 25** Two Patriot regiments of the Connecticut Line, unpaid and nearly starving, mutiny in their camps outside Morristown.	**JUNE 4** British General Lord Cornwallis assumes command of the British campaign in the South.
» French officer's sword			⌄ Siege of Charleston	**MAY 29** Tarleton's Legion inflict heavy losses on a force of Continentals at the Waxhaws, South Carolina.	**JUNE 7** Patriot New Jersey militia halt the advance of Hessian troops under General Wilhelm von Knyphausen toward Morristown, in the Battle of Connecticut Farms.
JANUARY 30 A British fleet, carrying troops under the command of General Clinton, arrives off British-held Savannah, Georgia—the first stage in seizing nearby Charleston.					**JUNE 23** Patriot forces thwart another British probe toward Morristown at Springfield.

"If you could see what **difficulties surround us** … you would be convinced … we have everything to dread. Indeed, I have **almost ceased to hope.**"

GEORGE WASHINGTON TO JOSEPH REED, MAY 28, 1780

JULY	AUGUST	SEPTEMBER	OCTOBER	NOVEMBER	DECEMBER

» Benedict Arnold

» John André sentenced to death on September 29

OCTOBER 2
Patriots hang British Major John André as a spy.

AUGUST 3
Patriot Major General Benedict Arnold is given command of the rebel fort at West Point.

SEPTEMBER 4
Marion's men trap and defeat a Loyalist force at Blue Savannah, South Carolina.

OCTOBER 7
Frontier Patriot militiamen kill British Major Patrick Ferguson and most of his 800 Loyalists at the Battle of Kings Mountain.

NOVEMBER 9
British forces led by Major James Weymess make a failed attack on Thomas Sumter's positions at Fishdam Ford.

DECEMBER 2
Major General Nathanael Greene takes command of the Patriot forces in the southern department.

JULY 10
Comte de Rochambeau arrives in Newport, Rhode Island with 7,000 French troops.

AUGUST 25
South Carolina rebel Francis Marion frees 150 Patriots captured at the Battle of Camden.

SEPTEMBER 14
Francis Marion and his guerrilla fighters defeat a Loyalist force at Black Mingo Creek in the South Carolina swamps.

» Ferguson rifle

DECEMBER 21
Britain declares war on the Netherlands, which has been covertly supplying arms to the rebels and selling naval stores to France.

SEPTEMBER 21
Benedict Arnold meets with British spymaster John André and agrees to surrender West Point to the British.

» Comte de Rochambeau

» Francis Marion crossing the Pee Dee River

JULY 12
Loyalist Captain Christian Huck, ordered to quell Patriot uprisings in South Carolina, is defeated and killed at Williamson's Plantation.

SEPTEMBER 25
André is captured in civilian clothes, whilst carrying incriminating documents. Benedict Arnold flees to safety on a British warship.

OCTOBER 11
The Great Hurricane damages British Admiral George Rodney's fleet at St. Lucia.

NOVEMBER 20
Thomas Sumter's Patriot forces repulse Tarleton's legion at Blackstock's Farm.

DECEMBER 21
Brigadier General Daniel Morgan begins a series of maneuvers into western South Carolina.

New York Theater

The year 1780 brought George Washington to the nadir of his fortunes and General Henry Clinton to the pinnacle of his powers. Yet neither commander was able to break a stalemate that had lasted for two grinding years.

BEFORE

Lack of supplies and the toll taken by severe winters had prevented Washington from making serious progress against the British in New York during 1779.

CITY ENCIRCLED

A military stalemate had prevailed after the clash at **Monmouth Court House** in June 1778 **« 196–97**. With the British holding New York, and the Continental Army positioned in a ragged ring around the city, the war had consisted mainly of raids. In August 1778, the Patriots and French bungled a joint attempt to capture the Rhode Island port of **Newport « 204–05**, but the British voluntarily abandoned the port the following year.

WASHINGTON AT MONMOUTH COURT HOUSE

GAINS ON THE HUDSON

In July 1779, Patriot General Anthony Wayne **took Stony Point**, and in August "Light Horse Harry" Lee **seized Paulus Hook « 236–37** for the Patriots. Such triumphs were short-lived, however, and neither side made the necessary breakthrough to end the deadlock in New York.

Building trust
Relations were guarded when Comte de Rochambeau (center left) first met Washington in September 1780. But after their meeting at Wethersfield, Connecticut, in May 1781 (pictured here), mutual regard prevailed.

The winter of 1779–80 was one of the worst on record. Snowstorms swept the heights about Morristown, New Jersey, Washington's headquarters, and snowdrifts blocked the roads, choking off supply lines. The Continental Army was out of food, and its men and horses were on the verge of starvation. At one point only 3,500 soldiers were still answering roll calls.

The spring thaw turned the roads into quagmires, increasing the misery, and some men could take it no longer. At Jockey Hollow, on May 25, two

> ## "Every idea … of our **distresses** will fall **short of the reality.**"
>
> GEORGE WASHINGTON TO JOSEPH REED, MAY 1780

regiments of the Connecticut Line mutinied, grabbing muskets and threatening to quit the camp. The men were eventually pacified without the use of force, but the episode set a troubling precedent.

Breaking the deadlock

Now that the war was a worldwide conflict, the British Army in New York was much reduced by the dispatch of detachments around the globe. Without the resources to confront and defeat the rebel forces, the British, like their adversaries, conducted a war of forage and raid. Homesteads in the lands between the opposing armies were terrorized by armed desperados.

Nevertheless, in the spring and summer of 1780, Hessian General Wilhelm von Knyphausen tried to lure Washington's army out of its Morristown base, through a series of sorties launched from Staten Island. The New Jersey militia rallied to turn back one attack at Connecticut Farms on June 7. On June 23, General Nathanael Greene's forces parried another thrust led by von Knyphausen at the Battle of Springfield, which was effectively the last significant engagement of the war in the North.

At the end of June, General Sir Henry Clinton, the British commander in chief, returned to New York from the South. He was anxious to end this seemingly interminable war, and spied an opportunity for doing so when intelligence reports informed him that a French fleet—carrying a large force of elite troops—was crossing the Atlantic. It was bound for Newport, the Rhode Island port that Clinton had abandoned two years previously.

Hope and despair

On July 5, French sails were seen off Chesapeake Bay, but then disappeared. Clinton was frantic to find and destroy the enemy fleet, but British ships under the command of Admiral Marriot Arbuthnot were slow to get underway, and on July 10, the French squadron slipped into an anchorage near the Rhode Island port. Clinton hoped to mount an attack on the town, but a shortage of men forced him to settle for a naval blockade.

For George Washington, the report that 5,500 French infantry, cavalrymen, and artillerymen had disembarked at Newport was excellent news. He hoped to combine forces with Comte de Rochambeau, the newly arrived French commander, and attack New York. But it wasn't until September that Washington and his aides crossed the Hudson and rode to Hartford, Connecticut to meet the French commander. Rochambeau, known to possess a brimming war

chest, was all smiles and politesse, but was under secret orders to avoid commitment to the tattered rebel army. Instead, Rochambeau emphasized that any future plans depended on the arrival of French naval reinforcements.

After this disappointing meeting, Washington received another shock; when he rode into West Point, New York, he learned that its commander, Benedict Arnold (see pp.260–61), had defected to join the British.

Clinton's vision

The fall of 1780 marked the passage of yet another fruitless campaigning season in the North. The main action was elsewhere, mostly in the South, where news of Cornwallis's emphatic victory over Horatio Gates at Camden was cheered by Clinton and mourned by Washington. When winter arrived, Washington once again had no food for his army, and his starving men plundered local settlers.

Buoyed by success, Clinton still planned to quash the rebellion. By December 1780, he was thinking about how the British could gain control of the Chesapeake Bay, and therefore of the Bay country, which would cut off Washington from his supplies and sever his communications with the South.

AFTER

In 1781, there were signs that the balance was begining to shift in the rebels' favor, as the Patriot alliance with the French began to bear fruit.

NEW LEADERS, NEW ALLIES

The early months of 1781 saw troops on both sides of the conflict concentrating on land and sea operations in **Virginia**. In June 1781, British Admiral Marriot Arbuthnot—Clinton's naval counterpart and arch rival—was replaced with Admiral Sir Thomas Graves. Summoned to support his compatriot, Rochambeau, French Admiral Comte de Grasse left the West Indies and arrived in the **Chesapeake Bay 300–01 »**, at the end of August, where he encountered the British fleet under Graves.

GERMAN GENERAL 1716–1800

WILHELM VON KNYPHAUSEN

Leader of the 1776 Hessian assault on Fort Washington, Baron Wilhelm von Knyphausen was the epitome of the German professional officer. Born in Luxembourg, this aloof but highly esteemed military leader, spent four decades in the service of Frederick the Great of Prussia before joining the forces of Hesse-Kassel fighting for the British in America in 1776. In 1778, he was appointed commander in chief of all German mercenaries in the War of Independence. He returned to Germany in 1782, where he became the military governor of Hesse-Kassel.

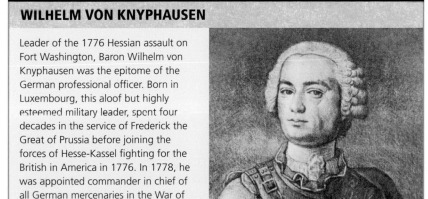

Suspicions confirmed
Militiamen John Paulding, David Williams, and Isaac Van Wart stopped and searched André near Tarrytown, New York. They found incriminating papers in his boot.

Betrayal at West Point

By 1780, General Benedict Arnold, once a Patriot hero, was questioning his loyalty to both the Congress and the Patriot cause. Appointed commander of the strategic stronghold of West Point, Arnold responded with an infamous act of treachery.

« BEFORE

A talented military commander, Benedict Arnold's career had been studded with both victories and disappointments.

OVERLOOKED HERO
Arnold had shown his skill in the **invasion of Canada ‹‹ 80–81** in 1775, and had designed the gondola fleet that **fought on Lake Champlain** in 1776. In spite of his abilities, however, Arnold was not promoted. Because of this, he tried to resign in 1777, but Washington blocked his resignation.

Later that year, Arnold was shot in the leg at **Saratoga ‹‹ 162–63**, a victory for which General Gates received the lion's share of the credit. In 1778, the injured Arnold was given a non-combat role as the military governor of Philadelphia, where he began to form connections with **Loyalist sympathizers**.

Washington badly wanted General Benedict Arnold back in the fight. He knew that Arnold was the best combat officer the Patriots had yet produced, and that he was unsuited to the sedentary role of military governor of Philadelphia. Yet by the summer of 1780, Arnold had still not fully recovered from the leg wound he had sustained at Saratoga, so Washington acquiesced to Arnold's pleas to be given command of West Point, the key to the strategic Hudson River. Arnold assumed command of West Point on August 3.

Washington pays a visit
A few weeks later, on the morning of September 24, as Washington was returning from a conference with the French commanders in Connecticut, he stopped at West Point for breakfast and found its commander gone. On further inspection, he found the fort in a deplorable condition: its garrison scattered, and the giant chain that prevented enemy vessels from sailing up the Hudson River in disrepair.

These worrying findings were, however, dwarfed by the events that were to unfold on Washington's return to Arnold's quarters. Washington was handed a packet of papers that had been taken from a "John Anderson," who had been caught trying to enter the British lines. They contained a pass for Mr. Anderson signed by Arnold, and reports on West Point's troop strength and artillery. It was clear that Arnold was a traitor.

There were a number of possible reasons for Arnold's treachery. Arnold had long resented the fact that his military achievements had not earned him promotion, and been angered by investigations into his financial affairs by the Continental Congress. Accused of benefiting financially from the provision of war-related supplies, he had been court-martialed in 1779 and told to pay the Congress £1,000 (around $190,000 today), for failing to account for his spending in 1775. Furthermore, Arnold's young wife, Peggy, had been accused of having Loyalist sympathies. Perhaps he simply desired to join the winning side—but whatever the reasons, it became clear that Arnold had made his decision more than a year previously.

Coded correspondence
Arnold and André exchanged coded letters using aliases. Arnold called himself "Monk," "Moore," or, as in this case, "Gustavus." André used the alias "John Anderson."

Code for £20,000, the sum Arnold wanted for surrendering West Point

Coded signature of Benedict Arnold

New York saw little action after Arnold's betrayal. Washington had planned to attack Clinton there in 1781, but chose instead to campaign in Virginia.

WAR MOVES TO VIRGINIA
In 1781, after facing General Greene at **Guilford Court House 292–93 »** General Lord Cornwallis decided to go to Virginia, to cut off Greene's supply chain. Washington pushed for an attack on New York City, but his French allies convinced him that **Virginia was a better prospect**. French Admiral de Grasse and his fleet landed off the Chesapeake Bay in early September, and were **confronted by the British 300–01 »**.

INGLORIOUS FATE
Having failed to deliver West Point, Arnold received only part of his reward, but was given his promised brigadier's commission in the British Army. He **landed in Virginia** in 1781 **304–05 »**, and was involved in attacks on Richmond and Petersburg. After the war, he and his wife moved to England. To this day, the name Benedict Arnold is synonymous with treachery.

The road to betrayal
In the summer of 1779, Arnold had begun a long exchange of coded letters with one of Peggy's former admirers, Major John André, a British adjutant general and spymaster under General Sir Henry Clinton. By the summer of 1780, André and Arnold had agreed that, for a brigadier's commission and £20,000 (around $3.8 million today), Arnold would surrender West Point and its garrison to the British. But that September, Arnold offered André an even more enticing catch—Washington himself, who he knew would be passing West Point.

Worried that Arnold might set a trap, Clinton insisted on André meeting Arnold face to face. Before dawn on September 21, a British sloop, HMS *Vulture*, sailed up the Hudson, and

the Patriot lines without a flag of truce and donned civilian clothes in order to ride overland to New York. Finally, and most incriminating of all, he carried a package of papers from Arnold, containing intelligence on West Point.

André had nearly reached the British lines when, on September 23, Patriot militiamen halted and searched him. Finding the package, they took him to their senior officer. Seeing Arnold's signature on "Anderson's" pass, the officer sent a note to Arnold at West Point. Unfortunately for Arnold, the officer also sent the package of papers by special messenger to Washington.

Patriot response
The betrayal was discovered just in time. Washington quickly shored up West Point's defenses. André was put on trial. The military tribunal—which included Marquis de Lafayette, Henry Knox, Nathanael Greene, and Baron von Steuben among its members—was openly sympathetic to the plight of the courteous and considerate young Englishman, but its verdict was a foregone conclusion. Caught without a flag of truce, wearing civilian clothes, and bearing papers containing military secrets on his person, André was sentenced to death as a spy on September 29.

Clinton tried bargaining to get his spymaster back. "Give us Arnold in exchange" was the Patriot response. But Clinton could not agree to this. Arnold had crossed over to the British side, and Clinton knew that any others who might follow suit would be deterred if Arnold was delivered up to certain death. André must be sacrificed, even if doing so "struck Sir Henry to the quick."

On October 2, Washington in his headquarters at Tappan, New Jersey, heard fifes and drums playing as André went to the gallows. The music was then replaced by the sound of men choking back tears. It was over. "Policy required a sacrifice," Washington wrote to Rochambeau on October 10, "but as he was more unfortunate than criminal in the affair ... we could not but lament it."

> "Having become a **cripple** in the **service of my country,** I little expected to meet [such] **ungrateful returns.**"

BENEDICT ARNOLD TO GEORGE WASHINGTON, MAY 1779

"John Anderson" was rowed ashore. Under the shadow of trees, he had a three-hour meeting with Arnold.

Incriminating evidence
Arnold's plot began to unravel when "Anderson"—Major John André—was unable to return to the *Vulture*, which Patriot batteries had forced to retreat downstream. As a result, André crossed

Arnold received the note in his quarters on the morning of September 24, only minutes before Washington's arrival. He informed his wife and told his staff he had business at West Point. He then ordered his bargemen to take him downriver to the waiting HMS *Vulture*, which he boarded, and was then carried to British-occupied New York City.

LOYALIST 1760–1804
PEGGY SHIPPEN
Margaret "Peggy" Shippen, daughter of a Loyalist sympathizer, became friends with John André during the British occupation of Philadelphia. She met Benedict Arnold, who was 20 years her senior, in 1778, and married him in April 1779. When Arnold's betrayal was discovered, Shippen played a role in facilitating his escape, feigning hysteria to buy him time. Although she denied any knowledge of her husband's plans, one of his surviving letters to André has annotations in Shippen's handwriting.

Protecting the Hudson
The Hudson River was of enormous strategic importance, and West Point was the key to its defense. As early as June 1779, Washington worried that a British attack on West Point might "open a new source of supplies to them and a new door to distress and disaffect the country."

257

The **Execution** of **John André**

Sentenced to death by a military tribunal for inciting American General Benedict Arnold to commit treason, the British spy Major John André hoped to be shot like a soldier. Instead, he was hanged in a field in Tappan, New York. He faced the gibbet as only a gallant officer and gentleman could, deeply impressing the large crowd of onlookers, including many former enemies.

"Major André walked from the stone house, in which he had been confined, between two of our subaltern officers, arm in arm … He betrayed no want of fortitude, but retained a complacent smile on his countenance, and politely bowed to several gentlemen whom he knew … When suddenly he came in view of the gallows, he involuntarily started backward, and made a pause. 'Why this emotion, Sir?' said an officer by his side. Instantly recovering his composure, he said, 'I am reconciled to my death, but I detest the mode.' While waiting and standing near the gallows, I observed some degree of trepidation; placing his foot on a stone, and rolling it over and choking in his throat, as if attempting to swallow. So soon, however, as he perceived that things were in readiness, he stepped quickly into the wagon, and … said, 'It will be but a momentary pang,' and taking from his pocket two white handkerchiefs, the provost marshal with one, loosely pinioned his arms, and with the other, the victim, after taking off his hat and stock, bandaged his own eyes with perfect firmness … The rope being appended to the gallows, he slipped the noose over his head and adjusted it to his neck, without the assistance of the awkward executioner. Colonel Scammel now informed him that he had an opportunity to speak, if he desired it; he raised the handkerchief from his eyes and said, 'I pray you to bear me witness that I meet my fate like a brave man.' The wagon being now removed from under him, he was suspended and instantly expired …**"**

CONTINENTAL ARMY SURGEON JAMES THACHER FROM *A MILITARY JOURNAL DURING THE AMERICAN REVOLUTIONARY WAR, FROM 1775 TO 1783*, 1823

Facing death
André made this self-portrait in prison on the evening before his execution, having learned of his fate two days previously. He claimed in a letter to Sir Henry Clinton to be "perfectly tranquil," a state of mind that this image attempts to capture.

DOUBLE AGENT Born 1741 Died 1801

Benedict **Arnold**

"Love to my country actuates my present conduct ..."

BENEDICT ARNOLD, IN A LETTER TO GEORGE WASHINGTON, SEPTEMBER 25, 1780

Reviled in the United States as a traitor and turncoat, Benedict Arnold was a general in the Continental Army who conspired against the Patriots and subsequently fought for the British. His positive attributes—boldness, energy, and courage—made him one of the most notable Patriot commanders in the War of Independence. However, he was also unscrupulous, arrogant, quarrelsome, and mercenary, faults that eventually undermined his commitment to the cause.

Arnold was born into the elite of Connecticut society, the son of a wealthy businessman. In his youth, his prospects were blighted by his father's decline into alcoholism and the collapse of the family fortune. He remained socially well connected, however, and built a successful commercial career in the port of New Haven, first as a pharmacist and then as a merchant operating ships trading with the West Indies and Quebec.

Like other American merchants, Arnold reacted strongly against the Sugar Tax and Stamp Tax in the mid-1760s, which he regarded as direct attacks upon his own business ventures. Evading duties imposed by the British, he became a smuggler. His attachment to the Patriot cause had its origins in self-interest, as well as in a temperamental reluctance to accept any authority other than his own.

Naturally belligerent, in spring 1775 he threw himself into the nascent war against Britain.

Soldiering on

Despite only minimal military training, Arnold had risen to the rank of brigadier general in the Continental Army by January 1776. His actions in the early years of the war showed initiative and great personal bravery. In the fall of 1775, he led an expedition along an arduous and wild route through Maine to Quebec, and in December was wounded in the failed assault on Quebec City. The following year, after retreating to Lake Champlain, he used his knowledge of ships to supervise the building of a makeshift fleet and then commanded it at the Battle of Valcour Island (see pp.128–29). Outnumbered and outgunned by British warships, he inflicted heavy losses on the enemy before

Oath of allegiance

Like all other Continental Army officers, Benedict Arnold was required to sign America's first oath of allegiance in 1778. He broke his oath comprehensively through his treacherous dealings with the British.

succumbing to inevitable defeat. Surviving by luck amid the carnage, Arnold escaped capture and led the remnants of his force to safety.

The climax of Arnold's military career, however, came at the Battle of Saratoga in 1777 (see pp.162–63). Boldly engaging the enemy at Freeman's Farm in the opening round of the battle, he received no support from the cautious General Gates. A violent argument ensued, which resulted in Gates stripping Arnold of his command. Not to be restrained, Arnold joined in the second round of the battle at Bemis Heights on his own initiative, storming into the heart of the fighting to decisive effect. A severe wound sustained in this action left him permanently disabled, with one leg shorter than the other.

Simmering tensions

Arnold was without any doubt an American military hero. But he was a man driven more by personal ambition than by wider ideals.

He constantly complained that he had been passed over for promotion or that others had stolen credit for his actions. His belligerence, which made him so bold and fearless in action, led him into vicious personal disputes with fellow officers, especially General Moses Hazen during the Patriot retreat from Quebec in 1776. Arnold and Hazen worked tirelessly to blacken one another's reputations. Hazen alleged that, during the invasion of Canada, Arnold had exploited his position of command for personal gain. No doubt he did pursue profit in the middle of war, though many others did likewise.

Similar accusations surfaced about Arnold's conduct in Philadelphia, where he was military commander after the British retreat in June 1778. Although officially cleared of these charges, he could not escape the stain to his reputation.

It was during his time in Philadelphia that the first seeds of betrayal were sewn in Arnold's mind. In his own eyes, the mistreatment he suffered at the hands of the Patriots was blatant and insufferable. He not only found himself threatened with prosecution for his business dealings, but was refused reimbursement of money that

Colonel Arnold

This portrait shows Benedict Arnold as a colonel in the Continental Army during the expedition to Canada in 1776. Arnold was an American military hero before earning notoriety as a traitor.

he had spent out of his own pocket on the war effort. In May 1779, he wrote to George Washington: "Having made every sacrifice of fortune and blood and become a cripple in the service of my country, I little expected to meet the ungrateful returns I have received from my countrymen." As military governor of Philadelphia, he was often in the society of pro-British Tories and found among them his second wife, Peggy Shippen. The Philadelphia radicals, by contrast, reviled him.

Switching sides

On top of these personal factors, Arnold was disillusioned by the spectacle of infighting between factions in Congress, and by the apparent incompetence of the Continental Army and state militias. During this stagnant period of the war, his belief in the success of the American cause

Tribute to an American traitor

Arnold is represented in a stained glass window at St. Mary's Church, Battersea, London, where he was interred. The conflicting array of flags is fitting for a man who fought on both sides in the war.

for decisive action, escaping capture by boarding the British sloop HMS *Vulture*, setting sail for New York. His £20,000 fee was reduced to £6,000 ($1,138,000 today) because he had failed to deliver West Point into British hands.

Arnold never accepted that his conduct had been dishonorable. In an open letter that he addressed "To the Inhabitants of America," published in October 1780, he appealed to his countrymen to restore their allegiance to the British Empire. Commissioned as a brigadier general in the British Army soon after this, he fought against the Patriots with the same ruthless energy he had shown on the other

"Judas sold only one man; Arnold three millions."

BENJAMIN FRANKLIN, IN A LETTER TO THE MARQUIS DE LAFAYETTE, MAY 14, 1781

evaporated. Always pursuing first and foremost his own advantage, he came to believe that his interests might be best served by changing sides.

In contact with British agents from spring 1779, he began supplying them with information written in code or invisible ink. Arnold was heavily in debt and the betrayal turned into a sordid negotiation over financial terms. He finally succeeded in raising his price from £10,000 ($1,920,000 today) to £20,000 ($3,800,000 today) after his appointment as commander of West Point (see pp.256–57). When his plot to hand West Point to the British was discovered through the arrest of his British spymaster, Major John André, Arnold showed his habitual capacity

side. He commanded a force that burned Richmond, Virginia, in January 1781, and carried out destructive raids in Connecticut in September of that year.

The taint of treachery stuck to Arnold, blighting his efforts to build a life in Britain after the war. He returned across the Atlantic, experiencing many changes in fortune as a merchant, privateer, and land speculator in Canada and the West Indies. On the island of Guadeloupe, he escaped imprisonment after the French authorities accused him of spying for the British.

Arnold died on June 14, 1801, after four days of delirium, and was buried without military honors.

TIMELINE

- **1741** Born January 14 in Norwich, Connecticut, the son of Benedict Arnold and Hannah Waterman King.
- **1757** Serves briefly in the Connecticut militia during the French and Indian War.
- **1764** Sets up a prosperous business as a merchant trading with the West Indies.
- **1767** Marries Margaret Mansfield; they have three children.
- **May–June 1775** Commissioned as a colonel in the Massachusetts militia, takes part in the capture of Fort Ticonderoga.
- **September–November 1775** Leads a Continental Army expedition to Quebec.
- **December 31, 1775** Wounded in failed assault on Quebec City.
- **January–April 1776** Promoted to brigadier general, commands at siege of Quebec.
- **October 11, 1776** Commands an American fleet at the Battle of Valcour Island.
- **April 1777** Fights against the British at Ridgefield, Connecticut.
- **August 1777** Relieves the siege of Fort Stanwix in the Mohawk River Valley.
- **September–October 1777** Plays a leading role at Saratoga, but clashes with General Gates and is wounded in the leg.
- **May 1778** Signs an oath of allegiance to the United States at Valley Forge.
- **June 1778** Given command of Philadelphia.
- **May 1779** Enters into contact with British spy chief Major John André.

BENEDICT ARNOLD PERSUADING ANDRÉ TO CONCEAL PAPERS IN HIS BOOT.

- **April 1780** In dispute with the Congress and rebuked by Washington, he resigns military command of Philadelphia.
- **August 1780** Assigned to command West Point, he agrees to surrender it to the British.
- **September 1780** Flees to British New York aboard HMS *Vulture* following the arrest of John André.
- **December 1780** Invades Virginia as a brigadier general in the British Army.
- **September 1781** Raids New London, Connecticut, and captures Fort Griswold.
- **1785–91** Settles in New Brunswick, Canada.
- **1793** Trading in the West Indies, escapes after arrest by French authorities on Guadeloupe.
- **1801** Dies on June 14 in London, England.

Caring for the **Wounded**

When the smoke from the battlefields cleared, the human cost of the fighting was revealed. It was the job of the regimental surgeon and his assistants to do what they could to assist the living and alleviate the sufferings of the dying.

After every battle, the field was strewn with the dead: soldiers killed outright when their heads were blown off, or their torsos eviscerated by cannonballs. But often twice as many men lay there alive and wounded—some writhing in agony, and often screaming for mercy. Those among the injured who could, limped to the rear of the field during battle. The more seriously wounded—especially officers—were carried off by their comrades, often in blankets, since there were no stretcher-bearers. Everyone else lay on the field through the heat of the afternoon or even through the night, many bleeding to death, or dying of exposure or thirst. However, as soon as possible after the battle, regimental surgeons and surgeons' mates moved among the bodies to aid the critically wounded. Surgeons from the two armies often worked side by side.

When the wounded were ready to be moved, they were piled into country carts or the army wagons used to transport ammunition and provisions. During the bone-jarring trip to a field hospital, the injured men suffered terrible pain. The British Lieutenant Thomas Anburey, who served in the Battle of Saratoga, recorded witnessing soldiers in "most excruciating torments, sending forth dreadful groans."

Kill or cure

Churches, barns, and private houses with a large parlor or dining room served as temporary hospitals, but sometimes the only building available was a cow-shed. There, the surgeon and his assistants presided over diabolical scenes. While the pile of severed limbs grew ever higher, they separated the soldiers most in need of assistance from those without hope of recovery, such as men shot in the head, near the heart, or in major blood vessels. Imminent death was also certain for anyone shot or bayoneted in the gut. In an era without antibacterial drugs, a bullet or blade perforating the stomach or intestines led to peritonitis—an invariably fatal inflammation caused by bacteria escaping from the digestive tract and entering the body.

Surgeons could sometimes save soldiers hacked by heavy cavalry sabers. Although often fearfully lacerated and permanently disfigured, such cases could often be patched up. Patriot fighter Captain John Stokes sustained broken teeth, a gashed nose, a sliced lip, a severed hand, the loss of a finger on the remaining hand, and an open scalp wound when one of

Banastre Tarleton's troopers sabered him at the Battle of Waxhaws in 1780. Stokes's wounds were dressed with tow—broken hemp fibers—and particles of the material clung to his brain for days. Nonetheless, he lived for many years afterward.

Firearms caused an estimated 60 percent of battle casualties. At close range, a lead musket ball, nearly an inch (2.5 cm) in diameter, flying at perhaps 500 ft (150 m) a second, made a terrific impact upon the body, driving deep into flesh and leaving only a small opening. Once the surgeon had stanched the bleeding, he would widen the opening to remove the ball, using a bullet probe, or even just his bloodstained fingers. It was common to find more than lead embedded in the wound: wadding, epaulettes, leather straps, or part of the soldier's uniform were often driven inside by the force of the blast. If a surgeon could not locate the ball—as was sometimes the case—he would sew up the wound regardless.

A grisly procedure

If a bullet had shattered arm or leg bones, destroying ligaments or joints, the limb was often amputated. This was a painful and dangerous procedure. Anesthesia had not yet been developed; the only palliatives available were rum or a tincture of opium called laudanum. Often, the stricken soldier was given a lead musket ball or a wooden stick to

> **Smallpox killed one in three of those who became infected. Washington wrote that it was more destructive to his army than the enemy's sword.**

America's first
The Pennsylvania Hospital, Philadelphia, was founded in 1751 with Benjamin Franklin's help. It treated British soldiers in the winter of 1777–78, but was used by the Patriots after the British Army evacuated Philadelphia.

Easing the pain
Doctors had a small number of drugs at their disposal. The inscriptions on these apothecary jars identify the medicines inside. "BALS: LOCAT," for example, stands for *Balsamum locatelli*, used to treat bruising.

BEFORE

In the 18th century, doctors had little understanding of how infections spread, and many soldiers died of disease as well as from their wounds.

LIMITED KNOWLEDGE
Although the idea was in decline by the 18th century, some physicians still believed that illness was caused by "four humors." The practice of **bloodletting** was fairly common, and without knowledge of sterilization, wounds often became infected. Diseases could spread fast, especially in **army camps ❮❮ 184–85** and **prisons ❮❮ 166–67**. There had, however, been some progress in surgical techniques, and human anatomy was well understood, thanks to the work of 16th-century surgeon Andreas Vesalius.

> "The wounded had **remained out all night ... some of them begged** they might **lay and die.**"
>
> LIEUTENANT THOMAS ANBUREY, AFTER THE BATTLE OF FREEMAN'S FARM, NEAR SARATOGA, 1777

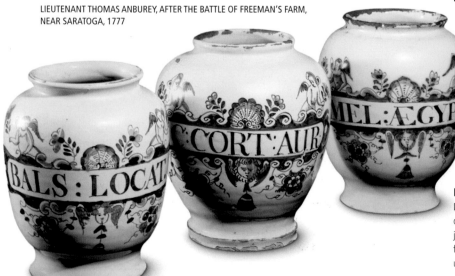

bite down on. Men subjected to torment of amputation often needed to be pinned to the operating table while the surgeon applied a tourniquet to major arteries, sliced through muscle, and then wielded his bone. An experienced surgeon could saw through bone in less than a minute, but the entire procedure could take a half hour. Under ideal circumstances, the surgeon finished by tying off severed blood vessels with ligatures, but there was rarely time for this. Instead the stump was often cauterized with a red-hot iron, sending many patients into shock. Without sterile instruments or dressings, infection was unavoidable, often leading to tetanus or gangrene. Only about a third of amputees survived the procedure.

Permanently scarred

The treatment of head wounds could entail a similarly traumatic ordeal, especially if the surgeon drilled out part of the skull—a process called trepanning—to relieve pressure on the brain, or drain blood. After British Lieutenant St. George Mansergh of the 52nd Foot was shot in the head at Germantown, the surgeon removed such a large portion of bone from the side of his skull that the wound never fully healed. For the rest of his life, Mansergh wore a silver plate over the hole, and was left "feeble, emaciated, and in almost constant pain," the poet Anna Seward observed.

Many soldiers died from their wounds. Others succumbed to the after effects. Some recovered to live long lives, and went to their graves with a musket ball still lodged somewhere in their frames.

A woman's touch
Nursing was dangerous, and those who took it up were exposed to disease. Some camp followers were offered rations and pay to become nurses; others were threatened with the loss of rations if they did not.

Military medicine did not improve until the mid-19th century, when scientific advances and better organization had an impact.

SLOW IMPROVEMENT
In 1793, Baron Dominique Jean Larrey placed surgical teams near the front lines during the **French Revolutionary Wars**, and introduced a form of triage. In the 19th century, ether (1846) and chloroform (1847) were used to ease the pain of surgery. The demands of the **American Civil War** (1861–65) led to the creation of an effective military medical corps.

AMERICAN PHYSICIAN 1746–1813

BENJAMIN RUSH

A signatory of the Declaration of Independence, Dr. Benjamin Rush attended the wounded at the battles of Princeton and Brandywine. In 1777, he became surgeon general of the middle department in the Continental Army, but resigned in 1778, accusing Director of Hospitals Dr. William Shippen of dereliction of duty. An advocate of bloodletting, Rush's *Directions for preserving the health of soldiers* remained in use for well over a century.

Medical Equipment

Eighteenth-century medicine was rudimentary: little was understood about bacteria or how diseases spread. Consequently, more soldiers died of disease than on the battlefield, and small wounds were frequently fatal.

[1] **Surgical manual** This French book provided instruction for major operations. The level of surgical training and experience among doctors was often low. [2] **Bone saw** Musket balls could smash a soldier's limbs, necessitating amputation. This saw would cut through the large arm or leg bones. [3] **Folding knife** Folding knives were carried for emergency use. [4] **Tongue depressor** Used to hold the patient's tongue in place, this device allowed examination of the mouth and throat. [5] **Folding knife** This multipurpose knife is enclosed in a paper-mache case. [6] **Fleam** With a choice of blades, this handheld metal instrument was used for phlebotomy—bloodletting. [7] **Falciform amputation knife** A surgeon would use this knife to cut in a circular motion, slicing away skin and muscle before sawing the bone. [8] **Scalpel** Like its modern counterpart, this extremely sharp knife would have been used in surgery. [9] **Amputation knife** Straight knives were used in amputations to cut soft tissue, leaving a flap of skin to fold over the stump. [10] **Lancet set** This case, designed to hold six lancets, is made of green sharkskin with a silver trim. [11] **Lancets** As is the case today, lancets were used to incise and dissect smaller tissue. [12] **Bloodletting set** This leather box contains equipment needed to bleed a patient, a process thought to remove impurities from the body. [13] **Surgical kit** Owned by Charles McKnight, a surgeon in the Continental Army, this kit contains saws, knives, and scalpels. [14] **Apothecary scale** Medicines and their ingredients were weighed out on scales. [15] **Cast-iron mortar and pestle** These were used to grind herbs and mix drugs. [16] **Traveling medicine chest** Typically these contained bottled remedies, ready for use, but no antiseptics, which, like anesthetics, were still unknown.

[1] SURGICAL MANUAL

[2] BONE SAW

[3] FOLDING KNIFE

[4] TONGUE DEPRESSOR

[5] FOLDING KNIFE

[7] FALCIFORM AMPUTATION KNIFE

[8] SCALPEL

[6] FLEAM

[9] AMPUTATION KNIFE

10 LANCET SET

11 LANCETS

12 BLOODLETTING SET

13 SURGICAL KIT

14 APOTHECARY SCALE

15 CAST-IRON MORTAR AND PESTLE

16 TRAVELING MEDICINE CHEST

The Siege of Charleston

In the spring of 1780, British Commander in Chief General Sir Henry Clinton and 8,500 troops left New York for the Carolinas. Assembling on the islands south of Charleston, the invasion force prepared to seize South Carolina's biggest city and leading port.

« BEFORE

Buoyed by the capture of Savannah in 1778, the British looked at ways to achieve a breakthrough in the South.

SOUTHERN OBJECTIVES

Britain's southern strategy began in 1778 with the **seizure of Savannah « 210–11.** A Franco-American attempt had failed to regain the town in 1779, and the Patriot commander in the South, General Benjamin Lincoln, had retreated to Charleston—the next target on General Sir Henry Clinton's list. Having been **repulsed outside Charleston in 1776 « 110–11,** Clinton was determined to succeed with a new attempt.

It was such a stormy passage from New York to South Carolina that it took 40 days before the British invasion force landed on the islands south of Charleston. The notoriously seasick Sir Henry Clinton yearned to set foot on dry land, but it was his German Jaegers who preceded him, debarking on the lightly inhabited Simmons Island. Wading chest-deep through the swamps, the redoubtable Germans met no resistance.

General Benjamin Lincoln had elected to move his Patriot force behind Charleston's protective works

The art of siege warfare

Over the course of the siege, the British dug a series of trenches to close the 800 yard (730 m) gap between themselves and the rebel lines, and to increase the power and accuracy of their artillery.

at the bottom of the peninsula formed by the Cooper River to the north and the Ashley to the south, positively inviting a siege. Perhaps he thought Fort Moultrie on Sullivan's Island would keep the Royal Navy at bay, or that they would be rescued by a French fleet, or that the swamps would defeat a landward approach.

Whatever Lincoln's reasoning, he was mistaken. Clinton crossed the Ashley River with ease, and was soon bearing down on the city. On April 1, his army began digging the first in a series of siege trenches.

Eight days later, as British artillerists mounted guns in the trenches, the Royal Navy's Admiral Arbuthnot ran the gauntlet past Fort Moultrie and brought eight ships of the line and six frigates into Charleston's inner harbor. The city was now vulnerable to cannonading from both land and sea.

Fight or flight

On April 10, under a flag of truce, Clinton offered terms, but Lincoln unwisely refused them. Even the Patriot Governor John Rutledge knew they were trapped. On April 13, he

and several members of the governing council escaped Charleston, aiming to resist from North Carolina. One lifeline still remained open, a track fording the Cooper River 30 miles (50 km) to the north at a crossroads called Monck's Corner, guarded by a mixed force of soldiers and militia.

The next day, April 14, the British closed this last lifeline. Two hard-charging and promising young British officers, Lieutenant Colonel Banastre Tarleton (see pp.272–73) and Major Patrick Ferguson attacked and routed the rebels there. Tarleton's Legion—a mixed force of cavalry and infantry raised from Pennsylvania Loyalists—acted with savagery, sabering one French officer after he surrendered. The city was now doomed. By April

Badge of honor
Among the British units serving at Charleston was the 71st Regiment of Foot—popularly known as Fraser's Highlanders—who marched overland from Savannah to join Clinton.

20, the siege works were within 250 yards (230 m) of the rebel defenses. By May 6, the lines were only 100 yards (90 m) apart, and Hessian sharpshooters were killing any defenders who showed their heads.

On May 9 and 10, Clinton unleashed a terrific bombardment. As mortar rounds and incendiary shells dropped on their rooftops, prominent Charlestonians begged Lincoln to come to terms. Their city was in shambles. Even the statue of William Pitt, the great prime minister and friend to the colonies, lost an arm to a cannonball. On May 12, after a 42-day siege,

Lincoln surrendered Charleston and its 5,000-man garrison.

Counting the cost

For the Patriots, it was a disaster. With no Continental army left in the South, the militia garrisons of Ninety-Six, Camden, Beaufort, and Georgetown also laid down their arms. They all received the same terms: Continental officers and men became prisoners of war, while civilians and militiamen were paroled, pledged on pain of death not to take up arms again.

For the British, it was their greatest victory of the war. In London, cannons were fired in celebration. Now that the South's main seaport was in hand, and with the effective restoration of Georgia to the Crown in 1778, the pacification of South Carolina could begin, a task entrusted to General Lord Cornwallis. "All the rebel grandees have come in," Clinton wrote triumphantly to a friend in England.

Then, just before sailing back to New York, Clinton made his one mistake. On June 3, as backcountry Loyalists were beginning to take revenge on the rebels, he issued a proclamation abrogating the terms of surrender. Parolees were ordered to pledge allegiance to the king and take up arms or be declared "rebels and enemies to their country." They had 17 days to come to a decision.

AMERICAN OFFICER 1733–1810
BENJAMIN LINCOLN

Although too often irresolute during the siege of Charleston, Major General Benjamin Lincoln was an "active, spirited, sensible Man," in George Washington's opinion. Born in Hingham, Massachusetts, Lincoln proved a reliable commander of New England militia—in spite of having no combat experience prior to the war—and was wounded at Saratoga. Paroled after the fiasco at Charleston, he stood at Washington's side when the British surrendered at Yorktown (see pp.306–07).

AFTER

With the surrender of an entire army at Charleston, Patriot military activity in the South collapsed.

FROM THE JAWS OF DEFEAT
Partisan warriors such as Francis Marion, Thomas Sumter, and Andrew Pickens picked up the fight, attacking British forces in a series of **guerrilla raids 268–69 ≫**. Patriot General **Horatio Gates was sent South** with a new army, but this new campaign got off to a disastrous start in August 1780 against Lord Cornwallis at the **Battle of Camden 274–75 ≫**. However, Patriot fortunes revived with the appointment of **Nathanael Greene** as the commander of the southern department in October 1780.

Guerilla War in South Carolina

Away from the sieges and battles of the main armies, South Carolina witnessed a different kind of warfare in the backcountry—guerrilla attacks by Patriots on British forts and Loyalist communities.

PATRIOT CAVALRYMAN 1756–1818

LT. COLONEL HENRY LEE

Henry Lee became Washington's favorite cavalryman, winning his nom de guerre "Light Horse Harry" through his superb horsemanship. Lee personally raised and equipped "Lee's Legion" and his successful raids on British supply trains kept the Continental Army fed in the hard winter of 1776–77. During the southern campaign, Lee proved as adept at guerrilla warfare as the Patriot partisans. He was the father of Confederate Commander Robert E. Lee.

On May 29, 1780, British Lieutenant Colonel Banastre Tarleton's Legion, otherwise known as Tarleton's Raiders, cornered Colonel Abraham Buford's Virginia Continentals at the Waxhaws, an area on the border of North and South Carolina. When Tarleton called on him to surrender, Buford refused. Within the hour, 113 Continental soldiers had been killed and 150 wounded, many of them sabered or bayoneted when they were already hurt and unable to resist or were trying to surrender. No quarter was given. "Tarleton's Quarter"—a term that became synonymous with massacre—heralded an escalation of the already vicious war in South Carolina.

A civil war
In blundering into the backcountry in the summer of 1780, the British Army stirred up a long-simmering local conflict and turned it into a full-blown civil war. After the fall of Charleston to the British in May, Loyalists from all over the state emerged to join the fight. Many of them were protecting land grants issued by the Crown; others were highwaymen and cutthroats who had long plagued the region, and joined the winning side in hope of plunder.

The Loyalists burned down houses and plantations, and soon Patriot posses were gathering in the night to hang those they saw as traitors. What really incensed the populace

was a proclamation by General Clinton on June 3, 1780, which called for South Carolinians to swear loyalty to the British, or be labeled "rebels and enemies." Faced with having to choose one side or the other, and risk reprisals for their choice, many people with no strong allegiance sought to join the Patriot bands haunting the woods.

In the feuding backcountry, father might fight against son, cousin against cousin, settling old scores. But these bands of men, called "partisans," now also directed their energies at the British Army. They

attacked outposts, raided supply convoys, and cut sentries' throats—frequently applying "Tarleton's Quarter." The British were forced to detach more and more soldiers to act as escorts and guards.

Partisan heroes
The most famous partisan was not a backcountry man at all. Francis Marion, known as the "Swamp Fox," was a Low Country planter who waged

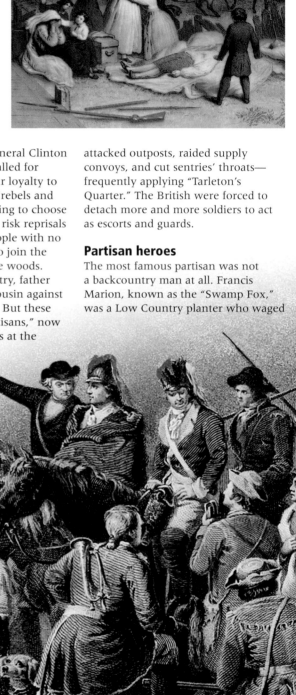

Mourning the massacre
Andrew Jackson, who later became the seventh president of the United States, witnessed Tarleton's massacre of the Waxhaws Continentals as a child of 13.

Guerrilla force
The "Swamp Fox" and his men crossed the Pee Dee River in South Carolina to harass the British. Some of Marion's volunteers were African American—like the man rowing the shallow boat in William Ranney's romanticized painting.

war from the marshes and forests of the South Carolina coasts. Marion worked with regular troops—such as Colonel Henry Lee, who led the Patriot equivalent of Tarleton's Legion. But Marion also surrounded himself with volunteers: armed with rough-hewn sabers fashioned from plantation wood saws, and guns with lethal No. 2 goose-shot that could tear men to pieces at close range. In November 1780, when Tarleton tried to catch him, Marion proved too elusive.

Thomas Sumter, on the other hand, was in many ways Marion's opposite. The "Carolina Gamecock" was both pugnacious and independent, and Cornwallis found him to be the "greatest plague" of all. Sumter promulgated "Sumter's Law," a

The wily "Swamp Fox" lived up to his name, eluding the British for seven hours on November 8, over a distance of 26 miles (48 km).

promise to pay his recruits with plunder taken from Loyalists. He was also known for "Sumter's fruit," the many supposed traitors he hanged from the nearest tree.

In August 1780, after the Battle of Camden (see pp.374–75) Tarleton surprised Sumter at Fishing Creek, killing many of his men. Sumter escaped bareback, with no hat, coat, or boots. However, the fight wasn't over. On November 20, at William Blackstock's farm, Sumter's riflemen shot at Tarleton's troops from behind outhouses and fences, strewing the road with bodies.

Marion and Sumter were not the only noted leaders. Andrew Pickens became the leading partisan in the western areas, winning victory at

Kettle Creek. North Carolina's William Davie reputedly killed more men with his saber than any other Patriot officer in the war. Georgia's Elijah Clarke teamed up with Isaac Shelby, one of the so-called Overmountain Men who later fought at Kings Mountain (see pp.280–81), to kill more than 60 Loyalists at the Battle of Musgrove's Mill in August 1780.

Redcoats diminished

By December, civil war had wrecked the backcountry, and British supply deliveries were so constricted that when Cornwallis settled into winter quarters near Winnsboro, South Carolina, his ragged men were nearly starving. By the time General Nathanael Greene arrived to oppose them, the British Army had been worn thin by guerrilla warfare.

AFTER

General Greene arrived in South Carolina to find the enemy army in a sorry state, but he struggled to make the most of this advantage.

RUN RAGGED
Building on the success of the partisans, Greene wore Cornwallis's army down further in the so-called **Race to the Dan**. Although his army fought hard at **Guilford Court House 292–93 »**, Greene failed to defeat Cornwallis. However, Greene's persistence caused Cornwallis to **move his forces to Virginia 304–05 »**, where he hoped to cut his enemy's supply lines.

"This **old fox,** the Devil himself could not **catch him.**"

BANASTRE TARLETON ON FRANCIS MARION, NOVEMBER 8, 1780

Impressions of the Swamp Fox

Francis Marion—the "Swamp Fox"—is seen as a Robin Hood of the southern forests, his band of brothers warring against a tyrannical king. In reality, he was an innovative guerrilla fighter whose mounted men regularly menaced British supply lines and isolated outposts. Cavalryman Henry "Light-Horse Harry" Lee, who served alongside Marion, left a vivid portrait of the man behind the legend.

"Marion was about forty-eight years of age, small in stature, hard in visage, healthy, abstemious and taciturn. Enthusiastically wedded to the cause of liberty, he deeply deplored the doleful condition of his beloved country ... Fertile in stratagem, he struck unperceived; and retiring to those hidden retreats, selected by himself, in the morasses of Pedee and Black River, he placed his corps not only out of the reach of his foe, but often out of the discovery of his friends.

An officer, with a small party, preceded [me] a few days march to find out Marion, who was known to vary his position in the swamps of Pedee: sometimes in South Carolina, sometimes in North Carolina, and sometimes on the Black River. With the greatest difficulty did this officer learn how to communicate with the brigadier; and that by the accident of hearing ... of a small provision party of Marion's... was conveyed to the general, who had changed his ground since his party left him, which occasioned many hours' search even before his own men could find him."

GENERAL HENRY LEE, FROM *MEMOIRS OF THE WAR IN THE SOUTHERN DEPARTMENT OF THE UNITED STATES*, 1869

Mythical meal
An apocryphal tale of Francis Marion sharing a meal of roasted sweet potatoes with a British officer was a popular vignette of the War of Independence. This version, the "Sweet Potato Picture," by John Blake White, appeared on the back of the Confederate $10 bill.

BRITISH MILITARY OFFICER Born 1754 Died 1833

Banastre Tarleton

"I have cut 170 officers and men to pieces."

BANASTRE TARLETON, IN A REPORT TO GENERAL CORNWALLIS, MAY 1780

The young British cavalry officer, Banastre Tarleton brought dash and energy to the conduct of the war in America. His performance compared favorably with the pedestrian and lackluster efforts of many British commanders, and the British public hailed him as a hero. His opponents, however, denounced him as a ruthless officer who laid waste to Patriot communities in pursuit of victory, paying no regard to the established rules of war.

Dissolute youth

Tarleton came from an unusual background for a British cavalryman. He was born in the fast-growing port of Liverpool, where his family had made its fortune in the Atlantic trade in sugar and slaves. His father intended for him to become a lawyer, but this was not a career likely to suit his son's wild temperament. On the death of his father, Tarleton inherited £5,000—equal to more than $1.2 million today—at the age of just 21. Within two years he had spent it on gambling and loose living. Despairing over his conduct, his widowed mother paid for him to join the army as a cornet, the lowest grade of cavalry officer, in the 1st King's Dragoon Guards.

Tarleton volunteered for service in the American war, but there is no reason to believe he had any high military ambitions. Once in America, he continued with the womanizing

and gambling that had brought him to grief in England. He had a moment of luck on December 13, 1776, when he was part of a patrol that captured American General Charles Lee after surprising him in his dressing gown at White's Tavern in Basking Ridge, New Jersey. Considered to have performed well in this notable coup, Tarleton was promoted to the rank of captain, but advancement depended on family influence.

In 1778, an infantry regiment, the Royal Liverpool Volunteers, was established in Tarleton's home city. His family obtained for him an offer of a lieutenant-colonel's rank in the new regiment, but when Tarleton discovered it was bound for the West Indies, where disease often made service a death sentence, he declined the offer. Instead, an obscure post was found for him in New York as lieutenant colonel of the British Legion—a new formation of Loyalist infantry and cavalry.

Battlefield commander

In 1780, this backwater role suddenly brought Tarleton into the limelight. Sent to join in the siege of Charleston, he led the Legion in bold actions at Monck's Corner and Lenud's Ferry that blocked the Patriots' escape routes from the city and won him praise from his superiors. He was then ordered to pursue a force of Virginia Continental Army troops, under the command of Colonel Abraham Buford, which was heading away from Charleston. Driving his men and horses at a relentless pace, Tarleton caught the Virginians at Waxhaws and cut them to pieces in a frenzied attack. The slaughter continued after the Patriots attempted to surrender.

"Even his fellow officers felt no love for Tarleton."

COLONEL RODERICK MACKENZIE, 1787

Cultivating a romantic image
The British portrait artist Sir Joshua Reynolds painted Tarleton on his return to England in 1782. Dressed in the uniform of the British Legion that he had led in America, he is every inch the dashing cavalry officer who captured the imagination of the British people.

Butchery in battle

An American engraving shows Tarleton's mounted Loyalists cutting down Patriot soldiers at Waxhaws in 1780. Patriot propagandists seized upon the "Waxhaws Massacre" as an example of their enemies' brutality and demonized Tarleton.

For British General Charles Cornwallis, Tarleton's conduct at Waxhaws confirmed his impression that he had found a young commander with the aggression and ruthlessness he needed to lead a counterinsurgency campaign in the South.

Reckless reputation

The British Legion became known as "Tarleton's Raiders" as they marauded across South Carolina, inflicting destruction on any farms or settlements deemed to support the Patriots. Their attacks on civilians and property served only to alienate the hearts and minds of the population from the Loyalist cause.

Tarleton sought to engage Patriot irregulars in fighting, in particular Francis Marion, the elusive "Swamp Fox." His efforts regarding Marion were frustrated, but he twice clashed with General Thomas Sumter's Carolina militia. At Fishing Creek in August 1780, he caught Sumter by surprise and routed his numerically superior force, but at Blackstock's Farm three months later Sumter was better prepared and inflicted heavy casualties on the Legion. This did not stop Tarleton from claiming success.

In fact, Tarleton's virtues as a battlefield commander were limited. He was fearless and aggressive, but invariably lacked subtlety and judgment and bold frontal attack was more or less the only tactic he understood. In the major British

victory at Camden in 1780, he served Cornwallis well by leading a shock cavalry charge against already shaken Continental troops. However, in January 1781, when Cornwallis gave him two battalions of infantry to augment his Volunteers in pursuit of a Patriot force commanded by General Daniel Morgan, such tactics backfired. With his usual energy, Tarleton succeeded in bringing Morgan to battle at Cowpens (see pp.290–91) but his immediate full-on frontal assault played into the hands of Morgan's defenses. The result was a catastrophic defeat from which Tarleton was fortunate to escape—more than 800 of his 1,050 soldiers were killed, wounded, or taken prisoner.

Surprisingly, this debacle did not noticeably damage Tarleton's standing or rein in his impetuous courage. He lost two fingers of his right hand while leading cavalry in the British pyrrhic victory at Guilford Court House in March 1781. In the subsequent campaign in Virginia, he narrowly failed to capture Thomas Jefferson in

a raid on the Virginia legislature at Charlottesville. His final action in the war was a skirmish with French cavalry at Gloucester Point during the siege of Yorktown. After the British surrender at Yorktown on October 19, 1781 (see pp.306–07), during which Tarleton was excluded from the usual courtesies extended to the defeated, he was paroled and returned to Britain.

Royal favorite

Lacking true war heroes, the British elite feted Tarleton. When his war record was attacked, he fought back in print with aggressive self-justification and denigration of Cornwallis. He drifted into the raffish circle of the Prince of Wales, eventually forming a liaison with the Prince's ex-mistress, the famous actress Mary Robinson. Taking up politics, he became the member of parliament for Liverpool, resolutely defending the slave trade—the origin of his family fortune—against its critics, aided by his wife, Priscilla Bertie, the illegitimate daughter of a duke, whom he married in 1798. He did not, however, officially leave the army, and rose effortlessly through the higher ranks to full general, despite playing almost no part in Britain's prolonged wars with France between 1793 and 1815. Tarleton lived to the ripe old age of 78. In American popular culture, he survives into the 21st century as a hated figure.

The Tarleton helmet

When leading the British Legion in the War of Independence, Tarleton introduced a new helmet made of leather, with a fur crest and a white plume. The Tarleton helmet was adopted by British dragoons from 1789 and was worn throughout the Napoleonic Wars in Europe (1803–15).

TIMELINE

- **1754** Born in Liverpool, England, on August 24, the son of wealthy merchant John Tarleton and his wife, Jane.

- **1770–71** Studies law.

- **1773** Inherits a large fortune from his father, which he quickly squanders.

- **April 1775** Mother purchases a junior officer's commission for him in the Dragoon Guards.

- **February 1776** Sails for the Carolinas.

- **August 1776** After the failure of the first siege of Charleston, joins the army in New York.

- **December 1776** Distinguishes himself in the capture of American General Charles Lee.

- **August 1777–June 1778** Takes part in the Philadelphia Campaign, including the battles of Brandywine and Monmouth.

- **July 1778** Promoted to lieutenant-colonel, he is given command of the Loyalist British Legion.

- **April-May 1780** Plays a prominent part in the siege of Charleston.

- **May 29,1780** Accused of the massacre of Patriot prisoners after the Battle of Waxhaws.

- **August 1780** Contributes to the British victory at Camden.

- **January 1781** Suffers a catastrophic defeat at the Battle of Cowpens.

- **March 1781** Loses two fingers at the Battle of Guilford Court House.

- **October 1781** One of the British officers who surrender at Yorktown.

- **1782** Back in Britain, he joins the circle of the Prince of Wales, courting the prince's former mistress, Mary Robinson.

TARLETON'S POSTWAR MISTRESS, MARY ROBINSON, PAINTED BY THOMAS GAINSBOROUGH

- **1787** Publishes *History of the Campaigns of 1780 and 1781*, a defense of his war record.

- **1790** Elected to parliament.

- **December 1798** Marries Priscilla Susan Bertie; they have one child.

- **1812** His parliamentary career ends; promoted to full general.

- **1816** Made a baronet; knighted 1820.

- **1833** Dies on January 15, in Herefordshire.

BEFORE

Since 1778, the British had poured effort and resources into conquering the southern colonies.

FIGHT FOR THE SOUTH

The need to conserve resources to counter the entry of France into the conflict led the British to shift the focus of their war effort to the South. The **capture of Savannah in 1778 ‹‹ 210–11** gave the British a base from which to re-establish their control of the region, and British dominance was reinforced when Lord Cornwallis's forces **seized Charleston ‹‹ 266–67** in spring 1780, decimating the Continental Army in the South.

PUNISHMENT AND REVENGE

After the fall of Charleston, a vicious, highly personal struggle developed between Loyalists and Patriots in the South, with atrocities committed by both sides. British Lieutenant Colonel **Banastre Tarleton** notoriously destroyed an American force at the **Waxhaws ‹‹ 268–69** in May 1780, but could not subdue his many enemies, including noted guerrilla fighters such as **Thomas Sumter** and **Francis Marion**.

FRANCIS MARION, THE "SWAMP FOX"

PATRIOT GENERAL 1721–80

JOHANN DE KALB

Johann von Robais, Baron de Kalb, was a Bavarian-born French officer who served as a major general in the Continental Army. He fought for France in Europe between 1740 and 1770, and first visited America on a secret mission in 1768, to investigate the strength of anti-British opinion in the colonies. De Kalb joined the Continental Army in the fall of 1777, and later commanded a division of Maryland and Delaware troops. Disappointed to be overlooked for the command of the forces in the South in 1780, he died from wounds sustained in the Battle of Camden.

Battle of Camden

Following the defeat at Charleston and the loss of its entire southern army, the Patriot leadership gave General Gates command of a new army in May 1780, with the aim of regaining the initiative in the South.

George Washington and the Continental Congress rarely agreed on military matters. After the fall of Charleston in 1780, the commander in chief preferred that the tough and resourceful General Johann de Kalb, who had been with the army at Valley Forge in 1777–78, continue to lead the only force that might counter Lord Cornwallis's astonishing progress through South Carolina. But the Continental Congress disagreed, preferring instead to appoint the "Hero of Saratoga," General Horatio Gates (see pp.278–79).

Amiable and polite, yet also vain and obtuse, Gates, a former British Army officer, took over de Kalb's corps of 3,000 men based in North Carolina on July 25. Two days later he marched this force of mainly raw militia, toward Camden, the principal British depot in the center of South Carolina. De Kalb advised taking a circuitous route, but Gates insisted on following a direct path, even though it took the army through lands destitute of forage save for green corn and green peaches that made many of his soldiers ill.

Welsh contribution

This insignia comes from the kit of a soldier in the 23rd Regiment of Foot, the Royal Welch Fusiliers, which fought at Camden. Twenty-four of its men were wounded during the battle.

Surprise encounter

On the evening of August 15, Gates stumbled into Cornwallis's army some 5 miles (8 km) north of Camden. Gates thought the earl was in Savannah, whereas Cornwallis had just ridden to Camden to take command of the 2,200 veteran Redcoats assembling there. By dawn on August 16, the armies were lined up, several hundred yards apart, across the road leading from Camden northward to Charlotte. Gates positioned General Mordecai Gist's 900 experienced Maryland and Delaware regulars, commanded by de Kalb, in the traditional post of honor on the right. His nervous Virginia and North Carolina militiamen lined up in the center and on the left. Some 600 yards (550 m) to the rear, in the middle of the road, Gates sat on his horse, reputed to be the fastest mount in the country. He listened as the guns fired to open the battle, confident of success.

Guns blazing

The Patriot artillery fired before the British had finished deploying. They made little impact, however, for Cornwallis had seen the militia to his front and, leaving Lord Francis Rawdon to hold the left, moved his best units to his right, opposite the Virginians and North Carolinians. With a cheer, his light infantry fired a volley and followed it with a bayonet charge.

The Virginians managed to loose a volley of their own before taking to their heels. The North Carolina militia did not even do that; they fled from the field, tossing their loaded muskets to the ground. Within minutes there was a total rout, as thousands ran for their lives. At the rear, Gates cantered around, then turned his charger, put spurs to its flank, and galloped toward Charlotte.

Meanwhile, in the smoke and chaos of battle, de Kalb almost certainly had no idea that the entire left wing had

fled. Furiously attacking Lord Rawdon's lines, his Marylanders and Delawares may even have thought victory was in sight. But the British regulars on the right wing, having routed the militia, simply wheeled left and attacked the Continentals in their exposed flank. Suddenly it was 600 men against 2,000 encircling Redcoats. De Kalb's horse was shot from beneath him, but the 59-year-old kept fighting, personally leading bayonet charges.

At that moment Banastre Tarleton's British Legion cavalry, having circled behind the Patriot lines, slammed into the rear of de Kalb's forces, and the Marylanders broke and ran

Camden ⎯⎯⎯

Swampy ground

De Kalb's Maryland and Delaware regulars

Battle lines

The disposition of inexperienced Virginia and North Carolina militia in opposition to the British regulars can be seen in this map of the battle drawn up by a British officer afterward. The swampy ground on each flank limited the possibility of extensive maneuvering.

to avoid the slashing sabers. Cannons, muskets, and colors were abandoned. De Kalb collapsed, fatally lacerated by 11 sword, bullet, and bayonet wounds. On Cornwallis's orders, the dying man was taken to a hospital in Camden.

The aftermath

Cornwallis had won a tremendous victory; another Patriot army had disintegrated. Tarleton led a pursuit that eventually covered 20 miles (32 km) along a road littered with broken wagons, dead horses, and cast-off equipment. Abandoned women and crying children were all that remained of the camp followers, while in the nearby swamps, militiamen were heading for home or dying lonely deaths.

Eight field pieces, 200 wagons, and about 1,000 Continentals were taken prisoner. Hundreds of rebels were dead; British losses were relatively light at 68 killed and 256 wounded. Two days later, Tarleton caught up with the Patriot fighter Thomas Sumter at Fishing Creek, where he killed 150 of Sumpter's militia and captured more than 50 of his wagons.

Horatio Gates proved impossible to catch. When one Patriot major, galloping alongside for a moment, asked what to do about the slain, he received a curt reply: "Let the dead bury the dead!" It was said that Gates did not draw rein until he reached Charlotte, a distance of 60 miles (100 km) from the battle. On a fresh horse, he then rode another 120 miles (200 km) to Hillsboro, North Carolina. General de Kalb—who died three days after the battle—was so well-respected by both sides that Cornwallis gave him a funeral with full military honors.

AFTER ⟫

For the Patriots, defeat at Camden made clear the need for changes at the top. New leadership led to improving fortunes in the fall of 1780.

CHANGING THE GAME

After Camden, Gates was removed from command in the South. He was replaced by **Nathanael Greene**, who reorganized his forces, and changed the nature of the war in the South. This enabled the Patriot militia to take on their Loyalist counterparts at **Kings Mountain 280–81** ⟫ in October 1780, and a few months later, British regulars led by Tarleton were confronted by Continentals commanded by Daniel Morgan at the **Battle of Cowpens 290–91** ⟫.

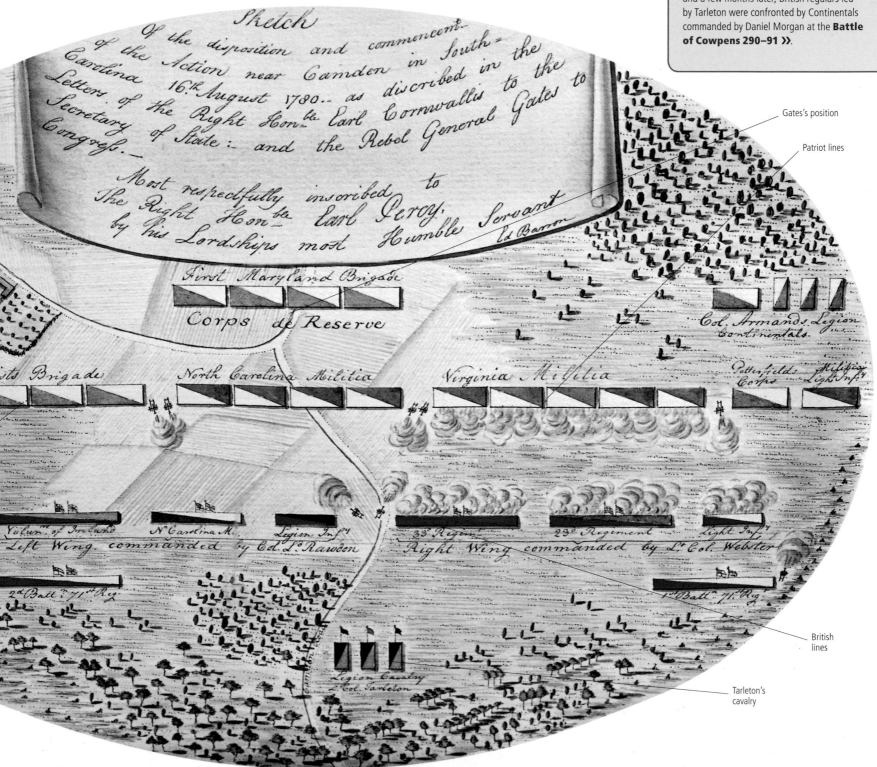

Gates's position

Patriot lines

British lines

Tarleton's cavalry

Felled at Camden
The dying Patriot General Johann de Kalb is spared another bayonet thanks to the pleas of his aide, the Chevalier du Buysson, in *The Battle of Camden—Death of de Kalb* by Alonzo Chappel.

UNITED STATES GENERAL Born 1728 Died 1806

Horatio **Gates**

> "Our business is to **defend the main chance;** to attack only… when a precious advantage offers."

HORATIO GATES, LETTER TO JOHN ADAMS, APRIL 23, 1776

Conspiracy theory
In 1777–78 General Gates lived in this house in York, Pennsylvania, then the seat of the Continental Congress. Reportedly, members of the "Conway Cabal" met here with Gates to conspire against Washington.

As the general in command at Saratoga, Horatio Gates led the American troops in their most important victory without foreign assistance in the whole course of the independence struggle. He was undoubtedly a good soldier and a dedicated supporter of the Patriot cause, yet his reputation has been tarnished by allegations that he plotted to supplant George Washington as commander in chief and by his dismal performance at the Battle of Camden later in the war.

Gates was born in Essex, England. His mother was employed in the household of the Duke of Bolton and she secured the nobleman's patronage for her son, allowing Gates to obtain a commission as an officer in a British infantry regiment at the age of 17. He saw action in Germany in the War of the Austrian Succession before crossing the Atlantic for the first time in 1749. He traveled as an aide to the newly appointed governor of Nova Scotia, Colonel

Edward Cornwallis, the uncle of the British general whom Gates would fight at Camden three decades later.

Climbing ranks
Gates took to life in North America, marrying there and becoming an officer in a volunteer company in New York. In 1755, at the start of the French and Indian War, he joined the ill-fated Braddock Expedition to the Ohio Valley alongside George Washington. Shot in the chest early in the Battle of the Monongahela in July 1755, he played no further combat role in the war, but he did build a reputation as an efficient military administrator. General Robert Monckton took Gates with him on an expedition to capture the French West Indian island of Martinique in 1762 and accorded him the honor of carrying the news of victory to Britain. When peace resumed in 1763, Gates held the rank of major, but without wealth or aristocratic contacts,

he could expect no further promotion in the British Army. He therefore sold his commission and emigrated to Virginia, settling down on a plantation.

Gates took no part in the agitation against Britain before 1775, but once the fighting started he hastened to seek

a place in the new Continental Army, which had a shortage of experienced officers. He was immediately accorded the rank of brigadier general. His organizational skills also made him the ideal choice for setting up the administrative systems required for

> "Was there ever such an instance of a **general running away**, as Gates had done, **from his whole army?**"

ALEXANDER HAMILTON, IN A LETTER TO JAMES DUANE, SEPTEMBER 6, 1780

the European-style regular army that Washington wished to establish.

In military matters Gates was always the advocate of caution, but in politics he adopted an aggressively anti-British stance, calling for America's full independence and cultivating the support of radicals such as Samuel Adams (see pp.34–35).

Cowardly conduct
Gates unquestionably wanted to win glory commanding in the field. He fought long and hard to replace General Philip Schuyler as commander of the army's Northern Department, eventually achieving his goal just in time for the Battle of Saratoga (see pp.162–63). Gates expected his defeat of the British at Saratoga to bring him glory, but his conduct of the battle, cautious and tentative, almost drove his subordinate Benedict Arnold to mutiny. Amid the bitterness and bickering that followed, the image of Gates as a victor in battle was lost. He did not hold another field command for three years.

In the aftermath of Saratoga, Gates became a pawn in other people's power games against Washington. He

A generous offer
Many observers believed that victory at Saratoga occurred more in spite of Gates's leadership than because of it, and the generous terms of surrender he agreed with Burgoyne outraged Washington and the Congress.

was appointed president of the Board of War in 1777, a post that effectively made him Washington's superior. At the same time, he was implicated in the attacks on Washington by senior officers of the so-called Conway Cabal—a group of senior officers and politicians who wanted Washington replaced as commander in chief. When Washington trounced his military and political opponents in the fall of 1778, Gates was forced to resign from the board.

Gates was recalled by Congress to face the crisis in the Carolinas in summer 1780. Here he acted with unusual impetuosity. In August, he left the comparative safety of North Carolina to march his army into South Carolina and seize the crossroads at Camden, where, he was surprised to encounter Cornwallis's army. Gates deployed his army ineptly, placing ill-trained militia to face hardened British regulars, and in the ensuing rout, instead of staying to rally his troops, he fled the field, riding 60 miles (95 km) to safety. Gates's enemies accused him of cowardice, while Congress ordered a board of inquiry to examine his performance. It never sat.

Gates, however, was not entrusted with further independent command and retired shortly after the war's end. After his first wife's death he married into money and gave up his plantation to live in Manhattan. Gates died there in 1806, and was buried at Trinity Church, on Wall Street.

Defeated general

This 1782 copy of a portrait by Charles Willson Peale was painted after Gates had been relieved of his command following the defeat at Camden in 1780.

TIMELINE

1728 Born in Maldon, England, on July 26, son of a customs collector and a housekeeper.

1745 Commissioned as an officer in the British Army.

1749 Travels to Nova Scotia as aide to Colonel Edward Cornwallis.

1754 Marries Elizabeth Phillips; they have a son, Robert.

July 1755 Wounded at the Battle of the Monongahela in the French and Indian War.

1762 Takes part in military expedition under Robert Monckton that seizes Martinique from the French; promoted to major.

1769 Quits the British Army.

1772 Emigrates from Britain to Virginia.

June 1775 Offers his services to the Congress, and is made a brigadier general in the Continental Army.

June 1776 Promoted to major general and given command of the Canadian Department.

December 1776 Misses Washington's raid on Trenton, claiming illness.

GATES'S EARLY MENTOR ROBERT MONCKTON

August 1777 Placed in command of the Northern Department after lengthy dispute with General Schuyler.

September–October 1777 Defeats Burgoyne at the Battle of Saratoga.

October 1777–January 1778 Implicated in the Conway Cabal plot against Washington.

November 1777 Becomes president of the Board of War, a post he holds until October 1778.

1779–80 Sidelined from the war effort, returns to his plantation in Virginia.

July 1780 Recalled to take command of the Southern Department of the Continental Army.

August 1780 Defeated by Cornwallis at the Battle of Camden.

October 1780 Death of his son in combat.

December 1780 Relieved of command of the southern department, he is threatened with a court of inquiry into the Camden defeat.

1782 Joins Washington's staff at Newburgh, New York.

1783 Death of his first wife, Elizabeth.

1784 Retires from military service.

1786 Marries wealthy widow Mary Vallence.

1790 Sells his Virginia plantation and frees his slaves; moves to Manhattan.

1800 Elected for a term in the New York legislature.

1806 Dies in Manhattan on April 10.

The **Battle** of **Kings Mountain**

When British Major Patrick Ferguson warned Patriot sympathizers in the Blue Ridge Mountains to put down their arms or he would "lay waste to their country with fire and sword," he set the stage for a ferocious battle that turned the war around.

◀ BEFORE

While the Patriot cause was beset by one disaster after another in the Carolinas, the British had made tremendous gains in the Deep South.

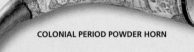

COLONIAL PERIOD POWDER HORN

LOYALIST SUCCESS

With the **fall of Charleston ❮❮ 268–69** and the capture of the Patriot garrison there, followed by a tremendous victory and the rout of General Horatio Gates's army at the **Battle of Camden ❮❮ 276–77**, Britain's "Southern Strategy" seemed to be vindicated. Although Lord Cornwallis had only 3,000 men, success at Camden and the apparent massacre at **Waxhaws ❮❮ 270–71** sent Loyalists flocking to his banner.

ON THE VERGE OF VICTORY

In September, Lord Cornwallis began advancing on Charlotte. His left flank was guarded by a Loyalist force commanded by Major Patrick Ferguson, a Scottish line officer of the 71st Regiment of Foot. His task was to recruit more Loyalists to the British army and intimidate any locals who resisted his advance.

On September 25, 1780, more than 1,000 frontier militiamen gathered at Sycamore Shoals on the Holston River in what is today Tennessee. They wore wide-brimmed hats and deerskin tunics and carried long hunting rifles. Most of them were veteran Indian fighters.

The Patriot militiamen had convened after a call had gone out for a general muster. After electing three colonels to be their principal leaders—John Sevier and Isaac Shelby from North Carolina and William Campbell from Virginia, who would be in overall command—they began saddling their

The fate of Ferguson

The climax of the battle, as depicted in this contemporary print, occurred when British Major Patrick Ferguson was shot out of his saddle. His riderless horse is seen bolting in the background.

horses. Since they all came from west of the Blue Ridge Mountains, they were called the Overmountain Men.

Taking up positions

Their opponent, Major Patrick Ferguson, referred to this militia as "backwater banditti," but the well-born Scotsman, the best shot in the British army until a wound had disabled his arm, was cautious. His spies told him that the militiamen were well-mounted and intending to fight. He decided to move his army to what he thought was an impregnable position on Kings Mountain, on the border between the Carolinas. There he would await reinforcements from Lord Cornwallis.

74 sets of brothers fought in the battle.

29 sets of fathers and sons took part. Some boys were just 15.

On reaching Kings Mountain, Ferguson pitched his tents and wrote that "all the Rebels in hell could not drive him" from the summit. In addition to having 1,000 Loyalist militiamen from the Carolinas, he had a crack force of 75 Provincial Rangers led by Captain Abraham DePeyster.

Meanwhile, after a difficult crossing of the Blue Ridge Mountains, the Overmountain Men arrived in the North Carolina Piedmont. There they met with fellow Patriots from the area, some of whom had brothers among Ferguson's Loyalists. It was a war between kith and kin, and the battle was fought almost entirely between Americans. Major Ferguson was the only Briton.

Trigger guard

34-inch (86.3 cm) barrel

Ramrod (used to push musket ball into position)

The Ferguson rifle
In addition to being a Loyalist leader, Patrick Ferguson invented the Ferguson rifle. Although considered superior to any shoulder arm then in existence, it was too costly to make in large numbers.

Ferguson knew the frontiersmen were coming. Nevertheless, shortly before 3 a.m. on October 7, he was surprised to hear his sentries shooting. Somehow 910 Patriots, handpicked by Campbell and on the best horses, had managed to approach within a quarter of a mile (0.4 km) and nearly encircle Kings Mountain without being spotted. As the Loyalist drums began beating, Colonel Campbell cried: "Here they are my brave boys; shout like hell and fight like devils!"

The fog of battle
With shrieks and whoops, the dismounted frontiersmen assaulted the hill. They were repulsed by volley after volley flaming from Brown Bess muskets. Then came an advancing wall

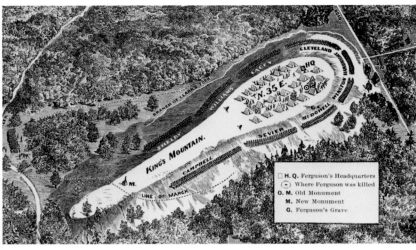

Map of the battle
In this 19th-century representation of the battle, Kings Mountain extends from southwest to northeast (where Ferguson's tents can be seen). Colonel Campbell's forces are seen ranged around the mountain's base.

□ H.Q. Ferguson's Headquarters
⊙ Where Ferguson was killed
O.M. Old Monument
M. New Monument
G. Ferguson's Grave

of sharpened steel as Ferguson's Provincial Rangers mounted first one bayonet charge, then a second, then a third. Sent reeling, many frontiersmen sheltered behind rocks and trees until they could clamber back up the hill. Campbell's Virginians were soon swarming over its southwest crest, where the plateau was more open, allowing them to level their long rifles to better advantage. The Rangers were quickly shot to pieces, and the Loyalist militiamen were forced back toward their tents.

As the battle turned in the Patriots' favor, Ferguson galloped through the smoke on his white charger. Frontier sharpshooters took aim, and at least six musket balls slammed into him, one smashing into his face. He was knocked from the saddle, but his foot caught in the stirrup as he fell. As his frightened horse bolted, it dragged the Scotsman across the rocky ground. He was dead by the time his orderly retrieved him.

Stopping the carnage
Taking charge, Captain DePeyster tried to rally the Loyalist troops, but they were running out of ammunition. As the fusillade directed at them intensified, DePeyster reluctantly ordered the raising of a white flag. Yet the enraged Patriots continued firing, and the confused Loyalist militia crowded into a draw. "It is murder to kill them now!" Colonel Campbell screamed, knocking his men's barrels away. "Cease firing! For God's sake, cease firing!"

The battle lasted for 65 minutes. As DePeyster and his surviving officers turned over their swords, the smoke cleared to reveal a scene of carnage. More than 200 groaning men had one surgeon between them to attend to their wounds. About 290 others were already dead or dying. Only 29 of them were Colonel Campbell's men.

The dead were buried in shallow trenches in the surrounding woods. For many years their bleached bones were found strewn around the battle ground. Major Ferguson's grave, however, was—and is—protected by a cairn of stones.

The unexpected victory at Kings Mountain lifted the spirits of those still fighting for independence and sent confidence plunging in those who thought rebellion was on the wane.

BRITISH TACTICS
The complete destruction of his left wing left Lord Cornwallis with no choice but to retreat. Charlotte was too close to the rebel-infested mountains, so he took his troops 60 miles (96 km) south for the winter, deep into South Carolina. He did not go north again until January 1781, when a **new Continental Army** arrived on the scene. That month **General Daniel Morgan** defeated **Banastre Tarleton at the Battle of Cowpens 284–85 »**, inflicting another blow to the Southern Strategy of the British.

NEWFOUND CONFIDENCE
Within a few weeks of the battle, the Overmountain Men disbanded, and most of them recrossed the Blue Ridge to defend their families against **Indian attacks.** But after Kings Mountain, young men who had been undecided about which side to join, flocked to the Patriots' banner. The road to **Yorktown 308–09 »** was only a few steps away.

When news of the victory reached **General Washington,** he said, "With soldiers like that, no wonder the frontiersmen won." Years later, as the battlefield itself lay neglected and overgrown, Thomas Jefferson remembered the battle as being the "turn of the tide of success."

"Never **see an enemy** without **bringing** him **down…**"
COLONEL ISAAC SHELBY, 1780

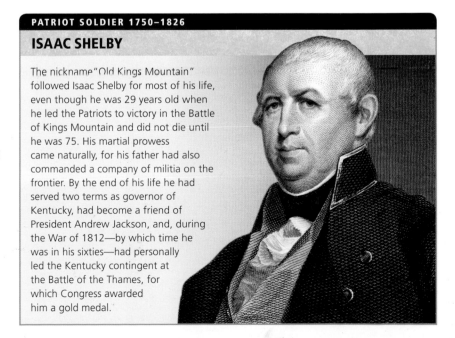

PATRIOT SOLDIER 1750–1826

ISAAC SHELBY

The nickname "Old Kings Mountain" followed Isaac Shelby for most of his life, even though he was 29 years old when he led the Patriots to victory in the Battle of Kings Mountain and did not die until he was 75. His martial prowess came naturally, for his father had also commanded a company of militia on the frontier. By the end of his life he had served two terms as governor of Kentucky, had become a friend of President Andrew Jackson, and, during the War of 1812—by which time he was in his sixties—had personally led the Kentucky contingent at the Battle of the Thames, for which Congress awarded him a gold medal.

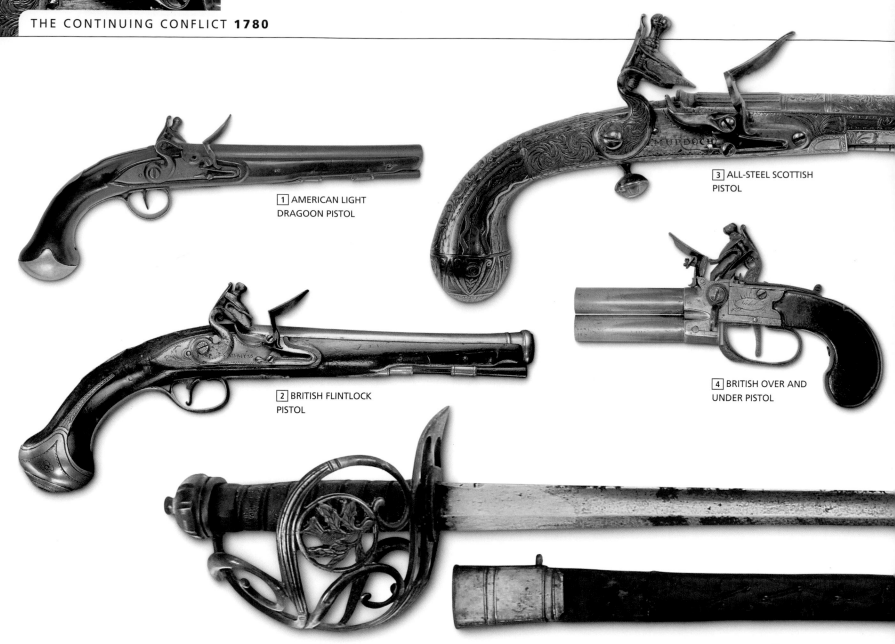

[1] AMERICAN LIGHT DRAGOON PISTOL

[3] ALL-STEEL SCOTTISH PISTOL

[2] BRITISH FLINTLOCK PISTOL

[4] BRITISH OVER AND UNDER PISTOL

[5] GEORGE WASHINGTON'S BATTLE SWORD

Pistols and Swords

Swords were carried by officers. They were purchased privately and ornate designs were something of a status symbol. The majority of pistols were also the property of their bearer, but a few were supplied to dragoons.

[1] **American light dragoon pistol** A copy of a British design, these pistols were issued to the Continental Light Dragoons. [2] **British flintlock pistol** Produced by gunsmith William Gabbitas, this was gifted to George Washington during the French and Indian War by General Edward Braddock. [3] **All-steel Scottish pistol** Many of these pistols were produced in Perthshire in Scotland; they were popular among the officers of the Scottish Highland regiments. [4] **British over and under pistol** British armorer Nicholson's design enabled this pocket pistol to be fired twice before it needed reloading. [5] **George Washington's battle sword** Forged in steel with a green-dyed ivory grip, this sword was carried by Washington throughout the war. [6] **American sword in scabbard** Individual blades varied greatly. This sword, owned by the Patriot officer of a Massachusetts regiment, has a wooden handle with a carved lion-head pommel. [7] **French short sword** Imported from France,

this weapon is marked "Artillery of Virginia." Artillerymen were sometimes provided with swords to use if their guns were in danger of being overrun. [8] **British infantry hanger** Regulations to standardize colors and clothing in 1768 stipulated that only sergeants, grenadiers, and musicians were allowed to carry this short sword. [9] **French small sword** Designed for thrusting, this light, silver-hilted blade belonged to a French officer. [10] **British infantry hanger** Carried by a sergeant of the 16th Regiment of Foot, which served in Florida, this sword has a dog's head pommel. [11] **Scottish sword and scabbard** Finished with thistle decoration on the guard, this sword belonged to an officer of the 71st Highlanders. [12] **Loyalist cavalry saber and scabbard** This saber, made in British-occupied New York for Loyalists, was designed for slashing, rather than thrusting. [13] **German hussar's saber** Long and heavy, the curved saber was designed for use on horseback.

[6] AMERICAN SWORD IN SCABBARD

[7] FRENCH SHORT SWORD

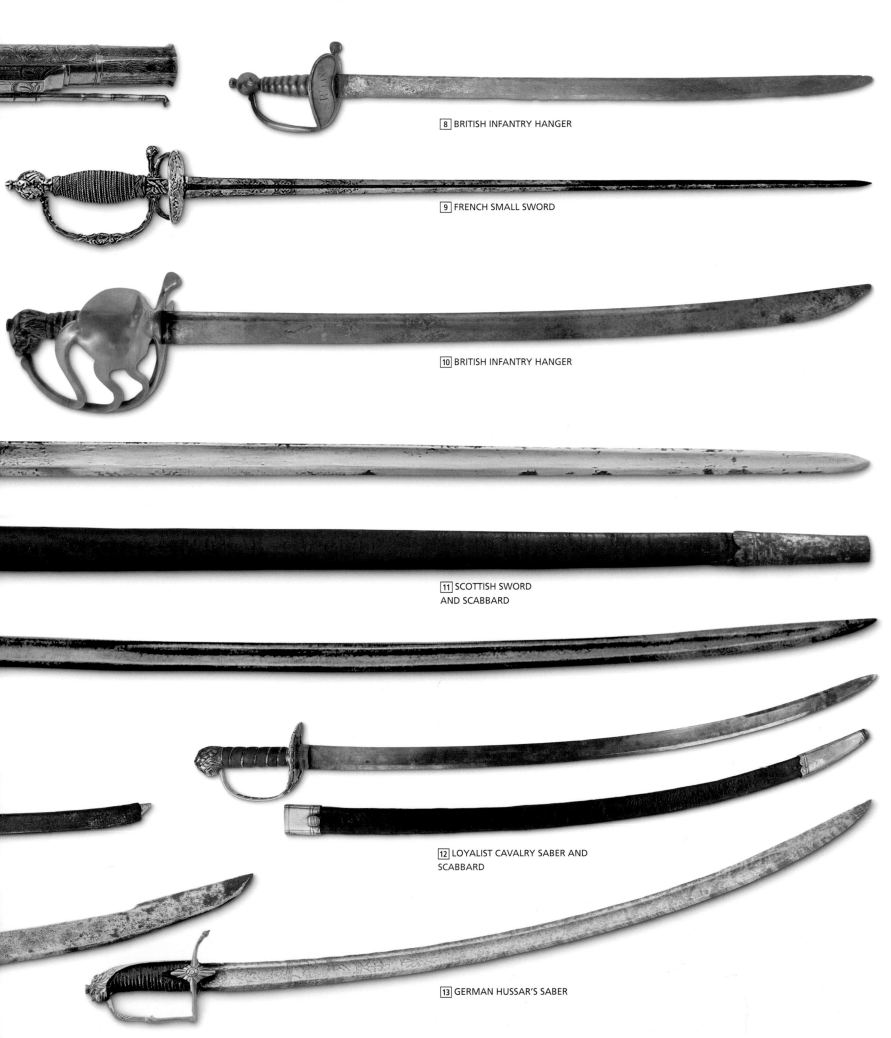

8 BRITISH INFANTRY HANGER

9 FRENCH SMALL SWORD

10 BRITISH INFANTRY HANGER

11 SCOTTISH SWORD
AND SCABBARD

12 LOYALIST CAVALRY SABER AND
SCABBARD

13 GERMAN HUSSAR'S SABER

8
AMERICA VICTORIOUS
1781–83

After a "devil of a whipping" at Cowpens, and run ragged by Nathanael Greene in North Carolina, the British attempted to regain the upper hand in Virginia. It was here that the Patriots and their French allies pounced, leading to a fateful showdown at Yorktown.

《 *The Surrender of Yorktown*
On October 19, 1781, the British marched out of Yorktown and delivered their flags to the victors. The defeat of Lord Cornwallis's entire Southern Army precipitated the end of the war, and peace negotiations swiftly followed.

ACTION 1781–83

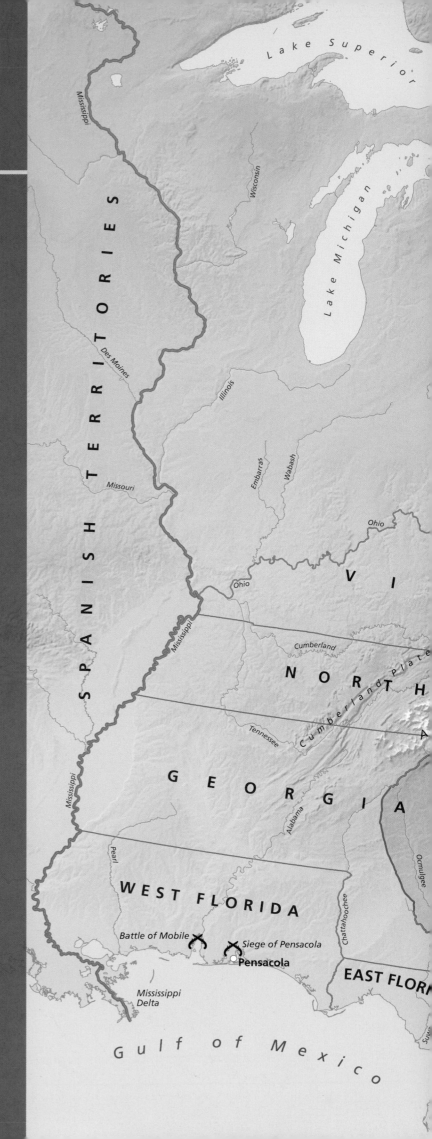

The year 1781 saw a new Patriot army in the South under the leadership of the tenacious Nathanael Greene. Although Patriot success at Cowpens in January was followed by technical defeats at Guilford Courthouse and Eutaw Springs, Greene's army inflicted heavy damage on its opponents, gradually eroding British control of the Carolinas and Georgia and forcing their commander, Lord Cornwallis, to open a new campaign in Virginia. Together with the superior efforts of the French Navy in the Chesapeake Bay, Greene's campaign helped unravel Britain's "southern strategy" and set the stage for the allied victory at Yorktown and the British surrender. Peace negotiations led to the Treaty of Paris in 1783, after which Washington resigned his commission as commander in chief.

1 The Battle of Eutaw Springs in September was the war's last major engagement in the Carolinas. 2 Franco-Patriot forces trapped the British at Yorktown in October, 1781 3 George Washington resigned his military commission in December 1783.

Newfoundland

Magdalen Islands

Prince Edward Island

NOVA SCOTIA

Louisbourg

Sable Island

Quebec

Montreal

MASSACHUSETTS

Halifax

Q U E B E C

Lake Huron

Georgian Bay

Ottawa

St. Lawrence

Saguenay

St. John

Penobscot

Bay of Fundy

Saint-Maurice

Lake Ontario

Lake Erie

Lake Champlain

Adirondack Mountains

Green Mountains

White Mountains

NEW HAMPSHIRE

ATLANTIC OCEAN

N E W   Y O R K

Albany

Hudson

Catskill Mountains

Boston
MASSACHUSETTS

Cape Cod

Mohawk

Susquehanna

Newburgh

CONNECTICUT

New York City

P E N N S Y L V A N I A

Allegheny

Delaware

Second Continental Congress

Princeton

Philadelphia

NEW JERSEY

Baltimore

DELAWARE

3

MARYLAND

KEY

— Border of Spanish territory (1763)

— 1763 Proclamation Line

— Colonial boundaries (1763)

○ Town / settlement

⚔ Battle / siege

🏰 Fort

🚢 Naval battle

🪶 Treaty / convention

⛺ Patriot winter camp

Ohio

Muskingum

Kanawha

Potomac

James

2

Battle of Yorktown

Yorktown

Norfolk

Chesapeake Bay

🚢 Battle of Cape Henry

🚢 Battle of the Chesapeake

V I R G I N I A

Roanoke

Dan

A L L E G H E N Y   M O U N T A I N S

A P P A L A C H I A N   M O U N T A I N S

B L U E   R I D G E

⚔ Battle of Guilford Court House

C A R O L I N A

⚔ Battle of Cowpens

Pee Dee

Cape Fear

⚔ Siege of Ninety-Six

⚔ Battle of Hobkirk's Hill

Camden

t Granby

🏰 Fort Motte

⚔ Siege of Augusta

🏰 Fort Watson

Orangeburg

⚔ Battle of Eutaw Springs

1

Charleston

Wilmington

SOUTH CAROLINA

annah

Johns

ma

N

0   100 km

0   100 miles

Mohawk

N E W   Y O R K

Albany

Hudson

Green Mountains

NEW HAMPSHIRE

Connecticut

Catskill Mountains

MASSACHUSETTS

Boston

Cape Cod

Susquehanna

Newburgh ⛺

CONNECTICUT

P E N N S Y L V A N I A

Morristown ⛺

Long Island

New York City

Newport

RHODE ISLAND

Delaware

Princeton

NEW JERSEY

Second Continental Congress 🪶

Philadelphia

ATLANTIC OCEAN

Baltimore

MARYLAND

DELAWARE

3

🪶 Washington resigns

0   100 km

0   100 miles

TIMELINE 1781–83

Battle of Cowpens ▪ **Cornwallis in Virginia** ▪ Southern forts besieged ▪ **Battle of the Chesapeake** ▪ Siege of Yorktown ▪ **Cornwallis surrenders** ▪ Peace negotiations ▪ **Newburgh address** ▪ Peace of Paris ▪ **Washington resigns his commission**

1781

JANUARY 1
Several regiments of the Pennsylvania Line threaten mutiny at Morristown, New Jersey.

MARCH 15
British forces under Lord Cornwallis engage Patriots under General Greene at Guilford Court House.

APRIL 7
Cornwallis withdraws his troops to Wilmington, North Carolina.

MAY 12
Lee and Marion capture Fort Motte, South Carolina, from the British.

MAY 20
Cornwallis arrives in Petersburg, Virginia, with a force of 1,500 men.

JULY 20
Cornwallis receives orders from General Sir Henry Clinton to establish a naval base in Virginia. He chooses to do so at Yorktown.

JANUARY 17
Brigadier General Daniel Morgan's army defeats British forces at the Battle of Cowpens.

APRIL 15
Patriot troops under Colonel "Light Horse Harry" Lee and Francis Marion begin an eight-day siege of Fort Watson, South Carolina.

⌄ Patriot cavalry at Guilford Court House

JUNE 6
British forces occupying Fort Augusta, Georgia, surrender to Patriot forces led by General Andrew Pickens and "Light Horse Harry" Lee.

SEPTEMBER 8
Greene surprises a British force at Eutaw Springs.

SEPTEMBER 30
The armies of Washington and Rochambeau arrive at Yorktown.

⌃ The British surrender at Yorktown

NOVEMBER 25
Word of Cornwallis's surrender at Yorktown reaches England.

JUNE 19
Greene abandons the 28-day siege of Fort Ninety-Six, having failed to secure its surrender.

» General Lord Cornwallis

OCTOBER 9
The French fire the first shot, formally opening the Siege of Yorktown.

OCTOBER 19
Cornwallis formally surrenders to Washington at Yorktown.

DECEMBER 12
A British squadron engages a French convoy in the Second Battle of Ushant, capturing 15 transports with troops bound for the East and West Indies.

JUNE 4
British forces under Banastre Tarleton raid Charlottesville, Virginia.

AUGUST 14
Washington receives news that Admiral de Grasse's French fleet has set sail for the Chesapeake Bay.

AUGUST 30
De Grasse's fleet arrives in the Chesapeake Bay.

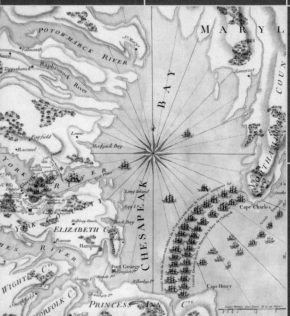

JANUARY 30
Greene and Morgan lead Cornwallis's forces on a chase through North Carolina in the so-called "Race to the Dan."

APRIL 25
Lord Rawdon seizes the initiative, attacking and defeating Greene's army near Camden, South Carolina, at the Battle of Hobkirk's Hill.

JULY 6
Brigadier General Anthony Wayne leads a detachment of Lafayette's army in an unsuccessful attack on Cornwallis's forces at Green Spring, Virginia.

SEPTEMBER 5
De Grasse defeats a British fleet under Rear Admiral Thomas Graves, securing the Chesapeake Bay and isolating Cornwallis's army at Yorktown.

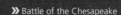
» Battle of the Chesapeake

> **"**These are times that tried men's souls, and they are over … the **greatest** and completest **revolution** the world ever knew, gloriously and happily **accomplished."**

THOMAS PAINE, *THE AMERICAN CRISIS*, 1783

1782

1783

FEBRUARY 27
The British parliament votes against continuing the war in America.

APRIL 4
Sir Guy Carleton replaces Henry Clinton as the commander of British forces in America.

NOVEMBER 30
Britain and the United States sign a preliminary peace treaty in Paris, which recognizes American independence.

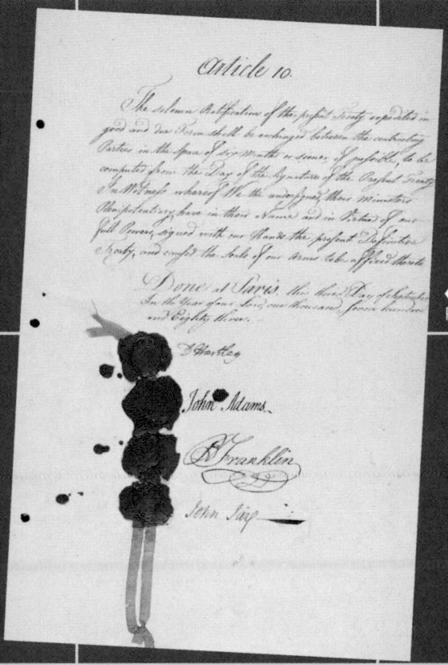

« The Treaty of Paris, 1783

SEPTEMBER 3
The Peace of Paris formally ends the War of Independence.

DECEMBER 4
Washington bids farewell to his officers at Fraunces Tavern, in New York.

MARCH 5
Parliament empowers the king to negotiate peace with the United States.

APRIL 12
Admiral Sir George Rodney's British fleet defeats Admiral de Grasse's French fleet in the Battle of the Saintes.

NOVEMBER 2
Washington issues his Farewell Orders to the Continental Army.

⌄ The Battle of the Saintes

FEBRUARY 3
Spain recognizes the United States as an independent nation.

DECEMBER 23
George Washington resigns his commission as commander in chief before the Congress.

⌄ Washington resigns at Annapolis

MARCH 15
General Washington addresses a group of his officers in Newburgh, New York, averting a potential rebellion against the authority of the Congress.

MARCH 20
Lord North resigns as prime minister following a vote of "no confidence."

MARCH 27
Lord Rockingham becomes prime minister of Britain and subsequently opens negotiations with American peace commissioners.

APRIL 12
Peace negotiations between the United States and Britain begin in Paris.

JUNE 11
British forces evacuate Savannah, Georgia.

DECEMBER 14
British forces evacuate Charleston, South Carolina.

APRIL 15
The Congress ratifies the Preliminary Articles of Peace with Britain.

Battle of Cowpens

The encounter between the forces of the reckless British officer Banastre Tarleton and the wily frontiersman Daniel Morgan near the town of Cowpens in North Carolina saw Tarleton make his usual all-out attack only to find Morgan well prepared.

The year 1780 had been disastrous for the Patriots in the South—until the Battle of Kings Mountain.

MOUNTING DEFEATS

In the summer of 1780, two American armies had been destroyed—one at the **Siege of Charleston ‹‹ 266–67**, and the other at the **Battle of Camden ‹‹ 274–75**. In the wake of these and other lesser successes, the British occupied all of Georgia and South Carolina, harried only by bands of partisans.

CHANGING FORTUNES

In October, news that frontier militia had destroyed a fifth of Cornwallis's army at the **Battle of Kings Mountain ‹‹ 280–81** boosted Patriot morale. Described as "Cornwallis's Trenton" by British Commander in Chief Sir Henry Clinton, in reference to the surprise defeat of British forces in New Jersey in 1776, for the Americans it was a sign that the tide could turn.

Brigadier General Daniel Morgan, had his orders. The "Old Wagoner" was to "annoy the enemy," as his commander Nathanael Greene put it. Morgan knew that he could elude any pursuit—but not when the Broad River, swollen by rain, was blocking his escape, as it was on January 16, 1781, just as British commander Banastre Tarleton (see pp.272–73) and his force of 1,000 men were nearly upon him. Morgan had to turn and fight, but he would do so on ground of his own choosing.

Hannah's Cowpens—so-called because it was used for fattening cattle before they were driven to market—was 5 miles (8 km) from the Broad River. It was a long, fenced, sloping, and parklike place, dotted with tall pines and oaks, and free of undergrowth. It featured two prominent hills, a smaller one backed by a bigger one, and beyond that, a swale in which Morgan could hide his cavalry. It was here that Morgan camped that night.

Visiting each campfire, Morgan offered his 1,100 men personal encouragement. All the frightened militia had to do, he emphasized, was keep calm and fire two volleys. They should then withdraw around the left and reform in the swale. The veteran

tactician planned a defense in depth to lure the British onward while blunting their momentum. He knew Tarleton would attack without reconnoitering.

Ready and waiting

In the clear dawn of January 17, Tarleton's dragoons were at the entrance to the Cowpens. Facing them, concealed among the scattered trees, was a thin line of riflemen from Morgan's militia, handpicked for their marksmanship. As these men opened fire, the dragoons prudently withdrew, but the impetuous Tarleton instantly

26 The age of Banastre Tarleton at Cowpens.

44 The age of "Old Wagoner" Daniel Morgan.

PATRIOT GENERAL 1736–1802

DANIEL MORGAN

Awarded a gold medal by the Congress for his victory at Cowpens, big, brawling Dan Morgan was known as the "Old Wagoner" because he was once a teamster on the Virginia frontier, hauling supplies to military outposts. During the French and Indian War, he was disciplined with 499 lashes from a cat-o'-nine tails after assaulting a British officer. He survived only to have all his left teeth shot out by an Indian bullet. During the War of Independence, Morgan attacked Quebec (see pp.80–81) with Benedict Arnold and played a key role in the Patriot victory at Saratoga (see pp.162–63).

Despite the stunning victory at Cowpens, the Patriot generals still had to retreat for a time in the face of Cornwallis's army.

CAT AND MOUSE
After Cowpens, Lord Cornwallis abandoned the pacification of South Carolina to chase Nathanael Greene into Virginia. Both armies then moved into North Carolina, where they confronted one another at **Guilford Court House 292–93 »**. The battle there was so costly to Cornwallis that his army was forced to rest and resupply at the port of Wilmington. While Cornwallis was there, Greene slipped past him and started the reconquest of South Carolina.

Clash of cavalry
Frederick Kemmelmeyer's painting of 1809 shows Colonel Washington and his men in action with British cavalry. At the end of the battle, Washington personally fought a British officer who may have been Tarleton.

deployed his tired foot soldiers, including the 7th Royal Fusiliers and the esteemed light infantry, in line of battle at the bottom of the grassy slope. With sharpshooters already thinning their ranks, the British line fired a volley, gave three cheers, and came forward into battle.

Fading back up the smaller of the two hills, the sharpshooters regrouped at the crest behind Morgan's second line: 300 militiamen from South Carolina, North Carolina, and Georgia who were commanded by a noted partisan, Colonel Andrew Pickens. The British came on. At 100 paces, while the Patriot sharpshooters aimed at the "epaulettes," or officers, the militia loosed their first volley. The red-coated line staggered, and many officers went down. The soldiers regrouped, only to be shredded by a second volley.

The militia duly began filing off to the left; but through the battle smoke it looked as though they were fleeing. Seizing a perceived opportunity, the 17th Dragoons, called the Death or Glory Boys, came pounding onto the field, slashing at the militiamen—only to be halted and scattered by a counterattack delivered by Colonel William Washington's horsemen from the swale behind the second hill.

Double envelopment
While the cavalry slugged it out, the largely leaderless British infantry, approaching the crest of the second, higher hill, met Morgan's third line composed of Lieutenant Colonel John Eager Howard's Continentals, flanked by militiamen from Virginia and Georgia, all kneeling and firing. The Redcoats nevertheless closed ranks and a roaring volley for volley fight ensued.

At this point, Tarleton ordered in his reserves, the 71st Highlanders, to outflank the Patriot right. Turning to oppose the oncoming Scots, the Virginians misunderstood an order and began to withdraw, taking the Marylanders with them. The British line surged ahead, trusting to the bayonet. As his men crossed to the reverse side of the hill, Morgan had them wheel around and fire a point-blank volley into the British as they came over the crest. An entire line was knocked to the ground, and the Patriots rolled forward.

While the Highlanders fought on, their leaderless comrades on the right fell back in disarray. Washington's cavalry again galloped out of the swale and promptly encircled them. Panicking at the sight of flashing sabers, the fusiliers and light

Heavy losses for Cornwallis
Patriot soldiers overwhelmed the British forces. The destruction of Cornwallis's light infantry battalion at Cowpens hobbled British forces for the rest of the southern campaign.

infantrymen began to surrender. Meanwhile, 100 yards (90 m) away, Pickens's militiamen were now returning to the battle on the Patriot right, putting them at the flank and rear of the embattled Highlanders. Surrounded, the gallant Scots had to lay down their arms. Designed or not, it had been a classic military maneuver—a double envelopment, or pincer movement.

> ## "The best troops were put under 'that boy' to be sacrificed."
> MAJOR McARTHUR, 71ST HIGHLANDER, ABOUT BANASTRE TARLETON, 1780

Tarleton thundered onto the field to try to retrieve the situation, but most of his Legion horsemen were already heading to the rear. Rallying a few dozen men, he mounted a brave but hopeless counterattack. Washington's troopers overwhelmed them, but in the melee Tarleton spurred away.

The battle was over. As the smoke cleared, 100 Redcoats—including 39 officers—lay dead, and another 229 wounded. At least 600 more were rounded up as prisoners. Morgan reported 12 dead and 60 wounded.

Morgan wasted no time celebrating his victory. He moved his troops across the Broad River before nightfall. The next day a crestfallen Tarleton, accompanied by a mere handful of survivors, arrived at Cornwallis's headquarters. Cornwallis stood resting against his sword as he listened to the report. Realizing that he had lost a quarter of his small army in a single hour of combat, the earl reportedly leaned on that sword so heavily that the blade snapped.

The North Carolina Campaign

Whether they were won or lost, each battle in the South during 1780 and 1781 seemed to leave the British forces weaker. At Guilford Court House, Cornwallis met an army more than twice the size of his own, but was determined to reverse his army's declining fortunes.

BEFORE

Despite early victories, Britain's southern strategy began to crumble during the fall of 1780.

GREENE TAKES CHARGE

After setbacks at Charleston and Camden, American forces fought back at **Kings Mountain ‹‹ 280–81** in October 1780. Nathanael Greene arrived to take command of the Continental Army troops in the South in December 1780, and decided to take the offensive immediately, forcing Lord Cornwallis to maneuver his army to confront them.

THE BATTLE OF COWPENS

In January 1781, Brigadier General Daniel Morgan defeated a British force under Lieutenant Colonel Banastre Tarleton at **Cowpens ‹‹ 292–93** by a tactical plan that maximized the abilities of the Patriot militia and a small force of experienced Continentals.

Furious at the loss of Cowpens in January 1781, Lord Cornwallis set off from Charleston in pursuit of General Nathanael Greene and frontiersman Daniel Morgan. Deprived by the Battle of Cowpens of his best light troops, Cornwallis resorted to drastic measures, and burned his baggage train to lighten his army and speed the chase. This fateful decision left the British without their tents during an unusually wet winter, adding exposure to the hardships of hunger and exhaustion in the weeks that followed.

Meanwhile, in a meeting with Morgan on January 30, 1781, Greene decided to consolidate his forces and head for Virginia in an attempt to lead Cornwallis progressively farther from his supply bases along the Carolina coast. The ensuing chase across North Carolina culminated in Greene's successful crossing of the rain-swollen Dan River near the Virginia–North Carolina border on February 14, with Cornwallis nipping at his heels, in what became known as the "Race to the Dan." Greene's army took all the available

Guilford Court House flag
Reputedly flown by a militia unit at Guilford Court House, the "stars and stripes" design of this regimental banner echoed elements of the national flag of the new American nation. The similarities in the flags identified the unit as Patriots.

Each star represented one of the 13 states

approached along the Salisbury Road from New Garden, 12 miles (19 km) to the southwest. They were first sighted by a screen of cavalry from Lee's Legion, who skirmished with the British vanguard and reported their approach to Greene. Mirroring Daniel Morgan's tactics at Cowpens, Greene

> ## "Another such victory would ruin the British Army."
>
> CHARLES JAMES FOX, BRITISH PARLIAMENTARY OPPOSITION LEADER, 1781

boats, making it almost impossible for Cornwallis's tired units to follow. Instead, having lost the race, he returned 50 miles (80 km) south to Hillsborough in search of supplies.

In a sense, the contest had been a draw. While Greene had escaped over the river to the safety of Virginia with his army intact, Cornwallis could claim to have driven him from the Carolinas, encouraging local Loyalist support. Aware of the importance of countering such views, Greene recrossed the Dan in late February. The two armies stalked each other warily, skirmishing periodically, while Greene awaited promised militia reinforcements from North Carolina and Virginia.

Time and place

On March 14, 1781, with a force of about 4,400 men, including recently arrived militia, Greene chose the ground around Guilford Court House to face Cornwallis. He did not have long to wait. At dawn on the following day, Cornwallis's 1,900-strong force,

Light Horse Harry
American cavalry under the command of Henry Lee, known as Light Horse Harry, were the first to engage Cornwallis's forces at Guilford Court House.

Short, sharp shock
For all the ferocity of the fighting and the heavy casualties on both sides, the Battle of Guilford Court House only lasted about 90 minutes before Greene pulled back to ensure he could fight another day.

arranged his forces on strong defensive ground in three lines that were roughly perpendicular to the road along which the British advanced.

The first American line comprised of North Carolina militia and artillery, posted behind a rail fence with 500 yards (460 m) of open ground to their front. Their flanks were secured on the right by Virginia riflemen, light infantry, and Lieutenant Colonel William Washington's band of cavalry; on the left, were Lee's Legion and more Virginia riflemen.

The second line, composed of Virginia militia, was about 300 yards (275 m) behind the first. Greene's third line—two Virginia Continental regiments on the right and two from Maryland on the left, with two six-pounder guns in the center—occupied the brow of a steeply wooded hill. Just behind the Marylanders was Guilford Court House. Greene's plan included no operational reserve.

Fast and furious
The battle began with an artillery exchange at about noon, as the British column emerged and deployed into lines on either side of the road: Highlanders and Hessian troops on the right, the 23rd and 33rd regiments on the left. The Guards, Grenadiers, and Jaegers followed in support. As the British line, led by Colonel James Webster, came into range, the North Carolinians fired and retired to the rear as planned.

Patriot riflemen continued to fire on the British from the wooded flanks as they advanced toward the second line and engaged it amid the dense woods. Cornwallis later recalled how the "excessive thickness of the woods rendered our bayonets little use and enabled the broken enemy to make frequent stands with an irregular fire." Even so, the right side of the Patriot second line began to give way. The British pressed on to attack the right of the third line, but were repelled by Greene's Virginia Continentals.

Lieutenant Colonel Stuart now led the British Guards into the American left, scattering one inexperienced regiment. Seeing the danger, William Washington led a devastating cavalry charge through the Guards' flank, followed up by a bayonet charge from Lieutenant Colonel John Eager Howard's Maryland Continentals.

At this critical moment, seeing the British attack falter, Cornwallis ordered his artillery to fire grapeshot into the melee. This calculated move felled friend and foe alike, but crucially served to check the Patriots' momentum and allowed the British to re-form for a new attack. With his first two lines scattered and the third depleted, although holding, Greene called for an orderly retreat rather than risk losing a third southern army in a year. Patriot casualties stood at 260, including 78 dead. Cornwallis retained the field, but at great cost. Suffering 500 casualties—amounting to over a quarter of his army—and destitute of supplies, two days later he marched off toward the coast at Wilmington, North Carolina.

> **The losses at Guilford Court House helped persuade Cornwallis that continuing the fight in the South was fruitless.**
>
> **CORNWALLIS DEPARTS**
> At Wilmington in early April 1781, Cornwallis learned that Greene had departed for South Carolina, his sights set on Camden. Believing he could not catch Greene in time to aid Lieutenant Colonel Francis Rawdon's British garrison there, Cornwallis resolved to take advantage of General Greene's "having left the back part of Virginia open" and join forces in the richest of the colonies with detachments led by Benedict Arnold and William Phillips. In October, Cornwallis would make a stand at **Yorktown 304–05 ≫**, albeit without Phillips, who died of typhus or malaria en route.
>
> **WILLIAM PHILLIPS**

Action at Guilford Court House

The British were technically the victors at Guilford Court House, despite being the much smaller army, but there was a disproportionately large number of British casualties—some 532 killed, wounded, or missing out of 2,100 men. At just 90 minutes, the battle was brief but intense, as survivors from both sides recalled.

❝General Greene came to Guilford Old Court House where he made a halt and hearing that the British was moving towards him he drew up his Men in three Lines about 100 yards behind each other ... I was posted in the front Line with scarce a complete Captain's Company ... We were posted behind a Fence & I told the Men to sit down until the British came near enough to shoot.

About 100 yards [away] I saw [a] British officer ... I asked Captain Forbes if he could take him down he said [he] could for [he] had a good Rifle. I told him let him come to within 50 yards and then take him down which he did it was a Captain of the British Army ... ❞

PATRIOT COLONEL JAMES MARTIN, COMMANDER OF THE 1ST REGIMENT, GUILFORD COUNTY MILITIA, FROM HIS 1832 WAR PENSION DEPOSITION

❝When arrived within forty yards of the enemy's line their whole force had their arms presented, and resting on a rail fence taking aim with the nicest precision ... a general pause took place; both parties surveyed each other for the moment with the most anxious suspense. [Then] Colonel Webster rode forward in the front of the 23rd regiment, and said, 'Come on, my brave Fuzileers.' They rushed forward amidst the enemy's fire; dreadful was the havoc on both sides. At last the Americans gave way, and the brigade advanced, to the attack of their second line.❞

BRITISH SERGEANT ROGER LAMB, 23RD WELSH FUSILIERS, DIARY ENTRY

Pitched battle
TThe First Maryland Regiment—depicted by Frederick Coffay Yohn recapturing field pieces at Guilford Court House—had gained experience on the battlefield in the Northern department of the war prior to 1780.

BRITISH GENERAL AND STATESMAN Born 1738 Died 1805

Charles **Cornwallis**

> "A **successful defense** in our **position** was perhaps **impossible.**"

GENERAL CORNWALLIS, WRITING ON YORKTOWN, 1783

British General Charles Cornwallis, despite achieving numerous victories, is chiefly remembered as the commander whose surrender at Yorktown in 1781 lost Britain its American colonies. However, the war in America was only one episode in a long career, during which he also served as a reforming imperial administrator in India and Ireland.

Personal privilege

Cornwallis was born into the British aristocracy, with relatives in the upper circles of public life on both his father's and mother's side. It was privilege that enabled him to become a Guards officer at 18 and an MP by the age of 21, but he was also an individual whose talents fully justified the positions he acquired. He developed his knowledge of warfare in theory, by studying at a military academy in Italy, and in practice by fighting in the Seven Years' War in Europe. In politics, sitting first in the House of Commons and then, after succeeding to his father's title, in the House of Lords, he pursued a liberal agenda, opposing the Stamp Act and other measures imposed on the American colonies. Yet his liberalism was tempered by a distaste for disorder and a devotion to his king and country.

> "I never saw **such fighting** since **God** made me."

CHARLES CORNWALLIS, AFTER THE BATTLE OF GUILFORD COURT HOUSE, 1781

In 1775, after the colonists rebelled, Cornwallis felt it his duty to volunteer for service in the American war.

Cornwallis served loyally under General William Howe, accepting his place as a subordinate general. He possessed a gift for organization

Empire builder

This painting by British portraitist Daniel Gardner shows Cornwallis in the early 1780s, around the time of his surrender at Yorktown. An aristocrat, Cornwallis devoted his life to the service of empire.

Trained in Europe

Cornwallis took part in the hard-won British victory at Minden in Germany in 1759. His thorough grounding in European warfare was of more limited use when faced with the less formal nature of American combat.

that he applied vigorously to the multiple problems of conducting military operations in North America. Cornwallis was popular with his troops because he strove to keep them properly clothed, fed, and housed, but as a field commander his talents were more mixed. His physical courage was unquestionable and his performance at several battles—including Long Island (see pp.118–19), Brandywine (see pp.170–71), and Monmouth (see pp.196–97)—was widely admired, but he allowed himself to be outsmarted by Washington at Princeton in 1777 (see pp.132–33).

Frustrated hopes

During the winter of 1778–79, Cornwallis suffered a personal tragedy in the death of his wife, Jemima, and returned to America in a somber and troubled state. He now found himself second in command to General Henry Clinton, and relations between the two men deteriorated rapidly, with detrimental effects on their conduct of the war. Cornwallis became the key figure entrusted with the southern strategy, which sought to restore Georgia's and the Carolinas' allegiance to Britain, and his victory over Horatio Gates at Camden in 1780 was among the greatest British successes of the war. But Cornwallis despised the Loyalist militia with whom he was supposed

to collaborate, and was upset by the failure of his counterinsurgency measures to suppress Patriot resistance and win Loyalist territory. His victorious but costly attack at Guilford Court House in March 1781 was born of frustration approaching despair.

Surrender document

Cornwallis signed the Articles of Capitulation at Yorktown on October 19, 1781, along with naval Captain Thomas Symonds. The terms allowed officers to return to Britain on parole.

With Clinton far off in New York, in spring 1781 Cornwallis made his own decision to march into Virginia. Bombarded with contradictory orders from Clinton, he adopted a defensive position at Yorktown that he knew to be weak and vulnerable. The lack of promised reinforcements and the

defeat of the Royal Navy by the French at Chesapeake Bay left Cornwallis in a hopeless situation, with no choice but to surrender.

Imperial successes

Despite his surrender at Yorktown, Cornwallis's reputation in Britain remained high. In 1786, he was chosen as governor general of British India, with a remit to reform the administration and stamp out corruption. He also fought a war against Tippu Sultan, the ruler of Mysore. His performance in India earned him the title of Marquess Cornwallis in 1792. By the time he returned to Britain in 1794 the country was at war with France. He was appointed Master of the Ordnance, with a responsibility for preparing the defense of Britain against an anticipated French invasion.

In 1798, Cornwallis was sent to govern Ireland, at a time when the country was seething with revolt and the French were planning military intervention in support of the rebels. The rebel forces were easily trounced, and Ireland joined the United Kingdom with the Act of Union in 1801. However, relations between the British and Irish were embittered, as George III denied Cornwallis's wish to grant Catholics equal rights.

By the end of his life, Cornwallis had become a distinguished figure, admired for his competence and character. He was entrusted with negotiating peace with Napoleon Bonaparte in 1802 and was once more sent to administer India in 1805. Struck down by a fever, he died that year at Ghazipur, near Benares (Varanasi). A mausoleum was erected at the site of his grave, overlooking the Ganges River.

TIMELINE

1738 Born December 31, in Grosvenor Square, London, eldest son of an earl.

1757 Commissioned as a Guards officer.

1759 Sees first action at the Battle of Minden, Prussia, in the Seven Years War.

1760 Elected a member of parliament.

1761–62 Promoted to lieutenant colonel, fights in a number of battles in Germany, during the Seven Years' War.

1762 Succeeds to the title of Earl Cornwallis, taking a seat in the House of Lords.

1768 Marries Jemima Tullekin Jones; they will have two children.

May 1776 Arrives in America.

August 1776 Fights in Battle of Long Island.

January 1777 He is outwitted by Washington at the Battle of Princeton.

August–December 1777 Plays a leading role in the Philadelphia Campaign, including battles of Brandywine and Germantown.

June–July 1778 Commands the British rearguard in the withdrawal from Philadelphia, fighting at the Battle of Monmouth.

December 1778 Returns to England because his wife is mortally ill; she dies February 1779.

July 1779 Returns to America.

March 1780 Successful Siege of Charleston.

August 1780 Inflicts a major defeat on the Americans at the Battle of Camden.

March 1781 Victory at Guilford Court House.

October 1781 Surrenders at Yorktown, Virginia; on parole, he returns to Britain.

1786 Appointed governor general of India.

1789–92 Commands forces in the Third Anglo-Mysore War against Tippu Sultan.

1794–98 Returns to Britain, serving as Master of the Ordnance.

1798–1801 Suppresses Irish Rebellion led by Wolf Tone.

1802 Negotiates the Treaty of Amiens with Napoleon Bonaparte.

1805 Reappointed governor general of India, dies on October 5 at Ghazipur.

STATUE OF CORNWALLIS, KOLKATA, INDIA

<< BEFORE

Success in Georgia and the Carolinas

In late 1780 and early 1781, American fortunes revived in the South. British detachments were defeated while Cornwallis's main army failed in its efforts to strike back decisively.

ACTION IN THE CAROLINAS
While Patriot militia and **guerrilla fighters << 268–69** had some success in the backcountry in 1780, the Continental Army suffered a string of defeats, notably at **Charleston << 266–67** and at **Camden << 274–75**. In a bid to turn the tide, George Washington appointed **Nathanael Greene** to command in the South. Part of Greene's army won a notable victory at **Cowpens << 290–91** the next month, and then his main force blunted a British attack at **Guilford Court House << 292–93** in **March**.

While the main Continental Army and its French allies pursued Cornwallis to Virginia in the spring of 1781, Nathanael Greene, Patriot commander in the South, focused on the Carolinas, mustering partisans and militia to attack a chain of well-fortified but isolated British outposts.

In March 1781, General Greene reported that he was "determined to carry the war immediately into South Carolina." By mid-April, he had reached the area around Camden. The British had about 8,000 troops in Georgia and the Carolinas, principally stationed in a chain of forts along the corridor created by the Santee, Congaree, and Saluda rivers. These tenuous extensions of British control from their coastal bases in Charleston and Savannah included Georgetown, Fort Watson, Fort Motte, Orangeburg, Fort Granby, and Fort Ninety-Six, as well as Fort Augusta in Georgia.

Faced with expiring enlistments of his Virginia and North Carolina militia, Greene took stock. In addition to 2,400 remaining Continentals, he could count on militia forces conducting partisan operations under Thomas Sumter in western North Carolina, Andrew Pickens in western South Carolina, and Francis Marion in the swamps around the Pee Dee River. Greene decided to detach "Light Horse Harry" Lee to join Marion and lay siege to the chain of forts. Meanwhile, he tried to summon Pickens and Sumter

Damage control
William Washington's cavalry and some Maryland infantrymen managed to save three American guns from capture during the chaotic Patriot withdrawal at Hobkirk's Hill.

Although the British won the battle, their casualties were heavy, and Rawdon decided to abandon Camden on May 10. Rawdon also planned to evacuate the British forts in the backcountry but his messengers to them were all intercepted—the forts were already besieged.

Attacking British forts

Beginning even before Hobkirk's Hill, Lee and Marion took Fort Watson (April 14–23), then Motte (May 8–12) and Granby (May 15) also fell, while Sumter took Orangeburg (May 11), leaving only Augusta and Ninety-Six in British hands. Lee and Pickens, joined by Georgia partisan Elijah Clarke, captured Augusta from Lieutenant Colonel Thomas Brown's Loyalist force on June 5, after mounting a bitter two-week siege.

Greene himself led the effort against Fort Ninety-Six in late May. Having

Alexander Stuart and encamped by an imposing brick mansion at Eutaw Springs. Heading for the British camp on the morning of September 8, Greene formed two lines, with militia in the first, followed by Continentals. Initially, the militia fared well against the single, hastily formed British line, but then gave way to a British counterattack.

Greene then fed his second line of troops into the fight, unhinging the British line and sending it into retreat, except for the British right under Major John Majoribanks, who stubbornly resisted from a blackjack thicket. Greene deployed his reserve of William Washington's cavalry against Majoribanks's position, but the horses struggled in the thicket. Unable to escape, Washington's cavalry was mauled by the British, suffering some 50 percent casualties.

Meanwhile, the Patriot infantry pursued the British retreat but, pausing to plunder the British camp, they gave the British time to seek the safety of the fortified mansion from where they counterattacked in turn.

"We fight, **get beat**, rise and **fight again.**"

NATHANAEL GREENE, LETTER TO THE CHEVALIER DE LA LUZERNE, JUNE 1781

heard that British reinforcements had landed at Charleston, Greene rushed a combined assault with Lee on June 18. This failed and, with the British relief column just a day's march away, the Patriots were forced to abandon the siege of Fort Ninety-Six. In fact, extreme heat, meager rations, and exhausting forced marches had taken their toll on the British, and Rawdon ordered the evacuation of the fort within days.

Eutaw Springs

Six weeks of rest and recovery followed during the height of the Carolina summer, but in early September Greene, joined by Pickens, Marion, and Sumter, again sought out the British—now under the command of Lieutenant Colonel

Full charge
Colonel William Washington orders the 3rd Continental Light Dragoons onward during the Patriot charge at Eutaw Springs. Washington was wounded and captured in the battle.

After an exhausting three-hour fight, Greene retired with more than 500 casualties—20 percent of his force. The British retained the field, but they had suffered more than 800 casualties in the battle and other nearby clashes— 40 percent of their number. Although

Greene had been denied the tactical victory he sought, by the year's end the only British positions in Georgia and the Carolinas were a force of Loyalists who regularly raided inland from Wilmington and the garrisons of the cities of Charleston and Savannah.

to help him confront the force of about 900 Loyalists and British regulars in Camden under Lieutenant Colonel Lord Rawdon.

Hobkirk's Hill

While Greene held Hobkirk's Hill north of Camden, awaiting reinforcements, Rawdon received word of Greene's plans from a deserter. Deciding to preempt Greene, Rawdon attacked at dawn on April 26. He pushed back the Patriot sentries, but Greene managed to deploy his troops. Seeing his line overlapping the British flanks, Greene changed his plan and decided to launch an immediate counterattack rather than await the British advance.

When a Maryland Continental battalion paused to fire a volley, the attack lost momentum, causing the American line to unravel completely. Captain James Smith's light infantry company—killed to a man—and William Washington's cavalry managed to cover Greene's retreat.

AFTER

The main theater of war moved to Virginia. By late summer 1781, the armies were converging on the deep harbor port at Yorktown on Chesapeake Bay.

CONVERGING ON VIRGINIA
While Lord Rawdon was occupied in the Carolinas, Lord Cornwallis **moved his army into Virginia 304–05 »** to link up with British units there. In response, George Washington and Rochambeau sent army reinforcements to Virginia, and a **French fleet under the Comte de Grasse 300–01 »** sailed for the Chesapeake.

LOYALISTS MOVE ON
Carolina Loyalists **312–13 »**, including many from Fort Ninety-Six, moved to **Nova Scotia**, Canada, after the war. They named their new hometown Rawdon, after Lord Rawdon, in gratitude for his relief of the fort.

LORD RAWDON FOUGHT AT BUNKER HILL AND NEW YORK AS WELL AS IN THE SOUTH

Battle of the Chesapeake

While the opposing armies focused their attentions on Virginia's Yorktown peninsula, French and British fleets vied for control of the bay surrounding it. In the battle that ensued between the two naval powers, luck and miscommunication both played a part.

« BEFORE

The French formally allied with the US in 1778, and Spain followed suit in 1779. They supplied fleets, armies, military supplies, and funds.

GENEROUS ALLIES

On May 28, 1781, Rochambeau wrote to Admiral de Grasse, apprising him of the allies' most pressing needs: **troops and money**. In response, de Grasse embarked 3,200 French troops from the West Indies, and sent 1.2 million livres ($9 million today)—borrowed from Bernardo de Galvez, the senior Spanish military commander (and later governor) of Cuba—before departing with his fleet for America.

BERNARDO DE GÁLVEZ

FRENCH ADMIRAL 1722–88

COMTE DE GRASSE

François-Joseph Paul, Comte de Grasse, was a French naval commander sent to assist the Patriots. After fighting at Ushant, off Brittany, in 1778, he joined d'Estaing's fleet in the West Indies. Promoted to admiral in 1781, de Grasse defeated Admiral Samuel Hood at Tobago, and fought in the Chesapeake Bay. After this, de Grasse returned to the West Indies, where he was captured and taken to London after his defeat in the 1782 Battle of the Saintes.

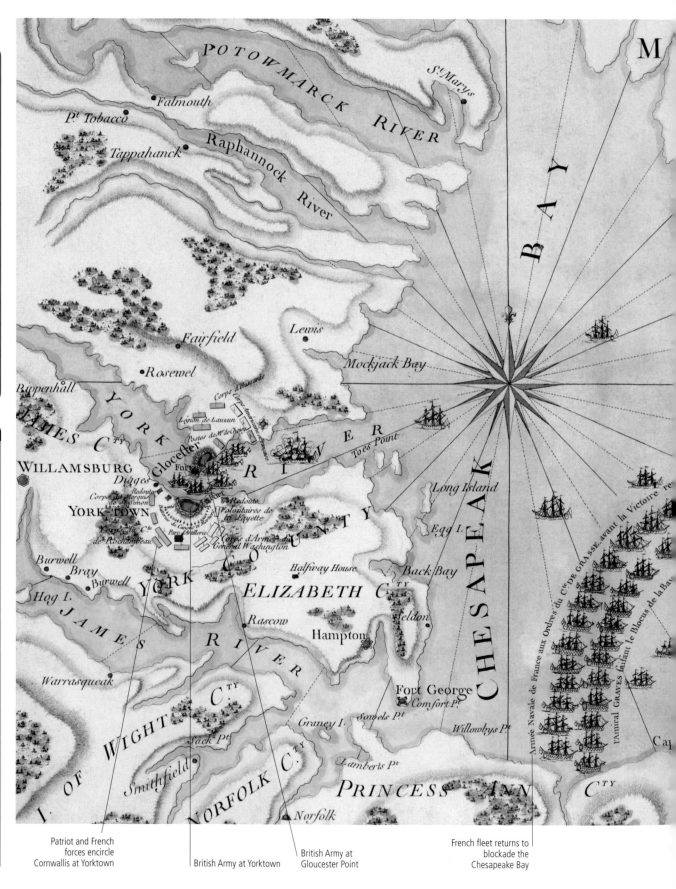

Patriot and French forces encircle Cornwallis at Yorktown

British Army at Yorktown

British Army at Gloucester Point

French fleet returns to blockade the Chesapeake Bay

In August 1781, Washington learned that Admiral de Grasse intended to sail from Cap-Français—now Cap-Haïtien, Haiti—to the Chesapeake Bay, where he intended to stay until October 15 in order to escape the hurricane season in the West Indies. On receiving this news, Washington shifted his focus to Virginia.

Meanwhile, in the West Indies, the departure of de Grasse's fleet did not go unnoticed, and a squadron under the command of Admiral Samuel Hood was dispatched in pursuit. Despite de Grasse's five-day headstart, Hood's copper-bottomed ships were faster and arrived in the Chesapeake Bay first. Finding no French fleet there, Hood departed for Sandy Hook, off New York, which allowed de Grasse to arrive uncontested off Cape Henry on August 30. Realizing that the French had eluded Hood, the new British naval commander in North America, Rear Admiral Thomas Graves, sailed for the Chesapeake on August 31 to do battle with de Grasse.

Battle in the capes

On the morning of September 5, a lookout on the French frigate *Aigrette* spotted the approaching British fleet, which contained 19 ships of the line. De Grasse swiftly ordered his 24 ships of the line to set sail. In their haste, the French were caught shorthanded: some 1,200–1,800 sailors were ashore or in boats landing troops and supplies. Because of this, the first four French ships to clear the Virginia Capes for the open sea were about 1 mile (1.6 km) ahead of the rest of the vanguard, but the British failed to make the most of their chance to cut the ships off from the rest of the French fleet.

Around noon, from his flagship HMS *London*, Graves ordered the British fleet to form a line of battle. As the last of the French fleet emerged from the bay at about 1:45 p.m., Graves ordered his line to turn their sterns through the wind to avoid shoals. This turned the whole fleet, reversing the order of sail: Hood, who had been commanding the vanguard, now commanded the British rear. After the maneuver, the opposing fleets found themselves on roughly parallel southeasterly courses. Giving orders from his flagship *Ville de Paris*, de Grasse attempted to close the gap between his vanguard and the remaining French ships of the line.

Mixed signals

Around 4 p.m., both vanguards opened fire, sustaining serious damage in the exchange. Then, in the heat of battle, British communications broke down. About this time, Graves later claimed, he ordered the signal for "line ahead" to be hauled down and replaced with the signal "engage closely." According to Hood, both signals flew from *London*'s masthead simultaneously for nearly an hour. Believing the "line ahead" signal to have precedence, Hood remained in formation, effectively precluding the British from getting their strongest ships into the fray. When Hood finally reported seeing "line ahead" hauled down, he set a course to close in on the French, but it was already too late.

Necessary ceasefire

The impending darkness ended the engagement after a long-range exchange between Hood's division and the French center. HMS *Terrible* was badly damaged, while *Diadème*, on the French side, fared little better, with 125 holes in its hull. Both fleets eyed each other warily out of range while making repairs. In a conference convened by Graves aboard *London*, Hood unsuccessfully advocated a return to the Chesapeake to support Lord Cornwallis's army.

As the fleets continued to maneuver eastward within sight of each other, de Grasse became increasingly concerned about his distance from the bay, and the possibility of being isolated. On September 8, de Grasse caught Graves off guard by escaping westward. By September 11, de Grasse had arrived back in the mouth of the Chesapeake Bay—ready to contribute to the Patriot campaign at Yorktown.

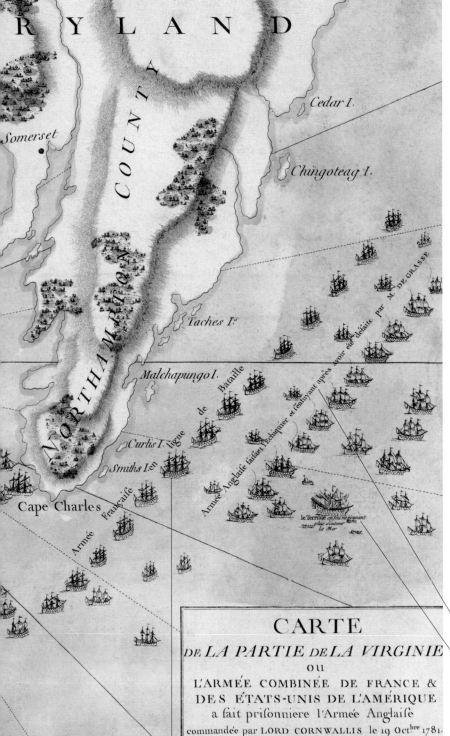

British ships of the line leave the capes after the battle

HMS *Terrible* scuttled by fire

Propaganda bravado

Although the mouth of the bay was indeed blockaded by the French fleet, this contemporary French map by Esnauts and Rapilly suggests a more perfect chain than was really formed. It also erroneously places the battle to the northeast of Cape Henry, not the southeast.

The French line of battle formed much closer to Cape Henry than this diagram suggests

AFTER »

The French, Spanish, and Dutch all continued to engage with British fleets at sea after 1781.

LAST BATTLES
Britain fought numerous naval battles in the West Indies and off India in 1782 and 1783, which only ended with the **Peace of Paris 312–13** ». Although de Grasse was the victor in 1781, the tables were turned in April 1782 when he surrendered the *Ville de Paris* to Hood at the **Battle of the Saintes**.

SURRENDER OF THE *VILLE DE PARIS* AT THE BATTLE OF THE SAINTES, OFF DOMINICA

Closing in
Jean-Antoine-Siméon Fort's painting was based on the notes of a topographer under Rochambeau called Berthier, who drew 111 maps of the campaign. Fort shows the French, in white, moving into Yorktown's outer defenses on September 30.

The **Yorktown Campaign**

In the summer of 1781, Cornwallis's plan to use Yorktown as the base for a new campaign in Virginia appeared to be unraveling. While a French fleet blockaded the bay, preventing reinforcements from landing, the French and Patriot armies targeted the British garrison.

With Britain's southern army much depleted from pursuing General Greene's army through the Carolinas, Lord Cornwallis decided to consolidate his remaining troops with those of General William Phillips in Virginia, in an effort to disrupt the flow of men and supplies to Greene. Arriving at Portsmouth on May 20, the combined British force now totaled more than 7,000 men. Initially angered that Cornwallis had moved to Virginia without his permission, Commander in Chief Sir Henry Clinton then revised his opinion and instructed Cornwallis to establish a naval base in Virginia. Cornwallis chose to fortify Yorktown, at the mouth of the Chesapeake Bay.

The allies' plans

Having received confirmation of the departure of Admiral de Grasse's French fleet from Cap-Français on August 14, Washington and the Comte de Rochambeau began planning a simultaneous land campaign in Virginia. Their proposal required marching some 2,500 Continentals and 5,400 French troops south in the war's largest operational movement to date. They devised multiple marching routes, to spread the demand for forage, while Washington also employed deception measures—collecting boats, building camp bake ovens, and planting false dispatches—to convince the British that their target was really New York.

The first Continental troops reached Williamsburg on September 19, with the rest arriving over the course of the week. Both armies set off on the final march to Yorktown on September 28. By this time, a French fleet blockaded Yorktown from the Chesapeake Bay.

BEFORE

Thwarted in his efforts to achieve victory in the South, Cornwallis decided to move the war to Virginia.

GREENE ELUDES THE BRITISH
Failure to defeat General Greene decisively at **Guilford Court House ‹‹ 292–93** convinced the British commander that he needed a new strategy for the South.

REINFORCEMENTS ARRIVE
In January 1781, **Patriot traitor Benedict Arnold** returned to the field **‹‹ 256–57**. On General Clinton's orders, he led British forces on a rampage through Virginia, burning both Richmond and Petersburg. Lafayette, originally sent to reinforce Greene in South Carolina, was diverted to Virginia to oppose them.

BENEDICT ARNOLD IN BRITISH UNIFORM

Storming the defenses
Patriots capture redoubt ten from British and German troops, which together with the French capture of redoubt nine, on October 14–15, enabled the allies to complete their siege lines.

At 3 p.m. on October 9, Washington granted the French the honor of starting the bombardment. Two hours later, the Patriot batteries joined in, and the first Patriot gun, laid by the commander in chief himself, scored a direct hit on Cornwallis's officers' mess. On October 10, French artillery attacked British ships in the York River, burning HMS *Charon* to the waterline with red-hot shot.

As the digging progressed, it became clear that the last trench, known as the second parallel, could not be completed without capturing two redoubts on the far left of the British

AFTER

Cornwallis had no choice but to surrender his army. His capitulation would set the wheels in motion for the end of the war.

THE END IN SIGHT
The morning after Abercrombie's attack, **Cornwallis sought to negotiate surrender**, effectively marking the end of the major land battles of the war **306–07 ››**. Some fighting continued elsewhere. Britain's Royal Navy won an important victory in the **Battle of the Saintes** off Dominica in April 1782, and successfully relieved the **Siege of Gibraltar** in the fall. The **peace treaties** between the European powers were less damaging to Britain as a result of these late successes **312–13 ››**.

the second parallel. On October 16, British Lieutenant Colonel Robert Abercrombie led an attack on two French batteries near the American lines, but succeeded in putting them out of action only temporarily.

The British War Council in New York could provide Cornwallis with no assistance. That same day, trapped between the allied armies and the French fleet in the Chesapeake Bay, the British commander ordered his forces to evacuate across the York River by boat. He hoped to attempt a breakout via Gloucester Point, but a sudden storm doomed his desperate move. Outnumbered roughly two to one, Cornwallis had run out of options.

> " Against so **powerful** an attack we **cannot hope** to make a very **long resistance**."
>
> CORNWALLIS, LETTER TO CLINTON, OCTOBER 11, 1781

Textbook siege
At the approach of the French and American armies on September 30, Cornwallis abandoned his outermost defensive works, perhaps believing them overextended. Under cover of darkness, the allies began mounting a formal siege, using the Vaubanian method. This process—designed in the 17th century—required them to dig a series of successively closer firing positions for artillery, connected by zigzag approach trenches.

Fatally trapped
If a British counter-sortie were to succeed, standard practice held that it must be before the completion of

line. On the night of October 14, Lieutenant Colonel Alexander Hamilton of the Continental Army led more than 400 light infantry against one redoubt, while 400 French chasseurs and grenadiers attacked the other. Both fell quickly, allowing work on the second parallel to begin.

Directing labor
Washington and de Rochambeau oversee the digging of trenches by French and American soldiers. Dug by hand, the trenches were plotted by a dozen engineer officers and took the allies three nights to complete.

Surrender at Yorktown

General Lord Cornwallis hoped to negotiate a surrender on favorable terms. Unfortunately for the British, Washington had a long memory and the talks dragged on for two days while the two generals hashed out the terms of capitulation.

BEFORE

At Yorktown, Cornwallis had found himself cut off on all sides, by the allied armies and the French fleet.

CORNWALLIS CAUGHT

In May 1781, Cornwallis had moved his army to Yorktown, Virginia, to establish a new springboard for campaigns in the South. Taking advantage of his isolation, Washington and his French counterpart, the Comte de Rochambeau **laid siege** to Cornwallis's base at Yorktown **«304–05** while a **French fleet mounted a blockade**. Cornwallis was trapped by land and sea.

At about 10 a.m. on October 17, 1781, a British officer waving a white handkerchief and a drummer beating a parley appeared on the British works at Yorktown. As the allies' guns fell silent, a Patriot officer greeted the pair, before blindfolding the British officer to take him behind Patriot lines. There, the British officer delivered Cornwallis's proposal to Washington: "a cessation of hostilities for twenty-four hours … to settle terms for the surrender."

Initial terms proposed by Cornwallis specified "that the Garrisons of York and Gloucester shall be Prisoners of War with the customary Honors," and that the British and German soldiers would be sent home, should they promise not to serve against America

or its allies. Cornwallis also proposed that "all Arms & public Stores" would be relinquished.

Difficult negotiations

Washington's response to Cornwallis was both harsh and unexpected: "The same Honors will be granted to the Surrendering Army as were granted to the Garrison of Charles Town." He referred to the ignominious terms offered by Sir Henry Clinton to General Benjamin Lincoln when

Lincoln surrendered his army at Charleston in May 1780. Cornwallis's men were refused parole and relegated to prisoner-of-war status.

A truce was observed while the negotiations proceeded. Washington chose Lieutenant Colonel John Laurens to represent the Patriots, while Rochambeau sent the Vicomte de Noailles to speak for the French. They met with the British delegation at the Moore House, near the York River, where negotiations dragged on as the

> " You must **be prepared** to **hear the worst.** "
>
> LORD CORNWALLIS TO GENERAL CLINTON, SEPTEMBER 16, 1781

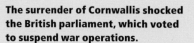
The surrender of Cornwallis shocked the British parliament, which voted to suspend war operations.

NEWS SPREADS

On October 24, a British fleet carrying 5,000 troops that had set sail from New York to relieve Cornwallis's army arrived at Cape Henry, where it learned of the defeat from a passing schooner. When the news reached Britain, parliament decided to **sue for peace 310–11 ❯❯**. However, until the **peace treaties** of 1783 **312–13 ❯❯**, battles continued to rage between British and European fleets off India and the West Indies.

THE FRENCH SAIL FOR THE WEST INDIES

Glorifying the victors
Rochambeau, in field dress, directs two white-clad soldiers in the foreground. The French commander commissioned a version of this painting, depicting him in formal dress, to hang in his château.

British pressed for better terms. One sticking point pertained to the fate of American Loyalists within British lines, who rightly feared that they would not be granted true prisoner-of-war status.

Triumph and defeat
At 11 a.m. on October 19, Cornwallis finally signed the terms of surrender, shortly followed by the British naval commander, Captain Thomas Symonds.

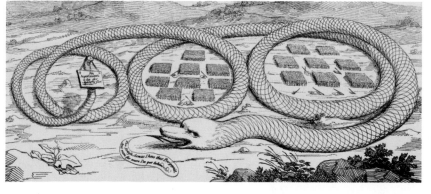

"The American Rattlesnake"
America coils itself around the armies of Burgoyne and Cornwallis, which were both imprisoned in America until 1783. The sign on the snake's tail boasts room for more armies, should the British choose to keep fighting.

Washington, Rochambeau, and French Admiral de Barras signed on behalf of the allies. Less than an hour passed before American and French troops took possession of the British fortifications at Yorktown, planting the flags of their respective nations with pride. Meanwhile, Cornwallis broke the news to his troops that they would not be paroled and sent home as hoped.

At around 3 p.m. on October 19, the unhappy British garrison marched out of Yorktown. The allies lined the route along Hampton Road to a field—now named Surrender Field—designated for the surrender ceremony. French troops lined the west side of the road, while the Americans stood on the east. The French were resplendent in their white coats—trimmed with colored facings according to their regiments—marking a stark contrast to their Patriot counterparts, who were ragged and motley, but who stood no less proud.

Breaching etiquette
Claiming that he was indisposed, the defeated Cornwallis would not attend the surrender, so the British column was led by his second in command, Brigadier General Charles O'Hara. He was followed by the British Guards, British infantry, British cavalry, and the Hessians. All marched, in accordance with Article III of the terms, with "Colors cased [furled] & Drums beating a British or German march."

The honors of war generally dictated that the surrendering army play an enemy march—in this case, American or French—while flying their own colors. The British were denied this right, just as Lincoln had been at Charleston. Under these terms, they would thus surrender without the honors of war. Although popular mythology holds that the British played "The World Turned Upside Down," the tune they played, if any, remains lost to history.

As the British approached, General O'Hara at first endeavored to approach Rochambeau, but was politely conducted, at Rochambeau's bidding, to General Washington. Crossing the road to Washington, General O'Hara apologized for Cornwallis's absence and attempted to present his sword in token surrender. The commander in chief refused it. Instead, Washington directed O'Hara to General Lincoln, his second in command, who had been on the reciprocal end of the ignominious surrender at Charleston in 1780.

The British column bore right into a field ringed by French Hussars, where 28 standard bearers presented their regimental colors. The defeated troops grounded their arms and equipment, and finally surrendered themselves. Now prisoners of the allied armies, they were sent to prison camps in Virginia and Maryland to wait for peace.

The **British Surrender**

James Thacher, a Massachusetts-born surgeon and writer, served in the Continental Army during the Yorktown campaign. A witness to the surrender, Thacher described the humbling of the British troops with great satisfaction, but criticized the absent Cornwallis for not submitting himself to the same experience.

"It was about two o'clock when the captive army advanced ... Every eye was prepared to gaze on Lord Cornwallis, the object of peculiar interest and solicitude; but he disappointed our anxious expectations; pretending indisposition, he made General O'Hara his substitute as the leader of his army. This officer was followed by the conquered troops in a slow and solemn step ... drums beating a British march ... At the head of the line, General O'Hara, elegantly mounted, advanced to his excellency the commander in chief, taking off his hat, and apologized for the non-appearance of Earl Cornwallis. With his usual dignity and politeness, his excellency pointed to Major-General Lincoln for directions, by whom the British army was conducted into a spacious field, where it was intended they should ground their arms.

The royal troops ... exhibited a decent and neat appearance ... but in their line of march we remarked a disorderly and unsoldierly conduct, their step was irregular, and their ranks frequently broken ... it was in the field ... that the spirit and pride of the British soldier was put to the severest test: here their mortification could not be concealed. Some of the platoon officers appeared to be exceedingly chagrined when giving the word "ground arms," and ... performed this duty in a very unofficer-like manner ... many of the soldiers manifested a sullen temper, throwing their arms on the pile with violence, as if determined to render them useless... After having grounded their arms and divested themselves of their accoutrements, the captive troops were conducted back to Yorktown.**"**

CONTINENTAL ARMY SURGEON JAMES THACHER, FROM *A MILITARY JOURNAL DURING THE AMERICAN REVOLUTIONARY WAR, FROM 1775 TO 1783* (1823)

Trumbull's flawed depiction
Artist and Continental Army officer John Trumbull was
not present for the surrender, and originally placed
Cornwallis on horseback at the center of this scene.
Criticized for his error, Trumbull changed the colors of
the figure's coat, placing Benjamin Lincoln there instead.

Negotiating Peace

The Patriot victory at Yorktown convinced British politicians that the American war could not be won. Meanwhile, war-weariness was damaging the morale of Continental troops. Few on either side wanted the conflict to continue, but making peace was far from easy.

« BEFORE

Once the War of Independence turned into a global conflict, Britain faced war on many fronts.

PRESSURE ON BRITAIN

Once Spain (1779) and the Netherlands (`1780) joined France (1778) on the side of the Patriots, Britain had to fight a global conflict, with its **colonial possessions under threat « 218–19**. In America, the Spanish consolidated control of the **Mississippi Valley** with the capture of Baton Rouge and Mobile in 1780, and secured West Florida with the **siege of Pensacola** in May 1781. The last major battle of the War of Independence took place at **Yorktown « 304–05** in October 1781.

Cornwallis's defeat at Yorktown was a fatal blow to the British war effort in America. The growing pressures turned the tide in parliament, which voted against continuation of the war in America on February 27, 1782, empowering the government to negotiate peace on March 5.

Changes in personnel also helped. Lord North's Tory ministry ended with a vote of no confidence in late March; he was replaced by the Whig Lord Rockingham. Similarly, Sir Guy Carleton replaced Sir Henry Clinton as the new British commander in America (the fourth of the war), with a mandate to suspend offensive operations during peace talks. These began in April.

The war news from the West Indies was slightly better than that at Yorktown. Admiral George Rodney's fleet defeated the French under Admiral Comte de Grasse, thwarting a planned invasion of Jamaica at the Battle of the Saintes in April 1782. But the increasing strain upon Britain's manpower and finances made further offensive efforts in America untenable. Both armies marshaled their resources, eyeing one another warily as they awaited the outcome of the negotiations.

Rebellion in the ranks

After countless hardships imposed by long years of hard campaigning with chronic shortages of nearly every kind—food, clothing, adquate shelter, and pay—schisms began to emerge in the Continental Army. In January 1781, the Pennsylvania Line threatened mutiny in winter quarters outside Morristown, New Jersey. Chief among their grievances was the fact that many soldiers who had enlisted in 1777 "for three years or the duration of the war," had received no pay during their time in the army, except for a $20 bounty (around $460 today) upon enlistment. These so-called "twenty dollar men" interpreted

Mending fences
Peacemakers stressed the common bonds between Britain and America. This British cartoon entitled *Reconciliation between Britannia and her Daughter America* makes fun of the sudden about-face.

> **"One or other of the Parties at War must take the first Step."**
>
> BENJAMIN FRANKLIN TO DAVID HARTLEY, 1782

the ambiguous terms of enlistment to mean that their three-year commitment to the army had run its course and stated their intention to return home.

The issue was resolved when Joseph Reed, president of the Pennsylvania Supreme Executive Council, appeared in person to negotiate a settlement with the mutinous soldiers. Under the agreement, the "twenty dollar men" were discharged and offered the option to reenlist for a second bounty. In the end, about half of the Pennsylvanians availed themselves of Reed's offer. During the negotiations, a British agent approached the conspirators on behalf of General Clinton, offering to provide the soldiers' back pay if they abandoned the rebel cause and joined the British side—an offer the Pennsylvanians universally rejected.

The Newburgh Conspiracy

A similar affair involving a number of Continental Army officers occurred in Newburgh, New York, in March 1783. With the government facing financial collapse—due, in part, to Congress's inability to generate revenue under the Articles of Confederation—officers' pay, too, was in arrears. In addition, the crisis also threatened promised officer pensions of half pay for life. A petition signed by several respected senior officers was sent to Congress with a vague threat of "fatal effects" if the situation was not resolved.

The crisis came to a climax when a number of anonymous letters were circulated through the camp, urging the army to send Congress an ultimatum. Alarmed, Washington called an officers' meeting for March 15, implying that a senior officer would chair the meeting instead of

him. During the proceedings, however, Washington entered the building where the meeting was taking place and asked a surprised General Gates, then presiding, for the opportunity to address his officers.

Urging the assembly not to let financial consideration jeopardize the liberties for which they had fought so hard, Washington began to read a letter from the Congress, but paused to retrieve his newly acquired reading glasses, saying "Gentlemen, you will permit me to put on my

spectacles, for I have not only grown gray but almost blind in the service of my country." This rare show of vulnerability by their commander in chief broke the tension in the room and reminded all those present that Washington, too, had shared their privations, and put an abrupt end to the affair.

Negotiations begin

The American delegation sent to Paris and charged with conducting the peace negotiations included Benjamin Franklin, John Adams, John Jay, and initially Henry Laurens, with

Mutiny for the bounty
Pennsylvania paid its soldiers a bounty of $20, compared to hundreds of dollars paid in other states. Pennsylvania resolved grievances with little bloodshed, but Washington ordered the execution of mutinous soldiers in New Jersey.

A fond farewell
By the time Washington resigned his command, his standing among his fellow officers was unrivaled. On December 4, 1783, he was given an emotional send-off at a farewell dinner at the Fraunces tavern.

David Hartley and Richard Oswald representing the British. On April 12, 1782, the opposing delegations began the long and contentious process of negotiating an end to the war that was now entering its eighth year.

It was clear that reaching agreements between the multiple nations involved would not be an easy process. Although France and the United States had a treaty of alliance, each nation still had its own interests to pursue. France and Spain had treaty obligations to each other, but Spain was not formally allied to the United States and had its own territorial interests to consider in North America. Even if Britain recognized American independence, the British had possessions they would wish to retain in Canada, the Caribbean, India, and other places. Balancing these conflicting requirements would take months of haggling.

AFTER ≫

After more than a year of negotiations, the Treaty of Paris was signed on September 3, 1783.

FRAUNCES TAVERN MEETINGS
For much of 1783, Fraunces Tavern, where Washington held his farewell feast, became the venue for meetings of the joint British–American board tasked to ensure that the British did not take "American property" with them when they left. In this case, "property" meant former slaves. In the end, most **Loyalist African Americans** interviewed by the board kept their freedom.

BECOMING PRESIDENT
George Washington was appointed as **president of the Constitutional Convention 328–29 ≫** to establish new forms of government for the country in 1787. When he became the **first president of the United States 334–35 ≫** in 1789, every member of the electoral college voted for him.

Treaty of Paris

The War of Independence was officially brought to an end on September 3, 1783, at the Hôtel de York in Paris, where treaties were signed by delegates of Britain, the United States, France, and Spain. The Americans were ready to make the most of their strong bargaining position.

The biggest challenge facing the American delegates during the long process of reaching a settlement with Britain was coming to agreement among themselves. Thomas Jefferson, delayed by bad weather, arrived too late to take part in the negotiations, and Henry Laurens arrived late (having been held prisoner by the British) and left before the final agreement was signed. The negotiations therefore fell mainly to the three remaining delegates: John Adams, Benjamin Franklin, and John Jay.

Personal differences

The Congress deliberately selected the delegates for their different views as well as their complementary abilities, making the challenge of presenting the British delegation with a united American front at times a daunting one. While popular longtime French ambassador Franklin provided insight into French interests, his fellow delegates—Jay and Adams—distrusted his pro-French bias.

John Adams, believing that the future success of the United States lay in an eventual rapprochement with its former colonial master, risked alienating French foreign minister the Comte de Vergennes, who

Signed and sealed

The Treaty of Paris, 1783, bears the signatures of John Adams and Benjamin Franklin, among others. Article 10 stipulated that ratification of the treaty was to take place within six months of its signature.

remarked that Adams "has an inflexibility, a pedantry, an arrogance … which render him incapable of negotiating political matters." For his part, Jay, in turn, harbored a lingering resentment of Spain, following a frustrating stint as the American envoy there during the last years of the war. Described, like Adams, as somewhat humorless, his lawyer's acumen reputedly made him the toughest American negotiator at the conference.

The task faced by the American delegation was difficult and delicate: they had to divine the national interests of the new nation with little input from home, while resisting the

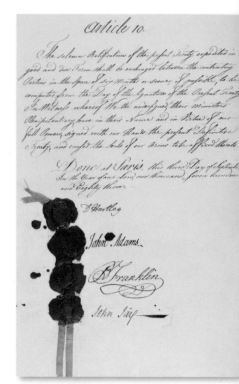

"Blessed are the Peacemakers"
This British cartoon, published in February 1783, lampooned preliminary peace talks taking place in France. "Spain" and "France" lead George III, followed by Britain's prime minister Lord Shelburne, to an inquisition, while "America," holding 13 lashes, pulls "Holland" along behind.

"There shall be a **firm and perpetual peace** between his **Brittanic Majesty** and the said states."

TREATY OF PARIS, 1783

efforts of the European powers to use them as pawns in a struggle for mastery in Europe and beyond.

Contentious points

In dealing with the British, the first major issue was the Americans' demand—championed by a dogged Jay—that Britain recognize the United States as an independent nation before further negotiations could take place. While the British eventually conceded this point, Franklin nearly overreached his hand with a bold suggestion that Britain cede Canada to the new nation as "war reparations." Britain refused.

As the negotiations wore on, sticking points included compensation for dispossessed Loyalists, fishing rights, and the establishment of the western border of the new nation. In the final agreement, the Americans prevailed on all three issues. Adams secured lucrative fishing rights for New England settlers off Newfoundland and Nova Scotia, a gain that was as much at the expense of France as of Britain. Moreover, the Americans managed to reduce the Loyalist compensation issue to a vague promise, agreeing only to "earnestly recommend" that each of the states pay restitution to their dispossessed Loyalists. In practice, this measure produced little effect.

New borders

Most importantly, to the mutual dismay of Spain and France, who both still harbored territorial ambitions of their own in North America, the Americans secured the Mississippi River as their western border. This included the Northwest Territory, long disputed between Britain and France, which became part of the new United States.

Britain also agreed to transfer sovereignty over East and West Florida back to Spain, but the boundaries agreed by this treaty, implying a return to those that existed before 1763, did not match those established by Britain's treaty with America, setting the stage for future disputes.

It was notable that the treaty said nothing about the Native American peoples. Far larger numbers of Native Americans had fought with the British than with the Patriots, having more to fear from an independent America than from continued British rule. Many, at war's end, refused to accept American sovereignty over their lands.

Officially at peace

The British and American delegations signed the initial terms of the treaty on November 30. Surprised at the favorable terms that the Americans had secured—and not pleased—Vergennes accused the Americans of a breach of faith by excluding France from their final negotiations with Britain. Franklin was given the task of smoothing Vergennes' ruffled feathers, essential if the Americans were to achieve their aims.

Despite protests from the Continental Congress that the delegation had ignored its instructions by negotiating separately with Britain without the advice and consent of the French, the Congress approved the terms of the treaty on April 15, 1783. The British signed preliminary agreements with France and Spain on January 20, 1783.

The Treaty of Paris between the United States and Britain, and the Treaties of Versailles between Britain, France, and Spain were signed by representatives of all parties on September 3, 1783. The Peace of Paris—the term given jointly to all of these documents—officially ended the War of Independence. The Congress ratified the Treaty of Paris on January 14, 1784, and the ratified copies were finally exchanged in May that year. The United States had won.

2.5 PERCENT of the colonial population, the so-called "United Empire Loyalists," left the country after the war under the provisions of the Treaty of Paris.

The American negotiators
Left to right: John Jay, John Adams, Benjamin Franklin, Henry Laurens, and William Temple Franklin, Franklin's grandson and secretary. This painting by Benjamin West was unfinished because the British peace commissioners refused to pose.

AFTER

In the coming years, the issues left unresolved by the Treaty of Paris brought more diplomatic maneuvers and the threat of conflict.

THE JAY TREATY
Agreed in 1794, the Jay Treaty improved American **trade relations with Britain** and secured the evacuation of the forts the British had kept in the Northwest, contrary to the Treaty of Paris. Opposition to the terms of the treaty, led by Thomas Jefferson, helped establish a **party political system 328–29 >>** in the United States.

TREATY OF MADRID
In 1795, a new agreement between the United States and Spain ended the **Florida boundary dispute 324–25 >>**. It also confirmed that Americans had the right to use the Mississippi and granted access to the Spanish-held ports at its mouth for trade.

Washington steps down
On December 23, 1783, Washington resigned his commission, a moment recorded for posterity in this painting by John Trumbull. The occasion was marked by a feast for 200 people, at which 13 toasts were made and 13 cannons discharged.

9

AFTERMATH: A STRONGER UNION

With the war over and the eyes of the world upon them, the victors had to build a nation, overcoming debt, destruction, and profound disagreements between states. Their most urgent task was to draw up a constitution.

≪ Leading the nation
George Washington stepped down from his role as commander of the armed forces at the end of the War of Independence, impressing international bystanders, including George III. But the American people wanted only one man to lead the nation in peace, and in 1789 Washington became the first

AFTER 1783

In the three decades following the Treaty of Paris, the United States expanded its territory and adopted the new Constitution. The Northwest Indian War delayed expansion to the West, but the American victory at Fallen Timbers in 1794 and the defeat of Tecumseh's Native American coalition opened new territories to American settlers. Thomas Jefferson's Louisiana Purchase in 1803 doubled the size of the United States, while the Quasi-War with France, the Tripolitan War, and the War of 1812 demonstrated that the new nation was capable of defending its interests against foreign powers. In domestic affairs, disputes between Alexander Hamilton and Thomas Jefferson led to the creation of two political parties, and tensions increased between the northern and southern states over the issue of slavery.

1 Seneca leader Red Jacket resisted the 1784 treaty between the United States and the Iroquois. 2 In May 1804, the Lewis and Clark Expedition set out to explore territory gained by the Louisiana Purchase. 3 During the War of 1812 the British attacked Washington, D.C.

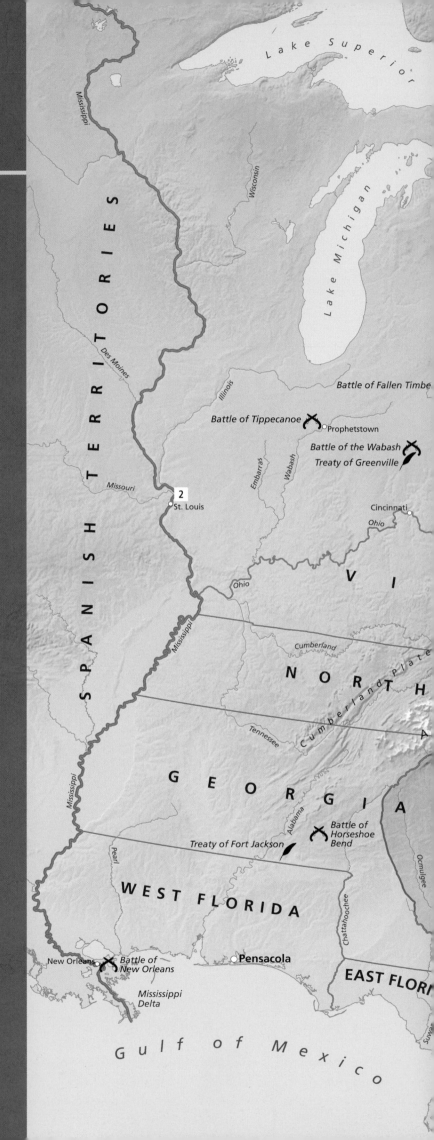

Newfoundland

Magdalen Islands

Prince Edward Island

Louisbourg

N O V A   S C O T I A

Sable Island

Quebec

St. Lawrence

Saguenay

St. John

Penobscot

Montreal

Ottawa

MASSACHUSETTS

Bay of Fundy

Halifax

Q U E B E C

Lake Champlain

White Mountains

NEW HAMPSHIRE

A T L A N T I C   O C E A N

Lake Ontario
1 Treaty of Fort Stanwix

Adirondack Mountains

Mohawk

Green Mountains

Connecticut

Fort Niagara

Battle of the Thames

Lake Erie

Battle of Lake Erie

N E W   Y O R K

Albany

Hudson

MASSACHUSETTS

Boston

Cape Cod

Catskill Mountains

CONNECTICUT

Newport
RHODE ISLAND

Allegheny

Treaty of Fort McIntosh

Whiskey Rebellion

P E N N S Y L V A N I A

Susquehanna

Washington's Inauguration
New York City

Delaware

Muskingum

Ohio

Princeton

Constitutional Convention
Philadelphia
NEW JERSEY

Baltimore

Battle of Bladensburg

3 Washington DC

DELAWARE

Kanawha

Potomac

MARYLAND

Chesapeake Bay

KEY

——— Border of Spanish territories

——— 1763 Proclamation Line

——— Colonial boundaries

○ Town / settlement

⚔ Battle / siege

🏰 Fort

🚢 Naval battle

🖋 Treaty / convention

⛺ Patriot winter camp

I N I A

James

Yorktown

Roanoke

Norfolk

Chesapeake-Leopard *Affair*

Dan

A R O L I N A

Watere

Pee Dee

Cape Fear

Camden

Wilmington

SOUTH CAROLINA

Augusta

Santee

Savannah

Cooper

Charleston

annah

Johns

N E W   Y O R K

Mohawk

Albany

Hudson

Green Mountains

Connecticut

NEW HAMPSHIRE

MASSACHUSETTS

Boston

Cape Cod

Catskill Mountains

Shays' Rebellion

CONNECTICUT

Newport
RHODE ISLAND

Susquehanna

Newburgh

Delaware

P E N N S Y L V A N I A

Washington's Inauguration
New York City

Long Island

Princeton
NEW JERSEY

A T L A N T I C
O C E A N

Constitutional Convention
Philadelphia

MARYLAND

Baltimore

Battle of Baltimore

3 Battle of *Bladensburg*
Washington DC

DELAWARE

0 ___ 100 km
0 ___ 100 miles

N

0 ___ 100 km
0 ___ 100 miles

TIMELINE AFTER 1783

Peace ratified ▪ **President Washington** ▪ The Bill of Rights ▪ **Economic crisis**
▪ European trade embargoes ▪ **Tripolitan War** ▪ Lewis and Clark expedition ▪ **French Quasi-War** ▪ Slave trade made illegal ▪ **The War of 1812** ▪ Native Americans cede lands

1784–89

JANUARY 14, 1784
The Treaty of Paris is ratified by the Confederation Congress, ending the War of Independence.

JUNE 2, 1784
The Continental Army is reduced in size by the Continental Congress.

AUGUST 19, 1784
The Congress moves from Annapolis, Maryland, to New York City.

JUNE 3, 1785
The sale of the Continental Navy's last vessel, the *Alliance*, is approved by the Confederation Congress.

AUGUST 29, 1786
Shays' Rebellion begins in western Massachusetts.

SEPTEMBER 11, 1786
The Annapolis Convention opens to discuss the Articles of Confederation.

FEBRUARY 28, 1787
The Confederation Congress calls for states to send representatives to a convention to revise the Articles of Confederation.

MAY 25, 1787
The Constitutional Convention begins in Philadelphia.

JULY 13, 1787
The Congress passes the Northwest Ordinance on settlement and statehood of the Northwest.

SEPTEMBER 17, 1787
Delegates sign the new Constitution in Philadelphia.

OCTOBER 27, 1787
The first of the Federalist essays is published in New York newspapers.

FEBRUARY 4, 1789
The Electoral College unanimously chooses George Washington to be the first president of the United States, electing John Adams as vice-president.

MARCH 4, 1789
The first Congress elected under the new Constitution convenes in New York City.

⌃ George Washington inaugural button

APRIL 30, 1789 George Washington is inaugurated as president.

JUNE 8, 1789
James Madison introduces legislation creating the Bill of Rights.

⌄ The US Constitution

1790–99

MAY 29, 1790
Rhode Island ratifies the Constitution—the last of the 13 states to do so.

OCTOBER 22, 1790
US forces under General Josiah Harmar are defeated at Pumpkin Fields, in the Northwestern Territories, by a Native American coalition under Little Turtle.

MARCH 4, 1791
Vermont becomes the 14th state of the Union.

NOVEMBER 4, 1791
The Northwest Native American coalition are victorious at the Battle of the Wabash.

DECEMBER 15, 1791
The Bill of Rights becomes part of the Constitution.

FEBRUARY 13, 1793
George Washington is unanimously elected by the Electoral College for a second term as president.

« Suppressing the Whiskey Rebellion

MARCH 1792
Widespread financial speculation produces an economic crisis in the United States.

JUNE 1, 1792
Kentucky becomes the 15th state of the Union.

JULY 16, 1794
The Whiskey Rebellion begins over taxation in western Pennsylvania.

AUGUST 20, 1794
General Anthony Wayne defeats a coalition of Native Americans at the Battle of Fallen Timbers.

⌄ The Battle of Fallen Timbers

NOVEMBER 19, 1794
The United States and Britain sign Jay's Treaty, resolving several disputes.

AUGUST 3, 1795
Defeated Native Americans in the Northwest sign the Treaty of Greenville, ceding lands to the United States.

OCTOBER 27, 1795
Spain and the United States sign the Treaty of San Lorenzo, which establishes a formal border between the United States and Spanish Florida.

"The **American war is over:** but this is far from being the case with the American revolution ... nothing but the **first act of the great drama is closed."**

DR. BENJAMIN RUSH, ADDRESS TO THE PEOPLE OF THE UNITED STATES, JANUARY 1787

1800–1809

1810–19

JULY 11, 1796
Tennessee becomes the 16th state of the Union.

SEPTEMBER 19, 1796
Washington issues his Farewell Address.

SEPTEMBER 30, 1800
The United States sign the Treaty of Mortefontaine with France to end the Quasi-War.

FEBRUARY 17, 1801
Thomas Jefferson is elected as the third president of the United States by the House of Representatives.

⌃ The whipping of a female slave, published by abolitionists

JANUARY 1, 1808
The slave trade becomes illegal in the United States.

MAY 1, 1810
Macon's Bill No.2 permits Americans to trade with Britain and France.

MARCH 27, 1814
Andrew Jackson defeats the Creeks at Horseshoe Bend, ending the Creek War.

AUGUST 9, 1814
The Creeks sign the Treaty of Fort Jackson.

⌃ President Washington

OCTOBER 1796
Revolutionary France orders the seizure of American merchant ships in response to Jay's Treaty.

FEBRUARY 17, 1801
Tripoli declares war on the United States.

MARCH 1, 1803
Ohio becomes the 17th state of the Union.

AUGUST 3, 1804
The United States Navy launches a series of attacks against Tripoli.

FEBRUARY 13, 1805
The Electoral College elect Thomas Jefferson to a second presidential term.

JUNE 3, 1805
The United States agree peace terms with Tripoli.

FEBRUARY 8, 1809
James Madison is elected as the fourth president of the United States.

NOVEMBER 7, 1811
US troops under William Henry Harrison defeat Tecumseh's allies at the Battle of Tippecanoe.

AUGUST 24, 1814
Occupying British forces burn public buildings in Washington, D.C.

SEPTEMBER 11, 1814
US forces defeat the British at the Battle of Lake Champlain.

MAY 2, 1803
The US acquires Louisiana from France in the so-called Louisiana Purchase.

FEBRUARY 8, 1797
John Adams is elected as the second president of the United States.

MAY 28, 1798
Congress authorizes the creation of an army in the event of war with France.

SEPTEMBER 23, 1806
Lewis and Clark return to St. Louis.

MARCH 1, 1809
The Embargo Act is repealed and replaced by the Non-Intercourse Act, which allows trade with any foreign nations except Britain and France.

⌃ A cartoon depicting the defeat of King George III by President James Madison

APRIL 30, 1812
Louisiana becomes the 18th state of the Union.

JUNE 18, 1812
The United States declares war on Britain.

SEPTEMBER 12, 1814
The Star Spangled Banner is flown at the Battle of Baltimore; Francis Scott Key writes the poem that will become the national anthem.

DECEMBER 24, 1814
The Treaty of Ghent ends the War of 1812.

JULY 7, 1798
The Quasi-War between the United States and France begins.

DECEMBER 14, 1799
George Washington dies at his home at Mount Vernon, Virginia.

⌃ Lewis and Clark's compass

MAY 14, 1804
Lewis and Clark's Expedition leaves St. Louis.

DECEMBER 22, 1807
Congress passes the Embargo Act, which makes it illegal for American merchant ships to trade with foreign nations.

SEPTEMBER 1809
Several Native American nations sign the Treaty of Fort Wayne, ceding land to the United States.

SEPTEMBER 10, 1813
A fleet commanded by Commodore Oliver Hazard Perry defeats British naval forces in the Battle of Lake Erie.

OCTOBER 5, 1813
Tecumseh is killed at the Battle of the Thames.

JANUARY 8, 1815
Andrew Jackson defeats the British in the last major battle of the War of 1812, at New Orleans.

BEFORE

Victory brought the fledgling United States many benefits, including new territories, but there were also debts to pay.

WASHINGTON'S EPAULETTES

TREATY GAINS
Under the terms of the **Treaty of Paris « 312–13**, Britain ceded the vast territory from the Appalachian Mountains to the Mississippi River, from the Great Lakes in the North to the border with Spanish Florida in the South. In return, the Americans agreed to **pay prewar debts** owed to British merchants and recommended that compensation be paid to Loyalists whose property had been seized by state governments. As the challenges of war gave way to those of peace, **Washington disbanded the Continental Army** and resigned his commission.

The Costs of War

American independence had been achieved at a high price for all parties, not only financially but also in terms of loss of life and social upheaval. The new nation would have to repair its physical and social fabric.

The financial cost of the war was immense for all the participants. The Continental Congress spent about $37 million ($850 million today) during the war, and the individual states a further $114 million (about $2.6 billion today). The Congress had procured much of its finance from foreign loans, and also borrowed from wealthy Americans. Additional money came from the issue of paper currency, which rapidly lost value, giving rise to the phrase "not worth a Continental." France spent approximately 1.3 billion livres (around $9.6 billion today) on the war. For Britain, the annual cost of the war was an average of £12 million ($2 billion today), most of which was borrowed, increasing the British national debt to £350 million ($60.2 billion today) by 1783—triple what it had been 20 years earlier. On top of these huge financial losses, each nation also had to assess the enormous human cost of the war.

Patriot losses
Of the 2.5 million people living in the Thirteen Colonies, 230,000 served in the Continental Army. An even larger number were in the militia. Official reports listed 4,435 Americans killed in action and 6,168 wounded, but more recent estimates put the number of killed at 8,000 and the wounded as high as 25,000. Another 10,000–40,000 Americans are believed to have died from disease while in military service. In addition, as many as 18,000 Patriots were taken prisoner, over half of whom died on board British prison ships (see pp.168–69).

France provided 13,000 troops to fight alongside the Continental Army, along with substantial naval forces. About 2,000 French soldiers and sailors were killed while directly assisting the rebellion. Many hundreds of Spanish troops were killed or wounded during campaigns in the Mississippi Valley and West Florida in 1780 and 1781.

British losses
Britain also suffered heavy losses. Of approximately 50,000 regular soldiers who fought in the war, at least 4,000 are believed to have died in battle,

Hail Britannia! Loyalist refugees arriving in Britain receive a symbolic welcome in this drawing of 1815. It shows the wide range of Americans who supported Britain in the war, including royal officials, clergymen, African Americans, and Native Americans.

along with 1,800 men from the various German states that provided troops to the British. About 3,000 American Loyalists are estimated to have been killed. At least 500 of Britain's Native American allies died in battle, as well as an unknown number of African Americans who supported the British.

However, a far larger number of British, Hessian, Loyalist, and African American troops died of disease—possibly as many as 33,000. More than 15,000 British, Loyalist, and Hessian troops were also captured, and lost to imprisonment. Many men who survived the prison camps chose to remain in America after their release.

Trails of destruction

The fighting destroyed a great deal of property in America, but not all of the destruction was the result of battle. In January 1776, for example, when a British naval bombardment set fire to the docks in Norfolk, Virginia, Patriot soldiers took advantage of the chaos to burn Loyalist homes and shops; the fires destroyed nearly 900 buildings.

Later that year, soon after the British occupation of New York City, a fire destroyed some 500 buildings. The British blamed Patriot sympathizers.

On a smaller scale, parties of Patriot and Loyalist militia, and sometimes regular troops, routinely set fire to their enemies' homes, mills, crops, ships in port, and other property. Wherever soldiers passed, livestock and crops were seized or destroyed to deny them to the enemy. Britain's Native American allies devastated frontier settlements, while settlers destroyed Native American villages. Many Americans returned to cities once occupied by the British to find their homes and property gone.

Loyalist exiles

Although some Loyalists made peace with their neighbors and returned to their homes, around 100,000 left the country to start new lives in Britain, Canada, and the British West Indies. Britain compensated Loyalist refugees with grants of unoccupied land, primarily in Canada, and by providing monetary payments, but this assistance reflected only a fraction of the Loyalists' financial losses. Many of those who left had been banished by state governments, or had their property confiscated as punishment for supporting the British. All 13 former colonies treated Loyalists harshly, but in those states where they were more numerous—such as New York, New Jersey, and South Carolina—Loyalists were often imprisoned and sometimes executed for the threat they posed to the new republic.

Native Americans and African Americans who had sided with the British also suffered. Both the United States government and several state governments forced Britain's Native American allies to cede vast tracts of land as the price of peace. Thousands were forced to abandon their ancestral homelands to the United States.

Several thousand African Americans in the South had joined the British in the hope of escaping slavery, but some were sold into bondage in the West Indies by unscrupulous British officers. Other former slaves received their freedom and settled in Canada. However, they were often denied land grants or assigned to the poorest tracts. Facing racial discrimination in many forms, some found their new lives so difficult that they eventually emigrated to Sierra Leone in Africa.

The hard road to Nova Scotia

A number of former slaves who fought as Loyalists were awarded land in Nova Scotia. They often experienced hardship in the cold climate where farming was difficult, and were rarely accepted as part of the Loyalist community because of racial prejudice.

> ## "Independence will disgrace Us, unless We are honest in Payment of the publick Debts."
>
> AMERICAN STATESMAN ELBRIDGE GERRY TO JOHN ADAMS, NOVEMBER 23, 1783

RED JACKET

Sagoyewatha (He Who Keeps Them Awake) of the Seneca nation fought with the British during the war. Given a red coat for his contribution, he became known as Red Jacket. In 1784, Red Jacket convinced the Six Nations council not to ratify the Treaty of Fort Stanwix, which included a huge cession of Iroquois lands. He signed the Treaty of Canandaigua in 1794, affirming "peace and friendship" between his people and the United States.

AFTER

War debts had a significant impact on the fortunes of the main protagonists in the conflict.

GOVERNMENT STRENGTHENED
After the war, the scale of the debt created financial problems for the United States and led many to support the adoption of a more effective system of government, with **stronger revenue-raising powers 324–25** **324–25 ≫**.

REVOLUTION AND RETRENCHMENT
The **French government** lacked the revenue to pay the war debts it had incurred in support of the Patriot cause. The resulting financial crisis was a significant contributing factor to the outbreak of the **French Revolution** in 1789.

Britain, despite its great expenditures and the loss of the Thirteen Colonies, **retained its position as a major European power** and strengthened its hold on its remaining colonies in North America by the settlement of thousands of Loyalist refugees in Canada.

The **Limits** of **Confederation**

The Treaty of Paris ended the war and gave the United States its independence, but the new nation found that peace did not bring an end to earlier difficulties, and difficult new problems emerged almost as soon as the fog of war had cleared.

BEFORE

The United States government established by the Continental Congress struggled to raise revenue through taxation.

LACK OF FUNDS

The weak central government established by the **Articles of Confederation** could ask the states to provide specific amounts of funds and troops but had no power to compel them to comply. Throughout the war, the Continental Congress was **chronically short of funds ‹‹ 322–23** resulting in a shortage of military supplies and soldiers going without pay. From 1778, the war effort was largely dependent upon **French loans ‹‹ 188–89**.

STATE RESISTANCE

In late 1782, after the states had contributed only $1.5 million ($30.2 million today) of the $8 million ($161 million today) requested by the Congress for its annual budget, Superintendent of Finance Robert Morris proposed amending the Articles to allow Congress to levy a **5 percent tax** on all imports. Twelve states approved the legislation, but **Rhode Island refused**, effectively blocking the measure.

The Confederation government lacked both the resources and the constitutional authority to deal with the many challenges it faced after independence. The Congress appeared so powerless that some representatives rarely attended its meetings, and others elected to the Congress chose not to serve. Such indifference further weakened the ability of the government to function effectively.

Tariffs on trade

The most serious difficulties facing the Congress were financial. The United States carried a large war debt and had no revenue with which to repay it. Superintendent of Finance Robert Morris became so frustrated with the Congress's failure to amend the Articles of Confederation to provide the government with a reliable source of income that he resigned in November 1784. A renewed effort to amend the Articles to impose a 5 percent tariff on imports was thwarted by New York in 1786. The economic recovery following the war was also uneven.

During the colonial era, Americans had profited from trading directly with the British West Indies, but after independence, the United States was barred from that market by Britain. Instead, Americans either had to sell their products at wholesale prices to British merchants or find new customers. Exports from the New England states, South Carolina, and Virginia declined: America's new trading partners in continental Europe did not purchase as much fish, rice, and tobacco as Britain and the West Indies had.

Southern plantations were also less productive than they had been before independence: thousands of slaves who had worked the land had fled, and the plantations themselves had

Territorial wrangles

Lacking the powers to promote economic recovery by addressing these issues, the Congress instead sought to raise funds by selling the western lands ceded by Britain to settlers. But there were serious obstacles to this plan. Farmers moving west of the Appalachians could sell their surplus crops only by shipping them down the Ohio River and its tributaries to the Mississippi, and exporting them from New Orleans. Spain made this impossible by closing the Mississippi

> **"These U. States must … establish a permanent capable government or submit to the horrors of anarchy."**
>
> HENRY LEE, IN A LETTER TO GEORGE WASHINGTON, SEPTEMBER 18, 1786

been devastated by the opposing armies. More populous northern states, such as Pennsylvania and New York, enjoyed better economic conditions due to their relatively large domestic markets, but interstate commerce was hampered because states taxed imports from their neighbors in order to protect their own economies.

and New Orleans to Americans. Even worse, it sent agents among the southwestern settlers urging them to unite their settlements with the Spanish colonies. Spanish officials also provided secret military aid to the southern Native American nations, hoping to prevent Americans from encroaching on Spanish territory.

The Congress assigned Secretary of Foreign Affairs John Jay to negotiate a new treaty with Spain. However, the negotiations foundered as a result of Spanish intransigence and the suspicions of southern representatives in the Congress who believed that Jay was sacrificing their interests to those of the northern states.

In the Northwest, the Miami, Mingo, Shawnee, Wyandot, and other Indian nations were opposing American settlement of the Ohio River valley. Eager to regain the goodwill of the Native Americans—whom Britain had alienated by handing over their land to the United States in the Treaty of Paris—British officials encouraged them to resist the Americans and supplied them with arms.

A further problem for the Congress in the years after the war was that Britain refused to evacuate its posts within US borders. The British argued that this violation of the peace treaty was

Advocate of reform
Superintendent of Finance Robert Morris (right), pictured with his assistant, advocated tariff-raising powers. Later in life, Morris went bankrupt and even served time in a debtors' prison.

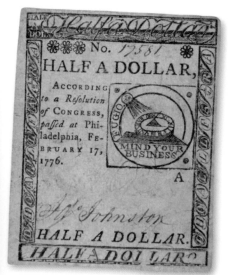

Not worth a dime
The Continental Congress issued millions of currency banknotes, but confidence in these bills soon evaporated and the money became almost worthless.

Through the looking glass
This cartoon reflects events leading up to the ratification of the new Constitution. The wagon represents Connecticut sinking under the weight of its debts, being pulled on the right by Anti-Federalists saying "Success to the Shays."

in retaliation for America's failure to ensure that debts to British merchants were honored and that Loyalists were reimbursed for their losses.

Reducing costs

The Confederation government was too weak to challenge Spain, Britain, or the Native American nations on any of these issues. To reduce its costs, in June 1784 the Congress had cut the size of the army to 80 enlisted men and a few commissioned officers. Divided between two bases—West Point, New York, and Fort Pitt, Pennsylvania—the force was barely capable of guarding military supplies.

With such limited resources, the United States could not respond to threats abroad. When pirates from Algiers seized two American merchant ships off Spain in 1785, the American negotiators could not pay the ransom demanded for the crews, and the pirates sold the American sailors into slavery. Even within its borders, the Congress lacked the means to keep order. When Shays' Rebellion broke out in western Massachusetts in 1786, state officials asked the Confederation Congress for aid, but Secretary of War Henry Knox did not have the resources to provide assistance.

DECISIVE MOMENT

SHAYS' REBELLION

By August 1786, poor economic conditions and high state taxes had driven many farmers in western Massachusetts into debt. When their creditors attempted to foreclose on their farms, the farmers armed themselves, prevented courts from convening, and stopped officials from arresting debtors. Led by Patriot veteran Daniel Shays, in January 1787 the rebels attempted to seize the Springfield arsenal but were defeated by militia from eastern Massachusetts under Benjamin Lincoln. The Congress's failure to come to the aid of Massachusetts convinced many Americans of the need for a central government.

AFTER ▸▸

In the wake of Shays' Rebellion moves to revise the Articles of Confederation gained momentum.

THE CONSTITUTIONAL CONVENTION
In May 1787, state delegates met at the **Constitutional Convention 328–29 ▸▸** to hammer out new Articles of Confederation and shape the future governance of the United States. If the new country was to survive, **Federalists and Anti-Federalists** had to reach a compromise.

UNDER THE SPOTLIGHT
Prominent Americans such as George Washington knew that European nations were carefully **watching the American experiment** in republican government, hoping it would fail and expecting to take advantage of the situation when the new nation collapsed.

PRESIDENT Born 1751 Died 1836

James **Madison**

"If men were **angels, no government** would be **necessary.**"

JAMES MADISON, *THE FEDERALIST*,1778

Often called "the Father of the Constitution," James Madison was a key figure in the transformation of the new United States from a loose confederation of states into a federal republic. His commitment to states' rights and individual freedom were balanced by his recognition of the need for a strong federal government. Madison's career culminated in two terms as the fourth President of the United States.

Like George Washington and Thomas Jefferson, Madison was born into the plantation-owning elite of the colony of Virginia. His father, James Madison Sr., was the largest landowner in Orange County, with some 4,000 acres (1,600 ha) and 100 slaves. Educated at a private boarding school and then at Princeton, he received, as he later wrote, "very early and strong impressions in favor of liberty both civil and religious."

In 1774, Madison joined his father on the Orange County Committee of Safety and even drilled with the militia, although his short stature and poor health rendered him unsuitable for military service. Instead he was to wage the fight for independence in assemblies, councils, and committees.

A commanding figure
A small, sickly man, Madison was neither charismatic nor an impressive orator. But the force of his intelligence made him a key figure in the formative years of the United States.

Political rise
In 1776, aged 25, Madison was elected to the fifth Virginia Convention. Over the following years his intelligence and dedication earned him a prominent position in the political life of his state and the nation. Sent as a delegate to the Continental Congress in 1780, he proved an effective political operator, working tirelessly on securing support for measures that strengthened the Confederation. After returning to take a seat in the Virginia state assembly, he succeeded in pushing through the Statute for Religious Freedom, originally drafted by Jefferson.

By 1786, Madison was deeply unhappy about the direction in which the US was developing. He believed that rivalry between the states might lead to the disintegration of the Confederation and even wars between states. He feared the potential effects of democracy, in which a majority could exert tyranny over minorities, especially "the minority of the opulent," who might be dispossessed by the majority of the common people.

Believing that only a properly constituted national government could save the Union and protect individual freedom, Madison became the prime

Expanding territory
When he was Secretary of State, Madison masterminded the Louisiana Purchase of land from France in 1803 and vastly expanded US territory. This 1804 map shows the extent of the new territories from Canada to Louisiana.

> "The **religion** ... of every man must be **left to ... the conscience** of every man."

JAMES MADISON, MEMORIAL AND REMONSTRANCE AGAINST RELIGIOUS ASSESSMENTS, 1785

mover behind the summoning of a Constitutional Convention in 1787 (see pp.328–29), and the driving force behind the framing of the US Constitution. He even persuaded George Washington to come out of retirement to preside over the Convention, realizing that the great man's prestige would ensure the attendance of others. Madison's Virginia Plan provided the basis for the Convention's deliberations and his efforts secured general agreement to the compromises required by conflicting state interests.

Constitutional catalyst
After the Convention had completed its work, Madison applied himself to its ratification, devoting his powerful intellect to the explanation, interpretation, and defense of the constitution in articles and essays known as the *Federalist Papers*, published in newspapers. Madison's prime concern in drawing up the constitution had been to create a federal government strong enough to hold together the new republic. Once the constitution was in place, he threw his efforts behind the defense of individual freedom, and in 1789, following his election to the House of Representatives, proposed the raft of amendments to the constitution that became the Bill of Rights.

From 1801 to 1817, Madison exercised great power, as Secretary of State under Jefferson and then as president. He vastly expanded the territory of the United States through the Louisiana Purchase, while maintaining his commitment to minimize the exercise of power and expenditure by the federal government. With Jefferson, he was responsible for the folly of the Embargo Act of 1807, an attempt to use economic pressure as an alternative to armed conflict. The embargo's failure resulted, in 1812, in Madison presiding over the first declaration of war by the US. The resulting conflict with Britain, the War of 1812, was mostly a disaster, revealing the weakness of American finances and military forces. Madison even suffered the indignity of having to flee the White House in 1814, when the British sacked the capital. Still, a late victory at the Battle of New Orleans, actually occurring after peace had been signed, enabled Americans to emerge from the war in a mood of exalted patriotism that boosted Madison's popularity to new heights.

After his last term as president, Madison retired to his estate at Montpelier in Orange County, from whence he issued commentaries on constitutional matters. Madison died at his home, six days before the 60th anniversary of the Declaration of Independence.

Up in flames
After defeating the Americans at Bladensburg in August 1814, the British burned down public buildings in Washington, including the White House and the Capitol. President Madison was forced to flee the city.

TIMELINE

1751 Born on March 16, in King George County, Virginia, son of tobacco planter John Madison Sr. and Nelly Conway Madison.

1762 Sent to Donald Robertson's boarding school in King and Queen County, Virginia.

1769–72 Attends the College of New Jersey (now Princeton University).

December 1774 Joins the local Committee of Safety in Orange County, Virginia.

October 1775 Commissioned as a colonel in the Orange County militia.

1776 Elected to the state Convention that draws up a constitution for Virginia.

1778 Appointed to the eight-member Virginia Council of State.

1780–83 Serves as a Virginian delegate to the Continental Congress in Philadelphia.

1784 Takes his seat as a representative to the Virginia state legislature.

January 1786 Plays a major role in the passage of the Virginia Statute for Religious Freedom.

September 1786 Attends the Annapolis Convention, which calls for a Constitutional Convention to be held in Philadelphia.

May–September 1787 Represents Virginia at the Constitutional Convention; his Virginia Plan forms the basis for the US Constitution.

1787–88 With Alexander Hamilton and John Jay, publishes the *Federalist Papers*, urging ratification of the Constitution.

1789 Elected to the House of Representatives, he proposes the amendments to the Constitution known as the Bill of Rights.

1791 With Thomas Jefferson, forms the anti-Federalist Democratic-Republican Party.

1794 Marries Dolley Payne Todd on September 15, following a brief courtship.

1798 Writes the Virginia Resolutions in response to the Alien and Sedition Acts.

1801–09 Serves as US secretary of state under President Thomas Jefferson.

DOLLEY PAYNE TODD

1803 Supervises the acquisition of territory from France in the Louisiana Purchase.

1809 Elected fourth President of the US.

June 1812 Signs declaration of war on Britain.

1813 Elected to second presidential term.

August 1814 Madison escapes the city as British forces sack Washington, D.C.

February 1815 Ratification of the Treaty of Ghent ends the war with Britain.

1817 Madison retires to Montpelier plantation in Orange County.

1836 Dies on June 28 at Montpelier and is interred in the Madison Family Cemetery.

BEFORE

Shays' Rebellion provided the impetus that the Confederation needed to create a more effective central government.

THE NEED FOR CHANGE
Advocates of a stronger central government had been working to revise the Articles of Confederation decided upon by the **Second Continental Congress** ≪ 62–63 even before **Shays' Rebellion** ≪ 324–25 reached its peak. The need to raise money, stand up to foreign powers, and keep internal order required concerted action. **James Madison**, fearful that the Confederation might disintegrate, called for a convention in Annapolis, Maryland, to discuss the reform of interstate trade.

DATES ARE SET
On September 11, 1786, delegates from New York, New Jersey, Pennsylvania, Delaware, and Virginia began discussions at Annapolis. On September 14, they resolved to meet in Philadelphia the following May to **revise the Articles of Confederation**.

> "A **Firm Union** will be of the utmost moment to the **peace and liberty** of the **States.**"
>
> ALEXANDER HAMILTON, FEDERALIST PAPER IX, NOVEMBER 21, 1787

AMERICAN WRITER AND HISTORIAN 1728–1814

MERCY OTIS WARREN

More active in politics than any other woman of her era, Mercy Otis Warren of Massachusetts wrote poems, essays, and plays in support of the Patriot position before and during the War of Independence.

In 1787, Warren took an Anti-Federalist stance, opposing the ratification of the Constitution. Writing under the pseudonym "A Columbian Patriot," her essay *Observations on the New Constitution and on the Federal and State Conventions* (1788) criticized the Constitution for what she considered a dangerous intermixing of executive and legislative authority. Despite her tireless efforts, Massachusetts ratified the Constitution on February 6, 1788.

The **Constitutional** Convention

Delegates at the Constitutional Convention, which met from May to September 1787, presented a range of very different views on the future government of the United States. Eventually a compromise was reached between the many competing visions.

The convention to revise the Articles of Confederation was scheduled to begin on May 14, 1787. However, due to the unpredictable nature of travel, several delegates were delayed and formal meetings could not start until May 25, when representatives from seven states were present. By July, delegates from 12 states had arrived. Rhode Island, suspicious of stronger central government, did not send delegates.

When the proceedings opened, those present unanimously elected George Washington to serve as president of the convention. They quickly abandoned attempts to revise the Articles of Confederation and opted instead to create a new form of government.

Fair representation
Several delegates had anticipated this development and prepared plans in advance. Edmund Randolph of Virginia introduced the first proposal—that states should be represented in Congress according to either their population or their wealth. Alexander Hamilton of New York proposed a system based on that of Britain, with a president for life, which the delegates

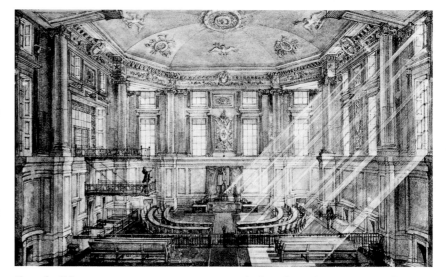

Place of enlightenment
New York City's Federal Hall, built in 1700, hosted the early meetings of the House of Representatives. A permanent home for the legislature—the Capitol in Washington, D.C.—was not opened until 1800. Federal Hall was subsequently demolished.

rejected. William Paterson of New Jersey suggested that each state should have an equal voice in Congress.

The resulting dispute between delegates from large states and those from smaller states provoked lengthy debate. Delegates from the small states, such as Delaware, Maryland, and New Jersey, argued that under the Virginia Plan, the three most populous states—Massachusetts, Pennsylvania, and Virginia—would dominate. The large states, in favor of the Virginia Plan, insisted that equality among the states would be unfair to their more sizable populations. Eventually, Roger Sherman of Connecticut proposed a compromise. The new Congress would consist of two bodies: the House of Representatives—in which states would be represented according to their population—and the Senate, in which each state would be represented equally. Legislation would be approved by a majority vote in both houses.

Extended powers
Other provisions of the new system gave the federal government substantial authority over the states,

including the rights to tax, regulate commerce, and invalidate state laws that conflicted with federal legislation. After much debate, the delegates also reached agreement on how executive authority should be exercised. Many representatives wanted more than one executive (president), with some suggesting that there should be three, each from a different region. Other delegates argued that such a system would be inefficient, because the presidents might disagree. The length of time the president should serve was also contentious. It was finally decided that there should be one president, elected for a four-year term, who would act as commander in chief of the armed forces to ensure civilian control over the military.

Distrusting democracy
The delegates sought to create a representative republic rather than a direct democracy, so steps were taken to limit the people's role in the new government. Some delegates believed that the Confederation, as well as the state governments, had suffered from too much democracy. They believed that most people were not well informed concerning political matters and would be too easily swayed by self-interest and emotion. They argued that voters should not be allowed to choose any federal representatives. However, Virginians James Madison

and George Mason insisted that the people were entitled to a direct role in government and should elect the members of the House of Representatives—and their views prevailed. Senators were to be chosen by state legislators, and the president and vice president by an electoral college. The delegates hoped this would provide stability in government and result in qualified people being chosen for office.

A third branch of government, which consisted of a supreme court and federal judiciary, nominated by the president, was also created.

Counting slaves

After heated discussion, the delegates rejected proposals to abolish slavery. Southern representatives did, however, want slaves to be included as part of a state's population for congressional districts, because this determined the number of electoral votes awarded to each state. Opponents of slavery argued that slaves should not be counted, since they were legally property. In the end, it was agreed that each slave would

Divided over slavery

Many delegates to the Constitutional Convention believed that slavery was at odds with the nation's ideals of liberty and equality, but to ensure agreement, it was allowed to continue.

Instrument of agreement

The US Constitution was signed with quill pens. Thomas Jefferson used quills from geese bred at his Monticello estate for his extensive writing.

equal three-fifths of a person in determining a state's population for congressional representation.

On September 17, 1787, the convention president George Washington and 39 delegates signed the Constitution of the United States. Some delegates had already left the convention, and three, including George Mason of Virginia, refused to sign because they feared that either states or individuals did not have enough rights, and that tyranny could result.

The opponents

The Constitution still had to be ratified by special state conventions, and would take effect only after nine states had approved it. Supporters of the Constitution, known as Federalists, met strong opposition. Many prominent Americans, who, like Mason, opposed the Constitution, became known as Anti-Federalists. They asserted that the new government favored the wealthy and powerful at the expense of ordinary citizens, that the federal government was too strong, and that the Constitution lacked a bill of rights. The Federalists countered with their own defense of the Constitution, notably set down in 85 letters to newspapers published from October 1787 to August 1788, written under the pen name "Publius" by James Madison, Alexander Hamilton, and John Jay. Its purpose was to sway New York voters.

By May 1788, only one more state's approval was needed for the Constitution to take effect. North Carolina and Rhode Island showed little interest in ratification, and Anti-Federalist feeling remained strong in New York and Virginia. Finally, on June 21, New Hampshire voted 57:47 in favor of ratification, and the Constitution was adopted as the supreme law of the United States.

The elections for the new federal offices created by the Constitution were held in the fall of 1788.

THE NEW CONGRESS

The new government became effective on March 4, 1789, when the first Congress elected under the Constitution convened in New York City. **George Washington was elected as president 334–35 ≫**. The Constitution was ratified by **North Carolina** in November 1789, and **Rhode Island** in May 1790.

LASTING LEGACY

The letters written by "Publius" still provide a brilliant analysis of **the US Constitution**.

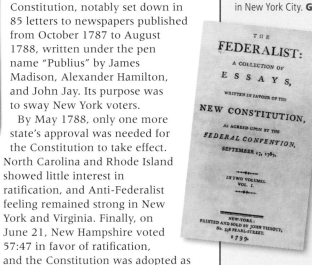

THE
FEDERALIST:
A COLLECTION OF
ESSAYS,
WRITTEN IN FAVOUR OF THE
NEW CONSTITUTION,
AS AGREED UPON BY THE
FEDERAL CONVENTION,
SEPTEMBER 17, 1787.

IN TWO VOLUMES.
VOL. I.

NEW-YORK:
PRINTED AND SOLD BY JOHN TIEBOUT,
No. 358 PEARL-STREET.
1799.

THE FEDERALIST, 1799 EDITION

Signing the Constitution

In September 1787, delegates from all 13 states except Rhode Island convened at the Pennsylvania State House in Philadelphia to sign the new Constitution, the result of three months' work. Despite some notable absences—Thomas Jefferson and John Adams were both serving abroad—39 out of 55 delegates signed the Constitution on September 17, following Franklin's speech in support of its adoption.

"I confess that there are several parts of this Constitution which I do not at present approve, but I am not sure I shall ever approve them: For having lived long, I have experienced many instances of being obliged by better information, or fuller consideration, to change opinions even on important subjects …

In these sentiments, Sir, I agree to this Constitution with all its faults … because I think a general Government necessary for us … I doubt too whether any other Convention we can obtain, may be able to make a better Constitution. For when you assemble a number of men to have the advantage of their joint wisdom, you inevitably assemble with those men, all their prejudices, their passions, their errors of opinion, their local interests, and their selfish views. From such an assembly can a perfect production be expected? It therefore astonishes me, Sir, to find this system approaching so near to perfection as it does; and I think it will astonish our enemies, who are waiting with confidence to hear that … our States are on the point of separation, only to meet hereafter for the purpose of cutting one another's throats. Thus I consent, Sir, to this Constitution … because I am not sure, that it is not the best …

[I] wish that every member of the Convention who may still have objections to it, would with me, on this occasion doubt a little of his own infallibility, and to make manifest our unanimity, put his name to this instrument."

BENJAMIN FRANKLIN, AS RECORDED IN JAMES MADISON'S NOTES OF DEBATES IN THE FEDERAL CONVENTION OF 1787, PUBLISHED IN 1840. MADISON STALLED THEIR PUBLICATION UNTIL EVERY DELEGATE HAD PASSED AWAY—HIMSELF INCLUDED

Scene at the Signing of the Constitution
In this painting of 1910 by Howard Chandler Christy, Washington, representing Virginia, stands on the stage, while Benjamin Franklin (in gray), for Pennsylvania, looks out of the painting from the floor. Alexander Hamilton (New York) whispers an aside in Franklin's ear.

We the People

of the U...

insure domestic Tranquility, provide for the common defence, prom...
and our Posterity, do ordain and establish this Constitution for the...

Article. I.

Section. 1. All legislative Powers herein granted shall be vested...
of Representatives.

Section. 2. The House of Representatives shall be composed of Me...
in each State shall have the Qualifications requisite for Electors of the most num...

No Person shall be a Representative who shall not have attaine...
and who shall not, when elected, be an Inhabitant of that State in which he...

Representatives and direct Taxes shall be apportioned among the se...
Numbers, which shall be determined by adding to the whole Number of free...
not taxed, three fifths of all other Persons. The actual Enumeration sha...
and within every subsequent Term of ten Years, in such Manner as they...
thirty Thousand, but each State shall have at Least one Representative;
entitled to chuse three, Massachusetts eight, Rhode-Island and Provid...
eight, Delaware one, Maryland six, Virginia ten, North Carolina fiv...

When vacancies happen in the Representation from any State...
The House of Representatives shall chuse their Speaker and othe...

Section. 3. The Senate of the United States shall be composed of two...
Senator shall have one Vote.

Immediately after they shall be assembled in Consequence of th...
of the Senators of the first Class shall be vacated at the Expiration of the...
Class at the Expiration of the sixth Year, so that one third may be chosen...
Recess of the Legislature of any State, the Executive thereof may make temp...
such Vacancies.

No Person shall be a Senator who shall not have attained to the...
not, when elected, be an Inhabitant of that State for which he shall be ch...
The Vice President of the United States shall be President of the Se...

d States, in Order to form a more perfect Union, establish Justice,
the general Welfare, and secure the Blessings of Liberty to ourselves
ed States of America.

Congress of the United States, which shall consist of a Senate and House

s chosen every second Year by the People of the several States, and the Electors
n Branch of the State Legislature.
he Age of twenty five Years, and been seven Years a Citizen of the United States,
l be chosen.

States which may be included within this Union, according to their respective
ons, including those bound to Service for a Term of Years, and excluding Indians
made within three Years after the first Meeting of the Congress of the United States,
by Law direct. The Number of Representatives shall not exceed one for every
until such enumeration shall be made, the State of New Hampshire shall be
Plantations one, Connecticut five, New York six; New Jersey four, Pennsylvania
th Carolina five, and Georgia three.
recutive Authority thereof shall issue Writs of Election to fill such Vacancies.
ies; and shall have the sole Power of Impeachment.
ors from each State, chosen by the Legislature thereof, for six Years; and each

t Election, they shall be divided as equally as may be into three Classes. The Seats
d Year, of the second Class at the Expiration of the fourth Year, and of the third
second Year; and if Vacancies happen by Resignation, or otherwise, during the
Appointments until the next Meeting of the Legislature, which shall then fill
f thirty Years, and been nine Years a Citizen of the United States, and who shall

but shall have no Vote, unless they be equally divided.
ore, in the Absence of the Vice President, or when he shall exercise the Office of

President Washington

The first challenge facing President Washington was how to make the transition from rebel military commander to civilian leader. He also had to assemble a group of men who could make the new nation viable—economically and politically.

MARTHA WASHINGTON

Born into a farming family in Virginia, Martha Washington had two children from a first marriage and considerable wealth when she wed George Washington in 1759. Martha actively supported him on military campaigns and encouraged the wives of other officers to do the same. She carried this sense of duty into her new role as First Lady, securing the affection of American citizens. She was buried with her husband at Mount Vernon.

« **BEFORE**

After achieving independence, the Americans had to organize themselves into a coherent country with an effective government.

TWO HOUSES
The **US Constitution** « **330–31** drawn up by delegates at the **Constitutional Convention** « **328–29** in 1787 split Congress into two bodies—the **House of Representatives** and the **Senate**, with a **president** exercising executive authority elected every four years.

FIRST CHOICE
The first presidential election in the United States was held from December 15, 1788, to January 10, 1789. **George Washington won the unanimous vote** of the Electoral College. John Adams, the runner-up, was chosen as vice president.

Washington waited until Congress verified the election results before setting off from his estate at Mount Vernon to the capital, New York. Two weeks later, on April 30, 1789, he was inaugurated as first president of the United States. The new president wished to act in strict accordance with the Constitution; rather than initiating policy, he chose to wait for the two houses of Congress to pass legislation. The Senate became mired in matters of protocol, but James Madison quickly emerged as the leader of the House of Representatives and began to address important issues. He succeeded in passing a tariff bill to provide the government with revenue, and then proposed 12 amendments to the Constitution. Two were dropped, but the remaining ten, which became known as the Bill of Rights, were adopted as part of the Constitution on December 16, 1791.

Key appointments
Congress rejected Washington's offer to serve without pay if the government covered his expenses, and instead provided him with an annual salary of $25,000 ($650,000 today). Senator Oliver Ellsworth of Connecticut took the lead in crafting legislation to put in place a federal judicial system. Washington appointed John Jay chief justice of the Supreme Court and made appointments to cabinet positions, including Alexander Hamilton as secretary of the treasury, Thomas Jefferson as secretary of state, and

Henry Knox as secretary of war. The government was soon functioning effectively, but disputes arose over Hamilton's financial proposals. From January 1790, he issued a series of recommendations, including the creation of a national bank. Hamilton believed his plans would strengthen the government's financial position by tying the interests of both states and wealthy investors to the government.

Jefferson and Madison both opposed Hamilton's proposals, particularly the bank plan, which they argued was unconstitutional. Hamilton asserted

Inaugural button
Commemorative buttons were sold as souvenirs of Washington's inauguration as the first president on April 30, 1789. Contrary to Washington's stated wishes, the ceremony became the occasion for great public celebration.

> **"** It is our true policy to **steer clear** of **permanent alliances** with any portion of the foreign world. **"**
>
> GEORGE WASHINGTON, FAREWELL ADDRESS, 1796

that a key clause in the Constitution, known as the "necessary and proper" clause, permitted the creation of a bank, establishing the doctrine of "implied powers" that is now widely accepted. Congress approved and Washington signed the bank bill. The First Bank of the United States was chartered on February 25, 1791. This fueled speculation in the stocks of other banks, which helped to foment an economic

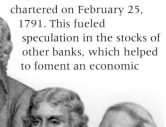

crisis. In those volatile circumstances, Washington felt it necessary to serve a second term as president. He was returned to office without opposition.

In 1793, Jefferson resigned from the cabinet, believing that Washington was ignoring his advice and relying solely on Hamilton. Jefferson, with the support of Madison, started to organize the opponents of Hamilton's Federalist party (supporters of a strong national government) into the Democratic Republican Party, and a two-party political system began to take shape.

Hamilton's excise tax on whiskey, introduced in 1791, sparked an uprising in western Pennsylvania in 1794, known as the Whiskey Rebellion. The tax hurt small farmers who distilled their surplus corn into whiskey and used it to barter for items they needed. When federal inspectors tried to force them to comply with the law, the farmers resisted. Washington called out militia from several states

The nation's first cabinet
Washington (seated on the left) formed his first cabinet in 1789–90. To his left are Secretary of War Henry Knox, Secretary of the Treasury Alexander Hamilton, Secretary of State Thomas Jefferson, and Attorney General Edmund Randolph.

to suppress the rebellion, and the opposition collapsed. Hamilton felt vindicated at this firm demonstration of federal power, but Jefferson denounced the government's actions as excessive and unnecessary.

Shaping foreign policy

In foreign affairs, Washington sought to reduce tensions with Britain. He dispatched John Jay to London to negotiate a treaty that would end Royal Navy seizures of American ships trading with France, reopen trade with the British West Indies, and require the British to evacuate their forts in the Northwest Territory. The British agreed only to withdraw from the forts and permit limited trade with the West Indies. The resulting Jay Treaty, ratified

in 1795, was criticized by Democratic-Republicans, who felt the treaty was abandoning American interests in order to seek favor with Britain.

The Treaty of San Lorenzo with Spain, ratified in 1796, was more popular. Spain agreed to open the Mississippi River and the port of New Orleans to United States commerce.

Partner in power

While George Washington established presidential precedents, his wife, Martha, became the model for First Ladies of the United States. Her main duty was to serve as hostess for state dinners. She disliked the role, remarking that instead of First Lady she should be called "Chief State Prisoner." Martha ignored Mercy

Otis Warren's suggestion that she use her position to campaign for women's voting rights, but did meet with Judith Sargent Murray, a vocal advocate for the equal education of women.

Upon leaving office in 1796, Washington issued his "Farewell Address," in which he advocated for avoiding involvement in European affairs. He also urged US citizens to put aside party divisions and work for the common good—a piece of advice that largely went unheeded by the men who succeeded him.

Taxing question

A government exciseman carrying two flagons of whiskey is waylaid by a devil in this cartoon championing the Whiskey Rebellion and opposing the tax-raising power of Congress.

Son of the soil

Washington surveys his beloved plantation at Mount Vernon, Virginia. The president visited his estate as often as he could during his terms in office and retired there after his presidency.

AFTER »

In March 1797, John Adams became the second president of the United States, with Thomas Jefferson as vice president. The two were sharply divided on political issues, and partisan disputes intensified.

CITIZEN CLAMPDOWN
Aiming to prevent foreign interference and unrest at home, President Adams pushed through the **Alien and Sedition Acts** of 1798 **342–43 »**. Opposition to these laws helped Jefferson to replace Adams as president in the 1800 election, and Jefferson went on to repeal the acts.

INDUSTRIAL PROGRESS
In December 1790, inventor and mechanic Samuel Slater brought the **Industrial Revolution** to the United States when he opened a **water-powered textile mill** in Rhode Island. Slater employed young women and girls to operate equipment that spun cotton fibers into thread, which was then sent to older women who wove it into fabric on household looms. Slater's experiment proved successful, and in succeeding years his **mills expanded** throughout New England.

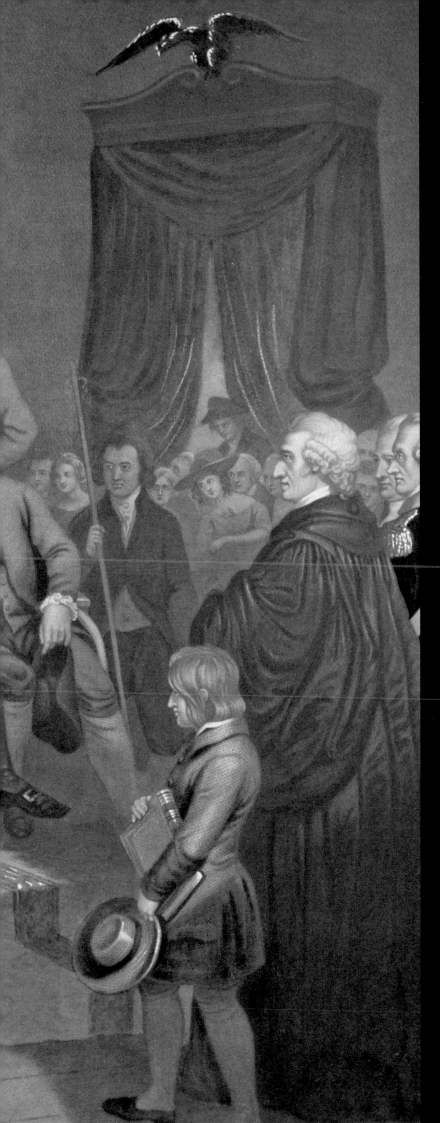

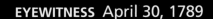

Washington's Inaugural Address

George Washington took his oath on a second floor balcony of New York's Federal Hall as crowds gathered below. Afterward, the new president made the first inaugural address to members of Congress and the Senate. Washington desired an inauguration "devoid of ceremony," but the day was full of pomp and grandeur.

"By the article establishing the Executive Department, it is made the duty of the President 'to recommend to your consideration, such measures as he shall judge necessary and expedient.' The circumstances under which I now meet you will acquit me from entering into that subject, farther than to refer to the Great Constitutional Charter under which you are assembled; and which ... designates the objects to which your attention is to be given ...

I dwell on this prospect with every satisfaction which an ardent love for my Country can inspire, since ... there exists in the economy and course of nature, an indissoluble union between virtue and happiness, between duty and advantage, between the genuine maxims of an honest and magnanimous policy ... and since the preservation of the sacred fire of liberty, and the destiny of the Republican model of Government, are ... staked, on the experiment entrusted to the hands of the American people.

Besides the ordinary objects submitted to your care, it will remain with your judgment to decide how far an exercise of the occasional power delegated by the Fifth article of the Constitution is rendered expedient ... I shall again give way to my entire confidence in your discernment and pursuit of the public good: For I assure myself that ... a reverence for the characteristic rights of freemen, and a regard for the public harmony, will sufficiently influence your deliberations ... "

GEORGE WASHINGTON, FROM THE RECORDS OF THE US SENATE, 1789

Washington addresses Congress
The victorious George Washington is depicted along with members of the Congress as he makes his inaugural address. In acknowledgment of his status as a victorious general, Washington carried a steel-hilted sword, but dressed as a civilian in a brown broadcloth suit with buttons engraved with an eagle.

The American West

Following independence, the British cession of land between the Appalachian Mountains and the Mississippi River, and from the Great Lakes to Spanish Florida, opened the door for white expansion. But settlers and the American army had to contend with opposition from the Native American nations.

The Native American nations that had allied with the British during the War of Independence were infuriated to learn that in the Treaty of Paris of 1783, Britain had ceded their lands to the Americans without consultation. The Native Americans believed they had had the upper hand in the frontier war when Britain made peace, and insisted that the British government had no authority to dispose of Native American territory. Many nations therefore continued to battle the new United States along its western frontier.

Expansion checked

Native American resistance created a big problem for the Confederation Congress, which had hoped to pay off debts by selling land in the west to settlers. Americans had little incentive to move west of the Appalachians, as Spain barred access to the Mississippi, secretly arming Native Americans in the South who were hostile to settlers. In the Northwest, the British supplied and armed Native American nations in the hope of restoring their damaged wartime alliance.

Native American resistance

In the fall of 1789, discussions between federal representatives and the Creek nation failed to produce an acceptable agreement on the disputed Georgia frontier, and it appeared that war was likely. The following year, however, Creek leader Alexander McGillivray, the son of a Scottish trader who had married into the Creek confederation, traveled to New York and signed a treaty with federal officials that settled the boundary. Kentucky, originally part of Virginia, became a state in 1792 despite strong opposition from Dragging Canoe and his Chickamauga followers. The militants, who had split from the Cherokee nation and absorbed people from other nations, resisted American expansion until the combination of Dragging Canoe's death and the impact of American raids led them to end hostilities.

Little Turtle's War

Native American opposition to westward expansion was more united in the Northwest Territory, where a coalition led by Miami chief Little Turtle and Shawnee chief Blue Jacket, along with Delaware, Mingo, Ottawa, Wyandot, and other nations pursued armed resistance to American settlement in a conflict known as the Northwest Indian War, or Little Turtle's War. In 1790, President Washington dispatched Brigadier General Josiah Harmar with 1,300 regulars and militia to crush the Native American coalition, but the coalition ambushed and defeated Harmar's forces.

The next year, Washington sent a larger expedition under Major General Arthur St. Clair. In November 1791, Native Americans attacked near the Wabash River and killed or wounded more than half of St. Clair's 1,400 men. The US government then opened negotiations with the coalition, while at the same time preparing an even more powerful force to invade Native American lands. After nearly three years of fruitless

Lewis and Clark compass
Meriwether Lewis ordered this pocket compass for the Corps of Discovery expedition that explored and mapped the West. William Clark kept it as a memento—it is one of the only instruments to survive the expedition.

<< B E F O R E

Throughout Colonial times, Native Americans had battled to defend their territory from European expansion.

TERRITORIAL SAFEGUARDS
Westward expansion by settlers during the colonial era had been limited by the **French and their Native American allies << 24–25**, and then by the **British prohibition of settlement** west of the Appalachian Mountains **<< 36–37**.
During the war, most Native American tribes had chosen to **side with the British << 228–29**, aware that a Patriot victory could threaten their traditional territories.

Going west

Following the 1795 Treaty of Greenville, thousands journeyed west to settle in the Ohio Territory. Many traveled overland by wagon; others went by water via the Ohio River.

flow of settlers to Ohio greatly increased and the territory became the 17th state in the Union in 1803.

Benefits of statehood

In addition to Native American attacks and the physical dangers of frontier life, prospective settlers worried that they would lose their hard-won political rights if they moved to the federally controlled territories, which had no elected legislature to protect them.

The Confederation Congress tried to address concerns about lack of representation with the Northwest Ordinance of 1787. The ordinance divided the region into territories, subdivided into townships, using a system created by Thomas Jefferson. Each township was to be 6 miles (10 km) square divided into 36 plots

those of the existing states. It stipulated that when the population reached 5,000 adult white males, the territory should elect a legislature, and have a governor and judges appointed by Congress. When the total population reached 60,000, the inhabitants could write a state constitution, submit it to Congress, and if approved, obtain statehood. The law also banned slavery in the territories and states created by the Northwest Ordinance.

The Louisiana Purchase

In 1803, President Thomas Jefferson nearly doubled the size of the United States by purchasing the Louisiana Territory, a broad swathe of land extending from Louisiana in the South to present-day Montana in the Northwest. The French emperor, Napoleon Bonaparte, had forced Spain to cede the land to France, but his plan to use the territory as a base for operations against the British in North America proved impossible to carry out. Instead—because Napoleon needed funds to finance his wars in Europe and also wished to keep Louisiana out of British hands—he offered to sell the vast colony to the United States. Jefferson agreed to purchase the territory for $15 million, and despite questions as to whether the deal was constitutional, the Senate ratified the treaty.

Jefferson announced the purchase on July 4, and the next day appointed Meriwether Lewis to lead an expedition to explore and map the new territory. Helped by his friend William Clark, Lewis set off from St. Louis, Missouri, in May 1804 and returned in September 1806, having reached the Pacific Ocean and twice crossed the Rocky Mountains.

WAR LEADER c.1747–1812
LITTLE TURTLE

Michikinikwa, meaning Little Turtle, was the war leader of the Miami nation during the War of Independence, during which he earned a reputation as a skilled military commander. His most notable success was the defeat of the Patriots in their attempt to capture Fort Detroit in November 1780.

After independence, Little Turtle was a leading figure in the coalition of Native American nations that fought white expansion in the Northwest Indian War. Following this conflict, Little Turtle became an advocate of peace with the United States. He opposed Shawnee leader Tecumseh's later effort to form a new Indian alliance, which cost him influence among the Miami nation.

> "Let us form **one body, one heart,** and **defend to the last warrior** our country."

TECUMSEH, SPEECH TO THE CHOCTAWS AND CHICKASAWS, 1811

discussions, President Washington ordered forces under Major General Anthony Wayne to attack the Native Americans. Wayne's 2,000 men defeated Blue Jacket and about 1,000 warriors at Fallen Timbers on August 20, 1794. Coalition leaders, including Little Turtle, signed the Treaty of Greenville in August 1795, ceding their remaining lands in Ohio along with territory in Indiana to the United States. With the end of Native American opposition, the

measuring 1 sq. mile (259 ha) to be made available to settlers at $1 ($26) per acre. Land in each township was to be made available for public education and Patriot war veterans.

The 1787 ordinance also added the means by which each territory could become a state with rights equal to

Bloody defeat

After their defeat at Fallen Timbers near modern-day Toledo, Ohio, the Native Americans fled to Fort Miami, a British outpost, but found the gates closed despite previous promises of support. The British could not risk angering the US while at war with Revolutionary France.

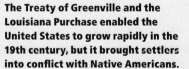

AFTER

The Treaty of Greenville and the Louisiana Purchase enabled the United States to grow rapidly in the 19th century, but it brought settlers into conflict with Native Americans.

REDUCING TENSION

The federal government attempted to reduce tensions on the frontier by providing the Native Americans with tools, livestock, and training to encourage them to **give up their traditional culture**. This policy also aimed to provide more land for settlers; as the Indians abandoned hunting in favor of farming, they needed less space. Some Native American nations, particularly in the South, attempted to **remain at peace** by trying to live like their new neighbors, but many nations in the Northwest, notably the Shawnee led by Tecumseh, **continued to resist**.

The Lewis and Clark Expedition
In 1804, following the Louisiana Purchase, Second Lieutenant William Clark and Captain Meriwether Lewis of the US Army set out on horseback to map the newly acquired land.

The Irrepressible Conflicts

In its first years as an independent nation, the United States attempted to protect its trading interests and establish its North American borders. In doing so, it antagonized former friends and raked up quarrels with old adversaries.

BEFORE

Victory in the war did not prevent the US from being caught up in Europe's conflicts, or save it from trouble on the western frontier.

ALLIANCES IN FLUX
While **Jay's Treaty of 1795 ≪ 324–25** created a better understanding between America and Britain, the changing international situation caused by the **French Revolution** brought America's alliance with France into question.

WESTWARD EXPANSION
On the western frontier, **Native American tribes** resisted American expansion, which was accelerated by the Treaty of Paris and the **Louisiana Purchase ≪ 338–39**.

Washington's advice to his successors to steer clear of entangling alliances with European powers proved hard to follow. Relations between the United States and France deteriorated rapidly in the mid-1790s, as the US repaired its relations with Britain, with which France was again at war. The election of Federalist John Adams as president in 1796, reinforced the breach between the former allies. Federalists had been supporters of Jay's Treaty with Britain in 1794, and the French perceived that

Pirates of the Mediterranean
On August 3, 1804, US Navy officer Stephen Decatur led an attack on a Tripolitan vessel off the Barbary Coast of North Africa. During hand-to-hand fighting, Decatur's own brother, James, was killed in the action.

the Adams administration would be anti-French and sympathetic to Britain.

In an attempt to force a change in US policy, French leaders authorized their naval vessels and privateers to seize US merchant ships trading with Britain in the Caribbean. Congress responded by increasing the size of the US Navy. Tensions led to the so-called Quasi-War, two years of naval skirmishes between the US and France, brought to an end by the Convention of Mortefontaine of 1800, negotiated by Adams in the interests of avoiding a full-blown conflict.

A domestic consequence of the build up to possible war with France was the passage of the temporary Alien and Sedition Acts, passed by Congress in

Action in the Quasi-War
The US frigate *Constellation* (left) bears down on the French *L'Insurgente* off the island of Nevis in the West Indies on February 9, 1799. *L'Insurgente* was captured after a brief battle.

1798, making it illegal to criticize the Federal government within the United States. This crude attempt to silence opposition to Federal policy had the opposite effect, and contributed to the victory of Anti-Federalist Thomas Jefferson in the 1800 elections.

Trade wars

One of the most pressing problems facing the US in the late 1790s was piracy by the so-called Barbary states—Tunis, Morocco, Algiers, and Tripoli—against US merchant shipping in the Mediterranean. Adams tried to deal with the problem by paying tribute to the leaders of these states, but when Tripoli declared war on the United States in May 1801, Thomas Jefferson imposed a naval blockade on the city. In August 1804, after the capture of USS *Philadelphia* off Tripoli, the US Navy bombarded Tripoli, and in the following April a US-led force captured the Tripolitan city of Derna. Worn down by the conflict, Tripoli made peace in June 1805, guaranteeing American access to the Mediterranean.

With the Napoleonic Wars raging in Europe, American merchant ships were also seized by the British and French as each side tried to disrupt the other's trade, and the British forced any British-born sailors they found on US ships into the Royal Navy. On June 22, 1807, HMS *Leopard* fired on the US navy frigate *Chesapeake* off the Virginia coast, causing several American casualties and seizing four crewmen The attack sparked calls for war with Britain, but Jefferson imposed an embargo on trade instead. This proved ineffective and was soon lifted.

Old troubles resurface

When James Madison succeeded Jefferson as president in 1809, he faced a new threat in the Old Northwest, where Shawnee chief Tecumseh and his brother, Tenskwatawa, a religious leader known as the Prophet, were organizing a new Indian coalition. Alarmed by this development, William Henry Harrison, the governor of Indiana Territory, assembled an army and marched on the brothers' base in Prophetstown while Tecumseh was in the South seeking recruits. On November 7, 1811, at the Battle of Tippecanoe,

Bloody nose
This 1813 cartoon shows King George III losing a fight with US President James Madison, thought to be a reference to American victories in the War of 1812.

THE BATTLE OF NEW ORLEANS

In November 1814, the British assembled a fleet at Jamaica and sailed to attack the port of New Orleans in one of the last battles of the War of 1812. Andrew Jackson reached the city on December 1 and hastily assembled a force of 4,000 defenders. British commander Sir Edward Pakenham assaulted the US fortifications on January 8, 1815, advancing in dense lines across open ground with 5,300 troops. They were repulsed with 2,037 casualties; American losses numbered only 71 men. The victory greatly boosted American morale and patriotic sentiment.

Harrison forced Tenskwatawa to abandon Prophetstown. When Tecumseh returned from the South, he decided to turn to the British in Canada for assistance.

In late 1811 and early 1812, Madison came under pressure from a group of southern and western congressmen known as "War Hawks," who demanded war with Britain to secure the western frontier and end British attacks on US shipping. When the British rejected a request to respect US trading rights, Madison asked Congress to declare war on Britain. The legislators did so on June 18, 1812.

A new war with Britain

The War of 1812 lasted 1,000 days (1812–14). Initially unprepared for war, the US Army suffered early defeats, notably at Detroit in August 1812. However, its fortunes changed after American warships under Commodore Oliver Hazard Perry defeated the Royal Navy on Lake Erie in September 1813, allowing American forces led by William Henry Harrison to invade Canada. In October, Harrison routed British troops at the Battle of the Thames in Ontario. The death of Britain's ally, Tecumseh, in

the battle effectively ended Native American resistance in the Northwest. At sea, American ships won a number of single-ship battles, but a naval blockade by the British severely disrupted trade and effectively bankrupted the Federal government. Exploiting their naval superiority, British forces landed in Chesapeake Bay in August 1814. They defeated the

Americans at Bladensburg, Maryland, on August 24, 1814, and went on to burn Washington, D.C. The offensive ended when the Royal Navy's attempt to capture Baltimore was thwarted by the valiant defenders of Fort McHenry on September 13–14.

In a final thrust, British forces attacked New Orleans on January 8, 1815. The city's defenders were led by Andrew Jackson, a recent victor in the Creek War, in which Creek Indians who favored adopting white culture and their American allies fought other Creeks opposed to white expansion. Unknown to Jackson or the British commanders at New Orleans, the War of 1812 had already ended. On Christmas Eve, 1814, American and British negotiators had signed the Treaty of Ghent, in Belgium.

Even so, Jackson's victory at New Orleans was a key factor in the demise of the Federalist Party, which had met in Hartford, Connecticut, from December 1814 to January 1815. The delegates, from five New England

states, demanded that Madison make peace with Britain. They also insisted that the Constitution be amended to curb the power of the southern and western states and discussed withdrawing from the American union if their demands were not met. The party's antiwar stance in the face of the American victory virtually wiped out its support.

> "We behold our **seafaring citizens** still the **daily victims of lawless violence**."
>
> PRESIDENT MADISON'S "WAR MESSAGE" TO CONGRESS, 1812

AFTER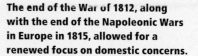

The end of the War of 1812, along with the end of the Napoleonic Wars in Europe in 1815, allowed for a renewed focus on domestic concerns.

A NEW POLITICS
Andrew Jackson's victory at New Orleans made him a **national hero**, and he became the dominant figure in American politics in the next decade. The War of 1812 ended serious Native American and foreign threats to the United States, but the national unity of the postwar era soon gave way to increasingly **bitter disputes** between northern and southern states over the issue of slavery.

SLAVES AND FREE MEN
Racial divisions in America generally became more institutionalized in the early 19th century. Free blacks, comprising 11 percent of the population in 1800, gradually **lost civil rights** they had held since the War of Independence. At the same time, the slave population greatly increased as "King Cotton" brought increasing wealth to the white South.

The Revolution Remembered

The War of Independence is a cornerstone of American history that has been celebrated and commemorated since its conclusion. It inspired countless patriotic memoirs, scholarship art, and fiction paying tribute to war heroes, the Founding Fathers, and liberty itself.

On July 3, 1776, John Adams wrote to inform his wife Abigail that the Continental Congress had approved the Declaration of Independence the previous day. Adams asserted that this event was the most important in all of American history, and predicted that future generations of Americans would celebrate July 2 "as the great anniversary Festival" with "Acts of Devotion to God … Pomp and Parade … Bells, Bonfires and Illuminations from one End of this Continent to the other."

Adams was correct in every way but one: Americans chose to celebrate July 4—the day that the Declaration of Independence was signed—as the founding date of their country, rather than July 2. Although Congress did not make July 4 an official national holiday until 1870, the date has always been the most important anniversary in the United States, and many individuals, organizations, and events have kept the memory of the war alive in the minds of the American people.

Celebrations down the years

The War of 1812 against Britain (see pp.342–43), often called the Second War of Independence, renewed

Fighting spirit
George Washington's portrait adorns this 19th century field drum. In 1777, Washington found his army's music to be so poor that he ordered the drum and fife players to practice more, or risk demotion.

interest in the struggle and caused an increase in celebrations marking July 4. Much of this attention focused on Patriot soldiers, and resulted in Congress passing an act in 1818 providing payments to impoverished veterans of the Continental Army.

In 1826, celebrations marking the 50th anniversary of independence were larger and more widespread than previous commemorations, with public events such as speeches, parades, dinners, and firework displays held all over the country. Coincidentally, two of the last surviving founders, John Adams and Thomas Jefferson, died on the 50th anniversary.

The highlight of the celebrations marking the 1876 Centennial was the Centennial Exhibition in Philadelphia. This event featured more than 250 pavilions showcasing American history and industrial achievements, along with displays sponsored by 37 foreign nations. The exhibition, which looked to the future as well as the past, reportedly drew almost nine million visitors.

In 1976, Americans marked the Bicentennial with a host of special events. The "Freedom Train" toured the country to display replicas of important historical artifacts. On a visit to Boston, President Gerald Ford praised American accomplishments, stating that "We kept the faith, liberty flourished, freedom lived."

BEFORE

The War of Independence ended in British surrender, the Treaty of Paris, and the recognition of the United States as an independent nation.

THE ROAD TO NATIONHOOD
Although the **First Continental Congress had declared independence in 1776** ≪ 112–13, King George III rejected the status of the US as an independent nation until after the British surrender, when he was forced to acknowledge them "to be free sovereign and independent states" in the resulting **peace treaty** ≪ 312–13. The new US Constitution was constructed by the **Constitutional Convention** ≪ 328–29 in 1787.

Celebrated in song
This sheet music cover was designed for the United States centennial in 1876, a milestone that inspired a fresh wave of art and music celebrating the story of the foundation of the Union.

Literature and art
Poets also helped keep the memory of the war vibrant. Ralph Waldo Emerson wrote the "Concord Hymn" in 1837 to memorialize the beginning of the struggle in Massachusetts, and in 1860 Henry Wadsworth Longfellow composed "Paul Revere's Ride."

Artists similarly found the War of Independence an appealing subject. John Singleton Copley, Charles Willson Peale, and Gilbert Stuart painted portraits of many of the Patriot leaders. John Trumbull produced paintings of several momentous scenes, including *The Declaration of Independence* and *The Surrender of Lord Cornwallis at Yorktown*. Emanuel Gottlieb Leutze painted *Washington Crosses the Delaware* (see pp.130–31), one of the most famous paintings of the war.

Historians were among the first to record and publicize the story of the fight for independence, but several participants, from ordinary soldiers to generals, provided firsthand accounts

Godlike status
The reverence and affection that Americans felt toward Washington was captured by Constantino Brumidi's fresco *Apotheosis of Washington* painted in 1865 for the central rotunda of the US Capitol.

George Washington

The American War of Independence was not only a key event in American history, but also in that of the world. It signaled the birth of a superpower.

AMERICA'S ORIGIN STORY

The first histories of the war, such as Mercy Otis Warren's *History of the Rise, Progress, and Termination of the American Revolution*, published in 1805–06, and David Ramsay's *History of the American Revolution*, in 1789, were produced so soon after the war that they became primary sources for hundreds of later histories, as well as movies, art, and literature. In the 20th century, the story of the revolution also became the **origin story of a global superpower**, as American influence spread throughout of the world.

MERCY OTIS WARREN, A CHRONICLER OF THE WAR

> "Here once the **embattled farmers** stood And **fired the shot** heard round the world."

RALPH WALDO EMERSON, "CONCORD HYMN," 1837

Old soldiers
In the late 19th century, several organizations were founded that emphasized members' family connections with the war. Taking their inspiration from the Society of the Cincinnati, founded as early as 1783 by officers of the Continental Army, other organizations sprang up—the Sons of the Revolution in 1875, the Sons of the American Revolution in 1889, the Daughters of the American Revolution in 1890, and the Children of the American Revolution in 1895. To this day, many of these organizations maintain museums and libraries, and work to promote greater understanding of the conflicts.

During the Civil War, both sides claimed to be the true heirs of the revolution and invoked the writings and speeches of its leading protagonists to justify their actions. The Confederate government even went as far as including an image of George Washington on his horse on its official seal.

In the 20th century, American leaders invoked the country's struggle for independence in both world wars, to inspire patriotism and encourage men and women to join the armed forces. One of the best known recruiting posters of 1943 depicts American soldiers marching past the ethereal figures of Washington's soldiers standing resolute at Valley Forge. It exclaimed "Americans will *always* fight for liberty."

in memoirs published in the early 19th century. In addition, biographers chronicled the lives of Patriot leaders. Among them were a five-volume biography of George Washington, which also provided a detailed history of the war, by Continental Army veteran and Supreme Court Chief Justice John Marshall, and Mason Locke Weems's *Life of George Washington*, first published in 1800. Frequently revised and reprinted, Weems's work proved a highly popular—if not always accurate—account of the war.

Two centuries of freedom
On July 4, 1976, spectators aboard vessels in New York Harbor and lining the shore watched a procession of tall ships from around the world sail past the Statue of Liberty, an icon of the nation's independence, in honor of America's Bicentennial.

In their Footsteps

Many sites relating to the War of Independence have been carefully preserved. Today, visitors can tour battlefields, military encampments, and the homes of important leaders who took part in the struggle for independence.

CONNECTICUT

Fort Griswold Battlefield State Park

American militia defended this fort against British attackers during a raid led by former American officer Benedict Arnold. After a stubborn defense, British troops stormed and captured the fort on September 6, 1781.
www.fortgriswold.org

Nathan Hale Homestead

This building, constructed in 1776 by the Hale family, replaced the house where Nathan Hale was born in 1755. Hale was captured by the British and hanged as a spy on September 22, 1776.
www.ctlandmarks.org/content/nathan-hale-homestead

Putnam Memorial State Park

During the winter of 1778–79, Continental Army troops under Major General Israel Putnam made their winter encampment at this site.
putnampark.org

DELAWARE

John Dickinson Plantation

A prominent political writer, member of the Continental Congress, and delegate to the Constitutional Convention, John Dickinson lived in the brick house built here in 1740.
history.delaware.gov/museums/jdp

FLORIDA

Castillo de San Marcos National Monument

St. Augustine served as the capital of British East Florida during the Revolution, and Fort St. Marks—as the British called it—was garrisoned by British troops and used as a base for raids into Georgia.
www.nps.gov/casa

GEORGIA

Fort Morris

Built to defend the port of Sunbury, Fort Morris withstood a British attack in November 1778, but was captured on January 9, 1779, by a British invasion force from East Florida.
gastateparks.org/FortMorris

Kettle Creek Battlefield

On February 14, 1779, several hundred Loyalists from the Carolinas marching to join the British Army were attacked and defeated here by American militia.
www.nps.gov/nr/feature/july/2011/Kettle_Creek_Battlefield

INDIANA

George Rogers Clark National Historical Park

Colonel George Rogers Clark led American troops on a winter expedition into the western territories. After a difficult march, his force captured British Fort Sackville on February 25, 1779.
www.nps.gov/gero/index.htm

KENTUCKY

Blue Licks Battlefield State Park

In one of the last battles of the War of Independence, on October 19, 1782, Native Americans allied with the British ambushed and defeated a force of Kentucky militia that included the famed frontiersman Daniel Boone.
parks.ky.gov/parks/resortparks/blue_licks

MAINE

Old Fort Western

This fort on the Kennebec River was the staging area for Benedict Arnold's troops when they began their wilderness march to attack the British stronghold at Quebec in the fall of 1775.
www.oldfortwestern.org

MARYLAND

Fort Frederick State Park

This fort was used to house British prisoners captured during the War of Independence, namely those taken at the Battles of Saratoga (1777) and Yorktown (1781).
dnr2.maryland.gov/publiclands/Pages/western/fortfrederick

Old Senate Chamber, Maryland State House

On December 23, 1783, General George Washington appeared before the Continental Congress here and resigned his commission as commander in chief of the Continental Army.
msa.maryland.gov/msa/mdstatehouse/html/old_chamber

MASSACHUSETTS

Adams National Historical Park

This site includes the birthplace and home of Massachusetts political leader and second president of the United States, John Adams. During the War of Independence, his wife—Abigail Adams—managed the Braintree farm.
www.nps.gov/adam/index

Freedom Trail

This 2.5–mile (4 km) route includes Boston's most important revolutionary sites: the Old South Meeting House, Old State House, the Boston Massacre Site, Paul Revere House, Old North Church, and the Bunker Hill Monument.
www.thefreedomtrail.org

Hancock-Clarke House

John Hancock and Samuel Adams were staying in this Lexington parsonage when Paul Revere awakened them during his famous ride through the countryside on April 19, 1775.
www.lexingtonhistory.org/historic-sites

Minute Man National Historical Park

This park includes the site of the North Bridge, where militiamen and British troops exchanged shots on April 19, 1775, the first day of the War of Independence. The park also includes the 5–mile (8 km) Battle Road, where Patriots clashed with British soldiers retreating to Boston.
www.nps.gov/mima/index

NEW HAMPSHIRE

John Paul Jones House

Patriot naval officer John Paul Jones resided in this house from 1781 to 1782, while he supervised construction of the ship of the line *America*, which was being built at Portsmouth.
portsmouthhistory.org/john-paul-jones-house

NEW JERSEY

Monmouth Battlefield State Park

On June 28, 1778, George Washington's Continental Army attacked British forces withdrawing from Philadelphia to New York. The battle was the last major engagement of the war in the North, and was ultimately inconclusive.
www.state.nj.us/dep/parksandforests/parks/monbat

Morristown National Historical Park

The Continental Army encamped at Morristown during the winter of 1779–80, enduring conditions even harsher than those experienced two years earlier at Valley Forge.
www.nps.gov/morr

Princeton Battlefield State Park

The Continental Army under George Washington engaged a British detachment on January 3, 1777, inflicting heavy losses on the royal forces.
www.state.nj.us/dep/parksandforests/parks/princeton

Trenton Battle Monument

After a daring crossing of the Delaware River the previous night, General George Washington and the Continental Army surrounded and attacked the Hessian garrison on December 26, 1776, winning a decisive victory.
www.state.nj.us/dep/parksandforests/historic/trentonbattlemonument

Washington Crossing State Park

On the night of December 25, 1776, George Washington and the Continental Army crossed the Delaware River at this site and prepared their march for a surprise attack on Trenton.
www.washingtoncrossingpark.org

NEW YORK

Fort Ticonderoga

American troops led by Ethan Allen and Benedict Arnold captured the fort on May 10, 1775. British forces under General John Burgoyne reoccupied the post on July 6, 1777, but it returned to American control when Burgoyne surrendered at Saratoga in October.
www.fortticonderoga.org

Fraunces Tavern

At the end of the War of Independence, George Washington dined with his officers here, bidding them goodbye before setting out for Annapolis, Maryland, to resign his commission.
frauncestavernmuseum.org

Fort Montgomery State Historic Site

British forces, including Loyalists and Hessians, attacked Fort Montgomery in October 1777. The capture of the fort, and

nearby Fort Clinton, allowed the British to dismantle the Hudson River Chain.
nysparks.com/historic-sites/28/details.aspx

New York Freedom Trail

This route encompasses 19 locations in the War of Independence, including historic buildings and the sites of the Battles of Brooklyn (August 27), Harlem Heights (September 16), and Fort Washington (November 17) in 1776.
www.nyfreedom.com

Oriskany Battlefield State Historic Site

On August 6, 1777, Patriot militia marching to relieve Fort Stanwix from a British siege were ambushed by Native Americans and Loyalists. Despite heavy losses, the surviving militia reached the fort and the British retreated.
nysparks.com/historic-sites/21/details.aspx

Saratoga National Historical Park

Burgoyne's British army was defeated at Freeman's Farm (September 19, 1777) and Bemis Heights (October 7, 1777). The British army surrendered on October 17; the American victory at Saratoga was the turning point of the War of Independence The national park includes the battlefield, Schuyler House, the Saratoga monument, and Victory Woods, where Burgoyne's army camped prior to the surrender.
www.nps.gov/sara

Washington's Headquarters State Historic Site

Washington resided at the farmhouse in Newburgh between April 1782 and August 1783, while the Continental Army was camped nearby. Washington was living there when he announced the Cessation of Hostilities.
www.nysparks.com/historic-sites/17/details.aspx

NORTH CAROLINA

Guilford Courthouse National Military Park

On March 15, 1781, British forces under Lord Cornwallis defeated Major General Nathanael Greene's American army after a long and bloody battle.
www.nps.gov/guco

Moores Creek National Battlefield

Loyalists attempting to reach the coast and unite with a British expeditionary force attacked American militia on February 27, 1776, and were defeated.
www.nps.gov/mocr

PENNSYLVANIA

Brandywine Battlefield State Park

General Sir William Howe's British army, attempting to capture Philadelphia, outflanked and defeated George Washington's Continental Army on September 11, 1777.
brandywinebattlefield.org

Cliveden (Benjamin Chew House)

Action at the 1777 Battle of Germantown took place at this colonial mansion, inside which Musgrave's 40th Regiment were ordered to barricade themselves, taking up positions at the windows.
www.cliveden.org/battle-of-germantown

Fort Mifflin

In November 1777, Fort Mifflin took a relentless bombardment from the Royal Navy. Around 350 Americans were killed, but the efforts of the troops gave Washington and his army crucial time to get to Valley Forge and regroup.
www.fortmifflin.us

General Gates House (part of the York County Colonial Complex)

General Horatio Gates lived in this house during the Second Continental Congress of 1778. For nine months, York served as the capital of the nascent United States.
www.yorkheritage.org

Independence National Historical Park

This Philadelphia park includes Independence Hall—where both the Declaration of Independence and the US Constitution were debated and signed—the Liberty Bell, and the Benjamin Franklin Museum.
www.nps.gov/inde

Valley Forge National Historical Park

During their encampment here over the winter of 1777–78, soldiers of the Continental Army suffered great hardships. However, they also benefited from a training program instituted by Baron von Steuben and emerged as a more effective fighting force.
www.nps.gov/vafo

RHODE ISLAND

Major General Nathanael Greene Homestead

The home of Nathanael Greene and his family was built in 1770. Greene was one of George Washington's most trusted generals and earned fame commanding Continental Army forces in the southern theater.
nathanaelgreenehomestead.org

SOUTH CAROLINA

Cowpens National Battlefield

On January 17, 1781, American forces under Brigadier General Daniel Morgan nearly annihilated a British detachment under Lieutenant Colonel Banastre Tarleton.
www.nps.gov/cowp

Eutaw Springs Battlefield Park

The bloody Battle of Eutaw Springs on September 8, 1781, was the last major engagement of the war in the South.
www.eutawvillesc.com/eutawsprings

Historic Camden Revolutionary War Site

This site includes historic buildings and exhibits focusing on the British occupation of Camden in 1780–81. Camden's location resulted in two major engagements nearby: the Battle of Camden (August 16, 1780) and the Battle of Hobkirk's Hill (April 25, 1781).
www.historic-camden.net

Kings Mountain National Military Park

Considered the turning point of the southern campaign, on October 7, 1780, Patriot militia surrounded and destroyed a Loyalist force under British Major Patrick Ferguson at Kings Mountain.
www.nps.gov/kimo

Ninety Six National Historic Site

The backcountry town was the scene of a battle between American patriots and Loyalists in 1775. In May–June 1781, the Loyalist garrison withstood a siege by General Greene's Continental Army but evacuated the post shortly afterward.
www.nps.gov/nisi

Overmountain Victory National Historic Trail

Those interested in following the route taken by the Overmountain Men, Patriot militia from west of the Appalachians, on their march to Kings Mountain can visit the Overmountain Victory National Historic Trail, which runs from Abingdon, Virginia, to the battle site.
www.nps.gov/ovvi

TENNESSEE

Sycamore Shoals State Park

Sycamore Shoals was where the Overmountain Men gathered on September 25, 1780, before marching to attack Major Patrick Ferguson's Loyalists at Kings Mountain.
tnstateparks.com/parks/about/sycamore-shoals

VERMONT

Bennington Battle Monument

Colonel John Stark and his militia encountered a detachment of British, German, and Loyalist troops and defeated them on August 16, 1777. The monument sits on the site of the store of supplies that the battle was fought over.
www.benningtonbattlemonument.com

Ethan Allen Homestead

Later a political writer, Ethan Allen was a hero of the War of Independence, notably capturing Fort Ticonderoga in 1775. Allen built this house after the war, in 1787, and spent the rest of his life there.
www.ethanallenhomestead.org

VIRGINIA

George Washington Birthplace National Monument

George Washington was born at this location in Westmoreland County on February 22, 1732.
www.nps.gov/gewa

Monticello

Thomas Jefferson's magnificent home near Charlottesville shows details of his varied career as a revolutionary leader, third president of the United States, farmer, and scientist.
www.monticello.org

Mount Vernon

Situated on the south bank of the Potomac River, Mount Vernon was George Washington's home as well as a working plantation.
www.mountvernon.org

Yorktown Battlefield (part of Colonial National Historical Park)

In the campaign that secured American victory in the War of Independence, George Washington and a combined French and American army besieged Cornwallis's British army at Yorktown. The site includes the battlefield, a monument, and Surrender Field, as well as Moore House, where the surrender documents were signed.
www.nps.gov/york

WASHINGTON, D.C.

Smithsonian Institution

The Smithsonian Institution's National Museum of American History houses many exhibits related to the War of Independence, including artifacts that once belonged to Patriot leaders such as George Washington and Thomas Jefferson.
americanhistory.si.edu

Society of the Cincinnati

Founded by Continental officers in 1783 with hereditary membership, the Society is the oldest War of Independence organization in existence. Its headquarters includes a museum and research library.
www.societyofthecincinnati.org

Index

Page numbers in **bold** refer to main subject entries

Acknowledgments

The publisher would like to thank the following people at the Smithsonian Institution for their kind assistance: **Kealy Gordon**, Product Development Manager; **Ellen Nanney**, Licensing Manager; **Brigid Ferraro**, Vice President, Education and Consumer Products; **Carol LeBlanc**, Senior Vice President, Education and Consumer Products; and **Chris Liedel**, President.

Special thanks go to **Agata Rutkowska**, Picture Library Assistant, Royal Collection Trust; **Chris Barker**, Assistant Curator, Royal Mint; **Dr. Alastair Massie**, Head of Academic Access, National Army Museum; **Don Troiani**; and **John Loughery**, for their help and advice.

The publisher would also like to thank **James Grinter** at Reeman Dansie for allowing us to photograph their collections. Reeman Dansie Auctioneers, No. 8 Wyncolls Road, Colchester CO4 9HU. www.reemandansie.com/

Dorling Kindersley would also like to thank: **Devika Awasthi**, **Sanjay Chauhan**, **Parul Gambhir**, **Namita**, **Anusri Saha**, **Chhaya Sajwan**, **Mahua Sharma**, **Upasana Sharma**, and **Alexander Lloyd** for design assistance; **Sneha Sunder Benjamin** and **Arpita Dasgupta** for editorial assistance; and **Aditya Katyal** and **Sakshi Saluja** for picture research support.

Picture Credits
The publisher would like to thank the following for their kind permission to reproduce their photographs:

(Key: a-above; b-below/bottom; c-center; f-far; l-left; r-right; t-top)

2-3 Getty Images: DEA / M. Seemuller. **4 Smithsonian Institution, Washington, DC:** (tc, cr). **SuperStock:** (br). **5 Anne S.K. Brown Military Collection, Brown University Library:** (br). **Dorling Kindersley:** Peter Keim (tc, tr). **Yale University Art Gallery:** (bl). **6 Alamy Images:** Don Klumpp (br). **Corbis:** Don Troiani (cra). **Smithsonian Institution, Washington, DC:** (cl, tc). **The Library of Congress, Washington DC:** (bl). **7 Bridgeman Images:** © Chicago History Museum, USA (br). **Corbis:** Heritage Images (cl). **Dorling Kindersley:** Peter Keim (tc). **Getty Images:** DEA / M. Seemuller (bl). **8 Bridgeman Images:** Pennsylvania Academy of the Fine Arts, Philadelphia, USA. **10-11 Mary Evans Picture Library:** Antiquarian Images. **12-13 Corbis:** The Gallery Collection (br). **Getty Images:** Stock Montage. **14 Corbis:** (bl); adoc-photos (clb). **The Library of Congress, Washington DC:** (fclb). **16 Alamy Images:** The National Trust Photolibrary (cl). **Bridgeman Images:** Château de Versailles, France (br). **Corbis:** GraphicaArtis (ca). **Smithsonian Institution, Washington, DC:** (cr). **17 Corbis:** Burstein Collection (cla). **Rex Shutterstock:** Everett Collection (bc). **TopFoto.co.uk:** The Granger Collection (cr). **18 Alamy Images:** North Wind Picture Archives (cl). **18-19 SuperStock:** (b). **19 Alamy Images:** North Wind Picture Archives (tr). **20-21 Corbis:** Francis G. Mayer. **22 Corbis:** (bl); Tyrone Turner/ National Geographic Creative (tr). **23 Smithsonian Institution, Washington, DC:** (bc). **TopFoto.co.uk:** The Granger Collection (t). **24-25 Bridgeman Images:** Private Collection (b). **25 Corbis:** Don Troiani (tc, br). **26-27 The Library of Congress, Washington DC. 28 Alamy Images:** Pictorial Press Ltd (c). **Bridgeman Images:** Petworth House, West Sussex, UK / National Trust Photographic Library (clb). **29 Getty Images:** Fotosearch (br). **Smithsonian Institution, Washington, DC:** (tc). **30 Bridgeman Images:** Peabody Essex Museum, Salem, Massachusetts, USA (bl). **Corbis:** (t). **31 Getty Images:** Archive Photos (bc); MPI (tr). **32-33 Corbis:** Burstein Collection. **34 Bridgeman Images:** Private Collection / Peter Newark American Pictures (r). **Corbis:** Joseph Sohm (bl). **35 Alamy Images:** Alastair Balderstone (br). **Bridgeman Images:** Private Collection / Peter Newark American Pictures (bc). **Corbis:** (tl). **36 Alamy Images:** North Wind Picture Archives (bl). **Smithsonian Institution, Washington, DC:** (cb). **36-37 Alamy Images:** North Wind Picture Archives (c). **37 The Library of Congress, Washington DC:** (cr). **38 Alamy Images:** Chronicle (cla); North Wind Picture Archives (bl). **Bridgeman Images:** Gilder Lehrman Collection, New York, USA (br). **38-39 Alamy Images:** Glasshouse Images (tr). **40-41 Corbis:** The Gallery Collection. **42-43 The Library of Congress, Washington DC:** (t). **43 Alamy Images:** North Wind Picture Archives (cr). **Bridgeman Images:** The Putnam Foundation, Timken Museum of Art, San Diego, USA (bl). **44-45 TopFoto.co.uk:** The Granger Collection. **46 Corbis:** Heritage Images (bl). **The Library of Congress, Washington DC:** (tr). **47 Bridgeman Images:** Private Collection / © Look and Learn; Private Collection / Photo © Christie's Images (cra). **48-49 Alamy Images:** North Wind Picture Archives. **Corbis:** The Gallery Collection (br). **50 Alamy Images:** World History Archive (clb). **Bridgeman Images:** Private Collection / Peter Newark American Pictures (bl). **Smithsonian Institution, Washington, DC:** (fbl). **52 Alamy Images:** North Wind Picture Archives (cla); Pictorial Press Ltd (c). **Bridgeman Images:** Private Collection (br). **The Lexington Historical Society:** (bl). **53 akg-images:** British Library (br). **Dorling Kindersley:** Peter Keim (cra). **Smithsonian Institution, Washington, DC:** (cb). **The US National Archives and Records Administration:** (cla). **54 The Library of Congress, Washington DC. 55 Alamy Images:** Stillman Rogers (br). **Corbis:** (tr). **The Lexington Historical Society:** (clb). **56-57 Alamy Images:** North Wind Picture Archives. **58 Alamy Images:** FineArt (bl). **The Library of Congress, Washington DC:** (cra). **59 Corbis:** (bl). **Smithsonian Institution, Washington, DC:** (t). **60-61 Bridgeman Images:** Private Collection. **62 Getty Images:** Emory Kristof (clb). **62-63 Alamy Images:** World History Archive. **63 Dorling Kindersley:** Peter Keim (crb). **The Library of Congress, Washington DC:** (tr). **64 Alamy Images:** The Print Collector (br). **65 Alamy Images:** Everett Collection Inc (tl); SuperStock (bc). **66 Corbis:** Don Troiani (tc, tr, ftr, cra, cla, cr, br). **Smithsonian Institution, Washington, DC:** (tl, c). **67 Corbis:** Don Troiani (tr, br). **Smithsonian Institution, Washington, DC:** (l). **68 Alamy Images:** North Wind Picture Archives (bl). **Bridgeman Images:** Private Collection/ Peter Newark Pictures (tr). **69 akg-images:** British Library. **70-71 Bridgeman Images:** Gilder Lehrman Collection, New York, USA. **72-73 Mary Evans Picture Library:** Library of Congress (t). **73 Mary Evans Picture Library:** (ca). **The US National Archives and Records Administration:** (crb). **74 Alamy Images:** Heritage Image Partnership Ltd (crb). **Bridgeman Images:** Cleveland Museum of Art, OH, USA / Gift of Mr. and Mrs. Lawrence S. Robbins (l). **75 Alamy Images:** coin Alan King (br). **Bridgeman Images:** Private Collection / © Look and Learn / Elgar Collection (c). **The Library of Congress, Washington DC:** (tl). **76 Bridgeman Images:** Harris, Charles Xavier (b.1856) / Virginia Historical Society, Richmond, Virginia, USA (bc). **The Colonial Williamsburg Foundation:** (cl). **77 Alamy Images:** Chronicle. **78 Mary Evans Picture Library:** Antiquarian Images. **79 Corbis:** Don Troiani (tr). **The Library of Congress, Washington DC:** (bl). **80 TopFoto.co.uk:** The Granger Collection (b). **81 Bridgeman Images:** Private Collection / Peter Newark American Pictures (cr). **Canadian War Museum (CWM):** (tc). **82-83 Yale University Art Gallery. 84-85 Bridgeman Images:** Collection of the New-York Historical Society, USA. **Corbis:** The Gallery Collection (br). **86 Alamy Images:** Niday Picture Library (clb). **Bridgeman Images:** Private Collection / Photo © Christie's Images (bl). **Corbis:** (fclb). **88 Alamy Images:** Maurice Savage (c). **Bridgeman Images:** Courtesy of the Director, National Army Museum, London, UK (br). **Smithsonian Institution, Washington, DC:** (tr). **The Library of Congress, Washington DC:** (bl). **89 Bridgeman Images:** © Chicago History Museum, USA (br). **Corbis:** (cra). **Getty Images:** DEA / M. Seemuller (cl); Science & Society Picture Library (cla). **90 Corbis:** Historical Picture Archive (t). **91 Bridgeman Images:** Private Collection (bl). **Smithsonian Institution, Washington, DC:** (br). **The Library of Congress, Washington DC:** (tr). **92 Alamy Images:** (tl). **Corbis:** Don Troiani (clb). **92-93 Alamy Images:** North Wind Picture Archives (b). **93 Corbis:** Don Troiani (tc). **94 Corbis:** Don Troiani (tl, tr). **Dorling Kindersley:** The 68th Durham Light Infantry (br); Queens's Rangers (cl). **Smithsonian Institution, Washington, DC:** (tc). **95 Corbis:** Don Troiani (l, tr, cra, cr, cb, crb, bc, br). **Smithsonian Institution, Washington, DC:** (ca). **96-97 Anne S.K. Brown Military Collection, Brown University Library. 98 Corbis:** (ca). **Smithsonian Institution, Washington, DC:** (crb). **The Library of Congress, Washington DC:** (bl). **99 The Library of Congress, Washington DC. 100 Corbis:** Rick Friedman (bl). **100-101 Bridgeman Images:** Private Collection / Peter Newark Pictures (tc). **101 Alamy Images:** Niday Picture Library (cr). **102-103 The Library of Congress, Washington DC. 104 Alamy Images:** Michele and Tom Grimm (c). **Corbis:** Don Troiani (ca). **Dorling Kindersley:** David Edge's Private Collection (tl). **104-105 Alamy Images:** Maurice Savage (c). **Corbis:** Don Troiani (tc). **105 Alamy Images:** North Wind Picture Archives (br); Maurice Savage (tc). **Corbis:** Don Troiani (tr, cra, cr, bl). **106 Alamy Images:** Everett Collection Inc (t). **106-107 Alamy Images:** INTERFOTO (b). **107 Alamy Images:** Classic Image (tl). **Mary Evans Picture Library:** Ashmolean Museum (tr). **108 Bridgeman Images:** Courtesy of the Director, National Army Museum, London, UK. **109 Alamy Images:** North Wind Picture Archives (bl); Lee Snider (tl). **Mary Evans Picture Library:** Antiquarian Images (cra). **110-111 United States Senate:** (b). **110 Alamy Images:** Niday Picture Library (bc). **The Library of Congress, Washington DC:** (tr). **111 The Library of Congress, Washington DC:** (tc). **112 Alamy Images:** North Wind Picture Archives (bc). **The Library of Congress, Washington DC:** (cl). **112-113 Getty Images:** DEA / M. Seemuller (b). **113 Corbis:** Ted Spiegel (tl). **114-115 Yale University Art Gallery. 116 Smithsonian Institution, Washington, DC. 117 Dreamstime.com:** Olivier Le Queinec (bc). **Photoshot:** LOOK (br). **Smithsonian Institution, Washington, DC:** (tl, c). **118 Corbis:** (cra). **TopFoto.co.uk:** Topham Picturepoint (bl). **119 Bridgeman Images:** Private Collection / Photo © Christie's Images (t). **120 Corbis:** (cr). **Getty Images:** Superstock (l). **121 Alamy Images:** Archive Images (tl). **Getty Images:** Travel Ink (cra). **122-123 Maryland State Archives. 124-125 Alamy Images:** Niday Picture Library (b). **125 Corbis:** Don Troiani (bc). **The Library of Congress, Washington DC:** (tl). **126-127 Getty Images:** The New York Historical Society. **128 Smithsonian Institution, Washington, DC. 129 Boston Public Library:** Leventhal Map Center (bl). **Bridgeman Images:** Collection of the New-York Historical Society, USA (tr). **130-131 Corbis. 132 The Library of Congress, Washington DC:** (bl). **132-133 Yale University Art Gallery:** (t). **133 Alamy Images:** Nikreates (bl). **134-135 Bridgeman Images:** Brown University Library, Providence, Rhode Island, USA. **Corbis:** The Gallery Collection (br). **136 Bridgeman Images:** Philadelphia History Museum at the Atwater Kent,/ Courtesy of Historical Society of Pennsylvania Collection (bl). **Getty Images:** Print Collector (clb). **Yale University Art Gallery:** (fbl). **138 Alamy Images:** PRISMA ARCHIVO (cb). **Corbis:** Leemage (cra).

Mary Evans Picture Library: (cl). **Smithsonian Institution, Washington, DC:** (bl). **139 Bridgeman Images:** Valley Forge Historical Society, USA (ca). **Corbis:** (br). **TopFoto.co.uk:** The Granger Collection (clb). **140 The Library of Congress, Washington DC**. **141 Mary Evans Picture Library:** (tr). **The New York Public Library:** (bl). **The Library of Congress, Washington DC:** (br). **142-143 Alamy Images:** North Wind Picture Archives. **144-145 Corbis:** Don Troiani (b). **144 Alamy Images:** The Art Archive (tr). **145 Alamy Images:** Heritage Image Partnership Ltd (tl); North Wind Picture Archives (cr). **146 Alamy Images:** Pictorial Press Ltd (bl). **Corbis:** Leemage (r). **147 Alamy Images:** North Wind Picture Archives (tc). **Corbis:** Leemage (crb). **148 Corbis:** (cl). **Wally Gobetz**. **149 Alamy Images:** Everett Collection Inc (ca). **Corbis:** Don Troiani (bl). **150-151 Corbis**. **152 Getty Images:** Hulton Archive (br). **TopFoto.co.uk:** The Granger Collection (t). **153 Corbis:** (br). **154-155 Corbis:** Don Troiani (c). **154 Alamy Images:** PRISMA ARCHIVO (bl). **155 Corbis:** Don Troiani (br). **Smithsonian Institution, Washington, DC:** (tr). **156-157 Getty Images:** Print Collector. **158 Corbis:** Don Troiani (tl, tc, clb). **Courtesy Susan Walters of Sue's Old Fashions & Melody Sciarratta of Magic Needle Constructions:** Melody Sciarratta (r). **159 Corbis:** Don Troiani (tl, bl, br, cr, cl, fcl). **160 Corbis:** Don Troiani (tr). **The Library of Congress, Washington DC:** (bl). **160-161 Alamy Images:** Universal Images Group Limited (b). **161 Bridgeman Images:** Private Collection / Photo © Christie's Images (tc). **162 Getty Images:** PhotoQuest (cla). **162-163 Alamy Images:** North Wind Picture Archives (bc). **163 Corbis:** Don Troiani (tc). **Brian Fulton:** (cr). **164-165 Yale University Art Gallery**. **166 Corbis:** (cla). **TopFoto.co.uk:** The Granger Collection (br). **167 Alamy Images:** Niday Picture Library (tc, br). **168-169 Alamy Images:** Niday Picture Library. **170-171 Bridgeman Images:** Valley Forge Historical Society, USA (b). **171 Smithsonian Institution, Washington, DC:** (tl, br). **172-173 Bridgeman Images:** Philadelphia History Museum at the Atwater Kent / Courtesy of Historical Society of Pennsylvania Collection. **174-175 akg-images:** North Wind Picture Archives. **Corbis:** The Gallery Collection (br). **176 Alamy Images:** Robert Garrigus (fclb). **The Library of Congress, Washington DC:** (bl). **TopFoto.co.uk:** The Granger Collection (clb). **178 Bridgeman Images:** Private Collection / Peter Newark American Pictures (br); Tallandier (c). **Corbis:** (cla); Don Troiani (cra). **Smithsonian Institution, Washington, DC:** (bl). **179 Alamy Images:** Heritage Image Partnership Ltd (cr). **Bridgeman Images:** Wilkins, Robert (c.1740-90) / Private Collection (bc). **Corbis:** Christie's Images (cla). **180 Smithsonian Institution, Washington, DC:** (cla). **The Library of Congress, Washington DC:** (b). **181 Bridgeman Images:** De Agostini Picture Library (tr). **Mary Evans Picture Library:** INTERFOTO / Nachum T. Gidal/ Ma (bl). **182-183 Bridgeman Images:** Allen Memorial Art Museum, Oberlin College, Ohio, USA / Gift of Charles F. Olney. **184 Smithsonian Institution, Washington, DC:** (bl). **184-185 SuperStock:** (bc). **185 Alamy Images:** JG Photography (br). **Bridgeman Images:** © Collection of the New-York Historical Society, USA (tr). **186-187 Bridgeman Images:** Private Collection / Ken Welsh. **188 Alamy Images:** Niday Picture Library (ca). **Smithsonian Institution, Washington, DC:** (bl). **188-189 Bridgeman Images:** Wilkins, Robert (c.1740-90) / Private Collection (b). **189 Alamy Images:** Heritage Image Partnership Ltd (tc). **190 Smithsonian Institution, Washington, DC**. **191 Alamy Images:** D Hale-Sutton (cr). **Smithsonian Institution, Washington, DC:** (bc). **TopFoto.co.uk:** The Granger Collection (tl). **192 Corbis:** Don Troiani (tr). **Smithsonian Institution, Washington, DC:** (b). **193 Getty Images:** Stock Montage (bc). **Smithsonian Institution, Washington, DC:** (tc). **194 Getty Images:** MPI (cl). **Mary Evans Picture Library:** Castle Howard Collection (clb). **194-195 Alamy Images:** GL Archive (b). **195 The Library of Congress, Washington DC:** (tl). **196 Alamy Images:** North Wind Picture Archives (cra). **Smithsonian Institution, Washington, DC:** (clb). **196-197 Corbis:** Don Troiani (cb). **197 Corbis:** (tr). **198-199 Bridgeman Images:** Private Collection/ Peter Newark American Pictures. **200 Smithsonian Institution, Washington, DC**. (bc). **200-201 Bridgeman Images:** Killerton, Devon, UK / National Trust Photographic Library / John Hammond (tc). **201 Photo Scala, Florence:** The Metropolitan Museum of Art / Art Resource (bl). **TopFoto.co.uk:** The Granger Collection (cr). **202 Bridgeman Images:** © Massachusetts Historical Society, Boston, MA, USA (l). **203 Bridgeman Images:** © Collection of the New-York Historical Society, USA (bc). **Smithsonian Institution, Washington, DC:** (tl, cr). **204 Getty Images:** MPI (c). **204-205 Alamy Images:** Universal Images Group Limited (b). **205 Alamy Images:** The Art Archive (cr). **The Library of Congress, Washington DC:** (tc). **206-207 The Library of Congress, Washington DC**. **208 Dreamstime.com:** Petrle (cra). **Smithsonian Institution, Washington, DC:** (ca). **208-209 Corbis:** Don Troiani (cb/Carbine, br). **Smithsonian Institution, Washington, DC:** (t, ca, c, cb). **209 Corbis:** Don Troiani (ca/Bayonet, crb, bl, br). **Smithsonian Institution, Washington, DC:** (ca, fcrb). **210 Corbis:** Don Troiani (tr). **Courtesy National Gallery of Art, Washington:** (bc). **TopFoto.co.uk:** The Granger Collection (cl). **210-211 The Library of Congress, Washington DC:** (b). **211 Corbis:** Don Troiani (tl). **212-213 Bridgeman Images:** © Chicago History Museum, USA. **Corbis:** The Gallery Collection (br). **214 Alamy Images:** North Wind Picture Archives (fclb). **Bridgeman Images:** © Collection of the New-York Historical Society, USA (clb). **The Library of Congress, Washington DC:** (bl). **216 Corbis:** (bl); Don Troiani (crb). **Getty Images:** Fotosearch (cla). **Smithsonian Institution, Washington, DC:** (cra). **217 akg-images:** (cr). **Anne S.K. Brown Military Collection, Brown University Library:** (cla). **Boston Public Library:** Courtesy of The Richard Brown's collection (cb). **The Library of Congress, Washington DC:** (bl). **218-219 Bridgeman Images:** Royal Ontario Museum, Toronto, Canada (b). **219 Corbis:** (tl). **Mary Evans Picture Library:** Library of Congress (tr). **220 Getty Images:** Heritage Images (cra). **TopFoto.co.uk:** The Granger Collection (cl). **221 Boston Public Library:** Courtesy of The Richard Brown's collection. **222 Smithsonian Institution, Washington, DC:** (tl, clb, bl, c). **222-223 Corbis:** Don Troiani (ca, c). **TopFoto.co.uk:** HIP (tl). **223 akg-images:** North Wind Picture Archives (r). **Corbis:** Don Troiani (clb). **Smithsonian Institution, Washington, DC:** (tc, bl, bc). **224-225 The Library of Congress, Washington DC**. **226 Alamy Images:** David Coleman (l). **Getty Images:** Interim Archives (crb). **227 Bridgeman Images:** Private Collection / Peter Newark American Pictures (tc). **TopFoto.co.uk:** The Granger Collection (br). **228-229 Getty Images:** Fotosearch (t). **228 Bridgeman Images:** De Agostini Picture Library / G. Dagli Orti (br). **229 Alamy Images:** Ivy Close Images (tr). **Darlington Digital Library, Special Collections, University Library System, University of Pittsburgh:** (br). **230-231 Corbis:** Tarker. **232 Corbis**. **233 Alamy Images:** William Manning (cr). **iStockphoto.com:** hstiver (cb). **The Art Archive:** Granger Collection (tl). **234 Bridgeman Images:** Peabody Essex Museum, Salem, Massachusetts, USA (cla). **Corbis:** Marilyn Angel Wynn / Nativestock Pictures (cb). **Photo Scala, Florence:** Marilyn Angel Wynn / Nativestock.com (bl). **Smithsonian Institution, Washington, DC:** (cra). **The Art Archive:** Granger Collection (c). **234-235 Bridgeman Images:** Peabody Essex Museum, Salem, Massachusetts, USA (ca). **Corbis:** Don Troiani (t). **235 American Museum of Natural History Library:** (cl). **236 Alamy Images:** North Wind Picture Archives. **237 Bridgeman Images:** © Collection of the New-York Historical Society, USA (br). **Corbis:** Don Troiani (ca). **The Library of Congress, Washington DC:** (bl). **238-239 akg-images**. **240 Alamy Images:** North Wind Picture Archives (bl). **Bridgeman Images:** Private Collection/ Peter Newark American Pictures (crb). **241 Alamy Images:** North Wind Picture Archives (bl). **The Trustees of the British Museum:** (cr). **Corbis:** Don Troiani (tr). **242-243 Alamy Images:** North Wind Picture Archives. **244 Smithsonian Institution, Washington, DC:** (cra). **244-245 Alamy Images:** dbimages (b). **245 The Library of Congress, Washington DC:** (tr). **246-247 Alamy Images:** Don Klumpp. **248-249 Alamy Images:** North Wind Picture Archives. **Corbis:** The Gallery Collection (br). **250 Bridgeman Images:** Brown University Library, Providence, Rhode Island, USA (fbl). **Getty Images:** DEA Picture Library (clb). **Yale University Art Gallery:** (bl). **252 Alamy Images:** North Wind Picture Archives (cra). **Corbis:** Don Troiani (cla). **Smithsonian Institution, Washington,** DC: (clb). **The Art Archive:** Granger Collection (bc). **253 Alamy Images:** Mira (bl); Rod Williams (cla). **Courtesy of The Old Print Shop, Inc:** (cra). **Smithsonian Institution, Washington, DC:** (cr). **The Art Archive:** Granger Collection (crb). **254 Alamy Images:** North Wind Picture Archives. **255 The New York Public Library:** (bl). **The Art Archive:** (cl). **256 The Library of Congress, Washington DC:** (t). **257 William L. Clements Library, The University Of Michigan:** (tc). **The Art Archive:** Granger Collection (bl). **Yale University Art Gallery:** (br). **258-259 Yale University Art Gallery**. **260 Bridgeman Images:** Brown University Library, Providence, Rhode Island, USA (r). **The US National Archives and Records Administration:** (clb). **261 Alamy Images:** Rod Williams (tc). **Corbis:** (cr). **262 Bridgeman Images:** Harriet Wynter Antiques, London, UK (bl). **The Art Archive:** Granger Collection (cra). **263 Alamy Images:** North Wind Picture Archives (bl). **Bridgeman Images:** Museo Nazionale di Capodimonte, Naples, Italy (t). **264 Alamy Images:** age fotostock (cra). **Getty Images:** The New York Historical Society (b). **265 Corbis:** Don Troiani (bc). **North Carolina Museum of History:** (crb). **Smithsonian Institution, Washington, DC:** (tl, tr, c, cr). **266-267 The Art Archive:** Granger Collection (b). **267 Corbis:** Don Troiani (tl). **Mary Evans Picture Library:** Thaliastock (cr). **268 Alamy Images:** Classic Image (bl). **The Tennessee Historical Society:** Tennessee State Library and Archives tr). **268-269 Yale University Art Gallery:** (b). **270-271 Bridgeman Images:** Brown University Library, Providence, Rhode Island, USA. **272 Bridgeman Images:** National Gallery, London, UK. **273 Alamy Images:** North Wind Picture Archives (tl); SuperStock (crb). **The Art Archive:** Gunshots (bc). **274 Alamy Images:** Classic Image (bc). **Corbis:** Don Troiani (c). **The Art Archive:** (cl). **275 Getty Images:** DEA Picture Library. **276-277 Alamy Images:** North Wind Picture Archives. **278 Alamy Images:** Philip Scalia (tr). **Getty Images:** Culture Club (bl). **279 Bridgeman Images:** De Agostini Picture Library. **Mary Evans Picture Library:** (cr). **280 Smithsonian Institution, Washington, DC:** (cla). **TopFoto.co.uk:** The Granger Collection (b). **281 Alamy Images:** Georgios Kollidas (br). **The New York Public Library:** Benson John Lossing (ca). **Smithsonian Institution, Washington, DC:** (t). **282 Corbis:** Don Troiani (tl, tr, crb, br). **Smithsonian Institution, Washington, DC:** (cla,cra). **282-283 Corbis:** Don Troiani (c). **Smithsonian Institution, Washington, DC:** (cb). **283 akg-images:** Interfoto / Hermann Historica (b). **Corbis:** Don Troiani (t, ca/British Infantry Hanger, cb). **Smithsonian Institution, Washington, DC:** (ca). **284-285 Bridgeman Images:** Bibliotheque Nationale, Paris, France / Archives Charmet. **Corbis:** The Gallery Collection (br). **286 Alamy Images:** North Wind Picture Archives (clb). **The Library of Congress, Washington DC:** (fbl). **Yale University Art Gallery:** (bl). **288 Bridgeman Images:** Private Collection (c). **The Art Archive:** (clb). **The Library of Congress, Washington DC:** (br). **Yale University Art Gallery:** (cra). **289 Alamy Images:** Niday Picture Library (clb). **Corbis:** (ca). **Yale University Art Gallery:** (br). **290 Yale University Art Gallery:** (t). **291 Alamy Images:** The Art Archive (br). **Getty Images:** Stock Montage (tc). **292 North Carolina Museum of History:** (tr).

The Art Archive: (bl). **293 Bridgeman Images:** New York Public Library, USA (b). **The Art Archive:** National Army Museum London / National Army Museum (tr). **294-295 Alamy Images:** North Wind Picture Archives. **296 Bridgeman Images:** Private Collection (r). **297 Alamy Images:** Angelo Hornak (br); North Wind Picture Archives (c). **Bridgeman Images:** Brown University Library, Providence, Rhode Island, USA (tl). **298 Pamela White:** (t). **299 Alamy Images:** North Wind Picture Archives (br). **Bridgeman Images:** National Army Museum, London (cr). **300 Alamy Images:** Heritage Image Partnership Ltd (bl). **Corbis:** (cl). **300-301 The Library of Congress, Washington DC:** (c). **301 Alamy Images:** Niday Picture Library (br). **302-303 Getty Images:** DEA / M. Seemuller. **304 Alamy Images:** The Art Archive. **305 Alamy Images:** North Wind Picture Archives (ca, br). **Mary Evans Picture Library:** Grosvenor Prints (bl). **306-307 The Art Archive:** Musée du Château de Versailles/ Gianni Dagli Orti (t). **307 Corbis:** (cr). **The Library of Congress, Washington DC:** (bl). **308-309 Yale University Art Gallery. 310 Bridgeman Images:** Private Collection / Peter Newark Pictures (bl). **310-311 Bridgeman Images:** © Chicago History Museum, USA (t). **311 Alamy Images:** North Wind Picture Archives (bl). **312 Bridgeman Images:** Private Collection/ Peter Newark Historical Pictures (cl). **Corbis:** (tr). **312-313 The Art Archive:** Granger Collection (b). **313 The Art Archive:** Winterthur Museum Delaware / Granger Collection (tr). **314-315 Yale University Art Gallery. 316-317 Bridgeman Images:** © Collection of the New-York Historical Society, USA. **317 Corbis:** The Gallery Collection (br). **318 Alamy Images:** North Wind Picture Archives (bl). **Smithsonian Institution, Washington, DC:** (fclb). **The Art Archive:** Buffalo Bill Center of the West, Cody, Wyoming / Buffalo Bill Center of the West/21.78 (clb). **320 Alamy Images:** North Wind Picture Archives (cra). **Smithsonian Institution, Washington, DC:** (c). **The Art Archive:** Granger Collection (crb). **The US National Archives and Records Administration:** (bl). **321 Alamy Images:** Niday Picture Library (cl). **Bridgeman Images:** Private Collection / Peter Newark American Pictures (ca). **Smithsonian Institution, Washington, DC:** (clb). **The Library of Congress, Washington DC:** (crb). **322 Smithsonian Institution, Washington, DC:** (tl). **322-323 Library and Archives Canada:** (b). **323 Courtesy of The Lewis Walpole Library, Yale University:** (tl). **Smithsonian Institution, Washington, DC:** (cr). **324 Smithsonian Institution, Washington, DC:** (bc). **The Art Archive:** Granger Collection (bl). **325 Alamy Images:** Everett Collection Inc (t); North Wind Picture Archives (bc). **326 Corbis. 327 Alamy Images:** Niday Picture Library (bc). **Corbis:** (tl, crb). **328 Alamy Images:** Universal Images Group Limited (cra). **Bridgeman Images:** Museum of Fine Arts, Boston, Massachusetts, USA / Bequest of Winslow Warren (bc). **329 Bridgeman Images:** Private Collection / Peter Newark American Pictures (b). **Smithsonian Institution,**

Washington, DC: (tc). **The Library of Congress, Washington DC:** (cra). **330-331 Corbis:** GraphicaArtis. **332-333 The US National Archives and Records Administration. 334 Alamy Images:** Bygone Collection (bc). **Smithsonian Institution, Washington, DC:** (cl, tr). **335 Corbis:** Leemage (t). **The Art Archive:** Granger Collection (b). **336-337 Courtesy of Mount Vernon Ladies' Association. 338 Corbis:** (t). **Smithsonian Institution, Washington, DC:** (br). **339 Alamy Images:** Chronicle (cr). **The Art Archive:** Granger Collection (bc). **340-341 The Art Archive:** Buffalo Bill Center of the West, Cody, Wyoming / Buffalo Bill Center of the West / 21.78. **342 Alamy Images:** GL Archive (b). **The Art Archive:** Granger Collection (tr). **343 The Library of Congress, Washington DC:** (tr, bl). **344 Corbis:** Don Troiani (ca). **The Art Archive:** Culver Pictures (bc). **344-345 Corbis:** John and Lisa Merrill (c). **345 Alamy Images:** North Wind Picture Archives (cr). **346-347 Press Association Images:** Ray Stubblebine. **348-349 Alamy Images:** Stillman Rogers.

Chapter tabs:
18-47 Smithsonian Institution, Washington, DC. 55-81 Smithsonian Institution, Washington, DC. 91-132 Dorling Kindersley: Peter Keim. **140-171 Dorling Kindersley:** Peter Keim. **180-211 Smithsonian Institution, Washington, DC. 218-245 Smithsonian Institution, Washington, DC. 253-283 Corbis:** Don Troiani. **291-313 Corbis:** Heritage Images. **322-349 Dorling Kindersley:** Peter Keim. **350-360 Corbis.**

Front and Back Endpapers: **Alamy Images:** The Art Archive

All other images © Dorling Kindersley
For further information see:
www.dkimages.com

CONSULTANT

Jennifer L. Jones is a curator and department chair at the Smithsonian's National Museum of American History. She is the objects curator for the *Price of Freedom: Americans at War* exhibition; the Gunboat *Philadelphia* exhibit; and the curator in charge of the Star Spangled Banner. Her publications include chapters in *Smithsonian's Civil War*. She is collaborating on an updated publication on the gunboat *Philadelphia* with the Lake Champlain Maritime Museum for summer 2016. She serves as an editorial consultant on many DK publications, as well as other Smithsonian co-branded publications. She has appeared on Smithsonian Channel programs *Civil War 360* and *A Star Spangled Story: Battle for America*.

David D. Miller III and Kathleen Golden are both Associate Curators, Armed Forces Division, National Museum of American History.

AUTHORS

James C. Bradford is Associate Professor of History at Texas A&M University, College Station, Texas. He specializes in early American and naval and maritime history. James co-edits the book series *New Perspectives on Maritime History and Nautical Archeology*.

R.G. Grant is a history writer who has published more than 30 books, many of them dealing with aspects of military conflict. He is the author of numerous Dorling Kindersley titles, including *Battle* (2009), *Commanders* (2010), and *World War I: The Definitive Visual History* in this series.

Jeremy Harwood worked in publishing for many years before becoming a full-time history writer. His particular interests include World War II as well as the War of Independence.

David Hatt read History at Peterhouse, Cambridge, and graduated in 2009. He is particularly interested in American history, and is the author of a dissertation on the Adams political dynasty.

Mark Collins Jenkins is the author of *The War of 1812 and the Rise of the US Navy*, and also contributed to Dorling Kindersley's *The American Civil War: A Visual History*. Mark is an independent historian who formerly worked with the National Geographic Society.

Paul D. Lockhart is Professor of History and Brage Golding Distinguished Professor of Research at Wright State University, Dayton, Ohio. His latest book is *The Whites of Their Eyes: Bunker Hill, the First American Army, and the Emergence of George Washington*.

Cdr. John J. Patterson VI is a distinguished naval aviator. Currently, he is a faculty member of the US Army War College, where he teaches strategy and campaign design. His work has been published in journals such as *Air & Space Power Journal*, *Parameters*, and *Proceedings*.

Jim Piecuch is Associate Professor of History at Kennesaw State University, Kennesaw, Georgia. He is the author of several books, numerous articles, and book chapters on America during the colonial and revolutionary periods.

John Ruddiman teaches early American history at Wake Forest University, Winston-Salem, North Carolina. His 2014 book, *Becoming Men of Some Consequence*, explores how young soldiers' expectations and actions shaped the Continental Army and the War of Independence.

James D. Scudieri served 30 years as a US Army logistician, including 10 years teaching in Army education. He is currently an historian at the US Army Heritage and Education Center.